1 KINGS

THE PREACHER'S OUTLINE & SERMON BIBLE®

OLD TESTAMENT

KING JAMES VERSION

Leadership Ministries Worldwide
Chattanooga, TN

THE PREACHER'S OUTLINE & SERMON BIBLE® 1 KINGS
KING JAMES VERSION

Published by Leadership Ministries Worldwide, Chattanooga, Tennessee

Please address all requests for information or permission to:
Leadership Ministries Worldwide
Ph.# (800) 987-8790 E-Mail: info@lmw.org
Web: lmw.org

Library of Congress Catalog Card Number: 96-75921
ISBN Softbound Edition: 978-1-57407-170-2

Printed in the United States of America

DEDICATED

To all the men and women of the world
who preach and teach the Gospel of
our Lord Jesus Christ and
to the Mercy and Grace of God

- Demonstrated to us in Christ Jesus our Lord.

  "In whom we have redemption through His blood, the forgiveness of sins, according to the riches of His grace." (Ep.1:7)

- Out of the mercy and grace of God, His Word has flowed. Let every person know that God will have mercy upon him, forgiving and using him to fulfill His glorious plan of salvation.

  "For God so loved the world, that he gave His only begotten Son, that whosoever believeth in Him should not perish, but have everlasting life. For God sent not his son into the world to condemn the world, but that the world through him might be saved." (Jn.3:16-17)

  "For this is good and acceptable in the sight of God our Saviour; who will have all men to be saved, and to come unto the knowledge of the truth." (1 Ti.2:3-4)

10/22

The Preacher's Outline & Sermon Bible® is written for God's servants to use in their study, teaching, and preaching of God's Holy Word...

- to share the Word of God with the world.
- to help believers, both ministers and laypersons, in their understanding, preaching, and teaching of God's Word.
- to do everything we possibly can to lead men, women, boys, and girls to give their hearts and lives to Jesus Christ and to secure the eternal life that He offers.
- to do all we can to minister to the needy of the world.
- to give Jesus Christ His proper place, the place the Word gives Him. Therefore, no work of Leadership Ministries Worldwide will ever be personalized.

ACKNOWLEDGMENTS AND BIBLIOGRAPHY

Every child of God is precious to the Lord and deeply loved. And every child as a servant of the Lord touches the lives of those who come in contact with him or his ministry. The writing ministries of the following servants have touched this work, and we are grateful that God brought their writings our way. We hereby acknowledge their ministries to us, being fully aware that there are so many others down through the years whose writings have touched our lives and who deserve mention, but the weaknesses of our minds have caused them to fade from memory. May our wonderful Lord continue to bless the ministry of these dear servants, and the ministry of us all as we diligently labor to reach the world for Christ and to meet the desperate needs of those who suffer so much.

THE REFERENCE WORKS

Archer, Gleason L. *A Survey of Old Testament Introduction*. Chicago, IL: Moody Bible Institute of Chicago, 1974.

———. *Encyclopedia of Bible Difficulties*. Grand Rapids, Michigan: Zondervan Publishing House, 1982.

Atlas of the World. Hammond Concise Edition. Maplewood, NJ: Hammond Inc., 1993.

Baker's Dictionary of Theology. Everett F. Harrison, Editor-in-Chief. Grand Rapids, MI: Baker Book House, 1960.

Barker, William P. *Everyone in the Bible*. Westwood, NJ: Fleming H. Revell Co., 1966.

Brown, Francis. *The New Brown-Driver-Briggs-Gesenius Hebrew-English Lexicon*. Peabody, MA: Hendrickson Publishers, 1979.

Cruden's Complete Concordance of the Old & New Testament. Philadelphia, PA: The John C. Winston Co., 1930.

Dake, Finis Jennings. *Dake's Annotated Reference Bible, The Holy Bible*. Lawrenceville, GA: Dake Bible Sales, Inc., 1963.

Easton's 1897 Bible Dictionary. Database NavPress Software, 1996.

Enhanced Nave's Topics. Database NavPress Software, 1991, 1994.

Frank, Harry Thomas, ed. *Atlas of the Bible Lands*. Maplewood, NJ: Hammond Incorporated, 1977.

Freedman, David Noel, ed., et. al. *The Anchor Bible Dictionary*. New York: Doubleday, 1992.

Funk & Wagnalls Standard Desk Dictionary. Lippincott & Crowell, Publishers, 1980, Vol.2.

Geisler, Norman. *A Popular Survey of the Old Testament*. Grand Rapids, MI: Baker Book House, 1977.

Good News Bible. Old Testament: © American Bible Society, 1976. New Testament: © American Bible Society, 1966, 1971, 1976. Collins World.

Good News for Modern Man, The New Testament. New York, NY: American Bible Society, 1971.

Goodrick, Edward W. and John R. Kohlenberger, III. *The NIV Exhaustive Concordance*. Grand Rapids, MI: Zondervan Publishing House, 1990.

Grun, Bernard. *The Timetables of History*. 3rd ed. New York: Simon & Schuster, 1991.

Harrison, Roland Kenneth. *Introduction to the Old Testament*. Grand Rapids, MI: Eerdmans Publishing Co., 1969.

Holman Bible Dictionary. Nashville, TN: Broadman & Holman Publishers, 1991. Database NavPress Software.

Hooper, Jerry L., ed. *The Holman Bible Atlas*. Philadelphia, PA: A.J. Holman Company, 1978.

Jauchen, John S., ed., et. al. *NIV Thompson Student Bible*. Indianapolis, IN: Kirkbride Bible Company, 1999.

Josephus, Flavius. *Complete Works*. Grand Rapids, MI: Kregel Publications, 1981.

Kaiser, Walter C. *A History of Israel*. Nashville, Tennessee: Broadman and Holman Publishers, 1998.

Kipfer, Barbara Ann, Ph.D. *Roget's 21st Century Thesaurus*. New York, NY: Dell Publishing, 1992.

Kohlenberger, John R. III. *The Interlinear NIV Hebrew-English Old Testament*. Grand Rapids, MI: Zondervan Publishing House, 1987.

Kouffman, Donald T. *The Dictionary of Religious Terms*. Westwood, NJ: Fleming H. Revell Co., 1967.

Life Application® Bible. Wheaton, IL: Tyndale House Publishers, Inc., 1991.

Life Application® Study Bible. New International Version. Tyndale House Publishers, Inc.: Wheaton, IL 1991, and Zondervan Publishing House: Grand Rapids, MI, 1984.

Lindsell, Harold and Woodbridge, Charles J. *A Handbook of Christian Truth*. Westwood, NJ: Fleming H. Revell Company, A Division of Baker Book House, 1953.

Living Quotations For Christians. Edited by Sherwood Eliot Wirt and Kersten Beckstrom. New York, NY: Harper & Row, Publishers, 1974.

Lockyer, Herbert. *All the Books and Chapters of the Bible*. Grand Rapids, MI: Zondervan Publishing House, 1966.

———. *All the Men of the Bible*. Grand Rapids, MI: Zondervan Publishing House, 1958.

———. *All the Miracles of the Bible*. Grand Rapids, MI: Zondervan Publishing House, 1961.

———. *All the Parables of the Bible*. Grand Rapids, MI: Zondervan Publishing House, 1963.

———. *The Women of the Bible*. Grand Rapids, MI: Zondervan Publishing House, 1967.

Martin, Alfred. *Survey of the Scriptures*, Part I, II, III. Chicago, IL: Moody Bible Institute of Chicago, 1961.

McDowell, Josh. *Evidence That Demands a Verdict*, Vol.1. San Bernardino, CA: Here's Life Publishers, Inc., 1979.

Miller, Madeleine S. & J. Lane. *Harper's Bible Dictionary*. New York, NY: Harper & Row Publishers, 1961.

Nave, Orville J. *Nave's Topical Bible*. Nashville, TN: The Southwestern Company. Copyright © by J.B. Henderson, 1921.

Nelson's Complete Book of Bible Maps & Charts. Nashville, TN: Thomas Nelson Publishers, Inc., 1996.

New American Standard Bible, Reference Edition. La Habra, CA: The Lockman Foundation, 1975.

New American Standard Bible, Updated Edition. La Habra, CA: The Lockman Foundation, 1995.

New Bible Dictionary, 3rd Edition. Leicester, England: Universities & Colleges Christian Fellowship, 1996.

New International Version Study Bible. Grand Rapids, MI: Zondervan Bible Publishers, 1985.

New Living Translation, Holy Bible. Wheaton, IL: Tyndale House Publishers, Inc., 1996.

Orr, William. *How We May Know That God Is*. Wheaton, IL: Van Kampen Press, n.d.

Owens, John Joseph. *Analytical Key to the Old Testament*, Vols.1, 2, 3. Grand Rapids, MI: Baker Book House, 1989.

Payne, J. Barton. *Encyclopedia of Biblical Prophecy*. New York, NY: Harper & Row, Publishers, 1973.

ACKNOWLEDGMENTS AND BIBLIOGRAPHY

THE REFERENCE WORKS

(continued)

Pilgrim Edition, Holy Bible. New York, NY: Oxford University Press, 1952.

Ridout, Samuel. *Lectures on the Tabernacle.* New York, NY: Loizeaux Brothers, Inc., 1914.

Silverman, David P. ed. *Ancient Egypt.* New York: Oxford University Press, 1997.

Smith, William. *Smith's Bible Dictionary.* Peabody, MA: Hendrickson Publishers, n.d.

Stone, Nathan J. *Names of God.* Chicago, IL: Moody Press, 1944.

Strong, James. *Strong's Exhaustive Concordance of the Bible.* Nashville, TN: Thomas Nelson, Inc., 1990.

——. *The Tabernacle of Israel.* Grand Rapids, MI: Kregel Publications, 1987.

Strong's Greek and Hebrew Dictionary as compiled by iExalt Software. Database NavPress Software, 1990-1993.

The Amplified Bible. Scripture taken from THE AMPLIFIED BIBLE, Old Testament copyright © 1965, 1987 by the Zondervan Publishing House. The Amplified New Testament copyright © 1958, 1987 by The Lockman Foundation. Used by permission.

The Evangelical Dictionary of Theology. Elwell, Walter A., Editor. Grand Rapids, MI: Baker Book House, 1984.

The Hebrew-Greek Key Study Bible, New International Version. Spiros Zodhiates, Th.D., Executive Editor. Chattanooga, TN: AMG Publishers, 1996.

The Holy Bible in Four Translations. Minneapolis, MN: Worldwide Publications. Copyright © The Iversen-Norman Associates: New York, NY, 1972.

The Illustrated Bible Atlas, with Historical Notes by F. F. Bruce. Grand Rapids, MI: Kregel Publications, 1994.

The Interlinear Bible, Vols.1, 2, 3. Translated by Jay P. Green, Sr. Grand Rapids, MI: Baker Book House, 1976.

The International Standard Bible Encyclopaedia, Edited by James Orr. Grand Rapids, MI: Eerdmans Publishing Co., 1939.

The NASB Greek/Hebrew Dictionary and Concordance. La Habra, CA: The Lockman Foundation, 1988.

The Nelson Study Bible, New King James Version. Nashville, TN: Thomas Nelson Publishers, Inc., 1997.

The New Compact Bible Dictionary. Edited by T. Alton Bryant. Grand Rapids, MI: Zondervan Publishing House, 1967. Used by permission of Zondervan Publishing House.

The New Scofield Reference Bible. Edited by C.I. Scofield. New York, NY: Oxford University Press, 1967.

The New Thompson Chain Reference Bible. Indianapolis, IN: B.B. Kirkbride Bible Co., Inc., 1964.

The New Unger's Bible Dictionary. Chicago, IL: Moody Press, 1998. Database NavPress Software, 1997.

The NIV Study Bible, New International Version. Grand Rapids, MI: Zondervan Publishing House, 1985.

The Open Bible. Nashville, TN: Thomas Nelson Publishers, 1975.

The Quest Study Bible. New International Version. Grand Rapids, MI: Zondervan Publishing House, 1994.

The Zondervan Pictorial Encyclopedia of the Bible, Vol.1. Merrill C. Tenney, Editor. Grand Rapids, MI: Zondervan Publishing House, 1982.

Theological Wordbook of the Old Testament. Edited by R. Laird Harris. Chicago, IL: Moody Bible Institute of Chicago, 1980.

Unger, Merrill F. & William White, Jr. *Nelson's Expository Dictionary of the Old Testament.* Nashville, TN: Thomas Nelson Publishers, 1980.

Vine, W.E., Merrill F. Unger, William White, Jr. *Vine's Complete Expository Dictionary of Old and New Testament Words.* Nashville, TN: Thomas Nelson Publishers, 1985.

Walton, John H. *Chronological and Background Charts of the Old Testament.* Grand Rapids, MI: Zondervan Publishing House, 1978.

Webster's Seventh New Collegiate Dictionary. Springfield, MA: G. & C. Merriam Company, Publishers, 1971.

Wilmington. Harold L. *The Outline Bible.* Wheaton, IL: Tyndale House Publishers, Inc., 1999.

Wilson, William. *Wilson's Old Testament Word Studies.* McLean, VA: MacDonald Publishing Company, n.d.

Wood, Leon. *A Survey of Israel's History.* Grand Rapids, MI: Zondervan Publishing House, 1982.

Young, Edward J. *An Introduction to the Old Testament.* Grand Rapids, MI: Eerdmans Publishing Co., 1964.

Young, Robert. *Young's Analytical Concordance to the Bible.* Grand Rapids, MI: Eerdmans Publishing Co., n.d.

Zondervan NIV Bible Library. Version 2.5. Grand Rapids, MI: Zondervan Publishing House.

THE COMMENTARIES

Baldwin, Joyce G. *1 & 2 Samuel.* "The Tyndale Old Testament Commentaries." Downers Grove, IL: Inter-Varsity Press, 1988.

Barnes' Notes, Exodus to Esther. F.C. Cook, Editor. Grand Rapids, MI: Baker Book House, n.d.

Bergen, Robert D. *1, 2 Samuel.* "The New American Commentary," Vol.7. Nashville, TN: Broadman & Holman Publishers, 1996.

Brueggemann, Walter. *1 Kings.* "Knox Preaching Guides." Atlanta, GA: John Knox Press, 1982.

Burroughs, P.E., D.D. *Old Testament Studies.* Nashville, TN: Sunday School Board, Southern Baptist Convention, 1915.

Chafin, Kenneth. *The Preacher's Commentary on 1, 2 Samuel.* Nashville, TN: Word Publishing, 1989, 2003.

Crockett, William Day. *A Harmony of Samuel, Kings, and Chronicles.* Grand Rapids, MI: Baker Book House, 1985.

Denton, Robert C. *The First and Second Books of the Kings. The First and Second Books of the Chronicles.* "The Layman's Bible Commentary," Vol.7. Atlanta, GA: John Knox Press, 1964.

DeVries, S.J. *1 Kings.* WBC. Waco, TX: Word, 1985.

Dilday, Russell. *The Preacher's Commentary on 1, 2 Kings.* Nashville, TN: Word Publishing, 1987, 2003.

Evans, Mary J. *1 and 2 Samuel.* "New International Biblical Commentary." Peabody, MA: Hendrickson Publishers, Inc., 2000.

Farrar, F.W. *The First Book of Kings.* Minneapolis, MN: Klock & Klock Christian Publishers, Inc., n.d.

Gill, John. *Gill's Commentary*, Vol.2. Grand Rapids, MI: Baker Book House, 1980.

THE COMMENTARIES

(continued)

Gray, John. *I & II Kings.* Second, Fully Revised, Edition. "The Old Testament Library." Philadelphia, PA: The Westminster Press, 1970.
Henry, Matthew. *Matthew Henry's Commentary*, 6 Vols. Old Tappan, NJ: Fleming H. Revell Co., n.d.
Hertzberg, Hans Wilhelm. *I & II Samuel.* Philadelphia, PA: Westminster Press, 1964.
Hobbs, T.R. *2 Kings.* "Word Biblical Commentary," Vol.13. Waco, TX: Word Books, 1985.
House, Paul R. *1, 2 Kings.* "The New American Commentary," Vol.8. Nashville, TN: Broadman & Holman Publishers, 1995.
Kaiser, Walter C., Jr. *A History of Israel.* Nashville, TN: Broadman & Holman Publishers, 1998.
Keil-Delitzsch. *Commentary on the Old Testament*, Vol.3. Grand Rapids, MI: Eerdmans Publishing Co., n.d.
Maclaren, Alexander. *Expositions of Holy Scripture*, 11 Vols. Grand Rapids, MI: Eerdmans Publishing Co., 1952-59.
McGee, J. Vernon. *Thru the Bible*, Vol.2. Nashville, TN: Thomas Nelson Publishers, 1981.
Morgan, G. Campbell. *Living Messages of the Books of the Bible*, Vol.1. Old Tappan, NJ: Fleming H. Revell, 1912.
Newsome, James D., Jr. *1 Samuel, 2 Samuel.* Atlanta, GA: John Knox Press, 1982.
Patterson, Richard D. and Hermann J. Austel. *1, 2 Kings.* "The Expositor's Bible Commentary," Vol.4. Grand Rapids, MI: Zondervan Publishing House, 1988.
Payne, D.F. *I and II Samuel*, DSB. Philadelphia, PA: Westminster Press, 1982.
Poole, Matthew. *Matthew Poole's Commentary on the Holy Bible.* Peabody, MA: Hendrickson Publishers, n.d.
Provan, Iain W. *1 and 2 Kings.* "New International Biblical Commentary." Peabody, MA: Hendrickson Publishers, Inc., 1995.
Rust, Eric C. *The First and Second Books of Samuel.* "The Layman's Bible Commentary," Vol.6. Atlanta, GA: John Knox Press, 1961.
Spurgeon, C.H. *Spurgeon's Sermon Notes. Genesis to Malachi.* Westwood, NJ: Fleming H. Revell Co., n.d.
The Interpreter's Bible, 12 Vols. New York, NY: Abingdon Press, 1956.
The Pulpit Commentary. 23 Vols. Edited by H.D.M. Spence & Joseph S. Exell. Grand Rapids, MI: Eerdmans Publishing Co., 1950.
Walvoord, John F. and Roy B. Zuck, Editors. *The Bible Knowledge Commentary, Old Testament.* Colorado Springs, CO: Chariot Victor Publishing, 1985.
Wiersbe, Warren W. *Be Responsible.* Colorado Springs, CO: Victor Books, 2000.
———. *Be Successful.* Colorado Springs, CO: Victor Books, 2001.
Wiseman, Donald J. *1 & 2 Kings.* "The Tyndale Old Testament Commentaries." Downers Grove, IL: Inter-Varsity Press, 1993.
Youngblood, Ronald F. *1 Samuel. 2 Samuel.* "The Expositor's Bible Commentary," Vol.3. Grand Rapids, MI: Zondervan Publishing House, 1990.

ABBREVIATIONS

&	= and	O.T.	= Old Testament
Bc.	= because	p./pp.	= page/pages
Concl.	= conclusion	Pt.	= point
Cp.	= compare	Quest.	= question
Ct.	= contrast	Rel.	= religion
e.g.	= for example	Rgt.	= righteousness
f.	= following	Thru	= through
Illust.	= illustration	v./vv.	= verse/verses
N.T.	= New Testament	vs.	= versus

THE BOOKS OF THE OLD TESTAMENT

Book	*Abbreviation*	*Chapters*
GENESIS	Gen. or Ge.	50
Exodus	Ex.	40
Leviticus	Lev. or Le.	27
Numbers	Num. or Nu.	36
Deuteronomy	Dt. or De.	34
Joshua	Josh. or Jos.	24
Judges	Judg. or Jud.	21
Ruth	Ruth or Ru.	4
1 Samuel	1 Sam. or 1 S.	31
2 Samuel	2 Sam. or 2 S.	24
1 Kings	1 Ki. or 1 K.	22
2 Kings	2 Ki. or 2 K.	25
1 Chronicles	1 Chron. or 1 Chr.	29
2 Chronicles	2 Chron. or 2 Chr.	36
Ezra	Ezra or Ezr.	10
Nehemiah	Neh. or Ne.	13
Esther	Est.	10
Job	Job or Jb.	42
Psalms	Ps.	150
Proverbs	Pr.	31

Book	*Abbreviation*	*Chapters*
Ecclesiastes	Eccl. or Ec.	12
The Song of Solomon	S. of Sol. or Song	8
Isaiah	Is.	66
Jeremiah	Jer. or Je.	52
Lamentations	Lam.	5
Ezekiel	Ezk. or Eze.	48
Daniel	Dan. or Da.	12
Hosea	Hos. or Ho.	14
Joel	Joel	3
Amos	Amos or Am.	9
Obadiah	Obad. or Ob.	1
Jonah	Jon. or Jona.	4
Micah	Mic. or Mi.	7
Nahum	Nah. or Na.	3
Habakkuk	Hab.	3
Zephaniah	Zeph. or Zep.	3
Haggai	Hag.	2
Zechariah	Zech. or Zec.	14
Malachi	Mal.	4

THE BOOKS OF THE NEW TESTAMENT

Book	*Abbreviation*	*Chapters*
MATTHEW	Mt.	28
Mark	Mk.	16
Luke	Lk. or Lu.	24
John	Jn.	21
The Acts	Acts or Ac.	28
Romans	Ro.	16
1 Corinthians	1 Cor. or 1 Co.	16
2 Corinthians	2 Cor. or 2 Co.	13
Galatians	Gal. or Ga.	6
Ephesians	Eph. or Ep.	6
Philippians	Ph.	4
Colossians	Col.	4
1 Thessalonians	1 Th.	5
2 Thessalonians	2 Th.	3

Book	*Abbreviation*	*Chapters*
1 Timothy	1 Tim. or 1 Ti.	6
2 Timothy	2 Tim. or 2 Ti.	4
Titus	Tit.	3
Philemon	Phile. or Phm.	1
Hebrews	Heb. or He.	13
James	Jas. or Js.	5
1 Peter	1 Pt. or 1 Pe.	5
2 Peter	2 Pt. or 2 Pe.	3
1 John	1 Jn.	5
2 John	2 Jn.	1
3 John	3 Jn.	1
Jude	Jude	1
Revelation	Rev. or Re.	22

HOW TO USE

The Preacher's Outline & Sermon Bible®

Follow these easy steps to gain maximum benefit from The POSB.

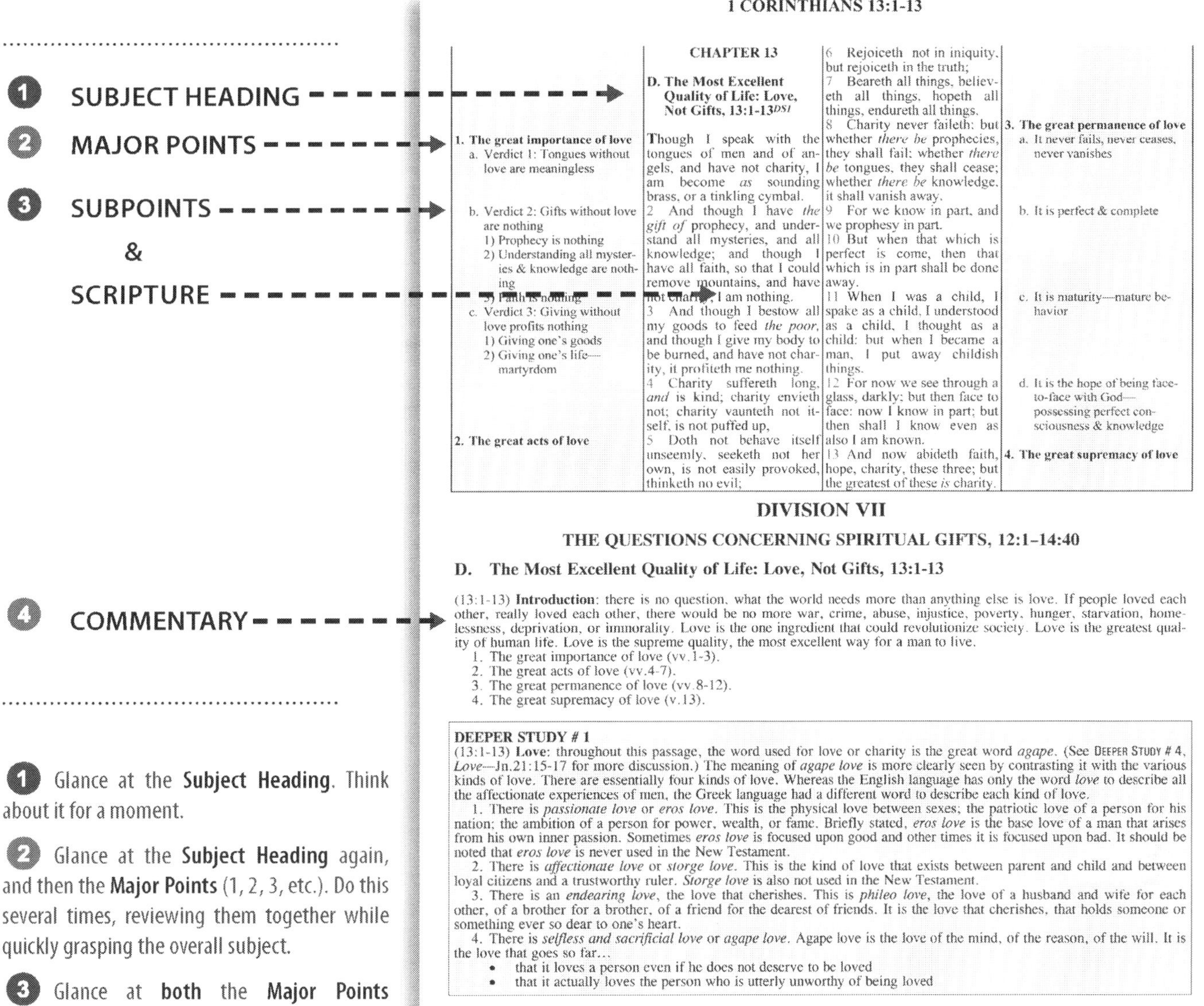

1 CORINTHIANS 13:1-13

Outline	Scripture	Scripture	Outline
	CHAPTER 13 **D. The Most Excellent Quality of Life: Love, Not Gifts, 13:1-13**[DS1]	6 Rejoiceth not in iniquity, but rejoiceth in the truth; 7 Beareth all things, believeth all things, hopeth all things, endureth all things.	
1. The great importance of love a. Verdict 1: Tongues without love are meaningless	Though I speak with the tongues of men and of angels, and have not charity, I am become *as* sounding brass, or a tinkling cymbal.	8 Charity never faileth: but whether *there be* prophecies, they shall fail; whether *there be* tongues, they shall cease; whether *there be* knowledge, it shall vanish away.	**3. The great permanence of love** a. It never fails, never ceases, never vanishes
b. Verdict 2: Gifts without love are nothing 1) Prophecy is nothing 2) Understanding all mysteries & knowledge are nothing 3) Faith is nothing	2 And though I have *the gift of* prophecy, and understand all mysteries, and all knowledge; and though I have all faith, so that I could remove mountains, and have not charity, I am nothing.	9 For we know in part, and we prophesy in part. 10 But when that which is perfect is come, then that which is in part shall be done away.	b. It is perfect & complete
c. Verdict 3: Giving without love profits nothing 1) Giving one's goods 2) Giving one's life—martyrdom	3 And though I bestow all my goods to feed *the poor*, and though I give my body to be burned, and have not charity, it profiteth me nothing.	11 When I was a child, I spake as a child, I understood as a child, I thought as a child: but when I became a man, I put away childish things.	c. It is maturity—mature behavior
2. The great acts of love	4 Charity suffereth long, *and* is kind; charity envieth not; charity vaunteth not itself, is not puffed up, 5 Doth not behave itself unseemly, seeketh not her own, is not easily provoked, thinketh no evil;	12 For now we see through a glass, darkly; but then face to face: now I know in part; but then shall I know even as also I am known. 13 And now abideth faith, hope, charity, these three; but the greatest of these *is* charity.	d. It is the hope of being face-to-face with God—possessing perfect consciousness & knowledge **4. The great supremacy of love**

DIVISION VII

THE QUESTIONS CONCERNING SPIRITUAL GIFTS, 12:1–14:40

D. The Most Excellent Quality of Life: Love, Not Gifts, 13:1-13

(13:1-13) **Introduction**: there is no question, what the world needs more than anything else is love. If people loved each other, really loved each other, there would be no more war, crime, abuse, injustice, poverty, hunger, starvation, homelessness, deprivation, or immorality. Love is the one ingredient that could revolutionize society. Love is the greatest quality of human life. Love is the supreme quality, the most excellent way for a man to live.

1. The great importance of love (vv.1-3).
2. The great acts of love (vv.4-7).
3. The great permanence of love (vv.8-12).
4. The great supremacy of love (v.13).

DEEPER STUDY # 1

(13:1-13) **Love**: throughout this passage, the word used for love or charity is the great word *agape*. (See DEEPER STUDY # 4, *Love*—Jn.21:15-17 for more discussion.) The meaning of *agape love* is more clearly seen by contrasting it with the various kinds of love. There are essentially four kinds of love. Whereas the English language has only the word *love* to describe all the affectionate experiences of men, the Greek language had a different word to describe each kind of love.

1. There is *passionate love* or *eros love*. This is the physical love between sexes; the patriotic love of a person for his nation; the ambition of a person for power, wealth, or fame. Briefly stated, *eros love* is the base love of a man that arises from his own inner passion. Sometimes *eros love* is focused upon good and other times it is focused upon bad. It should be noted that *eros love* is never used in the New Testament.

2. There is *affectionate love* or *storge love*. This is the kind of love that exists between parent and child and between loyal citizens and a trustworthy ruler. *Storge love* is also not used in the New Testament.

3. There is an *endearing love*, the love that cherishes. This is *phileo love*, the love of a husband and wife for each other, of a brother for a brother, of a friend for the dearest of friends. It is the love that cherishes, that holds someone or something ever so dear to one's heart.

4. There is *selfless and sacrificial love* or *agape love*. Agape love is the love of the mind, of the reason, of the will. It is the love that goes so far…

- that it loves a person even if he does not deserve to be loved
- that it actually loves the person who is utterly unworthy of being loved

1 Glance at the **Subject Heading**. Think about it for a moment.

2 Glance at the **Subject Heading** again, and then the **Major Points** (1, 2, 3, etc.). Do this several times, reviewing them together while quickly grasping the overall subject.

3 Glance at **both** the **Major Points** and **Subpoints** together while reading the **Scripture**. Do this slower than Step 2. Note how these points sit directly beside the related verse and simply restate what the Scripture is saying—in Outline form.

4 Next read the **Commentary**. Note that the *Major Point Numbers* in the Outline match those in the Commentary. A small raised number (**DS1, DS2, etc.**) at the end of a Subject Heading or Outline Point, directs you to a related **Deeper Study** in the Commentary.

Finally, read the **Thoughts** and **Support Scripture** (not shown).

As you read and re-read, pray that the Holy Spirit will bring to your attention exactly what you should preach and teach. May God bless you richly as you study and teach His Word.

The POSB contains everything you need for sermon preparation:

1. **The Subject Heading** describes the overall theme of the passage, and is located directly above the Scripture (keyed *alphabetically*).
2. **Major Points** are keyed with an outline *number* guiding you to related commentary. Note that the Commentary includes *"Thoughts"* (life application) and abundant Supporting Scriptures.
3. **Subpoints** explain and clarify the Scripture as needed.
4. **Commentary** is fully researched and developed for every point.
   - **Thoughts (in bold)** help apply the Scripture to real life.
   - **Deeper Studies** provide in-depth discussions of key words.

"Woe is unto me, if I preach not the gospel"
(1 Co.9:16)

TABLE OF CONTENTS
1 KINGS

PAGE

THE
FIRST BOOK OF THE KINGS

COMMONLY CALLED
THE THIRD BOOK OF THE KINGS

AUTHOR: Uncertain. There is no direct claim to authorship. However, there is strong evidence that a prophet wrote the Book of *First Kings*.

1. *First Kings* is written from the perspective of a prophet. Time and again the destructive results of an evil life of immorality, wickedness, lawlessness, violence, idolatry, and false worship are seen and warned against. In addition, there is a strong emphasis upon the temple and other religious subjects. The very purpose of the book is to give the Israelites a permanent history of their monarchy, a history of their kings from a *moral and spiritual* perspective. These facts point toward a prophet's having written *First Kings*.

2. *First Kings* was apparently written before the exile of the Southern Kingdom by Babylon. This fact is known because the phrase "to this day" is used repeatedly (1 K.8:8; 9:13, 21; 10:12; 12:19; 2 K.2:22; 8:22; 10:27; 14:7; 16:6; 17:23, 41; 20:17; 21:15). Although some scholars claim that this phrase could have easily been copied from one of the original sources, this seems most unlikely. For if the fact being spoken about was not true in his day, it seems far more logical to think he would have either worded the fact as *past history* or else just omitted the phrase from his record. Thus it seems that the bulk of *First Kings* was written before the exile.

3. The focus of the book is the *moral and spiritual* evaluation of the kings and the ministries of the prophets. Every king is measured against the righteous reign of David to which they should have all aspired. Every king is judged either as righteous or "evil in the sight of the LORD."

4. Jewish tradition actually says that Jeremiah the prophet wrote the book of *Kings*. Jeremiah lived during the days of Josiah and the other kings of Judah up to the destruction of Jerusalem and the Babylonian captivity. Some scholars say that the style of writing is like that in the book of *Jeremiah* and that much of the content of *First Kings* actually sounds like the book of *Jeremiah*. In fact, 2 Kings 24:18–25:30 is the same as Jeremiah 52. However, other scholars claim that the differences in writing styles between *Jeremiah* and *Kings* are significant.

Whatever the case concerning writing styles, Jeremiah was a priest and prophet who had access to the royal records of his day. He was also present and personally involved in the circles of government during the days of Jerusalem's fall. Among all the known persons of his day, he was certainly capable of writing a permanent history of the nation from a moral and spiritual perspective. However, it must be kept in mind that Jeremiah died in Egypt, not in Babylon (Je.43:6-7). Therefore, if he was the author, the historical fact mentioned at the end of *Second Kings* was obviously written and added to the book by someone in Babylon (2 K.25:27-30).

Although the author cannot be known for certain, the Divine Author is clearly known. The Holy Spirit of God *breathed* or *inspired* the great books of *First* and *Second Kings*. Through His inspiration, the Holy Spirit has given to the world a history of the very events God wanted recorded about the kings of Israel and the people they served. A study of these events shows us the great hope we can have in the LORD, for they were written to be both an example and a warning to us.

> **"For whatsoever things were written aforetime were written for our learning, that we through patience and comfort of the scriptures might have hope" (Ro.15:4).**
>
> **"Now all these things happened to them for examples: and they are written for our admonition, upon whom the ends of the world are come" (1 Co.10:11).**

DATE: Some of the book was written before 586 B.C., and the rest was written before 538 B.C. The Babylonian captivity took place in 586 B.C., so the major portion of *Kings* was written before this date, as is indicated by the above-mentioned phrase "to this day."

The return of King Jehoiachin from Babylon, which took place in the 37th year of his imprisonment (c.568 B.C.), is also mentioned. Hence the latter part of *Second Kings* was written sometime later. In determining just when, note that nothing whatsoever is mentioned about the return of the exiles from the Babylonian captivity in 538 B.C. Thus the books of *First* and *Second Kings* were probably written before 586 and 538 B.C.

TO WHOM WRITTEN: The Israelites in particular and the human race in general. *First Kings* was written in a time of civil, moral, and spiritual decline. Political unrest and disunity gripped the people and their leaders. Furthermore, the nation had split asunder, dividing into the Northern Kingdom of Israel and the Southern Kingdom of Judah. *First* and *Second Kings* were written to the Israelites...

- to teach them the utter necessity of building their lives and society upon the LORD and His commandments.
- to warn them of judgment to come unless they repented and returned to the LORD.

PURPOSE: Three purposes can be gleaned from the books of *First* and *Second Kings*:

1. The *Historical Purpose*:
   a. To record a permanent history of Israel's monarchy or kings from a moral, spiritual perspective. Beginning with Solomon and the tragic division of the nation, the author covers all the kings of both the Northern and Southern Kingdoms. He then ends with the utter destruction of Jerusalem and the Babylonian captivity.
   b. To explain the decline and utter destruction of Israel as a nation, pointing out why the people lost the promised land and were exiled, suffering a terrible plight.

c. To turn the Israelites back to the LORD, teaching both leaders and people the importance of building their lives and society upon the LORD. To be successful as a nation and people they must...
- obey God's law, His commandments
- reject all false worship, worshipping the LORD and Him alone
- govern with compassion, executing true justice and righteousness throughout the land

2. The *Doctrinal* or *Spiritual Purpose*:
a. To explain the reason for the plight of the Israelite people and their nation. The author shows that the wickedness of the kings and the people led to the destruction of their nation and the loss of their land, the promised land of God. The rulers and the people committed all forms of immorality, lawlessness, violence, idolatry, and false worship. Consequently, the LORD was left with no choice but to execute judgment upon the people.
b. To teach the importance of obedience to God. In covering the history of the kings, the author points out how obedience to God's law led to God's blessing, but disobedience led to His judgment. If the ruler and the people kept the covenant—their promise to believe and obey the LORD—they would be blessed by God. But if the people broke their covenant (promise), they would be judged and suffer the curses spelled out in the covenant (see outline and notes—Le.26:1-46; De.28:1-68).
c. To give the people hope and assurance that God would fulfill His wonderful promise to David (the Davidic covenant), the promise that David's kingdom would be an eternal kingdom. Despite the apostasy of various rulers and the people and the eventual destruction of the nation, the LORD had always kept His promises. Thus He would fulfill His promise to David, giving an eternal kingdom to those who truly believed and obeyed the LORD. This promise, of course, was to be fulfilled in Christ.
d. To stress the sovereignty of God. The author shows how God works behind the scene of world history. He uses the chain of natural events and the actions of men to bless the obedient and to judge the wicked.

3. The *Christological* or *Christ-Centered Purpose*: To stress the faithfulness of God in continuing the royal line of David despite the unbelief and sin of the people. God was faithful to His promise, the promise of the Davidic covenant (see outline and note—2 S.7:11-17 for more discussion). God was going to continue the dynasty, the royal line of David, just as He had promised. As the New Testament tells us, from the line of David arose the Messiah or Savior of the world. David's kingdom will last forever through the Lord Jesus Christ and the eternal kingdom He has established.

SPECIAL FEATURES:

1. *First* and *Second Kings* are "The Great Books That Were Originally One Book in the Hebrew Scriptures." The two books were known as *The Book of Kings*. However, when the Old Testament was translated into Greek (about 150 B.C.), the four books of *Samuel* and *Kings* were combined to give a complete history of Israel's kings and monarchy (titled *First, Second, Third* and *Fourth Kingdom*). Later, the two books of Samuel were again separated from *First and Second Kings,* which is the way the books are divided in many Bibles today. However, in the Vulgate and Latin Bibles they are called *First*, *Second*, *Third*, and *Fourth Kings*.

2. *First* and *Second Kings* are "The Great Books That Made Use of Other Written Sources in Recording the History of the Kings and the Divided Monarchy." The author used at least these sources:
⇒ *The Book of the Acts of Solomon* (1 K.11:41).
⇒ *The Book of the History of the Kings of Judah* (1 K.14:29; 15:7, 23; 22:45; 2 K.8:23; 12:19; 14:18; 15:6, 36; 16:19; 20:20; 21:17, 25; 23:28; 24:5).
⇒ *The Book of the History of the Kings of Israel* (1 K.15:31; 16:5, 14, 20, 27; 22:39; 2 K.1:18; 10:34; 13:8, 12; 14:15, 28; 15:21).

The author probably used other sources as well, such as the four sources used by the author of *First Chronicles*:
⇒ The court records of King David (1 Chr.27:24).
⇒ The records of Samuel the seer (1 Chr.29:29).
⇒ The records of Nathan the prophet (1 Chr.29:29).
⇒ The records of Gad the seer (1 Chr.29:29).

3. *First* and *Second Kings* are "The Great Books That Give the Official Account of the Monarchy's History, Its Rise to Glory Under Solomon and Its Division and Decline Under Various Kings."
4. *First* and *Second Kings* are "The Great Books That Cover Solomon's Wisdom, Wealth, and Wickedness" (1 K.1-11).
5. *First* and *Second Kings* are "The Great Books That Cover the Division of the Nation" (1 K.12–16).
6. *First* and *Second Kings* are "The Great Books That Lift Up the Reign of David as the Standard by Which All Other Kings Are to Be Measured" (1 K.9:4; 11:4, 6, 33, 38; 14:8; 15:3, 5, 11; 2 K.16:2; 18:3; 22:2).
7. *First* and *Second Kings* are "The Great Books That Stress Prophecy and Its Fulfillment" (2 S.7:13 with 1 K.8:20; 1 K.11:29-39 with 12:15; 1 K.13:1-34 with 2 K.23:16-18; and many others).
8. *First* and *Second Kings* are "The Great Books That Cover the Ministry of Elijah" (1 K.17–19).
9. *First* and *Second Kings* are "The Great Books That Stress the Prophets and Their Ministry."
⇒ Elijah, 1 K.17–19
⇒ Elisha, 2 K.1–13
⇒ Ahijah, 1 K.11:29-40; 14:5-18
⇒ Shemaiah, 1 K.12:22-24
⇒ Micaiah, 1 K.22:8-28
⇒ Jonah, 2 K.14:25
⇒ Isaiah, 2 K.19:1-7, 20-34
⇒ Huldah, 2 K.22:14-20

10. *First* and *Second Kings* are "The Great Books That Cover the Spiritual Erosion of Israel and Judah and the Result of Their Apostasy: The Great Captivity and Exile" (1 K.20–2 K.25).

11. *First* and *Second Kings* are "The Great Books That Stress the People's Disobedience to God—and Their Insane Rush to the Inevitable Judgment of Utter Destruction."

12. *First* and *Second Kings* are "The Great Books That Show That Society Reaps What It Sows." As long as the people of Israel lived righteous lives, obeying the commandments of God and worshipping God alone, they were successful. They were blessed more and more by God. But when the people committed sin and continued on in their sin, they stepped ever closer to the day when they would face the judgment of God (1 K.2:3; 8:33-34; 9:6-7).

13. *First* and *Second Kings* are "The Great Books That Teach a Necessary Truth: We Must Base Our Lives, Government, and Society upon the Word of God" (1 K.3:14; 6:12; 8:61; 11:38; 18:26; 21:26).

14. *First* and *Second Kings* are "The Great Books That Show the Faithfulness of God." Even when the people of Israel were not faithful to God, God was faithful to continue the royal line of David. And through the royal line of David, God sent His Son into the world. Jesus Christ is the promised Son of David, the King of kings and LORD of lords, the Messiah and Savior of the world (1 K.9:5; Mt.1:20; Re.22:16).

Timeline of Kings, Prophets and History*

The United Kingdom		
Bible Ref.	**Kings** (Years Reigned)	**Prophets**
		Samuel (1095–1015)
1 S.16:1-1 K.2:11; 1 Chr.11:1-30	**David** (40) (1011–971)	**Gad** (1015–950)
		Asaph (1004)
1 K.2:12-11:43; 1 Chr.28:1-2 Chr.9:31	**Solomon** (40) (971–931)	**Nathan** (1003–931) **Heman** (971)

The Divided Kingdom					
Southern Kingdom of Judah			Northern Kingdom of Israel		
Bible Ref.	**Kings** (Years Reigned)	**Prophets**	**Bible Ref.**	**Kings** (Years Reigned)	**Prophets**
1 K.12:1-24; 14:21-31; 2 Chr.9:31-12:16	**Rehoboam** (17) (931–913)		1 K.12:1-24; 12:25-14:20; 2 Chr.10:1-16	**Jeroboam I** (22) (931–910)	**Ahijah** (931–910)
1 K.15:1-8; 2 Chr.12:16-14:1	**Abijah** (3) (913–911)				**Man from Judah** (930)
1 K.15:9-24; 2 Chr.14:1-16:14	**Asa** (3) (911–870)		1 K.15:25-31	**Nadab** (2) (910–909)	**Shemaiah** (927)
		Iddo (910)	1 K.15:16-16:7; 2 Chr.16:1-6	**Baasha** (24) (909–886)	**Jehu** (886)
		Azariah (896)	1 K.16:6-14	**Elah** (2) (886–885)	
			1 K.16:9-20	**Zimri** (7 days) (885)	**Hanani** (870)
			1 K.16:21-28	**Omri** (12) (885–874)	
1 K.22:41-50; 2 K.3:6-14; 2 Chr.17:1-21:1	**Jehoshaphat** (25) (873–848)		1 K.16:28-22:40; 2 Chr.18:1-34	**Ahab** (22) (874–853)	**Elijah** (860–845)
			1 K.22:49-51; 2 K. 1:1-18; 2 Chr.20:35-37; 22:1-11	**Ahaziah** (2) (853–852)	**Micaiah** (853)
2 K.8:16-24; 2 Chr.21:1-20	**Jehoram** (8) (853–841)		2 K.1:17; 3:1-8:15	**Joram/Jehoram** (12) (852–841)	**Elisha** (850–795)
2 K.8:25-29; 9:27-29; 2 Chr.22:1-10	**Ahaziah** (2) (841)	**Obadiah** (845)			**Eliezer** (849–48)
2 K.11:1-16; 2 Chr.22:10-23:21	**Athaliah** (7) (841–835)		2 K.9:1-10:36; 2 Chr.22:7-9	**Jehu** (28) (841–814)	
2 K.11:17-12:21; 2 Chr.22:11-12; 24:1-27	**Joash/Jehoash** (40) (835–796)	**Joel** (830)	2 K.13:1-9	**Jehoahaz** (17) (814–798)	
2 K.14:1-20; 2 Chr.24:27-25:28	**Amaziah** (29) (796–767)		2 K.13:9-25; 14:8-16	**Jehoash** (16) (798–782)	**Zechariah** (797)
			2 K.14:23-29	**Jeroboam II** (41) (793–753)	**Jonah** (780–765)
2 K.14:21-22; 15:1-7; 2 Chr.26:1-23	**Azariah/Uzziah** (52) (792–740)				**Amos** (750)
		Hosea (788-723)	2 K.15:8-12	**Zechariah** (6 mos) (753)	
		Jonah (780-765)	2 K.15:13-15	**Shallum** (1 mo) (752)	
2 K.15:32-38; 2 Chr.26:23-27:9	**Jotham** (16) (750–731)		2.K.15:16-22	**Menahem** (10) (752–742)	

Date	History	
BC	**Foreign Kings**	**World Events**
1000		**David captures Jerusalem** (1004)
	Ashur-Rabi II (1010–970) *(Assyria)*	
	Hiram (1003–966) *(Tyre)*	**Foundation for the Temple** (966)
950	**Tiglath-Pileser II** (960–935) *(Assyria)*	**22nd Egyptian Dynasty** (945)
930		**Kingdom Divided** (930)
	Shishak I (945–924) *(Egypt)*	
		Assyria makes peace with Babylon (915)
900	**Ben-Hadad I** (900) *(Syria)*	**Jehoshaphat leads a revival** (865)
	Eth-Baal (887–856) *(Sidon)*	**Elijah's contest with prophets of Baal** (857)
		Elijah's mantle passed to Elisha (845)
850		
	Hazael (840) *(Syria)*	
		Carthage established (814)
		Joash repairs Temple (812)
800	**Ben-Hadad II** (798) *(Syria)*	**23rd Egyptian dynasty** (800)
	Ben-Hadad III (773) *(Syria)*	**Olympic games begin** (776)
		Rome founded (753)
750	**Rezin** (750) *(Syria)*	**Babylonian and Chinese calendar** (750)

The Divided Kingdom

Southern Kingdom of Judah			Northern Kingdom of Israel			Date	History	
Bible Ref.	**Kings** (Years Reigned)	**Prophets**	**Bible Ref.**	**Kings** (Years Reigned)	**Prophets**	**BC**	**Foreign Kings**	**World Events**
			2 K.15:23-26	**Pekahiah** (2) (742–740)			**Tiglath-Pil[n]eser III [or Pul]** (745–727) *(Assyria)*	**Assyria takes control of Northern Kingdom** (745–627)
		Isaiah (740–690)	2 K.15:27-31	**Pekah** (20) (752–732) . (752–740) (ruled only in Gile-ad) (740–732) (ruled in Samaria)			**Shalmaneser V** (727–722) *(Assyria)*	**Assyria invades Northern Israel** (732)
2 K.15:38-16:20; 2 Chr.27:9-27; Is.7:1-9:1	**Ahaz** (16) (735–715)	**Micah** (735–725) **Oded** (733)	2 K.17:1-23	**Hoshea** (9) (732–722)			**So** (727–716) *(Egypt)* **Sargon II** (710–705) *(Assyria)*	**Fall of Northern Kingdom** (722)
2 K.18:1-20:21; 2 Chr.28:27-32:33; Pr.25:1; Is.36:1-39:8	**Hezekiah** (29) (729–686)					**700**	**Sennacherib** (705–681) *(Assyria)* **Merodach-Baladan** (721–710, 705–704) *(Assyria)*	**Sennacherib defeats Egypt** (701) **Hezekiah's tunnel** (701)
2 K.20:21-21:18; 2 Chr.32:33-33:20	**Manasseh** (55) (696–642)	**Nahum** (663–612)					**Tirhakah** (690–664) *(Egypt)*	**185,000 Assyrians killed by God** (701)
2 K.21:18-26; 2 Chr.33:20-25	**Amon** (2) (642–640)					**650**	**Esarhaddon** (681–669) *(Assyria)*	**Sennacherib destroys Babylon** (689)
2 K.21:26-23:30; 2 Chr.33:25-35:27	**Josiah** (31) (640–609)	**Zephaniah** (640–609)					**Nabopolassar** (626–605) *(Assyria)*	**Josiah's reform** (621) **Nineveh destroyed** (612)
2 K.23:31-33; 2 Chr.36:1-4	**Jehoaz/Jehoahaz** (3 mos) (609)	**Jeremiah** (627–562)					**Neco** (610–595) *(Egypt)*	**Battle of Carchemish** (605) **1st group of exiles from Judah tak-en to Babylon** (605)
2 K.23:34-24:7; 2 Chr.36:5-8	**Jehoiakim** (11) (608–598)	**Habakkuk** (615–598)				**600**	**Nebuchadnezzar II** (605–562) *(Babylon)*	
2 K.24:8-17; 25:27-30; 2 Chr.36:8-10;	**Jehoiachin** (3 mos) (598–597)	**Daniel** (605–535)						2nd group of exiles from Judah taken to Babylon (597)
2 K.24:18-25:21; 2 Chr.36:10-14; Je.21:1-52:11	**Zedekiah/Mattaniah (11)** (597–586)	**Ezekiel** (593–571)					**Evil-Merodach** (562–560) *(Babylon)*	**Fall of Judah—Third group of ex-iles from Judah taken to Babylon** (586)
2 K.25:22-26; Je.40:5-41:18	**Gedaliah** (2 mos) (Appointed by Nebuchadnezzar) (586)					**550**	**Cyrus II** (559–530) *(Medo-Persia)*	**Fall of Babylon to Medo-Persian Empire** (539)
							Belshazzar (552–539) *(Babylon)*	**Cyrus II decrees that the Jews may return to the Holy Land** (538) **1st exiles return to Holy Land with Zerubbabel** (537)
		Haggai (520) **Zechariah** (520–518)						**1st Temple foundation laid** (536) **2nd Temple foundation laid** (520)
						500	**Darius I** (521–486) *(Medo-Persia)*	Temple completed (516) Republic of Rome est. (509)
								2nd return under Ezra (458)
		Malachi (430)				**450**	**Artaxerxes** (465–425) *(Persia)*	**3rd return under Nehemiah** (445)

The resources used for the Timeline in addition to the *Bible* are as follows:
[1] Archer, Gleason L. *Encyclopedia of Bible Difficulties*. (Grand Rapids, Michigan: Zondervan Publishing House), 1982.
[2] Freedman, David Noel, ed., et. al. *The Anchor Bible Dictionary*. (New York: Doubleday), 1992.
[3] Grun, Bernard. *The Timetables of History*. 3rd ed. (New York: Simon & Schuster), 1991.
[4] Kaiser, Walter C. *A History of Israel*. (Nashville, Tennessee: Broadman & Holman Publishers), 1998.
[5] Silverman, David P., ed. *Ancient Egypt*. (New York: Oxford University Press), 1997.

*Some dates are approximate.

1 KINGS

The Preacher's Outline and Sermon Bible® is unique. It differs from all other Study Bibles and Sermon Resource Materials in that every Passage and Subject is outlined right beside the Scripture. When you choose any *Subject* below and turn to the reference, you have not only the Scripture but also an outline of the Scripture and Subject *already prepared for you—verse by verse.*

For a quick example, choose one of the subjects below and turn over to the Scripture; you will find this to be a marvelous help for more *organized* and *streamlined* study.

In addition, every point of the Scripture and Subject is *fully developed in a Commentary with supporting Scripture* at the end of each point. Again, this arrangement makes sermon preparation much simpler and more efficient.

Note something else: the Subjects of *First Kings* have titles that are both Biblical and *practical.* The practical titles are often more appealing to people. This benefit is clearly seen for use on billboards, bulletins, church newsletters, etc.

A suggestion: for the *quickest* overview of *First Kings*, first read all the Division titles (I, II, III, etc.), then come back and read the individual outline titles.

Outline Of 1 Kings

Part One: The United Kingdom 1:1–11:43

I. The Rise and Reign of Solomon As King: Beginning in Glory and Ending in Shame, 1:1-11:43

A. The Plot of Adonijah and the Succession of Solomon to the Throne: A Picture of Rebellion and Mercy, 1:1-53
B. The Death of David and the Consolidation of Solomon's Power: A Picture of Death and of Justice, 2:1-46
C. The Request for Wisdom by Solomon and His Wise Justice: A Lesson on Wisdom and Discernment, 3:1-28
D. The Government or Political Administration of Solomon: A Picture of Capable Leaders, 4:1-34
E. The Preparations for Building the Temple: Making the Commitment to Build a Place of Worship, 5:1-18
F. The Building of the Temple: A Lesson on the Living Temple, the Believer in Whom God's Spirit Dwells, 6:1-38
G. The Palace Complex of Solomon and the Temple Furnishings: Being Diligent to Put God First, 7:1-51
H. The Dedication of the Temple (Part 1)—Solomon's Placement of the Ark in the Temple and His Message: A Picture of God's Presence and His Faithfulness, 8:1-21
I. The Dedication of the Temple (Part 2)—Solomon's Prayer of Dedication: A Picture of the Temple As the "House of Prayer," 8:22-53
J. The Dedication of the Temple (Part 3)—Solomon's Benediction: A Challenge for Obedience and Total Commitment, 8:54-66
K. The Second Appearance of God to Solomon and Solomon's Achievements: A Need to Be Obedient and Diligent in Life and Work, 9:1-28
L. The Wisdom, Wealth, and Power of Solomon: A Picture of Seeking Truth and of Being Materially Blessed by God, 10:1-29
M. The Shocking Decline and Death of Solomon: The Tragic Consequences of Extravagance, Shameful Indulgence, and Compromise, 11:1-43

Part Two: The Divided Kingdom 12:1–22:53

II. The Early History of the Divided Kingdom: Witnessing the Awful Rise of Idolatry and False Worship, 12:1–16:34

A. The Division of the Kingdom: A Picture of Arrogance and of God's Sovereign Judgment, 12:1-24
B. The Reign of Jeroboam I in Israel (Part 1): A Picture of Being a Stumbling Block to Others, 12:25–13:34
C. The Reign of Jeroboam I in Israel (Part 2): A Prophecy of God's Judgment, 14:1-20
D. The Reign of Rehoboam in Judah: A Sad, Detestable Life, 14:21-31
E. The Reign of Two Kings in Judah, Abijah (Abijam) and Asa, Father and Son: A Son Who Refused to Walk in the Evil Steps of His Father, 15:1-24
F. The Reign of Six Kings in Israel, from Nadab to Ahab: A Downward Spiral of Sin and Destruction, 15:25–16:34

III. The Ministry of Elijah and Other Prophets During the Reign of Ahab: Learning Who the Living and True God Is, 17:1–22:53

A. The Drought Predicted by Elijah: Judgment Due to Idolatry and False Worship, 17:1-24
B. The End of the Drought After Elijah's Contest with the Prophets of Baal: Proving Who the True and Living God Is, 18:1-46
C. The Escape of Elijah from Jezebel: Being Saved by the Living God from Disappointment, Discouragement, and Despair, 19:1-21
D. The Defeat of Syria or Aram by Ahab: Learning That the LORD Alone Is God, 20:1-43
E. The Terrible Crimes Against Naboth by Ahab and Jezebel: Facing Judgment Due to Horrible Evil, 21:1-29
F. The Death of Ahab: Proving the Surety of God's Judgment, 22:1-40
G. The Reigns of Jehoshaphat in Judah and Ahaziah in Israel: Learning the Importance of Parental Influence, 22:41-53

PART ONE: THE UNITED KINGDOM 1:1–11:43

DIVISION I

THE RISE AND REIGN OF SOLOMON AS KING: BEGINNING IN GLORY AND ENDING IN SHAME, 1:1–11:43

(1:1–11:43) **DIVISION OVERVIEW**: flowing from *Second Samuel*, *First Kings* continues the history of Israel's monarchy, the rule of the kings. There is a natural flow from *Second Samuel* into *First Kings*, from the reign of David to the rule of his son Solomon. *First Kings* opens with David still on the throne, but he is aged and critically ill. His health is rapidly declining. The transition of power to Solomon takes place, but it is far from smooth. Solomon's older brother Adonijah launches a plot to seize the throne; but before David dies, he is able to rally his strength enough to counter the plot and to make absolutely certain that Solomon is crowned king (ch.1).

After Solomon consolidated his power, the very first thing he did was seek the LORD for wisdom. Graciously, the LORD heard Solomon's prayer and flooded him with a spirit of unparalleled wisdom and discernment. Throughout the early years of his reign, Solomon used his God-given wisdom for good. He served the people...

- by making wise decisions and executing justice (ch.3)
- by structuring a strong political administration and government (ch.4)
- by making thorough preparations for building the temple and the palace complex and completing the construction of both, as well as the temple furnishings (chapters 5–7)
- by establishing worship within the temple and by challenging the people to be faithful in worshipping and serving the LORD (ch.8)
- by continuing to personally seek the LORD (9:1-9)
- by continuing to strengthen the nation economically, militarily, spiritually until Israel became one of the most powerful nations in the world, a fact acknowledged by the Queen of Sheba (9:10–10:29)

However, in the latter years of his life Solomon began to decline spiritually. Luxury and pleasure became his downfall. The LORD had blessed Solomon beyond measure, and he had achieved the summit of power and wealth, fame and influence. But shockingly, the end of his life took a tragic turn. During his adult life, luxury and pleasure gradually began to eat away at Solomon's character and commitment to the LORD. Sadly, by the end of his life he had turned away from serving the LORD and the people. He began to severely oppress the people through taxation and a compulsory draft into government service. Failing to persevere to the end, he forsook the LORD and gave himself up to a life of luxury, indulgence, immorality, and false worship. Having begun his life in glory, he ended it in shame.

THE RISE AND REIGN OF SOLOMON AS KING: BEGINNING IN GLORY AND ENDING IN SHAME, 1:1–11:43

A. The Plot of Adonijah and the Succession of Solomon to the Throne: A Picture of Rebellion and Mercy, 1:1-53

B. The Death of David and the Consolidation of Solomon's Power: A Picture of Death and of Justice, 2:1-46

C. The Request for Wisdom by Solomon and His Wise Justice: A Lesson on Wisdom and Discernment, 3:1-28

D. The Government or Political Administration of Solomon: A Picture of Capable Leaders, 4:1-34

E. The Preparations for Building the Temple: Making the Commitment to Build a Place of Worship, 5:1-18

DIVISION I
1:1–11:43

F. The Building of the Temple: A Lesson on the Living Temple, the Believer in Whom God's Spirit Dwells, 6:1-38

G. The Palace Complex of Solomon and the Temple Furnishings: Being Diligent to Put God First, 7:1-51

H. The Dedication of the Temple (Part 1)—Solomon's Placement of the Ark in the Temple and His Message: A Picture of God's Presence and His Faithfulness, 8:1-21

I. The Dedication of the Temple (Part 2)—Solomon's Prayer of Dedication: A Picture of the Temple As the "House of Prayer," 8:22-53

J. The Dedication of the Temple (Part 3)—Solomon's Benediction: A Challenge for Obedience and Total Commitment, 8:54-66

K. The Second Appearance of God to Solomon and Solomon's Achievements: A Need to Be Obedient and Diligent in Life and Work, 9:1-28

L. The Wisdom, Wealth, and Power of Solomon: A Picture of Seeking Truth and of Being Materially Blessed by God, 10:1-29

M. The Shocking Decline and Death of Solomon: The Tragic Consequences of Extravagance, Shameful Indulgence, and Compromise, 11:1-43

THE
FIRST BOOK OF THE KINGS

COMMONLY CALLED

THE THIRD BOOK OF THE KINGS

CHAPTER 1

PART I
THE UNITED KINGDOM
1:1–11:43

I. THE RISE & REIGN OF SOLOMON AS KING: BEGINNING IN GLORY & ENDING IN SHAME, 1:1–11:43

A. The Plot of Adonijah & the Succession of Solomon to the Throne: A Picture of Rebellion & Mercy, 1:1-53

1:28-53; see 1 Chr.29:21-25

1. The plot of Adonijah to become king: An act of pride, arrogance, & self-exaltation
- a. The reasons for Adonijah's plot
  - 1) David's health declined: He could not keep warm
    - His advisors suggested a common medical custom: To find a young virgin who could nurse David & lie next to him for body warmth
    - His advisors found Abishag, a beautiful Shunammite girl: She took care of David, but he was so weak he could not have sexual relations with her
  - 2) Adonijah was self-centered & exalted himself
  - 3) Adonijah had been spoiled (parental indulgence)
  - 4) Adonijah was handsome & charismatic
  - 5) Adonijah was the royal prince, next in line to be king
  - 6) Adonijah was supported by some powerful leaders
    - Joab, the army commander
    - Abiathar, the High Priest
- b. The opposition to Adonijah's plot

Now king David was old *and*
stricken in years; and they
covered him with clothes, but
he gat no heat.
2 Wherefore his servants
said unto him, Let there be
sought for my lord the king a
young virgin: and let her
stand before the king, and let
her cherish him, and let her
lie in thy bosom, that my lord
the king may get heat.
3 So they sought for a fair
damsel throughout all the
coasts of Israel, and found
Abishag a Shunammite, and
brought her to the king.
4 And the damsel *was* very
fair, and cherished the king,
and ministered to him: but
the king knew her not.
5 Then Adonijah the son of
Haggith exalted himself, saying,
I will be king: and he
prepared him chariots and
horsemen, and fifty men to
run before him.
6 And his father had not
displeased him at any time
in saying, Why hast thou
done so? and he also *was a*
very goodly *man;* and *his
mother* bare him after Absalom.
7 And he conferred with
Joab the son of Zeruiah, and
with Abiathar the priest: and
they following Adonijah
helped *him.*
8 But Zadok the priest, and
Benaiah the son of Jehoiada,
and Nathan the prophet, and
Shimei, and Rei, and the
mighty men which *belonged*
to David, were not with
Adonijah.
9 And Adonijah slew sheep
and oxen and fat cattle by the
stone of Zoheleth, which *is*
by En-rogel, and called all
his brethren the king's sons,
and all the men of Judah the
king's servants:
10 But Nathan the prophet,
and Benaiah, and the mighty
men, and Solomon his brother,
he called not.
11 Wherefore Nathan spake
unto Bath-sheba the mother
of Solomon, saying, Hast
thou not heard that Adonijah
the son of Haggith doth
reign, and David our lord
knoweth *it* not?
12 Now therefore come, let
me, I pray thee, give thee
counsel, that thou mayest
save thine own life, and the
life of thy son Solomon.
13 Go and get thee in unto
king David, and say unto
him, Didst not thou, my lord,
O king, swear unto thine
handmaid, saying, Assuredly
Solomon thy son shall reign
after me, and he shall sit upon
my throne? why then doth
Adonijah reign?
14 Behold, while thou yet
talkest there with the king, I
also will come in after thee,
and confirm thy words.
15 And Bath-sheba went in
unto the king into the chamber:
and the king was very
old; and Abishag the Shunammite
ministered unto the
king.
16 And Bath-sheba bowed,
and did obeisance unto the
king. And the king said,
What wouldest thou?
17 And she said unto him,
My lord, thou swarest by the
LORD thy God unto thine
handmaid, *saying,* Assuredly
Solomon thy son shall reign
after me, and he shall sit upon
my throne.
18 And now, behold, Adonijah
reigneth; and now, my lord
the king, thou knowest *it* not:
19 And he hath slain oxen
and fat cattle and sheep in
abundance, and hath called
Abiathar the priest, and Joab
the captain of the host: but

- c. The strategy of Adonijah
  - 1) He invited both the royal officials & the king's sons to a great feast
  - 2) His purpose: To unite the group to support his claim
  - 3) He did not invite the opposition

2. The counterplan of Nathan & Bathsheba to have Solomon crowned king: A willingness to work out God's will no matter the cost
- a. Nathan warned Bathsheba of Adonijah's plot & advised her
  - 1) That she & Solomon were in danger of being assassinated
  - 2) That she go before David to remind him of two facts
    - That he had sworn an oath that Solomon would be his successor, 2 S.12:24-25; 1 Chr. 22:8-10; 28:3-7
    - That Adonijah was plotting to take over the throne—immediately
  - 3) That he, Nathan, would confirm her story
- b. Bathsheba warned the bedridden David of Adonijah's plot
  - 1) She showed respect for David: Bowed & knelt before him
  - 2) She reminded David of his sworn oath: Solomon would be appointed king, the successor to the throne
  - 3) She warned David that Adonijah was plotting insurrection
    - Adonijah was holding a feast at that very moment—to mobilize support
    - Abiathar & Joab were supporting Adonijah's plot

4) She informed David that all Israel was excitedly waiting for him to appoint his successor

5) She appealed to David, stating that hers & Solomon's lives were at risk when he died—unless he acted quickly

c. Nathan entered the king's presence & confirmed Bathsheba's report

1) He showed the proper respect: Bowed

2) He asked David if he had appointed Adonijah king

- That Adonijah was holding a coronation feast at that very moment
- That he had invited all the king's sons, military leaders, & Abiathar the priest: They all were proclaiming him king

3) He informed David that he, Zadok, Benaiah, & Solomon had not been invited to the feast: Their lives were in danger

4) He again asked if David had acted alone in appointing Adonijah—without informing his closest advisors

3. The decisive command of King David that Solomon would indeed be king: An example of keeping oaths, one's word

a. David summoned Bathsheba & restated his sworn oath

1) David would carry out his promise that very day: Solomon would be immediately installed as king, 2 S.12:24-25; 1 Chr.22:9-10; 28:4-7

2) Bathsheba humbled herself & expressed the hope

Solomon thy servant hath he
not called.
20 And thou, my lord, O
king, the eyes of all Israel *are*
upon thee, that thou shouldest tell them who shall sit on
the throne of my lord the
king after him.
21 Otherwise it shall come to
pass, when my lord the
king shall sleep with his fathers, that I and my son Solomon shall be counted of-
fenders.
22 And, lo, while she yet
talked with the king, Nathan
the prophet also came in.
23 And they told the king,
saying, Behold Nathan the
prophet. And when he was
come in before the king, he
bowed himself before the
king with his face to the
ground.
24 And Nathan said, My
lord, O king, hast thou said,
Adonijah shall reign after
me, and he shall sit upon my
throne?
25 For he is gone down this
day, and hath slain oxen and
fat cattle and sheep in abundance, and hath called all the
king's sons, and the captains
of the host, and Abiathar the
priest; and, behold, they eat
and drink before him, and
say, God save king Adonijah.
26 But me, *even* me thy
servant, and Zadok the priest,
and Benaiah the son of Jehoiada, and thy servant Solomon, hath he not called.
27 Is this thing done by my
lord the king, and thou hast
not showed *it* unto thy servant, who should sit on the
throne of my lord the king after him?
28 Then king David an-
swered and said, Call me
Bath-sheba. And she came
into the king's presence, and
stood before the king.
29 And the king sware, and
said, *As* the LORD liveth, that
hath redeemed my soul out of
all distress,
30 Even as I sware unto thee
by the LORD God of Israel,
saying, Assuredly Solomon
thy son shall reign after me,
and he shall sit upon my
throne in my stead; even so
will I certainly do this day.
31 Then Bath-sheba bowed
with *her* face to the earth, and
did reverence to the king, and
said, Let my lord king David
live for ever.
32 And king David said,
Call me Zadok the priest, and
Nathan the prophet, and
Benaiah the son of Jehoiada.
And they came before the
king.
33 The king also said unto
them, Take with you the servants of your lord, and cause
Solomon my son to ride upon
mine own mule, and bring
him down to Gihon:
34 And let Zadok the priest
and Nathan the prophet
anoint him there king over Israel: and blow ye with the
trumpet, and say, God save
king Solomon.
35 Then ye shall come up after him, that he may come
and sit upon my throne; for
he shall be king in my stead:
and I have appointed him to
be ruler over Israel and over
Judah.
36 And Benaiah the son of
Jehoiada answered the king,
and said, Amen: the LORD
God of my lord the king say
so *too*.
37 As the LORD hath been
with my lord the king, even
so be he with Solomon, and
make his throne greater than
the throne of my lord king
David.
38 So Zadok the priest, and
Nathan the prophet, and
Benaiah the son of Jehoiada,
and the Cherethites, and the
Pelethites, went down, and
caused Solomon to ride upon
king David's mule, and
brought him to Gihon.
39 And Zadok the priest
took an horn of oil out of the
tabernacle, and anointed Solomon. And they blew the
trumpet; and all the people
said, God save king Solo-
mon.
40 And all the people came
up after him, and the people
piped with pipes, and re-
joiced with great joy, so that
the earth rent with the sound
of them.
41 And Adonijah and all the
guests that *were* with him
heard *it* as they had made an
end of eating. And when Joab
heard the sound of the trumpet, he said, Wherefore *is this*
noise of the city being in an

that David's kingdom would never end

b. David summoned the leaders he could depend upon & gave them clear, forceful instructions

1) They were to set Solomon on David's mule & go down to Gihon to publicly show that he was the designated king

2) They were to anoint Solomon as king

3) They were to sound the trumpet: Call the people together & proclaim him king

4) They were to place him on the throne as king, to begin his rule immediately: To reign as co-regent until David's death

c. David acted decisively & was strongly supported by the military commander, Benaiah

1) He prayed for God to decree it

2) He prayed God to be with Solomon: To make his kingdom even greater than David's

4. The climactic anointing of Solomon as king: A type of Christ, the Anointed Son of David

a. The officials placed Solomon on David's mule: Escorted him to Gihon, a site of major water supply & a public meeting place

b. The priest Zadok anointed Solomon as king before the people

c. The officials sounded the trumpet

d. The people rejoiced over the coronation

1) Followed Solomon & the officials back to the palace shouting for joy

2) Made so much noise the ground shook

e. The prince Adonijah & his guests heard the uproar & commotion off in the distance

f. The coronation of Solomon was immediately reported to Adonijah, that all the steps of installation had already taken place
   1) That King David himself had declared Solomon king
   2) That the king's officials had placed Solomon on the king's mule: Publicly demonstrated that Solomon was the designated king
   3) That Zadok had anointed Solomon king
   4) That the people had publicly & enthusiastically accepted the coronation & rejoiced in it
   5) That Solomon had already taken his seat on the royal throne
   6) That the royal officials had already extended their congratulations to David: Asked God to make Solomon's dynasty more famous & even greater than David's rule had been
   7) That the king had expressed his pleasure & rejoiced that he had lived to see Solomon reign

uproar?
42 And while he yet spake,
behold, Jonathan the son of
Abiathar the priest came: and
Adonijah said unto him,
Come in; for thou *art* a valiant man, and bringest good
tidings.
43 And Jonathan answered
and said to Adonijah, Verily
our lord king David hath
made Solomon king.
44 And the king hath sent
with him Zadok the priest,
and Nathan the prophet, and
Benaiah the son of Jehoiada,
and the Cherethites, and the
Pelethites, and they have
caused him to ride upon the
king's mule:
45 And Zadok the priest and
Nathan the prophet have
anointed him king in Gihon:
and they are come up from
thence rejoicing, so that the
city rang again. This is the
noise that ye have heard.
46 And also Solomon sitteth
on the throne of the kingdom.
47 And moreover the king's
servants came to bless our
lord king David, saying, God
make the name of Solomon
better than thy name, and
make his throne greater than
thy throne. And the king
bowed himself upon the bed.
48 And also thus said the
king, Blessed *be* the LORD
God of Israel, which hath
given *one* to sit on my throne
this day, mine eyes even seeing *it*.
49 And all the guests that
were with Adonijah were
afraid, and rose up, and went
every man his way.
50 And Adonijah feared because of Solomon, and arose,
and went, and caught hold on
the horns of the altar.
51 And it was told Solomon,
saying, Behold, Adonijah
feareth king Solomon: for, lo,
he hath caught hold on the
horns of the altar, saying, Let
king Solomon swear unto
me to day that he will not
slay his servant with the
sword.
52 And Solomon said, If
he will show himself a
worthy man, there shall not
an hair of him fall to the
earth: but if wickedness shall
be found in him, he shall
die.
53 So king Solomon sent,
and they brought him down
from the altar. And he came
and bowed himself to king
Solomon: and Solomon said
unto him, Go to thine house.

g. The plot of Adonijah was crushed
   1) His supporters fled, scattered, fearing for their lives
   2) Adonijah—gripped by fear—fled & grabbed hold of the horns of the altar: An act of seeking mercy & refuge
      • Adonijah's desperate act & plea for mercy was reported to Solomon
      • Solomon expressed a willingness to show mercy: He would place Adonijah on probation

h. The traitorous Adonijah was arrested & shown mercy
   1) Adonijah showed proper respect: He bowed
   2) Solomon sent him home, but on probation, v.52

PART I
THE UNITED KINGDOM
1:1–11:43

DIVISION I

THE RISE AND REIGN OF SOLOMON AS KING: BEGINNING IN GLORY AND ENDING IN SHAME, 1:1–11:43

A. The Plot of Adonijah and the Succession of Solomon to the Throne: A Picture of Rebellion and Mercy, 1:1-53

(1:1-53) **Introduction**: few experiences affect families and society as much as rebellion.

⇒ When a child rebels against a parent, the heart of the parent suffers pain, hurt, and sorrow. Sometimes the parent's heart is pierced, cut to the core, and utterly broken.

⇒ When a worker rebels against an employer, production slows and sometimes stops. Money is lost; contracts are left unfilled, and the company suffers.

⇒ When an employer reacts or rebels against workers, the workers suffer. They lose wages, and sometimes they are demoted or even fired.

⇒ When a person or group of people rebel against a just and righteous government, society always suffers. Often the result is multitudes of hungry, diseased, and exhausted refugees fleeing for their lives.

In the opening scene of this great book of *First Kings*, King David is immediately confronted with a rebellion plotted by his son Adonijah. Knowing that David had designated Solomon to succeed him upon the throne, Adonijah planned a coup or an uprising to seize the throne. And he launched his treason while his father was lying bedridden, presumably unable to personally squelch the revolt against his kingdom. But Adonijah's evaluation was incorrect, for he judged his father by his declining health and not by the strength of his spirit and mind. David was physically weak, but he had not lost his mental sharpness. His mind was obviously as sound as ever. Although bedridden, he was able to direct a counterplan to Adonijah's rebellion. He was able to make sure that Solomon was crowned king. This is the subject of this dramatic, suspenseful passage of Scripture: *The Plot of Adonijah and the Succession of Solomon to the Throne: A Picture of Rebellion and Mercy,* 1:1-53.

1. The plot of Adonijah to become king: an act of pride, arrogance, and self-exaltation (vv.1-10).
2. The counterplan of Nathan and Bathsheba to have Solomon crowned king: a willingness to work out God's will no matter the cost (vv.11-27).
3. The decisive command of King David that Solomon would indeed be king: an example of keeping oaths, one's word (vv.28-37).
4. The climactic anointing of Solomon as king: a type of Christ, the Anointed Son of David (vv.38-53).

1 (1:1-10) **Self-exaltation, Example of—Parents, Indulgence of Children, Example of—Indulgence, by Parents, Example of—Self-centered, Example of—Rebellion, Example of—Coup, Example of—David, Rebellion Against**: there was the plot of Adonijah to become king. His insurrection against his father David is a clear example of self-exaltation, arrogance, and pride. Scripture clearly shows this:

OUTLINE	SCRIPTURE	SCRIPTURE	OUTLINE
1. The plot of Adonijah to become king: An act of pride, arrogance, & self-exaltation a. The reasons for Adonijah's plot 1) David's health declined: He could not keep warm • His advisors suggested a common medical custom: To find a young virgin who could nurse David & lie next to him for body warmth • His advisors found Abishag, a beautiful Shunammite girl: She took care of David, but he was so weak he could not have sexual relations with her 2) Adonijah was self-centered & exalted himself 3) Adonijah had been spoiled	Now king David was old *and* stricken in years; and they covered him with clothes, but he gat no heat. 2 Wherefore his servants said unto him, Let there be sought for my lord the king a young virgin: and let her stand before the king, and let her cherish him, and let her lie in thy bosom, that my lord the king may get heat. 3 So they sought for a fair damsel throughout all the coasts of Israel, and found Abishag a Shunammite, and brought her to the king. 4 And the damsel *was* very fair, and cherished the king, and ministered to him: but the king knew her not. 5 Then Adonijah the son of Haggith exalted himself, saying, I will be king: and he prepared him chariots and horsemen, and fifty men to run before him. 6 And his father had not	displeased him at any time in saying, Why hast thou done so? and he also *was a* very goodly *man;* and *his mother* bare him after Absalom. 7 And he conferred with Joab the son of Zeruiah, and with Abiathar the priest: and they following Adonijah helped *him.* 8 But Zadok the priest, and Benaiah the son of Jehoiada, and Nathan the prophet, and Shimei, and Rei, and the mighty men which *belonged* to David, were not with Adonijah. 9 And Adonijah slew sheep and oxen and fat cattle by the stone of Zoheleth, which *is* by En-rogel, and called all his brethren the king's sons, and all the men of Judah the king's servants: 10 But Nathan the prophet, and Benaiah, and the mighty men, and Solomon his brother, he called not.	(parental indulgence) 4) Adonijah was handsome & charismatic 5) Adonijah was the royal prince, next in line to be king 6) Adonijah was supported by some powerful leaders • Joab, the army commander • Abiathar, the High Priest b. The opposition to Adonijah's plot c. The strategy of Adonijah 1) He invited both the royal officials & the king's sons to a great feast 2) His purpose: To unite the group to support his claim 3) He did not invite the opposition

a. Six factors encouraged Adonijah to rebel and seek the throne of his father.

1) Adonijah was encouraged to seize the throne because of David's declining health (vv.1-4). David was now about 70 years old (2 S.5:4-5) and his physical condition had become extremely weakened. Apparently his circulation was poor, so poor that he was not able to keep warm even when he was covered with blankets. The rigors and hardship of war, the strain and stress of rule and of facing so many crises down through the years had taken their toll upon David's body. Remember, the LORD had chosen David to be a warrior, to spend his life conquering the enemies of Israel and bringing peace to the nation. In addition to the rigors of war and the stress of ruling the nation, David had suffered a series of disasters in his own personal life as well as that of his family. The disasters included:[1]

⇒ his adultery with Bathsheba
⇒ his murder of Uriah, Bathsheba's husband
⇒ his son Amnon's rape of his half-sister Tamar
⇒ his son Amnon's murder by his other son Absalom, Tamar's full brother
⇒ his son Absalom's revolt
⇒ his unwise census with the resulting chastisement of God's plague upon the nation
⇒ his facing a second revolt by Shibni

1 Richard D. Patterson and Hermann J. Austel. *1, 2 Kings.* "The Expositor's Bible Commentary," Vol.4. (Grand Rapids, MI: Zondervan Publishing House, 1988), p.25.

Add to the strain of all these hardships the seven-plus years of living as a fugitive from the government, being fiercely pursued by King Saul. Few people are ever called upon to suffer as much strain and stress as David was. And the pressure and anxiety took their toll upon him physically, wearing him down and weakening his body. To help him, his advisors suggested a common medical custom of that day: to find a young virgin who could nurse him and lie next to him for body warmth (v.2). Josephus (AD 37-100?), the famous Jewish historian, and Galen (AD 130-200?), a Greek physician, both state that this was a common medical custom of that day.[2] Searching throughout the nation, the advisors found a beautiful young lady named Abishag. They brought her to King David, and she took care of the king as one of his concubines. Note that David was so weak that he was unable to have sexual relations with her. This fact stresses his rapidly declining health.

Standing in the wings of the palace, Adonijah took note of his father's declining health, that he was physically an invalid who could no longer defend himself. Knowing that someone would soon be crowned the new king of Israel, Adonijah was encouraged to make his move to seize the throne.

2) His father's declining health was not the only factor that drove the crown prince Adonijah to plot against the throne. The prince was a self-centered, arrogant, prideful person. He was a man who honored and elevated himself above others (v.5). Scripture clearly says that he exalted himself, made a deliberate decision to seize the throne. He emphatically declared, "I will be king" (v.5). Note that Adonijah acted like a king before he was king. He secured chariots and horses and fifty bodyguards to run ahead of him when he traveled throughout the land and the capital of Jerusalem.
3) A third reason Adonijah plotted against the throne gives clear insight into his character: he was a *spoiled* young man. All of his life he had been indulged, allowed to do basically what he wanted. Apparently, David had seldom disciplined or corrected him.
4) Another factor that encouraged Adonijah to seize the throne was his physical appearance: he was handsome and charismatic (v.6). He looked like a ruler and he related to the people as a ruler, just the kind of person the public wanted governing them.
5) Also, Adonijah was the royal prince, the son who was next in line to become king (v.6). Amnon had been the firstborn son of David, but Absalom, David's second son, had murdered him. Later, Absalom himself was killed by Joab's men. And a third son, Chileab, apparently died when he was young. Scripture says nothing about him other than giving his name. Thus Adonijah, the fourth son born to David, was now the crown prince, the next in line to become king. And although he knew that the LORD had appointed Solomon and that Solomon was David's choice to be crowned king, Adonijah was driven by the fact that he was the royal prince. By natural birth, he was supposed to be next in line to become king. To him, moral character, ability, and God's will had little if anything to do with the right to rule the nation as king. As a result, he plotted to seize the throne.
6) No doubt, one of the significant factors that encouraged Adonijah was the support of some powerful leaders (v.7). Both Joab the army commander and Abiathar the High Priest threw their support behind Adonijah's plot.

b. But there was also strong opposition to Adonijah's scheme to seize the throne (v.8). And the opposition included some powerful leaders:

⇒ Zadok was the second High Priest serving the nation at this time. He had joined David after Saul had been killed in battle (1 Chr.12:28), and he had also been loyal to David during Absalom's rebellion.
⇒ Benaiah was one of David's bravest soldiers and commanders and had eventually been placed over David's personal bodyguards, the Kerethites and Pelethites (2 S.8:18; 20:23; 23:20-23; 1 Chr.11:22-25).
⇒ Nathan was the prophet sent by God to confront David on three very important occasions: to share the Davidic covenant (2 S.7), to share the judgment of God upon David's sin with Bathsheba (2 S.12), and to share God's special love for Solomon at Solomon's birth (2 S.12:24-25).
⇒ Shimei and Rei are unknown; however, Shimei may have been the leader appointed by Solomon to be one of the twelve district governors (4:7, 18).
⇒ David's royal bodyguard also remained loyal to him.

c. The strategy of Adonijah was well planned and thought out (vv.9-10). Rallying the help of Joab and Abiathar, he invited all the royal officials and all the king's sons to a great feast. He hoped to unite the group to support his claim to be king (v.9). Since Joab was the commander of the armed forces as well as one of the ringleaders of the coup, the royal officials would have been heavily pressured to accept Adonijah as the new king. Note that the strategy excluded those closest to David, for Adonijah apparently sensed that they would have opposed his plot.

Thought 1. Adonijah is a clear picture of self-exaltation, arrogance, and pride. We, too, sometimes walk around full of conceit and self-importance, exalting ourselves over others, causing all kinds of problems:

⇒ We lose friends and alienate people. Few people want anything to do with us.
⇒ We lose opportunities at work such as promotions, raises, and job openings.
⇒ We degrade people, making them feel unworthy.
⇒ We irritate or anger people, including family members, neighbors, fellow workers, or even strangers.
⇒ We arouse opposition, people who become determined to retaliate or to seek revenge against us, putting us in our place.

---

2 John F. Walvoord and Roy B. Zuck, Editors. *The Bible Knowledge Commentary, Old Testament*. (Colorado Springs, CO: Chariot Victor Publishing, 1985), p.486.
Flavius Josephus. *Josephus Antiquities. Complete Works*. (Grand Rapids, MI: Kregel Publications, 1981), 7.19.3.

Pride, arrogance, and self-exaltation cause a host of problems both for us and for people who surround us. Acting superior or better than other people can cause problems ranging from minor alienation to revenge, from minor retaliation to murder and war. For this reason, God warns us against these terrible self-absorbing sins:

"And whosoever shall exalt himself shall be abased; and he that shall humble himself shall be exalted" (Mt.23:12).

"Love not the world, neither the things *that are* in the world. If any man love the world, the love of the Father is not in him. For all that *is* in the world, the lust of the flesh, and the lust of the eyes, and the pride of life, is not of the Father, but is of the world" (1 Jn.2:15-16).

"The wicked in *his* pride doth persecute the poor: let them be taken in the devices that they have imagined" (Ps.10:2).

"Therefore pride compasseth them about as a chain; violence covereth them *as* a garment" (Ps.73:6).

"Thou hast rebuked the proud *that are* cursed, which do err from thy commandments" (Ps.119:21).

"Be not wise in thine own eyes: fear the LORD, and depart from evil" (Pr.3:7).

"The fear of the LORD *is* to hate evil: pride, and arrogancy, and the evil way, and the froward mouth, do I hate" (Pr.8:13).

"*When* pride cometh, then cometh shame: but with the lowly *is* wisdom" (Pr.11:2).

"Pride *goeth* before destruction, and an haughty spirit before a fall" (Pr.16:18).

"He loveth transgression that loveth strife: *and* he that exalteth his gate seeketh destruction" (Pr.17:19).

"An high look, and a proud heart, *and* the plowing of the wicked, *is* sin" (Pr.21:4).

"Seest thou a man wise in his own conceit? *there is* more hope of a fool than of him" (Pr.26:12).

"He that is of a proud heart stirreth up strife: but he that putteth his trust in the LORD shall be made fat" (Pr.28:25).

"And I will punish the world for *their* evil, and the wicked for their iniquity; and I will cause the arrogancy of the proud to cease, and will lay low the haughtiness of the terrible" (Is.13:11).

"For thou hast said in thine heart, I will ascend into heaven, I will exalt my throne above the stars of God: I will sit also upon the mount of the congregation, in the sides of the north: I will ascend above the heights of the clouds; I will be like the most High. Yet thou shalt be brought down to hell, to the sides of the pit" (Is.14:13-15).

"Though thou exalt *thyself* as the eagle, and though thou set thy nest among the stars, thence will I bring thee down, saith the LORD" (Obad.4).

2 (1:11-27) **Willingness, to Serve God, Essential—Will of God, Duty—Service, Duty, Willingness to Serve—Nathan, Opposed Adonijah's Plot—Bathsheba, Opposed Adonijah's Plot—David, Rebellion Against**: there was the counterplan of Nathan and Bathsheba to have Solomon crowned king. This is a clear picture of being willing to work out God's will no matter the cost. In determining to oppose Adonijah, the prophet Nathan and Bathsheba were risking their lives, for the likelihood was that the rebellion would be successful because the army commander Joab was leading it. And most likely, Adonijah would assassinate his bedridden father King David as well as Nathan and Bathsheba. Of course, there was the possibility that Adonijah would have eliminated the entire family of David anyway, executed them in order to remove all threats to the throne. Whatever the case, these two loyal supporters of David took prompt, decisive action against Adonijah's plot. What happened paints a suspenseful scene of high drama:

OUTLINE	SCRIPTURE	SCRIPTURE	OUTLINE
2. The counterplan of Nathan & Bathsheba to have Solomon crowned king: A willingness to work out God's will no matter the cost a. Nathan warned Bathsheba of Adonijah's plot & advised her 1) That she & Solomon were in danger of being assassinated 2) That she go before David to remind him of two facts • That he had sworn an oath that Solomon would be his successor, 2 S.12:24-25; 1 Chr. 22:8-10; 28:3-7 • That Adonijah was plotting to take over the throne—immediately	11 Wherefore Nathan spake unto Bath-sheba the mother of Solomon, saying, Hast thou not heard that Adonijah the son of Haggith doth reign, and David our lord knoweth *it* not? 12 Now therefore come, let me, I pray thee, give thee counsel, that thou mayest save thine own life, and the life of thy son Solomon. 13 Go and get thee in unto king David, and say unto him, Didst not thou, my lord, O king, swear unto thine handmaid, saying, Assuredly Solomon thy son shall reign after me, and he shall sit upon my throne? why then doth Adonijah reign?	14 Behold, while thou yet talkest there with the king, I also will come in after thee, and confirm thy words. 15 And Bath-sheba went in unto the king into the chamber: and the king was very old; and Abishag the Shunammite ministered unto the king. 16 And Bath-sheba bowed, and did obeisance unto the king. And the king said, What wouldest thou? 17 And she said unto him, My lord, thou swarest by the LORD thy God unto thine handmaid, *saying,* Assuredly Solomon thy son shall reign after me, and he shall sit upon my throne.	3) That he, Nathan, would confirm her story b. Bathsheba warned the bedridden David of Adonijah's plot 1) She showed respect for David: Bowed & knelt before him 2) She reminded David of his sworn oath: Solomon would be appointed king, the successor to the throne

OUTLINE	SCRIPTURE	SCRIPTURE	OUTLINE
3) She warned David that Adonijah was plotting insurrection	18 And now, behold, Adonijah reigneth; and now, my lord the king, thou knowest *it* not:	bowed himself before the king with his face to the ground.	
• Adonijah was holding a feast at that very moment—to mobilize support • Abiathar & Joab were supporting Adonijah's plot	19 And he hath slain oxen and fat cattle and sheep in abundance, and hath called all the sons of the king, and the captain of the host: but Solomon thy servant hath he not called.	24 And Nathan said, My lord, O king, hast thou said, Adonijah shall reign after me, and he shall sit upon my throne?	2) He asked David if he had appointed Adonijah king
4) She informed David that all Israel was excitedly waiting for him to appoint his successor	20 And thou, my lord, O king the eyes of all Israel *are* upon thee, that thou shouldest tell them who shall sit on the throne of my lord the king after him.	25 For he is gone down this day, and hath slain oxen and fat cattle and sheep in abundance, and hath called all the king's sons, and the captains of the host, and Abiathar the priest; and, behold, they eat and drink before him, and say, God save king Adonijah.	• That Adonijah was holding a coronation feast at that very moment • That he had invited all the king's sons, military leaders, & Abiathar the priest: They all were proclaiming him king
5) She appealed to David, stating that hers & Solomon's lives were at risk when he died—unless he acted quickly	21 Otherwise it shall come to pass, when my lord the king shall sleep with his fathers, that I and my son Solomon shall be counted offenders.	26 But me, *even* me thy servant, and Zadok the priest, and Benaiah the son of Jehoiada, and thy servant Solomon, hath he not called.	3) He informed David that he, Zadok, Benaiah, & Solomon had not been invited to the feast: Their lives were in danger
c. Nathan entered the king's presence & confirmed Bathsheba's report	22 And, lo, while she yet talked with the king, Nathan the prophet also came in.	27 Is this thing done by my lord the king, and thou hast not showed *it* unto thy servant, who should sit on the throne of my lord the king after him?	4) He again asked if David had acted alone in appointing Adonijah—without informing his closest advisors
1) He showed the proper respect: Bowed	23 And they told the king, saying, Behold Nathan the prophet. And when he was come in before the king, he		

a. Once aware of the plot, Nathan promptly warned Bathsheba that Adonijah was planning to seize the throne (vv.11-14). She and Solomon were in danger of being assassinated. Therefore, she must immediately go before David and remind him of two facts:

⇒ that David had sworn an oath: Solomon was to be the successor to his throne (2 S.12:24-25; 1 Chr.22:9-10; 28:4-7).
⇒ that Adonijah was plotting to immediately take over the throne. In fact, all the preparations had already been made to launch the rebellion.

Nathan stated that while Bathsheba was presenting her case before David, he would interrupt her audience with David to confirm her story. He would strongly urge David to counteract Adonijah's plot to seize the throne.

b. Sensing the urgency of the situation, Bathsheba followed the advice of Nathan. She sought an audience with the bedridden king and warned him of Adonijah's plot (vv.15-21). As she approached David lying in bed, she showed the deepest respect for him by bowing and kneeling in his presence. Inviting her to explain what she wanted, she reminded David of his sworn oath that Solomon was to be king, the successor to his throne (v.17). Then, without exaggeration, she simply stated the facts, which no doubt stunned the bedridden king. Adonijah was plotting insurrection, to have himself proclaimed the successor to David's throne (vv.18-19). In fact, at that very moment Adonijah was holding a feast to mobilize support for his claim to the throne. And both Abiathar and Joab, the commander of the army, were supporting his plot.

Bathsheba then claimed that all Israel was anxiously waiting for David to appoint his successor (v.20). In desperation, Bathsheba finally appealed to her husband to save Solomon's life and hers, for they were at risk when David died—unless the ailing king acted quickly.

c. Just as Bathsheba was concluding her appeal, the king's servants informed him that Nathan the prophet was requesting an urgent audience with him (vv.22-27). As Nathan approached David, he too showed the proper respect to the king, bowing with his face to the ground. Immediately supporting Bathsheba's claim of a plot against the throne, Nathan asked David if he had appointed Adonijah king, for Adonijah was holding a coronation feast even as they were speaking (vv.22-25). He had invited all of David's sons, the military leaders, and Abiathar the High Priest to attend the feast. By this time, they were all proclaiming Adonijah to be the new king of Israel.

Nathan then informed David that neither he, nor Zadok, nor Benaiah, nor Solomon had been invited to the feast. Their lives were in imminent danger (v.26). Sounding desperate, Nathan asked if David had acted alone in appointing Adonijah—without informing his closest advisors (v.27).

Thought 1. This is a clear picture of being willing to work out God's will no matter the cost. It was God's will for Solomon to be the successor to David. God had clearly stated this (2 S.12:24-25; 1 Chr.22:8-10; 28:3-7). By seeking to counter the plot of Adonijah, Nathan and Bathsheba demonstrated a willingness to work out God's will—disregarding the cost to their own lives. Once we know God's will, we too must demonstrate willingness—a strong willingness—to carry out God's will.

⇒ When God moves upon our hearts to serve Him, we must willingly commit our lives and perform the service.
⇒ When the Spirit of God moves upon our hearts to help those around us, we must willingly help to meet the need.
⇒ When the Word of God commands us to live righteously, we must willingly live righteously before God.
⇒ When God gives us a commandment in the Holy Bible, we must *willingly* obey that commandment.

When God makes His will known concerning any behavior or any event, we must demonstrate a *willing* spirit, a readiness to do exactly what God says. We must earnestly seek to work out God's will. A *willing* spirit—a strong driving force to do God's will—must captivate our lives. This is the clear teaching of God's Holy Word:

"Jesus saith unto them, My meat is to do the will of him that sent me, and to finish his work" (Jn.4:34).

"I have glorified thee on the earth: I have finished the work which thou gavest me to do" (Jn.17:4).

"But none of these things move me, neither count I my life dear unto myself, so that I might finish my course with joy, and the ministry, which I have received of the LORD Jesus, to testify the gospel of the grace of God" (Ac.20:24).

"I beseech you therefore, brethren, by the mercies of God, that ye present your bodies a living sacrifice, holy, acceptable unto God, which is your reasonable service. And be not conformed to this world: but be ye transformed by the renewing of your mind, that ye may prove what is that good, and acceptable, and perfect, will of God" (Ro.12:1-2).

"So being affectionately desirous of you, we were willing to have imparted unto you, not the gospel of God only, but also our own souls, because ye were dear unto us" (1 Th.2:8).

"I have fought a good fight, I have finished *my* course, I have kept the faith: Henceforth there is laid up for me a crown of righteousness, which the LORD, the righteous judge, shall give me at that day: and not to me only, but unto all them also that love his appearing" (2 Ti.4:7-8).

"Wherefore we receiving a kingdom which cannot be moved, let us have grace, whereby we may serve God acceptably with reverence and godly fear" (He.12:28).

"And now, Israel, what doth the Lord thy God require of thee, but to fear the Lord thy God, to walk in all his ways, and to love him, and to serve the Lord thy God with all thy heart and with all thy soul" (De.10:12).

"Serve the LORD with fear, and rejoice with trembling" (Ps.2:11).

"If ye be willing and obedient, ye shall eat the good of the land" (Is.1:19).

3 (1:28-37) **Promises, Duty, to Keep—Vows, Duty, to Keep—Oaths, Duty, to Keep—David, Successor, Solomon—Solomon, Appointed King, by David**: there was the decisive command of King David: Solomon would indeed be king. Being informed of the threat against his throne, David's blood began to boil. No longer was the blood circulating slowly through his body, for his emotions had been aroused and his heart was beating rapidly. The king was ready to take decisive action. He would immediately install Solomon upon the throne before Adonijah could act. The scene of David's decisive action reaches the summit of suspenseful drama:

OUTLINE	SCRIPTURE	SCRIPTURE	OUTLINE
3. The decisive command of King David that Solomon would indeed be king: An example of keeping oaths, one's word a. David summoned Bathsheba & restated his sworn oath 1) David would carry out his promise that very day: Solomon would be immediately installed as king, 2 S.12:24-25; 1 Chr.22:9-10; 28:4-7 2) Bathsheba humbled herself & expressed the hope that David's kingdom would never end b. David summoned the leaders he could depend upon & gave them clear, forceful instructions	28 Then king David answered and said, Call me Bath-sheba. And she came into the king's presence, and stood before the king. 29 And the king sware, and said, *As* the LORD liveth, that hath redeemed my soul out of all distress, 30 Even as I sware unto thee by the LORD God of Israel, saying, Assuredly Solomon thy son shall reign after me, and he shall sit upon my throne in my stead; even so will I certainly do this day. 31 Then Bath-sheba bowed with *her* face to the earth, and did reverence to the king, and said, Let my lord king David live for ever. 32 And king David said, Call me Zadok the priest, and Nathan the prophet, and Benaiah the son of Jehoiada.	And they came before the king. 33 The king also said unto them, Take with you the servants of your lord, and cause Solomon my son to ride upon mine own mule, and bring him down to Gihon: 34 And let Zadok the priest and Nathan the prophet anoint him there king over Israel: and blow ye with the trumpet, and say, God save king Solomon. 35 Then ye shall come up after him, that he may come and sit upon my throne; for he shall be king in my stead: and I have appointed him to be ruler over Israel and over Judah. 36 And Benaiah the son of Jehoiada answered the king, and said, Amen: the LORD	1) They were to set Solomon on David's mule & go down to Gihon to publicly show that he was the designated king 2) They were to anoint Solomon as king 3) They were to sound the trumpet: Call the people together & proclaim him king 4) They were to place him on the throne as king, to begin his rule immediately: To reign as co-regent until David's death c. David acted decisively & was strongly supported by the military commander, Benaiah

OUTLINE	SCRIPTURE
1) He prayed for God to decree it 2) He prayed God to be with Solomon: To make his kingdom even greater than David's	God of my lord the king say so *too.* 37 As the LORD hath been with my lord the king, even so be he with Solomon, and make his throne greater than the throne of my lord king David.

a. Arousing all his mental faculties, David summoned Nathan back into the room and restated his sworn oath (vv.28-31). As was the custom of that day, Bathsheba left the room when Nathan arrived. Now, with anger and a spirit of urgency rushing through the veins of his body, David barked the order for Bathsheba to be recalled. When his dear wife returned, David restated the oath he had earlier sworn: as surely as the LORD lives—the LORD who had always delivered him—he would carry out his promise that very day. Solomon would immediately be installed as king (2 S.12:24-25; 1 Chr.22:9-10; 28:4-7). With deep gratitude for granting her request, Bathsheba prostrated herself before the bedridden king and expressed the hope that David's kingdom would never end (v.31).

b. After giving assurance to his wife, David immediately summoned the leaders he could depend upon (vv.32-35). Keep in mind that Zadok was the priest, Nathan the prophet, and Benaiah the commander of David's royal bodyguard. As soon as the three leaders arrived, David issued his clear, forceful instructions:

1) They were to act immediately: to set Solomon on David's own mule and lead him through the capital city of Jerusalem to the place of anointing. When kings rode on mules, they were symbolizing their role as servants to the people. David knew that the public would immediately recognize that Solomon was being anointed as king.
2) The leaders were to anoint Solomon as king when they arrived at the spring of Gihon. This was one of the two springs that provided most of the water for Jerusalem. The spring at En Rogel was the other major water supply, the place where Adonijah and his supporters were holding their celebration (v.9).
3) After anointing Solomon as king, the leaders were to sound the trumpets, calling the people together so they too could join in the proclamation of Solomon as king (v.34).
4) David's supporters were then to place Solomon on the throne as king, where he could begin his rule immediately. He was to be co-regent until David's death.

c. Note that David's decisive action was strongly supported by the military commander Benaiah (vv.36-37). This was of critical importance, for the commander Benaiah was responsible for executing David's orders. His immediate response was to burst forth with an "Amen!" And then he asked God to declare David's stated wish. He asked God to be with Solomon, making Solomon's kingdom even greater than David's.

Thought 1. David had been instructed by God to appoint Solomon as his successor to the throne. This is clearly seen in the following Scripture:

"And David comforted Bath-sheba his wife, and went in unto her, and lay with her: and she bare a son, and he called his name Solomon: and the LORD loved him. And he sent by the hand of Nathan the prophet; and he called his name Jedidiah, because of the LORD" (2 S.12:24-25).

"But the word of the LORD came to me, saying, Thou hast shed blood abundantly, and hast made great wars: thou shalt not build an house unto my name, because thou hast shed much blood upon the earth in my sight. Behold, a son shall be born to thee, who shall be a man of rest; and I will give him rest from all his enemies round about: for his name shall be Solomon, and I will give peace and quietness unto Israel in his days. He shall build an house for my name; and he shall be my son, and I *will be* his father; and I will establish the throne of his kingdom over Israel for ever" (1 Chr.22:8-10).

"But God said unto me, Thou shalt not build an house for my name, because thou *hast been* a man of war, and hast shed blood. Howbeit the LORD God of Israel chose me before all the house of my father to be king over Israel for ever: for he hath chosen Judah *to be* the ruler; and of the house of Judah, the house of my father; and among the sons of my father he liked me to make *me* king over all Israel: And of all my sons, (for the LORD hath given me many sons,) he hath chosen Solomon my son to sit upon the throne of the kingdom of the LORD over Israel. And he said unto me, Solomon thy son, he shall build my house and my courts: for I have chosen him *to be* my son, and I will be his father. Moreover I will establish his kingdom for ever, if he be constant to do my commandments and my judgments, as at this day" (1 Chr.28:3-7).

Now it was up to David to make sure that God's will was executed, carried out. Despite being bedridden, he had to make sure that Solomon was anointed and crowned king.

The lesson for us is straightforward: just as David kept his vow, so we must keep our vows and oaths. When we make promises to people, we must keep our promises. We must do exactly what we say, keeping our every word. One of the most valuable possessions we have is *trust*. Can people trust us? Depend upon what we say? Know that our promises will be fulfilled? Just think what happens when our word is broken, when our vows or promises cannot be trusted. What happens…

- when a wife cannot trust the vows of her husband?
- when a child cannot trust the promises of his or her parent?
- when an employer cannot trust the word of an employee?

- when an employee cannot trust the promise of an employer?
- when a student cannot trust the word of a teacher?
- when a neighbor cannot trust the word of a neighbor?
- when a businessperson cannot trust the word of his partner or associate?
- when the public cannot trust the word of a politician or government representative?

All kinds of problems arise when we fail to keep our word and promises, the vows we make to people. Listen to what the Word of God has to say about keeping our word and the oaths we make:

> **"But let your communication be, Yea, yea; Nay, nay: for whatsoever is more than these cometh of evil" (Mt.5:37).**
>
> **"Wherefore putting away lying, speak every man truth with his neighbour: for we are members one of another" (Ep.4:25).**
>
> **"Let your speech *be* alway with grace, seasoned with salt, that ye may know how ye ought to answer every man" (Col.4:6).**
>
> **"For he that will love life, and see good days, let him refrain his tongue from evil, and his lips that they speak no guile" (1 Pe.3:10).**
>
> **"But the fearful, and unbelieving, and the abominable, and murderers, and whoremongers, and sorcerers, and idolaters, and all liars, shall have their part in the lake which burneth with fire and brimstone: which is the second death" (Re.21:8).**
>
> **"If a man vow a vow unto the LORD, or swear an oath to bind his soul with a bond; he shall not break his word, he shall do according to all that proceedeth out of his mouth" (Nu.30:2).**
>
> **"When thou shalt vow a vow unto the LORD thy God, thou shalt not slack to pay it: for the LORD thy God will surely require it of thee; and it would be sin in thee. But if thou shalt forbear to vow, it shall be no sin in thee. That which is gone out of thy lips thou shalt keep and perform; *even* a freewill offering, according as thou hast vowed unto the LORD thy God, which thou hast promised with thy mouth" (De.23:21-23).**
>
> **"Thou shalt destroy them that speak leasing [lying]: the LORD will abhor the bloody and deceitful man" (Ps.5:6).**
>
> **"Keep thy tongue from evil, and thy lips from speaking guile" (Ps.34:13).**
>
> **"He that worketh deceit shall not dwell within my house: he that telleth lies shall not tarry in my sight" (Ps.101:7).**
>
> **"Lying lips *are* abomination to the LORD: but they that deal truly *are* his delight" (Pr.12:22).**
>
> **"*It is* a snare to the man *who* devoureth *that which is* holy, and after vows to make enquiry" (Pr.20:25).**
>
> **"The getting of treasures by a lying tongue *is* a vanity tossed to and fro of them that seek death" (Pr.21:6).**
>
> **"Whoso keepeth his mouth and his tongue keepeth his soul from troubles" (Pr.21:23).**
>
> **"When thou vowest a vow unto God, defer not to pay it; for *he hath* no pleasure in fools: pay that which thou hast vowed. Better *is it* that thou shouldest not vow, than that thou shouldest vow and not pay. Suffer not thy mouth to cause thy flesh to sin; neither say thou before the angel, that it *was* an error: wherefore should God be angry at thy voice, and destroy the work of thine hands?" (Ec.5:4-6).**
>
> **"These *are* the things that ye shall do; Speak ye every man the truth to his neighbour; execute the judgment of truth and peace in your gates" (Zec.8:16).**
>
> **"The law of truth was in his mouth, and iniquity was not found in his lips: he walked with me in peace and equity, and did turn many away from iniquity" (Mal.2:6).**

4 (1:38-53) **Anointing, of Solomon—Solomon, Anointed as King—Solomon, Type of Christ—Mercy, Example of, Solomon**: there was the climactic anointing of Solomon as king. His anointing was a type of Jesus Christ, the anointed Son of David who was to be the Messiah and Savior of the world. Picture the thrilling moment of Solomon's coronation as king:

OUTLINE	SCRIPTURE	SCRIPTURE	OUTLINE
4. The climactic anointing of Solomon as king: A type of Christ, the Anointed Son of David a. The officials placed Solomon on David's mule: Escorted him to Gihon, a site of major water supply & a public meeting place b. The priest Zadok anointed Solomon as king before the people	38 So Zadok the priest, and Nathan the prophet, and Benaiah the son of Jehoiada, and the Cherethites, and the Pelethites, went down, and caused Solomon to ride upon king David's mule, and brought him to Gihon. 39 And Zadok the priest took an horn of oil out of the tabernacle, and anointed	Solomon. And they blew the trumpet; and all the people said, God save king Solomon. 40 And all the people came up after him, and the people piped with pipes, and rejoiced with great joy, so that the earth rent with the sound of them. 41 And Adonijah and all the	c. The officials sounded the trumpet d. The people rejoiced over the coronation 1) Followed Solomon & the officials back to the palace shouting for joy 2) Made so much noise the ground shook e. The prince Adonijah & his

OUTLINE	SCRIPTURE	SCRIPTURE	OUTLINE
guests heard the uproar & commotion off in the distance	guests that *were* with him heard *it* as they had made an end of eating. And when Joab heard the sound of the trum-pet, he said, Wherefore *is this* noise of the city being in an uproar?	better than thy name, and make his throne greater than thy throne. And the king bowed himself upon the bed.	Solomon's dynasty more famous & even greater than David's rule had been
f. The coronation of Solomon was immediately reported to Adonijah, that all the steps of installation had already taken place	42 And while he yet spake, behold, Jonathan the son of Abiathar the priest came: and Adonijah said unto him, Come in; for thou *art* a valiant man, and bringest good tidings.	48 And also thus said the king, Blessed *be* the LORD God of Israel, which hath given *one* to sit on my throne this day, mine eyes even seeing *it*.	7) That the king had expressed his pleasure & rejoiced that he had lived to see Solomon reign
1) That King David himself had declared Solomon king	43 And Jonathan answered and said to Adonijah, Verily our lord king David hath made Solomon king.	49 And all the guests that *were* with Adonijah were afraid, and rose up, and went every man his way.	g. The plot of Adonijah was crushed 1) His supporters fled, scattered, fearing for their lives
2) That the king's officials had placed Solomon on the king's mule: Publicly demonstrated that Solomon was the designated king	44 And the king hath sent with him Zadok the priest, and Nathan the prophet, and Benaiah the son of Jehoiada, and the Cherethites, and the Pelethites, and they have caused him to ride upon the king's mule:	50 And Adonijah feared because of Solomon, and arose, and went, and caught hold on the horns of the altar. 51 And it was told Solomon, saying, Behold, Adonijah feareth king Solomon: for, lo, he hath caught hold on the horns of the altar, saying, Let king Solomon swear unto me to day that he will not slay his servant with the sword.	2) Adonijah—gripped by fear—fled & grabbed hold of the horns of the altar: An act of seeking mercy & refuge • Adonijah's desperate act & plea for mercy was reported to Solomon
3) That Zadok had anointed Solomon king 4) That the people had publicly & enthusiastically accepted the coronation & rejoiced in it	45 And Zadok the priest and Nathan the prophet have anointed him king in Gihon: and they are come up from thence rejoicing, so that the city rang again. This is the noise that ye have heard.	52 And Solomon said, If he will show himself a worthy man, there shall not an hair of him fall to the earth: but if wickedness shall be found in him, he shall die.	• Solomon expressed a willingness to show mercy: He would place Adonijah on probation
5) That Solomon had already taken his seat on the royal throne	46 And also Solomon sitteth on the throne of the kingdom.	53 So king Solomon sent, and they brought him down from the altar. And he came and bowed himself to king Solomon: and Solomon said unto him, Go to thine house.	h. The traitorous Adonijah was arrested & shown mercy 1) Adonijah showed proper respect: He bowed 2) Solomon sent him home, but on probation, v.52
6) That the royal officials had already extended their congratulations to David: Asked God to make	47 And moreover the king's servants came to bless our lord king David, saying, God make the name of Solomon		

a. The three faithful officials quickly carried out David's instructions. They placed Solomon on David's mule; and with the royal palace guard leading the way, they escorted him through the city streets of Jerusalem. Their destination was Gihon, one of the major public meeting places of the capital. Obviously, most of the citizens of the city had fallen in behind Solomon's processional as he was escorted through the city streets.

b. As soon as the processional reached its destination, Zadok the priest anointed Solomon as king before the multitude of people (v.39). The people knew beyond question that Solomon was David's choice to be king, for they had seen Solomon riding David's own mule, declaring himself to be the appointed servant of the people. And now they had witnessed with their own eyes the anointing of Solomon by Zadok the priest. A priest anointed only the kings who continued the dynasty of a ruler (1 K.1:39; 2 K.11:12). When an outsider was anointed as king, it was always a prophet who performed the ceremony (1 S.9:16; 16:12; 1 K.19:15-18; 2 K.9:1-13).

c. Once Solomon had been officially anointed, the leaders blew the trumpets announcing his coronation (v.39).

d. After the trumpets sounded, the people rejoiced over the coronation, shouting out, "Long live King Solomon!" The people followed Solomon and the officials back to the palace, playing their musical instruments and shouting and singing for joy. They made so much noise that the very ground itself shook with the sound of their rejoicing.

e. The uproar and commotion was so loud that Adonijah and his guests heard the noise off in the distance (v.41). Joab immediately asked if any of the guests knew what the noise in the city meant.

f. Just as Joab was speaking, Jonathan, the son of Abiathar the priest, arrived at the feast and announced the shocking news to Adonijah and his guests: Solomon had just been installed as king (vv.42-48). And all the steps of the coronation had been taken:

⇒ David himself had declared Solomon king.

⇒ Zadok the priest, Nathan the prophet, Benaiah the military commander, and the royal guard had placed Solomon on the king's mule and publicly demonstrated that he was the newly designated king (v.44).

⇒ Zadok the high priest had also anointed Solomon king at Gihon, one of the major public meeting places of the city (v.45).

⇒ The people had publicly and enthusiastically accepted the coronation and rejoiced in it.

⇒ Solomon had even taken his seat on the royal throne.

⇒ The royal officials had already extended their congratulations to David, even asking God to make Solomon's dynasty more famous and more great than David's own rule.
⇒ And finally, the king had expressed his pleasure, rejoicing that he had lived to see Solomon crowned as his successor (v.48).

g. The plot of Adonijah was now crushed (vv.49-52). His supporters fled and scattered, fearing for their lives. Adonijah himself—gripped by fear—fled to the sacred tent and grabbed hold of the bloodstained horns of the altar (v.50). Seeking refuge by such an act was allowed for those who had committed *unintentional crimes* (Ex.21:12-14). However, there was no question, no doubt that Adonijah's crime was deliberate and deceitful. In this desperate act, he was pleading for mercy, and his plea was immediately reported to Solomon (v.51). In response, Solomon expressed a willingness to show mercy (v.52). He would place Adonijah on probation, letting him live so long as he renounced his claims to the throne.

h. Sending guards to arrest the traitorous Adonijah, Solomon had him brought before the throne (v.53). As Adonijah approached Solomon, he showed proper respect by bowing before the king. After discussing the insurrection with his half-brother, Solomon sent him home but placed him on probation. He must renounce all claims to the throne and never again give any indication whatsoever of conspiracy or rebellion.

Thought 1. The anointing of Solomon is a type of Christ, the anointed Son of David. Throughout Holy Scripture, the anointing of certain people points to the Anointed One of God Himself, the promised Messiah and Savior of the world. Note two clear lessons for us:

(1) Jesus Christ is the anointed Son of David, the promised Messiah and Savior of the world.

"The book of the generation of Jesus Christ, the son of David, the son of Abraham" (Mt.1:1).

"And all the people were amazed, and said, Is not this the son of David?" (Mt.12:23).

"And, behold, a woman of Canaan came out of the same coasts, and cried unto him, saying, Have mercy on me, O LORD, *thou* Son of David; my daughter is grievously vexed with a devil" (Mt.15:22).

"And the multitudes that went before, and that followed, cried, saying, Hosanna to the Son of David: Blessed *is* he that cometh in the name of the LORD; Hosanna in the highest" (Mt.21:9).

"And many charged him that he should hold his peace: but he cried the more a great deal, *Thou* Son of David, have mercy on me" (Mk.10:48).

"And Jesus answered and said, while he taught in the temple, How say the scribes that Christ is the Son of David?" (Mk.12:35).

"Hath not the scripture said, That Christ cometh of the seed of David, and out of the town of Bethlehem, where David was?" (Jn.7:42).

"Paul, a servant of Jesus Christ, called *to be* an apostle, separated unto the gospel of God, (Which he had promised afore by his prophets in the holy scriptures,) Concerning his Son Jesus Christ our LORD, which was made of the seed of David according to the flesh; And declared *to be* the Son of God with power, according to the spirit of holiness, by the resurrection from the dead" (Ro.1:1-4).

"Remember that Jesus Christ of the seed of David was raised from the dead according to my gospel" (2 Ti.2:8).

(2) If we wish to be saved from sin, death, and judgment to come, we must accept Jesus Christ as our personal Messiah and Savior. This is the declaration of God's Holy Word:

"For God so loved the world, that he gave his only begotten Son, that whosoever believeth in him should not perish, but have everlasting life" (Jn.3:16).

"For God sent not his Son into the world to condemn the world; but that the world through him might be saved" (Jn.3:17).

"Jesus said unto her, I am the resurrection, and the life: he that believeth in me, though he were dead, yet shall he live" (Jn.11:25).

"I am come a light into the world, that whosoever believeth on me should not abide in darkness" (Jn.12:46).

"But these are written, that ye might believe that Jesus is the Christ, the Son of God; and that believing ye might have life through his name" (Jn.20:31).

"Him hath God exalted with his right hand *to be* a Prince and a Saviour, for to give repentance to Israel, and forgiveness of sins" (Ac.5:31).

"That if thou shalt confess with thy mouth the LORD Jesus, and shalt believe in thine heart that God hath raised him from the dead, thou shalt be saved. For with the heart man believeth unto righteousness; and with the mouth confession is made unto salvation" (Ro.10:9-10).

"This *is* a faithful saying, and worthy of all acceptation, that Christ Jesus came into the world to save sinners; of whom I am chief" (1 Ti.1:15).

"Wherefore he is able also to save them to the uttermost that come unto God by him, seeing he ever liveth to make intercession for them" (He.7:25).

CHAPTER 2

B. The Death of David & the Consolidation of Solomon's Power: A Picture of Death & of Justice, 2:1-46

2:10-12; see 1 Chr.3:4; 29:26-28

1. The charge of David to Solomon: Be strong, obey the LORD, execute justice, & show yourself a real man—stand for right, not wrong

- a. Be strong (courageous), De. 31:7-8; Jos.1:1-7; 23:6-8
- b. Keep the charge of the LORD
  - 1) Walk in His ways, requirements
  - 2) Obey His law & commandments—His Word
  - 3) The results
    - You will prosper, be successful
    - God will fulfill His promises: David's kingdom will be eternal (fulfilled in Christ, the Son of David, whose kingdom is eternal), 2 S.7:11-16; 1 Chr. 17:11-14; Ac.2:22-36; 3:25-26; 15:15-17; Ga.3:25-29; Re.3:21
- c. Execute justice: A picture of the need for justice
  - 1) Justice needed to be executed upon Joab
    - He disobeyed orders & killed two commanders in peacetime: Abner & Amasa, 2 S.3:22-27; 20:8-13
    - He conspired with Adonijah, 1:7, 19, 41; 2:28
    - His punishment was left up to Solomon, but he was to be watched, not left alone in peace
  - 2) Justice needed to be shown on behalf of Barzillai
    - His sons needed to be shown kindness
    - The reason: They supported David, 2 S.17:27-29
  - 3) Justice needed to be executed upon Shimei
    - He had cursed God's anointed & threatened David's life, 2 S.16:11
    - His punishment was left up to Solomon, but he was to be watched in his old age & executed

Now the days of David drew
nigh that he should die; and
he charged Solomon his son,
saying,
2 I go the way of all the
earth: be thou strong therefore, and show thyself a man;
3 And keep the charge of
the LORD thy God, to walk in
his ways, to keep his statutes,
and his commandments, and
his judgments, and his testimonies, as it is written in
the law of Moses, that thou
mayest prosper in all that
thou doest, and whither-
soever thou turnest thyself:
4 That the LORD may con-
tinue his word which he
spake concerning me, saying,
If thy children take heed to
their way, to walk before me
in truth with all their heart
and with all their soul, there
shall not fail thee (said he) a
man on the throne of Israel.
5 Moreover thou knowest also what Joab the son of Zeruiah did to me, *and* what he
did to the two captains of the
hosts of Israel, unto Abner
the son of Ner, and unto
Amasa the son of Jether,
whom he slew, and shed the
blood of war in peace, and
put the blood of war upon
his girdle that *was* about his
loins, and in his shoes that
were on his feet.
6 Do therefore according to
thy wisdom, and let not his
hoar head go down to the
grave in peace.
7 But show kindness unto the
sons of Barzillai the Gilea-
dite, and let them be of those
that eat at thy table: for so
they came to me when I fled
because of Absalom thy
brother.
8 And, behold, *thou hast*
with thee Shimei the son of
Gera, a Benjamite of Ba-
hurim, which cursed me with
a grievous curse in the day
when I went to Mahanaim:
but he came down to meet
me at Jordan, and I sware to
him by the LORD, saying, I
will not put thee to death with
the sword.
9 Now therefore hold him
not guiltless: for thou *art* a
wise man, and knowest what
thou oughtest to do unto him;
but his hoar head bring thou
down to the grave with blood.

2. The death of David: Hope in God's eternal rest, Ac.2:25-17

- a. He was buried in Jerusalem
- b. He reigned as king 40 years
  - Seven years in Hebron
  - Thirty-three years in Jerusalem
- c. He left a firmly established kingdom for Solomon

10 So David slept with his
fathers, and was buried in the
city of David.
11 And the days that David
reigned over Israel *were* forty
years: seven years reigned he
in Hebron, and thirty and
three years reigned he in Jerusalem.
12 Then sat Solomon upon
the throne of David his father; and his kingdom was
established greatly.

3. The second plot of Adonijah & his execution: A picture of judgment falling upon those who oppose God's kingdom

- a. Adonijah made a clever but foolish appeal to Bathsheba: His appeal revealed that his ambition to be king was still very much alive
  - 1) His exaggerated claim: That all Israel had expected him to be appointed king
  - 2) His deceptive claim: That he submitted, accepted Solomon as the LORD's choice
  - 3) His one request as a compensation for not receiving the crown: That King Solomon give Abishag, David's concubine & nurse, to be his wife (to possess the king's concubine was to have a claim to the throne)
- b. Bathsheba agreed & secured an audience before Solomon
  - 1) She was deeply respected by Solomon
    - He stood up to meet her
    - He bowed to her
    - He had a throne brought to her
  - 2) She presented Adonijah's request: Almost word for word

13 And Adonijah the son of
Haggith came to Bath-sheba
the mother of Solomon. And
she said, Comest thou peaceably? And he said, Peace-
ably.
14 He said moreover, I have
somewhat to say unto thee.
And she said, Say on.
15 And he said, Thou knowest that the kingdom was
mine, and *that* all Israel set
their faces on me, that I
should reign: howbeit the
kingdom is turned about, and
is become my brother's: for it
was his from the LORD.
16 And now I ask one petition of thee, deny me not.
And she said unto him, Say
on.
17 And he said, Speak, I
pray thee, unto Solomon the
king, (for he will not say thee
nay,) that he give me Abishag the Shunammite to wife.
18 And Bath-sheba said,
Well; I will speak for thee
unto the king.
19 Bath-sheba therefore
went unto king Solomon, to
speak unto him for Adonijah.
And the king rose up to meet
her, and bowed himself unto
her, and sat down on his
throne, and caused a seat to
be set for the king's mother;
and she sat on his right
hand.
20 Then she said, I desire
one small petition of thee; I
pray thee, say me not nay.
And the king said unto her,
Ask on, my mother: for I will
not say thee nay.

c. Solomon sharply rebuked his mother
   1) He questioned why she would make such a request
   2) He saw through the scheming plot of Adonijah: Stated Bathsheba might as well request the kingdom for Adonijah as well as for Joab & Abiathar
   3) He declared that Adonijah had condemned himself with his request
   4) He pronounced the verdict with an irrevocable oath: Death

d. He ordered Benaiah to execute Adonijah

4. The dismissal & banishment of the High Priest Abiathar: A lesson on being disqualified for service, 1 Co.9:27

a. He was banished to his home
b. He deserved to die for backing Adonijah's revolt, 1:7, 19
c. He was shown mercy because of his service to David
d. He was permanently removed from the priesthood: A fulfillment of prophecy, 1 S.2:30-35

5. The execution of Joab: The consequences of disobeying clear commands

a. Joab—one of the conspirators—understood his fate: He fled to the altar for refuge
b. Solomon received news that Joab was seeking refuge in the worship center: He ordered Benaiah to go & execute the conspirator
   1) Benaiah confronted Joab:

21 And she said, Let Abishag the Shunammite be given to Adonijah thy brother to wife.

22 And king Solomon answered and said unto his mother, And why dost thou ask Abishag the Shunammite for Adonijah? ask for him the kingdom also; for he *is* mine elder brother; even for him, and for Abiathar the priest, and for Joab the son of Zeruiah.

23 Then king Solomon sware by the LORD, saying, God do so to me, and more also, if Adonijah have not spoken this word against his own life.

24 Now therefore, *as* the LORD liveth, which hath established me, and set me on the throne of David my father, and who hath made me an house, as he promised, Adonijah shall be put to death this day.

25 And king Solomon sent by the hand of Benaiah the son of Jehoiada; and he fell upon him that he died.

26 And unto Abiathar the priest said the king, Get thee to Anathoth, unto thine own fields; for thou *art* worthy of death: but I will not at this time put thee to death, because thou barest the ark of the Lord GOD before David my father, and because thou hast been afflicted in all wherein my father was afflicted.

27 So Solomon thrust out Abiathar from being priest unto the LORD; that he might fulfil the word of the LORD, which he spake concerning the house of Eli in Shiloh.

28 Then tidings came to Joab: for Joab had turned after Adonijah, though he turned not after Absalom. And Joab fled unto the tabernacle of the LORD, and caught hold on the horns of the altar.

29 And it was told king Solomon that Joab was fled unto the tabernacle of the LORD; and, behold, *he is* by the altar. Then Solomon sent Benaiah the son of Jehoiada, saying, Go, fall upon him.

30 And Benaiah came to the tabernacle of the LORD, and said unto him, Thus saith the king, Come forth. And he said, Nay; but I will die here. And Benaiah brought the king word again, saying, Thus said Joab, and thus he answered me.

31 And the king said unto him, Do as he hath said, and fall upon him, and bury him; that thou mayest take away the innocent blood, which Joab shed, from me, and from the house of my father.

32 And the LORD shall return his blood upon his own head, who fell upon two men more righteous and better than he, and slew them with the sword, my father David not knowing *thereof, to wit,* Abner the son of Ner, captain of the host of Israel, and Amasa the son of Jether, captain of the host of Judah.

33 Their blood shall therefore return upon the head of Joab, and upon the head of his seed for ever: but upon David, and upon his seed, and upon his house, and upon his throne, shall there be peace for ever from the LORD.

34 So Benaiah the son of Jehoiada went up, and fell upon him, and slew him: and he was buried in his own house in the wilderness.

35 And the king put Benaiah the son of Jehoiada in his room over the host: and Zadok the priest did the king put in the room of Abiathar.

36 And the king sent and called for Shimei, and said unto him, Build thee an house in Jerusalem, and dwell there, and go not forth thence any whither.

37 For it shall be, *that* on the day thou goest out, and passest over the brook Kidron, thou shalt know for certain that thou shalt surely die: thy blood shall be upon thine own head.

38 And Shimei said unto the king, The saying *is* good: as my lord the king hath said, so will thy servant do. And Shimei dwelt in Jerusalem many days.

39 And it came to pass at the end of three years, that

Ordered him to come out
   2) Joab refused: Stated he would die there
   3) Benaiah reported Joab's words to Solomon

c. Solomon ordered the execution of Joab in the worship center
   1) To remove any personal or national guilt for failing to execute justice
      - Because Joab committed senseless murder
      - Because Joab killed two commanders—Abner & Amasa—without the knowledge & orders of David
   2) To make sure that Joab finally bore the responsibility for his evil
   3) To bring God's peace on the leaders & the nation

d. Benaiah executed Joab: Buried him at his home

6. The execution of Shimei: A picture of judgment, reaping what one sows

a. Shimei was placed under city-arrest, confined, & restricted to Jerusalem—not allowed to travel anywhere else
   1) He was warned: If he violated the restriction, he would die
   2) He accepted the terms
   3) He lived by the confinement for a long time

b. Shimei broke the restriction three years later

1) He had two slaves who fled for their freedom 2) He learned where they were, then pursued & returned them	two of the servants of Shimei ran away unto Achish son of Maachah king of Gath. And they told Shimei, saying, Behold, thy servants *be* in Gath. 40 And Shimei arose, and saddled his ass, and went to Gath to Achish to seek his servants: and Shimei went, and brought his servants from Gath.	and thou saidst unto me, The word *that* I have heard *is* good. 43 Why then hast thou not kept the oath of the LORD, and the commandment that I have charged thee with? 44 The king said moreover to Shimei, Thou knowest all the wickedness which thine heart is privy to, that thou didst to David my father:	3) Why, then, had he broken his sworn vow & the king's order? d. Shimei heard the fateful verdict from King Solomon: Death 1) Because of the wrong he had done to Solomon's father, David
c. Shimei was immediately summoned by Solomon for questioning	41 And it was told Solomon that Shimei had gone from Jerusalem to Gath, and was come again.	therefore the LORD shall return thy wickedness upon thine own head;	
1) Had he not been warned & ordered to swear that he understood the restriction, "If he left the city, he would die"? 2) Had he not vowed by oath to obey the restriction?	42 And the king sent and called for Shimei, and said unto him, Did I not make thee to swear by the LORD, and protested unto thee, saying, Know for a certain, on the day thou goest out, and walkest abroad any whither, that thou shalt surely die?	45 And king Solomon *shall be* blessed, and the throne of David shall be established before the LORD for ever. 46 So the king commanded Benaiah the son of Jehoiada; which went out, and fell upon him, that he died. And the kingdom was established in the hand of Solomon.	2) Because he had been a threat long enough: God would now bless & secure David's dynasty forever e. Solomon gave the order to Benaiah: Execute Shimei f. Solomon's kingdom was now firmly established: All threats to the throne were removed

DIVISION I

THE RISE AND REIGN OF SOLOMON AS KING: BEGINNING IN GLORY AND ENDING IN SHAME, 1:1–11:43

B. The Death of David and the Consolidation of Solomon's Power: A Picture of Death and of Justice, 2:1-46

(2:1-46) **Introduction**: death is a surety, inevitable. Once we are born, death is the only event we are ever sure of experiencing. Death cannot be escaped: we must die. Death is part of the human experience.

The great tragedy is this: many people fear death—and rightly so, if a person has never trusted Jesus Christ as his or her Savior. But if a person is a genuine believer, death will be the most wonderful event ever experienced by the person. When the true believer crosses the portals of death, he moves...

- from corruption to incorruption
- from being perishable to being imperishable
- from a body of dishonor to a body of glory
- from a body of weakness to a body of power
- from a natural body to a spiritual body

The natural body is the body we now possess, the body that will die and be laid in the grave to deteriorate and return to dust. But the spiritual body is the body we will possess once we cross the portals of death, the body that will be permanent. With the spiritual body we will never again have to die, but instead we will live in the presence of God in all the majesty, glory, and splendor of heaven itself. And we will live in God's presence forever and ever.

Death holds no fear, no dread for the genuine, committed believer who faithfully walks day by day in the Lord Jesus Christ. The faithful, obedient believer lives in expectation and hope of eternal life.

This was the great hope of King David. And in this chapter, David dies. The greatest of all Israel's kings passes from the scene of human history. But not the impact of his life. The great faith and hope of David's heart lives on today just as it has down through the eons of human history. But David's death is not the only death covered in this chapter. Four other deaths are recorded, the deaths of men who posed a threat to the dynasty of David and to the reign of his son King Solomon. As long as these four men lived, there was the possibility of an insurrection against the throne. There was the threat of a rebellion, a coup against King Solomon. To consolidate the power of Solomon's throne and to secure the nation Israel, these four men and the threat they presented had to be handled. This is the subject of this great passage of Scripture: *The Death of David and the Consolidation of Solomon's Power: A Picture of Death and of Justice*, 2:1-46.

1. The charge of David to Solomon: be strong, obey the LORD, execute justice, and show yourself a real man: Stand for right, not wrong (vv.1-9).
2. The death of David: hope in God's eternal rest (vv.10-12).
3. The second plot of Adonijah and his execution: a picture of judgment falling upon those who oppose God's kingdom (vv.13-25).
4. The dismissal and banishment of the high priest Abiathar: a lesson on being disqualified for service (vv.26-27).
5. The execution of Joab: the consequences of disobeying clear commands (vv.28-34).
6. The execution of Shimei: a picture of judgment, reaping what one sows (vv.35-46).

1 (2:1-9) **Strong, Duty—Courage, Duty—Walk, Spiritual, Duty—Obedience, Duty—Commandments, of God, Duty—Law, of God, Duty—Obedience, Results—Justice, Duty—David, Charges of, to Solomon—Manhood, Duty—Man, Duty**: there was the final charge of David to Solomon, a charge given in three parts: sound *manly* advice, sound *spiritual* advice, and sound *political* advice. The Scripture covers David's charge in detail:

OUTLINE	SCRIPTURE	SCRIPTURE	OUTLINE
1. The charge of David to Solomon: Be strong, obey the LORD, execute justice, & show yourself a real man—stand for right, not wrong a. Be strong (courageous), De. 31:7-8; Jos.1:1-7; 23:6-8 b. Keep the charge of the LORD 1) Walk in His ways, requirements 2) Obey His law & commandments—His Word 3) The results • You will prosper, be successful • God will fulfill His promises: David's kingdom will be eternal (fulfilled in Christ, the Son of David, whose kingdom is eternal), 2 S.7:11-16; 1 Chr. 17:11-14; Ac.2:22-36; 3:25-26; 15:15-17; Ga.3:25-29; Re.3:21 c. Execute justice: A picture of the need for justice 1) Justice needed to be executed upon Joab • He disobeyed orders & killed two commanders in peacetime: Abner & Amasa, 2 S.3:22-27;	Now the days of David drew nigh that he should die; and he charged Solomon his son, saying, 2 I go the way of all the earth: be thou strong therefore, and show thyself a man; 3 And keep the charge of the LORD thy God, to walk in his ways, to keep his statutes, and his commandments, and his judgments, and his testimonies, as it is written in the law of Moses, that thou mayest prosper in all that thou doest, and whither-soever thou turnest thyself: 4 That the LORD may continue his word which he spake concerning me, saying, If thy children take heed to their way, to walk before me in truth with all their heart and with all their soul, there shall not fail thee (said he) a man on the throne of Israel. 5 Moreover thou knowest also what Joab the son of Zeruiah did to me, *and* what he did to the two captains of the hosts of Israel, unto Abner the son of Ner, and unto Amasa the son of Jether, whom he slew, and shed the	blood of war in peace, and put the blood of war upon his girdle that *was* about his loins, and in his shoes that *were* on his feet. 6 Do therefore according to thy wisdom, and let not his hoar head go down to the grave in peace. 7 But show kindness unto the sons of Barzillai the Gileadite, and let them be of those that eat at thy table: for so they came to me when I fled because of Absalom thy brother. 8 And, behold, *thou hast* with thee Shimei the son of Gera, a Benjamite of Bahurim, which cursed me with a grievous curse in the day when I went to Mahanaim: but he came down to meet me at Jordan, and I sware to him by the LORD, saying, I will not put thee to death with the sword. 9 Now therefore hold him not guiltless: for thou *art* a wise man, and knowest what thou oughtest to do unto him; but his hoar head bring thou down to the grave with blood.	20:8-13 • He conspired with Adonijah, 1:7, 19, 41; 2:28 • His punishment was left up to Solomon, but he was to be watched, not left alone in peace 2) Justice needed to be shown on behalf of Barzillai • His sons needed to be shown kindness • The reason: They supported David, 2 S.17:27-29 3) Justice needed to be executed upon Shimei • He had cursed God's anointed & threatened David's life, 2 S.16:11 • His punishment was left up to Solomon, but he was to be watched in his old age & executed

a. David charged Solomon to be strong, to prove himself to be a *real* man (vv.1-2). In ruling Israel Solomon would face enormous problems, pressures, and threats. As he confronted these, he needed to be strong and courageous, proving himself to be a *real* man who stood for right, never wrong.

Moreover, he must keep the major charge of the LORD: to walk in the ways of the LORD and keep His commandments, always obeying His Word. Note that David spelled out the various parts of the Mosaic law, which included four different sets of laws:

⇒ God's statutes (decrees) and commandments
⇒ God's judgments (laws) and testimonies (requirements)

b. David reminded Solomon that if he kept the commandments of God, he would prosper and be successful in all that he did and wherever he went. God would fulfill the great promises He had given to David in the *Davidic covenant,* in particular the promise of an eternal dynasty. His descendants would always rule upon the throne of Israel (2 S.7:1-17; 1 Chr.17:11-14; Ac.2:22-36; 3:25-26; 15:15-17; Ga.3:25-29; Re.3:21). But keep this fact in mind: this promise was conditional. As men, David's descendants would always rule Israel if they obeyed God. But if they failed to obey God, they would no longer be given the privilege to rule. However, within the Davidic covenant was the promise of God to send His own Son to sit upon the throne of David (2 S.7:13-14). God promised that the Messiah or Savior would come from David's seed—his descendants—and this was an eternal promise. The Messiah did come from the descendants of David, and David is a clear type of Christ who is the Son of David, the Messiah and Savior of the world. In the words of Matthew Henry:

> *God had promised David that the Messiah should come from his loins, and that promise was absolute: but the promise that there should not fail him* a man on the throne of Israel *was conditional—if his seed behave themselves as they should. If Solomon, in his day, fulfil the condition, he does his part towards the perpetuating of the promise. The condition is that he walk before God in all his institutions, in sincerity, with zeal and resolution; and...that he* take heed to his way.[1]

[1] Matthew Henry. *Matthew Henry's Commentary*, Vol.2. (Old Tappan, NJ: Fleming H. Revell Co., n.d.), pp.585-586.

c. David also gave Solomon some good political advice, charging him to execute justice throughout the land (vv.5-9). In particular, Solomon needed to deal with several men whom David had been unable to handle for various reasons.

1) Justice needed to be executed upon Joab, the commander of David's army throughout his reign (vv.5-6). Joab had always been a mixed blessing for David. He was a brilliant military strategist, fiercely loyal and a wise counselor, a man whom David deeply respected (2 S.19:1-8). But Joab also created some embarrassing problems and political difficulties for David. For example...
   - Joab killed Abner, the commander-in-chief of Israel whom David had enlisted to help reunite Israel with Judah. By killing Abner, Joab jeopardized the reunification efforts (2 S.3:1-39).
   - Joab also murdered the commander Amasa, whom David had appointed to handle a revolt by the Israelites led by the traitor Sheba (2 S.20:1-26).
   - When Absalom rebelled against his father David, Joab killed Absalom against David's orders (2 S.18:1-18).
   - Just recently, in opposition to Solomon, Joab had supported the coup of Adonijah (1 K.1:1-53).

   Because of Joab's loyalty to David, David had always chosen not to execute Joab. However, when Joab killed Absalom, David had him removed from the position of commander-in-chief of the armed forces (20:4). But he never had Joab executed for the crimes he had committed. The execution of justice upon Joab was now being left up to Solomon (v.6). Solomon was to deal with Joab as he saw fit. But if he allowed the commander to live, Solomon needed to watch him closely; for the commander had proven to be a dangerous opponent to Solomon (1:7, 19, 25, 41).
2) Justice also demanded that certain people be rewarded, in particular the family of Barzillai (v.7). His sons needed to be shown kindness, for this family had supported David during his flight from the revolt of Absalom (2 S.17:27-29).
3) Justice also needed to be executed upon Shimei, a descendant of King Saul (vv.8-9). During David's flight from Absalom, Shimei had cursed and threatened David's life (2 S.16:5-14). Then, after the revolt of Absalom had been put down and David was returning back to the palace, Shimei met David and begged for forgiveness and pardon (2 S.19:16-23). Because of the wonderful victory God had just given, David showed mercy. He pardoned Shimei and swore by oath that he would not personally put him to death. However, Shimei could become a troublemaker for Solomon, for David knew that his repentance had been a sham. By being a descendant of Saul, he would support any rebel who sought to overthrow the throne of David's dynasty. Consequently, Solomon had to keep close watch over Shimei and execute justice upon him as soon as possible.

Thought 1. There are at least three lessons for us in David's charge to Solomon:

(1) We must be strong in the LORD, prove to be *real* men and *real* women who stand for what is right, always rejecting what is wrong. A person who is strong in the LORD will take a stand, standing up for righteousness and standing against all wickedness and evil. When we see a person standing up against wickedness, we are looking at a *real* man or a *real* woman, a person who has courage to stand up for truth and righteousness. We must be *real* men and *real* women, strong and courageous in the LORD.

> **"Watch ye, stand fast in the faith, quit you like men, be strong" (1 Co.16:13).**
>
> **"Finally, my brethren, be strong in the Lord, and in the power of his might. Put on the whole armour of God, that ye may be able to stand against the wiles of the devil. For we wrestle not against flesh and blood, but against principalities, against powers, against the rulers of the darkness of this world, against spiritual wickedness in high *places*. Wherefore take unto you the whole armour of God, that ye may be able to withstand in the evil day, and having done all, to stand" (Ep.6:10-13).**
>
> **"Only let your conversation [behavior] be as it becometh the gospel of Christ: that whether I come and see you, or else be absent, I may hear of your affairs, that ye stand fast in one spirit, with one mind striving together for the faith of the gospel; And in nothing terrified by your adversaries: which is to them an evident token of perdition, but to you of salvation, and that of God" (Ph.1:27-28).**
>
> **"Thou therefore, my son, be strong in the grace that is in Christ Jesus" (2 Ti.2:1).**
>
> **"Be strong and of a good courage, fear not, nor be afraid of them: for the LORD thy God, he *it is* that doth go with thee; he will not fail thee, nor forsake thee" (De.31:6).**
>
> **"Be strong and of a good courage: for unto this people shalt thou divide for an inheritance the land, which I sware unto their fathers to give them" (Jos.1:6).**
>
> **"Be ye strong therefore, and let not your hands be weak: for your work shall be rewarded" (2 Chr.15:7).**
>
> **"Arise; for *this* matter *belongeth* unto thee: we also *will be* with thee: be of good courage, and do *it*" (Ezr.10:4).**
>
> **"Behold, God *is* my salvation; I will trust, and not be afraid: for the LORD JEHOVAH *is* my strength and *my* song; he also is become my salvation" (Is.12:2).**
>
> **"Say to them *that are* of a fearful heart, Be strong, fear not: behold, your God will come *with* vengeance, *even* God *with* a recompence; he will come and save you" (Is.35:4).**

(2) We must keep the major charge of the LORD: walk in His ways and keep His commandments. We must obey God, do exactly as He says.

> **"Not every one that saith unto me, Lord, Lord, shall enter into the kingdom of heaven; but he that doeth the will of my Father which is in heaven" (Mt.7:21).**
>
> **"For whosoever shall do the will of my Father which is in heaven, the same is my brother, and sister, and mother" (Mt.12:50).**

"And he said unto him, Why callest thou me good? *there is* none good but one, *that is*, God: but if thou wilt enter into life, keep the commandments" (Mt.19:17).

"Jesus answered and said unto him, If a man love me, he will keep my words: and my Father will love him, and we will come unto him, and make our abode with him" (Jn.14:23).

"If ye keep my commandments, ye shall abide in my love; even as I have kept my Father's commandments, and abide in his love" (Jn.15:10).

"For this is the love of God, that we keep his commandments: and his commandments are not grievous" (1 Jn.5:3).

"Blessed are they that do his commandments, that they may have right to the tree of life, and may enter in through the gates into the city" (Re.22:14).

"Thou shalt keep therefore his statutes, and his commandments, which I command thee this day, that it may go well with thee, and with thy children after thee, and that thou mayest prolong *thy* days upon the earth, which the LORD thy God giveth thee, for ever" (De.4:40).

"Ye shall diligently keep the commandments of the LORD your God, and his testimonies, and his statutes, which he hath commanded thee" (De.6:17).

"This book of the law shall not depart out of thy mouth; but thou shalt meditate therein day and night, that thou mayest observe to do according to all that is written therein: for then thou shalt make thy way prosperous, and then thou shalt have good success" (Jos.1:8).

"But take diligent heed to do the commandment and the law, which Moses the servant of the LORD charged you, to love the LORD your God, and to walk in all his ways, and to keep his commandments, and to cleave unto him, and to serve him with all your heart and with all your soul" (Jos.22:5).

(3) We must execute justice upon the earth. If we allow immorality, lawlessness, and violence to run rampant throughout society, society will disintegrate and eventually collapse.

⇒ Neighbors will distrust and fear their neighbors.
⇒ Workers will distrust and fear their employers.
⇒ Students will distrust and fear their fellow students and teachers.
⇒ Buyers will distrust and fear their suppliers (businesses).
⇒ Citizens will distrust and fear their politicians.

Distrust and fear will grip the lives of people, and they will begin to live behind closed doors. People will even fear walking the streets because so many are living immoral, lawless, and violent lives.

Justice must be established and executed upon this earth. And the only way to build a just society is for each of us to live a life of morality and righteousness, treating his or her family fairly and being kind and loving to everyone. Fair treatment, kindness, and brotherly love—these are the foundation stones of a just and righteous society. Listen to what the Word of God says about justice:

"Then Peter opened his mouth, and said, Of a truth I perceive that God is no respecter of persons: But in every nation he that feareth him, and worketh righteousness, is accepted with him" (Ac.10:34-35).

"Render therefore to all their dues: tribute to whom tribute *is due;* custom to whom custom; fear to whom fear; honour to whom honour" (Ro.13:7).

"Masters, give unto *your* servants that which is just and equal; knowing that ye also have a Master in heaven" (Col.4:1).

"I charge *thee* before God, and the Lord Jesus Christ, and the elect angels, that thou observe these things without preferring one before another, doing nothing by partiality" (1 Ti.5:21).

"Ye shall do no unrighteousness in judgment: thou shalt not respect the person of the poor, nor honour the person of the mighty: *but* in righteousness shalt thou judge thy neighbour" (Le.19:15).

"That which is altogether just shalt thou follow, that thou mayest live, and inherit the land which the LORD thy God giveth thee" (De.16:20).

"Thou shalt not pervert the judgment of the stranger, *nor* of the fatherless; nor take a widow's raiment to pledge" (De.24:17).

"The God of Israel said, the Rock of Israel spake to me, He that ruleth over men *must be* just, ruling in the fear of God" (2 S.23:3).

"And said to the judges, Take heed what ye do: for ye judge not for man, but for the LORD, who *is* with you in the judgment" (2 Chr.19:6).

"How long will ye judge unjustly, and accept the persons of the wicked? Selah" (Ps.82:2).

"Defend the poor and fatherless: do justice to the afflicted and needy" (Ps.82:3).

"The LORD executeth righteousness and judgment for all that are oppressed" (Ps.103:6).

"By the blessing of the upright the city is exalted: but it is overthrown by the mouth of the wicked" (Pr.11:11).

"Righteousness exalteth a nation: but sin *is* a reproach to any people" (Pr.14:34).

"*It is* an abomination to kings to commit wickedness: for the throne is established by righteousness" (Pr.16:12).

"Mercy and truth preserve the king: and his throne is upholden by mercy" (Pr.20:28).

"To do justice and judgment *is* more acceptable to the LORD than sacrifice" (Pr.21:3).

"Take away the wicked *from* before the king, and his throne shall be established in righteousness" (Pr.25:5).

"The king by judgment establisheth the land: but he that receiveth gifts overthroweth it" (Pr.29:4).

"The king that faithfully judgeth the poor, his throne shall be established for ever" (Pr.29:14).

"An unjust man *is* an abomination to the just: and *he that is* upright in the way is abomination to the wicked" (Pr.29:27).

"Thus saith the LORD, Keep ye judgment, and do justice: for my salvation is near to come, and my righteousness to be revealed" (Is.56:1).

2 (2:10-12) **Death, of David—Hope, for What, Eternal Rest—Eternal Life, Hope for**: there was the death of David and his wonderful hope in God's eternal rest. David died at about age 70 and was buried in the city of Jerusalem (2 S.5:4-5). He had reigned as king for forty years, seven years in Hebron and thirty-three years in Jerusalem. Just how long the co-regency with Solomon lasted is not known. Some commentators feel it was for a couple of years, but most feel it was only for a brief period of time. Whatever the case, when David died he left a firmly established kingdom for Solomon. Solomon was king, the sole ruler over all Israel, and the nation was united under his leadership.

OUTLINE	SCRIPTURE	SCRIPTURE	OUTLINE
2. The death of David: Hope in God's eternal rest, Ac.2:25-17 a. He was buried in Jerusalem b. He reigned as king 40 years • Seven years in Hebron • Thirty-three years in	10 So David slept with his fathers, and was buried in the city of David. 11 And the days that David reigned over Israel *were* forty years: seven years reigned he in Hebron,	and thirty and three years reigned he in Jerusalem. 12 Then sat Solomon upon the throne of David his father; and his kingdom was established greatly.	Jerusalem c. He left a firmly established kingdom for Solomon

Thought 1. This passage says that David "slept [rested] with his fathers." The New Testament says that David had the great hope that his flesh would "rest [live] in hope" because the LORD would not leave his "soul in hell [the grave]" (Ac.2:25-27). David had hope of living eternally with the LORD. And the same hope fills the hearts of all believers.

If we believe—trust the *eternal* Son of David, the Lord Jesus Christ—we will live eternally. For God accepts all who trust His Son. No matter who a person is or what a person has done, if that individual accepts Jesus Christ as his Savior, the person is forgiven his sins and accepted by God. The person lives eternally in the very presence of God. This was the hope of David. And it can become the hope of us all. What we have to do is exactly what David did: trust the *promised seed*, the Messiah and Savior of the world, the Lord Jesus Christ.

"And as Moses lifted up the serpent in the wilderness, even so must the Son of man be lifted up: That whosoever believeth in him should not perish, but have eternal life" (Jn.3:14-15).

"For God so loved the world, that he gave his only begotten Son, that whosoever believeth in him should not perish, but have everlasting life. For God sent not his Son into the world to condemn the world; but that the world through him might be saved" (Jn.3:16-17).

"He that believeth on the Son hath everlasting life: and he that believeth not the Son shall not see life; but the wrath of God abideth on him" (Jn.3:36).

"And this is life eternal, that they might know thee the only true God, and Jesus Christ, whom thou hast sent" (Jn.17:3).

"For the wages of sin *is* death; but the gift of God *is* eternal life through Jesus Christ our Lord" (Ro.6:23).

"These all died in faith, not having received the promises, but having seen them afar off, and were persuaded of *them,* and embraced *them,* and confessed that they were strangers and pilgrims on the earth" (He.11:13).

"And I heard a voice from heaven saying unto me, Write, Blessed *are* the dead which die in the Lord from henceforth: Yea, saith the Spirit, that they may rest from their labours; and their works do follow them" (Re.14:13).

3 (2:13-25) **Judgment, Surety of—Adonijah, Death of—Bathsheba, Rebuke of—Solomon, Rebuke of His Mother**: there was the second plot of Adonijah and his execution. Adonijah's ambition for the throne had not died. This is clearly seen in this passage:

OUTLINE	SCRIPTURE	SCRIPTURE	OUTLINE
3. The second plot of Adonijah & his execution: A picture of judgment falling upon those who oppose God's kingdom a. Adonijah made a clever but foolish appeal to Bathsheba: His appeal revealed that his ambition to be king was still very much alive 1) His exaggerated claim: That all Israel had	13 And Adonijah the son of Haggith came to Bathsheba the mother of Solomon. And she said, Comest thou peaceably? And he said, Peaceably. 14 He said moreover, I have somewhat to say unto thee. And she said, Say on. 15 And he said, Thou knowest that the kingdom was	mine, and *that* all Israel set their faces on me, that I should reign: howbeit the kingdom is turned about, and is become my brother's: for it was his from the LORD. 16 And now I ask one petition of thee, deny me not. And she said unto him, Say on. 17 And he said, Speak, I	expected him to be appointed king 2) His deceptive claim: That he submitted, accepted Solomon as the LORD's choice 3) His one request as a compensation for not receiving the crown: That King Solomon give Abishag,

OUTLINE	SCRIPTURE	SCRIPTURE	OUTLINE
David's concubine & nurse, to be his wife (to possess the king's concubine was to have a claim to the throne)	pray thee, unto Solomon the king, (for he will not say thee nay,) that he give me Abishag the Shunammite to wife.	22 And king Solomon answered and said unto his mother, And why dost thou ask Abishag the Shunammite for Adonijah? ask for him the kingdom also; for he *is* mine elder brother; even for him, and for Abiathar the priest, and for Joab the son of Zeruiah.	c. Solomon sharply rebuked his mother 1) He questioned why she would make such a request 2) He saw through the scheming plot of Adonijah: Stated Bathsheba might as well request the kingdom for Adonijah as well as for Joab & Abiathar
	18 And Bath-sheba said, Well; I will speak for thee unto the king.		
b. Bathsheba agreed & secured an audience before Solomon 1) She was deeply respected by Solomon • He stood up to meet her • He bowed to her • He had a throne brought to her	19 Bath-sheba therefore went unto king Solomon, to speak unto him for Adonijah. And the king rose up to meet her, and bowed himself unto her, and sat down on his throne, and caused a seat to be set for the king's mother; and she sat on his right hand.	23 Then king Solomon sware by the LORD, saying, God do so to me, and more also, if Adonijah have not spoken this word against his own life.	3) He declared that Adonijah had condemned himself with his request
2) She presented Adonijah's request: Almost word for word	20 Then she said, I desire one small petition of thee; I *pray thee,* say me not nay. And the king said unto her, Ask on, my mother: for I will not say thee nay.	24 Now therefore, *as* the LORD liveth, which hath established me, and set me on the throne of David my father, and who hath made me an house, as he promised, Adonijah shall be put to death this day.	4) He pronounced the verdict with an irrevocable oath: Death
	21 And she said, Let Abishag the Shunammite be given to Adonijah thy brother to wife.	25 And king Solomon sent by the hand of Benaiah the son of Jehoiada; and he fell upon him that he died.	d. He ordered Benaiah to execute Adonijah

a. Adonijah requested an audience with Solomon's mother, Bathsheba. Being granted the audience, he made a clever, foolish appeal to her (vv.13-17). Although Bathsheba did not see what Adonijah was really after, his appeal indicated that his ambition to be king was still very much alive. In making his unusual request of her, he made an exaggerated claim. He declared that by having been the crown prince, the kingdom had rightfully belonged to him; and everyone had expected him to be appointed king. But when the situation changed and Solomon was crowned king, he willingly accepted Solomon as the LORD's choice (v.15).

Note this fact about Adonijah's claim: all Israel had not supported him in his efforts to become king. He was in the process of deceiving Bathsheba and attempting to deceive Solomon, for his desire and ambition to become king was once again being aroused within his soul. His craving ambition is clearly exposed in his request. Adonijah is painting a picture of the great loss he has suffered by not being chosen king so that Bathsheba will grant his request. To offset his great loss for not receiving the crown, he makes one bold request: that King Solomon give Abishag, David's concubine and nurse, to be his wife (vv.16-17). Adonijah wants Bathsheba to appeal to Solomon to grant this one request as a *compensation,* a *payment* for not being crowned king.

This was a foolish request on the part of Adonijah, revealing his inability to rule. For taking one of the king's concubines was an act that laid claim to the throne. In ancient times, taking possession of a king's harem meant that a person was laying claim to the throne of a nation (2 S.3:7-10; 12:8; 16:21-22).

b. Bathsheba agreed to the request of Adonijah and secured an audience with her son Solomon (vv.18-21). Note Solomon's deep respect for his mother (v.19). When she entered the court, he stood up and then bowed before her. And he had a throne brought for her to sit upon.

As soon as she sat down upon the throne, Bathsheba presented Adonijah's request to Solomon, almost word for word (vv.20-21).

c. But no sooner had Bathsheba made her request than Solomon sharply rebuked his mother (vv.22-24). He questioned why she would make such a request, that she might as well request the whole kingdom for Adonijah. Solomon saw through the scheming purpose of his half-brother. The king knew that Adonijah was laying the groundwork, as small as it might seem in this particular request, for a future plot to take over the throne. Solomon declared that Adonijah had condemned himself with his request, and he pronounced the verdict with an irrevocable oath: Adonijah was to be executed (vv.23-24). Turning to his military commander Benaiah, Solomon issued the fatal order to execute the traitor Adonijah (v.25). The commander carried out the king's order immediately.

Thought 1. Adonijah's rebellion against King Solomon is a clear picture of a person's rebellion against the King of kings and LORD of lords, God Himself. If we rebel against God, keep Him from ruling in our lives, we will face the condemnation of God. We will hear the terrifying verdict: eternal death. Justice will be executed against us and we will be condemned to live eternally apart from God, condemned to live in hell itself. There are only two choices: living with God or living apart from God, in a place the Lord Jesus Christ Himself called hell.

One thing determines our destiny, what we do with God. Do we allow God to be the King of our lives or do we rebel against God and take our lives into our own hands? Do we live righteously as the King commands or do we live wicked lives in rebellion against the King? God demands that we live moral and righteous lives, loving our neighbors as ourselves. But if we live immoral and wicked lives and mistreat and hate our neighbors, we will face the judgment of God. This is the clear declaration of God's Holy Word:

"For the Son of man shall come in the glory of his Father with his angels; and then he shall reward every man according to his works" (Mt.16:27).

"And this is the condemnation, that light is come into the world, and men loved darkness rather than light, because their deeds were evil" (Jn.3:19).

"And to you who are troubled rest with us, when the Lord Jesus shall be revealed from heaven with his mighty angels, In flaming fire taking vengeance on them that know not God, and that obey not the gospel of our Lord Jesus Christ" (2 Th.1:7-8).

"The Lord knoweth how to deliver the godly out of temptations, and to reserve the unjust unto the day of judgment to be punished" (2 Pe.2:9).

"And Enoch also, the seventh from Adam, prophesied of these, saying, Behold, the Lord cometh with ten thousands of his saints, To execute judgment upon all, and to convince all that are ungodly among them of all their ungodly deeds which they have ungodly committed, and of all their hard *speeches* which ungodly sinners have spoken against him" (Jude 14-15).

"And I saw a great white throne, and him that sat on it, from whose face the earth and the heaven fled away; and there was found no place for them. And I saw the dead, small and great, stand before God; and the books were opened: and another book was opened, which is *the book* of life: and the dead were judged out of those things which were written in the books, according to their works. And the sea gave up the dead which were in it; and death and hell delivered up the dead which were in them: and they were judged every man according to their works. And death and hell were cast into the lake of fire. This is the second death. And whosoever was not found written in the book of life was cast into the lake of fire" (Re.20:11-15).

4 (2:26-27) **Disqualification, for Service—Discipline, Duty—Chastisement, Duty—Dismissal, Duty—Abiathar, Disqualified**: there was the dismissal and banishment of the High Priest Abiathar for political reasons. Remember Abiathar had supported Adonijah's rebellion against Solomon's being crowned king (1:7, 19, 25). Although Scripture does not mention it in the present passage, perhaps Abiathar and Joab were behind Adonijah's deceptive appeal for Solomon to grant him David's concubine Abishag. Whatever the case, Abiathar had become a political risk to the throne and to the peace and security of the nation. For this reason, Solomon banished him to his home in Anathoth, which was about three and one half miles north of Jerusalem. In reality, the High Priest deserved to die for backing Adonijah's revolt, but he was shown mercy because of his years of service to David. However, he was disqualified from service, removed from the priesthood. And note: this was a clear fulfillment of prophecy (1 S.2:30-35).

OUTLINE	SCRIPTURE	SCRIPTURE	OUTLINE
4. The dismissal & banishment of the High Priest Abiathar: A lesson on being disqualified for service, 1 Co.9:27 a. He was banished to his home b. He deserved to die for backing Adonijah's revolt, 1:7, 19 c. He was shown mercy because of his service to David	26 And unto Abiathar the priest said the king, Get thee to Anathoth, unto thine own fields; for thou *art* worthy of death: but I will not at this time put thee to death, because thou barest the ark of the Lord GOD before David my father, and because thou	hast been afflicted in all wherein my father was afflicted. 27 So Solomon thrust out Abiathar from being priest unto the LORD; that he might fulfil the word of the LORD, which he spake concerning the house of Eli in Shiloh.	d. He was permanently removed from the priesthood: A fulfillment of prophecy, 1 S.2:30-35

Thought 1. There is a much-needed lesson for us in this point: a believer can be disqualified from service. No matter who we are—pastor, teacher, evangelist, priest, minister, missionary, godly servant, leader, ruler—we can become unfit, unworthy to serve. All kinds of sin—including immorality and lawlessness—can disqualify us. Making too many mistakes can disqualify us, or not adequately preparing can disqualify us from having a fruitful, productive service. Whatever our position or service, we can become disqualified. This is the clear teaching of God's Holy Word:

"And cast ye the unprofitable servant into outer darkness: there shall be weeping and gnashing of teeth" (Mt.25:30; see also 25:14-30).

"Every branch in me that beareth not fruit he taketh away: and every *branch* that beareth fruit, he purgeth it, that it may bring forth more fruit" (Jn.15:2).

"If a man abide not in me, he is cast forth as a branch, and is withered; and men gather them, and cast *them* into the fire, and they are burned" (Jn.15:6).

"It is reported commonly *that there is* fornication among you, and such fornication as is not so much as named among the Gentiles, that one should have his father's wife....To deliver such an one unto Satan for the destruction of the flesh, that the spirit may be saved in the day of the Lord Jesus. Your glorying *is* not good. Know ye not that a little leaven leaveneth the whole lump" (1 Co.5:1, 5-6; see also 5:1-13).

"But I keep under my body, and bring *it* into subjection: lest that by any means, when I have preached to others, I myself should be a castaway" (1 Co.9:27).

"For this cause many *are* weak and sickly among you, and many sleep. For if we would judge ourselves, we should not be judged. But when we are judged, we are chastened of the Lord, that we should not be condemned with the world" (1 Co.11:30-32).

"Of whom is Hymenaeus and Alexander; whom I have delivered unto Satan, that they may learn not to blaspheme" (1 Ti.1:20).

"(For if a man know not how to rule his own house, how shall he take care of the church of God?" (1 Ti.3:5).

"A man that is an heretick after the first and second admonition reject" (Tit.3:10).

5 (2:28-34) **Disobedience, Consequences of—Commandments, Disobeying, Consequences—Execution, Example of, Joab—Joab, Execution of**: there was the execution of Joab. Was Joab involved in the latest scheme of Adonijah? Was he seeking to lay the groundwork for claiming the throne of Israel for Adonijah? Perhaps. But whatever the case, he was definitely involved in the first rebellion of Adonijah (1:7, 9, 19, 25, 41). As long as he lived, he would be a constant threat to the stability of the throne and the nation. What to do with Joab was one of the major decisions Solomon had to make right after being crowned king. Note what happened:

OUTLINE	SCRIPTURE	SCRIPTURE	OUTLINE
5. The execution of Joab: The consequences of disobeying clear commands a. Joab—one of the conspirators—understood his fate: He fled to the altar for refuge	28 Then tidings came to Joab: for Joab had turned after Adonijah, though he turned not after Absalom. And Joab fled unto the tabernacle of the LORD, and caught hold on the horns of the altar.	the innocent blood, which Joab shed, from me, and from the house of my father. 32 And the LORD shall return his blood upon his own head, who fell upon two men more righteous and better than he, and slew them with the sword, my father David not knowing *thereof, to wit,* Abner the son of Ner, captain of the host of Israel, and Amasa the son of Jether, captain of the host of Judah.	or national guilt for failing to execute justice • Because Joab committed senseless murder • Because Joab killed two commanders—Abner & Amasa—without the knowledge & orders of David
b. Solomon received news that Joab was seeking refuge in the worship center: He ordered Benaiah to go & execute the conspirator	29 And it was told king Solomon that Joab was fled unto the tabernacle of the LORD; and, behold, *he is* by the altar. Then Solomon sent Benaiah the son of Jehoiada, saying, Go, fall upon him.		
1) Benaiah confronted Joab: Ordered him to come out 2) Joab refused: Stated he would die there 3) Benaiah reported Joab's words to Solomon	30 And Benaiah came to the tabernacle of the LORD, and said unto him, Thus saith the king, Come forth. And he said, Nay; but I will die here. And Benaiah brought the king word again, saying, Thus said Joab, and thus he answered me.	33 Their blood shall therefore return upon the head of Joab, and upon the head of his seed for ever: but upon David, and upon his seed, and upon his house, and upon his throne, shall there be peace for ever from the LORD.	2) To make sure that Joab finally bore the responsibility for his evil 3) To bring God's peace on the leaders & the nation
c. Solomon ordered the execution of Joab in the worship center 1) To remove any personal	31 And the king said unto him, Do as he hath said, and fall upon him, and bury him; that thou mayest take away	34 So Benaiah the son of Jehoiada went up, and fell upon him, and slew him: and he was buried in his own house in the wilderness.	d. Benaiah executed Joab: Buried him at his home

a. When the news of Adonijah's execution reached Joab, he fully understood his own fate (v.28). As quickly as he could, he fled to the altar for refuge, grabbing hold of the horns of the altar (v.28). Remember, the altar was a place of refuge, the place where a man offered his sacrifice in order to be reconciled to God. Through the sacrifice, the man's sins were forgiven; and he was granted the refuge and mercy of God, granted God's acceptance and protection. By seeking refuge at the altar, Joab was hoping for Solomon's mercy and forgiveness, acceptance and protection.

b. When Solomon received news that Joab was seeking refuge in the worship center, he immediately ordered Benaiah to go and execute the conspirator (v.29). Confronting Joab, Benaiah ordered him to come out of the worship center; but Joab refused, stating that he would die there at the foot of the altar (v.30).

For some reason, perhaps because of the sanctity of the worship center, Benaiah refused to execute Joab at the altar. He quickly returned to King Solomon with Joab's refusal to leave the altar of rescue.

c. Without hesitation, Solomon ordered the execution of Joab in the worship center (vv.31-33). And Solomon stated three clear reasons for Joab's execution:

1) Joab was to be executed in order to remove all guilt from the throne, for David had earlier failed to execute justice against the commander (vv.31-32). If Solomon had failed to execute Joab, Solomon himself—as well as his father—would have been guilty of injustice. Remember, Joab had earlier committed senseless murder, killing both Abner and Amasa, and David had refused to execute justice against him (2 S.3:23-27; 20:8-13).
2) Joab was to be executed to make sure that he finally bore the responsibility for his evil (v.33). It was he who had killed the two commanders; consequently, the guilt of their blood rested on his head. For this reason, he deserved the penalty of death.
3) Joab was to be executed to bring God's peace on the leaders and on the nation of Israel (v.33). As long as a murderer ran loose in Israel (or in any nation for that matter), there would be a lack of peace within society. People feel restless, uneasy, suspicious, and distrustful, always looking over their shoulders, in particular as they walk about at night. And when the murderer is a leader within the nation, there is always the threat of a plot to overthrow the government. God's peace never rests upon a society when a murderer is running loose. For this reason, Joab was to be executed.

d. Following the clear instructions of Solomon, the commander Benaiah went into the worship center and executed Joab at the foot of the altar (v.34). When his body was removed, he was buried in his own tomb on his own property, which was located near Bethlehem (2 S.2:32).

e. With the death of the commander-in-chief Joab and the removal of the High Priest Abiathar, Solomon promoted Benaiah to be the new commander-in-chief and Zadok to be the leading High Priest of Israel (v.35). Rather quickly, the major officials of Solomon's government were being set in place. Solomon was beginning to demonstrate wisdom and organizational skills that were to make him famous throughout the world and down through the centuries.

Thought 1. There is a clear lesson for us in the execution of Joab. He was executed for two clear reasons: rebelling against the king and disobeying the commandments of the king. On several occasions Joab had deliberately acted on his own, going against the clear command of his superior, King David.

The LORD is our superior, the LORD of the universe and the LORD of all living creatures. When we disobey Him, we suffer the consequences just as Joab did in disobeying King David. Disobedience brings consequences. If we disobey God, break His commandments, we will suffer the consequences. Listen to what God says about disobedience:

"And that servant, which knew his lord's will, and prepared not *himself,* neither did according to his will, shall be beaten with many *stripes*" (Lu.12:47).

"But unto them that are contentious, and do not obey the truth, but obey unrighteousness, indignation and wrath" (Ro.2:8).

"Let no man deceive you with vain words: for because of these things cometh the wrath of God upon the children of disobedience" (Ep.5:6).

"And to you who are troubled rest with us, when the Lord Jesus shall be revealed from heaven with his mighty angels, In flaming fire taking vengeance on them that know not God, and that obey not the gospel of our Lord Jesus Christ: Who shall be punished with everlasting destruction from the presence of the Lord, and from the glory of his power" (2 Th.1:7-9).

"For if the word spoken by angels was stedfast, and every transgression and disobedience received a just recompence of reward; How shall we escape, if we neglect so great salvation; which at the first began to be spoken by the Lord, and was confirmed unto us by them that heard *him*" (He.2:2-3).

"The Lord knoweth how to deliver the godly out of temptations, and to reserve the unjust unto the day of judgment to be punished" (2 Pe.2:9).

"And a curse, if ye will not obey the commandments of the LORD your God, but turn aside out of the way which I command you this day, to go after other gods, which ye have not known" (De.11:28).

"But if ye will not obey the voice of the LORD, but rebel against the commandment of the LORD, then shall the hand of the LORD be against you, as *it was* against your fathers" (1 S.12:15).

"And I will punish the world for *their* evil, and the wicked for their iniquity; and I will cause the arrogancy of the proud to cease, and will lay low the haughtiness of the terrible" (Is.13:11).

6 (2:35-46) **Judgment, Results of—Reaping, What One Sows—Sowing, Results of—Shimei, Execution of**: there was the execution of Shimei, a clear picture of coming judgment, of reaping exactly what one sows. Remember Shimei had cursed and threatened David, God's anointed ruler (2 S.16:5-14). Because he was from the family of Saul, he was a potential threat in stirring up an insurrection against Solomon. For this reason, Solomon had to deal with the potential threat of Shimei. Scripture graphically describes what he did:

OUTLINE	SCRIPTURE	SCRIPTURE	OUTLINE
6. The execution of Shimei: A picture of judgment, reaping what one sows	35 And the king put Benaiah the son of Jehoiada in his room over the host: and Zadok the priest did the king put in the room of Abiathar.	so will thy servant do. And Shimei dwelt in Jerusalem many days.	
a. Shimei was placed under city-arrest, confined, & restricted to Jerusalem—not allowed to travel anywhere else	36 And the king sent and called for Shimei, and said unto him, Build thee an house in Jerusalem, and dwell there, and go not forth thence any whither.	39 And it came to pass at the end of three years, that two of the servants of Shimei ran away unto Achish son of Maachah king of Gath. And they told Shimei, saying, Behold, thy servants *be* in Gath.	b. Shimei broke the restriction three years later 1) He had two slaves who fled for their freedom 2) He learned where they were, then pursued & returned them
1) He was warned: If he violated the restriction, he would die	37 For it shall be, *that* on the day thou goest out, and passest over the brook Kidron, thou shalt know for certain that thou shalt surely die: thy blood shall be upon thine own head.	40 And Shimei arose, and saddled his ass, and went to Gath to Achish to seek his servants: and Shimei went, and brought his servants from Gath.	
2) He accepted the terms 3) He lived by the confinement for a long time	38 And Shimei said unto the king, The saying *is* good: as my lord the king hath said,	41 And it was told Solomon that Shimei had gone from Jerusalem to Gath, and was come again.	c. Shimei was immediately summoned by Solomon for questioning

OUTLINE	SCRIPTURE	SCRIPTURE	OUTLINE
1) Had he not been warned &ordered to swear that he understood the restriction, "If he left the city, he would die"? 2) Had he not vowed by oath to obey the restriction? 3) Why, then, had he broken his sworn vow & the king's order? d. Shimei heard the fateful	42 And the king sent and called for Shimei, and said unto him, Did I not make thee to swear by the LORD, and protested unto thee, saying, Know for a certain, on the day thou goest out, and walkest abroad any whither, that thou shalt surely die? and thou saidst unto me, The word *that* I have heard *is* good. 43 Why then hast thou not kept the oath of the LORD, and the commandment that I have charged thee with? 44 The king said moreover	to Shimei, Thou knowest all the wickedness which thine heart is privy to, that thou didst to David my father: therefore the LORD shall return thy wickedness upon thine own head; 45 And king Solomon *shall be* blessed, and the throne of David shall be established before the LORD for ever. 46 So the king commanded Benaiah the son of Jehoiada; which went out, and fell upon him, that he died. And the kingdom was established in the hand of Solomon.	verdict from King Solomon: Death 1) Because of the wrong he had done to Solomon's father, David 2) Because he had been a threat long enough: God would now bless & secure David's dynasty forever e. Solomon gave the order to Benaiah: Execute Shimei f. Solomon's kingdom was now firmly established: All threats to the throne were removed

a. Summoning Shimei to the royal court, Solomon placed the scoundrel under city-arrest in Jerusalem, forbidding him to travel anywhere else (vv.36-38). Solomon's reason was to keep Shimei from stirring up insurrection. After all, Shimei, a very influential and powerful man, was a descendant of Saul. The king warned him never to cross the Kidron Valley, just outside the city of Jerusalem. If he ever violated this restriction, he would be executed and his blood would be on his own head. Note that Shimei accepted the terms and lived by the confinement for a long period of time.

b. But eventually, some three years later, Shimei broke the restriction, which showed a very low view of Solomon's authority (vv.39-40). Two slaves had escaped and fled for their freedom from his estate. When he learned where they were, he personally pursued and returned them.

c. When Solomon received word of Shimei's offense, the king immediately summoned him to court for questioning (vv.41-43). Just as a brilliant attorney would spell out the charges against a criminal, Solomon laid out the clear charges against Shimei:

⇒ Had Shimei not been warned and ordered to swear that he understood the restriction: if he ever left the city he would die?
⇒ Had Shimei not vowed by oath to obey the restriction?
⇒ Why, then, had Shimei broken his sworn vow and the king's order?

The implication of the charges was clear: Shimei could not be trusted. No matter what restriction Solomon placed upon this scoundrel, Shimei had a low view of authority, in particular Solomon's authority.

d. Solomon pronounced the verdict upon Shimei: execution (vv.44-45). He was to be executed because of the wrong he had done to King Solomon's father, David. Now he would reap what he had sown. The LORD would repay him for his wrongdoing. But the scoundrel was to be executed for another reason as well: because he had been a threat long enough. As long as Shimei lived, he would be a threat to the throne and to David's dynasty (v.45). It was now time for God to bless and secure David's dynasty forever.

e. Solomon then gave the order to the commander Benaiah: execute Shimei (v.46). Immediately, the commander carried out the order.

f. With the leaders of the rebellion or coup now dead, Solomon's kingdom could finally be consolidated—firmly and solidly established. All the leaders involved in Adonijah's uprising—both the military and the religious leaders—were now executed. And the one person who could have stirred up support for Saul's dynasty and aroused an insurrection against King Solomon had also been executed. So far as was known, every potential threat to a unified kingdom had been removed. Thus the way was fully open for God to fulfill His promise to David, the promise that he would have an eternal descendant sitting upon the throne. Of course, this was a direct prophecy of the *promised seed,* the coming Messiah and Savior of the world who would be the Ideal Son of David (Is.9:1-7; 11:1-9; Je.23:1-8; Mi.5:2; Mt.1:1-17; Lu.3:23-27).

Thought 1. The execution of Shimei is a clear picture of judgment, of reaping exactly what one sows.
⇒ If a worker fails to produce, he will be demoted or fired.
⇒ If a person steals, he will face the bar of justice.
⇒ If a person commits murder, he will face imprisonment or execution.
⇒ If a person overeats or abuses his body any other way, he will suffer ill health.
⇒ If a husband commits adultery, he will reap a damaged home life and family.

If we sow wrong behavior of any kind, we will reap judgment—either in this life or in the life to come. Reaping what we sow is one of the basic laws of the universe. And the truth of the law is written across the pages of history down through the years. Listen to what God's Holy Word says:

"Tribulation and anguish, upon every soul of man that doeth evil, of the Jew first, and also of the Gentile" (Ro.2:9).

"For the wages of sin *is* death; but the gift of God *is* eternal life through Jesus Christ our Lord" (Ro.6:23).

"For to be carnally minded *is* death; but to be spiritually minded *is* life and peace" (Ro.8:6).

"Now the works of the flesh are manifest, which are *these;* Adultery, fornication, uncleanness, lasciviousness, Idolatry, witchcraft, hatred, variance, emulations, wrath, strife, seditions, heresies, Envyings, murders, drunkenness, revellings, and such like: of the which I tell you before, as I have also told *you* in time past, that they which do such things shall not inherit the kingdom of God" (Ga.5:19-21).

"Be not deceived; God is not mocked: for whatsoever a man soweth, that shall he also reap. For he that soweth to his flesh shall of the flesh reap corruption; but he that soweth to the Spirit shall of the Spirit reap life everlasting" (Ga.6:7-8).

"For if the word spoken by angels was stedfast, and every transgression and disobedience received a just recompence of reward; How shall we escape, if we neglect so great salvation; which at the first began to be spoken by the Lord, and was confirmed unto us by them that heard *him*" (He.2:2-3).

"For if after they have escaped the pollutions of the world through the knowledge of the Lord and Saviour Jesus Christ, they are again entangled therein, and overcome, the latter end is worse with them than the beginning. For it had been better for them not to have known the way of righteousness, than, after they have known *it,* to turn from the holy commandment delivered unto them. But it is happened unto them according to the true proverb, The dog *is* turned to his own vomit again; and the sow that was washed to her wallowing in the mire" (2 Pe.2:20-22).

"Even as I have seen, they that plow iniquity, and sow wickedness, reap the same" (Jb.4:8).

"The wicked man travaileth with pain all *his* days, and the number of years is hidden to the oppressor" (Jb.15:20).

"Fools because of their transgression, and because of their iniquities, are afflicted" (Ps.107:17).

"Good understanding giveth favour: but the way of transgressors *is* hard" (Pr.13:15).

"He that soweth iniquity shall reap vanity: and the rod of his anger shall fail" (Pr.22:8).

CHAPTER 3

C. The Request for Wisdom by Solomon & His Wise Justice: A Lesson on Wisdom & Discernment, 3:1-28

3:4-15; see 2 Chr.1:2-13

1. A glimpse into the attitude of Solomon: Planting the seeds that lead to a worldly, carnal life
   a. An attitude that allowed him to make an alliance with Egypt & to marry an unbeliever
   b. An attitude that drove him to undertake massive, extravagant building projects
   c. An attitude that was divided spiritually
      1) The people still sacrificed & worshipped at the high places
      2) Solomon loved the LORD & obeyed the law
      3) But Solomon worshipped in the high places, not only in the tent before the Ark of God, 15; Le.17:3-4; De.12:5-6

2. A request for wisdom: A lesson on the assurance of answered prayer
   a. Solomon worshipped God: Traveled to Gibeon to offer sacrifices
   b. Solomon was confronted by God in a dream: God appeared in a dream & told Solomon to ask for whatever he wanted
   c. Solomon acknowledged two great facts
      1) That God had been very kind to his father David: Because of David's righteousness & upright heart
      2) That God had given a son to continue David's dynasty
   d. Solomon displayed a very essential spirit: Humility
      1) He had a deep sense of helplessness & inadequacy for the task given him
      2) He sensed a desperate need: God's chosen people were too great for him to serve
   e. Solomon made a striking request
      1) The request: For an understanding, discerning heart
      2) The reason: That he might govern God's people & discern between good & evil
   f. Solomon pleased the LORD immensely with his request
      1) The LORD reviewed, confirmed Solomon's request
         • It was not for long life
         • It was not for wealth
         • It was for an understanding, discerning heart
      2) The LORD made an astounding promise to Solomon
         • He would be given a wise & discerning heart—one that never had been nor ever would be surpassed
         • He would be given wealth & honor—above all his contemporaries
         • He would also be given a long life: But this promise was conditional, based upon obedience
   g. Solomon awoke from his dream & returned to Jerusalem
      1) He was stirred to worship before the Ark because of God's promise
      2) He gave a feast for his court officials

3. A demonstration of wise judgment or discernment: The importance of wisdom
   a. The difficult case of two prostitutes came before Solomon: They lived together & bore sons just three days apart
      1) There were no witnesses to the birth
      2) One woman's son died during the night: Because she rolled over on him
      3) This careless woman awoke during the night, quietly got up, & switched sons while the other

And Solomon made affinity
with Pharaoh king of Egypt,
and took Pharaoh's daughter,
and brought her into the city
of David, until he had made
an end of building his own
house, and the house of the
LORD, and the wall of Jerusalem round about.
2 Only the people sacri-
ficed in high places, because
there was no house built unto
the name of the LORD, until
those days.
3 And Solomon loved
the LORD, walking in the
statutes of David his
father: only he sacrificed
and burnt incense in high
places.
4 And the king went to
Gibeon to sacrifice there; for
that *was* the great high place:
a thousand burnt offerings
did Solomon offer upon that
altar.
5 In Gibeon the LORD ap-
peared to Solomon in a
dream by night: and God
said, Ask what I shall give
thee.
6 And Solomon said, Thou
hast showed unto thy servant
David my father great mercy,
according as he walked before thee in truth, and in
righteousness, and in uprightness of heart with thee; and
thou hast kept for him this
great kindness, that thou hast
given him a son to sit on his
throne, as *it is* this day.
7 And now, O LORD my
God, thou hast made thy
servant king instead of David
my father: and I *am but* a little child: I know not *how* to
go out or come in.
8 And thy servant *is* in the
midst of thy people which
thou hast chosen, a great
people, that cannot be numbered nor counted for multitude.
9 Give therefore thy servant an understanding heart to
judge thy people, that I may
discern between good and
bad: for who is able to
judge this thy so great a people?
10 And the speech pleased
the Lord, that Solomon had
asked this thing.
11 And God said unto him,
Because thou hast asked this
thing, and hast not asked for
thyself long life; neither hast
asked riches for thyself, nor
hast asked the life of thine
enemies; but hast asked for
thyself understanding to discern judgment;
12 Behold, I have done according to thy words: lo, I
have given thee a wise and an
understanding heart; so that
there was none like thee before thee, neither after thee
shall any arise like unto thee.
13 And I have also given
thee that which thou hast not
asked, both riches, and honour: so that there shall not be
any among the kings like unto thee all thy days.
14 And if thou wilt walk in
my ways, to keep my statutes
and my commandments, as
thy father David did walk,
then I will lengthen thy days.
15 And Solomon awoke;
and, behold, *it was* a dream.
And he came to Jerusalem,
and stood before the ark of
the covenant of the LORD,
and offered up burnt offerings, and offered peace offerings, and made a feast to all
his servants.
16 Then came there two
women, *that were* harlots,
unto the king, and stood before him.
17 And the one woman said,
O my lord, I and this woman
dwell in one house; and I was
delivered of a child with her
in the house.
18 And it came to pass the
third day after that I was delivered, that this woman was
delivered also: and we *were*
together; *there was* no
stranger with us in the house,
save we two in the house.
19 And this woman's child
died in the night; because she
overlaid it.
20 And she arose at mid-
night, and took my son from
beside me, while thine handmaid slept, and laid it in her

woman slept 4) The mother of the living son discovered the switching of the baby boys the next morning 5) Each woman was now claiming the living son as her own b. The extraordinary discernment of Solomon 1) He reviewed the facts of the case 2) He applied the principle of maternal instinct & love to get to the truth	bosom, and laid her dead child in my bosom. 21 And when I rose in the morning to give my child suck, behold, it was dead: but when I had considered it in the morning, behold, it was not my son, which I did bear. 22 And the other woman said, Nay; but the living *is* my son, and the dead *is* thy son. And this said, No; but the dead *is* thy son, and the living *is* my son. Thus they spake before the king. 23 Then said the king, The one saith, This *is* my son that liveth, and thy son *is* the dead: and the other saith, Nay; but thy son *is* the dead, and my son *is* the living. 24 And the king said, Bring me a sword. And they brought a sword before the	king. 25 And the king said, Divide the living child in two, and give half to the one, and half to the other. 26 Then spake the woman whose the living child *was* unto the king, for her bowels yearned upon her son, and she said, O my lord, give her the living child, and in no wise slay it. But the other said, Let it be neither mine nor thine, *but* divide *it*. 27 Then the king answered and said, Give her the living child, and in no wise slay it: she *is* the mother thereof. 28 And all Israel heard of the judgment which the king had judged; and they feared the king: for they saw that the wisdom of God *was* in him, to do judgment.	• Called for a sword • Ordered the child to be cut in two with one half given to each mother • The true mother of the child was immediately gripped by her maternal love & concern for the baby: Cried out, begging for the king to give the child to the other woman c. The verdict of Solomon: The baby was to be given to the loving, compassionate woman d. The impact of Solomon's wisdom: The entire nation held him in awe, recognized his God-given ability to rule wisely & justly

DIVISION I

THE RISE AND REIGN OF SOLOMON AS KING: BEGINNING IN GLORY AND ENDING IN SHAME, 1:1–11:43

C. The Request for Wisdom by Solomon and His Wise Justice: A Lesson on Wisdom and Discernment, 3:1-28

(3:1-28) **Introduction**: Does wisdom dwell on the earth today? Are there many wise men and women within society serving in governmental, business, educational, and other leadership positions? Are there many husbands and wives who possess genuine wisdom, who develop wise relationships between themselves and with their children?

Wisdom is the ability to understand and to discern what to do, how to do it, and when to do it. Wisdom knows what to do and does it. Wisdom knows right from wrong, and always does what is right. Wisdom recognizes wickedness and has nothing to do with sin and evil. Wisdom knows what responsible behavior is and lives responsibly, turning away from all acts of irresponsibility.

Wisdom was the great concern of Solomon. Remember that Solomon had just consolidated the power of his throne. He had shattered a rebellion, a coup against the throne by his half-brother Adonijah. And he had executed all the powerful, influential conspirators who had supported the uprising of Adonijah. The nation was now unified under his leadership, and peace swept through the land. Solomon's father, King David, had recently died, and Solomon sat all alone upon the throne of the nation. Sensing deep inadequacy and helplessness to handle the task laid out before him, he felt the need to seek the face of the LORD. He desperately needed wisdom, a very special ability to understand and to discern what to do as he governed the great nation Israel. This is the subject of this great passage of Scripture: *The Request for Wisdom by Solomon and His Wise Justice: A Lesson on Wisdom and Discernment*, 3:1-28.

1. A glimpse into the attitude of Solomon: planting the seeds that leads to a worldly, carnal life (vv.1-3).
2. A request for wisdom: a lesson on the assurance of answered prayer (vv.4-15).
3. A demonstration of wise judgment or discernment: the importance of wisdom (vv.16-28).

1 (3:1-3) **Carnality, Caused by—Mind, Carnal, Caused by—Attitude, Carnal, Caused by—Attitude, Carnal, Example of—Carnality, Example of—Solomon, Carnality—High Places, Discussed**: a glimpse into the attitude of Solomon during the early years of his reign is given by Scripture. And the seeds that lead to a worldly, carnal life are already seen implanted in the heart of Solomon. Three attitudes in particular are spelled out:

OUTLINE	SCRIPTURE	SCRIPTURE	OUTLINE
1. A glimpse into the attitude of Solomon: Planting the seeds that lead to a worldly, carnal life a. An attitude that allowed him to make an alliance with Egypt & to marry an unbeliever	And Solomon made affinity with Pharaoh king of Egypt, and took Pharaoh's daughter, and brought her into the city of David, until he had made an end of building his own	house, and the house of the LORD, and the wall of Jerusalem round about. 2 Only the people sacrificed in high places, because there was no house built unto the	b. An attitude that drove him to undertake massive, extravagant building projects c. An attitude that was divided spiritually 1) The people still sacrificed

OUTLINE	SCRIPTURE	SCRIPTURE	OUTLINE
& worshipped at the high places 2) Solomon loved the LORD & obeyed the law	name of the LORD, until those days. 3 And Solomon loved the LORD, walking in the stat-	utes of David his father: only he sacrificed and burnt incense in high places.	3) But Solomon worshipped in the high places, not only in the tent before the Ark of God, 15; Le.17:3-4; De.12:5-6

a. Solomon had an attitude that allowed him to make a political alliance with Egypt and to marry an unbeliever (v.1). Under David's reign and now Solomon's, Israel had gained worldwide prominence—so much so that even Egypt was willing to make a peace alliance with Solomon. By this pact, Solomon was able to secure the southern border of the nation. His marriage to Pharaoh's daughter was obviously a political marriage, a marriage that sealed the alliance.

But note this fact: Solomon was marrying an unbeliever, bringing an unbeliever into the palace as his wife. He was exposing himself and the nation to her false gods and false religion. He was not as careful as he should have been in protecting himself and the Israelites from idolatrous beliefs. A worldly, carnal seed was already planted in the attitude and heart of Solomon.

b. Solomon had an industrious attitude that drove him to undertake massive, extravagant building projects (v.1). He was industrious, and for this he was to be commended. For it was his industrious spirit that drove him to complete the building of his own palace, the temple of the LORD, and the wall that surrounded the entire city of Jerusalem. Once he had completed these building projects, he built a special house or palace for his wife (7:1-51). But note this fact: several factors suggest an extravagant, indulgent, and unrestrained attitude and spirit within Solomon:

⇒ the ornate, costly structure and furnishings of his buildings (7:1-51; 9:10-28; 10:14-29)
⇒ the heavy taxation he placed on the people in order to complete his projects (10:14)
⇒ the labor policies he adopted, which included *forced*, *slave* labor and *drafted* labor (9:20-23)

The extravagance of Solomon, this seed of carnality that was planted within his heart, was to lead to a life of luxury, pleasure, compromise, and disobedience (9:10-28; 11:1-43).

c. Solomon had an attitude that was divided spiritually (vv.2-3). He allowed the people to continue worshipping at the high places throughout Israel. High places were usually open-air sanctuaries where altars and shrines were constructed for worship. These open-air sanctuaries had been constructed by the Canaanites on various hilltops throughout all Israel, including the countryside, towns, and cities. However, God had forbidden the Israelites to use the pagan altars and high places for worship of the LORD (Nu.33:52; De.7:5; 12:2-6, 13). The reason for this prohibition, this commandment, was to prevent the infiltration of false worship into Israel. If they worshipped at the high places, there would be the danger, even a tendency, to allow the infiltration of false belief and practices into their lives. Thus they were to destroy the high places and never participate in the worship of false gods. They were not to take over the pagan altars and high places that had been used by the nations they conquered. They were to construct worship centers only at the places chosen by God.

Solomon loved the LORD and obeyed the commandments of the LORD. But in this one area he failed: he worshipped the LORD at the high places, not only in the tent or worship center before the Ark of God. The seed of a worldly, carnal worship had been implanted in the life of Solomon.

Thought 1. The lesson for us is self-evident: we must guard against the seeds of a worldly, carnal life. When the urges of our flesh are aroused, we must restrain and subject them. We must keep our bodies under control. If we fail to discipline our bodies, the urges of our flesh will run wild, urges such as...

- eating a third or fourth helping
- committing immorality
- reading pornographic literature
- looking when we should control our eyes
- stealing or shoplifting
- deceiving or lying
- becoming angry or hostile
- seeking revenge or retaliation
- assaulting or murdering
- misusing or abusing
- subjecting or enslaving

The lust and arousal of the flesh will lead to a carnal life. For this reason, we must control, discipline ourselves. We must guard, protect ourselves against carnality, a fleshly, worldly life. This is the strong teaching of God's Holy Word:

"And that which fell among thorns are they, which, when they have heard, go forth, and are choked with cares and riches and pleasures of *this* life, and bring no fruit to perfection" (Lu.8:14).

"And I will say to my soul, Soul, thou hast much goods laid up for many years; take thine ease, eat, drink, *and* be merry. But God said unto him, *Thou* fool, this night thy soul shall be required of thee: then whose shall those things be, which thou hast provided? So *is* he that layeth up treasure for himself, and is not rich toward God" (Lu.12:19-21).

"Jesus answered them and said, Verily, verily, I say unto you, Ye seek me, not because ye saw the miracles, but because ye did eat of the loaves, and were filled" (Jn.6:26).

"For they that are after the flesh do mind the things of the flesh; but they that are after the Spirit the things of the Spirit. For to be carnally minded *is* death; but to be spiritually minded *is* life and peace. Because the carnal mind *is* enmity against God: for it is not subject to the law of God, neither indeed can be. So then they that are in the flesh cannot please God" (Ro.8:5-8).

"For, brethren, ye have been called unto liberty; only *use* not liberty for an occasion to the flesh, but by love serve one another" (Ga.5:13).

"Envyings, murders, drunkenness, revellings, and such like: of the which I tell you before, as I have also told *you* in time past, that they which do such things shall not inherit the kingdom of God" (Ga.5:21).

"For many walk, of whom I have told you often, and now tell you even weeping, *that they are* the enemies of the cross of Christ: Whose end *is* destruction, whose God *is their* belly, and *whose* glory *is* in their shame, who mind earthly things" (Ph.3:18-19).

"But she that liveth in pleasure is dead while she liveth" (1 Ti.5:6).

"Forasmuch then as Christ hath suffered for us in the flesh, arm yourselves likewise with the same mind: for he that hath suffered in the flesh hath ceased from sin; That he no longer should live the rest of *his* time in the flesh to the lusts of men, but to the will of God. For the time past of *our* life may suffice us to have wrought the will of the Gentiles, when we walked in lasciviousness, lusts, excess of wine, revellings, banquetings, and abominable idolatries: Wherein they think it strange that ye run not with *them* to the same excess of riot, speaking evil of *you:* Who shall give account to him that is ready to judge the quick and the dead" (1 Pe.4:1-5).

"Love not the world, neither the things *that are* in the world. If any man love the world, the love of the Father is not in him. For all that *is* in the world, the lust of the flesh, and the lust of the eyes, and the pride of life, is not of the Father, but is of the world" (1 Jn.2:15-16).

"He that loveth pleasure *shall be* a poor man: he that loveth wine and oil shall not be rich" (Pr.21:17).

"For the drunkard and the glutton shall come to poverty: and drowsiness shall clothe *a man* with rags" (Pr.23:21).

2 (3:4-15) **Wisdom, Prayer for—Prayer, Answered—Assurance, of Answered Prayer—Solomon, Prayer of**: Solomon began his reign in worship and prayer, sensing a deep need for wisdom to lead and govern the nation. With his power now consolidated and all the nation unified in supporting him, Solomon could now celebrate his inaugural ceremony or coronation service (2 Chr.1:1-13). What happened at the ceremony changed Solomon's life forever:

OUTLINE	SCRIPTURE	SCRIPTURE	OUTLINE
2. A request for wisdom: A lesson on the assurance of answered prayer a. Solomon worshipped God: Traveled to Gibeon to offer sacrifices	4 And the king went to Gibeon to sacrifice there; for that *was* the great high place: a thousand burnt offerings did Solomon offer upon that altar.	people? 10 And the speech pleased the Lord, that Solomon had asked this thing.	cern between good & evil f. Solomon pleased the LORD immensely with his request
b. Solomon was confronted by God in a dream: God appeared in a dream & told Solomon to ask for whatever he wanted	5 In Gibeon the LORD appeared to Solomon in a dream by night: and God said, Ask what I shall give thee.	11 And God said unto him, Because thou hast asked this thing, and hast not asked for thyself long life; neither hast asked riches for thyself, nor hast asked the life of thine enemies; but hast asked for thyself understanding to discern judgment;	1) The LORD reviewed, confirmed Solomon's request • It was not for long life • It was not for wealth • It was for an understanding, discerning heart
c. Solomon acknowledged two great facts 1) That God had been very kind to his father David: Because of David's righteousness & upright heart 2) That God had given a son to continue David's dynasty	6 And Solomon said, Thou hast showed unto thy servant David my father great mercy, according as he walked before thee in truth, and in righteousness, and in uprightness of heart with thee; and thou hast kept for him this great kindness, that thou hast given him a son to sit on his throne, as *it is* this day.	12 Behold, I have done according to thy words: lo, I have given thee a wise and an understanding heart; so that there was none like thee before thee, neither after thee shall any arise like unto thee. 13 And I have also given thee that which thou hast not asked, both riches, and honour: so that there shall not be any among the kings like unto thee all thy days.	2) The LORD made an astounding promise to Solomon • He would be given a wise & discerning heart—one that never had been nor ever would be surpassed • He would be given wealth & honor—above all his contemporaries
d. Solomon displayed a very essential spirit: Humility 1) He had a deep sense of helplessness & inadequacy for the task given him 2) He sensed a desperate need: God's chosen people were too great for him to serve	7 And now, O LORD my God, thou hast made thy servant king instead of David my father: and I *am but* a little child: I know not *how* to go out or come in. 8 And thy servant *is* in the midst of thy people which thou hast chosen, a great people, that cannot be numbered nor counted for multitude.	14 And if thou wilt walk in my ways, to keep my statutes and my commandments, as thy father David did walk, then I will lengthen thy days.	• He would also be given a long life: But this promise was conditional, based upon obedience
e. Solomon made a striking request 1) The request: For an understanding, discerning heart 2) The reason: That he might govern God's people & dis-	9 Give therefore thy servant an understanding heart to judge thy people, that I may discern between good and bad: for who is able to judge this thy so great a	15 And Solomon awoke; and, behold, *it was* a dream. And he came to Jerusalem, and stood before the ark of the covenant of the LORD, and offered up burnt offerings, and offered peace offerings, and made a feast to all his servants.	g. Solomon awoke from his dream & returned to Jerusalem 1) He was stirred to worship before the Ark because of God's promise 2) He gave a feast for his court officials

a. Solomon traveled to Gibeon to worship God and to conduct the inaugural ceremony (v.4). Attending the ceremony were the officials of the royal court, the military commanders, the judges and governors of the nation, the clan leaders, and, no doubt, a vast multitude of citizens (v.4; 2 Chr.1:1-13). A thousand burnt offerings were sacrificed to the LORD, indicating a huge and joyful occasion in celebrating the crowning of Solomon as king. It should be noted that the Tabernacle itself was located at Gibeon during these days of Solomon's reign (2 Chr.1:3). Once the worship service had been conducted, Solomon and the multitude of people retired to their tents and campsites for the night.

b. After having fallen asleep, Solomon was suddenly confronted by the LORD who appeared to him in a dream (v.5). Being very pleased with the worship and sacrifices Solomon had offered, the LORD told Solomon to ask for or make any request he wanted.

c. But note what Solomon did: instead of making an immediate request, he acknowledged two great facts (v.6). His heart was overflowing with gratitude to the LORD for His wonderful goodness to him as king. For that reason he expressed his gratitude and thankfulness for what the LORD had done:

⇒ that God had been very kind to his father David because David had been faithful to the LORD and lived a righteous and upright life
⇒ that God had given a son to continue David's dynasty

Solomon knew that he had been given the privilege of ruling only by the grace of God and only because his father David had lived a righteous life. With a heart full of praise and thanksgiving, Solomon expressed his gratitude to the LORD for the wonderful privilege of ruling and sitting upon the throne of David.

d. Solomon also expressed a very essential attitude or spirit—that of humility (v.7). He was gripped by a deep, intense sense of helplessness and inadequacy for the awesome task given him. Knowing how inexperienced he was in government, Solomon referred to himself as being "only a little child." Within the halls of government, he simply did not know how to go out or come in, how to find his way around, how to carry out his duties and perform his task as king. Solomon was gripped by a sense of desperate need, for God's chosen people were too numerous and too great a people for him to serve. He was helpless, too unqualified for the task.

e. Having shared his gratitude and his sense of inadequacy, Solomon then made a striking request of the LORD (vv.8-9). He requested an understanding, discerning heart so that he might govern God's people and discern between good and evil, right and wrong. Without this wisdom—the wisdom of an understanding and discerning heart—Solomon stated that he would not be able to govern the great nation Israel, the people of the LORD. Keep in mind that Solomon had become the ruler of the nation once led by great leaders such as Abraham, Isaac, Jacob, Moses, Joshua, Samuel, and his father King David.[1]

By an understanding and discerning heart, Solomon meant a heart that could understand issues and discern the truth, a heart that could judge between…

- good and bad
- right and wrong
- truth and falsehood
- righteousness and evil

He was asking for a heart that would listen and be patient with all sides of an issue and that could discern and judge the truth. He needed a tender, patient heart and a sharp mind that had the ability to reason and think issues through.

f. Solomon's striking request pleased the LORD immensely (vv.10-14). Responding to Solomon, the LORD reviewed and confirmed Solomon's request. He had not requested what most people would have: health and a long life, wealth and prosperity. Instead, Solomon had requested an understanding, discerning heart so that he might minister justice among the people. Because of Solomon's wise and humble request, the LORD made an astounding promise to Solomon:

⇒ he would be given a wise and discerning heart, a heart that never had been nor ever would be surpassed (v.12).
⇒ he would be given wealth and honor above all his contemporaries (v.13).
⇒ he would also be given a long life, but this promise was conditional: it was based upon obedience. Solomon must walk in the ways of the LORD and obey the LORD's commandments.

g. When the encounter with the LORD was over, Solomon immediately awoke from his dream and returned to Jerusalem (v.15). He was stirred to worship before the Ark of God because of God's wonderful promises to him. After standing there before the Ark, he offered two types of sacrifices to the LORD:

⇒ He offered burnt sacrifices, which symbolized the atonement, that he had been reconciled to God through the substitute sacrifice.
⇒ He offered fellowship or peace offerings, which symbolized that he wished to grow in the peace and fellowship of God, ever seeking a deeper life with the LORD (see outline and notes—Le.1:1–7:38 for more discussion).

After his personal worship before the Ark of God, Solomon held a great feast for his court officials (v.15). What a memorable experience his inaugural ceremony had been, an experience that led to a dramatic, life-changing encounter with the LORD!

> **Thought 1**. There is an encouraging lesson for us in this worship experience of Solomon. When we are facing desperate and critical situations or are feeling incapable and sensing deep, intense inadequacy, we can cry out to the LORD and He will answer us. The LORD will meet our desperate need, and He will help equip us to handle the difficult situation. The LORD will empower us, making us sufficient and adequate so that we can handle the task. Never will the LORD abandon us and leave us to plow through life by ourselves.

---

[1] Paul R. House. *1, 2 Kings*. "The New American Commentary." (Nashville, TN: Broadman & Holman Publishers, 1995), p.110.

Prayer is the answer. When we pray, the LORD hears and answers us, meeting our need. Whatever the need is, the LORD will hear our cry and answer our prayer, strengthening and empowering us to conquer whatever problems confront us. This is the clear teaching of God's Holy Word:

"Therefore I say unto you, What things soever ye desire, when ye pray, believe that ye receive *them,* and ye shall have *them*" (Mk.11:24).

"And I say unto you, Ask, and it shall be given you; seek, and ye shall find; knock, and it shall be opened unto you" (Lu.11:9).

"If ye abide in me, and my words abide in you, ye shall ask what ye will, and it shall be done unto you" (Jn.15:7).

"Hitherto have ye asked nothing in my name: ask, and ye shall receive, that your joy may be full" (Jn.16:24).

"So that we may boldly say, The Lord *is* my helper, and I will not fear what man shall do unto me" (He.13:6).

"Confess *your* faults one to another, and pray one for another, that ye may be healed. The effectual fervent prayer of a righteous man availeth much" (Ja.5:16).

"And whatsoever we ask, we receive of him, because we keep his commandments, and do those things that are pleasing in his sight" (1 Jn.3:22).

"The LORD *is* my strength and my shield; my heart trusted in him, and I am helped: therefore my heart greatly rejoiceth; and with my song will I praise him" (Ps.28:7).

"But I *am* poor and needy; *yet* the Lord thinketh upon me: thou *art* my help and my deliverer; make no tarrying, O my God" (Ps.40:17).

"He shall call upon me, and I will answer him: I *will be* with him in trouble; I will deliver him, and honour him" (Ps.91:15).

"Fear thou not; for I *am* with thee: be not dismayed; for I *am* thy God: I will strengthen thee; yea, I will help thee; yea, I will uphold thee with the right hand of my righteousness" (Is.41:10).

"Fear not: for I have redeemed thee, I have called *thee* by thy name; thou *art* mine. When thou passest through the waters, I *will be* with thee; and through the rivers, they shall not overflow thee: when thou walkest through the fire, thou shalt not be burned; neither shall the flame kindle upon thee" (Is.43:1-2).

"And it shall come to pass, that before they call, I will answer; and while they are yet speaking, I will hear" (Is.65:24).

"And ye shall seek me, and find *me,* when ye shall search for me with all your heart" (Je.29:13).

3 (3:16-28) **Wisdom, Example of—Judgment, Example of—Discernment, Example of—Understanding, Example of—Justice, Example of**: Solomon immediately demonstrated the wisdom God had supernaturally given him, a clear example of sharp, intelligent discernment. The case brought before Solomon is one of the most well-known stories in the Bible, and the case tested Solomon's wisdom. It revealed that the LORD had definitely given Solomon unusual insight into human nature. Note the difficult, perplexing case:

OUTLINE	SCRIPTURE	SCRIPTURE	OUTLINE
3. A demonstration of wise judgment or discernment: The importance of wisdom a. The difficult case of two prostitutes came before Solomon: They lived together & bore sons just three days apart 1) There were no witnesses to the births 2) One woman's son died during the night: Because she rolled over on him 3) This careless woman awoke during the night, quietly got up, & switched sons while the other	16 Then came there two women, *that were* harlots, unto the king, and stood before him. 17 And the one woman said, O my lord, I and this woman dwell in one house; and I was delivered of a child with her in the house. 18 And it came to pass the third day after that I was delivered, that this woman was delivered also: and we *were* together; *there was* no stranger with us in the house, save we two in the house. 19 And this woman's child died in the night; because she overlaid it. 20 And she arose at midnight, and took my son from beside me, while thine handmaid slept, and laid it in her	bosom, and laid her dead child in my bosom. 21 And when I rose in the morning to give my child suck, behold, it was dead: but when I had considered it in the morning, behold, it was not my son, which I did bear. 22 And the other woman said, Nay; but the living *is* my son, and the dead *is* thy son. And this said, No; but the dead *is* thy son, and the living *is* my son. Thus they spake before the king. 23 Then said the king, The one saith, This *is* my son that liveth, and thy son *is* the dead: and the other saith, Nay; but thy son *is* the dead, and my son *is* the living. 24 And the king said, Bring me a sword. And they	woman slept 4) The mother of the living son discovered the switching of the baby boys the next morning 5) Each woman was now claiming the living son as her own b. The wise discernment of Solomon 1) He reviewed the facts of the case 2) He applied the principle of maternal instinct & love to

OUTLINE	SCRIPTURE	SCRIPTURE	OUTLINE
get to the truth • Called for a sword • Ordered the child to be cut in two with one half given to each mother • The true mother of the child was immediately gripped by her maternal love & concern for the baby: Cried out, begging for the king to give the child to the other woman	brought a sword before the king. 25 And the king said, Divide the living child in two, and give half to the one, and half to the other. 26 Then spake the woman whose the living child *was* unto the king, for her bowels yearned upon her son, and she said, O my lord, give her the living child, and in no wise slay it. But the other	said, Let it be neither mine nor thine, *but* divide *it.* 27 Then the king answered and said, Give her the living child, and in no wise slay it: she *is* the mother thereof. 28 And all Israel heard of the judgment which the king had judged; and they feared the king: for they saw that the wisdom of God *was* in him, to do judgment.	c. The verdict of Solomon: The baby was to be given to the loving, compassionate woman d. The impact of Solomon's wisdom: The entire nation held him in awe, recognized his God-given ability to rule wisely & justly

a. The difficult case involved two prostitutes who lived together (vv.17-22). The two women bore sons just three days apart, but there were no witnesses present during the births. During the night one woman's son died because she carelessly rolled over on him (v.19). Perhaps she had been in a drunken stupor. Whatever the case, this careless woman awoke during the night, quietly got up, and switched sons while the other woman slept (v.20).

When the other woman arose the next morning to nurse her son, she discovered he was dead. But when she closely observed him, she noticed that he was not the son she had borne (v.21).

b. The perplexing case that needed to be solved was just this: To whom did the living son belong? Each woman was now claiming the living son as her own. Note the wisdom, the sharp understanding and discernment of Solomon (vv.23-26). He reviewed the facts of the case and then applied the principle of maternal instinct and love to get to the truth. He tested the women by calling for a sword and ordering the child to be cut in two, with one half given to each mother (vv.24-25). But immediately the true mother, gripped by her maternal love and concern for the baby, cried out, begging for the king to give the child to the other woman. A startling contrast between the nature of the two women was immediately exposed. One woman was revealing a cruel heart, a cruelty that was willing to allow the child to be killed. And the other woman was revealing a maternal instinct and love for the child (v.26).

c. Justice could now be executed. Solomon gave the verdict: the baby was to be given to the loving, compassionate woman (v.27). She had proven beyond any doubt that she was the true mother of the living child.

d. Note the impact of Solomon's wisdom: the entire nation held him in awe, recognizing his God-given ability to rule wisely and justly throughout the nation. The people respected their king and held him in the highest esteem, knowing that such wisdom could come only from God Himself.

Thought 1. One of the greatest needs of the human race is *wisdom*. Wisdom is the ability to understand and to discern what to do, how to do it, and when to do it. If we know what to do, how to do it, and when to do it—we are wise. We possess wisdom. A wise person understands and discerns between...

- right and wrong
- good and bad
- righteousness and evil
- honesty and dishonesty
- truth and falsehood
- morality and immorality
- diligence and slothfulness
- hard work and laziness
- pride and humility
- righteous anger and wicked anger
- fair treatment and unfair treatment
- genuine love and infatuation

Wisdom even discerns between the good and the excellent, the acceptable and the best. Wisdom is one of the greatest qualities in all the earth, a quality that we must all possess. Without wisdom, society disintegrates and eventually collapses. No government, no society, and no family can survive without wisdom. In order to walk through life successfully, we must grow in understanding, be able to discern what to do, how to do it, and when to do it. We must discern between the good and the bad, the truth and the deception in order to succeed and live fruitful and productive lives. This is the clear teaching of God's Holy Word:

"Therefore whosoever heareth these sayings of mine, and doeth them, I will liken him unto a wise man, which built his house upon a rock: And the rain descended, and the floods came, and the winds blew, and beat upon that house; and it fell not: for it was founded upon a rock. And every one that heareth these sayings of mine, and doeth them not, shall be likened unto a foolish man, which built his house upon the sand: And the rain descended, and the floods came, and the winds blew, and beat upon that house; and it fell: and great was the fall of it" (Mt.7:24-27).

"That the God of our Lord Jesus Christ, the Father of glory, may give unto you the spirit of wisdom and revelation in the knowledge of him" (Ep.1:17).

"For this cause we also, since the day we heard *it,* do not cease to pray for you, and to desire that ye might be filled with the knowledge of his will in all wisdom and spiritual understanding" (Col.1:9).

"And that from a child thou hast known the holy scriptures, which are able to make thee wise unto salvation through faith which is in Christ Jesus" (2 Ti.3:15).

"If any of you lack wisdom, let him ask of God, that giveth to all *men* liberally, and upbraideth not; and it shall be given him" (Ja.1:5).

"But the wisdom that is from above is first pure, then peaceable, gentle, *and* easy to be intreated, full of mercy and good fruits, without partiality, and without hypocrisy" (Ja.3:17).

"And unto man he said, Behold, the fear of the Lord, that *is* wisdom; and to depart from evil *is* understanding" (Jb.28:28).

"Happy *is* the man *that* findeth wisdom, and the man *that* getteth understanding. For the merchandise of it *is* better than the merchandise of silver, and the gain thereof than fine gold" (Pr.3:13-14).

"Get wisdom, get understanding: forget *it* not; neither decline from the words of my mouth" (Pr.4:5).

"Wisdom *is* the principal thing; *therefore* get wisdom: and with all thy getting get understanding" (Pr.4:7).

"For wisdom *is* better than rubies; and all the things that may be desired are not to be compared to it" (Pr.8:11).

"Buy the truth, and sell *it* not; *also* wisdom, and instruction, and understanding" (Pr.23:23).

"Then I saw that wisdom excelleth folly, as far as light excelleth darkness" (Ec.2:13).

"For *God* giveth to a man that *is* good in his sight wisdom, and knowledge, and joy: but to the sinner he giveth travail, to gather and to heap up, that he may give to *him that is* good before God. This also *is* vanity and vexation of spirit" (Ec.2:26).

1. **Solomon's administrative officials: The need for capable leaders**
   a. The chief officials or cabinet
      1) High Priest: Azariah
      2) Secretaries of State: Elihoreph & Ahijah
      3) Recorder: Jehoshaphat
      4) Chief commander: Benaiah
      5) Former High Priests: Zadok & Abiathar, 2:26-27; 2 S.8:17
      6) District Supervisor: Azariah
      7) Personal advisor & priest: Zabud
      8) Palace supervisor: Ahishar
      9) Supervisor of forced labor: Adoniram
   b. The 12 district governors over all Israel: Were the leaders who supplied provisions for the royal palace—each district responsible for one month a year
      1) Ben-Hur
      2) Ben-Deker
      3) Ben-Hesed
      4) Ben-Abinadab: Son-in-law of Solomon
      5) Baana
      6) Ben-Geber
      7) Ahinadab

CHAPTER 4

D. The Government or Political Administration of Solomon: A Picture of Capable Leaders, 4:1-34

So king Solomon was king
over all Israel.
2 And these *were* the princes which he had; Azariah the
son of Zadok the priest,
3 Elihoreph and Ahiah, the
sons of Shisha, scribes; Jehoshaphat the son of Ahilud,
the recorder.
4 And Benaiah the son of
Jehoiada *was* over the host:
and Zadok and Abiathar *were*
the priests:
5 And Azariah the son of
Nathan *was* over the officers:
and Zabud the son of Nathan
was principal officer, *and* the
king's friend:
6 And Ahishar *was* over the
household: and Adoniram the
son of Abda *was* over the
tribute.
7 And Solomon had twelve
officers over all Israel, which
provided victuals for the king
and his household: each man
his month in a year made
provision.
8 And these *are* their
names: The son of Hur, in
mount Ephraim:
9 The son of Dekar, in
Makaz, and in Shaalbim, and
Beth-shemesh, and Elon-
beth-hanan:
10 The son of Hesed, in
Aruboth; to him *pertained*
Sochoh, and all the land of
Hepher:
11 The son of Abinadab, in
all the region of Dor; which
had Taphath the daughter of
Solomon to wife:
12 Baana the son of Ahilud;
to him pertained Taanach and
Megiddo, and all Beth-shean,
which is by Zartanah beneath
Jezreel, from Beth-shean to
Abel-meholah, *even* unto *the*
place that is beyond Jok-
neam:
13 The son of Geber, in Ramoth-gilead; to him *per-*
tained the towns of Jair the
son of Manasseh, which *are*
in Gilead; to him *also per-*
tained the region of Argob,
which is in Bashan, three
score great cities with walls
and brasen bars:
14 Ahinadab the son of Iddo
had Mahanaim:
15 Ahimaaz *was* in Naphtali;
he also took Basmath the
daughter of Solomon to
wife:
16 Baanah the son of Hushai
was in Asher and in Aloth:
17 Jehoshaphat the son of
Paruah, in Issachar:
18 Shimei the son of Elah, in
Benjamin:
19 Geber the son of Uri *was*
in the country of Gilead, *in*
the country of Sihon king of
the Amorites, and of Og king
of Bashan; and *he was* the
only officer which *was* in the
land.
20 Judah and Israel *were*
many, as the sand which *is* by
the sea in multitude, eating
and drinking, and making
merry.
21 And Solomon reigned
over all kingdoms from the
river unto the land of the
Philistines, and unto the
border of Egypt: they
brought presents, and served
Solomon all the days of his
life.
22 And Solomon's pro-
vision for one day was thirty
measures of fine flour, and
threescore measures of
meal,
23 Ten fat oxen, and twenty
oxen out of the pastures, and
an hundred sheep, beside
harts, and roebucks, and fal-
lowdeer, and fatted fowl.
24 For he had dominion over
all *the region* on this side the
river, from Tiphsah even to
Azzah, over all the kings on
this side the river: and he had
peace on all sides round
about him.
25 And Judah and Israel
dwelt safely, every man under his vine and under his fig
tree, from Dan even to Beer-
sheba, all the days of Solomon.
26 And Solomon had forty
thousand stalls of horses for
his chariots, and twelve thousand horsemen.
27 And those officers provided victual for king Solomon, and for all that came
unto king Solomon's table,
every man in his month: they
lacked nothing.
28 Barley also and straw for
the horses and dromedaries
brought they unto the place
where *the officers* were,

      8) Ahimaaz: Son-in-law of Solomon
      9) Baana
      10) Jehoshaphat
      11) Shimei
      12) Geber

2. **Solomon's rule of peace & prosperity: A picture of God blessing His people**
   a. The blessings promised to Abraham, Ge.12:1-9
   b. The territory of Solomon's rule
      1) Stretched from the Euphrates River (NE) to the borders of the Philistines (W) & Egypt (SW)
      2) Was subjected & paid tribute to Solomon
   c. The daily provisions necessary to sustain the court of Solomon
      1) Flour: 150 bushels
      2) Meal: 300 bushels
      3) Oxen: 10
      4) Cattle: 20
      5) Sheep or goats: 100
      6) Deer, gazelles, roebucks, & choice fowl
      7) The supplies came from the kingdoms west of the Euphrates from Tiphsah (N) to Gaza (S)
      8) The peace & security of the nation during Solomon's reign
   d. The military power of Solomon: 40,000 stalls for horses & 12,000 horsemen
   e. The district officers, each in his own month, supplied provisions for Solomon, 7-19
      1) For his royal court
      2) For his horses

	every man according to his charge.	was in all nations round about.	• Calcol • Darda
3. Solomon's superior wisdom: A picture of God equipping the believer for his task a. The source of Solomon's wisdom: God b. The greatness of Solomon's wisdom: Incomparable 1) Greater than the wisdom of the East & of Egypt	29 And God gave Solomon wisdom and understanding exceeding much, and largeness of heart, even as the sand that *is* on the sea shore. 30 And Solomon's wisdom excelled the wisdom of all the children of the east country, and all the wisdom of Egypt.	32 And he spake three thousand proverbs: and his songs were a thousand and five. 33 And he spake of trees, from the cedar tree that *is* in Lebanon even unto the hyssop that springeth out of the wall: he spake also of beasts, and of fowl, and of creeping things, and of fishes.	c. The span of his wisdom 1) Proverbs: 3000 2) Songs: 1005 3) Botany: A careful observer of plant life 4) Zoology: Studied & expounded on animal life
2) Greater than any man—even greater than the four wisest men of that day... • Ethan: Author of Ps.89 • Heman: Author of Ps.88	31 For he was wiser than all men; than Ethan the Ezrahite, and Heman, Solomon's and Chalcol, and Darda, the sons of Mahol: and his fame	34 And there came of all people to hear the wisdom of Solomon, from all kings of the earth, which had heard of his wisdom.	d. The impact of Solomon's wisdom over the world: His wisdom was sought after by many national leaders of his day

DIVISION I

THE RISE AND REIGN OF SOLOMON AS KING: BEGINNING IN GLORY AND ENDING IN SHAME, 1:1–11:43

D. The Government or Political Administration of Solomon: A Picture of Capable Leaders, 4:1-34

(4:1-34) **Introduction**: today there is a dire need for good leaders. A shortage of qualified, courageous leaders exists throughout the world. As a result, weaknesses exist in the major institutions of society, weaknesses within...

- government
- businesses
- churches
- social clubs
- charity organizations
- ministries
- educational institutions
- families
- the military

The solution to the scarcity of leadership is simple: leaders must be trained. The basic qualities of leadership are these: initiative, skill, knowledge, understanding, wisdom, decisiveness, and a heart filled with the great qualities of character. To say that a person has character implies that he or she possesses the great qualities of love, joy, peace, patience, gentleness, goodness, faithfulness, meekness, and self-control (Gal.5:22-23). If a person has these qualities of character and leadership, the person is a very capable leader.

Leadership is the focus of this present passage of Scripture. Solomon had just squashed the rebellious uprising led by his half-brother Adonijah. And he had executed all the powerful, influential leaders who were supporting the coup. Furthermore, he had been able to consolidate his power and bring peace to the nation. Accordingly, the nation had just held its inaugural celebration. Now it was time for Solomon to form his government, to search for capable leaders to fill the administrative positions of his government. This is the subject of this important passage of Scripture: *The Government or Political Administration of Solomon: A Picture of Capable Leaders*, 4:1-34.

1. Solomon's administrative officials: the need for capable leaders (vv.1-19).
2. Solomon's rule of peace and prosperity: a picture of God blessing His people (vv.20-28).
3. Solomon's superior wisdom: a picture of God equipping the believer for his task (vv.29-34).

1 (4:1-19) **Leaders, Godly, Need for—Officials, of Solomon's Government—Government, Officials of, Solomon—Solomon, Officials of—Solomon, Government of**: there was the appointment of Solomon's administrative officials. Appointing these officials demonstrated Solomon's ability to organize and govern a large nation. Delegating authority is definitely a sign of wise leadership.

The Expositor's Bible Commentary points out that when Saul was crowned king, Israel was only a loose confederation of tribes. But through the military victories he achieved, Saul had slowly molded the nation into a kingdom. However, the government was modest and simple, with no central bureaucracy or lavish court. And he had never instituted a system of taxation.

However under David, Israel became a fully established nation or kingdom. His achievements were numerous:

⇒ He conquered enemy after enemy, building a great empire that extended Israel's borders from the Euphrates River in the northeast to the borders of the Philistines in the west and down to the borders of Egypt in the southwest (4:21).

⇒ He captured Jerusalem and established it as the permanent capital of Israel.

⇒ He built a palace (2 S.5:11), and he organized a royal court with a large number of chief officials to help him govern the nation.

⇒ He instituted some system of taxation among the Israelites and enforced a tribute system upon the nations he conquered.

⇒ He laid the groundwork and amassed the wealth for his son Solomon to build the temple.[1]

---

[1] Richard D. Patterson and Hermann J. Austel. *1, 2 Kings*, p.49.

Solomon indeed inherited a great kingdom from his father David. His task was to be that of consolidating and strengthening the nation. His ability to undertake such a task is seen in the administrative officials he appointed to serve in the royal court.

a. Solomon appointed nine chief officials or cabinet members of the royal court (vv.2-6). The fact that he instituted the *king's cabinet* or *royal officials* shows his administrative skills in developing a strong government. The cabinet positions were as follows:

1) The position of High Priest held by Azariah (v.2). Under David's reign, there had been two High Priests, Zadok and Abiathar. Remember that Abiathar had just been dismissed and banished from the High Priest's position because of his support of Adonijah's uprising (2:26-27). Zadok was elderly when Solomon became king and apparently died soon thereafter. Azariah was the grandson of Zadok (1 Chr.6:8-9). Remember that in Scripture the designation of "son" also refers to grandson in the family line.
2) The two positions of Secretary of State held by Elihoreph and Ahijah (v.3). These two secretaries kept all the official records dealing with foreign nations and managed the trade and commerce affairs between other nations and the military alliances. Simply stated, they handled both the economic and the military alliances with other nations.
3) The position of Recorder held by Jehoshaphat (v.3). He kept all the records dealing with the kingdom and nation of Israel. He was the historian or recorder of Solomon's court. He kept all the official documents of the administration and handled all the public notices of royal commands.
4) The position of Commander-in-chief held by Benaiah (v.4). He commanded all the armies of Israel.
5) The positions of two former High Priests were obviously just honorary positions or honorary recognition being made by the author of *First Kings* (v.4). These two priests had served David faithfully throughout the years, so much so that they deserved recognition for the contribution they had made. But the chief High Priest serving in the cabinet of Solomon's court was Azariah.
6) The position of District Supervisor held by Azariah, a son of Nathan the prophet (v.5). He was placed in charge of the twelve district governors who supplied provisions for the royal palace.
7) The position of personal advisor and priest to Solomon held by Zabud (v.5). This position was also known simply as the "the king's friend." Zabud was the son of Nathan the prophet.
8) The position of palace supervisor held by Ahishar (v.6). He was the steward of the palace. He oversaw the servants and other workers there as well as the buildings and the grounds.
9) The position of supervisor of forced labor held by Adoniram (v.6). Under Solomon's administration, this was a very important position because of the public building projects Solomon undertook. Thousands and thousands of laborers were needed; thus, Solomon had to institute a position of forced labor management.

b. Solomon appointed twelve district governors who were to rule over all Israel. It would have been impossible for Solomon to rule the nation without appointing district governors, capable men who could govern the people on a local basis. It was these governors who were responsible for raising the money to support the central government and to supply provisions for the royal palace (vv.7-19). Each district was responsible for supplying provisions one month each year. Note these facts about the districts:

⇒ The districts did not correspond to the territories and boundaries of the twelve tribes.
⇒ Two of the governors were sons-in-law of Solomon (vv.11, 15).
⇒ Some districts included far more territory than others, which indicates that Solomon gave more territory to the most capable leaders.
⇒ Judah is not listed as one of the twelve districts. Most likely, this was because Solomon himself ruled from Jerusalem in the tribe of Judah.

The names of the twelve district governors and the territories assigned them are given in the Scripture and outline below:

OUTLINE	SCRIPTURE	SCRIPTURE	OUTLINE
1. Solomon's administrative officials: The need for capable leaders a. The chief officials or cabinet 1) High Priest: Azariah	So king Solomon was king over all Israel. 2 And these were the princes which he had; Azariah the son of Zadok the priest,	tribute. 7 And Solomon had twelve officers over all Israel, which provided victuals for the king and his household: each man his month in a year made provision.	b. The 12 district governors over all Israel: Were the leaders who supplied provisions for the royal palace—each district responsible for one month a year
2) Secretaries of State: Elihoreph & Ahijah 3) Recorder: Jehoshaphat	3 Elihoreph and Ahiah, the sons of Shisha, scribes; Jehoshaphat the son of Ahilud, the recorder.	8 And these *are* their names: The son of Hur, in mount Ephraim:	1) Ben-Hur
4) Chief commander: Benaiah 5) Former High Priests: Zadok & Abiathar, 2:26-27; 2 S.8:17	4 And Benaiah the son of Jehoiada was over the host: and Zadok and Abiathar were the priests:	9 The son of Dekar, in Makaz, and in Shaalbim, and Beth-shemesh, and Elon-beth-hanan:	2) Ben-Deker
6) District Supervisor: Azariah 7) Personal advisor & priest: Zabud	5 And Azariah the son of Nathan was over the officers: and Zabud the son of Nathan was principal officer, and the king's friend:	10 The son of Hesed, in Aruboth; to him *pertained* Sochoh, and all the land of Hepher:	3) Ben-Hesed
8) Palace supervisor: Ahishar 9) Supervisor of forced labor: Adoniram	6 And Ahishar was over the household: and Adoniram the son of Abda *was* over the	11 The son of Abinadab, in all the region of Dor; which had Taphath the daughter of Solomon to wife:	4) Ben-Abinadab: Son-in-law of Solomon

OUTLINE	SCRIPTURE	SCRIPTURE	OUTLINE
5) Baana	12 Baana the son of Ahilud; *to him pertained* Taanach and Megiddo, and all Beth-shean, which is by Zartanah beneath Jezreel, from Beth-shean to Abel-meholah, *even* unto *the place that is* beyond Jokneam:	*had* Mahanaim:	
		15 Ahimaaz *was* in Naphtali; he also took Basmath the daughter of Solomon to wife:	8) Ahimaaz: Son-in-law of Solomon
		16 Baanah the son of Hushai *was* in Asher and in Aloth:	9) Baana
		17 Jehoshaphat the son of Paruah, in Issachar:	10) Jehoshaphat
6) Ben-Geber	13 The son of Geber, in Ramoth-gilead; to him *pertained* the towns of Jair the son of Manasseh, which *are* in Gilead; to him *also pertained* the region of Argob, which is in Bashan, three score great cities with walls and brasen bars:	18 Shimei the son of Elah, in Benjamin:	11) Shimei
		19 Geber the son of Uri *was* in the country of Gilead, *in* the country of Sihon king of the Amorites, and of Og king of Bashan; and *he was* the only officer which *was* in the land.	12) Geber
7) Ahinadab	14 Ahinadab the son of Iddo		

Thought 1. The major lesson for us in this point is that of capable leadership. If there has ever been a day when capable, courageous leaders were needed, it is today. Look at the leadership in most governments, both national and local. Look at the leadership in businesses, schools, and universities, as well as in the families of our nation. What kinds of people are filling the leadership positions within these institutions of society? Good people or bad people? Honorable people or evil people? An honest evaluation demands this answer: there are both good and bad leaders throughout our nation.

Sadly, there has been a breakdown in the character, integrity, righteousness, and morality of many leaders. And when it comes to possessing the courage to stand up for what is right without compromise, the backbone of many a leader has collapsed. Listen to what God's Holy Word says about capable leaders:

"For *the kingdom of heaven is* as a man travelling into a far country, *who* called his own servants, and delivered unto them his goods. And unto one he gave five talents, to another two, and to another one; to every man according to his several ability; and straightway took his journey" (Mt.25:14-15; see also vv.16-30).

"And that servant, which knew his lord's will, and prepared not *himself,* neither did according to his will, shall be beaten with many *stripes*" (Lu.12:47).

"...For unto whomsoever much is given, of him shall be much required: and to whom men have committed much, of him they will ask the more" (Lu.12:48).

"And he called his ten servants, and delivered them ten pounds, and said unto them, Occupy till I come" (Lu.19:13).

"So then every one of us shall give account of himself to God" (Ro.14:12).

"Moreover it is required in stewards [leaders], that a man be found faithful" (1 Co.4:2).

"O Timothy, keep that which is committed to thy trust, avoiding profane *and* vain babblings, and oppositions of science falsely so called" (1 Ti.6:20).

"As every man hath received the gift, *even so* minister the same one to another, as good stewards of the manifold grace of God" (1 Pe.4:10).

"Cursed *be* he that perverteth the judgment of the stranger, fatherless, and widow. And all the people shall say, Amen" (De.27:19).

"Be of good courage, and let us play the men for our people, and for the cities of our God: and the LORD do that which seemeth him good" (2 S.10:12).

"The God of Israel said, the Rock of Israel spake to me, He that ruleth over men *must be* just, ruling in the fear of God" (2 S.23:3).

"And said to the judges, Take heed what ye do: for ye judge not for man, but for the LORD, who *is* with you in the judgment" (2 Chr.19:6).

"Be wise now therefore, O ye kings: be instructed, ye judges of the earth. Serve the LORD with fear, and rejoice with trembling" (Ps.2:10-11).

"By the blessing of the upright the city is exalted: but it is overthrown by the mouth of the wicked" (Pr.11:11).

"Righteousness exalteth a nation: but sin *is* a reproach to any people" (Pr.14:34).

"*It is* an abomination to kings to commit wickedness: for the throne is established by righteousness" (Pr.16:12).

"Mercy and truth preserve the king: and his throne is upholden by mercy" (Pr.20:28).

"Take away the wicked *from* before the king, and his throne shall be established in righteousness" (Pr.25:5).

"The king by judgment establisheth the land: but he that receiveth gifts overthroweth it" (Pr.29:4).

"The king that faithfully judgeth the poor, his throne shall be established for ever" (Pr.29:14).

"Woe unto them that decree unrighteous decrees, and that write grievousness *which* they have prescribed" (Is.10:1).

2 (4:20-28) **Prosperity, Example of—Peace, Example of—Israel, Prosperity of—Israel, Peace of—Blessings, of God, Example of—Israel, Blessings of**: there was Solomon's rule of peace and prosperity, a clear picture that God was richly blessing His people. Under Solomon's leadership, the nation reached its summit in economic, military, and political strength. The Israelites were now a large population, a unified nation of strong, secure, and prosperous people. Scripture paints a graphic description of Israel's welfare during this period of their history:

OUTLINE	SCRIPTURE	SCRIPTURE	OUTLINE
2. Solomon's rule of peace & prosperity: A picture of God blessing His people a. The blessings promised to Abraham, Ge.12:1-9 b. The territory of Solomon's rule 1) Stretched from the Euphrates River (NE) to the borders of the Philistines (W) & Egypt (SW) 2) Was subjected & paid tribute to Solomon c. The daily provisions necessary to sustain the court of Solomon 1) Flour: 150 bushels 2) Meal: 300 bushels 3) Oxen: 10 4) Cattle: 20 5) Sheep or goats: 100 6) Deer, gazelles, roebucks, & choice fowl 7) The supplies came from the kingdoms west of the Euphrates from Tiphsah	20 Judah and Israel *were* many, as the sand which *is* by the sea in multitude, eating and drinking, and making merry. 21 And Solomon reigned over all kingdoms from the river unto the land of the Philistines, and unto the border of Egypt: they brought presents, and served Solomon all the days of his life. 22 And Solomon's provision for one day was thirty measures of fine flour, and threescore measures of meal, 23 Ten fat oxen, and twenty oxen out of the pastures, and an hundred sheep, beside harts, and roebucks, and fallowdeer, and fatted fowl. 24 For he had dominion over all *the region* on this side the river, from Tiphsah even to	Azzah, over all the kings on this side the river: and he had peace on all sides round about him. 25 And Judah and Israel dwelt safely, every man under his vine and under his fig tree, from Dan even to Beersheba, all the days of Solomon. 26 And Solomon had forty thousand stalls of horses for his chariots, and twelve thousand horsemen. 27 And those officers provided victual for king Solomon, and for all that came unto king Solomon's table, every man in his month: they lacked nothing. 28 Barley also and straw for the horses and dromedaries brought they unto the place where *the officers* were, every man according to his charge.	(N) to Gaza (S) 8) The peace & security of the nation during Solomon's reign d. The military power of Solomon: 40,000 stalls for horses & 12,000 horsemen e. The district officers, each in his own month, supplied provisions for Solomon, 7-19 1) For his royal court 2) For his horses

a. The promises given by God to Abraham were fulfilled during this period of Solomon's reign (v.20; see also v.21). This verse definitely points back to the Abrahamic Covenant, the promises God had given to the patriarch (see outline and notes—Ge.12:1c-3; 15:1-21 for more discussion). Just as God had promised, the Israelites had become as numerous as the stars in the sky (Ge.15:5, 18). And they were blessed with prosperity beyond measure, eating and drinking and rejoicing in God's wonderful blessings.

b. The territory of Solomon's rule stretched from the Euphrates River in the north and east to the borders of the Philistines in the west and down to Egypt in the southwest. In addition, all the countries that had been subjected to Solomon's rule paid tribute as subjects of Israel. As businessmen, salesmen, and others traveled throughout this enlarged territory of Solomon's rule and the known world of that day, they would no doubt sometimes bear witness about the only true and living God. Therefore, the witness to the Lord during Solomon's early days as king was most likely very strong.

c. The daily provisions necessary to sustain the court of Solomon were enormous (vv.22-24). Judging from the food supply listed here, estimates among commentators range from 14,000 to 32,000 people who were sustained by these daily provisions. Note that the taxes and provisions came from all the kingdoms west of the Euphrates from Tiphsah in the north to Gaza in the south. Throughout the lifetime of Solomon, the Israelites lived in peace and security (v.25). No nation threatened them. The statement in this verse that the people lived in safety under their own vine and fig trees was a picturesque way to describe their prosperity and security. Both the vine and the fig tree were symbols of the nation Israel and pictured the fruitfulness of the Promised Land.[2]

d. The military power of Solomon included 40,000 stalls for horses and 12,000 horsemen (v.26). It should be noted that some Greek manuscripts say 4,000 stalls (see 2 Chr.9:25). Solomon actually had 1,400 chariots (10:26; 2 Chr.1:14). A chariot needed three horses, so if this number is to be used in determining the accuracy of the manuscript, then the correct number would come closer to the 4,000 stalls as opposed to the 40,000. Whatever the case, the military power of Solomon had reached a pinnacle of strength in the history of Israel.

e. The district officers, each in his own month, supplied provisions for Solomon (vv.27-28). The provisions were used to sustain Solomon's royal court and his horses.

> **Thought 1**. This is a clear picture of God richly blessing His people. Just as God blessed Israel, so He will bless any people who will trust and follow Him. One of the great promises of God is that of meeting our *daily* needs. If we will live righteously and godly in this present world—truly trusting and following God—He promises to meet any and all of our needs, no matter what situation or problem or trial we are facing:
>
> ⇒ hunger ⇒ discouragement
> ⇒ thirst ⇒ distress
> ⇒ disease ⇒ pressure
> ⇒ injury ⇒ divorce

[2] John F. Walvoord and Roy B. Zuck, Editors. *The Bible Knowledge Commentary, Old Testament*, p.497.

⇒ addiction ⇒ financial difficulty
⇒ depression ⇒ bankruptcy

A need cannot be listed that God is not longing to meet. But God is not an indulgent grandfather who gives license to sinful, disobedient, and evil sons and daughters. God rewards faithfulness and obedience and judges wickedness and disobedience. But the wonderful truth to know is this glorious promise: the Lord will meet our needs and pour out upon us blessing after blessing. This is the clear promise of God's Holy Word:

"But seek ye first the kingdom of God, and his righteousness; and all these things shall be added unto you" (Mt.6:33).

"Give, and it shall be given unto you; good measure, pressed down, and shaken together, and running over, shall men give into your bosom. For with the same measure that ye mete withal it shall be measured to you again" (Lu.6:38).

"And ye shall serve the LORD your God, and he shall bless thy bread, and thy water; and I will take sickness away from the midst of thee" (Ex.23:25).

"If ye walk in my statutes, and keep my commandments, and do them; Then I will give you rain in due season, and the land shall yield her increase, and the trees of the field shall yield their fruit. And your threshing shall reach unto the vintage, and the vintage shall reach unto the sowing time: and ye shall eat your bread to the full, and dwell in your land safely" (Le.26:3-5).

"Keep therefore the words of this covenant, and do them, that ye may prosper in all that ye do" (De.29:9).

"And thou shalt return and obey the voice of the LORD, and do all his commandments which I command thee this day. And the LORD thy God will make thee plenteous in every work of thine hand, in the fruit of thy body, and in the fruit of thy cattle, and in the fruit of thy land, for good: for the LORD will again rejoice over thee for good, as he rejoiced over thy fathers" (De.30:8-9).

"Then shalt thou prosper, if thou takest heed to fulfil the statutes and judgments which the LORD charged Moses with concerning Israel: be strong, and of good courage; dread not, nor be dismayed" (1 Chr.22:13).

"Blessed *is* the man that walketh not in the counsel of the ungodly, nor standeth in the way of sinners, nor sitteth in the seat of the scornful. But his delight *is* in the law of the LORD; and in his law doth he meditate day and night. And he shall be like a tree planted by the rivers of water, that bringeth forth his fruit in his season; his leaf also shall not wither; and whatsoever he doeth shall prosper" (Ps.1:1-3).

"*Oh* how great *is* thy goodness, which thou hast laid up for them that fear thee; *which* thou hast wrought for them that trust in thee before the sons of men!" (Ps.31:19).

"Thou visitest the earth, and waterest it: thou greatly enrichest it with the river of God, *which* is full of water: thou preparest them corn, when thou hast so provided for it" (Ps.65:9).

"Blessed *be* the Lord, *who* daily loadeth us *with benefits, even* the God of our salvation. Selah" (Ps.68:19).

"He should have fed them also with the finest of the wheat: and with honey out of the rock should I have satisfied thee" (Ps.81:16).

"Then shall he give the rain of thy seed, that thou shalt sow the ground withal; and bread of the increase of the earth, and it shall be fat and plenteous: in that day shall thy cattle feed in large pastures" (Is.30:23).

"Bring ye all the tithes into the storehouse, that there may be meat in mine house, and prove me now herewith, saith the LORD of hosts, if I will not open you the windows of heaven, and pour you out a blessing, that *there shall* not *be room* enough *to receive it*" (Mal.3:10).

3 (4:29-34) **Equip - Equipping, Duty—Preparation, Duty—Task, Equipped for—Wisdom, Superior, Example of—Solomon, Wisdom, Example of**: these few verses give a descriptive account of Solomon's superior wisdom. His wisdom was limitless, too vast to be measured. This is exactly what Scripture says:

OUTLINE	SCRIPTURE	SCRIPTURE	OUTLINE
3. Solomon's superior wisdom: A picture of God equipping the believer for his task a. The source of Solomon's wisdom: God b. The greatness of Solomon's wisdom: Incomparable 1) Greater than the wisdom of the East & of Egypt 2) Greater than any man—even greater than the four wisest men of that day… • Ethan: Author of Ps.89 • Heman: Author of Ps.88 • Calcol	29 And God gave Solomon wisdom and understanding exceeding much, and largeness of heart, even as the sand that *is* on the sea shore. 30 And Solomon's wisdom excelled the wisdom of all the children of the east country, and all the wisdom of Egypt. 31 For he was wiser than all men; than Ethan the Ezrahite, and Heman, and Chalcol, and Darda, the sons of Mahol: and his fame was in all nations round	about. 32 And he spake three thousand proverbs: and his songs were a thousand and five. 33 And he spake of trees, from the cedar tree that *is* in Lebanon even unto the hyssop that springeth out of the wall: he spake also of beasts, and of fowl, and of creeping things, and of fishes. 34 And there came of all people to hear the wisdom of Solomon, from all kings of the earth, which had heard of his wisdom.	• Darda c. The span of his wisdom 1) Proverbs: 3000 2) Songs: 1005 3) Botany: A careful observer of plant life 4) Zoology: Studied & expounded on animal life d. The impact of Solomon's wisdom over the world: His wisdom was sought after by many national leaders of his day

a. The source of Solomon's wisdom was God Himself (v.29). God had promised Solomon great wisdom, and God fulfilled His promise. He gave Solomon great wisdom and understanding and knowledge or intellectual powers, which in some versions is called "largeness of heart" (KJV, NKJV). Note what Scripture says: his wisdom and understanding and breadth of knowledge were limitless, too vast to be measured. His wisdom was as measureless as the sands on the seashore. But keep this fact in mind: the source of his limitless wisdom was God.

b. Also, the greatness of Solomon's knowledge was incomparable (vv.30-31). His knowledge was greater than the wisdom of the east and of Egypt. This is a phenomenal claim when considering the enormous amount of wisdom resulting from literature produced by Babylon, Egypt, and other nations within the East.

Solomon's wisdom was greater than any man's, even greater than the four wisest men of his day:

⇒ Ethan, who was the author of Psalm 89
⇒ Heman, who was the author of Psalm 88
⇒ Calcol and Darda, who are listed in the genealogical records of 1 Chr.2:6. Nothing is known about these two men, but they had become famous for their wisdom, so famous that they were known as two of the wisest men alive during the days of Solomon.

c. The span of Solomon's wisdom was and still is incomprehensible (vv.32-33). During his lifetime, Solomon achieved the following:

⇒ He wrote 3,000 proverbs.
⇒ He composed 1,005 songs.
⇒ He became a careful student of botany, observing and learning the details of plant life (v.33).
⇒ He became a student of zoology, studying and expounding on animal life.

The commentator Russell Dilday says this:

> *The crown of Solomon's gifts...was...his wisdom. His "largeness of heart" referred to in verse 29 points to his broad interest in poetry, botany, biology, ornithology, ichthyology, astronomy, arithmetic, and medicine. The wisdom of Egypt in verse 30 refers to geometry, astronomy, and the preparation of ointments and medicines.*
>
> *Jewish tradition (as well as the Koran) credits Solomon with the ability to converse in the language of every beast, fowl, fish, plant, and demon. Ancient rankings put the cedar tree at the top of the list of plants and hyssop at the lowest level; thus Solomon's botanical interests were all-inclusive.*[3]

d. Solomon's wisdom made an impact worldwide (v.34). Many national leaders of his day and time sought after his wisdom. He had what might be called an encyclopedic knowledge and limitless wisdom and understanding. No wonder his fame spread worldwide and has continued to spread down through the ages, even to the present day of human history.

Thought 1. God equipped Solomon for the task assigned him. So it is with us: whatever task we are called to, God will equip us to perform the work. No matter how helpless or inadequate we may feel, God will equip us to fulfill our calling.

⇒ If God calls us into the ministry, God will equip us to do the work of the ministry.
⇒ If God calls us to be missionaries or evangelists, God will equip us to go forth bearing the testimony of Christ to the world.
⇒ If God calls us to enter business, God will equip us to manage the business.
⇒ If God calls us to seek or to take a certain job or position, God will equip us to do that job or fill the position.
⇒ If God calls us to seek additional education or to become better trained, God will equip us to learn and to better prepare ourselves.
⇒ If God calls us to minister to a neighbor—whether diseased, bedridden, or needing a friend—God will equip us to reach out and meet the need of the neighbor.
⇒ If we personally need to become a better husband or wife, God will equip and help us.
⇒ If we need the strength to turn from some wicked, sinful behavior, God will equip and empower us.

Whatever needs we may be confronting, whatever tasks set before us, whatever job or undertaking we face—God will equip us, giving us the strength and ability to do what is needed. This is the clear teaching of God's Holy Word:

"And unto one he gave five talents, to another two, and to another one; to every man according to his several ability; and straightway took his journey" (Mt.25:15).

"But the Comforter, *which is* the Holy Ghost, whom the Father will send in my name, he shall teach you all things, and bring all things to your remembrance, whatsoever I have said unto you" (Jn.14:26).

"But ye shall receive power, after that the Holy Ghost is come upon you: and ye shall be witnesses unto me both in Jerusalem, and in all Judaea, and in Samaria, and unto the uttermost part of the earth" (Ac.1:8).

"Having then gifts differing according to the grace that is given to us, whether prophecy, *let us prophesy* according to the proportion of faith; Or ministry, *let us wait* on *our* ministering: or he that teacheth, on teaching; Or he that exhorteth, on exhortation: he that giveth, *let him do it* with simplicity; he that ruleth, with diligence; he that showeth mercy, with cheerfulness" (Ro.12:6-8).

---

[3] Russell Dilday. *1, 2 Kings*. "Mastering the Old Testament," p.76-77.

"But God hath chosen the foolish things of the world to confound the wise; and God hath chosen the weak things of the world to confound the things which are mighty" (1 Co.1:27).

"Now there are diversities of gifts, but the same Spirit. And there are differences of administrations, but the same Lord. And there are diversities of operations, but it is the same God which worketh all in all. But the manifestation of the Spirit is given to every man to profit withal. For to one is given by the Spirit the word of wisdom; to another the word of knowledge by the same Spirit; To another faith by the same Spirit; to another the gifts of healing by the same Spirit; To another the working of miracles; to another prophecy; to another discerning of spirits; to another *divers* kinds of tongues; to another the interpretation of tongues" (1 Co.12:4-10).

"That he would grant you, according to the riches of his glory, to be strengthened with might by his Spirit in the inner man" (Ep.3:16).

"Now unto him that is able to do exceeding abundantly above all that we ask or think, according to the power that worketh in us" (Ep.3:20).

"And he gave some, apostles; and some, prophets; and some, evangelists; and some, pastors and teachers" (Ep.4:11).

"Strengthened with all might, according to his glorious power, unto all patience and longsuffering with joyfulness" (Col.1:11).

"For God hath not given us the spirit of fear; but of power, and of love, and of a sound mind" (2 Ti.1:7).

"Who through faith subdued kingdoms, wrought righteousness, obtained promises, stopped the mouths of lions, Quenched the violence of fire, escaped the edge of the sword, out of weakness were made strong, waxed valiant in fight, turned to flight the armies of the aliens" (He.11:33-34).

"But the anointing which ye have received of him abideth in you, and ye need not that any man teach you: but as the same anointing teacheth you of all things, and is truth, and is no lie, and even as it hath taught you, ye shall abide in him" (1 Jn.2:27).

"Be strong and of a good courage, fear not, nor be afraid of them: for the LORD thy God, he *it is* that doth go with thee; he will not fail thee, nor forsake thee" (De.31:6).

"For thou hast girded me with strength to battle: them that rose up against me hast thou subdued under me" (2 S.22:40).

"But they that wait upon the LORD shall renew *their* strength; they shall mount up with wings as eagles; they shall run, and not be weary; *and* they shall walk, and not faint" (Is.40:31).

"Fear thou not; for I *am* with thee: be not dismayed; for I *am* thy God: I will strengthen thee; yea, I will help thee; yea, I will uphold thee with the right hand of my righteousness" (Is.41:10).

"And I will put my spirit within you, and cause you to walk in my statutes, and ye shall keep my judgments, and do *them*" (Eze.36:27).

CHAPTER 5

E. The Preparations for Building the Temple: Making the Commitment to Build a Place of Worship, 5:1-18

5:1-16; see 2 Chr.2:1-18

1. Solomon's commitment to build the temple: A picture of surrendering to the call of God
   a. Hiram sent envoys to Solomon: To congratulate the new king on his succession & to continue peaceful relations
   b. Solomon sought to expand the peace treaty to include a trade agreement
      1) Solomon desired to build a temple for the LORD
         • Because his father David had been unable to build the temple due to constant warfare
         • Because the LORD had now given rest, peace from all enemies
         • Because he was committed to the LORD's call: God had instructed Solomon's father David to build a temple to the LORD'S name, 2 S.7:12-13; 1 Chr. 22:8-10; Zec.6:12-13
      2) Solomon desired to enter a trade agreement with Hiram
         • To secure building materials—the cedars of Lebanon—for the temple
         • To secure skilled laborers

2. Solomon's trade treaty with Hiram: A picture of keeping, preserving the peace
   a. Hiram enthusiastically accepted Solomon's proposal & laid out the terms for the trade agreement
      1) He would cut & supply the cypress & fir (cedar or pine) logs
         • Haul & ship them to the port of Solomon's choice
         • Separate them for Solomon to haul away
      2) Solomon would pay by supplying provisions for the royal household
   b. Hiram fulfilled his part of the trade agreement
   c. Solomon paid Hiram as agreed
      1) Provided 100,000 to 125,000 bushels of wheat
      2) Provided 115,000 gallons of olive oil
      3) Provided yearly
   d. Solomon was given a special wisdom, enabling him to preserve peaceful relations with Phoenicia

3. Solomon's labor force: A picture of fair & diligent labor
   a. The work force for the timber: 30,000 men
      1) Worked in shifts of 10,000
      2) Spent one month working in Lebanon & two months at home
      3) Were under the supervision of Adoniram
   b. The work force for the temple foundation
      1) 70,000 carriers
      2) 80,000 stone cutters
      3) 3,300 supervisors
   c. The foundation: Was constructed of large, costly blocks of stone—hewn, squared, shaped, dressed to fit perfectly
   d. The skilled craftsmen were provided by Solomon & Hiram: Some were secured from Geba or Byblos & were also enlisted to help in preparing the timber & stone

And Hiram king of Tyre sent his servants unto Solomon; for he had heard that they had anointed him king in the room of his father: for Hiram was ever a lover of David.

2 And Solomon sent to Hiram, saying,

3 Thou knowest how that David my father could not build an house unto the name of the LORD his God for the wars which were about him on every side, until the LORD put them under the soles of his feet.

4 But now the LORD my God hath given me rest on every side, *so that there is* neither adversary nor evil occurrent.

5 And, behold, I purpose to build an house unto the name of the LORD my God, as the LORD spake unto David my father, saying, Thy son, whom I will set upon thy throne in thy room, he shall build an house unto my name.

6 Now therefore command thou that they hew me cedar trees out of Lebanon; and my servants shall be with thy servants: and unto thee will I give hire for thy servants according to all that thou shalt appoint: for thou knowest that *there is* not among us any that can skill to hew timber like unto the Sidonians.

7 And it came to pass, when Hiram heard the words of Solomon, that he rejoiced greatly, and said, Blessed *be* the LORD this day, which hath given unto David a wise son over this great people.

8 And Hiram sent to Solomon, saying, I have considered the things which thou sentest to me for: *and* I will do all thy desire concerning timber of cedar, and concerning timber of fir.

9 My servants shall bring *them* down from Lebanon unto the sea: and I will convey them by sea in floats unto the place that thou shalt appoint me, and will cause them to be discharged there, and thou shalt receive *them:* and thou shalt accomplish my desire, in giving food for my household.

10 So Hiram gave Solomon cedar trees and fir trees *according to* all his desire.

11 And Solomon gave Hiram twenty thousand measures of wheat *for* food to his household, and twenty measures of pure oil: thus gave Solomon to Hiram year by year.

12 And the LORD gave Solomon wisdom, as he promised him: and there was peace between Hiram and Solomon; and they two made a league together.

13 And king Solomon raised a levy out of all Israel; and the levy was thirty thousand men.

14 And he sent them to Lebanon ten thousand a month by courses: a month they were in Lebanon, *and* two months at home: and Adoniram *was* over the levy.

15 And Solomon had threescore and ten thousand that bare burdens, and fourscore thousand hewers in the mountains;

16 Beside the chief of Solomon's officers which *were* over the work, three thousand and three hundred, which ruled over the people that wrought in the work.

17 And the king commanded, and they brought great stones, costly stones, *and* hewed stones, to lay the foundation of the house.

18 And Solomon's builders and Hiram's builders did hew *them,* and the stonesquarers: so they prepared timber and stones to build the house.

DIVISION I

THE RISE AND REIGN OF SOLOMON AS KING: BEGINNING IN GLORY AND ENDING IN SHAME, 1:1–11:43

E. The Preparations for Building the Temple: Making the Commitment to Build a Place of Worship, 5:1-18

(5:1-18) **Introduction**: during the course of our lives, most of us become involved in, or at least exposed to, some building project. The project may be a house, a hut, a porch, a landscaped yard or area, an office, a tree house or playground, a highway or driveway, a church or temple or synagogue. Everywhere we look, there is some building or construction that someone has done or is doing. In every building project one thing is essential: preparation. Preparations have to be made for the project to turn out as it should. A foundation can be built upon sand, but it will crack and sink. A building can be constructed without a design or blueprints, but the structure will begin to squeak and the walls or floors or ceilings or roof will become uneven and weaken. Without preparation, a building can become a shack.

The present passage has to do with Solomon's preparations for building the temple. Remember, he had just consolidated his power and selected the leaders to fill the administrative positions of his government. Now he set out to achieve the burning passion of his heart, that of building the temple to honor the name of the LORD his God, to provide a house of worship for the citizens of Israel. But before he could begin the construction, he had to lay the preparations for the massive building project. This is the subject of this chapter of Holy Scripture: *The Preparations for Building the Temple: Making the Commitment to Build a Place of Worship*, 5:1-18.

1. Solomon's commitment to build the temple: a picture of surrendering to the call of God (vv.1-6).
2. Solomon's trade treaty with Hiram: a picture of keeping, preserving the peace (vv.7-12).
3. Solomon's labor force: a picture of fair and diligent labor (vv.13-18).

1 (5:1-6) **Surrender, Spiritual, Example of—Yielding, Spiritual, Example of—Commitment, Example of—Solomon, Commitment of**: Solomon was totally committed to building the temple to honor the name of the LORD. Building the temple had consumed the heart of David, Solomon's father. But the LORD had other missions for David to undertake; consequently, the LORD would not allow David to build a house of worship. However, the LORD promised that David's son would build the temple that David had envisioned for the people of God. Once God indicated that Solomon was to be the successor, David began to focus his attention upon Solomon, preparing him for the throne and for building a house of worship for God's people. *The Expositor's Bible Commentary* gives an excellent description of David's preparation of Solomon that is well worth quoting in its entirety.

> *There can be no doubt that much of Solomon's early spiritual vitality and dedication to God may be attributed to David's deep personal relationship to his Lord and his desire to honor him. Proverbs 4:3, 9 indicates...that David spent time with Solomon as he was growing up, teaching and admonishing him from the Word of God. It is not clear just how strongly David instructed his other sons, [but]...it is probable that since David knew from the time of Solomon's birth that he was to be his successor, he gave him special instruction to prepare him for kingship.*
>
> *It is clear from 1 Chronicles 22–29 that David did everything in his power to smooth the way for Solomon to follow him as king, not only in drawing up the plans (cf. 1 Chron 28:11-19) for the temple, amassing the necessary materials and funds (cf., e.g., 1 Chron 22:14-16) and soliciting the help and cooperation of Israel's leadership (cf., e.g., 1 Chron 22:17-19), but also in admonishing and encouraging Solomon to carry out faithfully the task committed to him (cf. 1 Chron.22:6-13; 28:9-20). In Solomon, David found a responsive and humble heart. Amnon, Absalom, and Adonijah, Solomon's three older brothers, were spiritually and morally deficient; but Solomon had a heart prepared by God, and he responded willingly to David's instruction.*
>
> *David's legacy to Solomon was thus much more than a great kingdom with secure borders, tributary nations, and considerable wealth and prestige. Far more importantly he instilled in Solomon a love for God and his Word. He gave to Solomon a proper orientation to life and leadership and was himself an outstanding role model, despite his failures, of a man whose heart truly beat for God.*[1]

Obviously, Solomon had been an excellent student, learning all he could from his father. His strong commitment to fulfill his father's desire to build the temple shows just how much Solomon listened to David. Solomon was totally committed to completing the desire of his father. He sought to honor the LORD by building a house of worship for the people. In chapter 5, the preparations for building the temple began:

OUTLINE	SCRIPTURE	SCRIPTURE	OUTLINE
1. Solomon's commitment to build the temple: A picture of surrendering to the call of God a. Hiram sent envoys to Solomon: To congratulate the new king on his succession & to continue peaceful relations b. Solomon sought to expand the peace treaty to include a trade agreement 1) Solomon desired to build a temple for the LORD	And Hiram king of Tyre sent his servants unto Solomon; for he had heard that they had anointed him king in the room of his father: for Hiram was ever a lover of David. 2 And Solomon sent to Hiram, saying, 3 Thou knowest how that David my father could not build an house unto the name of the LORD his God for the wars which were about him	on every side, until the LORD put them under the soles of his feet. 4 But now the LORD my God hath given me rest on every side, *so that there is* neither adversary nor evil occurrent. 5 And, behold, I purpose to build an house unto the name of the LORD my God, as the LORD spake unto David my father, saying, Thy son, whom I will set upon thy	• Because his father David had been unable to build the temple due to constant warfare • Because the LORD had now given rest, peace from all enemies • Because he was committed to the LORD's call: God had instructed Solomon's father David to build a temple to the LORD's name, 2 S.7:12-13;

[1] Richard D. Patterson and Hermann J. Austel. *1, 2 Kings*, p.34.

OUTLINE	SCRIPTURE	SCRIPTURE	OUTLINE
1 Chr. 22:8-10; Zec.6:12-13 2) Solomon desired to enter a trade agreement with Hiram	throne in thy room, he shall build an house unto my name. 6 Now therefore command thou that they hew me cedar trees out of Lebanon; and my servants shall be with thy	servants: and unto thee will I give hire for thy servants according to all that thou shalt appoint: for thou knowest that *there is* not among us any that can skill to hew timber like unto the Sidonians.	• To secure building materials—the cedars of Lebanon—for the temple • To secure skilled laborers

a. King Hiram of Phoenicia sent envoys to congratulate Solomon on his succession to the throne and to continue peaceful relations with Israel (v.1). Remember that King Hiram and David had been allies and friends and that King Hiram had supplied the materials for David to build his palace (2 S.5:11). Thus it was only natural that King Hiram wanted to continue friendly relationships with the son of David, Solomon.

b. Solomon seized this opportunity by suggesting that the two nations *expand* the peace treaty to include a trade agreement (vv.2-6). Sending a message back with the envoys to King Hiram, Solomon expressed two desires:

1) Solomon desired to build a temple for the LORD (vv.3-5). He spelled out three reasons why he was undertaking the massive project:
   ⇒ Because his father David had been unable to build the temple due to constant warfare
   ⇒ Because the LORD had now given peace and rest to Israel from all enemies
   ⇒ Because he was personally committed to the LORD's call, the LORD's instructions that had been given to his father David to build a temple (2 S.7:12-13; 1 Chr.22:8-10; see also Zec.6:12-13).

2) Closing out his letter to King Hiram, Solomon expressed a desire to enter a trade agreement with Phoenicia (v.6). He wished to secure building materials, the cedars of Lebanon, for the temple. He also wished to secure skilled laborers, but he suggested that Israel also provide laborers who would work right beside the skilled laborers of King Hiram. Note that the amount of payment for the materials and laborers was to be set by King Hiram.

Thought 1. Solomon's commitment to build the temple is a strong lesson for us—a lesson on being surrendered to the call of God. No greater call can be given a person than the call of God, for God is the great Creator and Sovereign Ruler of the universe. Therefore, when God calls any of us to do anything, we must respond immediately...

- to serve in the ministry
- to go to the mission fields of the world
- to serve as an evangelist
- to minister to the sick and suffering of this world
- to help the needy
- to minister to the discouraged and depressed
- to be a friend to the lonely
- to enter business in order to make money to help the needy and to carry the gospel around the world
- to become a godly teacher to educate the student and untrained of this world
- to enter the medical field to minister to humanity as we all age, become diseased, and eventually die
- to enter the various professions and labor markets of this world in order to meet needs and provide services needed by society

There is no excuse for delay, hesitation, reservation, or refusal. When God calls us to any task, a resounding "Yes!" must be the response of our hearts. We must surrender, yield to God's call—no matter what the call is. This is the clear declaration of Holy Scripture:

"For whosoever shall do the will of my Father which is in heaven, the same is my brother, and sister, and mother" (Mt.12:50).

"Then Peter began to say unto him, Lo, we have left all, and have followed thee" (Mk.10:28).

"And after these things he went forth, and saw a publican, named Levi, sitting at the receipt of custom: and he said unto him, Follow me. And he left all, rose up, and followed him" (Lu.5:27-28).

"And he said to them all, If any man will come after me, let him deny himself, and take up his cross daily, and follow me" (Lu.9:23).

"If any man come to me, and hate not his father, and mother, and wife, and children, and brethren, and sisters, yea, and his own life also, he cannot be my disciple. And whosoever doth not bear his cross, and come after me, cannot be my disciple" (Lu.14:26-27).

"So likewise, whosoever he be of you that forsaketh not all that he hath, he cannot be my disciple" (Lu.14:33).

"And he said unto them, Verily I say unto you, There is no man that hath left house, or parents, or brethren, or wife, or children, for the kingdom of God's sake, Who shall not receive manifold more in this present time, and in the world to come life everlasting" (Lu.18:29-30).

"I must work the works of him that sent me, while it is day: the night cometh, when no man can work" (Jn.9:4).

"Ye have not chosen me, but I have chosen you, and ordained you, that ye should go and bring forth fruit, and that your fruit should remain: that whatsoever ye shall ask of the Father in my name, he may give it you" (Jn.15:16).

"For we cannot but speak the things which we have seen and heard" (Ac.4:20).

"But the Lord said unto him, Go thy way: for he is a chosen vessel unto me, to bear my name before the Gentiles, and kings, and the children of Israel" (Ac.9:15).

"But rise, and stand upon thy feet: for I have appeared unto thee for this purpose, to make thee a minister and a witness both of these things which thou hast seen, and of those things in the which I will appear unto thee" (Ac.26:16).

"I beseech you therefore, brethren, by the mercies of God, that ye present your bodies a living sacrifice, holy, acceptable unto God, *which is* your reasonable service" (Ro.12:1).

"We then that are strong ought to bear the infirmities of the weak, and not to please ourselves" (Ro.15:1).

"But God hath chosen the foolish things of the world to confound the wise; and God hath chosen the weak things of the world to confound the things which are mighty; And base things of the world, and things which are despised, hath God chosen, *yea,* and things which are not, to bring to nought things that are: That no flesh should glory in his presence" (1 Co.1:27-29).

"I am crucified with Christ: nevertheless I live; yet not I, but Christ liveth in me: and the life which I now live in the flesh I live by the faith of the Son of God, who loved me, and gave himself for me" (Ga.2:20).

"Brethren, if a man be overtaken in a fault, ye which are spiritual, restore such an one in the spirit of meekness; considering thyself, lest thou also be tempted. Bear ye one another's burdens, and so fulfil the law of Christ" (Ga.6:1-2).

"And let us not be weary in well doing: for in due season we shall reap, if we faint not. As we have therefore opportunity, let us do good unto all *men,* especially unto them who are of the household of faith" (Ga.6:9-10).

"Not with eyeservice, as menpleasers; but as the servants of Christ, doing the will of God from the heart" (Ep.6:6).

"Yea doubtless, and I count all things *but* loss for the excellency of the knowledge of Christ Jesus my Lord: for whom I have suffered the loss of all things, and do count them *but* dung, that I may win Christ" (Ph.3:8).

"Now the LORD had said unto Abram, Get thee out of thy country, and from thy kindred, and from thy father's house, unto a land that I will show thee" (Ge.12:1).

"And the LORD looked upon him, and said, Go in this thy might, and thou shalt save Israel from the hand of the Midianites: have not I sent thee" (Jud.6:14).

"I delight to do thy will, O my God: yea, thy law *is* within my heart" (Ps.40:8).

"My son, give me thine heart, and let thine eyes observe my ways" (Pr.23:26).

"Also I heard the voice of the Lord, saying, Whom shall I send, and who will go for us? Then said I, Here *am* I; send me" (Is.6:8).

2 (5:7-12) **Peace, Duty—Solomon, Alliances of—Trade, Example of—Treaties, Example of—Alliances, Example of**: in making preparations for building the temple, Solomon established a major trade agreement with King Hiram of Phoenicia. Hiram enthusiastically accepted Solomon's proposal and laid out the terms for the trade agreement (v.7). He agreed to cut and supply the cypress and fir (cedar, pine) logs (vv.8-9). He would ship them from the Lebanon mountains to the Mediterranean Sea by floating them in rafts to the port of Solomon's choice. There he would separate them for Solomon's workers to haul away. All labor costs were Solomon's responsibility. He would have to pay the wages for all workers. In addition, Solomon would have to pay for the wood by providing food for Hiram's royal household as well as for the laborers harvesting the timber.

As noted by the author, Hiram fulfilled his part of the trade agreement, and so did Solomon (vv.10-11). Solomon provided 100,000 to 125,000 bushels of wheat and 115,000 gallons of olive oil. And he continued to do this yearly. Besides the wheat and olive oil for Hiram's court, Solomon also provided barley and wine for labor costs (2 Chr.2:10).

Note once again, this event shows how God fulfilled His promise to Solomon. He gave him very special wisdom in management and diplomacy. Wisely, Solomon preserved the peaceful relations with King Hiram and even expanded the relations to include the trade agreement, trade that provided the necessary materials to build the temple. The longing thrust of David's heart to build a *house for the LORD* had been passed along to Solomon. And now the driving commitment of Solomon was to complete the temple for the LORD.

OUTLINE	SCRIPTURE	SCRIPTURE	OUTLINE
2. Solomon's trade treaty with Hiram: A picture of keeping, preserving the peace a. Hiram enthusiastically accepted Solomon's proposal & laid out the terms for the trade agreement 1) He would cut & supply the cypress & fir (cedar or pine) logs	7 And it came to pass, when Hiram heard the words of Solomon, that he rejoiced greatly, and said, Blessed *be* the LORD this day, which hath given unto David a wise son over this great people. 8 And Hiram sent to Solomon, saying, I have considered the things which thou sentest to me for: *and* I will do all thy desire concerning	timber of cedar, and concerning timber of fir. 9 My servants shall bring *them* down from Lebanon unto the sea: and I will convey them by sea in floats unto the place that thou shalt appoint me, and will cause them to be discharged there, and thou shalt receive *them:* and thou shalt accomplish my desire, in giving food	• Haul & ship them to the port of Solomon's choice • Separate them for Solomon to haul away 2) Solomon would pay by supplying provisions for the royal household

OUTLINE	SCRIPTURE	SCRIPTURE	OUTLINE
b. Hiram fulfilled his part of the trade agreement c. Solomon paid Hiram as agreed 1) Provided 100,000 to 125,000 bushels of wheat	for my household. 10 So Hiram gave Solomon cedar trees and fir trees *according to* all his desire. 11 And Solomon gave Hiram twenty thousand measures of wheat *for* food to his household, and twenty	measures of pure oil: thus gave Solomon to Hiram year by year. 12 And the LORD gave Solomon wisdom, as he promised him: and there was peace between Hiram and Solomon; and they two made a league together.	2) Provided 115,000 gallons of olive oil 3) Provided yearly d. Solomon was given a special wisdom, enabling him to preserve peaceful relations with Phoenicia

Thought 1. The lesson for us is very practical: we must seek peace and preserve peace throughout society. Far too often we give way to strife and division—arguing, grumbling, and griping. In some cases we even engage in combat. Every place we look, there is strife and division. There is an *absence of peace*...

- in far too many homes between husband and wife, parent and child
- in far too many schools where students disrupt and rebel, and teachers and staff fail to discipline
- in far too many workplaces where employees develop hard feelings toward one another
- in businesses where employers and employees mistreat each other or are treated unfairly
- in communities where neighbors differ and offend, reacting toward one another
- in social and charitable organizations where people differ and take opposing positions, reacting against one another
- in far too many churches where beliefs and opinions, likes and dislikes arouse complaints and murmurings among members, giving rise to discord
- in far too many political parties and governments where so many seek power to the point of lying, stealing, and cheating—and even combat and war—to the detriment of its citizens and the nation itself

Peace should permeate, rule, and reign throughout society. But in far too many cases, strife and division enter the lives of people and society. Yet the teaching of God's Word is clear: we are not to live in strife and division. We are to live in peace, and we are to preserve peace between ourselves and others. Listen to what God says:

"Blessed *are* the peacemakers: for they shall be called the children of God" (Mt.5:9).

"For to be carnally minded *is* death; but to be spiritually minded *is* life and peace" (Ro.8:6).

"For the kingdom of God is not meat and drink; but righteousness, and peace, and joy in the Holy Ghost" (Ro.14:17).

"Let us therefore follow after the things which make for peace, and things wherewith one may edify another" (Ro.14:19).

"Now the God of peace *be* with you all. Amen" (Ro.15:33).

"For God is not *the author* of confusion, but of peace, as in all churches of the saints" (1 Co.14:33).

"Finally, brethren, farewell. Be perfect, be of good comfort, be of one mind, live in peace; and the God of love and peace shall be with you" (2 Co.13:11).

"But the fruit of the Spirit is love, joy, peace, longsuffering, gentleness, goodness, faith" (Ga.5:22).

"Endeavouring to keep the unity of the Spirit in the bond of peace" (Ep.4:3).

"*Let* nothing *be done* through strife or vainglory; but in lowliness of mind let each esteem other better than themselves" (Ph.2:3).

"I beseech Euodias, and beseech Syntyche, that they be of the same mind in the Lord" (Ph.4:2).

"And to esteem them very highly in love for their work's sake. *And* be at peace among yourselves" (1 Th.5:13).

"Flee also youthful lusts: but follow righteousness, faith, charity, peace, with them that call on the Lord out of a pure heart" (2 Ti.2:22).

"And the servant of the Lord must not strive; but be gentle unto all *men,* apt to teach, patient" (2 Ti.2:24).

"Follow peace with all *men,* and holiness, without which no man shall see the Lord" (He.12:14).

"But the wisdom that is from above is first pure, then peaceable, gentle, *and* easy to be intreated, full of mercy and good fruits, without partiality, and without hypocrisy" (Ja.3:17).

"Acquaint now thyself with him, and be at peace: thereby good shall come unto thee" (Jb.22:21).

"Depart from evil, and do good; seek peace, and pursue it" (Ps.34:14).

"Deceit *is* in the heart of them that imagine evil: but to the counsellors of peace *is* joy" (Pr.12:20).

[3] (5:13-18) **Work, Duty—Labor, Duty—Diligence, Duty—Solomon, Labor Force—Temple, Organization of Labor**: Solomon raised a large labor force to build the temple, and the massive labor force was necessary. In order to secure enough workers, Solomon had to institute a *national draft* or conscription policy. This involuntary recruiting of forced labor was very unpopular and distasteful to the Israelites. Eventually, it was to become one of the major complaints of the people and one of the causes for the division of the nation (12:4-19). A detailed description is given of the labor force drafted by Solomon:

OUTLINE	SCRIPTURE	SCRIPTURE	OUTLINE
3. Solomon's labor force: A picture of fair & diligent labor a. The work force for the timber: 30,000 men 1) Worked in shifts of 10,000 2) Spent one month working in Lebanon & two months at home 3) Were under the supervision of Adoniram b. The work force for the temple foundation 1) 70,000 carriers 2) 80,000 stone cutters 3) 3,300 supervisors	13 And king Solomon raised a levy out of all Israel; and the levy was thirty thousand men. 14 And he sent them to Lebanon ten thousand a month by courses: a month they were in Lebanon, *and* two months at home: and Adoniram *was* over the levy. 15 And Solomon had threescore and ten thousand that bare burdens, and fourscore thousand hewers in the mountains; 16 Beside the chief of Solo-	mon's officers which *were* over the work, three thousand and three hundred, which ruled over the people that wrought in the work. 17 And the king commanded, and they brought great stones, costly stones, *and* hewed stones, to lay the foundation of the house. 18 And Solomon's builders and Hiram's builders did hew *them,* and the stonesquarers: so they prepared timber and stones to build the house.	c. The foundation: Was constructed of large, costly blocks of stone—hewn, squared, shaped, dressed to fit perfectly d. The skilled craftsmen were provided by Solomon & Hiram: Some were secured from Geba or Byblos & were also enlisted to help in preparing the timber & stone

a. The awesome task of securing the timbers from Lebanon demanded a work force of 30,000 men (vv.13-14). All of these laborers were drafted (conscripted) from Israelite men. The men worked in shifts of 10,000 a month, so each man spent one month working in Lebanon and two months working at home at his own job or in his own fields. This meant that a man was forced to spend four months a year in Lebanon, leaving eight months a year when he could be at home with his family and available to work at his own employment. Adoniram was in charge of the Lebanon work force.

b. The work force for the temple foundation was massive. There were 70,000 common laborers who carried materials from place to place, and 80,000 stonecutters who worked in the mountains. Thirty-three hundred supervisors oversaw the labor force.

c. The foundation of the temple was constructed of large, costly blocks of stone. The stone was hewn, squared, shaped, and dressed to fit perfectly (v.17).

d. Skilled craftsmen were provided by Solomon and Hiram, and some were even secured from Gebal or Byblos, which was about 60 miles north of Tyre (v.18).

Thought 1. The lesson for us is that of diligent labor. Whatever our task, we are to be hardworking and faithful, completing the work at hand. Far too many workers are idle, lazy, and unproductive. Being employed is a great privilege, and having the health to go to a job is a privilege. Therefore, we are to work diligently with a grateful heart for the privilege of being employed. As long as the work is legitimate—moral and ethical—we are providing a service for society and helping to meet the needs of people. Through our jobs...

- we are being productive in making our contribution to society
- we are producing for the benefit and welfare, the growth and development of one another
- we are providing income to meet the needs of our own families
- we are helping one another by generating provisions and supplies that we all need or want

For this reason, we must not be shiftless or slothful in our work. On the contrary, we must be industrious and diligent, producing all we can and making the greatest possible contribution to society. This is the strong teaching of God's Holy Word:

"Not slothful in business; fervent in spirit; serving the Lord" (Ro.12:11).

"Moreover it is required in stewards, that a man be found faithful" (1 Co.4:2).

"Let him that stole steal no more: but rather let him labour, working with *his* hands the thing which is good, that he may have to give to him that needeth" (Ep.4:28).

"And whatsoever ye do in word or deed, *do* all in the name of the Lord Jesus, giving thanks to God and the Father by him" (Col.3:17).

"And whatsoever ye do, do *it* heartily, as to the Lord, and not unto men" (Col.3:23).

"Now them that are such we command and exhort by our Lord Jesus Christ, that with quietness they work, and eat their own bread" (2 Th.3:12).

"Nevertheless we, according to his promise, look for new heavens and a new earth, wherein dwelleth righteousness. Wherefore, beloved, seeing that ye look for such things, be diligent that ye may be found of him in peace, without spot, and blameless. And account *that* the longsuffering of our Lord *is* salvation; even as our beloved brother Paul also according to the wisdom given unto him hath written unto you" (2 Pe.3:13-14).

"And the LORD God took the man, and put him into the garden of Eden to dress it and to keep it" (Ge.2:15).

"And she said, I pray you, let me glean and gather after the reapers among the sheaves: so she came, and hath continued even from the morning until now, that she tarried a little in the house" (Ru.2:7).

"Go to the ant, thou sluggard; consider her ways, and be wise" (Pr.6:6).

"He becometh poor that dealeth *with* a slack hand: but the hand of the diligent maketh rich" (Pr.10:4).

"He that gathereth in summer *is* a wise son: *but* he that sleepeth in harvest *is* a son that causeth shame" (Pr.10:5).

"He that tilleth his land shall be satisfied with bread: but he that followeth vain *persons is* void of understanding" (Pr.12:11).

"The soul of the sluggard desireth, and *hath* nothing: but the soul of the diligent shall be made fat" (Pr.13:4).

"Wealth *gotten* by vanity shall be diminished: but he that gathereth by labour shall increase" (Pr.13:11).

"In all labour there is profit: but the talk of the lips *tendeth* only to penury" (Pr.14:23).

"Love not sleep, lest thou come to poverty; open thine eyes, *and* thou shalt be satisfied with bread" (Pr.20:13).

"She seeketh wool, and flax, and worketh willingly with her hands" (Pr.31:13).

"She maketh fine linen, and selleth *it;* and delivereth girdles unto the merchant" (Pr.31:24).

"Whatsoever thy hand findeth to do, do *it* with thy might; for *there is* no work, nor device, nor knowledge, nor wisdom, in the grave, whither thou goest" (Ec.9:10).

CHAPTER 6

F. The Building of the Temple: A Lesson on the Living Temple, the Believer in Whom God's Spirit Dwells, 6:1-38

6:1-28; see 2 Chr.3:1-14

1. The date when construction of the temple began—480 years after the Exodus: Stresses the importance of God's temple, the body of the believer, 1 Co.6:19-20
   a. Was in the 4th year of Solomon's reign
   b. Was the temple of the LORD

2. The outer structure of the temple: Stresses the importance of a solid, spiritual foundation
   a. The overall size: 90 ft. long, 30 ft. wide, & 45 ft. high
   b. The front porch or portico: 30 ft. long, 15 ft. wide
   c. The recessed windows
   d. The three-floor structure: Built on two or three sides for chambers or side rooms
      1) The 1st floor: 7½ ft. wide
      2) The 2nd floor: 9 ft. wide
      3) The 3rd floor: 10½ ft. wide
      4) The narrow, three-floor building surrounded, but was separated from—not attached to—the temple
   e. The holiness of the temple: Was respected during construction
      1) Materials were precut
      2) The reason: For quietness, a sense of awe & reverence
   f. The door or entrance was built on the south side, & a winding stairway led up to the second & third floors
   g. The roof: Was covered with beams & cedar planks

And it came to pass in the four hundred and eightieth year after the children of Israel were come out of the land of Egypt, in the fourth year of Solomon's reign over Israel, in the month Zif, which *is* the second month, that he began to build the house of the LORD.

2 And the house which king Solomon built for the LORD, the length thereof *was* threescore cubits, and the breadth thereof twenty *cubits,* and the height thereof thirty cubits.

3 And the porch before the temple of the house, twenty cubits *was* the length thereof, according to the breadth of the house; *and* ten cubits *was* the breadth thereof before the house.

4 And for the house he made windows of narrow lights.

5 And against the wall of the house he built chambers round about, *against* the walls of the house round about, *both* of the temple and of the oracle: and he made chambers round about:

6 The nethermost chamber *was* five cubits broad, and the middle *was* six cubits broad, and the third *was* seven cubits broad: for without *in the wall* of the house he made narrowed rests round about, that *the beams* should not be fastened in the walls of the house.

7 And the house, when it was in building, was built of stone made ready before it was brought thither: so that there was neither hammer nor axe *nor* any tool of iron heard in the house, while it was in building.

8 The door for the middle chamber *was* in the right side of the house: and they went up with winding stairs into the middle *chamber,* and out of the middle into the third.

9 So he built the house, and finished it; and covered the house with beams and boards of cedar.

10 And *then* he built chambers against all the house, five cubits high: and they rested on the house *with* timber of cedar.

11 And the word of the LORD came to Solomon, saying,

12 *Concerning* this house which thou art in building, if thou wilt walk in my statutes, and execute my judgments, and keep all my commandments to walk in them; then will I perform my word with thee, which I spake unto David thy father:

13 And I will dwell among the children of Israel, and will not forsake my people Israel.

14 So Solomon built the house, and finished it.

15 And he built the walls of the house within with boards of cedar, both the floor of the house, and the walls of the ceiling: *and* he covered *them* on the inside with wood, and covered the floor of the house with planks of fir.

16 And he built twenty cubits on the sides of the house, both the floor and the walls with boards of cedar: he even built *them* for it within, *even* for the oracle, *even* for the most holy *place.*

17 And the house, that *is,* the temple before it, was forty cubits *long.*

18 And the cedar of the house within *was* carved with knops and open flowers: all *was* cedar; there was no stone seen.

19 And the oracle he prepared in the house within, to set there the ark of the covenant of the LORD.

20 And the oracle in the forepart *was* twenty cubits in length, and twenty cubits in breadth, and twenty cubits in the height thereof: and he overlaid it with pure gold; and so covered the altar *which was of* cedar.

21 So Solomon overlaid the house within with pure gold: and he made a partition by the chains of gold before the oracle; and he overlaid it with gold.

22 And the whole house he

   h. The chambers or side rooms of the three-floor structure: 7½ ft. high

3. The conditional promises of God concerning the temple: Stresses that the temple or church building is not sufficient by itself; obedience is necessary
   a. The condition: Must obey God's Word
   b. The promises
      1) Would use Solomon to fulfill His promises
      2) Would live among the Israelites: Grant His presence & guidance

4. The interior of the temple: Stresses the importance of communion with God
   a. The walls & floors
      1) The walls: Were lined with cedar
      2) The floor: Was covered with fir or pine
   b. The inner sanctuary or the Most Holy Place: Was partitioned off with cedar boards
      1) The location
         • Was 30 ft. from the rear of the temple
         • Left 60 ft. for the main hall
      2) The interior: Was covered with cedar, & all woodwork was delicately carved with no stone exposed
      3) The purpose: To house the Ark of the Covenant
      4) The size: Was a cube—30 ft. long, 30 ft. wide, 30 ft. high
      5) The interior covering: Was pure gold
      6) The altar of incense: Was overlaid with gold
   c. The inside of the temple: Was covered with pure gold
      1) The chains that protected the entrance to the Most Holy Place: Made of gold
      2) The whole interior was

covered with gold
   3) The altar of incense was also covered with gold

d. The two cherubim for the inner sanctuary
   1) Made of olive wood: 15 ft. high
   2) Made each wing 7½ ft. wide or 15 ft. from wing tip to wing tip
   3) Made the two cherubim identical in size & shape
   4) Made each cherubim 15 ft. high
   5) Were positioned in the Most Holy Place, facing the door
   6) Were placed so their wings reached from one wall to the other: Symbolized the protective holiness of God, Ge.3:24; Eze.1:4-14, 22-28
   7) Were overlaid with gold

e. The walls inside: Were delicately carved with cherubim, palm trees, & open flowers

f. The floors: Were covered with gold

overlaid with gold, until he had finished all the house: also the whole altar that *was* by the oracle he overlaid with gold.

23 And within the oracle he made two cherubims *of* olive tree, *each* ten cubits high.

24 And five cubits *was* the one wing of the cherub, and five cubits the other wing of the cherub: from the uttermost part of the one wing unto the uttermost part of the other *were* ten cubits.

25 And the other cherub *was* ten cubits: both the cherubims *were* of one measure and one size.

26 The height of the one cherub *was* ten cubits, and so *was it* of the other cherub.

27 And he set the cherubims within the inner house: and they stretched forth the wings of the cherubims, so that the wing of the one touched the *one* wall, and the wing of the other cherub touched the other wall; and their wings touched one another in the midst of the house.

28 And he overlaid the cherubims with gold.

29 And he carved all the walls of the house round about with carved figures of cherubims and palm trees and open flowers, within and without.

30 And the floor of the house he overlaid with gold, within and without.

31 And for the entering of the oracle he made doors *of* olive tree: the lintel *and* side posts *were* a fifth part *of the wall.*

32 The two doors also *were of* olive tree; and he carved upon them carvings of cherubims and palm trees and open flowers, and overlaid *them* with gold, and spread gold upon the cherubims, and upon the palm trees.

33 So also made he for the door of the temple posts of olive tree, a fourth part *of the wall.*

34 And the two doors *were of* fir tree: the two leaves of the one door *were* folding, and the two leaves of the other door *were* folding.

35 And he carved *thereon* cherubims and palm trees and open flowers: and covered *them* with gold fitted upon the carved work.

36 And he built the inner court with three rows of hewed stone, and a row of cedar beams.

37 In the fourth year was the foundation of the house of the LORD laid, in the month Zif:

38 And in the eleventh year, in the month Bul, which *is* the eighth month, was the house finished throughout all the parts thereof, and according to all the fashion of it. So was he seven years in building it.

g. The two doors & door posts (jambs) of the Most Holy Place
   1) Were made of olive wood
   2) Were delicately carved & overlaid with gold

h. The two doors for the main entrance
   1) Made doorposts (jambs) of olive wood
   2) Made two large doors of fir or pine
   3) Were delicately carved & overlaid with gold

i. The inner courtyard: Was constructed with three layers (courses) of dressed stone & one layer of trimmed cedar beams

5. The time spent in completing the temple: A lesson on being steadfast, on persevering & completing the task given by God
   a. The specifications of David were carried out, 1 Chr. 28:11-12
   b. The temple took seven years to complete

DIVISION I

THE RISE AND REIGN OF SOLOMON AS KING: BEGINNING IN GLORY AND ENDING IN SHAME, 1:1–11:43

F. The Building of the Temple: A Lesson on the Living Temple, the Believer in Whom God's Spirit Dwells, 6:1-38

(6:1-38) **Introduction**: when we think of a church, a temple, a synagogue, or a mosque, we usually think of a building—brick and mortar. But not God. As important as the buildings of our church or worship center are, the primary interest of God is the *living temple*. The *living temple* is the believer's body in which God's Spirit dwells. The *indwelling presence* of the Holy Spirit is one of the great teachings of God's Holy Word. Once a person is saved by faith in the Lord Jesus Christ, the Spirit of God enters the life of the new believer. The body of the believer actually becomes the temple of God's Holy Spirit. Imagine the very Spirit of God Himself dwelling, abiding, living, and being present within the body of the believer. A phenomenal, awesome truth! God's Spirit abides within us in order to guide us as we walk day by day, teaching and empowering us to conquer and overcome throughout life. The Spirit of God grows us into the image of Christ, conforming us to His very character. And the fruit of His character—of His Spirit—includes these wonderful qualities:

⇒ love
⇒ joy
⇒ peace
⇒ patience
⇒ gentleness
⇒ goodness
⇒ faithfulness
⇒ meekness
⇒ self-control

No greater gift could ever be received than the Spirit of God dwelling within our bodies. God's Spirit within us is the guarantee, the seal of our salvation. God's Spirit gives us the hope and power to live a full and victorious life. He empowers us to conquer all the temptations and trials of this world, even death itself. He then gives us the power to live eternally in the presence of God.

Because of what the Spirit of God gives to the believer—because of the wonderful fruit He bears in the life of the believer—we see why the primary interest of God is not bricks and mortar but instead the *living temple*. For it is the *living temple*, the body of the believer, in whom God's very own Spirit dwells.

"And I will pray the Father, and he shall give you another Comforter, that he may abide with you for ever; *Even* the Spirit of truth; whom the world cannot receive, because it seeth him not, neither knoweth him: but ye know him; for he dwelleth with you, and shall be in you" (Jn.14:16-17).

"But ye are not in the flesh, but in the Spirit, if so be that the Spirit of God dwell in you. Now if any man have not the Spirit of Christ, he is none of his" (Ro.8:9).

"Know ye not that ye are the temple of God, and *that* the Spirit of God dwelleth in you?" (1 Co.3:16).

"What? know ye not that your body is the temple of the Holy Ghost *which is* in you, which ye have of God, and ye are not your own? For ye are bought with a price: therefore glorify God in your body, and in your spirit, which are God's" (1 Co.6:19-20).

"Who hath also sealed us, and given the earnest [guarantee] of the Spirit in our hearts" (2 Co.1:22).

"That good thing which was committed unto thee keep by the Holy Ghost which dwelleth in us" (2 Ti.1:14).

"But the anointing which ye have received of him abideth in you, and ye need not that any man teach you: but as the same anointing teacheth you of all things, and is truth, and is no lie, and even as it hath taught you, ye shall abide in him" (1 Jn.2:27).

"And I will put my spirit within you, and cause you to walk in my statutes, and ye shall keep my judgments, and do *them*" (Eze.36:27).

The primary interest of God is not brick and mortar: it is the *living* temple. God is seeking people who will give their lives to Him so He can infill them with the presence and power of His precious Spirit. This is: *The Building of the Temple: A Lesson on the Living Temple, the Believer in Whom God's Spirit Dwells,* 6:1-38.

1. The date when construction of the temple began—480 years after the Exodus: stresses the importance of God's temple, the body of the believer, 1 Co.6:19-20 (v.1).
2. The outer structure of the temple: stresses the importance of a solid, spiritual foundation (vv.2-10).
3. The conditional promises of God concerning the temple: stresses that the temple or church building is not sufficient by itself; obedience is necessary (vv.11-13).
4. The interior of the temple: stresses the importance of communion with God (vv.14-36).
5. The time spent in completing the temple: a lesson on being steadfast, on persevering and completing the task given by God (vv.37-38).

1 (6:1) **Temple, Construction of—Temple, Dates of—Exodus, Date of**: the date when construction of the temple began was 480 years after the exodus of Israel out of Egypt. This was the fourth year of Solomon's reign over Israel in the month of Ziv, which was the second month of Israel's calendar. This is one of the most important verses in the Bible for determining certain events in Israel's history. The beginning of Solomon's reign was about 971–970 B.C., which means that the fourth year of his reign would have been 967–966 B.C. Thus, the date of the exodus would have been 1447–1446 BC. *The Expositor's Bible Commentary* says this:

> *This verse is one of the major pieces of internal evidence for the dating of the Exodus. Thiele's date (p. 205) for the end of Solomon's reign is 931/932 B.C. This puts the beginning of his forty-year reign at 971/970 and the fourth year at 967/966 and the date of the Exodus at 1447/1446. This date accords well with other biblical evidence (Judg 11:26 and the length of the time of the Judges) as with external historical evidence (for a good summary treatment, see Wood, Survey, pp. 88-109; G.A. Archer, Encyclopedia of Bible Difficulties [Grand Rapids: Zondervan, 1982], pp. 223-34; and Bruce Waltke, "Palestinian Artifactual Evidence Supporting the Early Date of the Exodus," BS 129 [1972]: 33-47).*[1]

The point to see is that Solomon began to build the temple of the LORD. At long last, the burning passion of his father's and his own heart was beginning to be fulfilled. Construction on the temple of the LORD had begun, begun 480 years after the exodus from Egyptian slavery. Not only had the people received their inheritance in the promised land, but now, at long last, they were also to have the promised worship center, the temple of the LORD. *The Expositor's Bible Commentary* gives an excellent discussion on the meaning and symbolism of the temple, a discussion that is well worth quoting in its entirety:

> *The temple was in reality a permanent tabernacle as far as its symbolism and typology are concerned. It is basically the dwelling place of God with his people. There is a spiritual and symbolic continuity that transcends the structure itself. Whether it be (1) a tent in the wilderness, (2) the splendid, awe-inspiring structure Solomon built, (3) the relatively simple building erected by the returned exiles, (4) the lavish and ornate edifice it became through*

---

[1] Richard D. Patterson and Hermann J. Austel. *1, 2 Kings,* p.61.

Herod's efforts, or (5) its future millennial form, it is the house of God, where God condescends to meet his people. This is seen, for example, in the exchange between David and God in 2 Samuel 7, in which God is described as living among his people in a tent, moving with them from place to place. Later David's son would build a house for God's name. From God's perspective there is no essential difference, whether the house be a tent or a splendid structure of stone and cedar. Perhaps even clearer is Haggai 2:3, 7, 9. Solomon's temple had been destroyed. Now, seventy years later, a new building had been put up—two different buildings; yet in v.3 both together are referred to as "this house." Verse 9 also sees one house, with its "latter glory...greater than the former" (NASB). God's house had had great glory in Solomon's time. In Haggai's time it was poor by comparison, but Haggai stated that the time would come when its glory would far outshine the former.

When Hebrews 9 compares the earthly sanctuary (v.1) with the perfect, heavenly one (v.11), it is the tabernacle that is discussed in terms of its symbolism and typology. This is because it is in connection with the tabernacle, for which Moses received specific construction specifications from the Lord, that the proper procedure for sacrifice and worship is given. Since the tabernacle is the forerunner of the temple, the same manner of sacrifice and ritual procedure pertained to both.

Basically the tabernacle was a miškān ("dwelling place"). This obviously does not mean that God depends on man to put a roof over his head. What it does mean is that God condescends to identify himself with his people, a graciously intimate association in which God makes it possible for men to approach him. This latter aspect is emphasized in the second [name]—'ōhel mō? ēd ("Tent of Meeting"). God has made provision for a meeting between God and man. This coming together is clearly seen as taking place by God's appointment, at the place and time of his designation, and in a manner prescribed by him. It is the one place where formal approach to God is to be made.

A third designation—'ōhel hā? ēdût ("tent of the testimony")—is an ever-present testimony to the covenant God had made with his people. It reminded them of the privileges and promises as well as their responsibilities relating to that covenant.

The fourth frequently found name is the miqdāš ("sanctuary," "Holy Place"). This points to the majesty and the separateness of God as contrasted to the sinfulness and unworthiness of man. It is to be remembered that, though God is indeed gracious, it is not a light thing to come into his presence. It can only be possible by the God-appointed means of sacrifice and cleansing, and that with a sincere heart, not carelessly or frivolously.

The general symbolism of the temple as the place that God indwells is continued in the church age in the temple that is the individual believer's body and in the temple that is the corporate body of believers, the church.[2]

OUTLINE	SCRIPTURE	SCRIPTURE	OUTLINE
1. The date when construction of the temple began—480 years after the Exodus: Stresses the importance of God's temple, the body of the believer,	And it came to pass in the four hundred and eightieth year after the children of Israel were come out of the land of Egypt, in the fourth	year of Solomon's reign over Israel, in the month Zif, which *is* the second month, that he began to build the house of the LORD.	**1 Co.6:19-20** a. Was in the 4th year of Solomon's reign b. Was the temple of the LORD

Thought 1. The stress of this point is the temple of the LORD, the body of the believer that is to honor the Name of the LORD. In God's sovereign plan throughout all eternity, God had the design of the temple in His mind and upon His heart.

"At that day ye shall know that I am in my Father, and ye in me, and I in you" (Jn.14:20).

"I in them, and thou in me, that they may be made perfect in one; and that the world may know that thou hast sent me, and hast loved them, as thou hast loved me" (Jn.17:23).

"Know ye not that ye are the temple of God, and that the Spirit of God dwelleth in you" (1 Co.3:16).

"What? know ye not that your body is the temple of the Holy Ghost which is in you, which ye have of God, and ye are not your own" (1 Co.6:19).

"And what agreement hath the temple of God with idols? for ye are the temple of the living God; as God hath said, I will dwell in them, and walk in them; and I will be their God, and they shall be my people" (2 Co.6:16).

"I am crucified with Christ: nevertheless I live; yet not I, but Christ liveth in me: and the life which I now live in the flesh I live by the faith of the Son of God, who loved me, and gave himself for me" (Ga.2:20).

"And are built upon the foundation of the apostles and prophets, Jesus Christ himself being the chief corner stone; In whom all the building fitly framed together groweth unto an holy temple in the Lord: In whom ye also are builded together for an habitation of God through the Spirit" (Ep.2:20-22).

"To whom God would make known what is the riches of the glory of this mystery among the Gentiles; which is Christ in you, the hope of glory" (Col.1:27).

"But Christ as a son over his own house; whose house are we, if we hold fast the confidence and the rejoicing of the hope firm unto the end" (He.3:6).

"Ye also, as lively stones, are built up a spiritual house, an holy priesthood, to offer up spiritual sacrifices, acceptable to God by Jesus Christ" (1 Pe.2:5).

"Behold, I stand at the door, and knock: if any man hear my voice, and open the door, I will come in to him, and will sup with him, and he with me" (Re.3:20).

---

2 Richard D. Patterson and Hermann J. Austel. *1, 2 Kings*, p.60-61.

2 (6:2-10) **Foundation, Spiritual, Importance of—Life, Foundation of—Temple, Structure of**: the details of the outer structure of the temple are discussed in these verses. These dimensions cover the *main structure* of the temple. Note the Scripture and outline:

OUTLINE	SCRIPTURE	SCRIPTURE	OUTLINE
2. The outer structure of the temple: Stresses the importance of a solid, spiritual foundation a. The overall size: 90 ft. long, 30 ft. wide, & 45 ft. high	2 And the house which king Solomon built for the LORD, the length thereof *was* threescore cubits, and the breadth thereof twenty *cubits,* and the height thereof thirty cubits.	narrowed rests round about, that *the beams* should not be fastened in the walls of the house.	attached to—the temple
b. The front porch or portico: 30 ft. long, 15 ft. wide	3 And the porch before the temple of the house, twenty cubits *was* the length thereof, according to the breadth of the house; *and* ten cubits *was* the breadth thereof before the house.	7 And the house, when it was in building, was built of stone made ready before it was brought thither: so that there was neither hammer nor axe *nor* any tool of iron heard in the house, while it was in building.	e. The holiness of the temple: Was respected during construction 1) Materials were precut 2) The reason: For quietness, a sense of awe & reverence
c. The recessed windows	4 And for the house he made windows of narrow lights.	8 The door for the middle chamber *was* in the right side of the house: and they went up with winding stairs into the middle *chamber,* and out of the middle into the third.	f. The door or entrance was built on the south side, & a winding stairway led up to the second & third floors
d. The three-floor structure: Built on two or three sides for chambers or side rooms	5 And against the wall of the house he built chambers round about, *against* the walls of the house round about, *both* of the temple and of the oracle: and he made chambers round about:	9 So he built the house, and finished it; and covered the house with beams and boards of cedar.	g. The roof: Was covered with beams & cedar planks
1) The 1st floor: 7½ ft. wide 2) The 2nd floor: 9 ft. wide 3) The 3rd floor: 10½ ft. wide 4) The narrow, three-floor building surrounded, but was separated from—not	6 The nethermost chamber *was* five cubits broad, and the middle *was* six cubits broad, and the third *was* seven cubits broad: for without *in the wall* of the house he made	10 And *then* he built chambers against all the house, five cubits high: and they rested on the house *with* timber of cedar.	h. The chambers or side rooms of the three-floor structure: 7½ ft. high

a. The overall size of the temple was not large (v.2). It was only ninety feet long, thirty feet wide, and forty-five feet high, consisting of 2,700 square feet of floor space. But the temple, which will be seen in later Scripture, was strikingly beautiful because of its furnishings (7:15-50).

b. The front porch or portico was thirty feet long by fifteen feet wide (v.3). Note that this was an additional fifteen feet added to the length of the temple, making the temple 105 feet long when the porch was added.

c. The recessed windows were apparently placed high on the wall, close to the ceiling (v.4).

d. There was a three-floor structure built on two or three sides for chambers or side rooms (v.5). The chambers or side rooms were probably used by the priests for storage and perhaps for counseling or performing other ministerial services when needed. The dimensions were these:

⇒ The first floor was seven and a half feet wide
⇒ The second floor was nine feet wide
⇒ The third floor was ten and a half feet wide

But note: they allowed no ceiling beam of the three-floor structure to be inserted into the temple walls. Rather, ledges were built out from the temple wall so that the ceiling beams could rest on them. Nothing could be inserted into the temple walls because of the presence and holiness of God. The temple was holy, the very dwelling place for the presence of God.

e. Note how the holiness of the temple was respected during construction (vv.7-8). All materials were precut away from the temple site because of the holiness of the temple. A sense of quietness, awe, and reverence was observed.

f. The door or entrance was built on the south side, and winding stairways led up to the second and third floors (v.8).

g. The roof was constructed out of beams or cedar planks (v.9). Obviously, some kind of ceiling material was used on top of the cedar planks to protect against water.

h. The chambers or side rooms of the three-floor structure were only seven and a half feet high (v.10).

Thought 1. The outer structure of the temple stresses the importance of a solid foundation to support the floor, walls, and roof of the temple. This is a striking picture for us, emphasizing the significance of building a strong foundation to life. Unless our lives are built upon the foundation of Christ, we are doomed to destruction. Without Christ we are separated from God. And without God there is no hope, not in this world nor in the next. Without God, we will never experience…

- the fullness of life
- the complete purpose, significance, and meaning of life
- the *spiritual rest*, the full assurance and confidence that all things are well
- the perfect peace and security that comes only from a personal relationship with God
- the love, joy, and rejoicing that can only be aroused by God's Spirit within the human soul

A spiritual foundation is desperately needed in our lives. We must base our lives upon the foundation of Christ, the only living stone ever laid by God Himself. And God longs to take our lives and lay them upon Christ, *cementing* them to Him, making us a part of the living structure He is building, even the temple of the LORD Himself. Listen to what God has to say about building our lives upon the foundation of the Lord Jesus Christ:

"Therefore whosoever heareth these sayings of mine, and doeth them, I will liken him unto a wise man, which built his house upon a rock: And the rain descended, and the floods came, and the winds blew, and beat upon that house; and it fell not: for it was founded upon a rock. And every one that heareth these sayings of mine, and doeth them not, shall be likened unto a foolish man, which built his house upon the sand: And the rain descended, and the floods came, and the winds blew, and beat upon that house; and it fell: and great was the fall of it" (Mt.7:24-27).

"Jesus saith unto them, Did ye never read in the scriptures, The stone which the builders rejected, the same is become the head of the corner: this is the Lord's doing, and it is marvellous in our eyes" (Mt.21:42).

"This is the stone which was set at nought of you builders, which is become the head of the corner" (Ac.4:11).

"For other foundation can no man lay than that is laid, which is Jesus Christ" (1 Co.3:11).

"And are built upon the foundation of the apostles and prophets, Jesus Christ himself being the chief corner stone" (Ep.2:20).

"Laying up in store for themselves a good foundation against the time to come, that they may lay hold on eternal life" (1 Ti.6:19).

"Nevertheless the foundation of God standeth sure, having this seal, The Lord knoweth them that are his. And, Let every one that nameth the name of Christ depart from iniquity" (2 Ti.2:19).

"Wherefore also it is contained in the scripture, Behold, I lay in Sion a chief corner stone, elect, precious: and he that believeth on him shall not be confounded" (1 Pe.2:6).

"Therefore thus saith the Lord God, Behold, I lay in Zion for a foundation a stone, a tried stone, a precious corner stone, a sure foundation: he that believeth shall not make haste" (Is.28:16).

[3] (6:11-13) **Obedience, Essential—Church, Needs of—Temple, Needs of—Promises, of God, to Solomon—Solomon, Encounters with the LORD—Encounters, with the LORD**: there were the conditional promises of God given to Solomon, promises concerning the temple. At some point during the construction of the temple, the LORD apparently sent a prophet to Solomon with a striking message: the temple was not sufficient for worship by itself; obedience was also necessary. As important as building the temple was, it alone was not enough, not in God's eyes: Solomon must obey God's Word, keeping the commandments of God. If he obeyed God, then the LORD promised to do two great things:

⇒ The LORD would use Solomon to fulfill the promises He had given to David, that David would have a lasting dynasty and that his son Solomon would build the temple.

⇒ The LORD Himself would live among the Israelites, grant His presence and guidance, never leaving nor abandoning them (v.13).

Apart from obedience, Solomon would never receive the promises made by God. And apart from obedience, the temple would have no meaning or significance for God's people. For the temple by itself was not sufficient to secure God's approval and acceptance. Obedience was necessary for pure worship.

OUTLINE	SCRIPTURE	SCRIPTURE	OUTLINE
3. The conditional promises of God concerning the temple: Stresses that the temple or church building is not sufficient by itself; obedience is necessary a. The condition: Must obey God's Word	11 And the word of the LORD came to Solomon, saying, 12 *Concerning* this house which thou art in building, if thou wilt walk in my statutes, and execute my judgments, and keep all my command-	ments to walk in them; then will I perform my word with thee, which I spake unto David thy father: 13 And I will dwell among the children of Israel, and will not forsake my people Israel.	b. The promises 1) Would use Solomon to fulfill His promises 2) Would live among the Israelites: Grant His presence & guidance

Thought 1. The lesson for us is just as striking as it was to Solomon. A church building is not enough, not sufficient by itself, not in the LORD's eyes. Obedience is necessary. Keeping the commandments of God, approaching God with a clean, pure heart is what makes us acceptable to Him. A worshiper entering the church with a sinful, wicked heart is not acceptable, not until he repents and turns to the LORD, forsaking his sin. No matter how ornate or beautiful a church is, the worshiper is acceptable to God only if he comes with a pure heart and clean life, only if he is willing to obey the LORD and to keep His commandments. This is the clear teaching of God's Holy Word:

"Not every one that saith unto me, Lord, Lord, shall enter into the kingdom of heaven; but he that doeth the will of my Father which is in heaven. Many will say to me in that day, Lord, Lord, have we not prophesied in thy name? and in thy name have cast out devils? and in thy name done many wonderful works? And then will I profess unto them, I never knew you: depart from me, ye that work iniquity" (Mt.7:21-23).

"For whosoever shall do the will of my Father which is in heaven, the same is my brother, and sister, and mother" (Mt.12:50).

"And he answered and said unto them, My mother and my brethren are these which hear the word of God, and do it" (Lu.8:21).

"Jesus answered and said unto him, If a man love me, he will keep my words: and my Father will love him, and we will come unto him, and make our abode with him" (Jn.14:23).

"If ye keep my commandments, ye shall abide in my love; even as I have kept my Father's commandments, and abide in his love" (Jn.15:10).

"Blessed *are* they that do his commandments, that they may have right to the tree of life, and may enter in through the gates into the city" (Re.22:14).

"O that there were such an heart in them, that they would fear me, and keep all my commandments always, that it might be well with them, and with their children for ever!" (De.5:29).

"This day the LORD thy God hath commanded thee to do these statutes and judgments: thou shalt therefore keep and do them with all thine heart, and with all thy soul" (De.26:16).

"And Samuel said, Hath the LORD *as great* delight in burnt offerings and sacrifices, as in obeying the voice of the LORD? Behold, to obey *is* better than sacrifice, *and* to hearken than the fat of rams" (1 S.15:22).

"And if thou wilt walk in my ways, to keep my statutes and my commandments, as thy father David did walk, then I will lengthen thy days" (1 K.3:14).

4 (6:14-36) **Communion, Importance of—Fellowship, With God, Importance of—Temple, Interior of, Discussed**: once the exterior of the temple had been completed, the workers began to focus upon the interior. Note how the focus of the interior is upon the inner sanctuary or Most Holy Place. This stresses the importance of communion or fellowship with God.

OUTLINE	SCRIPTURE	SCRIPTURE	OUTLINE
4. The interior of the temple: Stresses the importance of communion with God a. The walls & floors 1) The walls: Were lined with cedar 2) The floor: Was covered with fir or pine	14 So Solomon built the house, and finished it. 15 And he built the walls of the house within with boards of cedar, both the floor of the house, and the walls of the ceiling: *and* he covered *them* on the inside with wood, and covered the floor of the house with planks of fir.	oracle; and he overlaid it with gold. 22 And the whole house he overlaid with gold, until he had finished all the house: also the whole altar that *was* by the oracle he overlaid with gold.	Holy Place: Made of gold 2) The whole interior was covered with gold 3) The altar of incense was also covered with gold
b. The inner sanctuary or the Most Holy Place: Was partitioned off with cedar boards 1) The location • Was 30 ft. from the rear of the temple	16 And he built twenty cubits on the sides of the house, both the floor and the walls with boards of cedar: he even built *them* for it within, *even* for the oracle, *even* for the most holy *place.*	23 And within the oracle he made two cherubims *of* olive tree, *each* ten cubits high. 24 And five cubits *was* the one wing of the cherub, and five cubits the other wing of the cherub: from the uttermost part of the one wing unto the uttermost part of the other *were* ten cubits.	d. The two cherubim for the inner sanctuary 1) Made of olive wood: 15 ft. high 2) Made each wing 7½ ft. wide or 15 ft. from wing tip to wing tip
• Left 60 ft. for the main hall	17 And the house, that *is,* the temple before it, was forty cubits *long.*	25 And the other cherub *was* ten cubits: both the cherubims *were* of one measure and one size.	3) Made the two cherubim identical in size & shape
2) The interior: Was covered with cedar, & all woodwork was delicately carved with no stone exposed	18 And the cedar of the house within *was* carved with knops and open flowers: all *was* cedar; there was no stone seen.	26 The height of the one cherub *was* ten cubits, and so *was it* of the other cherub.	4) Made each cherubim 15 ft. high
3) The purpose: To house the Ark of the Covenant	19 And the oracle he prepared in the house within, to set there the ark of the covenant of the LORD.	27 And he set the cherubims within the inner house: and they stretched forth the wings of the cherubims, so that the wing of the one touched the *one* wall, and the wing of the other cherub touched the other wall; and their wings touched one another in the midst of the house.	5) Were positioned in the Most Holy Place, facing the door 6) Were placed so their wings reached from one wall to the other: Symbolized the protective holiness of God, Ge.3:24; Eze.1:4-14, 22-28
4) The size: Was a cube—30 ft. long, 30 ft. wide, 30 ft. high 5) The interior covering: Was pure gold 6) The altar of incense: Was overlaid with gold	20 And the oracle in the forepart *was* twenty cubits in length, and twenty cubits in breadth, and twenty cubits in the height thereof: and he overlaid it with pure gold; and so covered the altar *which was of* cedar.	28 And he overlaid the cherubims with gold.	7) Were overlaid with gold
c. The inside of the temple: Was covered with pure gold 1) The chains that protected the entrance to the Most	21 So Solomon overlaid the house within with pure gold: and he made a partition by the chains of gold before the	29 And he carved all the walls of the house round about with carved figures of	e. The walls inside: Were delicately carved with cherubim, palm trees, & open flowers

OUTLINE	SCRIPTURE	SCRIPTURE	OUTLINE
	cherubims and palm trees and open flowers, within and without.	33 So also made he for the door of the temple posts of olive tree, a fourth part *of the wall.*	h. The two doors for the main entrance 1) Made doorposts (jambs) of olive wood
f. The floors: Were covered with gold	30 And the floor of the house he overlaid with gold, within and without.	34 And the two doors *were of* fir tree: the two leaves of the one door *were* folding, and the two leaves of the other door *were* folding.	2) Made two large doors of fir or pine
g. The two doors & door posts (jambs) of the Most Holy Place 1) Were made of olive wood 2) Were delicately carved & overlaid with gold	31 And for the entering of the oracle he made doors *of* olive tree: the lintel *and* side posts *were* a fifth part *of the wall.* 32 The two doors also *were of* olive tree; and he carved upon them carvings of cherubims and palm trees and open flowers, and overlaid *them* with gold, and spread gold upon the cherubims, and upon the palm trees.	35 And he carved *thereon* cherubims and palm trees and open flowers: and covered *them* with gold fitted upon the carved work.	3) Were delicately carved & overlaid with gold
		36 And he built the inner court with three rows of hewed stone, and a row of cedar beams.	i. The inner courtyard: Was constructed with three layers (courses) of dressed stone & one layer of trimmed cedar beams

a. The walls were lined with cedar paneling stretching all the way from the floor to the ceiling, and the floor was covered with fir or pine (v.15). Both woods were very valuable in the ancient world, just as cedar paneling is today.

b. The inner sanctuary or the Most Holy Place was petitioned off with cedar boards (vv.16-20). The Most Holy Place was partitioned off at the rear of the temple and was thirty feet deep. It was paneled with cedar from floor to ceiling (v.16). This left sixty feet for the main hall, which was twice the size of the Most Holy Place. The interior of the main hall was covered with cedar as well as the Most Holy Place, and all woodwork of the temple was delicately carved, with no stone whatsoever exposed for the worshiper to see (v.18).

The purpose of the Most Holy Place was to house the Ark of the Covenant, which was a symbol of the very presence of God Himself (v.19; Ex.25:21-22; Jos.3:13; 1 S.4:4; 2 S.6:2; 1 K.8:10-11).

The dimensions of the Most Holy Place were thirty feet long, thirty feet wide, and thirty feet high—a perfect cube (v.20). The interior covering was overlaid with pure gold, as well as the altar of incense.

c. In fact, the entire interior was covered with pure gold (vv.21-22). This included the chains that protected the entrance to the Most Holy Place.

d. The two cherubim for the Most Holy Place were made of olive wood fifteen feet high, with a wing span of seven and one-half feet each, or fifteen feet from wing tip to wing tip (vv.23-28). This meant that the wings of the two cherubim stretched from one wall of the sanctuary to the other. Solomon made the two cherubim identical in size and shape and placed them in the Most Holy Place, facing the door so their wings would reach from one wall to the other. This was a clear symbol of the protective holiness of God. Standing there, the cherubim were the guardians of God's Holy Presence (Ge.3:24; Eze.1:4-14, 22-28). The cherubim were also overlaid with gold (v.28).

e. All the walls of the temple were delicately carved with cherubim, palm trees, and open flowers (v.29).

f. Solomon also covered the floors of both the inner and outer sanctuaries with gold (v.30).

g. The two doors and doorposts (jambs) of the Most Holy Place were made of olive wood (vv.31-32). These two were delicately carved and overlaid with gold.

h. The two large doors for the main entrance had doorposts constructed of olive wood; whereas the two doors themselves were made of fir or pine. They were delicately carved and overlaid with gold (vv.33-34).

i. The inner courtyard was constructed with three layers of dressed stone and one layer of trimmed cedar beams (v.36).

Thought 1. The sanctuary symbolized the very presence of God Himself, the place where the worshiper was to meet God, commune and fellowship with Him. Above all else, the one thing God wants from us is communion and fellowship with Him. God created us primarily for fellowship. He wanted communion with a creature who had a free will, who could choose either to fellowship or not to fellowship with God.

- The LORD wants us drawing near Him with broken hearts, contrite spirits, calling upon Him from the depths of our being.
- The Lord wants us seeking Him in prayer, asking Him to meet our needs and to help us through the problems, difficulties, and trials of life.
- The Lord wants us praising Him and giving thanks when He meets our needs and supplies whatever provisions we lack.
- The Lord wants to walk with us through the good times as well as the bad. God never wants us to walk alone facing the seductive temptations of this world and the difficult, distressing trials that so often confront us.
- The Lord wants to be right by our side, taking care of us and looking after us, sustaining us. God wants to infuse power within our hearts and minds, power to conquer, triumph, and overcome any and all enemies who oppose us or hate us or assault us. God wants to walk with us, empowering us to live victoriously as we walk day by day throughout life.

Communion with God, fellowship with God, drawing close to God—this is the desire of the LORD'S heart. Listen to what He says about communion and fellowship with Him:

"For where two or three are gathered together in my name, there am I in the midst of them" (Mt.18:20).

"Go ye therefore, and teach all nations, baptizing them in the name of the Father, and of the Son, and of the Holy Ghost: Teaching them to observe all things whatsoever I have commanded you: and, lo, I am with you alway, *even* unto the end of the world. Amen" (Mt.28:19-20).

"And it came to pass, that, while they communed *together* and reasoned, Jesus himself drew near, and went with them" (Lu.24:15).

"And they said one to another, Did not our heart burn within us, while he talked with us by the way, and while he opened to us the scriptures?" (Lu.24:32).

"I am the vine, ye *are* the branches: He that abideth in me, and I in him, the same bringeth forth much fruit: for without me ye can do nothing" (Jn.15:5).

"If ye abide in me, and my words abide in you, ye shall ask what ye will, and it shall be done unto you" (Jn.15:7).

"If ye keep my commandments, ye shall abide in my love; even as I have kept my Father's commandments, and abide in his love" (Jn.15:10).

"I in them, and thou in me, that they may be made perfect in one; and that the world may know that thou hast sent me, and hast loved them, as thou hast loved me" (Jn.17:23).

"God *is* faithful, by whom ye were called unto the fellowship of his Son Jesus Christ our Lord" (1 Co.1:9).

"I am crucified with Christ: nevertheless I live; yet not I, but Christ liveth in me: and the life which I now live in the flesh I live by the faith of the Son of God, who loved me, and gave himself for me" (Ga.2:20).

"That Christ may dwell in your hearts by faith; that ye, being rooted and grounded in love, May be able to comprehend with all saints what *is* the breadth, and length, and depth, and height; And to know the love of Christ, which passeth knowledge, that ye might be filled with all the fulness of God" (Ep.3:17-19).

"To whom God would make known what is the riches of the glory of this mystery among the Gentiles; which is Christ in you, the hope of glory" (Col.1:27).

"For the law made nothing perfect, but the bringing in of a better hope *did*; by the which we draw nigh unto God" (He.7:19).

"Let us draw near with a true heart in full assurance of faith, having our hearts sprinkled from an evil conscience, and our bodies washed with pure water" (He.10:22).

"Draw nigh to God, and he will draw nigh to you. Cleanse *your* hands, *ye* sinners; and purify *your* hearts, *ye* double minded" (Ja.4:8).

"That which we have seen and heard declare we unto you, that ye also may have fellowship with us: and truly our fellowship *is* with the Father, and with his Son Jesus Christ" (1 Jn.1:3).

"And he that keepeth his commandments dwelleth in him, and he in him. And hereby we know that he abideth in us, by the Spirit which he hath given us" (1 Jn.3:24).

"Behold, I stand at the door, and knock: if any man hear my voice, and open the door, I will come in to him, and will sup with him, and he with me" (Re.3:20).

"And, behold, I *am* with thee, and will keep thee in all *places* whither thou goest, and will bring thee again into this land; for I will not leave thee, until I have done *that* which I have spoken to thee of" (Ge.28:15).

"And he said, My presence shall go *with thee*, and I will give thee rest" (Ex.33:14).

"I have set the LORD always before me: because *he is* at my right hand, I shall not be moved" (Ps.16:8).

"The LORD *is* nigh unto them that are of a broken heart; and saveth such as be of a contrite spirit" (Ps.34:18).

"But *it is* good for me to draw near to God: I have put my trust in the Lord GOD, that I may declare all thy works" (Ps.73:28).

"The LORD *is* nigh unto all them that call upon him, to all that call upon him in truth" (Ps.145:18).

"When thou passest through the waters, I *will be* with thee; and through the rivers, they shall not overflow thee: when thou walkest through the fire, thou shalt not be burned; neither shall the flame kindle upon thee" (Is.43:2).

"*Am* I a God at hand, saith the LORD, and not a God afar off" (Je.23:23).

5 (6:37-38) **Steadfast, Example of—Perseverance, Example of—Work, Diligence—Temple, Completion of**: the temple took seven years to complete. The foundation was laid in the fourth year of Solomon's reign and completed in the eleventh year of his reign, making a difference of seven years. But the long years of exhausting, hard labor had been worth it. And what a day of rejoicing it must have been when Solomon walked out to find that the last decorative touches were being made to the temple. There Solomon stood, gazing at the temple of the LORD that, at long last, was ready for worship. Standing there, Solomon must have recalled the rejoicing of his father's heart in the last days of his life:

"Thine, O LORD, *is* the greatness, and the power, and the glory, and the victory, and the majesty: for all *that is* in the heaven and in the earth *is thine*; thine *is* the kingdom, O LORD, and thou art exalted as head above all. Both riches and honour *come* of thee, and thou reignest over all; and in thine

hand *is* power and might; and in thine hand *it is* to make great, and to give strength unto all. Now therefore, our God, we thank thee, and praise thy glorious name" (1 Chr.29:11-13).

OUTLINE	SCRIPTURE	SCRIPTURE	OUTLINE
5. The time spent in completing the temple: A lesson on being steadfast, on persevering & completing the task given by God a. The specifications of David were carried out, 1 Chr.	37 In the fourth year was the foundation of the house of the LORD laid, in the month Zif: 38 And in the eleventh year, in the month Bul, which *is*	the eighth month, was the house finished throughout all the parts thereof, and according to all the fashion of it. So was he seven years in building it.	28:11-12 b. The temple took seven years to complete

Thought 1. After Solomon had persevered for seven long years, the temple was completed. The lesson for us is perseverance, steadfastness, sticking to the task until it is completed. Whatever task God has given us, we must persevere in it. All around us are critical needs, innumerable needs, too many for any of us to slack off. We must never become complacent in our homes or churches or society. People are crying out all over the world in desperate need, with problems and difficulties such as...

- hunger
- homelessness
- poverty
- sickness
- depression
- terminal illness
- loss of a loved one
- loneliness
- purposelessness
- addiction
- lack of education
- discrimination
- prejudice
- financial difficulty

The cry of the hour is for us as Christians to be committed to meeting these needs and for us to be steadfast, persevering in our commitment. Listen to what the LORD says about steadfastness and perseverance:

"And ye shall be hated of all *men* for my name's sake: but he that endureth to the end shall be saved" (Mt.10:22).

"As the Father hath loved me, so have I loved you: continue ye in my love" (Jn.15:9).

"Therefore, my beloved brethren, be ye stedfast, unmovable, always abounding in the work of the Lord, forasmuch as ye know that your labour is not in vain in the Lord" (1 Co.15:58).

"Stand fast therefore in the liberty wherewith Christ hath made us free, and be not entangled again with the yoke of bondage" (Ga.5:1).

"And let us not be weary in well doing: for in due season we shall reap, if we faint not" (Ga.6:9).

"Only let your conversation [behavior, conduct] be as it becometh the gospel of Christ: that whether I come and see you, or else be absent, I may hear of your affairs, that ye stand fast in one spirit, with one mind striving together for the faith of the gospel" (Ph.1:27).

"Prove all things; hold fast that which is good" (1 Th.5:21).

"Seeing then that we have a great high priest, that is passed into the heavens, Jesus the Son of God, let us hold fast *our* profession" (He.4:14).

"Let us hold fast the profession of *our* faith without wavering; (for he *is* faithful that promised" (He.10:23).

"Wherefore seeing we also are compassed about with so great a cloud of witnesses, let us lay aside every weight, and the sin which doth so easily beset *us*, and let us run with patience the race that is set before us" (He.12:1).

"Blessed *is* the man that endureth temptation: for when he is tried, he shall receive the crown of life, which the Lord hath promised to them that love him" (Ja.1:12).

"Behold, we count them happy which endure. Ye have heard of the patience of Job, and have seen the end of the Lord; that the Lord is very pitiful, and of tender mercy" (Ja.5:11).

"Wherefore gird up the loins of your mind, be sober, and hope to the end for the grace that is to be brought unto you at the revelation of Jesus Christ" (1 Pe.1:13).

"For this *is* thankworthy, if a man for conscience toward God endure grief, suffering wrongfully" (1 Pe.2:19).

"Be sober, be vigilant; because your adversary the devil, as a roaring lion, walketh about, seeking whom he may devour: Whom resist stedfast in the faith, knowing that the same afflictions are accomplished in your brethren that are in the world" (1 Pe.5:8-9).

"Ye therefore, beloved, seeing ye know *these things* before, beware lest ye also, being led away with the error of the wicked, fall from your own stedfastness. But grow in grace, and *in* the knowledge of our Lord and Saviour Jesus Christ. To him *be* glory both now and for ever. Amen" (2 Pe.3:17-18).

"Behold, I come quickly: hold that fast which thou hast, that no man take thy crown" (Re.3:11).

"But cleave unto the LORD your God, as ye have done unto this day" (Jos.23:8).

"The righteous also shall hold on his way, and he that hath clean hands shall be stronger and stronger" (Jb.17:9).

"My foot hath held his steps, his way have I kept, and not declined" (Jb.23:11).

CHAPTER 7

G. The Palace Complex of Solomon & the Temple Furnishings: Being Diligent to Put God First, 7:1-51

7:15-22; see 2 Chr.3:15-17
7:23-26; see 2 Chr.4:2-5
7:40-51; see 2 Chr.4:11-5:1

1. The construction of Solomon's palace complex (built after the temple): A picture of putting God first
- a. The first building: The "Palace of the Forest of Lebanon," see 10:17; Is.22:8
  - 1) The size: 150 ft. long, 75 ft. wide, 45 ft. high
  - 2) The support columns: Four rows of cedar columns supporting cedar beams—45 beams, 15 to a row
  - 3) The roof: Cedar boards
  - 4) The windows: Three tiers on each side, placed high on the walls
  - 5) The doorways
    - • Were rectangular frames
    - • Were 3 doors on each wall
- b. The second section—a connecting colonnade or covered porch
  - 1) Was 15 ft. long, 45 ft. wide
  - 2) Was connected to adjacent buildings by a portico with pillars & a covered roof
- c. The third section—the throne hall or Hall of Justice: Was covered with cedar
- d. The fourth section—the living quarters for Solomon: Was built away from the public rooms
- e. The fifth section—the living quarters for Solomon's wife, Pharaoh's daughter
- f. The basic material: Was high-grade stones
  - 1) Were cut to an exact size
  - 2) Were smoothed on both their inner & outer surfaces
- g. The foundations: Were laid with large stones, 12–15 ft. in size
- h. The building stones & beams: Were high grade stone & cedar beams
- i. The large outer courtyard: Was surrounded by a wall built of three layers of dressed stone & one layer of cedar beams (as was the inner courtyard)

2. The skilled craftsman who was reared by his widowed mother: A picture of overcoming hardships
- a. His name: Hiram of Tyre
- b. His hardship: The child of a mixed marriage, reared by his widowed mother
- c. His conquest of hardships: Had become a skilled craftsman
- d. His diligent labor: Did all that Solomon assigned him

3. The outside furnishings of the temple: An example of diligent labor
- a. Hiram cast two bronze pillars for the portico (27 ft. x 18 ft.): Pictured God's power
  - 1) He made two bronze capitals (decorative tops) to set on the pillars (7½ ft. high)
    - • Each capital was decorated with latticework & seven interwoven chains
    - • Two rows of pomegranates encircled the latticework to add to the decorative appearance
    - • The capitals were bowl-shaped, looking like lilies, 6 ft. high
    - • Each capital had two rows of pomegranates encircling it, a total of 200 pomegranates
  - 2) The two pillars were set at the sides of the temple's entrance & named
    - • Jakin: *God establishes*
    - • Boaz: *In God is strength*

But Solomon was build-
ing his own house thirteen
years, and he finished all his
house.
2 He built also the house of
the forest of Lebanon; the
length thereof *was* an hundred cubits, and the breadth
thereof fifty cubits, and the
height thereof thirty cubits,
upon four rows of cedar pillars, with cedar beams upon
the pillars.
3 And *it was* covered with
cedar above upon the beams,
that *lay* on forty five pillars,
fifteen *in* a row.
4 And *there were* windows
in three rows, and light *was*
against light *in* three ranks.
5 And all the doors and
posts *were* square, with the
windows: and light *was*
against light *in* three ranks.
6 And he made a porch of
pillars; the length thereof *was*
fifty cubits, and the breadth
thereof thirty cubits: and the
porch was before them: and
the *other* pillars and the thick
beam *were* before them.
7 Then he made a porch for
the throne where he might
judge, *even* the porch of
judgment: and *it was* covered
with cedar from one side of
the floor to the other.
8 And his house where he
dwelt *had* another court within the porch, *which* was of
the like work. Solomon
made also an house for Pharaoh's daughter, whom he had
taken *to wife,* like unto this
porch.
9 All these *were of* costly
stones, according to the
measures of hewed stones,
sawed with saws, within and
without, even from the foundation unto the coping, and
so on the outside toward the
great court.
10 And the foundation *was*
of costly stones, even great
stones, stones of ten cubits,
and stones of eight cubits.
11 And above *were* costly
stones, after the measures of
hewed stones, and cedars.
12 And the great court round
about *was* with three rows of
hewed stones, and a row of
cedar beams, both for the inner court of the house of the
LORD, and for the porch of
the house.
13 And king Solomon sent
and fetched Hiram out of
Tyre.
14 He *was* a widow's son of
the tribe of Naphtali, and his
father *was* a man of Tyre, a
worker in brass: and he was
filled with wisdom, and understanding, and cunning to
work all works in brass. And
he came to king Solomon,
and wrought all his work.
15 For he cast two pillars of
brass, of eighteen cubits high
apiece: and a line of twelve
cubits did compass either of
them about.
16 And he made two chapi-
ters *of* molten brass, to set
upon the tops of the pillars:
the height of the one chapiter
was five cubits, and the
height of the other chapiter
was five cubits:
17 *And* nets of checker
work, and wreaths of chain
work, for the chapiters which
were upon the top of the pillars; seven for the one chapiter, and seven for the other
chapiter.
18 And he made the pillars,
and two rows round about
upon the one network, to
cover the chapiters that *were*
upon the top, with pome-
granates: and so did he for
the other chapiter.
19 And the chapiters that
were upon the top of the pillars *were* of lily work in the
porch, four cubits.
20 And the chapiters upon
the two pillars *had pome-*
granates also above, over
against the belly which *was*
by the network: and the pomegranates *were* two hundred
in rows round about upon the
other chapiter.
21 And he set up the pillars
in the porch of the temple:
and he set up the right pillar,
and called the name thereof Jachin: and he set up the
left pillar, and he called the

3) The work on the pillars was diligently completed

b. Hiram made a large round water tank or a laver called *the Sea*: Pictured cleansing

1) He made it of cast metal: 7½ ft. deep, 45 ft. in circumference

2) He encircled the tank or laver with two rows of decorative gourds, right below the rim

3) He stood the tank or laver on a base of 12 bronze oxen, all facing outward: 3 faced north, 3 west, 3 south, & 3 east

4) He made the wall about 3 inches thick & its rim was shaped like a cup, like a lily blossom: It held about 11,000 gallons of water

c. Hiram made 10 bronze carts (6 ft. long, 6 ft. wide, 4½ ft. high) & 10 bronze basins: Stressed a need for cleansing

1) They were made with side panels, braced with crossbars: Were decorated with carved lions, bulls, cherubim, & wreaths

2) Each had 4 bronze wheels & bronze axles, & 4 posts at the corners to support the basins: Were decorated with carved wreaths

3) Each had a circular frame on the top to hold the basin (1½ ft. deep, 2¼ ft. across): Were decorated with carved wreaths

4) The panels were square, not round

name thereof Boaz.
22 And upon the top of the
pillars *was* lily work: so was
the work of the pillars finished.
23 And he made a molten
sea, ten cubits from the one
brim to the other: *it was*
round all about, and his
height *was* five cubits: and a
line of thirty cubits did compass it round about.
24 And under the brim of it
round about *there were* knops
compassing it, ten in a cubit,
compassing the sea round
about: the knops *were* cast in
two rows, when it was cast.
25 It stood upon twelve oxen, three looking toward the
north, and three looking toward the west, and three
looking toward the south, and
three looking toward the east:
and the sea *was set* above
upon them, and all their hinder parts *were* inward.
26 And it *was* an hand
breadth thick, and the brim
thereof was wrought like the
brim of a cup, with flowers
of lilies: it contained two
thousand baths.
27 And he made ten bases of
brass; four cubits *was* the
length of one base, and four
cubits the breadth thereof,
and three cubits the height of
it.
28 And the work of the bases *was* on this *manner:* they
had borders, and the borders
were between the ledges:
29 And on the borders that
were between the ledges
were lions, oxen, and cherubims: and upon the ledges
there was a base above: and
beneath the lions and oxen
were certain additions made
of thin work.
30 And every base had four
brasen wheels, and plates of
brass: and the four corners
thereof had undersetters: under the laver *were* undersetters molten, at the side of
every addition.
31 And the mouth of it within the chapiter and above
was a cubit: but the mouth
thereof *was* round *after* the
work of the base, a cubit and
an half: and also upon the
mouth of it *were* gravings
with their borders, foursquare, not round.

32 And under the borders
were four wheels; and the axletrees of the wheels *were*
joined to the base: and the
height of a wheel *was* a cubit
and a half a cubit.
33 And the work of the
wheels was like the work of a
chariot wheel: their axletrees,
and their naves, and their felloes, and their spokes, *were*
all molten.
34 And *there were* four undersetters to the four corners
of one base: *and* the undersetters *were* of the very base
itself.
35 And in the top of the base
was there a round compass of
half a cubit high: and on the
top of the base the ledges
thereof and the borders
thereof *were* of the same.
36 For on the plates of the
ledges thereof, and on the
borders thereof, he graved
cherubims, lions, and palm
trees, according to the proportion of every one, and additions round about.
37 After this *manner* he
made the ten bases: all of
them had one casting, one
measure, *and* one size.
38 Then made he ten lavers
of brass: one laver contained
forty baths: *and* every laver
was four cubits: *and* upon
every one of the ten bases
one laver.
39 And he put five bases on
the right side of the house,
and five on the left side of
the house: and he set the sea
on the right side of the house
eastward over against the
south.
40 And Hiram made the lavers, and the shovels, and the
basons. So Hiram made an
end of doing all the work that
he made king Solomon for
the house of the LORD:
41 The two pillars, and the
two bowls of the chapiters
that *were* on the top of the
two pillars; and the two
networks, to cover the two
bowls of the chapiters which
were upon the top of the
pillars;
42 And four hundred pomegranates for the two networks,
even two rows of pomegranates for one network, to cover
the two bowls of the chapiters that *were* upon the pillars;

5) The axles were cast as one unit with the cart under the panels: Then the wheels (2¼ ft. diameter) were placed on the axles

- The wheels were like chariot wheels
- The axles, rims, spokes, & hubs were cast metal

6) Each had 4 handles, one at each corner & a 9 in. rim around the top: These were cast as one unit with the cart

7) Each cart had cherubim, lions, & palm trees carved where there was room, with wreaths all around

8) Each was cast in the same mold & made identical

9) Each cast held a bronze basin
- Each was 6 ft. across
- Each held 220 gallons of water

10) The carts & the Sea were set in the temple
- 5 carts on the south
- 5 carts on the north
- The Sea at the southeast corner

d. Hiram made the smaller basins, shovels, & bowls

e. Hiram completed the task assigned him: Pictured faithful & diligent work

1) He made the following
- The two pillars
- The bowl-shaped capitals
- The two networks of chains that decorated the capitals
- The 400 decorative pomegranates

• The 10 water carts & basins • The tank or Sea & the 12 oxen supporting it • The smaller basins (pots), shovels, & bowls 2) He made all these of burnished bronze • Were cast in clay molds in the Jordan Valley: Between Succoth & Zarethan • Were never weighed because the items or utensils were too numerous	43 And the ten bases, and ten lavers on the bases; 44 And one sea, and twelve oxen under the sea; 45 And the pots, and the shovels, and the basons: and all these vessels, which Hiram made to king Solomon for the house of the LORD, *were of* bright brass. 46 In the plain of Jordan did the king cast them, in the clay ground between Succoth and Zarthan. 47 And Solomon left all the vessels *unweighed,* because they were exceeding many: neither was the weight of the brass found out.	49 And the candlesticks of pure gold, five on the right *side,* and five on the left, before the oracle, with the flowers, and the lamps, and the tongs *of* gold, 50 And the bowls, and the snuffers, and the basons, and the spoons, and the censers *of* pure gold; and the hinges *of* gold, *both* for the doors of the inner house, the most holy *place, and* for the doors of the house, *to wit,* of the temple.	c. The 10 gold lampstands: Christ, the Light of the world d. The gold utensils e. The gold sockets for the doors
4. The inside furnishings of the temple: A symbol of prayer & of Christ a. The gold altar of incense: Prayer b. The gold table of showbread: Christ, the Bread of Life	48 And Solomon made all the vessels that *pertained* unto the house of the LORD: the altar of gold, and the table of gold, whereupon the showbread *was,*	51 So was ended all the work that king Solomon made for the house of the LORD. And Solomon brought in the things which David his father had dedicated; *even* the silver, and the gold, and the vessels, did he put among the treasures of the house of the LORD.	**5. The treasury of the temple: A lesson on turning away from greed & covetousness & giving to the LORD** a. Solomon did not personally covet the wealth dedicated to the temple by his father b. Solomon gave the treasure to the LORD

DIVISION I

THE RISE AND REIGN OF SOLOMON AS KING: BEGINNING IN GLORY AND ENDING IN SHAME, 1:1–11:43

G. The Palace Complex of Solomon and the Temple Furnishings: Being Diligent to Put God First, 7:1-51

(7:1-51) **Introduction**: God demands priority in our lives. He is to be put first. And when we put God first, He promises to take care of us, looking after every affair and detail of our lives. He promises to provide food, clothing, and shelter—the very basic necessities of life (Mt.6:33). No matter what we face, God promises to empower us, to give us the strength to conquer and to walk through the trying times of life. By the power of God, we can triumph over…

- trials or tribulations
- difficulties or problems
- hardships or misfortunes
- temptations or seductions
- enticements or passions

But there is a requirement of us. God's triumphant, conquering power is conditional: we must put God first in our lives. We must turn our lives over to Him and let Him control them. Unless our lives are under His control, His power cannot be present to help us.

Putting God first is the practical subject of this passage. Solomon built the temple of the LORD, and then he built his palace. He put the LORD and the LORD'S temple first, before his own residence. Throughout the points of this chapter, note how Solomon always put God first. *The Palace Complex of Solomon and the Temple Furnishings: Being Diligent to Put God First,* 7:1-51.

1. The construction of Solomon's palace complex (built after the temple): a picture of putting God first (vv.1-12).
2. The skilled craftsman who was reared by his widowed mother: a picture of overcoming hardships (vv.13-14).
3. The outside furnishing of the temple: an example of diligent labor (vv.15-47).
4. The inside furnishings of the temple: a symbol of prayer and of Christ (vv.48-50).
5. The treasury of the temple: a lesson on turning away from greed and covetousness and giving to the LORD (v.51).

1 (7:1-12) **Claims, of God, Upon Life—Priority, Duty—Believer, Duty—God, Claims of—Palace, of Solomon**: there was the construction of Solomon's palace complex. And note: the palace was built after the temple's completion, a clear picture of putting God first. It took Solomon thirteen years to build the palace complex, almost twice as long as it took to build the temple. But remember that the palace was a large complex that included several interconnected buildings. And the palace complex was enclosed within a large outer courtyard that was surrounded by a wall (v.12).

In studying Solomon's palace, a question needs to be asked: Is the seed of carnality—extravagance and indulgence—seen in the ornate structure of the palace? The commentator Paul R. House says this:

Solomon has built himself an impressive home. Is this project self-indulgence or another example of God's blessing? The author does not comment, though readers must wonder if this extravagance is in keeping with Moses' declaration that kings "must not accumulate large amounts of silver and gold" (Deut 17:17). At least it is quite possible that DeVries is correct in writing: "He did everything imaginable to show that, as Yahweh was a great God, he was a great king. What is displayed here is far more Solomon's 'riches and honor' than his 'wisdom.' He was undoubtedly the piety of worldly success."[1,2]

Whatever the case, it should be noted that the temple and palace were included in the large outer courtyard (v.12). In noting this fact, *The Expositor's Bible Commentary* gives an excellent statement:

This was no doubt intended to give visual expression to the fact that the king was to act on behalf of God. He himself was to walk in God's ways and, as shepherd of the people, lead them and direct them to God. As such he was a type of Christ, the Son of David, who will rule the earth from Jerusalem and who even now is seated at the right hand of God.[3]

Keep in mind that the Hall of Justice was also built within the palace complex. Thus the palace was in constant use not only by the royal family but also by the royal court officials and citizens of the nation. Altogether there were five sections or five parts to the palace complex:

OUTLINE	SCRIPTURE	SCRIPTURE	OUTLINE
1. The construction of Solomon's palace complex (built after the temple): A picture of putting God first	But Solomon was building his own house thirteen years, and he finished all his house.	judge, *even* the porch of judgment: and *it was* covered with cedar from one side of the floor to the other.	Was covered with cedar
a. The first building: The "Palace of the Forest of Lebanon," see 10:17; Is.22:8 1) The size: 150 ft. long, 75 ft. wide, 45 ft. high 2) The support columns: Four rows of cedar columns supporting cedar beams—45 beams, 15 to a row	2 He built also the house of the forest of Lebanon; the length thereof *was* an hundred cubits, and the breadth thereof fifty cubits, and the height thereof thirty cubits, upon four rows of cedar pillars, with cedar beams upon the pillars.	8 And his house where he dwelt *had* another court within the porch, *which* was of the like work. Solomon made also an house for Pharaoh's daughter, whom he had taken *to wife,* like unto this porch.	d. The fourth section—the living quarters for Solomon: Was built away from the public rooms e. The fifth section—the living quarters for Solomon's wife, Pharaoh's daughter
3) The roof: Cedar boards 4) The windows: Three tiers on each side, placed high on the walls	3 And *it was* covered with cedar above upon the beams, that *lay* on forty five pillars, fifteen *in* a row. 4 And *there were* windows *in* three rows, and light *was* against light *in* three ranks.	9 All these *were of* costly stones, according to the measures of hewed stones, sawed with saws, within and without, even from the foundation unto the coping, and so on the outside toward the great court.	f. The basic material: Was high-grade stones 1) Were cut to an exact size 2) Were smoothed on both their inner & outer surfaces
5) The doorways • Were rectangular frames • Were 3 doors on each wall	5 And all the doors and posts *were* square, with the windows: and light *was* against light *in* three ranks.	10 And the foundation *was of* costly stones, even great stones, stones of ten cubits, and stones of eight cubits.	g. The foundations: Were laid with large stones, 12–15 ft. in size
b. The second section—a connecting colonnade or covered porch 1) Was 15 ft. long, 45 ft. wide 2) Was connected to adjacent buildings by a portico with pillars & a covered roof	6 And he made a porch of pillars; the length thereof *was* fifty cubits, and the breadth thereof thirty cubits: and the porch was before them: and the *other* pillars and the thick beam *were* before them.	11 And above *were* costly stones, after the measures of hewed stones, and cedars. 12 And the great court round about *was* with three rows of hewed stones, and a row of cedar beams, both for the inner court of the house of the LORD, and for the porch of the house.	h. The building stones & beams: Were high grade stone & cedar beams i. The large outer courtyard: Was surrounded by a wall built of three layers of dressed stone & one layer of cedar beams (as was the inner courtyard)
c. The third section—the throne hall or Hall of Justice:	7 Then he made a porch for the throne where he might		

a. The first section of the palace complex was the large building known as the "Palace of the Forest of Lebanon" (10:17; Is.22:8). This particular building was not located in Lebanon, but in Jerusalem. It was given this name because of the extensive use of cedar that had been imported from Lebanon. Note that this structure was 11,250 square feet, almost four times larger than the temple (6:2). It was apparently used as an armory, for the 300 shields of gold were kept there (10:17). Also other military weapons were stored there (Is.22:8).

b. The second section was a connecting colonnade or covered porch (v.6). This colonnade or covered porch sat in front of the Palace of the Forest of Lebanon and apparently connected the palace to the Hall of Justice (v.7). Note that the overhanging roof of the colonnade was supported by pillars, pillars that were no doubt huge.

c. The third section was the Hall of Justice where Solomon's throne sat. From this palace complex, Solomon ruled the nation and sat as supreme judge executing justice for the nation.

1 Paul R. House. *1, 2 Kings*, pp.130-131.
2 S.J. DeVries. *1 Kings*. WBC. (Waco: Word, 1985), p.103.
3 Richard D. Patterson and Hermann J. Austel. *1, 2 Kings*, p.69.

d. The fourth section was the personal living quarters for Solomon himself (v.8). His personal palace was built somewhat away from the public buildings.

e. The fifth section was the palace for Solomon's wife, Pharaoh's daughter (v.8). Note that her residence was built just like Solomon's.

f. The basic material used in the construction of the palace complex was high-grade stone (v.9). These stones were cut to an exact size and smoothed on both their inner and outer surfaces.

g. The foundations of all buildings were laid with large stones, some measuring as much as twelve to fifteen feet (v.10).

h. The building stones and beams were constructed of high-grade stone and cedar beams (v.11).

i. The large outer courtyard was surrounded by a wall constructed of three layers of dressed stone and one layer of cedar beams (v.12). Note also that the same materials were used in the construction of the inner courtyard of the temple.

Thought 1. Remember that Solomon built God's temple first, then he built his own palace. He put God first. What a strong testimony for us. We too must put God first in our lives. Putting God first is exactly what God demands. He is the Creator and Sovereign Majesty of the universe, and we are His creation. God is the One who deserves the first recognition, honor, praise, worship, gift, and service—not man.

When we arise in the morning, God deserves our first thought, our first word, and our first act. We must learn to put God first in all that we think, say, or do.

Just think of all the blessings of life. God has given us so much and done so much for us. Every good and perfect gift has come from the LORD (Ja.1:17). Through creation and the laws that operate the universe, God has given us...

- life
- food
- water
- the beauty of the earth
- each other, companionship
- camaraderie or fellowship
- love
- joy

The list could go on and on. In addition, the LORD gives us *inner strength* to conquer and walk through all the temptations and trials of life—no matter how difficult. Every good and perfect gift of human life has come down from above, from the Father of lights, from the LORD God Himself. He deserves to be put first in our lives. This is the clear teaching of God's Holy Word:

"But seek ye first the kingdom of God, and his righteousness; and all these things shall be added unto you" (Mt.6:33).

"For whosoever will save his life shall lose it: and whosoever will lose his life for my sake shall find it" (Mt.16:25).

"Jesus said unto him, Thou shalt love the Lord thy God with all thy heart, and with all thy soul, and with all thy mind. This is the first and great commandment" (Mt.22:37-38).

"Then Peter began to say unto him, Lo, we have left all, and have followed thee" (Mk.10:28).

"And after these things he went forth, and saw a publican, named Levi, sitting at the receipt of custom: and he said unto him, Follow me. And he left all, rose up, and followed him" (Lu.5:27-28).

"And he said to *them* all, If any *man* will come after me, let him deny himself, and take up his cross daily, and follow me" (Lu.9:23).

"If any *man* come to me, and hate not his father, and mother, and wife, and children, and brethren, and sisters, yea, and his own life also, he cannot be my disciple. And whosoever doth not bear his cross, and come after me, cannot be my disciple" (Lu.14:26-27).

"So likewise, whosoever he be of you that forsaketh not all that he hath, he cannot be my disciple" (Lu.14:33).

"And he said unto them, Verily I say unto you, There is no man that hath left house, or parents, or brethren, or wife, or children, for the kingdom of God's sake, Who shall not receive manifold more in this present time, and in the world to come life everlasting" (Lu.18:29-30).

"Jesus saith unto him, I am the way, the truth, and the life: no man cometh unto the Father, but by me" (Jn.14:6).

"Yea doubtless, and I count all things *but* loss for the excellency of the knowledge of Christ Jesus my Lord: for whom I have suffered the loss of all things, and do count them *but* dung, that I may win Christ" (Ph.3:8).

"Do not err, my beloved brethren. Every good gift and every perfect gift is from above, and cometh down from the Father of lights, with whom is no variableness, neither shadow of turning. Of his own will begat he us with the word of truth, that we should be a kind of firstfruits of his creatures" (Ja.1:16-18).

"Because all the firstborn *are* mine; *for* on the day that I smote all the firstborn in the land of Egypt I hallowed unto me all the firstborn in Israel, both man and beast: mine shall they be: I *am* the LORD" (Nu.3:13).

"That thou shalt take of the first of all the fruit of the earth, which thou shalt bring of thy land that the LORD thy God giveth thee, and shalt put *it* in a basket, and shalt go unto the place which the LORD thy God shall choose to place his name there" (De.26:2).

"And Elijah said unto her, Fear not; go *and* do as thou hast said: but make me thereof a little cake first [putting God first], and bring *it* unto me, and after make for thee and for thy son" (1 K.17:13).

2 (7:13-14) **Hardship, Overcoming, Example of—Misfortune, Overcoming, Example of—Parents, Poverty, Children Overcoming—Children, Hardships of, Overcoming—Hiram, Example of, Overcoming Hardships—Temple, Craftsman of**: there was the skilled craftsman Hiram who was reared by his widowed mother. In seeking a master craftsman to build the furnishings of the temple, once again Solomon turned to his friend Hiram in Tyre. The King recommended Hiram, who was probably the most skilled craftsman in bronze of that day and time. Scripture says that he was highly skilled, a man filled with wisdom, understanding, and ability in handling all kinds of bronze works. He was also skilled in working with gold, silver, iron, stone, wood, and various dyes and fine linen (2 Chr.2:14). His ability was very much like that of Bezalel, who had made the furnishings of the Tabernacle during the days of Moses (Ex.31:1-11; 35:30-31).

Hiram was the child of a mixed marriage and was reared by his widowed mother. Being widowed in the ancient world was an extreme hardship, for women had little status in society and were totally dependent upon either their fathers or husbands for their livelihood. When a woman with small children became widowed, she had no way to secure employment or to earn a living. She was at the mercy of society for survival unless she had a compassionate relative who would help her. Consequently, Hiram had most likely faced terrible hardship growing up as a child. But he had conquered the hardship and become a skilled craftsman, obviously the most capable craftsman in Phoenicia.

OUTLINE	SCRIPTURE	SCRIPTURE	OUTLINE
2. The skilled craftsman who was reared by his widowed mother: A picture of overcoming hardships a. His name: Hiram of Tyre b. His hardship: The child of	13 And king Solomon sent and fetched Hiram out of Tyre. 14 He was a widow's son of the tribe of Naphtali, and his father was a man of Tyre, a	worker in brass: and he was filled with wisdom, and understanding, and cunning to work all works in brass. And he came to king Solomon, and wrought all his work.	a mixed marriage, reared by his widowed mother c. His conquest of hardships: Had become a skilled craftsman d. His diligent labor: Did all that Solomon assigned him

Thought 1. Having overcome the poverty and hardship of his childhood, Hiram stands as a powerful example for us. Hardship and misfortune can be overcome by the power of God. We will confront all kinds of adversity and affliction as we walk throughout life, adversity such as...

- disease
- accidents
- financial difficulties
- discouragement
- depression
- loneliness
- purposelessness
- prejudice
- ridicule
- loss of employment
- the death of a loved one
- being outcast or shunned

No matter what the hardship or misfortune, it can be overcome. We can conquer the adversity, triumph over the affliction. We can be victorious over all the trials and tribulations, temptations and bondages of this life. This is the wonderful promise of God's Holy Word:

"But seek ye first the kingdom of God, and his righteousness; and all these things shall be added unto you" (Mt.6:33).

"Who shall separate us from the love of Christ? *shall* tribulation, or distress, or persecution, or famine, or nakedness, or peril, or sword?...Nay, in all these things we are more than conquerors through him that loved us. For I am persuaded, that neither death, nor life, nor angels, nor principalities, nor powers, nor things present, nor things to come, Nor height, nor depth, nor any other creature, shall be able to separate us from the love of God, which is in Christ Jesus our Lord" (Ro.8:35, 37-39).

"And the Lord shall deliver me from every evil work, and will preserve *me* unto his heavenly kingdom: to whom *be* glory for ever and ever. Amen" (2 Ti.4:18).

"So that we may boldly say, The Lord *is* my helper, and I will not fear what man shall do unto me" (He.13:6).

"Casting all your care upon him; for he careth for you" (1 Pe.5:7).

"For whatsoever is born of God overcometh the world: and this is the victory that overcometh the world, *even* our faith. Who is he that overcometh the world, but he that believeth that Jesus is the Son of God?" (1 Jn.5:4-5).

"The eternal God *is thy* refuge, and underneath *are* the everlasting arms: and he shall thrust out the enemy from before thee; and shall say, Destroy *them*" (De.33:27).

"Thou hast also given me the shield of thy salvation: and thy right hand hath holden me up, and thy gentleness hath made me great" (Ps.18:35).

"The LORD *is* my strength and my shield; my heart trusted in him, and I am helped: therefore my heart greatly rejoiceth; and with my song will I praise him" (Ps.28:7).

"But I *am* poor and needy; *yet* the Lord thinketh upon me: thou *art* my help and my deliverer; make no tarrying, O my God" (Ps.40:17).

"For thou hast been a strength to the poor, a strength to the needy in his distress, a refuge from the storm, a shadow from the heat, when the blast of the terrible ones *is* as a storm *against* the wall" (Is.25:4).

"Fear thou not; for I *am* with thee: be not dismayed; for I *am* thy God: I will strengthen thee; yea, I will help thee; yea, I will uphold thee with the right hand of my righteousness" (Is.41:10).

"And I will bring the blind by a way *that* they knew not; I will lead them in paths *that* they have not known: I will make darkness light before them, and crooked things straight. These things will I do unto them, and not forsake them" (Is.42:16).

"...Fear not: for I have redeemed thee, I have called *thee* by thy name; thou *art* mine. When thou passest through the waters, I *will be* with thee; and through the rivers, they shall not overflow thee: when thou walkest through the fire, thou shalt not be burned; neither shall the flame kindle upon thee" (Is.43:1-2).

Thought 2. Note this fact about Hiram as well. Despite his difficult circumstances as a child—being reared in poverty by a single mother—he turned his negative experience into a positive one. He did not give way to self-pity, low self-esteem, discouragement, complacency, or lethargy. He did not use his difficult childhood days as an excuse for being irresponsible and unproductive in life. Nor did he become bitter. Instead, he used the difficult days as a motivating force to better himself. He was driven to educate himself by learning a trade and by becoming the best worker he could be. Hiram became just what every one of us is to be: a diligent and hard worker.

"Not slothful in business; fervent in spirit; serving the Lord" (Ro.12:11).

"Let him that stole steal no more: but rather let him labour, working with *his* hands the thing which is good, that he may have to give to him that needeth" (Ep.4:28).

"And whatsoever ye do in word or deed, *do* all in the name of the Lord Jesus, giving thanks to God and the Father by him" (Co.3:17).

"And whatsoever ye do, do *it* heartily, as to the Lord, and not unto men" (Co.3:23).

"For even when we were with you, this we commanded you, that if any would not work, neither should he eat. For we hear that there are some which walk among you disorderly, working not at all, but are busybodies. Now them that are such we command and exhort by our Lord Jesus Christ, that with quietness they work, and eat their own bread" (2 Th.3:10-12).

"Go to the ant, thou sluggard; consider her ways, and be wise" (Pr.6:6).

"He becometh poor that dealeth *with* a slack hand: but the hand of the diligent maketh rich" (Pr.10:4).

"He that gathereth in summer *is* a wise son: *but* he that sleepeth in harvest *is* a son that causeth shame" (Pr.10:5).

"Whatsoever thy hand findeth to do, do *it* with thy might; for *there is* no work, nor device, nor knowledge, nor wisdom, in the grave, whither thou goest" (Ec.9:10).

3 (7:15-47) **Labor, Duty—Diligence, Example of—Temple, Furnishings—Furnishings, of the Temple—Hiram, Skilled Craftsman—Craftsman, Example of**: there were the furnishings of the temple made by Hiram of Tyre. These furnishings included four major items and their accessories.

a. Hiram cast two bronze pillars for the portico of the temple (vv.15-22). Apparently these pillars were freestanding, not attached to the temple. As Scripture says, they were "by" or "at" or "near" or "in the front of" the portico or entrance of the temple (v.21; 2 Chr.3:17). The freestanding pillars were quite large, twenty-seven feet tall and eighteen feet in circumference (v.15). On top of the pillars were two bronze capitals (decorative tops) which were seven and a half feet tall. The Scripture and outline give a clear picture of what the pillars looked like:

OUTLINE	SCRIPTURE	SCRIPTURE	OUTLINE
3. The outside furnishings of the temple: An example of diligent labor a. Hiram cast two bronze pillars for the portico (27 ft. x 18 ft.): Pictured God's power 1) He made two bronze capitals (decorative tops) to set on the pillars (7½ ft. high) • Each capital was decorated with latticework & seven interwoven chains • Two rows of pomegranates encircled the latticework to add to the decorative appearance	15 For he cast two pillars of brass, of eighteen cubits high apiece: and a line of twelve cubits did compass either of them about. 16 And he made two chapiters *of* molten brass, to set upon the tops of the pillars: the height of the one chapiter *was* five cubits, and the height of the other chapiter *was* five cubits: 17 *And* nets of checker work, and wreaths of chain work, for the chapiters which *were* upon the top of the pillars; seven for the one chapiter, and seven for the other chapiter. 18 And he made the pillars, and two rows round about upon the one network, to cover the chapiters that *were* upon the top, with pome-	granates: and so did he for the other chapiter. 19 And the chapiters that *were* upon the top of the pillars *were* of lily work in the porch, four cubits. 20 And the chapiters upon the two pillars *had pomegranates* also above, over against the belly which *was* by the network: and the pomegranates *were* two hundred in rows round about upon the other chapiter. 21 And he set up the pillars in the porch of the temple: and he set up the right pillar, and called the name thereof Jachin: and he set up the left pillar, and he called the name thereof Boaz. 22 And upon the top of the pillars *was* lily work: so was the work of the pillars finished.	• The capitals were bowl-shaped, looking like lilies, 6 ft. high • Each capital had two rows of pomegranates encircling it, a total of 200 pomegranates 2) The two pillars were set at the sides of the temple's entrance & named • Jakin: *God establishes* • Boaz: In God is strength 3) The work on the pillars was diligently completed

Thought 1. The two bronze pillars stood at the entrance to the temple. As a worshiper approached the temple, one of the first sights he saw was the towering, massive pillars. These pillars symbolized strength, God's power. Being twenty-seven feet high and eighteen feet in circumference, the pillars were awe-inspiring and gave a sense of strength and power. Listen to what God's Word says about His strength and power:

"But Jesus beheld *them,* and said unto them, With men this is impossible; but with God all things are possible" (Mt.19:26).

"For with God nothing shall be impossible" (Lu.1:37).

"God *is* my strength *and* power: and he maketh my way perfect" (2 S.22:33).

"Both riches and honour *come* of thee, and thou reignest over all; and in thine hand *is* power and might; and in thine hand *it is* to make great, and to give strength unto all" (1 Chr.29:12).

"I know that thou canst do every *thing,* and *that* no thought can be withholden from thee" (Jb.42:2).

"The LORD *is* their strength, and he *is* the saving strength of his anointed" (Ps.28:8).

"God *is* our refuge and strength, a very present help in trouble" (Ps.46:1).

"My flesh and my heart faileth: *but* God *is* the strength of my heart, and my portion for ever" (Ps.73:26).

"Blessed *is* the man whose strength *is* in thee; in whose heart *are* the ways *of them*" (Ps.84:5).

"Yea, before the day *was* I *am* he; and *there is* none that can deliver out of my hand: I will work, and who shall let it?" (Is.43:13).

b. Hiram made a large round water tank or a laver called *the Sea* (vv.23-26). This laver corresponded to the laver in the Tabernacle, but it was much larger: seven and one-half feet deep and forty-five feet in circumference. The Scripture gives a detailed description:

OUTLINE	SCRIPTURE	SCRIPTURE	OUTLINE
b. Hiram made a large round water tank or a laver called *the Sea*: Pictured cleansing 1) He made it of cast metal: 7½ ft. deep, 45 ft. in circumference 2) He encircled the tank or laver with two rows of decorative gourds, right below the rim 3) He stood the tank or laver	23 And he made a molten sea, ten cubits from the one brim to the other: it was round all about, and his height was five cubits: and a line of thirty cubits did compass it round about. 24 And under the brim of it round about there were knops compassing it, ten in a cubit, compassing the sea round about: the knops were cast in two rows, when it was cast. 25 It stood upon twelve oxen,	three looking toward the north, and three looking toward the west, and three looking toward the south, and three looking toward the east: and the sea was set above upon them, and all their hinder parts were inward. 26 And it was an hand breadth thick, and the brim thereof was wrought like the brim of a cup, with flowers of lilies: it contained two thousand baths.	on a base of 12 bronze oxen, all facing outward: 3 faced north, 3 west, 3 south, & 3 east 4) He made the wall about 3 inches thick & its rim was shaped like a cup, like a lily blossom: It held about 11,000 gallons of water

The laver was used by the priests for washing and cleaning themselves after the sacrifices. Thus it is a symbol of the cleansing from sin that is so desperately needed by us all. Before we can ever become acceptable to God, we must be cleansed by the blood of Christ Himself. Once we have been cleansed, God accepts us.

"Husbands, love your wives, even as Christ also loved the church, and gave himself for it; That he might sanctify and cleanse it with the washing of water by the word" (Ep.5:25-26).

"How much more shall the blood of Christ, who through the eternal Spirit offered himself without spot to God, purge your conscience from dead works to serve the living God?" (He.9:14).

"But if we walk in the light, as he is in the light, we have fellowship one with another, and the blood of Jesus Christ his Son cleanseth us from all sin" (1 Jn.1:7).

"Come now, and let us reason together, saith the LORD: though your sins be as scarlet, they shall be as white as snow; though they be red like crimson, they shall be as wool" (Is.1:18).

c. Hiram made ten large carts and ten large basins to hold water for the various temple rituals (vv.27-39). These carts were moveable, so the priest could maneuver all around the courtyard cleaning the animals to be sacrificed and cleaning the other items that were needed in the various temple rituals. Again, a detailed description is given by Scripture:

OUTLINE	SCRIPTURE	SCRIPTURE	OUTLINE
c. Hiram made 10 bronze carts (6 ft. long, 6 ft. wide, 4½ ft. high) & 10 bronze basins: Stressed a need for cleansing 1) They were made with side panels, braced with crossbars: Were decorated with	27 And he made ten bases of brass; four cubits was the length of one base, and four cubits the breadth thereof, and three cubits the height of it. 28 And the work of the bases was on this manner: they had borders, and the borders	were between the ledges: 29 And on the borders that were between the ledges were lions, oxen, and cherubims: and upon the ledges there was a base above: and beneath the lions and oxen were certain additions made of thin work.	carved lions, bulls, cherubim, & wreaths

OUTLINE	SCRIPTURE	SCRIPTURE	OUTLINE
2) Each had 4 bronze wheels & bronze axles, & 4 posts at the corners to support the basins: Were decorated with carved wreaths	30 And every base had four brasen wheels, and plates of brass: and the four corners thereof had undersetters: under the laver *were* undersetters molten, at the side of every addition.	itself. 35 And in the top of the base *was there* a round compass of half a cubit high: and on the top of the base the ledges thereof and the borders thereof *were* of the same.	
3) Each had a circular frame on the top to hold the basin (1½ ft. deep, 2¼ ft. across): Were decorated with carved wreaths 4) The panels were square, not round	31 And the mouth of it within the chapiter and above *was* a cubit: but the mouth thereof *was* round *after* the work of the base, a cubit and an half: and also upon the mouth of it *were* gravings with their borders, four square, not round.	36 For on the plates of the ledges thereof, and on the borders thereof, he graved cherubims, lions, and palm trees, according to the proportion of every one, and additions round about.	7) Each cart had cherubim, lions, & palm trees carved where there was room, with wreaths all around
5) The axles were cast as one unit with the cart under the panels: Then the wheels (2¼ ft. diameter) were placed on the axles	32 And under the borders *were* four wheels; and the axletrees of the wheels *were joined* to the base: and the height of a wheel *was* a cubit and a half a cubit.	37 After this *manner* he made the ten bases: all of them had one casting, one measure, *and* one size. 38 Then made he ten lavers of brass: one laver contained forty baths: *and* every laver	8) Each was cast in the same mold & made identical 9) Each cast held a bronze basin
• The wheels were like chariot wheels • The axles, rims, spokes, & hubs were cast metal	33 And the work of the wheels was like the work of a chariot wheel: their axletrees, and their naves, and their felloes, and their spokes, *were* all molten.	was four cubits: *and* upon every one of the ten bases one laver. 39 And he put five bases on the right side of the house, and five on the left side of	• Each was 6 ft. across • Each held 220 gallons of water 10) The carts & the Sea were set in the temple
6) Each had 4 handles, one at each corner & a 9 in. rim around the top: These were cast as one unit with the cart	34 And *there were* four undersetters to the four corners of one base: *and* the undersetters *were* of the very base	the house: and he set the sea on the right side of the house eastward over against the south.	• 5 carts on the south • 5 carts on the north • The Sea at the southeast corner

Thought 1. As the carts and basins were wheeled around the courtyard, they painted a clear picture for the worshipers and priests: the need for cleansing from the sin and corruption of this world. And cleansing came only through the blood of the sacrifice. Keep in mind that the animal sacrifice was a type of the coming *Ideal Sacrifice,* the coming Messiah and Savior of the world, the Lord Jesus Christ. Being the *Ideal*, the *Pattern*, Christ's sacrificial death paid the penalty for all sin. And His payment can cover and stand for our sins. We can be cleansed from the penalty of sin by the *Ideal Sacrifice* of Christ.

"So Christ was once offered to bear the sins of many; and unto them that look for him shall he appear the second time without sin unto salvation" (He.9:28).

"Who his own self bare our sins in his own body on the tree, that we, being dead to sins, should live unto righteousness: by whose stripes ye were healed" (1 Pe.2:24).

"For Christ also hath once suffered for sins, the just for the unjust, that he might bring us to God, being put to death in the flesh, but quickened by the Spirit" (1 Pe.3:18).

"And ye know that he was manifested to take away our sins; and in him is no sin" (1 Jn.3:5).

"But he *was* wounded for our transgressions, *he was* bruised for our iniquities: the chastisement of our peace *was* upon him; and with his stripes we are healed" (Is.53:5).

"Therefore will I divide him *a portion* with the great, and he shall divide the spoil with the strong; because he hath poured out his soul unto death: and he was numbered with the transgressors; and he bare the sin of many, and made intercession for the transgressors" (Is.53:12).

d. Hiram made the smaller basins, shovels, and bowls (v.40[a]). Apparently the basins and shovels were used for removing the ashes from the Altar of Sacrifice, and the sprinkling bowls were used either in rituals that required less water or else for catching the blood of the sacrifices.

OUTLINE	SCRIPTURE
d. Hiram made the smaller basins, shovels, & bowls	40 And Hiram made the lavers, and the shovels, and the basons.

Thought 1. In the smaller basins and sprinkling bowls, the symbol of cleansing and the blood of the sacrifice are again seen. Our cleansing comes only through the sacrifice, the blood of the Lord Jesus Christ.

"For this is my blood of the new testament, which is shed for many for the remission of sins" (Mt.26:28).

"Take heed therefore unto yourselves, and to all the flock, over the which the Holy Ghost hath made you overseers, to feed the church of God, which he hath purchased with his own blood" (Ac.20:28).

"Much more then, being now justified by his blood, we shall be saved from wrath through him" (Ro.5:9).

"How much more shall the blood of Christ, who through the eternal Spirit offered himself without spot to God, purge your conscience from dead works to serve the living God" (He.9:14).

"Forasmuch as ye know that ye were not redeemed with corruptible things, *as* silver and gold, from your vain conversation *received* by tradition from your fathers; But with the precious blood of Christ, as of a lamb without blemish and without spot" (1 Pe.1:18-19).

"And from Jesus Christ, *who is* the faithful witness, *and* the first begotten of the dead, and the prince of the kings of the earth. Unto him that loved us, and washed us from our sins in his own blood" (Re.1:5).

e. Hiram completed the task assigned him, building all the bronze furnishings of the temple (vv.40[b]-47). Scripture summarizes the work he had done at the request of Solomon:

OUTLINE	SCRIPTURE	SCRIPTURE	OUTLINE
e. Hiram completed the task assigned him: Pictured faithful & diligent work 1) He made the following • The two pillars • The bowl-shaped capitals • The two networks of chains that decorated the capitals • The 400 decorative pomegranates	40 And Hiram made the lavers, and the shovels, and the basons. So Hiram made an end of doing all the work that he made king Solomon for the house of the LORD: 41 The two pillars, and the *two* bowls of the chapiters that *were* on the top of the two pillars; and the two networks, to cover the two bowls of the chapiters which *were* upon the top of the pillars; 42 And four hundred pomegranates for the two networks, *even* two rows of pomegranates for one network, to cover the two bowls of the chapiters	that *were* upon the pillars; 43 And the ten bases, and ten lavers on the bases; 44 And one sea, and twelve oxen under the sea; 45 And the pots, and the shovels, and the basons: and all these vessels, which Hiram made to king Solomon for the house of the LORD, *were of* bright brass. 46 In the plain of Jordan did the king cast them, in the clay ground between Succoth and Zarthan. 47 And Solomon left all the vessels *unweighed,* because they were exceeding many: neither was the weight of the brass found out.	• The 10 water carts & basins • The tank or Sea & the 12 oxen supporting it • The smaller basins (pots), shovels, & bowls 2) He made all these of burnished bronze • Were cast in clay molds in the Jordan Valley: Between Succoth & Zarethan • Were never weighed because the items or utensils were too numerous

Thought 1. In completing the task assigned to him, Hiram is a strong model of faithfulness, of being a diligent worker. Likewise, whatever task is given to us, we must be faithful and diligent in accomplishing it. When we arise daily and go to our jobs, we must work hard and faithfully, doing the very best we can—just as Hiram did.

"Not slothful in business; fervent in spirit; serving the Lord" (Ro.12:11).

"Let him that stole steal no more: but rather let him labour, working with *his* hands the thing which is good, that he may have to give to him that needeth" (Ep.4:28).

"And whatsoever ye do in word or deed, *do* all in the name of the Lord Jesus, giving thanks to God and the Father by him" (Col.3:17).

"And whatsoever ye do, do *it* heartily, as to the Lord, and not unto men" (Col.3:23).

"Now them that are such we command and exhort by our Lord Jesus Christ, that with quietness they work, and eat their own bread" (2 Th.3:12).

"And the LORD God took the man, and put him into the garden of Eden to dress it and to keep it" (Ge.2:15).

"In the sweat of thy face shalt thou eat bread, till thou return unto the ground; for out of it wast thou taken: for dust thou *art,* and unto dust shalt thou return" (Ge.3:19).

"Go to the ant, thou sluggard; consider her ways, and be wise" (Pr.6:6).

"He that tilleth his land shall be satisfied with bread: but he that followeth vain *persons is* void of understanding" (Pr.12:11).

"Whatsoever thy hand findeth to do, do *it* with thy might; for *there is* no work, nor device, nor knowledge, nor wisdom, in the grave, whither thou goest" (Ec.9:10).

4 (7:48-50) **Prayer, Symbolized by—Christ, Symbolized by—Temple, Furnishings of—Furnishings, of Temple—Showbread, Table of, Symbol of—Lampstand, Symbol of**: there were the inside furnishings of the temple. Scripture gives a list of these gold furnishings:

OUTLINE	SCRIPTURE	SCRIPTURE	OUTLINE
4. The inside furnishings of the temple: A symbol of prayer & of Christ a. The gold altar of incense: Prayer b. The gold table of showbread: Christ, the Bread of Life c. The 10 gold lampstands: Christ, the Light of the world	48 And Solomon made all the vessels that *pertained* unto the house of the LORD: the altar of gold, and the table of gold, whereupon the showbread *was,* 49 And the candlesticks of pure gold, five on the right *side,* and five on the left, before the oracle, with the flowers, and the lamps, and	the tongs *of* gold, 50 And the bowls, and the snuffers, and the basons, and the spoons, and the censers *of* pure gold; and the hinges *of* gold, *both* for the doors of the inner house, the most holy *place, and* for the doors of the house, *to wit,* of the temple.	d. The gold utensils e. The gold sockets for the doors

a. The first furnishing was the golden altar or the Altar of Incense (v.48). This altar filled the sanctuary with a sweet-smelling aroma. Twice a day, in the morning and evening, the High Priests burned incense on the altar. As the aroma of the incense arose and filled the temple, it symbolized the prayers and unbroken communion of God's people ascending up to God, pleasing Him (see outline and note—Ex.30:1-6 for more discussion).

> **"Ask, and it shall be given you; seek, and ye shall find; knock, and it shall be opened unto you" (Mt.7:7).**
> **"Praying always with all prayer and supplication in the Spirit, and watching thereunto with all perseverance and supplication for all saints" (Ep.6:18).**
> **"Pray without ceasing" (1 Th.5:17).**
> **"Seeing then that we have a great high priest, that is passed into the heavens, Jesus the Son of God, let us hold fast *our* profession. For we have not an high priest which cannot be touched with the feeling of our infirmities; but was in all points tempted like as *we are, yet* without sin" (He.4:14-15).**
> **"Seek the LORD and his strength, seek his face continually" (1 Chr.16:11).**

b. The second furnishing was the golden Table of Showbread (v.48). The showbread is also known as the Bread of the Presence referring to the presence of God, and the Bread of the Face referring to the face of God. The showbread is also called the Holy Bread or the Consecrated Bread (1 S.21:4-6). Twelve loaves of bread were placed upon the table representing the twelve tribes of Israel. This symbolized that the tribes of Israel were always sitting before the presence and face of God. By setting the bread upon the table the tribes were acknowledging that they always needed the presence of God, His provision and protection. They needed Him to provide their bread and food and to continue to look after and care for them. Of course, this is a clear symbol of the Lord Jesus Christ as the Bread of Life. Christ is both the Provider and Protector of His people (see outline and notes—Ex.25:23-30 for more discussion). This is exactly what Scripture declares:

> **"But seek ye first the kingdom of God, and his righteousness; and all these things shall be added unto you" (Mt.6:33).**
> **"For the bread of God is he which cometh down from heaven, and giveth life unto the world" (Jn.6:33).**
> **"I am that bread of life" (Jn.6:48).**
> **"And Jesus said unto them, I am the bread of life: he that cometh to me shall never hunger; and he that believeth on me shall never thirst" (Jn.6:35).**
> **"But my God shall supply all your need according to his riches in glory by Christ Jesus" (Ph.4:19).**

c. The third furnishing was the ten gold lampstands (v.49). In the Tabernacle built by Moses there was only one lampstand. But now Solomon had ten lampstands built. The lampstands provided the only light in the Holy Place. Thus, the lampstand was a symbol of God and of the Lord Jesus Christ as the Light of the world. It was the light of the lampstand that showed people how to approach God, that allowed them to move about the temple. So it is with God who is the Light of the world. He shows a person how to approach and worship Him. And Christ Himself came into the world to give light and illumination so that we might know and serve God. Christ alone is able to bring people out of the darkness of sin and death and give them the light of salvation and life, both now and forever (see outline and notes Ex.25:31-40 for more discussion).

> **"Then spake Jesus again unto them, saying, I am the light of the world: he that followeth me shall not walk in darkness, but shall have the light of life" (Jn.8:12).**
> **"I am come a light into the world, that whosoever believeth on me should not abide in darkness" (Jn.12:46).**
> **"Jesus saith unto him, I am the way, the truth, and the life: no man cometh unto the Father, but by me" (Jn.14:6).**
> **"This then is the message which we have heard of him, and declare unto you, that God is light, and in him is no darkness at all" (1 Jn.1:5).**
> **"The LORD *is* my light and my salvation; whom shall I fear? the LORD *is* the strength of my life; of whom shall I be afraid?" (Ps.27:1).**

d. The fourth furnishing for the inside of the temple was the gold utensils and other implements necessary for the various rituals of worship (vv.49-50). These are spelled out in the two verses of Scripture above.

e. The fifth furnishing was the gold sockets for the doors of both the Most Holy Place and the main hall of the temple (v.50). Note this fact: even the sockets of the doors were gold. Only the best was being used in the temple of the LORD.

5 (7:51) **Covetousness, Turning Away from, Example of—Greed, Turning Away from, Example of—Stewardship, Example of—Giving, to the LORD, Example of—Tithes and Offerings, Example of—Temple, Treasury of**: there was the treasury of the temple. All the silver and gold and some very special items that David had dedicated to the LORD were placed into the treasury. David had instructed Solomon to place this wealth in the temple, for he had dedicated it, given it to the LORD. It was to be used in the LORD's service and, no doubt, in the maintenance of the temple. Note this fact: Solomon did not personally covet the wealth dedicated to the temple by his father. In this instance, he had turned away from greed and covetousness, following the instructions of his father and giving the treasure to the LORD.

OUTLINE	SCRIPTURE	SCRIPTURE	OUTLINE
5. The treasury of the temple: A lesson on turning away from greed & covetousness & giving to the LORD a. Solomon did not personally	51 So was ended all the work that king Solomon made for the house of the Lord. And Solomon brought in the things which David his	father had dedicated; even the silver, and the gold, and the vessels, did he put among the treasures of the house of the Lord.	covet the wealth dedicated to the temple by his father b. Solomon gave the treasure to the LORD

Thought 1. What a strong example of stewardship for us. Tithing, giving to the LORD, supporting the LORD'S work, getting the gospel out to the world, and meeting the needs of people—all this and so much more is demanded of us. The church cannot survive and the gospel cannot be taken to the world and the needs of people cannot be met without tithes and offerings. One of the greatest needs facing the church and Christian ministries is the need for money. Covetousness and greed have gripped the hearts of so many, there simply is not enough money to do the tasks assigned us. Because of this, the needs of people are not being met:

⇒ The hungry are not being fed.
⇒ The homeless are not being sheltered.
⇒ The orphans are not being sufficiently cared for.
⇒ The handicapped or disabled are not being properly treated.
⇒ Many of the aged are impoverished and dying without adequate care.
⇒ Many people are unemployed and are struggling for survival.
⇒ Many single parents cannot provide the basic necessities for their children.
⇒ Many of the poor are going without medical attention.
⇒ Many children and youth are working to support their families and missing an education.
⇒ Many people are poverty stricken and destitute but are being ignored by society.
⇒ Many people are experiencing desperate financial difficulties and see no way out.
⇒ Many churches and missions do not have adequate staff to handle all the needs.
⇒ Many throughout the world are dying without hearing the truth of the gospel, the wonderful salvation found only in the Lord Jesus Christ.

We must turn away from covetousness and greed and learn to give. And we must give sacrificially, for God holds us accountable—not for what we give but for what we keep. For this reason, we must reject the spirit of greed and covetousness:

"Lay not up for yourselves treasures upon earth, where moth and rust doth corrupt, and where thieves break through and steal: But lay up for yourselves treasures in heaven, where neither moth nor rust doth corrupt, and where thieves do not break through nor steal" (Mt.6:19-20).

"And, behold, one came and said unto him, Good Master, what good thing shall I do, that I may have eternal life?...Jesus said unto him, If thou wilt be perfect, go *and* sell that thou hast, and give to the poor, and thou shalt have treasure in heaven: and come *and* follow me. But when the young man heard that saying, he went away sorrowful: for he had great possessions. Then said Jesus unto his disciples, Verily I say unto you, That a rich man shall hardly enter into the kingdom of heaven. And again I say unto you, It is easier for a camel to go through the eye of a needle, than for a rich man to enter into the kingdom of God" (Mt.19:16, 21-24).

"And he said unto them, Take heed, and beware of covetousness: for a man's life consisteth not in the abundance of the things which he possesseth" (Lu.12:15).

"Sell that ye have, and give alms; provide yourselves bags which wax not old, a treasure in the heavens that faileth not, where no thief approacheth, neither moth corrupteth" (Lu.12:33).

"I have showed you all things, how that so labouring ye ought to support the weak, and to remember the words of the Lord Jesus, how he said, It is more blessed to give than to receive" (Ac.20:35).

"Upon the first *day* of the week let every one of you lay by him in store, as *God* hath prospered him, that there be no gatherings when I come" (1 Co.16:2).

"But this *I say,* He which soweth sparingly shall reap also sparingly; and he which soweth bountifully shall reap also bountifully" (2 Co.9:6).

"Every man according as he purposeth in his heart, *so let him give;* not grudgingly, or of necessity: for God loveth a cheerful giver" (2 Co.9:7).

"Mortify therefore your members which are upon the earth; fornication, uncleanness, inordinate affection, evil concupiscence, and covetousness, which is idolatry: For which things' sake the wrath of God cometh on the children of disobedience" (Col.3:5-6).

"For the love of money is the root of all evil: which while some coveted after, they have erred from the faith, and pierced themselves through with many sorrows" (1 Ti.6:10).

"Your gold and silver is cankered; and the rust of them shall be a witness against you, and shall eat your flesh as it were fire. Ye have heaped treasure together for the last days" (Js.5:3).

"Thou shalt not covet thy neighbour's house, thou shalt not covet thy neighbour's wife, nor his manservant, nor his maidservant, nor his ox, nor his ass, nor any thing that *is* thy neighbour's" (Ex.20:17).

"Every man *shall give* as he is able, according to the blessing of the LORD thy God which he hath given thee" (De.16:17).

"He that is greedy of gain troubleth his own house; but he that hateth gifts shall live" (Pr.15:27).

"He that loveth silver shall not be satisfied with silver; nor he that loveth abundance with increase: this *is* also vanity" (Ec.5:10).

"For from the least of them even unto the greatest of them every one *is* given to covetousness; and from the prophet even unto the priest every one dealeth falsely" (Je.6:13).

"*As* the partridge sitteth *on eggs,* and hatcheth *them* not; *so* he that getteth riches, and not by right, shall leave them in the midst of his days, and at his end shall be a fool" (Je.17:11).

"And they come unto thee as the people cometh, and they sit before thee *as* my people, and they hear thy words, but they will not do them: for with their mouth they show much love, *but* their heart goeth after their covetousness" (Eze.33:31).

"And they covet fields, and take *them* by violence; and houses, and take *them* away: so they oppress a man and his house, even a man and his heritage" (Mi.2:2).

"Woe to him that coveteth an evil covetousness to his house, that he may set his nest on high, that he may be delivered from the power of evil?" (Hab.2:9).

"Bring ye all the tithes into the storehouse, that there may be meat in mine house, and prove me now herewith, saith the LORD of hosts, if I will not open you the windows of heaven, and pour you out a blessing, that *there shall* not *be room* enough *to receive it*" (Mal.3:10).

1. Solomon's placement of the Ark in the temple: A picture of God's presence among His people
- a. The king summoned all the leadership of Israel to assemble in Jerusalem
  - 1) The purpose: To move the Ark into the temple
  - 2) The time of year: The month of Ethanim (Sept.–Oct.), during the Festival of Tabernacles, Le.23:33-36
- b. The priests carried the Ark & the Tabernacle with all its furnishings up to the temple
- c. The king & leaders offered a large number of sacrifices before the Ark, 2 S.6:13
- d. The priests placed the Ark in the inner sanctuary of the temple, the Most Holy Place: Set it beneath the wings of the cherubim (symbolized holiness & power)
  - 1) The wings of the cherubim overshadowed the Ark & its carrying poles
  - 2) The carrying poles were extremely long: Their ends could be seen from the Holy Place
  - 3) The Ark contained only the two stone tablets of the Law (placed there by Moses): A forceful reminder of God's covenant, His commandments & man's duty to obey

CHAPTER 8

H. The Dedication of the Temple (Part 1)—Solomon's Placement of the Ark in the Temple & His Message: A Picture of God's Presence & His Faithfulness, 8:1-21

8:1-21; see 2 Chr.5:2–6:11

Then Solomon assembled the
elders of Israel, and all the
heads of the tribes, the chief
of the fathers of the children
of Israel, unto king Solomon
in Jerusalem, that they might
bring up the ark of the covenant of the LORD out of the
city of David, which *is* Zion.
2 And all the men of Israel
assembled themselves unto
king Solomon at the feast in
the month Ethanim, which *is*
the seventh month.
3 And all the elders of Israel came, and the priests took
up the ark.
4 And they brought up the
ark of the LORD, and the tabernacle of the congregation,
and all the holy vessels that
were in the tabernacle, even
those did the priests and the
Levites bring up.
5 And king Solomon, and
all the congregation of Israel,
that *were* assembled unto
him, were with him before
the ark, sacrificing sheep and
oxen, that could not be told
nor numbered for multitude.
6 And the priests brought in
the ark of the covenant of the
LORD unto his place, into the
oracle of the house, to the
most holy *place, even* under
the wings of the cherubims.
7 For the cherubims spread
forth *their* two wings over
the place of the ark, and the
cherubims covered the ark
and the staves thereof above.
8 And they drew out the
staves, that the ends of the
staves were seen out in the
holy *place* before the oracle,
and they were not seen without: and there they are unto
this day.
9 *There was* nothing in the
ark save the two tables of
stone, which Moses put there
at Horeb, when the LORD
made *a covenant* with the
children of Israel, when they
came out of the land of Egypt.
10 And it came to pass,
when the priests were come
out of the holy *place,* that the
cloud filled the house of the
LORD,
11 So that the priests could
not stand to minister because
of the cloud: for the glory of
the LORD had filled the house
of the LORD.
12 Then spake Solomon,
The LORD said that he would
dwell in thick darkness.
13 I have surely built thee an
house to dwell in, a settled
place for thee to abide in for
ever.
14 And the king turned his
face about, and blessed all
the congregation of Israel:
(and all the congregation of
Israel stood;)
15 And he said, Blessed *be*
the LORD God of Israel,
which spake with his mouth
unto David my father, and
hath with his hand fulfilled *it,*
saying,
16 Since the day that I
brought forth my people Israel out of Egypt, I chose no
city out of all the tribes of Israel to build an house, that
my name might be therein;
but I chose David to be over
my people Israel.
17 And it was in the heart of
David my father to build an
house for the name of the
LORD God of Israel.
18 And the LORD said unto
David my father, Whereas it
was in thine heart to build an
house unto my name, thou
didst well that it was in thine
heart.
19 Nevertheless thou shalt
not build the house; but
thy son that shall come
forth out of thy loins, he shall
build the house unto my
name.
20 And the LORD hath per-
formed his word that he
spake, and I am risen up in
the room of David my father,
and sit on the throne of Israel, as the LORD promised,
and have built an house for
the name of the LORD God of
Israel.
21 And I have set there a
place for the ark, wherein *is*
the covenant of the LORD,
which he made with our fathers, when he brought them
out of the land of Egypt.

  - 4) The priests withdrew from the Holy Place
- e. The cloud of God's presence & His glory filled the temple
  - 1) The priests were unable to continue their service: Due to the radiance (brightness, light) of God's glory, Ex.40:33-35
  - 2) The explanation of Solomon: The LORD had said He would dwell in a dark cloud; thus Solomon had built the temple to give God a place to manifest His presence

2. Solomon's message to the people at the dedication of the temple: A lesson on God's faithfulness
- a. Solomon first praised the LORD for His faithfulness to David
- b. Solomon then explained why the LORD had a special encounter with David
  - 1) Because God had never chosen a place where a temple should be built to honor God's Name
  - 2) Because God had not chosen David to build the temple but to rule & establish God's people
  - 3) Because David longed for & was determined to build a temple to honor the LORD'S Name
  - 4) Because the LORD wanted to commend David for his desire to build the temple & to give a great promise to David
    - He was not the person chosen to build the temple
    - He could, however, be assured: The temple would be built—by his own son
- c. Solomon declared the faithfulness of the LORD
  - 1) The LORD had kept His promise: Placed him, David's son, on the throne
  - 2) Solomon had built the temple for the Name of the LORD, the God of Israel
  - 3) Solomon had provided a place for the Ark: The Ark that held the law or covenant, the agreement between God & His people

DIVISION I

THE RISE AND REIGN OF SOLOMON AS KING: BEGINNING IN GLORY AND ENDING IN SHAME, 1:1–11:43

H. The Dedication of the Temple (Part 1)—Solomon's Placement of the Ark in the Temple and His Message: A Picture of God's Presence and His Faithfulness, 8:1-21

(8:1-21) **Introduction**: *The Expositor's Bible Commentary* gives an introduction on the dedication of the temple that is well worth quoting in its entirety.

> *With the completion of the temple and with all the furniture in place, the crowning event was about to take place, the placement of the ark into its permanent home. For Israel it marked the beginning of a new era: Now, more than ever before, there was a feeling of permanence. The ark was no longer housed in a temporary shelter in Jerusalem; the dichotomy in the sanctuary, with the ark in Jerusalem and the tabernacle at Gibeon, was ended.*
>
> *To mark this great occasion with the dignity and solemnity it deserved, Solomon assembled all the elders of Israel with the tribal and family chiefs. As God's anointed shepherd, he involved all Israel through its elders and chiefs in the moving of the ark, and the dedication of the temple. This involved more than mere pomp and ceremony. Solomon was very much in earnest about the spiritual significance of this occasion; and he desired that the heart of all Israel be knit together in the dedication of the temple and, more importantly, in the dedication of their hearts to God.*[1]

This is the great subject of this passage: The Dedication of the Temple (Part 1)—Solomon's Placement of the Ark in the Temple and His Message: A Picture of God's Presence and His Faithfulness, 8:1-21.

1. Solomon's placement of the Ark in the temple: a picture of God's presence among His people (vv.1-13).
2. Solomon's message at the dedication of the temple: a lesson on God's faithfulness (vv.14-21).

1 (8:1-13) **Presence, of God, Example of—Glory, of God, Manifestation of—Presence, of God, Promises of—Temple, Dedication of—Ark, Placed in the Temple**: there was Solomon's placement of the Ark in the temple. All the final touches by the construction workers had been completed, and all the furnishings had been placed in the temple. At last, the long-awaited moment had arrived. The Ark of God could be placed into the temple and a great ceremony would commemorate the occasion. Scripture describes the wonderful celebration of worship:

OUTLINE	SCRIPTURE	SCRIPTURE	OUTLINE
1. Solomon's placement of the Ark in the temple: A picture of God's presence among His people a. The king summoned all the leadership of Israel to assemble in Jerusalem 1) The purpose: To move the Ark into the temple 2) The time of year: The month of Ethanim (Sept.–Oct.), during the Festival of Tabernacles, Le.23:33-36 b. The priests carried the Ark & the Tabernacle with all its furnishings up to the temple c. The king & leaders offered a large number of sacrifices before the Ark, 2 S.6:13	Then Solomon assembled the elders of Israel, and all the heads of the tribes, the chief of the fathers of the children of Israel, unto king Solomon in Jerusalem, that they might bring up the ark of the covenant of the LORD out of the city of David, which *is* Zion. 2 And all the men of Israel assembled themselves unto king Solomon at the feast in the month Ethanim, which *is* the seventh month. 3 And all the elders of Israel came, and the priests took up the ark. 4 And they brought up the ark of the LORD, and the tabernacle of the congregation, and all the holy vessels that *were* in the tabernacle, even those did the priests and the Levites bring up. 5 And king Solomon, and all the congregation of Israel, that *were* assembled unto him, were with him before the ark, sacrificing sheep and	oxen, that could not be told nor numbered for multitude. 6 And the priests brought in the ark of the covenant of the LORD unto his place, into the oracle of the house, to the most holy *place, even* under the wings of the cherubims. 7 For the cherubims spread forth *their* two wings over the place of the ark, and the cherubims covered the ark and the staves thereof above. 8 And they drew out the staves, that the ends of the staves were seen out in the holy *place* before the oracle, and they were not seen without: and there they are unto this day. 9 *There was* nothing in the ark save the two tables of stone, which Moses put there at Horeb, when the LORD made *a covenant* with the children of Israel, when they came out of the land of Egypt. 10 And it came to pass, when the priests were come	d. The priests placed the Ark in the inner sanctuary of the temple, the Most Holy Place: Set it beneath the wings of the cherubim (symbolized holiness & power) 1) The wings of the cherubim overshadowed the Ark & its carrying poles 2) The carrying poles were extremely long: Their ends could be seen from the Holy Place 3) The Ark contained only the two stone tablets of the Law (placed there by Moses): A forceful reminder of God's covenant, His commandments & man's duty to obey 4) The priests withdrew from the Holy Place

[1] Richard D. Patterson and Hermann J. Austel. *1, 2 Kings*, p.79.

OUTLINE	SCRIPTURE	SCRIPTURE	OUTLINE
e. The cloud of God's presence & His glory filled the temple 1) The priests were unable to continue their service: Due to the radiance (brightness, light) of God's glory, Ex.40:33-35	out of the holy *place,* that the cloud filled the house of the LORD, 11 So that the priests could not stand to minister because of the cloud: for the glory of the LORD had filled the house of the	LORD. 12 Then spake Solomon, The LORD said that he would dwell in thick darkness. 13 I have surely built thee an house to dwell in, a settled place for thee to abide in for ever.	2) The explanation of Solomon: The LORD had said He would dwell in a dark cloud; thus Solomon had built the temple to give God a place to manifest His presence

a. Solomon summoned all the leadership of Israel to Jerusalem for the momentous dedication service (vv.1-2). Formal invitations were sent out, and all the leadership of the nation was summoned to participate in moving the Ark into the temple. Placing the Ark in the temple was to be the crowning event of the dedication service. As Matthew Henry says, without the Ark, the temple was like a body without a soul, or a candlestick without a candle, or a house without an inhabitant. All the cost that had gone into the temple was lost if God's presence did not dwell therein.[2] Remember, the Tabernacle had been erected in Gibeon, but the Ark had been kept in a temporary shelter that had been pitched on Mount Zion in Jerusalem (2 S.6:17).

Note that the dedication service took place in the month of Ethanim, which was the seventh month of the Jewish year (v.2). Although the major structure of the temple had been completed eleven months earlier (6:38), it had apparently taken an additional eleven months to put the final touches on the temple and to complete the furnishings. Moreover, some time was needed to summon the leadership of Israel and for them to make plans to attend the dedication service.

Note also when the dedication service was conducted: during the Feast or Festival of Tabernacles (Le.23:33-36). This festival celebrated the wilderness wanderings when the people of God had to live in tents on their way to the promised land. It also celebrated the gathering of the harvest at the end of the year; therefore it was to be a period of thanksgiving to God for the harvest. Now, finally, the people could celebrate the feast, knowing that God had brought them home to the promised land and had given them rest from the days of their wilderness wanderings (see outline and note—Le.23:33-44; De.12:8-11). Thus the festival of Tabernacles was an ideal occasion to celebrate the dedication of the temple. Once all the leaders and people had gathered in Jerusalem, the wonderful, long-awaited celebration began.

b. As God's law dictated, the priests themselves carried the Ark and the Tabernacle with all its furnishings up to the temple (vv.3-4).

c. Leading the processional were King Solomon and the leaders of the nation (v.5). And apparently, as they led the processional, a large number of sacrifices were being offered ahead of the Ark. Remember, when David brought the Ark to Jerusalem, he had offered a sacrifice every six steps taken by the priests who were carrying the Ark (2 S.6:13). Obviously, Solomon was following the example of his father.

d. When the priests reached the temple, they placed the Ark in the inner sanctuary, the Most Holy Place. They set it beneath the wings of the cherubim, the statues symbolizing the angelic beings who surround God's holy throne. Standing there overshadowing the Ark, the cherubim pictured God's holiness and power. Note these facts about the Ark:

1) The wings of the cherubim overshadowed, spread out over the Ark and its carrying poles (v.7).
2) The carrying poles were extremely long (v.8). Their ends could be seen when the doors of the Holy Place were opened. Although the Ark was in its permanent sanctuary, the poles were to remain in the rings of the Ark, never to be removed (Ex.25:15).
3) The Ark contained only the two stone tablets of the law that had been placed there by Moses himself (v.9). Apparently the pot of manna and Aaron's rod that budded, which had also been placed in the Ark years before (Ex.16:33-34; Nu.17:10), had been removed during the intervening years.
4) After arranging the Ark in its proper place, the priests withdrew from the Holy Place (v.10).

e. After the priests had completely withdrawn and the doors had been closed, the most wonderful event happened. The cloud of God's presence, His majestic glory filled the temple (v.10). Just as the cloud of God's presence and majestic glory had covered the Tabernacle when it was dedicated, so now the same phenomenal experience was given to God's people at the dedication of the temple. Note that the priests were unable to continue their service due to the radiance and splendor, the brilliant light of God's glory (v.11; Ex.40:33-35). Overwhelmed by the spectacular event, Solomon was gripped with a deep sense of awe and reverence. He did his best to explain to the assembly what was happening, declaring that the LORD had said He would dwell in a dark cloud. In fact, it was for this very purpose that Solomon had built the temple, to give God a place to manifest His presence forever (vv.12-13). The LORD had indeed shown that He approved of the temple. He accepted the worship of Solomon and the Israelites.

> **Thought 1**. Above all needs, we need the presence of God in our lives. For, "If God be for us, who can be against us?" (Ro.8:31). And, "Greater is He who is in us than he who is in the world" (1 Jn.4:4). When God is present with us, we experience His love, joy, peace, patience, gentleness, goodness, and self-control. When God is with us, we have purpose, meaning, and significance, and also a deep sense of assurance and confidence that all things will be worked out for good (Ro.8:28). Through God's presence, we receive the power of God, the power to conquer and overcome, to triumph and gain the victory over all hardships and misfortunes, temptations and trials, wickedness and evil. Even death itself has no hold over us if God's presence is with us. For the moment we come to the portals of death, God is there to instantaneously transfer us into His presence. The body will lie down and die, but we will be immediately in His glorious presence. Listen to the wonderful promises of God's presence:
> (1) God's presence assures us of living in the promised land of heaven itself.

---

[2] Matthew Henry. *Matthew Henry's Commentary*, Vol.2, p.613.

"For God so loved the world, that he gave his only begotten Son, that whosoever believeth in him should not perish, but have everlasting life" (Jn.3:16).

"In my Father's house are many mansions: if *it were* not so, I would have told you. I go to prepare a place for you. And if I go and prepare a place for you, I will come again, and receive you unto myself; that where I am, *there* ye may be also" (Jn.14:2-3).

"And I heard a voice from heaven saying unto me, Write, Blessed *are* the dead which die in the Lord from henceforth: Yea, saith the Spirit, that they may rest from their labours; and their works do follow them" (Re.14:13).

"And, behold, I am with thee, and will keep thee in all *places* whither thou goest, and will bring thee again into this land; for I will not leave thee, until I have done *that* which I have spoken to thee of" (Ge.28:15).

(2) God's presence assures us of rest, which means peace of heart, mind, and soul, and the full assurance of being taken care of and being given eternal life by God. The spiritual rest of God means security and stability, provision and protection, assurance and confidence, fulfillment and satisfaction, meaning and purpose in life.

"Take my yoke upon you, and learn of me; for I am meek and lowly in heart: and ye shall find rest unto your souls" (Mt.11:29).

"Behold, I stand at the door, and knock: if any man hear my voice, and open the door, I will come in to him, and will sup with him, and he with me" (Re.3:20).

"And he said, My presence shall go *with thee*, and I will give thee rest" (Ex.33:14).

"The LORD *is* my shepherd; I shall not want. He maketh me to lie down in green pastures: he leadeth me beside the still waters. He restoreth my soul: he leadeth me in the paths of righteousness for his name's sake. Yea, though I walk through the valley of the shadow of death, I will fear no evil: for thou *art* with me; thy rod and thy staff they comfort me. Thou preparest a table before me in the presence of mine enemies: thou anointest my head with oil; my cup runneth over. Surely goodness and mercy shall follow me all the days of my life: and I will dwell in the house of the LORD for ever" (Ps.23:1-6).

(3) God's presence assures us of courage and of strength to stand against the enemies of this life.

"When thou goest out to battle against thine enemies, and seest horses, and chariots, *and* a people more than thou, be not afraid of them: for the LORD thy God *is* with thee, which brought thee up out of the land of Egypt" (De.20:1).

"Fear thou not; for I *am* with thee: be not dismayed; for I *am* thy God: I will strengthen thee; yea, I will help thee; yea, I will uphold thee with the right hand of my righteousness" (Is.41:10).

(4) God's presence assures us of victory over all trials, even over all the helpless and hopeless circumstances of life.

"Fear not: for I have redeemed thee, I have called *thee* by thy name; thou *art* mine. When thou passest through the waters, I *will be* with thee; and through the rivers, they shall not overflow thee: when thou walkest through the fire, thou shalt not be burned; neither shall the flame kindle upon thee" (Is.43:1-2).

(5) God's presence assures us that He will never leave us, that He will always be with us.

"Teaching them to observe all things whatsoever I have commanded you: and, lo, I am with you alway, *even* unto the end of the world. Amen"(Mt.28:20).

"*Let your* conversation [behavior, conduct] *be* without covetousness; *and be* content with such things as ye have: for he hath said, I will never leave thee, nor forsake thee" (He.13:5).

2 (8:14-21) **Faithfulness, of God, Results, Prophecy Fulfilled—Temple, Prophecy of, Fulfilled—Solomon, Message of, at Temple Dedication**: there was Solomon's message to the people at the dedication of the temple. Standing there stunned at the spectacular demonstration of God's radiant glory descending upon the temple, Solomon eventually regained his composure enough to begin speaking. Turning around from gazing at the temple, Solomon began to address the people. Exactly what he said is given by the Scripture:

OUTLINE	SCRIPTURE	SCRIPTURE	OUTLINE
2. Solomon's message to the people at the dedication of the temple: A lesson on God's faithfulness a. Solomon first praised the LORD for His faithfulness to David	14 And the king turned his face about, and blessed all the congregation of Israel: (and all the congregation of Israel stood;) 15 And he said, Blessed *be* the LORD God of Israel, which spake with his mouth	unto David my father, and hath with his hand fulfilled *it*, saying, 16 Since the day that I brought forth my people Israel out of Egypt, I chose no city out of all the tribes of Israel to build an house, that	b. Solomon then explained why the LORD had a special encounter with David 1) Because God had never chosen a place where a temple should be built to honor God's Name 2) Because God had not

OUTLINE	SCRIPTURE	SCRIPTURE	OUTLINE
chosen David to build the temple but to rule & establish God's people 3) Because David longed for & was determined to build a temple to honor the LORD'S Name 4) Because the LORD wanted to commend David for his desire to build the temple & to give a great promise to David • He was not the person chosen to build the temple • He could, however, be assured: The temple	my name might be therein; but I chose David to be over my people Israel. 17 And it was in the heart of David my father to build an house for the name of the LORD God of Israel. 18 And the LORD said unto David my father, Whereas it was in thine heart to build an house unto my name, thou didst well that it was in thine heart. 19 Nevertheless thou shalt not build the house; but thy son that shall come forth out of thy loins, he shall	build the house unto my name. 20 And the LORD hath performed his word that he spake, and I am risen up in the room of David my father, and sit on the throne of Israel, as the LORD promised, and have built an house for the name of the LORD God of Israel. 21 And I have set there a place for the ark, wherein *is* the covenant of the LORD, which he made with our fathers, when he brought them out of the land of Egypt.	would be built—by his own son c. Solomon declared the faithfulness of the LORD 1) The LORD had kept His promise: Placed him, David's son, on the throne 2) Solomon had built the temple for the Name of the LORD, the God of Israel 3) Solomon had provided a place for the Ark: The Ark that held the law or covenant, the agreement between God & His people

a. Solomon first praised the LORD for His faithfulness (v.15). All praise and honor were due to the LORD, for it was He who had chosen to honor the temple with His presence. And by dwelling within the temple, God was fulfilling the wonderful promise He had made to Solomon's father, King David.

b. Solomon then explained the wonderful promise given by the LORD to David (vv.15-19). Appearing to David, the LORD revealed that He had never *chosen* a place where a temple should be built, but He had *chosen* a king who was to establish God's people as a great nation. That king was David (v.16). Nevertheless, a burning passion consumed David's heart, a passion to build the temple himself in order to honor the LORD's Name (v.17). But contrary to David's wish, the LORD instructed David not to build the temple. His task upon earth was to establish Israel as the great and powerful nation God had chosen His people to be.

However, the LORD did commend David for his desire to construct a temple to honor the LORD's Name (v.18). And more than just a commendation, the LORD gave a wonderful promise to David. Although he was not the person to build the temple, David could rest assured, the temple would be built—built by his very own son who would succeed him upon the throne (v.19). This, of course, was a reference to Solomon himself.

c. Having stated the wonderful promise of God that a temple would definitely be built, Solomon declared the faithfulness of the LORD (vv.20-21). The LORD had kept the promise He had so wonderfully made. The LORD had placed him, David's son, on the throne. And he, Solomon, had built the temple for the Name of the LORD, the God of Israel. He had provided a place for the Ark of God, the Ark that held the covenant of the LORD, the very agreement between God and His people.

Thought 1. God is faithful. He fulfills His promises, does exactly what He says. Never has God failed, not even in a single promise. Every promise God has ever made, He has fulfilled. Of this we can be assured: the LORD will never fail us, never, no, never. If we love and obey the LORD, the LORD promises to help us through all the difficulties and problems, trials and tribulations, temptations and seducements that confront us. He will give us the power to conquer and to overcome. He is faithful, faithful to do exactly what He promises. Listen to what God's Holy Word says about His faithfulness:

"God *is* faithful, by whom ye were called unto the fellowship of his Son Jesus Christ our Lord" (1 Co.1:9).

"But the Lord is faithful, who shall stablish you, and keep *you* from evil" (2 Th.3:3).

"If we believe not, *yet* he abideth faithful: he cannot deny himself" (2 Ti.2:13).

"Wherein God, willing more abundantly to show unto the heirs of promise the immutability of his counsel, confirmed *it* by an oath: That by two immutable things, in which *it was* impossible for God to lie, we might have a strong consolation, who have fled for refuge to lay hold upon the hope set before us" (He.6:17-18).

"Let us hold fast the profession of *our* faith without wavering; (for he is faithful that promised" (He.10:23).

"Wherefore let them that suffer according to the will of God commit the keeping of their souls *to him* in well doing, as unto a faithful Creator" (1 Pe.4:19).

"Know therefore that the LORD thy God, he *is* God, the faithful God, which keepeth covenant and mercy with them that love him and keep his commandments to a thousand generations" (De.7:9).

"Blessed *be* the LORD, that hath given rest unto his people Israel, according to all that he promised: there hath not failed one word of all his good promise, which he promised by the hand of Moses his servant" (1 K.8:56).

"Thy mercy, O LORD, *is* in the heavens; *and* thy faithfulness *reacheth* unto the clouds" (Ps.36:5).

"I will sing of the mercies of the LORD for ever: with my mouth will I make known thy faithfulness to all generations" (Ps.89:1).

I. The Dedication of the Temple (Part 2)—Solomon's Prayer of Dedication: A Picture of the Temple As the "House of Prayer," 8:22-53

8:22-53; see 2 Chr.6:12-40

1. Solomon's reverent posture: A lesson on reverence before God
- a. He stood before the altar
- b. He spread out his hands

2. Solomon's acknowledgment of the LORD's uniqueness & supremacy: A lesson on God's faithfulness & love
- a. God alone keeps His covenant (promises) & shows unfailing love to those who obey Him, De.7:8-9
- b. God had kept His promise to David, that David's son would succeed him & build the temple, 2 S.7:12-13

3. Solomon's ten requests in prayer: A strong lesson on seeking the LORD
- a. First, that God would keep all His promises
  - 1) That David's throne would be established forever, 2 S.7:11-16; esp.13,16
  - 2) That God would fulfill His Word, His promises to David
- b. Second, that God would watch over & always hear the prayers of His people
  - 1) The fact: No temple—not even the universe—can contain God's presence
  - 2) The four specific pleas of Solomon: That God would hear the prayer of His servant
    - For God to send His mercy
    - For God to watch over the temple—night & day—the temple where the Name of God is honored
    - For God to hear the prayers of His people

22 And Solomon stood be-
fore the altar of the LORD in
the presence of all the congregation of Israel, and
spread forth his hands toward
heaven:
23 And he said, LORD God
of Israel, *there is* no God like
thee, in heaven above, or
on earth beneath, who keep-
est covenant and mercy
with thy servants that walk
before thee with all their
heart:
24 Who hast kept with thy
servant David my father that
thou promisedst him: thou
spakest also with thy mouth,
and hast fulfilled *it* with thine
hand, as *it is* this day.
25 Therefore now, LORD
God of Israel, keep with thy
servant David my father that
thou promisedst him, saying,
There shall not fail thee a
man in my sight to sit on the
throne of Israel; so that thy
children take heed to their
way, that they walk before
me as thou hast walked before me.
26 And now, O God of Israel, let thy word, I pray thee,
be verified, which thou
spakest unto thy servant David my father.
27 But will God indeed
dwell on the earth? behold,
the heaven and heaven of
heavens cannot contain thee;
how much less this house
that I have builded?
28 Yet have thou respect unto the prayer of thy servant,
and to his supplication, O
LORD my God, to hearken
unto the cry and to the prayer, which thy servant prayeth
before thee to day:
29 That thine eyes may be
open toward this house night
and day, *even* toward the
place of which thou hast said,
My name shall be there: that
thou mayest hearken unto the
prayer which thy servant
shall make toward this place.
30 And hearken thou to the
supplication of thy servant,
and of thy people Israel,
when they shall pray toward
this place: and hear thou in
heaven thy dwelling place:
and when thou hearest, forgive.
31 If any man trespass
against his neighbour, and an
oath be laid upon him to
cause him to swear, and the
oath come before thine altar
in this house:
32 Then hear thou in heaven,
and do, and judge thy servants, condemning the wicked,
to bring his way upon his
head; and justifying the
righteous, to give him according to his righteousness.
33 When thy people Israel
be smitten down before the
enemy, because they have
sinned against thee, and shall
turn again to thee, and confess thy name, and pray, and
make supplication unto thee
in this house:
34 Then hear thou in heaven,
and forgive the sin of thy
people Israel, and bring them
again unto the land which
thou gavest unto their fathers.
35 When heaven is shut up,
and there is no rain, because
they have sinned against
thee; if they pray toward this
place, and confess thy name,
and turn from their sin, when
thou afflictest them:
36 Then hear thou in heaven,
and forgive the sin of thy
servants, and of thy people
Israel, that thou teach them
the good way wherein they
should walk, and give rain
upon thy land, which thou
hast given to thy people for
an inheritance.
37 If there be in the land
famine, if there be pestilence,
blasting, mildew, locust, *or* if
there be caterpillar; if their
enemy besiege them in the
land of their cities; whatsoever plague, whatsoever
sickness *there be;*
38 What prayer and supplication soever be *made* by any
man, *or* by all thy people Israel, which shall know every
man the plague of his own
heart, and spread forth his
hands toward this house:
39 Then hear thou in heav-
en thy dwelling place, and
forgive, and do, and give to
every man according to his
ways, whose heart thou
knowest; (for thou, *even* thou

- For God to forgive His people
- c. Third, that God would execute justice among the people
  - 1) Judge the disputes between people
  - 2) Condemn the guilty & establish the innocence of the righteous
- d. Fourth, that God would hear the prayer of the defeated
  - 1) The circumstance: When defeated by an enemy because of sin & God's chastisement
  - 2) The remedy: Repentance & confession
  - 3) The request: Forgive & restore to the promised land
- e. Fifth, that God would hear the prayer of those suffering drought
  - 1) The circumstance: When being chastised because of sin
  - 2) The remedy: Confession & repentance
  - 3) The request: Forgive & teach the right way to live & send rain on the land of the inheritance (the promised land)
- f. Sixth, that God would hear the prayer of those suffering financial disaster or disease
  - 1) The circumstance: Financial loss due to some disaster, disease, or enemy attack
  - 2) The remedy:
    - Seeking God, praying & pleading with Him
    - Being aware & repenting of one's own afflicted (sinful) heart
  - 3) The request of God
    - To forgive
    - To execute justice, reward each person for exactly what he does: God alone can, for He

alone knows the heart

4) The reason: That the people may fear & obey God, live for Him

g. Seventh, that God would hear the prayer of the foreigner (Gentile) who worships the LORD

1) The circumstance: When the foreigner hears about the LORD—that His mighty hand & outstretched arm saves—and he turns to the LORD
2) The request: Hear & answer the request of the foreigner
3) The reason: That the Name of the LORD might be taken worldwide; That all people may know & fear the LORD & worship Him

h. Eighth, that God would hear the prayer of soldiers for victory over their enemies
1) The circumstance: Conflict, war being justly fought (sent by God)

2) The request: Hear & uphold the cause—give victory

i. Ninth, that God would hear the prayer of the sinner who is captured by the enemy
1) The circumstance: A believer sins & is chastised by God—allowed to be defeated & captured by an enemy
2) The remedy: A change of heart
• Confessing & pleading

only, knowest the hearts of
all the children of men;)
40 That they may fear thee
all the days that they live in
the land which thou gavest
unto our fathers.
41 Moreover concerning a
stranger, that *is* not of thy
people Israel, but cometh out
of a far country for thy
name's sake;
42 (For they shall hear of
thy great name, and of thy
strong hand, and of thy
stretched out arm;) when he
shall come and pray toward
this house;
43 Hear thou in heaven thy
dwelling place, and do according to all that the
stranger calleth to thee for:
that all people of the earth
may know thy name, to fear
thee, as *do* thy people Israel;
and that they may know that
this house, which I have
builded, is called by thy
name.
44 If thy people go out to
battle against their enemy,
whithersoever thou shalt send
them, and shall pray unto the
LORD toward the city which
thou hast chosen, and *toward*
the house that I have built for
thy name:
45 Then hear thou in heaven
their prayer and their supplication, and maintain their
cause.
46 If they sin against thee,
(for *there is* no man that sinneth not,) and thou be angry
with them, and deliver them
to the enemy, so that they
carry them away captives unto the land of the enemy, far
or near;
47 *Yet* if they shall bethink
themselves in the land whither they were carried captives,
and repent, and make supplication unto thee in the land of
them that carried them captives, saying, We have
sinned, and have done perversely, we have committed
wickedness;
48 And *so* return unto thee
with all their heart, and with
all their soul, in the land of
their enemies, which led
them away captive, and pray
unto thee toward their land,
which thou gavest unto their
fathers, the city which thou
hast chosen, and the house
which I have built for thy
name:
49 Then hear thou their
prayer and their supplication
in heaven thy dwelling place,
and maintain their cause,
50 And forgive thy people
that have sinned against thee
and all their transgressions
wherein they have transgressed against thee, and give
them compassion before them
who carried them captive,
that they may have compassion on them:
51 For they *be* thy people,
and thine inheritance, which
thou broughtest forth out of
Egypt, from the midst of the
furnace of iron:
52 That thine eyes may be
open unto the supplication of
thy servant, and unto the
supplication of thy people Israel, to hearken unto them in
all that they call for unto
thee.
53 For thou didst separate
them from among all the
people of the earth, *to be*
thine inheritance, as thou
spakest by the hand of Moses
thy servant, when thou
broughtest our fathers out of
Egypt, O Lord GOD.

with God for deliverance

• Repenting—turning back to God wholeheartedly

• Praying for restoration to the promised land

3) The request to God
• To hear & vindicate them—uphold their cause
• To forgive

• To stir the enemy to show mercy

4) The reason: They are God's people, His inheritance—saved by Him

j. Tenth, that God would see & answer every prayer—all the pleas of His servant & people
1) The circumstance: Any & all cases of need

2) The reason
• They are God's own inheritance
• God Himself taught this fact through Moses & the great deliverance from Egypt (a symbol of the world)

DIVISION I

THE RISE AND REIGN OF SOLOMON AS KING: BEGINNING IN GLORY AND ENDING IN SHAME, 1:1–11:43

I. The Dedication of the Temple (Part 2)—Solomon's Prayer of Dedication: A Picture of the Temple As the "House of Prayer," 8:22-53

(8:22-53) **Introduction**: hardships and misfortunes, difficulties and problems, trials and tribulations, disasters and catastrophes, temptations and seductions, enticements and sinful passions—some of these events confront every one of us as we walk throughout life. When we are confronted by any difficult circumstance, there is an answer: prayer. Seeking the face of God for help. For when we seek God, He hears and answers our prayers. If we are genuine—believing and trusting God with our whole heart—God always hears us. He empowers us to walk through any trial or temptation of this life. Prayer—true prayer—is the greatest force upon this earth. It is the basic principle of the universe by which God has chosen to work and move events. His sovereign power takes action when God hears a person praying.

Prayer is the focus of this present Scripture. Solomon is standing on a platform before the assembly of Israel's leaders and many of the citizens. A crowning, memorable event is taking place: the temple is being dedicated to the LORD. Solomon had just delivered his message to the people. Now he is ready to offer up the prayer of dedication, one of the longest and most magnificent intercessory prayers in all of Scripture. This is: *The Dedication of the Temple (Part 2)—Solomon's Prayer of Dedication: A Picture of the Temple As the "House of Prayer,"* 8:22-53.

1. Solomon's reverent posture: a lesson on reverence before God (v.22).
2. Solomon's acknowledgment of the LORD's uniqueness and supremacy: a lesson on God's faithfulness and love (vv.23-24).
3. Solomon's ten requests in prayer: a strong lesson on seeking the LORD (vv.25-53).

1 (8:22) **Reverence, Example of—Awe, Example of—Posture, in Prayer**: there was Solomon's reverent posture in prayer. For the dedication service, Solomon had built a bronze platform seven and one-half feet long, seven and one-half feet wide, and four and one-half feet high (2 Chr.6:13). It was upon this platform that he stood in prayer before the people. Note that he begins this prayer standing, but ends in a kneeling position (vv.22, 54). Sometime during the prayer, Solomon's heart was so broken before the LORD that he sank to a kneeling position. He fell to his knees in a humble, reverent submission to the LORD (v.54).

For now, as he stood before the altar of the LORD in the presence of the whole assembly, he lifted up his hands toward heaven, outstretched in prayer. By stretching out his hands toward heaven, he was symbolizing...

- that he was totally dependent upon the LORD
- that the LORD alone could answer the request he was about to ask in prayer
- that absolutely nothing could be done apart from the LORD
- that he was humbly submitting himself and his people to the LORD

Standing there before the assembly of Israel, Solomon was both the *representative* and the *shepherd* of his people before the LORD.[1] This is one of the great prayers of Holy Scripture.

OUTLINE	SCRIPTURE	SCRIPTURE	OUTLINE
1. Solomon's reverent posture: A lesson on reverence before God	22And Solomon stood before the altar of the LORD in the presence of all the congrega-	tion of Israel, and spread forth his hands toward heaven:	a. He stood before the altar b. He spread out his hands

Thought 1. When we approach God, we must approach Him in *reverence* and *awe*, for the LORD is the great Creator and Sustainer of the universe. To Him we owe our lives, all we are and have. Every blessing we have ever received—every good and perfect gift of human life—has come from the hands of God (Jas.1:17). To the LORD belong all glory and majesty, dominion and power forever and ever. Amen. Thus when we approach Him, He is due the utmost reverence.

But this is often not the case. God is often approached rudely and even flippantly, with irreverence and disrespect. For example, some people have referred to God as "the man upstairs." Others look upon God as only a type of *grandfather*, a gray-haired superior who exists to meet our needs and demands. Even some worship services have become little more than social fellowships or clubs with a sermon tacked on the end, a sermon through which the members sit squirming and restless, impatiently waiting for it to end. And for many, prayer has become little more than an inconvenience, a rushed time to make quick requests for family members or for immediate personal needs.

Such irreverence is an *insult* to God. It is *profane*—an unholy, ungodly, sinful approach to God. This is never the way the LORD God of the universe—the Creator and Sovereign Majesty who rules and reigns over all—should be approached. Listen to what the Holy Word of God says about reverence for God:

"After this manner therefore pray ye: Our Father which art in heaven, Hallowed be thy name" (Mt.6:9).

"And fear not them which kill the body, but are not able to kill the soul: but rather fear him which is able to destroy both soul and body in hell" (Mt.10:28).

"And the Jews' passover was at hand, and Jesus went up to Jerusalem, And found in the temple those that sold oxen and sheep and doves, and the changers of money sitting: And when he had made a scourge of small cords, he drove them all out of the temple, and the sheep, and the oxen; and poured out the changers' money, and overthrew the tables; And said unto them that sold doves, Take these things hence; make not my Father's house an house of merchandise" (Jn.2:13-16).

"Ye shall keep my sabbaths, and reverence my sanctuary: I *am* the LORD" (Le.19:30).

"Speak unto Aaron and to his sons, that they separate themselves from the holy things of the children of Israel, and that they profane not my holy name *in those things* which they hallow unto me: I *am* the LORD" (Le.22:2).

"And now, Israel, what doth the Lord thy God require of thee, but to fear the LORD thy God, to walk in all his ways, and to love him, and to serve the LORD thy God with all thy heart and with all thy soul" (De.10:12).

"...that thou mayest fear this glorious and fearful name, THE LORD THY GOD" (De.28:58).

"And the captain of the LORD's host said unto Joshua, Loose thy shoe from off thy foot; for the place whereon thou standest is holy. And Joshua did so" (Jos.5:15).

[1] Richard D. Patterson and Hermann J. Austel. *1, 2 Kings*, p.84.

"Now therefore fear the LORD, and serve him in sincerity and in truth" (Jos.24:14).

"Stand in awe, and sin not: commune with your own heart upon your bed, and be still. Selah" (Ps.4:4).

"Give unto the LORD the glory due unto his name; worship the LORD in the beauty of holiness" (Ps.29:2).

"Let all the earth fear the LORD: let all the inhabitants of the world stand in awe of him" (Ps.33:8).

"O magnify the LORD with me, and let us exalt his name together" (Ps.34:3).

"Be thou exalted, O God, above the heavens; *let* thy glory *be* above all the earth" (Ps.57:5).

"God is greatly to be feared in the assembly of the saints, and to be had in reverence of all *them that are* about him" (Ps.89:7).

"Let them exalt him also in the congregation of the people, and praise him in the assembly of the elders" (Ps.107:32).

"Keep thy foot when thou goest to the house of God, and be more ready to hear, than to give the sacrifice of fools: for they consider not that they do evil" (Ec.5:1).

"Let us hear the conclusion of the whole matter: Fear God, and keep his commandments: for this *is* the whole *duty* of man" (Ec.12:13).

"Sanctify the LORD of hosts himself; and *let* him *be* your fear, and *let* him *be* your dread" (Is.8:13).

"O LORD, thou *art* my God; I will exalt thee, I will praise thy name; for thou hast done wonderful *things; thy* counsels of old *are* faithfulness *and* truth" (Is.25:1).

"For thus saith the high and lofty One that inhabiteth eternity, whose name *is* Holy; I dwell in the high and holy *place,* with him also *that is* of a contrite and humble spirit, to revive the spirit of the humble, and to revive the heart of the contrite ones" (Is.57:15).

"And I will sanctify my great name, which was profaned among the heathen, which ye have profaned in the midst of them; and the heathen shall know that I *am* the LORD, saith the Lord GOD, when I shall be sanctified in you before their eyes" (Eze.36:23).

"Daniel answered and said, Blessed be the name of God for ever and ever: for wisdom and might are his" (Da.2:20).

"But the LORD *is* in his holy temple: let all the earth keep silence before him" (Hab.2:20).

2 (8:23-24) **Faithfulness, of God—God, Faithfulness of—God, Love of—Love, of God—Prayer, of Solomon—God, Uniqueness of—God, None Like God**: there was Solomon's acknowledgment of the LORD's *uniqueness* and *supremacy*. Standing there with his hands stretched up toward heaven, Solomon acknowledged that there is no God other than the LORD Himself (Yahweh, Jehovah). There is none other, not in heaven above nor on earth below. Two things aroused Solomon to declare God's *uniqueness* and *supremacy*:

a. It is God alone who keeps His covenant (promises) and shows unfailing love to those who obey him (v.23). God is faithful. When He makes a promise, He keeps His promise. But note: His promises are conditional, given only to those who wholeheartedly obey Him. God's faithfulness never changes. But it is conditional. A person must obey God and obey Him wholeheartedly to receive God's promises. If a person is obedient, God's unfailing love will pour out the richest blessings upon the obedient believer. This is exactly what God's Holy Word says:

"And the LORD passed by before him, and proclaimed, The LORD, The LORD God, merciful and gracious, longsuffering, and abundant in goodness and truth, Keeping mercy for thousands, forgiving iniquity and transgression and sin, and that will by no means clear *the guilty;* visiting the iniquity of the fathers upon the children, and upon the children's children, unto the third and to the fourth *generation*" (Ex.34:6-7).

"Know therefore that the LORD thy God, he *is* God, the faithful God, which keepeth covenant and mercy with them that love him and keep his commandments to a thousand generations; And repayeth them that hate him to their face, to destroy them: he will not be slack to him that hateth him, he will repay him to his face. Thou shalt therefore keep the commandments, and the statutes, and the judgments, which I command thee this day, to do them. Wherefore it shall come to pass, if ye hearken to these judgments, and keep, and do them, that the LORD thy God shall keep unto thee the covenant and the mercy which he sware unto thy fathers: And he will love thee, and bless thee" (De.7:9-13).

b. God had kept His promise to David, that he would have a lasting dynasty and that his son Solomon would succeed him and build the temple (2 Sa.7:12-13). In standing there before the temple with his hands lifted up to God in prayer, Solomon was the proof that God had kept His promise to David. The LORD had set David's son Solomon on the throne and Solomon had built the temple. The LORD was faithful, and His faithfulness was being declared by Solomon.

OUTLINE	SCRIPTURE	SCRIPTURE	OUTLINE
2. Solomon's acknowledgment of the LORD's uniqueness & supremacy: A lesson on God's faithfulness & love a. God alone keeps His covenant (promises) & shows unfailing love to those who	23 And he said, LORD God of Israel, *there is* no God like thee, in heaven above, or on earth beneath, who keepest covenant and mercy with thy servants that walk before thee with all their	heart: 24 Who hast kept with thy servant David my father that thou promisedst him: thou spakest also with thy mouth, and hast fulfilled *it* with thine hand, as *it is* this day.	obey Him, De.7:8-9 b. God had kept His promise to David, that David's son would succeed him & build the temple, 2 S.7:12-13

Thought 1. God keeps His Word, doing exactly what He says and promises. His promises are as sure, as certain as the heavens and the earth. As long as heaven and earth exist, God will fulfill His promises to us. Even when heaven and earth pass away and the new heavens and earth are created, God will keep His promises. He is faithful—absolutely faithful—in doing exactly what He says. We can trust God, believe Him, and take Him at His Word. He will never fail to meet every need we have.

> **"For verily I say unto you, Till heaven and earth pass, one jot or one tittle shall in no wise pass from the law, till all be fulfilled" (Mt.5:18).**
>
> **"Heaven and earth shall pass away: but my words shall not pass away" (Lu.21:33).**
>
> **"God *is* faithful, by whom ye were called unto the fellowship of his Son Jesus Christ our Lord" (1 Co.1:9).**
>
> **"Wherein God, willing more abundantly to show unto the heirs of promise the immutability of his counsel, confirmed *it* by an oath: That by two immutable things, in which *it was* impossible for God to lie, we might have a strong consolation, who have fled for refuge to lay hold upon the hope set before us" (He.6:17-18).**
>
> **"Know therefore that the LORD thy God, he *is* God, the faithful God, which keepeth covenant and mercy with them that love him and keep his commandments to a thousand generations" (De.7:9).**
>
> **"Blessed *be* the LORD, that hath given rest unto his people Israel, according to all that he promised: there hath not failed one word of all his good promise, which he promised by the hand of Moses his servant" (1 K.8:56).**
>
> **"Thy mercy, O LORD, *is* in the heavens; *and* thy faithfulness *reacheth* unto the clouds" (Ps.36:5).**
>
> **"I will sing of the mercies of the LORD for ever: with my mouth will I make known thy faithfulness to all generations" (Ps.89:1).**
>
> **"Fear thou not; for I *am* with thee: be not dismayed; for I *am* thy God: I will strengthen thee; yea, I will help thee; yea, I will uphold thee with the right hand of my righteousness" (Is.41:10).**
>
> **"...Fear not: for I have redeemed thee, I have called *thee* by thy name; thou *art* mine. When thou passest through the waters, I *will be* with thee; and through the rivers, they shall not overflow thee: when thou walkest through the fire, thou shalt not be burned; neither shall the flame kindle upon thee" (Is.43:1-2).**
>
> **"And *even* to *your* old age I *am* he; and *even* to hoar [gray] hairs will I carry *you:* I have made, and I will bear; even I will carry, and will deliver *you*" (Is.46:4).**

3 (8:25-53) **Prayer, Request of, Listed—Prayer, Dedication Prayers, Example of—Solomon, Prayer of**: there were Solomon's ten requests in prayer. Pouring out his heart before God, Solomon became a prayer warrior, interceding for his people. Note that this prayer is one of the longest in Scripture:

OUTLINE	SCRIPTURE	SCRIPTURE	OUTLINE
3. Solomon's ten requests in prayer: A strong lesson on seeking the LORD a. First, that God would keep all His promises 1) That David's throne would be established forever, 2 S.7:11-16; esp.13,16	25 Therefore now, LORD God of Israel, keep with thy servant David my father that thou promisedst him, saying, There shall not fail thee a man in my sight to sit on the throne of Israel; so that thy children take heed to their way, that they walk before me as thou hast walked before me.	29 That thine eyes may be open toward this house night and day, *even* toward the place of which thou hast said, My name shall be there: that thou mayest hearken unto the prayer which thy servant shall make toward this place.	• For God to watch over the temple—night & day—the temple where the Name of God is honored
2) That God would fulfill His Word, His promises to David	26 And now, O God of Israel, let thy word, I pray thee, be verified, which thou spakest unto thy servant David my father.	30 And hearken thou to the supplication of thy servant, and of thy people Israel, when they shall pray toward this place: and hear thou in heaven thy dwelling place: and when thou hearest, forgive.	• For God to hear the prayers of His people • For God to forgive His people
b. Second, that God would watch over & always hear the prayers of His people 1) The fact: No temple—not even the universe—can contain God's presence	27 But will God indeed dwell on the earth? behold, the heaven and heaven of heavens cannot contain thee; how much less this house that I have builded?	31 If any man trespass against his neighbour, and an oath be laid upon him to cause him to swear, and the oath come before thine altar in this house:	c. Third, that God would execute justice among the people 1) Judge the disputes between people
2) The four specific pleas of Solomon: That God would hear the prayer of His servant • For God to send His mercy	28 Yet have thou respect unto the prayer of thy servant, and to his supplication, O LORD my God, to hearken unto the cry and to the prayer, which thy servant prayeth before thee to day:	32 Then hear thou in heaven, and do, and judge thy servants, condemning the wicked, to bring his way upon his head; and justifying the righteous, to give him according to his righteousness.	2) Condemn the guilty & establish the innocence of the righteous
		33 When thy people Israel	d. Fourth, that God would hear

OUTLINE	SCRIPTURE	SCRIPTURE	OUTLINE
the prayer of the defeated 1) The circumstance: When defeated by an enemy because of sin & God's chastisement 2) The remedy: Repentance & confession 3) The request: Forgive & restore to the promised land	be smitten down before the enemy, because they have sinned against thee, and shall turn again to thee, and con- fess thy name, and pray, and make supplication unto thee in this house: 34 Then hear thou in heaven, and forgive the sin of thy people Israel, and bring them again unto the land which thou gavest unto their fathers.	stranger calleth to thee for: that all people of the earth may know thy name, to fear thee, as *do* thy people Israel; and that they may know that this house, which I have builded, is called by thy name. 44 If thy people go out to battle against their enemy, whithersoever thou shalt send them, and shall pray unto the	foreigner 3) The reason: That the Name of the LORD might be taken worldwide; That all people may know & fear the LORD & worship Him h. Eighth, that God would hear the prayer of soldiers for victory over their enemies
e. Fifth, that God would hear the prayer of those suffering drought 1) The circumstance: When being chastised because of sin 2) The remedy: Confession & repentance 3) The request: Forgive & teach the right way to live & send rain on the land of the inheritance (the promised land)	35 When heaven is shut up, and there is no rain, because they have sinned against thee; if they pray toward this place, and confess thy name, and turn from their sin, when thou afflictest them: 36 Then hear thou in heaven, and forgive the sin of thy servants, and of thy people Is- rael, that thou teach them the good way wherein they should walk, and give rain upon thy land, which thou hast given to thy people for an inheritance.	LORD toward the city which thou hast chosen, and *toward* the house that I have built for thy name: 45 Then hear thou in heaven their prayer and their suppli- cation, and maintain their cause. 46 If they sin against thee, (for *there is* no man that sin- neth not,) and thou be angry with them, and deliver them to the enemy, so that they carry them away captives un- to the land of the enemy, far	1) The circumstance: Conflict, war being justly fought (sent by God) 2) The request: Hear & uphold the cause—give victory i. Ninth, that God would hear the prayer of the sinner who is captured by the enemy 1) The circumstance: A believer sins & is chastised by God—allowed to be defeated & captured by an
f. Sixth, that God would hear the prayer of those suffering financial disaster or disease 1) The circumstance: Financial loss due to some disaster, disease, or enemy attack 2) The remedy: • Seeking God, praying & pleading with Him • Being aware & repenting of one's own afflicted (sinful) heart 3) The request of God • To forgive • To execute justice, reward each person for exactly what he does: God alone can, for He alone knows the heart	37 If there be in the land famine, if there be pestilence, blasting, mildew, locust, *or* if there be caterpillar; if their enemy besiege them in the land of their cities; whatso- ever plague, whatsoever sickness *there be;* 38 What prayer and suppli- cation soever be *made* by any man, *or* by all thy people Is- rael, which shall know every man the plague of his own heart, and spread forth his hands toward this house: 39 Then hear thou in heaven thy dwelling place, and for- give, and do, and give to eve- ry man according to his ways, whose heart thou knowest; (for thou, *even* thou only, knowest the hearts of all the children of men;)	or near; 47 *Yet* if they shall bethink themselves in the land whith- er they were carried captives, and repent, and make suppli- cation unto thee in the land of them that carried them cap- tives, saying, We have sinned, and have done per- versely, we have committed wickedness; 48 And *so* return unto thee with all their heart, and with all their soul, in the land of their enemies, which led them away captive, and pray unto thee toward their land, which thou gavest unto their fathers, the city which thou hast chosen, and the house which I have built for thy name:	enemy 2) The remedy: A change of heart • Confessing & pleading with God for deliverance • Repenting—turning back to God wholeheartedly • Praying for restoration to the promised land
4) The reason: That the people may fear & obey God, live for Him g. Seventh, that God would hear the prayer of the foreigner (Gentile) who worships the LORD 1) The circumstance: When the foreigner hears about the LORD—that His mighty hand & outstretched arm saves—and he turns to the LORD 2) The request: Hear & answer the request of the	40 That they may fear thee all the days that they live in the land which thou gavest unto our fathers. 41 Moreover concerning a stranger, that *is* not of thy people Israel, but cometh out of a far country for thy name's sake; 42 (For they shall hear of thy great name, and of thy strong hand, and of thy stretched out arm;) when he shall come and pray toward this house; 43 Hear thou in heaven thy dwelling place, and do according to all that the	49 Then hear thou their pray- er and their supplication in heaven thy dwelling place, and maintain their cause, 50 And forgive thy people that have sinned against thee and all their transgressions wherein they have trans- gressed against thee, and give them compassion before them who carried them cap- tive, that they may have compassion on them: 51 For they *be* thy people, and thine inheritance, which thou broughtest forth out of Egypt, from the midst of the furnace of iron:	3) The request to God • To hear & vindicate them—uphold their cause • To forgive • To stir the enemy to show mercy 4) The reason: They are God's people, His inheritance—saved by Him

OUTLINE	SCRIPTURE	SCRIPTURE	OUTLINE
j. Tenth, that God would see & answer every prayer—all the pleas of His servant & people 1) The circumstance: Any & all cases of need 2) The reason	52 That thine eyes may be open unto the supplication of thy servant, and unto the supplication of thy people Israel, to hearken unto them in all that they call for unto thee. 53 For thou didst separate	them from among all the people of the earth, *to be* thine inheritance, as thou spakest by the hand of Moses thy servant, when thou broughtest our fathers out of Egypt, O Lord GOD.	• They are God's own inheritance • God Himself taught this fact through Moses & the great deliverance from Egypt (a symbol of the world)

a. First, Solomon asked God to keep all His promises (vv.25-26). In particular, he asked God to keep His promise to establish David's dynasty forever (2 S.7:11-16, esp.13, 16). He requested God to fulfill His Word, His promises to David. But again note: Solomon recognized that the promise was conditional. In giving the promise to David, the LORD had laid down the condition: only if David's sons took heed, guarded their walk before God, would the promise be fulfilled. David's successors must obey God if they were to rule upon the throne of Israel. Of course, David's descendants are not ruling in Israel today, for they failed to walk faithfully before the LORD. Nevertheless, the promise was fulfilled in the Ideal Son of David, the Messiah and Savior of the world, the Lord Jesus Christ.

b. Second, Solomon asked God to watch over His people and to always hear their prayers (vv.27-30). In a rhetorical, thought provoking question, Solomon actually declared the *true meaning* of the temple. The temple was not built and did not exist to *contain* the presence of God. It was built to *honor* the Name of God. Heaven, even the highest heaven, could not contain the presence of God. How much less could the temple Solomon had built?

Having declared the meaning, Solomon cried out with three specific pleas:

⇒ for God to watch over the temple night and day, the temple where the very Name of God was honored (v.29)
⇒ for God to hear the prayers of His people Israel (v.30)
⇒ for God to forgive His people Israel (v.30)

c. Third, Solomon asked God to execute justice among the people (vv.31-32). Solomon wanted God to judge the disputes between people, condemning the guilty and establishing the innocence of the righteous. When neighbor mistreated neighbor, it was a violation of God's law that said "love your neighbor as yourself" (Le.19:18). And loving one's neighbor was the second greatest commandment given by God (Mk.12:28-34). Thus when there was a failure to love one's neighbor through some sin or wrongdoing, Solomon prayed that God would discern and reveal the truth about the two contending parties. He prayed that God would execute justice among the citizens of Israel.

d. Fourth, Solomon asked God to hear the prayers of the defeated (vv.33-34). Who were the defeated? Solomon was thinking of Israel as a whole being defeated by an enemy nation, defeated because of some sin they had committed that resulted in God's chastisement falling upon them. But a person can also be defeated by personal circumstances, and this was certainly included in Solomon's prayer. An angry neighbor, financial difficulty, loss of property, rebellious children, disease, accident, the death of a loved one, and a host of other hardships and misfortunes can *defeat* a person. And sometimes difficult circumstances are due to sinful, wicked behavior—not always, but sometimes.

Whether defeat is caused by some national calamity or personal circumstance, the remedy is repentance and confession. Solomon cried out for the LORD to forgive if the people repented and confessed their sin. And in dealing with the national calamity, he asked the LORD to restore the people to the promised land, to bring them back to the land God had given them. In ancient days, a conquering nation enslaved the defeated enemy and took them back home to the conquering nation as slaves. Thus Solomon was asking God to remember His people when they repented and confessed their sins, to forgive and free them from captivity, allowing them to return to the promised land.

e. Fifth, Solomon asked God to hear the prayers of those suffering drought (vv.35-36). Again, Solomon was thinking of a drought caused by the chastisement of God against the sin of His people. No doubt, the drought represents any calamity coming upon the earth that would affect the harvest season. If the calamity was due to the sins of the people, the remedy was confession and repentance.

Knowing this, Solomon cried out for God to forgive their sin and to restore them to the promised land. But this was not all that Solomon asked, for there was another critical issue: the people needed to be taught the right way to live. This was essential in order to keep God's hand of judgment from continuing to fall upon His people, a judgment that would bring other calamities upon them and the land. If the people were living obedient lives, the LORD would look after them and take care of them. He would fulfill all His promises to bless and meet their needs. Thus, it was essential for them to live as they should, living holy and righteous lives.

f. Sixth, Solomon asked God to hear the prayers of those suffering financial disaster or disease (vv.37-40). Note the disastrous circumstances Solomon listed:

⇒ famine
⇒ pestilence or plague
⇒ crop disease
⇒ crop destruction by locusts or grasshoppers
⇒ attack by an enemy nation

Then, being all inclusive, Solomon cried out, pleading that whatever disaster or disease might come—if God's people sought Him and repented of their sin—that He forgive them and execute justice. Note that Solomon acknowledged that God alone knew the hearts of all men. For this reason, the people must learn to fear and obey God, living for Him as they should in the promised land.

The emphasis here is on individual responsibility and acknowledgment of sin. If a person acknowledged his sin and turned to the LORD in obedience, Solomon was asking God to stop the devastation, the disaster or disease that had fallen upon His people. Again, the purpose for his petition was that the people might fear and obey God and learn to live for Him.

g. Seventh, Solomon asked God to hear the prayer of the foreigner (Gentile) who worshipped the LORD (vv.41-43). Throughout the world there would be people who would hear about the LORD and want to be saved. They would hear and see the hand of God's salvation working in and through Israel. Consequently, they would turn to the LORD, seeking and praying for Him to save them. Solomon asked God to hear and answer the request of the foreigner. And note why: that the Name of the LORD might be taken worldwide, that all people everywhere might know and fear the LORD and worship Him. Remember that God had promised Abraham all nations would be blessed through him (Ge.12:1-3).

h. Eighth, Solomon asked God to hear the prayers of soldiers (and the nation) who would be praying for God to give victory over their enemies (vv.44-45). Why should God hear the prayer of a soldier for victory, uphold the cause of one army or nation over another? Because God's people, God's soldiers, are genuine believers who seek the face of the *true and living God*. In the case of the Israelites of Solomon's day, many were *genuine believers* who prayed to the LORD while looking toward the city of Jerusalem and toward the temple that had been built to honor the LORD's Name.

i. Ninth, Solomon asked God to hear the prayer of the sinner who had been captured by the enemy (vv.46-51). The point of this request concerns some national sin or deportation of the nation as a whole to a foreign conqueror. But the point is applicable to the individual believer as well.

1) The circumstance is that of Israel's being guilty of national sin and being chastised by God, being defeated and enslaved by a foreign enemy. The enemy then deported the population, taking the Israelites to some foreign land, whether far or near (v.46).
2) The remedy to their terrible circumstance would be to undergo a change of heart. A change of heart would involve taking three strong actions:
   ⇒ confessing and pleading with God for deliverance (v.47)
   ⇒ repenting and turning back to God wholeheartedly (v.48)
   ⇒ praying for restoration, for being returned to the promised land (v.48)
3) If the Israelites had a change of heart, Solomon asked that God would hear and vindicate them, upholding their cause. He asked God to forgive them and to stir the enemy to show mercy by freeing them and allowing them to return to the promised land (vv.49-50). This would be exactly what happened, as the book of *Ezra* shows.
4) Note the reason Solomon made this request: because they were God's people, His inheritance who had been saved by Him. He had set them free from the enslavement of Egypt (the world).

Remember that this request is applicable to the individual as well as to the nation of Israel as a whole. The commentator Paul R. House has an excellent comment on this particular request of Solomon that is well worth quoting:

> *Solomon's prayer takes on particular importance for the author's audience. Remember that 1, 2 Kings was written for people who had lost the land in the very manner Solomon describes. For them, then, this seventh petition acts as a call to repentance and a program for prayer. It teaches the readers how to restore their relationship with God. At the same time, it provides hope that exile is not God's final word for Israel. The chosen people can return to the promised land when they return to the covenant Lord who gave them the land. In this way Solomon's prayer redeems the time for the book's original, hurting audience.*[2]

j. Tenth, Solomon asked God to answer every prayer of His servant Solomon and of all His people (vv.52-53). He asked God to open His eyes to all the pleas of His people and to listen to them whenever they cried out to the LORD. He was asking God to keep His eyes open for people who were praying and seeking His face and to keep His ears open for any prayer that was ascending up to Him from any of His people. He was begging God to hear any and all cases of need among His people. There are two reasons why Solomon made this all-inclusive request:
⇒ because the LORD had chosen Israel from all the nations of the world to be His own inheritance.
⇒ because the LORD Himself had taught this fact through Moses and demonstrated it through the great deliverance from Egyptian slavery (a symbol of the world).

Thought 1. What a breathtaking prayer! What a prayer warrior! This is a dynamic example of intercessory prayer. God hears and answers prayer. If we truly trust the LORD and are willing to follow Him, God will hear our prayers and meet any need we have:

⇒ stress	⇒ loneliness	⇒ disaster
⇒ pressure	⇒ broken relationships	⇒ abuse
⇒ distress	⇒ financial difficulty	⇒ assault
⇒ discouragement	⇒ disease	⇒ murder
⇒ purposelessness	⇒ accident	⇒ loss of a loved one

All kinds of needs arise in our lives. And the answer to meeting these needs is prayer, seeking the LORD with genuine hearts, crying out to Him for help. When we cry out with genuine hearts, God hears and answers our prayers:

"Ask, and it shall be given you; seek, and ye shall find; knock, and it shall be opened unto you" (Mt.7:7).

"If ye abide in me, and my words abide in you, ye shall ask what ye will, and it shall be done unto you" (Jn.15:7).

---

[2] Paul R. House. *1, 2 Kings*, pp.146-147.

"Hitherto have ye asked nothing in my name: ask, and ye shall receive, that your joy may be full" (Jn.16:24).

"Praying always with all prayer and supplication in the Spirit, and watching thereunto with all perseverance and supplication for all saints" (Ep.6:18).

"Is any among you afflicted? let him pray. Is any merry? let him sing psalms. Is any sick among you? let him call for the elders of the church; and let them pray over him, anointing him with oil in the name of the Lord" (Ja.5:13-14).

"Confess *your* faults one to another, and pray one for another, that ye may be healed. The effectual fervent prayer of a righteous man availeth much" (Ja.5:16).

"And whatsoever we ask, we receive of him, because we keep his commandments, and do those things that are pleasing in his sight" (1 Jn.3:22).

"If my people, which are called by my name, shall humble themselves, and pray, and seek my face, and turn from their wicked ways; then will I hear from heaven, and will forgive their sin, and will heal their land" (2 Chr.7:14).

"He shall call upon me, and I will answer him: I *will be* with him in trouble; I will deliver him, and honour him" (Ps.91:15).

"Then shalt thou call, and the LORD shall answer; thou shalt cry, and he shall say, Here I *am.* If thou take away from the midst of thee the yoke, the putting forth of the finger, and speaking vanity" (Is.58:9).

"And it shall come to pass, that before they call, I will answer; and while they are yet speaking, I will hear" (Is.65:24).

"And ye shall seek me, and find *me,* when ye shall search for me with all your heart" (Je.29:13).

"And I will bring the third part through the fire, and will refine them as silver is refined, and will try them as gold is tried: they shall call on my name, and I will hear them: I will say, It *is* my people: and they shall say, The LORD *is* my God" (Zec.13:9).

CHAPTER 8

J. The Dedication of the Temple (Part 3)—Solomon's Benediction: A Challenge for Obedience & Total Commitment, 8:54-66

8:62-66; see 2 Chr.7:4-10

1. Solomon's praise to the Lord: A lesson on God's rest
   a. His posture in giving the benediction
      1) He arose from praying before the altar
      2) He stood & gave the benediction in a loud voice
   b. His praise to the Lord for keeping His promise to give His people rest

2. Solomon's earnest hope & expectation, Ph.1:20
   a. That the LORD be with His people, never leave nor forsake them
   b. That the LORD turn their hearts to focus upon Him
      • To walk in His ways
      • To obey Him
   c. That his prayer be answered, kept near the LORD—continually day & night
      1) So that God would uphold the cause of His servant & the people—meet their needs each day

54 And it was *so,* that when
Solomon had made an end of
praying all this prayer and
supplication unto the LORD,
he arose from before the altar
of the LORD, from kneeling
on his knees with his hands
spread up to heaven.
55 And he stood, and
blessed all the congregation
of Israel with a loud voice,
saying,
56 Blessed *be* the LORD, that
hath given rest unto his people Israel, according to all
that he promised: there hath
not failed one word of all his
good promise, which he
promised by the hand of Moses his servant.
57 The LORD our God
be with us, as he was
with our fathers: let him
not leave us, nor forsake
us:
58 That he may incline our
hearts unto him, to walk in all
his ways, and to keep his
commandments, and his statutes, and his judgments, which
he commanded our fathers.
59 And let these my words,
wherewith I have made supplication before the LORD,
be nigh unto the LORD our
God day and night, that he
maintain the cause of his
servant, and the cause of his
people Israel at all times, as
the matter shall require:
60 That all the people of the
earth may know that the
LORD *is* God, *and that there
is* none else.
61 Let your heart therefore
be perfect with the LORD our
God, to walk in his statutes,
and to keep his commandments, as at this day.
62 And the king, and all Israel with him, offered sacrifice before the LORD.
63 And Solomon offered a
sacrifice of peace offerings,
which he offered unto the
LORD, two and twenty thousand oxen, and an hundred
and twenty thousand sheep.
So the king and all the children of Israel dedicated the
house of the LORD.
64 The same day did the
king hallow the middle of the
court that *was* before the
house of the LORD: for there
he offered burnt offerings,
and meat offerings, and the
fat of the peace offerings: because the brasen altar that
was before the LORD *was* too
little to receive the burnt offerings, and meat offerings,
and the fat of the peace offerings.
65 And at that time Solomon
held a feast, and all Israel
with him, a great congregation, from the entering in of
Hamath unto the river of
Egypt, before the LORD our
God, seven days and seven
days, *even* fourteen days.
66 On the eighth day he
sent the people away: and
they blessed the king, and
went unto their tents joyful
and glad of heart for all
the goodness that the LORD
had done for David his servant, and for Israel his people.

      2) So that a strong witness would go out to the whole world—proclaiming that the LORD alone is God
   d. That the people would be *totally* committed & obedient to the Lord

3. Solomon's sacrifices to the LORD: A picture of seeking God through the substitute sacrifice of Christ
   a. The large number of sacrifices
      1) 22,000 cattle
      2) 120,000 sheep
   b. The dedication of the central area of the courtyard: To accommodate the large number of sacrifices because the altar area by itself was too small
   c. The great assembly of people attending the festival: People as far away as Lebo Hamath in the north & from the Wadi (river) of Egypt in the south
   d. The importance of the festival: Lasted 14 days
   e. The dismissal of the people & their great joy
      1) They blessed the king
      2) They traveled home filled with joy & rejoicing: Because of the goodness of God & the memorable dedication of the temple

DIVISION I

THE RISE AND REIGN OF SOLOMON AS KING: BEGINNING IN GLORY AND ENDING IN SHAME, 1:1–11:43

J. The Dedication of the Temple (Part 3)—Solomon's Benediction: A Challenge for Obedience and Total Commitment, 8:54-66

(8:54-66) **Introduction**: commitment is essential in life. No matter what our employment is and no matter what task lies out before us, to get the job done and to complete the task, commitment is necessary. Without commitment, no job and no task gets done, not adequately and not sufficiently. Commitment is needed, is absolutely necessary...

- in our marriages and rearing of children
- in our relationships with friends and fellow workers
- in our loyalty and duty to government, school, church, employment, and civic organizations

Without commitment, inefficiency, disorganization, and disintegration take place. In fact, the lack of commitment often destroys our families and organizations and sometimes even human life itself. For that reason, commitment is necessary at all levels of society. Just think what betrayal of a nation means. If we are not loyal and committed to our nation, the consequences can be catastrophic. Think of the damage done by spies and traitors down through history. If we are not loyal to our families, we hurt them deeply, often ruining marriages and shattering the lives of innocent children. And if enough of us are not loyal to our employers, we can even destroy businesses. Commitment is an absolute essential in all of our relationships and dealings.

Commitment or loyalty to the LORD is the theme of this passage of Scripture. Remember the temple is being dedicated by Solomon and the assembly of Israel. Solomon had already given his message to the people and led them in the dedicatory prayer. Now he offers the benediction, his closing blessing upon the people. This is: *The Dedication of the Temple (Part 3)—Solomon's Benediction: A Challenge for Obedience and Total Commitment,* 8:54-66.

1. Solomon's praise to the Lord: a lesson on God's rest (vv.54-56).
2. Solomon's earnest hope and expectation, Ph.1:20 (vv.57-61).
3. Solomon's sacrifices to the LORD: a picture of seeking God through the substitute sacrifice of Christ (vv.62-66).

1 (8:54-56) **Rest, Spiritual, Promise of, Fulfilled—Spiritual Rest, Promise of, Fulfilled—Promises, Rest, Fulfilled—God, Promises of, Rest—Israel, Promises to, Rest—Praise, for What, Rest**: Solomon praised the LORD for the *rest* He had given to His people. Solomon had just finished his memorable prayer on behalf of the people. Now he arose from kneeling before the altar, standing to his feet. With his heart filled with praise, he gave the benediction in a loud voice. He praised the LORD for giving *rest* to His people just as He had promised (v.56). The key word is "rest."

Throughout their history the Israelites had never had a permanent resting place. They had lived an unsettled, itinerant lifestyle. Since the birth of their nation through Abraham, they had been pilgrims and sojourners upon earth. They had wandered about from campsite to campsite, never being able to settle down or own property.

But God had given the Israelites a wonderful promise, the promise of an inheritance in the *promised land* of Canaan. This promise was fulfilled under Joshua. Under his leadership they had received their inheritance, established roots, built homes, and become permanent residents. However, the worship center of the Israelites had never been fixed, never *rested* in one place. Their worship was still held in the *temporary tent* of the Tabernacle. A permanent building had never been constructed.

Under Solomon, though, both the people and their worship center had secured *rest*. The people now had the promised *inheritance* of *physical* and *spiritual rest* in the promised land. Finally, both they and their worship center were firmly established and secure. Physically, they were safeguarded from their enemies and living in peace. They could work at their jobs and carry on their daily activities without ever again having to worry about being uprooted. Moreover, they had *spiritual rest,* for their worship could now be held in the temple, the central worship center of the nation. This was the *rest* of God for which Solomon praised the LORD.

OUTLINE	SCRIPTURE	SCRIPTURE	OUTLINE
1. Solomon's praise to the Lord: A lesson on God's rest a. His posture in giving the benediction 1) He arose from praying before the altar 2) He stood & gave the benediction in a loud	54And it was *so,* that when Solomon had made an end of praying all this prayer and supplication unto the LORD, he arose from before the altar of the LORD, from kneeling on his knees with his hands spread up to heaven. 55 And he stood, and blessed all the congregation of Israel	with a loud voice, saying, 56 Blessed *be* the LORD, that hath given rest unto his people Israel, according to all that he promised: there hath not failed one word of all his good promise, which he promised by the hand of Moses his servant.	voice b. His praise to the Lord for keeping His promise to give His people rest

Thought 1. There is a strong lesson for us in this point: we must trust God for spiritual *rest*. God's *rest* for us means peace of heart and peace of mind, which can only come from God. Spiritual *rest* means...

- the inner sense of purpose, meaning, significance, fulfillment, satisfaction, and confidence
- the assurance that all things are well and will be taken care of by God
- the inner sense of peace and security, no matter what hardship or misfortune, trial or temptation, assault or attack may confront us
- the assurance that we will conquer death and inherit the *promised land,* living eternally with God

How do we secure "spiritual rest"? By coming to the LORD. We must trust and obey Him. If we trust Him and obey His commandments, He will give us a sense of *rest* that literally floods our souls. Listen to what His Holy Word says:

"Come unto me, all *ye* that labour and are heavy laden, and I will give you rest. Take my yoke upon you, and learn of me; for I am meek and lowly in heart: and ye shall find rest unto your souls" (Mt.11:28-29).

"Through the tender mercy of our God; whereby the dayspring from on high hath visited us, To give light to them that sit in darkness and *in* the shadow of death, to guide our feet into the way of peace" (Lu.1:78-79).

"Peace I leave with you, my peace I give unto you: not as the world giveth, give I unto you. Let not your heart be troubled, neither let it be afraid" (Jn.14:27).

"These things I have spoken unto you, that in me ye might have peace. In the world ye shall have tribulation: but be of good cheer; I have overcome the world" (Jn.16:33).

"Harden not your hearts, as in the provocation, in the day of temptation in the wilderness: When your fathers tempted me, proved me, and saw my works forty years. Wherefore I was grieved with that generation, and said, They do alway err in *their* heart; and they have not known my ways. So I sware in my wrath, They shall not enter into my rest" (He.3:8-11).

"And to whom sware he that they should not enter into his rest, but to them that believed not? So we see that they could not enter in because of unbelief" (He.3:18-19).

"Let us therefore fear, lest, a promise being left *us* of entering into his rest, any of you should seem to come short of it. For unto us was the gospel preached, as well as unto them: but the word preached did not profit them, not being mixed with faith in them that heard *it.* For we which have believed do enter into rest, as he said, As I have sworn in my wrath, if they shall enter into my rest: although the works were finished from the foundation of the world" (He.4:1-3).

"There remaineth therefore a rest to the people of God. For he that is entered into his rest, he also hath ceased from his own works, as God *did* from his. Let us labour therefore to enter into that rest, lest any man fall after the same example of unbelief" (He.4:9-11).

"And I heard a voice from heaven saying unto me, Write, Blessed *are* the dead which die in the Lord from henceforth: Yea, saith the Spirit, that they may rest from their labours; and their works do follow them" (Re.14:13).

"And he said, My presence shall go *with thee,* and I will give thee rest" (Ex.33:14).

"I will both lay me down in peace, and sleep: for thou, LORD, only makest me dwell in safety" (Ps.4:8).

"Return unto thy rest, O my soul; for the LORD hath dealt bountifully with thee" (Ps.116:7).

"And it shall come to pass in the day that the LORD shall give thee rest from thy sorrow, and from thy fear, and from the hard bondage wherein thou wast made to serve" (Is.14:3).

"To whom he said, This *is* the rest *wherewith* ye may cause the weary to rest; and this *is* the refreshing: yet they would not hear" (Is.28:12).

"For thus saith the Lord GOD, the Holy One of Israel; In returning and rest shall ye be saved; in quietness and in confidence shall be your strength: and ye would not" (Is.30:15).

2 (8:57-61) **Hope, Source—Expectation, Source—Presence, of God, Seeking—Obedience, Prayer for—Benediction, of Solomon, at Temple Dedication—Temple, Dedication of, Benediction**: Solomon's benediction included four points, points that expressed the great hope and expectation of his heart. Scripture spells out this deep hope and expectation:

OUTLINE	SCRIPTURE	SCRIPTURE	OUTLINE
2. Solomon's earnest hope & expectation, Ph.1:20 a. That the LORD be with His people, never leave nor forsake them b. That the LORD turn their hearts to focus upon Him • To walk in His ways • To obey Him c. That his prayer be answered, kept near the LORD—continually day & night 1) So that God would uphold	57 The LORD our God be with us, as he was with our fathers: let him not leave us, nor forsake us: 58 That he may incline our hearts unto him, to walk in all his ways, and to keep his commandments, and his statutes, and his judgments, which he commanded our fathers. 59 And let these my words, wherewith I have made supplication before the LORD, be nigh unto the LORD our	God day and night, that he maintain the cause of his servant, and the cause of his people Israel at all times, as the matter shall require: 60 That all the people of the earth may know that the LORD *is* God, *and that there is* none else. 61 Let your heart therefore be perfect with the LORD our God, to walk in his statutes, and to keep his commandments, as at this day.	the cause of His servant & the people—meet their needs each day 2) So that a strong witness would go out to the whole world—proclaiming that the LORD alone is God d. That the people would be *totally* committed & obedient to the Lord

a. Solomon expressed the hope that the LORD would be with His people, never leave nor forsake them (v.57). He knew that the presence of God was an absolute essential if the people were to keep the *rest* of God. Living in peace, security, and prosperity; never lacking anything; having a deep sense of purpose, fulfillment, and satisfaction; being victorious over all the hardships and misfortunes of life; all this and so much more would all be dependent upon the LORD's presence. If the LORD was present with them, they would neither lack nor fail in life. They would be empowered to conquer, overcome, succeed, and be victorious in life.

"For where two or three are gathered together in my name, there am I in the midst of them" (Mt.18:20).

"...lo, I am with you alway, *even* unto the end of the world. Amen" (Mt.28:20).

"So that we may boldly say, The Lord *is* my helper, and I will not fear what man shall do unto me" (He.13:6).

"And, behold, I *am* with thee, and will keep thee in all *places* whither thou goest, and will bring thee again into this land; for I will not leave thee, until I have done *that* which I have spoken to thee of" (Ge.28:15).

"And he said, My presence shall go *with thee,* and I will give thee rest" (Ex.33:14).

"When thou goest out to battle against thine enemies, and seest horses, and chariots, *and* a people more than thou, be not afraid of them: for the LORD thy God *is* with thee, which brought thee up out of the land of Egypt" (De.20:1).

"The LORD *is* my strength and my shield; my heart trusted in him, and I am helped: therefore my heart greatly rejoiceth; and with my song will I praise him" (Ps.28:7).

"But I *am* poor and needy; *yet* the Lord thinketh upon me: thou *art* my help and my deliverer; make no tarrying, O my God" (Ps.40:17).

"Fear thou not; for I *am* with thee: be not dismayed; for I *am* thy God: I will strengthen thee; yea, I will help thee; yea, I will uphold thee with the right hand of my righteousness" (Is.41:10).

"When thou passest through the waters, I *will be* with thee; and through the rivers, they shall not overflow thee: when thou walkest through the fire, thou shalt not be burned; neither shall the flame kindle upon thee" (Is.43:2).

b. Solomon's great hope was that the LORD would turn their hearts to focus upon Him (v.58). In fact, the LORD would be with them and grant His presence only if the people did focus upon Him, walking in His ways and obeying Him. It was an absolute essential for the people to keep the commandments of God if the people wanted the *rest*, the blessings of God. Their relationship with God began with God in their hearts, with their hearts turning to Him. And that involved obedience, a commitment to walk in all of His ways and to keep all of His commandments.

"Not every one that saith unto me, Lord, Lord, shall enter into the kingdom of heaven; but he that doeth the will of my Father which is in heaven. Many will say to me in that day, Lord, Lord, have we not prophesied in thy name? and in thy name have cast out devils? and in thy name done many wonderful works? And then will I profess unto them, I never knew you: depart from me, ye that work iniquity" (Mt.7:21-23).

"And he said unto him, Why callest thou me good? *there is* none good but one, *that is,* God: but if thou wilt enter into life, keep the commandments" (Mt.19:17).

"For this is the love of God, that we keep his commandments: and his commandments are not grievous" (1 Jn.5:3).

"Thou shalt keep therefore his statutes, and his commandments, which I command thee this day, that it may go well with thee, and with thy children after thee, and that thou mayest prolong *thy* days upon the earth, which the LORD thy God giveth thee, for ever" (De.4:40).

"Ye shall diligently keep the commandments of the LORD your God, and his testimonies, and his statutes, which he hath commanded thee" (De.6:17).

"This day the LORD thy God hath commanded thee to do these statutes and judgments: thou shalt therefore keep and do them with all thine heart, and with all thy soul" (De.26:16).

"This book of the law shall not depart out of thy mouth; but thou shalt meditate therein day and night, that thou mayest observe to do according to all that is written therein: for then thou shalt make thy way prosperous, and then thou shalt have good success" (Jos.1:8).

"And Samuel said, Hath the LORD *as great* delight in burnt offerings and sacrifices, as in obeying the voice of the LORD? Behold, to obey *is* better than sacrifice, *and* to hearken than the fat of rams" (1 S.15:22).

"And keep the charge of the LORD thy God, to walk in his ways, to keep his statutes, and his commandments, and his judgments, and his testimonies, as it is written in the law of Moses, that thou mayest prosper in all that thou doest, and whithersoever thou turnest thyself" (1 K.2:3).

"That they might set their hope in God, and not forget the works of God, but keep his commandments" (Ps.78:7).

c. Solomon's great hope was that his prayer would be answered, kept very near to the heart of the LORD—continually day and night (vv.59-60). He wanted God to hear the prayer that he had just prayed for two reasons:

⇒ So that God would uphold the cause of His servant and people by meeting their daily needs.

⇒ So that a strong witness would go out to the whole world, proclaiming that the LORD alone is God (v.60). Solomon's heart burned with a passion for all the peoples of the earth to know the LORD personally. They needed to know that He and He alone is the LORD God of the universe.

Remember that Solomon's heart was bursting with joy and rejoicing in the LORD, for the LORD had descended upon the Tabernacle in a spectacular manifestation of His presence (8:10-13). The LORD had accepted the temple as the place that was to honor His Name. And the LORD had done so much for Israel by giving them the promised *rest* in the promised land, the inheritance that He had promised ever since the day of Abraham. Such a wonderful knowledge of the LORD and such a wonderful experience of His blessings—all this Solomon wanted the whole world to know and experience.

"And ye also shall bear witness, because ye have been with me from the beginning" (Jn.15:27).

"But ye shall receive power, after that the Holy Ghost is come upon you: and ye shall be witnesses unto me both in Jerusalem, and in all Judaea, and in Samaria, and unto the uttermost part of the earth" (Ac.1:8).

"For we cannot but speak the things which we have seen and heard" (Ac.4:20).

"Go, stand and speak in the temple to the people all the words of this life. And when they heard *that,* they entered into the temple early in the morning, and taught. But the high priest came, and they

that were with him, and called the council together, and all the senate of the children of Israel and sent to the prison to have them brought" (Ac.5:20-21).

"For thou shalt be his witness unto all men of what thou hast seen and heard" (Ac.22:15).

"For God hath not given us the spirit of fear; but of power, and of love, and of a sound mind" (2 Ti.1:7).

"But sanctify the Lord God in your hearts: and *be* ready always to *give* an answer to every man that asketh you a reason of the hope that is in you with meekness and fear" (1 Pe.3:15).

"Ye *are* my witnesses, saith the LORD, and my servant whom I have chosen: that ye may know and believe me, and understand that I *am* he: before me there was no God formed, neither shall there be after me" (Is.43:10).

d. Solomon hoped and expected the people to be totally committed and obedient to the LORD (v.61). In closing the benediction, Solomon pleaded with the Israelites to be faithful, fully committed to their covenant with the LORD. In the words of Paul R. House:

Each new generation must choose to follow the LORD. Abraham, Moses, Joshua and David have shown Solomon and his subjects how to obey the LORD, but they must now follow their ancestors' example.[1]

"Not every one that saith unto me, Lord, Lord, shall enter into the kingdom of heaven; but he that doeth the will of my Father which is in heaven. Many will say to me in that day, Lord, Lord, have we not prophesied in thy name? and in thy name have cast out devils? and in thy name done many wonderful works? And then will I profess unto them, I never knew you: depart from me, ye that work iniquity" (Mt.7:21-23).

"I beseech you therefore, brethren, by the mercies of God, that ye present your bodies a living sacrifice, holy, acceptable unto God, *which is* your reasonable service. And be not conformed to this world: but be ye transformed by the renewing of your mind, that ye may prove what is that good, and acceptable, and perfect, will of God" (Ro.12:1-2).

"I am crucified with Christ: nevertheless I live; yet not I, but Christ liveth in me: and the life which I now live in the flesh I live by the faith of the Son of God, who loved me, and gave himself for me" (Ga.2:20).

"For Moses had said, Consecrate yourselves to day to the LORD, even every man upon his son, and upon his brother; that he may bestow upon you a blessing this day" (Ex.32:29).

"And thou shalt love the LORD thy God with all thine heart, and with all thy soul, and with all thy might" (De.6:5).

"This book of the law shall not depart out of thy mouth; but thou shalt meditate therein day and night, that thou mayest observe to do according to all that is written therein: for then thou shalt make thy way prosperous, and then thou shalt have good success" (Jos.1:8).

"Now therefore fear the LORD, and serve him in sincerity and in truth: and put away the gods which your fathers served on the other side of the flood, and in Egypt; and serve ye the LORD. And if it seem evil unto you to serve the LORD, choose you this day whom ye will serve; whether the gods which your fathers served that *were* on the other side of the flood, or the gods of the Amorites, in whose land ye dwell: but as for me and my house, we will serve the LORD" (Jos.24:14-15).

"...And who *then* is willing to consecrate his service this day unto the LORD?" (1 Chr.29:5).

"Blessed *are* they that keep his testimonies, *and that* seek him with the whole heart" (Ps.119:2).

"My son, give me thine heart, and let thine eyes observe my ways" (Pr.23:26).

3 (8:62-66) **Sacrifice, of Animals, Example of—Christ, Sacrifice of, Symbolized by—Animal Sacrifice, Symbol of—Animal Sacrifice, Example of, Temple Dedication—Temple, Dedication of**: Solomon offered thousands of sacrifices to the LORD at the conclusion of the temple's dedication. Remember, the dedication service had been planned around the Festival of Tabernacles. Scripture describes an incredible scene:

OUTLINE	SCRIPTURE	SCRIPTURE	OUTLINE
3. Solomon's sacrifices to the LORD: A picture of seeking God through the substitute sacrifice of Christ a. The large number of sacrifices 1) 22,000 cattle 2) 120,000 sheep b. The dedication of the central	62 And the king, and all Israel with him, offered sacrifice before the LORD. 63 And Solomon offered a sacrifice of peace offerings, which he offered unto the LORD, two and twenty thousand oxen, and an hundred and twenty thousand sheep. So the king and all the children of Israel dedicated the house of the LORD. 64 The same day did the king	hallow the middle of the court that *was* before the house of the LORD: for there he offered burnt offerings, and meat offerings, and the fat of the peace offerings: because the brasen altar that *was* before the LORD *was* too little to receive the burnt offerings, and meat offerings, and the fat of the peace offerings. 65 And at that time Solomon held a feast, and all Israel	area of the courtyard: To accommodate the large number of sacrifices because the altar area by itself was too small c. The great assembly of people attending the festival: People

[1] Paul R. House. *1, 2 Kings*, p.148.

OUTLINE	SCRIPTURE	SCRIPTURE	OUTLINE
as far away as Lebo Hamath in the north & from the Wadi (river) of Egypt in the south d. The importance of the festival: Lasted 14 days e. The dismissal of the people	with him, a great congregation, from the entering in of Hamath unto the river of Egypt, before the LORD our God, seven days and seven days, *even* fourteen days. 66 On the eighth day he sent	the people away: and they blessed the king, and went unto their tents joyful and glad of heart for all the goodness that the LORD had done for David his servant, and for Israel his people.	& their great joy 1) They blessed the king 2) They traveled home filled with joy & rejoicing: Because of the goodness of God & the memorable dedication of the temple

a. A large, almost incomprehensible number of sacrifices were made (v.63). About 22,000 oxen and 120,000 sheep were sacrificed in offerings to the LORD. Priests were obviously using auxiliary altars over a period of two weeks (v.65).

b. Solomon consecrated, set apart the central area of the courtyard in front of the temple so that sacrifices could be made there (v.64). An area had to be consecrated to the LORD for sacrifices to be allowed. The major bronze altar, upon which sacrifices were usually made, was just too small to handle all the offerings being made by the multitudes who had attended the dedication service.

c. A huge assembly of people was attending the festival (v.65). They had come from as far away as Lebo Hamath in the north to the Wadi (river) of Egypt in the south.

d. The importance of this particular festival cannot be overstated, for it was the very festival at which the temple was dedicated (v.65). Because of its significance and the mass of people who had attended, the festival was extended from the required seven days to fourteen days, a full two weeks.

e. On the following day—the fifteenth day—Solomon dismissed the people (v.66). Note the joy that was flooding their hearts. Before leaving they blessed the king, then began their journey home. As they traveled home they were filled with joy and rejoicing because of the goodness of God and the memorable dedication of the temple.

Thought 1. The sacrifice of animals always picture the atonement or reconciliation between God and man. It was an offering that symbolized the perfect sacrifice, the *sacrificial substitute* that would take the place of man, bear his sins, and bear the judgment of God against sins. Simply stated, atonement means to redeem, to pay the price for. The perfect atonement, the substitute without defect and without blemish, is Jesus Christ, God's very own Son. Jesus Christ paid the price, the penalty of sin for man. He is the perfect sacrifice and substitute who died for man, on behalf of man, in the place of man, instead of man. This is exactly what God's Holy Word declares:

"The next day John seeth Jesus coming unto him, and saith, Behold the Lamb of God, which taketh away the sin of the world" (Jn.1:29).

"I am the good shepherd: the good shepherd giveth his life for the sheep" (Jn.10:11).

"For when we were yet without strength, in due time Christ died for the ungodly" (Ro.5:6).

"Purge out therefore the old leaven, that ye may be a new lump, as ye are unleavened. For even Christ our passover is sacrificed for us" (1 Co.5:7).

"Who gave himself for our sins, that he might deliver us from this present evil world, according to the will of God and our Father" (Ga.1:4).

"And walk in love, as Christ also hath loved us, and hath given himself for us an offering and a sacrifice to God for a sweetsmelling savour" (Ep.5:2).

"Who gave himself for us, that he might redeem us from all iniquity, and purify unto himself a peculiar people, zealous of good works" (Tit.2:14).

"But we see Jesus, who was made a little lower than the angels for the suffering of death, crowned with glory and honour; that he by the grace of God should taste death for every man" (He.2:9).

"Forasmuch as ye know that ye were not redeemed with corruptible things, *as* silver and gold, from your vain conversation *received* by tradition from your fathers; But with the precious blood of Christ, as of a lamb without blemish and without spot" (1 Pe.1:18-19).

"Who his own self bare our sins in his own body on the tree, that we, being dead to sins, should live unto righteousness: by whose stripes ye were healed" (1 Pe.2:24).

"For Christ also hath once suffered for sins, the just for the unjust, that he might bring us to God, being put to death in the flesh, but quickened by the Spirit" (1 Pe.3:18).

"Hereby perceive we the love *of God,* because he laid down his life for us: and we ought to lay down *our* lives for the brethren" (1 Jn.3:16).

"...Unto him that loved us, and washed us from our sins in his own blood" (Re.1:5).

"But he *was* wounded for our transgressions, *he was* bruised for our iniquities: the chastisement of our peace *was* upon him; and with his stripes we are healed" (Is.53:5).

1. God's encounter with Solomon: The blessings for obedience & the judgment for disobedience
- a. God's timing: After all projects were completed
- b. God's appearance: Was the same as at Gibeon, at night in a dream, 3:4-15
- c. God's assurance of answered prayer
  - 1) He had consecrated the temple by putting His Name there forever
  - 2) He would always keep His eyes & heart on the temple
- d. God's promise of blessings—if obedient
  - 1) The condition: Must walk in integrity, righteousness, & obedience
  - 2) The promise: A permanent dynasty—his sons would rule after him, 3:4-15; 6:11-13
- e. God's warning of judgment—if disobedient
  - 1) The warning against apostasy, turning away
    - By disobeying
    - By false worship
  - 2) The judgment
    - Will be cut off from the promised land
    - Will see the temple & worship rejected by God
    - Will be mocked & ridiculed by people
    - Will suffer terrible destruction: So much that people will hiss & mock & question & be appalled at so terrible a destruction
    - Will bear the terrible testimony of apostasy & idolatry: Because they had turned away from the LORD who had saved them & had embraced false gods & false worship

CHAPTER 9

K. The Second Appearance of God to Solomon & Solomon's Achievements: A Need to Be Obedient & Diligent in Life & Work, 9:1-28

9:1-9; see 2 Chr.7:11-22
9:10-28; see 2 Chr.8:1-18

And it came to pass, when
Solomon had finished the
building of the house of the
LORD, and the king's house,
and all Solomon's desire
which he was pleased to do,
2 That the LORD appeared to
Solomon the second time, as
he had appeared unto him at
Gibeon.
3 And the LORD said unto
him, I have heard thy prayer
and thy supplication, that
thou hast made before me: I
have hallowed this house,
which thou hast built, to put
my name there for ever; and
mine eyes and mine heart
shall be there perpetually.
4 And if thou wilt walk before me, as David thy father
walked, in integrity of heart,
and in uprightness, to do according to all that I have
commanded thee, *and* wilt
keep my statutes and my
judgments:
5 Then I will establish the
throne of thy kingdom upon
Israel for ever, as I promised
to David thy father, saying,
There shall not fail thee a
man upon the throne of
Israel.
6 *But* if ye shall at all turn
from following me, ye or
your children, and will not
keep my commandments *and*
my statutes which I have set
before you, but go and serve
other gods, and worship
them:
7 Then will I cut off Israel
out of the land which I have
given them; and this house,
which I have hallowed for
my name, will I cast out of
my sight; and Israel shall be a
proverb and a byword among
all people:
8 And at this house, *which*
is high, every one that passeth
by it shall be astonished, and
shall hiss; and they shall say,
Why hath the LORD done thus
unto this land, and to this
house?
9 And they shall answer, Because they forsook the LORD
their God, who brought forth
their fathers out of the land of
Egypt, and have taken hold
upon other gods, and have
worshipped them, and served
them: therefore hath the
LORD brought upon them all
this evil.
10 And it came to pass at the
end of twenty years, when
Solomon had built the two
houses, the house of the
LORD, and the king's house,
11 (*Now* Hiram the king of
Tyre had furnished Solomon
with cedar trees and fir trees,
and with gold, according to
all his desire,) that then king
Solomon gave Hiram twenty
cities in the land of Galilee.
12 And Hiram came out
from Tyre to see the cities
which Solomon had given
him; and they pleased him
not.
13 And he said, What cities
are these which thou hast
given me, my brother? And
he called them the land of
Cabul unto this day.
14 And Hiram sent to the
king sixscore talents of gold.
15 And this *is* the reason
of the levy which king Solomon raised; for to build the
house of the LORD, and his
own house, and Millo, and
the wall of Jerusalem, and
Hazor, and Megiddo, and
Gezer.
16 *For* Pharaoh king of
Egypt had gone up, and taken
Gezer, and burnt it with fire,
and slain the Canaanites that
dwelt in the city, and given it
for a present unto his daughter, Solomon's wife.
17 And Solomon built
Gezer, and Beth-horon the
nether,
18 And Baalath, and Tadmor
in the wilderness, in the land,
19 And all the cities of store
that Solomon had, and cities
for his chariots, and cities for
his horsemen, and that which
Solomon desired to build in
Jerusalem, and in Lebanon,
and in all the land of his dominion.
20 *And* all the people *that*
were left of the Amorites,
Hittites, Perizzites, Hivites,
and Jebusites, which *were* not

2. Solomon's pursuits & achievements: A picture of faithfulness, diligence, & hard work
- a. He built the temple & royal palace
- b. He sought to build a strong treasury: By replenishing the depleted funds or gold
  - 1) He gave King Hiram 20 border towns as collateral
  - 2) Hiram inspected the towns
    - Considered them useless
    - Taunted & teased Solomon
    - Called the towns "Cabul" (worthless) & returned them, 2 Chr.8:1-2
  - 3) Hiram had given Solomon 4 metric tons of gold
- c. He pursued a strong construction & public works program: By building & rebuilding
  - 1) The temple & palace
  - 2) The fortified terraces
  - 3) The wall of Jerusalem
  - 4) The cities of Hazor, Megiddo, & Gezer
    - Gezer was conquered & destroyed by Pharaoh & given as a wedding gift to his daughter when she married Solomon
    - Gezer was rebuilt
  - 5) The city of Lower Beth Horon
  - 6) The cities of Baalath & Tadmor
  - 7) The cities that served as supply centers
  - 8) The cities that housed his chariots & horses
- d. He drafted a huge labor or work force
  - 1) Drafted, recruited labor from the conquered nations

• The surviving descendants • The tragic fact: Forced or slave labor was still widely practiced up to the writing of *1 Kings*	of the children of Israel, 21 Their children that were left after them in the land, whom the children of Israel also were not able utterly to destroy, upon those did Solomon levy a tribute of bondservice unto this day.	then did he build Millo. 25 And three times in a year did Solomon offer burnt offerings and peace offerings upon the altar which he built unto the LORD, and he burnt incense upon the altar that *was* before the LORD. So he finished the house.	ace built especially for her f. He sought to establish a strong religious foundation for the nation: The Feasts of Unleavened Bread, Pentecost, & Tabernacles, Ex.23:14-19; De.16:16-17
2) Temporarily drafted the Israelites • Not as permanent slaves, but as temporary forced laborers, 5:13-18 • Not just as laborers but as soldiers, officers, government officials, & supervisors of the work projects	22 But of the children of Israel did Solomon make no bondmen: but they *were* men of war, and his servants, and his princes, and his captains, and rulers of his chariots, and his horsemen. 23 These *were* the chief of the officers that *were* over Solomon's work, five hundred and fifty, which bare rule over the people that wrought in the work.	26 And king Solomon made a navy of ships in Eziongeber, which is beside Eloth, on the shore of the Red sea, in the land of Edom. 27 And Hiram sent in the navy his servants, shipmen that had knowledge of the sea, with the servants of Solomon.	g. He built a fleet of ships for commercial purposes 1) A joint venture with King Hiram
e. He built the Millo, a fortified system of terraces within Jerusalem: After Pharaoh's daughter moved into the pal-	24 But Pharaoh's daughter came up out of the city of David unto her house which *Solomon* had built for her:	28 And they came to Ophir, and fetched from thence gold, four hundred and twenty talents, and brought *it* to king Solomon.	2) An example of the trade: Solomon received 420 talents of gold (16 tons) from trade with Ophir

DIVISION I

THE RISE AND REIGN OF SOLOMON AS KING: BEGINNING IN GLORY AND ENDING IN SHAME, 1:1–11:43

K. The Second Appearance of God to Solomon and Solomon's Achievements: A Need to Be Obedient and Diligent in Life and Work, 9:1-28

(9:1-28) **Introduction**: we all have some duty, some obligation to every person we know and to society in general. We do not live on an island, isolated from every other person. Even if we were isolated, we would still be obligated, have the duty to provide for our own survival. Duties or obligations permeate every aspect of our lives. For example:

⇒ We have a duty to be friendly and kind to everyone we know.

⇒ We have the obligation to cultivate friendliness and kindness within society—within our communities, workplaces, schools, and the halls of justice and government.

When considering the workplace, look at our obligation to be good employees, working hard and diligently. We must always give a fair day's work for a full day's wages. When it comes to our schools, think about the duties of the teachers and those of the students. Within our families, think about the duties, the obligations of every family member to be faithful, loyal, kind, supportive, and loving, and to contribute toward building a strong family.

In considering any area of life, we have personal obligations toward all the people and relationships involved. If a relationship revolves around us, we have a duty to strengthen and build this relationship. By faithfully fulfilling our duties and obligations, we strengthen society.

The concern of the present passage of Scripture is the duties and obligations that faced King Solomon. Solomon was obligated to obey God and to be a faithful, diligent, hardworking king on behalf of the Israelites. Before God, Solomon was obligated to fulfill his task, and to fulfill it faithfully and diligently. This is the subject of the present passage of Scripture: *The Second Appearance of God to Solomon and Solomon's Achievements: A Need to Be Obedient and Diligent in Life and Work,* 9:1-28.

1. God's encounter with Solomon: the blessings for obedience and the judgment for disobedience (vv.1-9).
2. Solomon's economic pursuits and achievements: a picture of faithfulness, diligence, and hard work (vv.10-28).

1 (9:1-9) **Obedience, Results of—Disobedience, Results of, Judgment—Vision, of Solomon—Prayer, Answered, Example of—Judgment, Warning of—Temple, Consecrated by God—Judgment, of Israel, Warning**: God encountered Solomon a second time after Solomon had spent twenty years completing his building projects. He had been reigning over Israel for a total of twenty-four years (v.10; 6:1; 7:1). It seems as though God needed to give Solomon a warning, for Solomon was beginning to disobey the LORD. He was engaging in false worship and allowing his heart to turn away from the LORD (11:4, 9). In an attempt to stop Solomon from turning away and slipping into apostasy, God issued a strong warning. Scripture gives the details of God's appearance, His warning:

OUTLINE	SCRIPTURE	SCRIPTURE	OUTLINE
1. God's encounter with Solomon: The blessings for obedience & the judgment for disobedience a. God's timing: After all projects were completed b. God's appearance: Was the same as at Gibeon, at night in a dream, 3:4-15 c. God's assurance of answered prayer 1) He had consecrated the temple by putting His Name there forever 2) He would always keep His eyes & heart on the temple d. God's promise of blessings—if obedient 1) The condition: Must walk in integrity, righteousness, & obedience 2) The promise: A permanent dynasty—his sons would rule after him, 3:4-15; 6:11-13	And it came to pass, when Solomon had finished the building of the house of the LORD, and the king's house, and all Solomon's desire which he was pleased to do, 2 That the LORD appeared to Solomon the second time, as he had appeared unto him at Gibeon. 3 And the LORD said unto him, I have heard thy prayer and thy supplication, that thou hast made before me: I have hallowed this house, which thou hast built, to put my name there for ever; and mine eyes and mine heart shall be there perpetually. 4 And if thou wilt walk be- fore me, as David thy father walked, in integrity of heart, and in uprightness, to do ac- cording to all that I have commanded thee, *and* wilt keep my statutes and my judgments: 5 Then I will establish the throne of thy kingdom upon Israel for ever, as I promised to David thy fa- ther, saying, There shall not fail thee a man upon the	throne of Israel. 6 *But* if ye shall at all turn from following me, ye or your children, and will not keep my commandments *and* my statutes which I have set before you, but go and serve other gods, and worship them: 7 Then will I cut off Israel out of the land which I have given them; and this house, which I have hallowed for my name, will I cast out of my sight; and Israel shall be a proverb and a byword among all people: 8 And at this house, *which* is high, every one that passeth by it shall be astonished, and shall hiss; and they shall say, Why hath the LORD done thus unto this land, and to this house? 9 And they shall answer, Because they forsook the LORD their God, who brought forth their fathers out of the land of Egypt, and have taken hold upon other gods, and have worshipped them, and served them: therefore hath the LORD brought upon them all this evil.	e. God's warning of judgment—if disobedient 1) The warning against apostasy, turning away • By disobeying • By false worship 2) The judgment • Will be cut off from the promised land • Will see the temple & worship rejected by God • Will be mocked & ridiculed by people • Will suffer terrible destruction: So much that people will hiss & mock & question & be appalled at so terrible a destruction • Will bear the terrible testimony of apostasy & idolatry: Because they had turned away from the LORD who had saved them & had embraced false gods & false worship

a. God encountered Solomon after all his building projects were completed, including the temple and the palace complexes (v.1). Having completed these projects was a significant achievement for Solomon and, no doubt, was a significant relief for him. The pressure of such mammoth building projects was now lifted from his shoulders. It was a pivotal time in Solomon's life. For this reason, it was an ideal time for God to confront Solomon and to issue a warning to him. God could now renew the covenant relationship with Solomon, assure him of God's presence if obedient but of God's judgment if disobedient.

b. God had already honored Solomon with His presence by appearing to him at Gibeon in a dream (3:4-15). Now He was honoring him with His presence a second time, just as He had done before (v.2). God appeared to Solomon for the purpose of assuring him that his prayer had been answered (v.3). Note that God Himself had *consecrated* the temple by putting His name there forever. It was not consecrated as a place of worship because of the ceremonies, rituals, and services held by the people. It was set apart and made holy for one reason and one reason only: because God accepted the temple as a place where His Name could be honored. As long as the Israelites honored God's Name in the temple, He would always keep His eyes and heart on the temple. He would watch over its care and welfare, holding it ever so dear to His heart.

c. God's second purpose for appearing to Solomon was that of promising to bless him personally. But to be blessed, he had to remain obedient to the LORD (v.4). God's blessing was conditional. Solomon must walk with integrity, living a life of righteousness and obedience just as his father David had. If he obeyed the commandments of the LORD, he could expect the most wonderful promise: a permanent dynasty. His sons would rule upon the throne of Israel after him (3:12-14; 6:11-13).

d. God also had a third purpose for appearing to Solomon, that of warning him of judgment if he disobeyed the LORD (vv.6-9). In particular, God revealed the shocking judgments that would fall upon Solomon and his people if they committed apostasy. If they turned away from God or engaged in false worship or idolatry, they would suffer the hand of God's judgment (v.6). Note that the judgments are applicable to any generation of people who disobey and turn to false worship:

⇒ They would be cut off from the promised land.
⇒ They would see their temple (church) and worship rejected by God.
⇒ They would be mocked and ridiculed by people (v.7).
⇒ They would suffer terrible destruction, so much destruction that some people would hiss and mock, whereas others would question and be appalled at the devastation of their land (v.8).
⇒ They would bear the shameful testimony of apostasy and idolatry. They would be accused of hypocrisy because they had turned away from the LORD and had embraced false gods and false worship (v.9).

These are the frightening consequences that result from false worship, from turning away from the LORD and committing apostasy against Him. The judgments spelled out are serious, very serious. Some commentators say that the word *cut off* (karat, v.7) often means that a person is cut off or excluded from the fellowship of God's people (Le.17:4, 9; Nu.19:20). The word *reject* (sillah, v.7) is the very same word used for a man who divorces his wife. Thus the idea seems to be that the person will be divorced, cut off, separated from the LORD—a very serious warning. And the word *byword* (masal, v.7) indicates a terrible calamity coming upon a person (De.28:37; Ps.64:3; Je.24:9).[1]

Thought 1. Just as Solomon was warned by God, so we are warned. God demands obedience, demands that we keep His commandments. If we keep them, we will be blessed. But if we disobey God, ignore and fail to keep His commandments, we will face the hand of His judgment. Listen to what God's Holy Word says about obedience and disobedience:

(1) If we obey God, we will receive the blessings of God.

"Therefore whosoever heareth these sayings of mine, and doeth them, I will liken him unto a wise man, which built his house upon a rock: And the rain descended, and the floods came, and the winds blew, and beat upon that house; and it fell not: for it was founded upon a rock" (Mt.7:24-25).

"For whosoever shall do the will of my Father which is in heaven, the same is my brother, and sister, and mother" (Mt.12:50).

"Jesus answered and said unto him, If a man love me, he will keep my words: and my Father will love him, and we will come unto him, and make our abode with him" (Jn.14:23).

"If ye keep my commandments, ye shall abide in my love; even as I have kept my Father's commandments, and abide in his love" (Jn.15:10).

"But whoso looketh into the perfect law of liberty, and continueth *therein,* he being not a forgetful hearer, but a doer of the work, this man shall be blessed in his deed" (Ja.1:25).

"And whatsoever we ask, we receive of him, because we keep his commandments, and do those things that are pleasing in his sight" (1 Jn.3:22).

"Blessed *are* they that do his commandments, that they may have right to the tree of life, and may enter in through the gates into the city" (Re.22:14).

"Now therefore, if ye will obey my voice indeed, and keep my covenant, then ye shall be a peculiar treasure unto me above all people: for all the earth *is* mine" (Ex.19:5).

"O that there were such an heart in them, that they would fear me, and keep all my commandments always, that it might be well with them, and with their children for ever!" (De.5:29).

"This book of the law shall not depart out of thy mouth; but thou shalt meditate therein day and night, that thou mayest observe to do according to all that is written therein: for then thou shalt make thy way prosperous, and then thou shalt have good success" (Jos.1:8).

(2) If we disobey God, the hand of God's chastisement and judgment will fall upon us.

"And every one that heareth these sayings of mine, and doeth them not, shall be likened unto a foolish man, which built his house upon the sand: And the rain descended, and the floods came, and the winds blew, and beat upon that house; and it fell: and great was the fall of it" (Mt.7:26-27).

"But fornication, and all uncleanness, or covetousness, let it not be once named among you, as becometh saints; Neither filthiness, nor foolish talking, nor jesting, which are not convenient: but rather giving of thanks. For this ye know, that no whoremonger, nor unclean person, nor covetous man, who is an idolater, hath any inheritance in the kingdom of Christ and of God. Let no man deceive you with vain words: for because of these things cometh the wrath of God upon the children of disobedience" (Ep.5:3-6).

"And to you who are troubled rest with us, when the Lord Jesus shall be revealed from heaven with his mighty angels, In flaming fire taking vengeance on them that know not God, and that obey not the gospel of our Lord Jesus Christ: Who shall be punished with everlasting destruction from the presence of the Lord, and from the glory of his power" (2 Th.1:7-9).

"For if the word spoken by angels was stedfast, and every transgression and disobedience received a just recompence of reward; How shall we escape, if we neglect so great salvation; which at the first began to be spoken by the Lord, and was confirmed unto us by them that heard *him*" (He.2:2-3).

"And a curse, if ye will not obey the commandments of the LORD your God, but turn aside out of the way which I command you this day, to go after other gods, which ye have not known" (De.11:28).

"But if ye will not obey the voice of the LORD, but rebel against the commandment of the LORD, then shall the hand of the LORD be against you, as *it was* against your fathers" (1 S.12:15).

2 (9:10-28) **Diligence, Example of—Wealth, Example of—Hard Work, Example of—Achievement, Example of—Pursuit, Example of—Solomon, Achievements of**: Solomon's pursuits and achievements are covered in the remaining section of this chapter. Under Solomon, Israel became the most wealthy, powerful, and dominant nation of that day and time. Just how Solomon achieved this wealth and power is explained in the seven points covered by the Scripture:

---

1 Richard D. Patterson and Hermann J. Austel. *1, 2 Kings*, p.94.
Also Paul R. House. *1, 2 Kings*, p.151.

<table>
<tr><th>OUTLINE</th><th>SCRIPTURE</th><th>SCRIPTURE</th><th>OUTLINE</th></tr>
<tr>
<td>2. Solomon's pursuits & achievements: A picture of faithfulness, diligence, & hard work
a. He built the temple & royal palace
b. He sought to build a strong treasury: By replenishing the depleted funds or gold
1) He gave King Hiram 20 border towns as collateral
2) Hiram inspected the towns
• Considered them useless
• Taunted & teased Solomon
• Called the towns "Cabul" (worthless) & returned them, 2 Chr.8:1-2
3) Hiram had given Solomon 4 metric tons of gold
c. He pursued a strong construction & public works program: By building & rebuilding
1) The temple & palace
2) The fortified terraces
3) The wall of Jerusalem
4) The cities of Hazor, Megiddo, & Gezer
• Gezer was conquered & destroyed by Pharaoh & given as a wedding gift to his daughter when she married Solomon
• Gezer was rebuilt
5) The city of Lower Beth Horon
6) The cities of Baalath & Tadmor
7) The cities that served as supply centers
8) The cities that housed his chariots & horses
d. He drafted a huge labor or</td>
<td>10 And it came to pass at the
end of twenty years, when
Solomon had built the two
houses, the house of the
LORD, and the king's house,
11 (Now Hiram the king of
Tyre had furnished Solomon
with cedar trees and fir trees,
and with gold, according to
all his desire,) that then king
Solomon gave Hiram twenty
cities in the land of Galilee.
12 And Hiram came out
from Tyre to see the cities
which Solomon had given him;
and they pleased him not.
13 And he said, What cities
are these which thou hast
given me, my brother? And
he called them the land of
Cabul unto this day.
14 And Hiram sent to the
king sixscore talents of gold.
15 And this is the reason
of the levy which king Solo-
mon raised; for to build the
house of the LORD, and his
own house, and Millo, and
the wall of Jerusalem, and
Hazor, and Megiddo, and
Gezer.
16 For Pharaoh king of
Egypt had gone up, and taken
Gezer, and burnt it with fire,
and slain the Canaanites that
dwelt in the city, and given it
for a present unto his daugh-
ter, Solomon's wife.
17 And Solomon built
Gezer, and Beth-horon the
nether,
18 And Baalath, and Tadmor
in the wilderness, in the land,
19 And all the cities of store
that Solomon had, and cities
for his chariots, and cities for
his horsemen, and that which
Solomon desired to build in
Jerusalem, and in Lebanon,
and in all the land of his do-
minion.
20 And all the people that</td>
<td>were left of the Amorites,
Hittites, Perizzites, Hivites,
and Jebusites, which were
not of the children of Israel,
21 Their children that were
left after them in the land,
whom the children of Israel
also were not able utterly to
destroy, upon those did Sol-
omon levy a tribute of bond-
service unto this day.
22 But of the children of Is-
rael did Solomon make no
bondmen: but they were men
of war, and his servants, and
his princes, and his captains,
and rulers of his chariots, and
his horsemen.
23 These were the chief of
the officers that were over
Solomon's work, five hun-
dred and fifty, which bare
rule over the people that
wrought in the work.
24 But Pharaoh's daughter
came up out of the city of
David unto her house which
Solomon had built for her:
then did he build Millo.
25 And three times in a year
did Solomon offer burnt of-
ferings and peace offerings
upon the altar which he built
unto the LORD, and he burnt
incense upon the altar that
was before the LORD. So he
finished the house.
26 And king Solomon made
a navy of ships in Ezion-
geber, which is beside Eloth,
on the shore of the Red sea,
in the land of Edom.
27 And Hiram sent in the
navy his servants, shipmen
that had knowledge of the
sea, with the servants of Sol-
omon.
28 And they came to Ophir,
and fetched from thence
gold, four hundred and twen-
ty talents, and brought it to
king Solomon.</td>
<td>work force
1) Drafted, recruited labor from the conquered nations
• The surviving descendants
• The tragic fact: Forced or slave labor was still widely practiced up to the writing of 1 Kings
2) Temporarily drafted the Israelites
• Not as permanent slaves, but as temporary forced laborers, 5:13-18
• Not just as laborers but as soldiers, officers, government officials, & supervisors of the work projects
e. He built the Millo, a fortified system of terraces within Jerusalem: After Pharaoh's daughter moved into the palace built especially for her
f. He sought to establish a strong religious foundation for the nation: The Feasts of Unleavened Bread, Pentecost, & Tabernacles, Ex.23:14-19; De.16:16-17
g. He built a fleet of ships for commercial purposes
1) A joint venture with King Hiram
2) An example of the trade: Solomon received 420 talents of gold (16 tons) from trade with Ophir</td>
</tr>
</table>

a. Solomon built the temple and royal palace complex (v.10). Both construction achievements were wonders to behold in the ancient world, as has been explained in earlier Scriptures (see outline and notes—1 K.6:1-38; 7:1-51).

b. Solomon sought to build a strong treasury by replenishing the depleted funds and gold that had been used in the massive building projects (vv.11-14). During the twenty years of construction, he apparently ran short of funds and became indebted to King Hiram of Tyre. For this reason, he gave King Hiram twenty border towns close to the capital Tyre in exchange for additional materials and gold. These were offered either as payment or as collateral until such time as Solomon could secure the funds to repay King Hiram.

When King Hiram inspected the towns, he considered them useless, taunting and teasing Solomon over giving him such worthless cities. Later Scripture indicates that he returned the cities to Solomon, expecting payment instead of the cities (2 Chr.8:1-2). Some form of payment was expected, for Hiram had given Solomon four metric tons or 9,000 pounds of gold.

It was the close relationship with King Hiram that enabled Solomon to continue and complete his building projects. In light of this fact, Solomon owed a great deal to his friend Hiram, for without his help it is unlikely Solomon could have achieved fame as a great builder. The commentator Paul R. House suggests that this particular episode shows a "conniving side" of Solomon, suggesting that he perhaps was not entirely trustworthy at this point of his life.[2]

c. Solomon pursued a strong construction and public works program that included the following (vv.15-19):
1) Solomon built the temple and palace mentioned in point one above (v.15).
2) Solomon built the Millo in the city of Jerusalem. This was either fortified terraces or a tower.
3) Solomon reinforced the wall of Jerusalem and perhaps added sections to it.
4) Solomon built the cities of Hazor, Megiddo, and Gezer (vv.15-17). The latter, Gezer, had been conquered and destroyed by Pharaoh and given as a wedding gift to his daughter when she married Solomon. After the marriage, Solomon rebuilt the city.
5) Solomon built the city of Lower Beth Horon (v.17).
6) Solomon built the cities of Baalath and Tadmor, which were two cities in the wilderness or desert located in the tribe of Judah (v.18).
7) In addition, Solomon built several cities to serve as supply centers (v.19).
8) Solomon also had cities built to house his chariots and horses (v.19).

d. All the building projects undertaken by Solomon required a huge labor or work force (v.20). These he drafted or recruited from the conquered nations, the nations Israel had failed to exterminate (vv.20-21). These were permanent laborers, workers who were forced to work year-round in the building projects. And note this tragic fact: forced or slave labor was still widely practiced up "to this day," referring to the day of the author himself.

However, Solomon did not make slaves of the Israelites (vv.22-23). He drafted them in a temporary work force with the unskilled serving as laborers and the skilled as soldiers, officers, government officials, and supervisors of the work projects. The Israelites were drafted to work in government service one out of every three months, which amounted to one fourth of a year, a heavy demand that was bound to cause stress and strain and take its toll upon families, businesses, farms, and relationships (see outline and note—1 K.5:13-18 for more discussion).

e. Solomon built the Millo, a fortified terrace (mounds or rampart) built up with earth and stones within the city of Jerusalem (v.24). Note that he built this after he had married Pharaoh's daughter and moved her into the palace built especially for her (7:8).

f. Solomon also sought to establish a strong religious foundation for the nation (v.25). As soon as the temple was finished, Solomon obviously began to focus the worship of the people at the temple. To do this, he instituted the three major feasts of the Israelites (see outline and notes—Ex.23:14-17; De.16:16-17 for more discussion):

⇒ There was the feast of unleavened bread, which celebrated God's great deliverance from Egyptian slavery through the blood of the Passover lamb. This feast reminded the people of their hasty exodus from Egypt.

⇒ There was the Feast of Harvest or Feast of Weeks, which celebrated the first fruits of the harvest. This pointed to the beginning of the law on Mount Sinai.

⇒ There was the Feast of Tabernacles, a weeklong feast when the people built simple hut-like structures and spent the week in them. This was to remind the people of their wilderness wanderings during the forty years when they had to live in tents as they journeyed to the promised land.

g. Lastly, Solomon built a fleet of ships for commercial purposes (vv.26-28). This was a joint venture with King Hiram, with Israel building the ships and King Hiram providing the sailors to man the ships. As an example of the commercial trade, Solomon received 420 talents or sixteen tons of gold from trading with Ophir (v.28). Apparently the ships made a round-trip journey to Ophir every three years (10:22).

Thought 1. This lesson is a clear picture of Solomon's faithfulness to the LORD and to the people of Israel. It shows his diligence and hard work to bring about a strong economy and to maintain the peace of the nation. His devotion, steadfastness, and fervor are dynamic examples for us. Whatever tasks we undertake, we must be faithful to finish the work. No matter what the demands are, we must work hard and be diligent, doing whatever is necessary to complete the job.

Looking around at the work force today, a person can become discouraged. Far too many workers appear lazy and lack initiative. They react against instruction and expose sour, negative attitudes. They do as little as they can and show limited appreciation for the privilege of having a job. As a result, their contribution to the service of society is minimal. With such behavior, God is very displeased. God demands that we be faithful, diligent, and hard-working, doing the best we can and making a significant contribution to society—not slothful or lazy. This is the clear teaching of God's Holy Word:

"Not slothful in business; fervent in spirit; serving the Lord" (Ro.12:11).

"Moreover it is required in stewards, that a man be found faithful" (1 Co.4:2).

"Therefore, my beloved brethren, be ye stedfast, unmovable, always abounding in the work of the Lord, forasmuch as ye know that your labour is not in vain in the Lord" (1 Co.15:58).

"Let him that stole steal no more: but rather let him labour, working with *his* hands the thing which is good, that he may have to give to him that needeth" (Ep.4:28).

"And whatsoever ye do in word or deed, *do* all in the name of the Lord Jesus, giving thanks to God and the Father by him" (Col.3:17).

"And whatsoever ye do, do *it* heartily, as to the Lord, and not unto men" (Col.3:23).

"Now them that are such we command and exhort by our Lord Jesus Christ, that with quietness they work, and eat their own bread" (2 Th.3:12).

---

[2] Paul R. House. *1, 2 Kings*, p.157.

"Nevertheless we, according to his promise, look for new heavens and a new earth, wherein dwelleth righteousness. Wherefore, beloved, seeing that ye look for such things, be diligent that ye may be found of him in peace, without spot, and blameless" (2 Pe.3:13-14).

"And the LORD God took the man, and put him into the garden of Eden to dress it and to keep it" (Ge.2:15).

"In the sweat of thy face shalt thou eat bread, till thou return unto the ground; for out of it wast thou taken: for dust thou *art,* and unto dust shalt thou return" (Ge.3:19).

"Go to the ant, thou sluggard; consider her ways, and be wise" (Pr.6:6).

"He becometh poor that dealeth *with* a slack hand: but the hand of the diligent maketh rich" (Pr.10:4).

"He that gathereth in summer *is* a wise son: *but* he that sleepeth in harvest *is* a son that causeth shame" (Pr.10:5).

"He that tilleth his land shall be satisfied with bread: but he that followeth vain *persons is* void of understanding" (Pr.12:11).

"The soul of the sluggard desireth, and *hath* nothing: but the soul of the diligent shall be made fat" (Pr.13:4).

"In all labour there is profit: but the talk of the lips *tendeth* only to penury" (Pr.14:23).

"Love not sleep, lest thou come to poverty; open thine eyes, *and* thou shalt be satisfied with bread" (Pr.20:13).

"Whatsoever thy hand findeth to do, do *it* with thy might; for *there is* no work, nor device, nor knowledge, nor wisdom, in the grave, whither thou goest" (Ec.9:10).

CHAPTER 10

L. The Wisdom, Wealth, & Power of Solomon: A Picture of Seeking Truth & of Being Materially Blessed by God, 10:1-29

10:1-13; see 2 Chr.9:1-12
10:14-29; see 2 Chr.1:14-17; 9:13-28

1. The Queen of Sheba's testimony about Solomon's wisdom: A picture of seeking truth, Mt.12:42
- a. Her purpose: To test Solomon, seeking answers to the great questions of life
- b. Her great caravan: Camels carried trade goods of spices, gold, & jewels—a trip of 1500 miles from SW Arabia or Yemen to Jerusalem
- c. Her discovery: Solomon excelled in wisdom
  - 1) She discussed all that was on her mind & he answered all her questions
  - 2) She was overwhelmed with the wisdom of Solomon & the splendor of everything
    - The royal palace
    - The banquet feasts
    - The officials & servants & their royal clothing
    - The approach to God through the burnt offering or substitute sacrifice: A symbol of Christ
- d. Her admission to Solomon
  - 1) The report of his achievements & wisdom were true
  - 2) The report had been difficult to believe—until she came & saw for herself: In fact, half was not known; his wisdom & wealth far exceeded the report
  - 3) The officials of his court were very privileged: To be continually exposed to his wise counsel & instructions
- e. Her praise to the LORD
  - 1) For choosing Solomon to rule Israel
  - 2) For the LORD's eternal love for Israel
  - 3) For establishing Solomon as king to maintain justice & righteousness
- f. Her expression of appreciation to Solomon
  - 1) Her gifts: 120 talents (9000 pounds) of gold; large quantities of spices, & precious jewels
  - 2) Her gifts added to the enormous wealth Solomon had gained from his trade agreement with King Hiram: Gold, almugwood, & precious jewels
    - The almugwood was used to make support beams for the temple & palace & to make musical instruments
    - The quantity of almugwood imported was more than ever before or after
- g. Her desires & requests met
  - 1) Solomon gave & traded whatever she wanted
  - 2) The queen returned home with her caravan

2. The Scriptures' testimony about Solomon's wealth: A picture of God's material blessing
- a. His yearly tax revenues were enormous: 666 talents (about 25 tons) of gold plus the tolls or tariffs from traders & rulers
- b. His 500 ceremonial shields were made of hammered gold
  - 1) The 200 large shields: Each had 15 pounds of gold
  - 2) The 300 small shields: Each had 4 pounds of gold
  - 3) The shields were kept in the Palace of the Forest of Lebanon
- c. His ivory throne was overlaid with pure gold
  - 1) It had 6 steps
  - 2) It had a back with a rounded top
  - 3) It had armrests with one lion figure standing beside each
  - 4) It had 12 lion figures on the steps, one at both ends of each step
  - 5) Its splendor exceeded any ever made
- d. His drinking cups & household utensils were made of pure gold: Not made of silver, because silver was so common it was of little value, 27

And when the queen of Sheba heard of the fame of Solomon concerning the name
of the LORD, she came to
prove him with hard ques-
tions.
2 And she came to Jerusalem
with a very great train, with
camels that bare spices, and
very much gold, and precious
stones: and when she was
come to Solomon, she com-
muned with him of all that
was in her heart.
3 And Solomon told her all
her questions: there was not
any thing hid from the king,
which he told her not.
4 And when the queen of
Sheba had seen all Solo-
mon's wisdom, and the
house that he had built,
5 And the meat of his table,
and the sitting of his servants, and the attendance of
his min-isters, and their apparel, and his cupbearers,
and his ascent by which he
went up unto the house of
the LORD; there was no
more spirit in her.
6 And she said to the king, It
was a true report that I heard
in mine own land of thy acts
and of thy wisdom.
7 Howbeit I believed not the
words, until I came, and
mine eyes had seen *it:* and,
behold, the half was not told
me: thy wisdom and pros-
perity exceedeth the fame
which I heard.
8 Happy *are* thy men, happy
are these thy servants, which
stand continually before thee,
and that hear thy wisdom.
9 Blessed be the LORD thy
God, which delighted in
thee, to set thee on the
throne of Israel: because the
LORD loved Israel for ever,
therefore made he thee
king, to do judgment and
justice.
10 And she gave the king an
hundred and twenty talents
of gold, and of spices very
great store, and precious
stones: there came no more
such abundance of spices as
these which the queen of
Sheba gave to king Solomon.
11 And the navy also of
Hiram, that brought gold from
Ophir, brought in from
Ophir great plenty of almug
trees, and precious stones.
12 And the king made of
the almug trees pillars for the
house of the LORD, and for the
king's house, harps also and
psalteries for singers: there
came no such almug trees,
nor were seen unto this day.
13 And king Solomon gave
unto the queen of Sheba all
her desire, whatsoever she
asked, beside *that* which
Solomon gave her of his
royal bounty. So she turned
and went to her own coun-
try, she and her servants.
14 Now the weight of gold
that came to Solomon in one
year was six hundred threescore and six talents of gold.
15 Beside *that he had* of the
merchantmen, and of the
traffick of the spice merchants, and of all the kings
of Arabia, and of the governors of the country.
16 And king Solomon made
two hundred targets of beat-
en gold: six hundred *shekels*
of gold went to one target.
17 And he made three hun-
dred shields of beaten gold;
three pound of gold went to
one shield: and the king put
them in the house of the forest of Lebanon.
18 Moreover the king made
a great throne of ivory, and
overlaid it with the best
gold.
19 The throne had six steps,
and the top of the throne *was*
round behind: and *there*
were stays on either side on
the place of the seat, and
two lions stood beside the
stays.
20 And twelve lions stood
there on the one side and on
the other upon the six steps:
there was not the like made
in any kingdom.
21 And all king Solomon's
drinking vessels *were of* gold,
and all the vessels of the
house of the forest of Lebanon *were of* pure gold; none
were of silver: it was nothing
accounted of in the days of

e. His fleet of merchant (deep sea) ships were very valuable, 9:26-28 1) A joint venture with King Hiram 2) A very profitable trade in metals & animals f. His wealth & wisdom exceeded that of all the kings of the earth 1) All sought an audience with him: Seeking his wise counsel (to improve their economies & welfare) 2) All brought gifts that added enormously to his wealth g. His wealth included 1400 chariots & 12,000 horses:	Solomon. 22 For the king had at sea a navy of Tharshish with the navy of Hiram: once in three years came the navy of Tharshish, bringing gold, and silver, ivory, and apes, and peacocks. 23 So king Solomon exceeded all the kings of the earth for riches and for wisdom. 24 And all the earth sought to Solomon, to hear his wisdom, which God had put in his heart. 25 And they brought every man his present, vessels of silver, and vessels of gold, and garments, and armour, and spices, horses, and mules, a rate year by year. 26 And Solomon gathered together chariots and horse	men: and he had a thousand and four hundred chariots, and twelve thousand horsemen, whom he bestowed in the cities for chariots, and with the king at Jerusalem. 27 And the king made silver *to be* in Jerusalem as stones, and cedars made he *to be* as the sycamore trees that *are* in the vale, for abundance. 28 And Solomon had horses brought out of Egypt, and linen yarn: the king's merchants received the linen yarn at a price. 29 And a chariot came u and went out of Egypt for six hundred *shekels* of silver, and an horse for an hundred and fifty: and so for all the kings of the Hittites, and for the kings of Syria, did they bring *them* out by their means.	All kept in chariot cities (built for this very purpose, 9:19) h. His wealth was so great that silver became as common as stones & cedar as common as sycamore trees i. His import & export business was lucrative: Traded horses & chariots 1) Secured from Egypt & the city of Keveh or Kue • A chariot cost 600 pieces of silver • A horse cost 150 pieces of silver 2) Exported & sold to the Hittite & Aramean kings

DIVISION I

THE RISE AND REIGN OF SOLOMON AS KING: BEGINNING IN GLORY AND ENDING IN SHAME, 1:1–11:43

L. The Wisdom, Wealth, and Power of Solomon: A Picture of Seeking Truth and of Being Materially Blessed by God, 10:1-29

(10:1-29) **Introduction**: What is the purpose of life? Who are we? Where did we really come from? Did we come through a process called evolution? Or from the hand of God? Or from nothing, just appearing out of nowhere? Also, why are we here upon earth? And where are we going? What is our end, the end of mankind?

The great philosophical questions of life cross the minds of most of us sometime during our lives. And each of us begins to wonder: What is the purpose of it all? What am I really here for? Where am I going after death? Is there life after death as preachers say, or is it the end of life as atheists say?

In thinking about these issues, many people wish they had the answers and knew the truth. They say to themselves, "If I only knew, I would know what to do and how to behave, know whether I could live as I wanted as the atheists and agnostics say or whether I must live a life of self-control, discipline, and righteousness as the preachers say."

Seeking after the truth is what the present Scripture focuses upon. One of the most fascinating stories in all the Bible is seen in the Queen of Sheba's search for truth. And in her search, she gives a strong testimony to the wisdom of Solomon and his relationship to the LORD. This is: *The Wisdom, Wealth, and Power of Solomon: A Picture of Seeking Truth and of Being Materially Blessed by God,* 10:1-29.

1. The Queen of Sheba's testimony about Solomon's wisdom: a picture of seeking truth (vv.1-13).
2. The Scriptures' testimony about Solomon's wealth: a picture of God's material blessing (vv.14-29).

1 (10:1-13) **Truth, Seeking—Insight, Seeking—Wisdom, Seeking, Example of—Queen of Sheba, Example of, Seeking Truth—Spiritual Insight, Seeking, Example of**: there was the Queen of Sheba's testimony about Solomon's wisdom. This is an intriguing story that later drew comments from the Lord Jesus when He was upon earth. In condemning the Pharisees for their unbelief, Jesus commended the Queen of Sheba for having traveled from the uttermost part of the earth to seek wisdom and truth from Solomon (Mt.12:42). Her traveling such a great distance shows just how much Solomon's fame and strong testimony for the LORD had impacted the world of his day. Scripture gives a graphic description of the queen's seeking truth from Solomon:

OUTLINE	SCRIPTURE	SCRIPTURE	OUTLINE
1. The Queen of Sheba's testimony about Solomon's wisdom: A picture of seeking truth, Mt.12:42 a. Her purpose: To test Solomon, seeking answers to the great questions of life	And when the queen of Sheba heard of the fame of Solomon concerning the name of the LORD, she came to prove him with hard questions.	2 And she came to Jerusalem with a very great train, with camels that bare spices, and very much gold, and precious stones: and when she was come to Solomon, she communed	b. Her great caravan: Camels carried trade goods of spices, gold, & jewels—a trip of 1500 miles from SW Arabia or Yemen to Jerusalem c. Her discovery: Solomon

OUTLINE	SCRIPTURE	SCRIPTURE	OUTLINE
excelled in wisdom 1) She discussed all that was on her mind & he answered all her questions	with him of all that was in her heart. 3 And Solomon told her all her questions: there was not *any* thing hid from the king, which he told her not.	thee, to set thee on the throne of Israel: because the LORD loved Israel for ever, therefore made he thee king, to do judgment and justice.	rule Israel 2) For the LORD's eternal love for Israel 3) For establishing Solomon as king to maintain justice & righteousness
2) She was overwhelmed with the wisdom of Solomon & the splendor of everything • The royal palace • The banquet feasts • The officials & servants & their royal clothing • The approach to God through the burnt offering or substitute sacrifice: A symbol of Christ	4 And when the queen of Sheba had seen all Solomon's wisdom, and the house that he had built, 5 And the meat of his table, and the sitting of his servants, and the attendance of his ministers, and their apparel, and his cupbearers, and his ascent by which he went up unto the house of the LORD; there was no more spirit in her.	10 And she gave the king an hundred and twenty talents of gold, and of spices very great store, and precious stones: there came no more such abundance of spices as these which the queen of Sheba gave to king Solomon. 11 And the navy also of Hiram, that brought gold from Ophir, brought in from Ophir great plenty of almug trees, and precious stones.	f. Her expression of appreciation to Solomon 1) Her gifts: 120 talents (9000 pounds) of gold; large quantities of spices, & precious jewels 2) Her gifts added to the enormous wealth Solomon had gained from his trade agreement with King Hiram: Gold, almugwood, & precious jewels
d. Her admission to Solomon 1) The report of his achievements & wisdom were true 2) The report had been difficult to believe—until she came & saw for herself: In fact, half was not known; his wisdom & wealth far exceeded the report	6 And she said to the king, It was a true report that I heard in mine own land of thy acts and of thy wisdom. 7 Howbeit I believed not the words, until I came, and mine eyes had seen *it:* and, behold, the half was not told me: thy wisdom and prosperity exceedeth the fame which I heard.	12 And the king made of the almug trees pillars for the house of the LORD, and for the king's house, harps also and psalteries for singers: there came no such almug trees, nor were seen unto this day.	• The almugwood was used to make support beams for the temple & palace & to make musical instruments • The quantity of almugwood imported was more than ever before or after
3) The officials of his court were very privileged: To be continually exposed to his wise counsel & instructions e. Her praise to the LORD 1) For choosing Solomon to	8 Happy *are* thy men, happy *are* these thy servants, which stand continually before thee, *and* that hear thy wisdom. 9 Blessed be the Lord thy God, which delighted in	13 And king Solomon gave unto the queen of Sheba all her desire, whatsoever she asked, beside *that* which Solomon gave her of his royal bounty. So she turned and went to her own country, she and her servants.	g. Her desires & requests met 1) Solomon gave & traded whatever she wanted 2) The queen returned home with her caravan

a. The purpose for the queen's visit was to test Solomon, to seek answers to the great questions of life (v.1). Within diplomatic circles of that day, it was the practice to test the wisdom of an official by posing hard questions to him. But in the queen's case, her purpose far exceeded this mental combat. Note what the verse said: she had heard about Solomon's fame and his relation to "the Name of the LORD." This reference to the LORD and the statement of Jesus Christ in Mt.12:42 strongly indicate that she was seeking spiritual insight from the wisdom of Solomon. Seeking the answers to the great questions of life obviously aroused a hunger in her heart to know the truth.

b. The great caravan of the queen included camels carrying large quantities of spices, gold, and precious jewels (v.2). Note that Sheba was a country some 1,500 miles from Israel, located in southwest Arabia or modern-day Yemen. For a woman to travel by chariot or camel on a journey of 1,500 miles in the ancient world, even if she was a queen, was a staggering event, perhaps unheard of in the ancient world. Whatever the case, this is a strong indication of the deep, spiritual hunger within her soul. If all she wanted was intellectual combat, no doubt she could have found challenging diplomats much closer to her home. Keep in mind also that the queen was not the wife of a king who was ruling the nation Sheba: she herself was the ruler.

c. In her own words, the queen's discovery far exceeded anything she could have imagined: Solomon excelled in wisdom (vv.2-5). She discussed all that was on her mind. As pointed out, she was obviously seeking truth and insight, answers to the great, perplexing questions of life. No doubt, the questions included those asked by every generation: What is the source, purpose, meaning, significance, and end of life? Or, to state it another way:

⇒ Who are we?
⇒ Where did we come from?
⇒ Why are we here?
⇒ Where are we going?

Solomon answered all of her questions, and nothing was too hard for him to explain to her. She was overwhelmed with the wisdom of Solomon and the splendor of everything she saw, including...

- the royal palace
- the banquet feast
- the organization of the officials, the government, the servants, and their royal clothing
- the magnificence of the entryway by which the king entered the temple. Note: her being overwhelmed may refer to the king's humble approach to God through the burnt offering or substitute sacrifice. Keep in mind that the burnt offering or substitute sacrifice was a symbol of Christ. (See NIV and other translations of the Hebrew.)

d. Overwhelmed, the Queen of Sheba admitted to Solomon that the report of his achievements and wisdom was certainly true (vv.6-8). Prior to her coming, the report had been difficult to believe. But now, since she had come, she saw for herself. In fact, half was not known: Solomon's wisdom and wealth far exceeded any report she had ever heard (v.7). Thereupon she exclaimed how happy the officials of his court must be because of their great privilege, the privilege of being continually exposed to his wise counsel and understanding (v.8).

e. Then note what the Queen of Sheba did: she gave praise to the LORD God of Solomon (v.9). She was declaring that Solomon's God, the LORD Himself, deserved to be honored for three reasons:

⇒ for choosing Solomon to rule the Israelites
⇒ for the Lord's eternal love for Israel, a love demonstrated in the covenant relationship that He established with the Israelites
⇒ for establishing Solomon as king for the purpose of maintaining justice and righteousness within Israel

Note how the Queen of Sheba acknowledged that God had established a very special covenant relationship with Israel, that He had chosen them to be His people because of their faith in Him. Keep in mind that King Hiram had also acknowledged the LORD's hand upon the Israelites. Both of these rulers acknowledged a fact that King Solomon and the Israelites were soon to forget (see outline and notes—1 K.11:1-43 for more discussion).

f. The Queen of Sheba gave King Solomon a number of gifts that were of enormous value: 120 talents or 9,000 pounds of gold, large quantities of spices, and precious jewels (vv.10-12). In fact, she gave more spices than Solomon ever received on any other single occasion. Spices were used for seasoning food and drink as well as for providing a fresh and pleasing fragrance for the home, worship services, and places of business. They were also used in embalming bodies.

The gifts added to the enormous wealth Solomon had gained from his trade agreement with King Hiram (vv.11-12). The trade agreement had included gold, almugwood, and some precious jewels. The almugwood had been used to make support beams for the temple and the palace and to make musical instruments. In fact, more almugwood had been imported than ever before or after.

g. The queen's desires and requests were met by Solomon (v.13). He gave and traded whatever she wanted. Afterward, she returned home with her caravan.

Thought 1. The commentator Russell Dilday has an excellent application on the Queen of Sheba's visit to Solomon, an application that is well worth quoting in its entirety:

Here is another of those biblical references to God's missionary purpose for His chosen people. The story of a foreign queen drawn to the wisdom of Israel from a distant land is a picture of the true relation Israel was to have with other nations in God's plan. They were not to be competing with other nations for wealth and military power. They were not to be at war with other nations, but they were chosen to point other nations to God. They were to be a light to enlighten the Gentiles.

It is obvious that the queen came for some purpose more serious than exchanging riddles with the wise king. A journey of fifteen hundred miles is too long and the rigors of travel in that century across desert lands too demanding for such a trivial purpose. The gifts were too great, the cost too high for her to have come just to satisfy her curiosity about the rumors she had heard. She must have been a serious seeker after deeper truth. She must have had a yearning, a hunger for God that drove her to Jerusalem. She came to Solomon tortured by eternal questions, and apparently the king was so anxious to show her the secular glories of his kingdom that he forgot the noble purpose for which he and the nation had been chosen. It's a tragedy easily repeated by individuals and churches today.

When Jesus used the queen of Sheba as an illustration in Matthew 12, He pointed to the fact that she was a seeker, and that she was to be commended for her quest. At great sacrifice, humility, and effort she made her way to the best source of truth available to her. The passage has a lesson for desperate seekers today. A greater than Solomon has come. His wisdom is infinitely greater. His power is greater. He is the way and the truth. Every question has its ultimate answer in Him. He is the satisfaction of every yearning. And when we meet Him, we too find that the half has not been told. He is greater than our highest expectations.[1]

"And when he was gone forth into the way, there came one running, and kneeled to him, and asked him, Good Master, what shall I do that I may inherit eternal life?" (Mk.10:17).

"And he sought to see Jesus who he was; and could not for the press, because he was little of stature" (Lu.19:3).

"And all the people came early in the morning to him in the temple, for to hear him" (Lu.21:38).

"So when the Samaritans were come unto him, they besought him that he would tarry with them: and he abode there two days" (Jn.4:40).

"The same came therefore to Philip, which was of Bethsaida of Galilee, and desired him, saying, Sir, we would see Jesus" (Jn.12:21).

"And I, if I be lifted up from the earth, will draw all *men* unto me" (Jn.12:32).

"Immediately therefore I sent to thee; and thou hast well done that thou art come. Now therefore are we all here present before God, to hear all things that are commanded thee of God" (Ac.10:33).

"And when the Jews were gone out of the synagogue, the Gentiles besought that these words might be preached to them the next sabbath" (Ac.13:42).

"These were more noble than those in Thessalonica, in that they received the word with all readiness of mind, and searched the Scriptures daily, whether those things were so" (Ac.17:11).

---

[1] Russell Dilday, *1, 2 Kings*, p.124.

"But if from thence thou shalt seek the LORD thy God, thou shalt find *him,* if thou seek him with all thy heart and with all thy soul" (De.4:29).

"My soul thirsteth for God, for the living God: when shall I come and appear before God?" (Ps.42:2).

"O God, thou *art* my God; early will I seek thee: my soul thirsteth for thee, my flesh longeth for thee in a dry and thirsty land, where no water is" (Ps.63:1).

"Seek the LORD, and his strength: seek his face evermore" (Ps.105:4).

"Seek ye the LORD while he may be found, call ye upon him while he is near" (Is.55:6).

"And ye shall seek me, and find *me,* when ye shall search for me with all your heart" (Je.29:13).

"Sow to yourselves in righteousness, reap in mercy; break up your fallow ground: for *it is* time to seek the LORD, till he come and rain righteousness upon you" (Ho.10:12).

"For thus saith the LORD unto the house of Israel, Seek ye me, and ye shall live" (Am.5:4).

"Seek ye the LORD, all ye meek of the earth, which have wrought his judgment; seek righteousness, seek meekness: it may be ye shall be hid in the day of the LORD'S anger" (Zep.2:3).

2 (10:14-29) **Blessings, Material, of God—Material Blessings, of God, Example of—Wealth, Example of—Riches, Example of—Solomon, Wealth of**: there is the Scripture's testimony about the enormous wealth of Solomon. This is a striking picture of God's material blessings upon Solomon:

OUTLINE	SCRIPTURE	SCRIPTURE	OUTLINE
2. The Scriptures' testimony about Solomon's wealth: A picture of God's material blessing a. His yearly tax revenues were enormous: 666 talents (about 25 tons) of gold plus the tolls or tariffs from traders & rulers b. His 500 ceremonial shields were made of hammered gold 1) The 200 large shields: Each had 15 pounds of gold 2) The 300 small shields: Each had 4 pounds of gold 3) The shields were kept in the Palace of the Forest of Lebanon c. His ivory throne was overlaid with pure gold 1) It had 6 steps 2) It had a back with a rounded top 3) It had armrests with one lion figure standing beside each 4) It had 12 lion figures on the steps, one at both ends of each step 5) Its splendor exceeded any ever made d. His drinking cups & household utensils were made of pure gold: Not made of silver, because silver was so common it was of little value, 27 e. His fleet of merchant (deep sea) ships were very valuable, 9:26-28	14 Now the weight of gold that came to Solomon in one year was six hundred threescore and six talents of gold. 15 Beside *that he had* of the merchantmen, and of the traffick of the spice merchants, and of all the kings of Arabia, and of the governors of the country. 16 And king Solomon made two hundred targets of beaten gold: six hundred *shekels* of gold went to one target. 17 And he made three hundred shields of beaten gold; three pound of gold went to one shield: and the king put them in the house of the forest of Lebanon. 18 Moreover the king made a great throne of ivory, and overlaid it with the best gold. 19 The throne had six steps, and the top of the throne *was* round behind: and *there were* stays on either side on the place of the seat, and two lions stood beside the stays. 20 And twelve lions stood there on the one side and on the other upon the six steps: there was not the like made in any kingdom. 21 And all king Solomon's drinking vessels *were of* gold, and all the vessels of the house of the forest of Lebanon *were of* pure gold; none *were of* silver: it was nothing accounted of in the days of Solomon. 22 For the king had at sea a navy of Tharshish with the navy of Hiram: once in three	years came the navy of Tharshish, bringing gold, and silver, ivory, and apes, and peacocks. 23 So king Solomon exceeded all the kings of the earth for riches and for wisdom. 24 And all the earth sought to Solomon, to hear his wisdom, which God had put in his heart. 25 And they brought every man his present, vessels of silver, and vessels of gold, and garments, and armour, and spices, horses, and mules, a rate year by year. 26 And Solomon gathered together chariots and horsemen: and he had a thousand and four hundred chariots, and twelve thousand horsemen, whom he bestowed in the cities for chariots, and with the king at Jerusalem. 27 And the king made silver *to be* in Jerusalem as stones, and cedars made he *to be* as the sycamore trees that *are* in the vale, for abundance. 28 And Solomon had horses brought out of Egypt, and linen yarn: the king's merchants received the linen yarn at a price. 29 And a chariot came up and went out of Egypt for six hundred *shekels* of silver, and an horse for an hundred and fifty: and so for all the kings of the Hittites, and for the kings of Syria, did they bring *them* out by their means.	1) A joint venture with King Hiram 2) A very profitable trade in metals & animals f. His wealth & wisdom exceeded that of all the kings of the earth 1) All sought an audience with him: Seeking his wise counsel (to improve their economies & welfare) 2) All brought gifts that added enormously to his wealth g. His wealth included 1400 chariots & 12,000 horses: All kept in chariot cities (built for this very purpose, 9:19) h. His wealth was so great that silver became as common as stones & cedar as common as sycamore trees i. His import & export business was lucrative: Traded horses & chariots 1) Secured from Egypt & the city of Keveh or Kue • A chariot cost 600 pieces of silver • A horse cost 150 pieces of silver 2) Exported & sold to the Hittite & Aramean kings

a. Solomon's yearly tax revenues were enormous, including 666 talents or about 25 tons of gold plus the tolls or tariffs from traders and rulers passing through Israel (v.15). Many of the nations of that day had to travel through Israel in order to trade with one another, for example, Egypt, Syria, Arabia and much of the Mediterranean world. Just the tariffs or tolls from the merchants of these nations would be huge.

b. Solomon also had 500 ceremonial shields made of hammered gold (vv.16-17). 200 large shields had five pounds of gold each, and 300 smaller shields had four pounds of gold each. The shields were kept in the Palace of the Forest of Lebanon (7:1-5).

c. Solomon imported enough ivory to make an ivory throne, which he overlaid with pure gold (vv.18-20). Note that the throne had six steps, and its back had a rounded top. It also had armrests, with one lion figure or statue standing beside each armrest. Twelve lion statues stood on the steps, one at both ends of each step (v.20). Note that its splendor is said to have exceeded any other throne ever made.

d. Even Solomon's drinking cups and household utensils were made of pure gold (v.21). Nothing in his household was made of silver because silver had become so plentiful that it had lost most of its value (v.27). This statement must have astounded the first readers, for remember, the book of Kings was being written to the Israelites who were in exile, poverty-stricken, owning little if anything. The contrast between Solomon's wealth and their own poverty was obviously incomprehensible to them. But keep in mind why they were in exile: because of sin and rebellion against God. They had failed to heed the warning that God had just given to Solomon (9:6-9). The glory and wealth of Solomon's reign was lost forever because of their sin, disobedience, and apostasy against God.[2]

e. Solomon built a fleet of merchants or deep sea ships for commercial purposes (v.22; 9:26-28). This was a joint venture with King Hiram that proved to be very profitable for trading in metals and animals.

f. Solomon's wealth and wisdom exceeded that of all the kings of the earth, clear evidence that God had kept His promise to Solomon (vv.23-25; 3:12; 4:29-34). Just as the queen of Sheba had sought the wisdom of Solomon, so other leaders sought his counsel. Obviously, the purpose behind most leaders' visiting Solomon was to improve the economy and welfare of their own nations. But with the visit of each dignitary, gifts were brought that added enormously to the wealth of Solomon (v.25).

g. Solomon's wealth included 1,400 chariots and 12,000 horses (v.26). All of these were kept in chariot cities that had been built for this very purpose (9:19).

h. Solomon's wealth had become so enormous that silver became as common as stones and the previously priceless cedar lumber as common as the lumber from sycamore trees (v.27).

i. Solomon's import and export business was very lucrative and involved the trading of horses and chariots that had been secured from Egypt and Kue (vv.28-29). A chariot cost 600 pieces of silver, and a horse 150 pieces. They were exported and sold to the Hittite and Aramean (Syrian) kings for profit.

Thought 1. Solomon's enormous wealth is a clear picture of God's material blessings upon His people. If we seek first the kingdom of God and His righteousness, He will meet all of our material needs. This is the clear promise of the Lord Jesus Christ.

"But seek ye first the kingdom of God, and his righteousness; and all these things shall be added unto you" (Mt. 6:33).

The phrase "all these things" refers to food, shelter, and clothing. If God provides food for the birds of the air, how much more will He provide food for us. And if God clothes the lilies of the field, how much more will He clothe us?

There is no need for which the LORD cannot make provision. And He will meet every need of the person who truly seeks first His kingdom and His righteousness. If we seek Him first and are confronted with hunger, God promises to see that we receive food. And if we find ourselves without adequate clothing, and we are seeking Him first, God promises to provide adequate clothing. But this is not all: if we are without shelter, and we are seeking Him first, God promises to provide shelter for us. We may never receive the wealth of Solomon, for God's purpose for us may be far different than to be the ruler of a nation. But God will always see that we have the necessities of life—food, clothing, and shelter—if we will only seek Him first, His kingdom and righteousness. This is the clear promise of God's Holy Word:

"But seek ye first the kingdom of God, and his righteousness; and all these things shall be added unto you" (Mt.6:33).

"Give, and it shall be given unto you; good measure, pressed down, and shaken together, and running over, shall men give into your bosom. For with the same measure that ye mete withal it shall be measured to you again" (Lu.6:38).

"But my God shall supply all your need according to his riches in glory by Christ Jesus" (Ph.4:19).

"And ye shall serve the LORD your God, and he shall bless thy bread, and thy water; and I will take sickness away from the midst of thee" (Ex.23:25).

"If ye walk in my statutes, and keep my commandments, and do them; Then I will give you rain in due season, and the land shall yield her increase, and the trees of the field shall yield their fruit. And your threshing shall reach unto the vintage, and the vintage shall reach unto the sowing time: and ye shall eat your bread to the full, and dwell in your land safely" (Le.26:3-5).

"And thou shalt return and obey the voice of the LORD, and do all his commandments which I command thee this day. And the LORD thy God will make thee plenteous in every work of thine hand,

[2] Paul R. House. *1, 2 Kings*, p.164.

in the fruit of thy body, and in the fruit of thy cattle, and in the fruit of thy land, for good: for the LORD will again rejoice over thee for good, as he rejoiced over thy fathers" (De.30:8-9).

"The LORD *is* my shepherd; I shall not want. He maketh me to lie down in green pastures: he leadeth me beside the still waters. He restoreth my soul: he leadeth me in the paths of righteousness for his name's sake. Yea, though I walk through the valley of the shadow of death, I will fear no evil: for thou *art* with me; thy rod and thy staff they comfort me. Thou preparest a table before me in the presence of mine enemies: thou anointest my head with oil; my cup runneth over. Surely goodness and mercy shall follow me all the days of my life: and I will dwell in the house of the LORD for ever" (Ps.23:1-6).

"*Oh* how great *is* thy goodness, which thou hast laid up for them that fear thee; *which* thou hast wrought for them that trust in thee before the sons of men!" (Ps.31:19).

"Blessed *be* the Lord, *who* daily loadeth us *with benefits, even* the God of our salvation. Selah" (Ps.68:19).

"Bring ye all the tithes into the storehouse, that there may be meat in mine house, and prove me now herewith, saith the LORD of hosts, if I will not open you the windows of heaven, and pour you out a blessing, that *there shall* not *be room* enough *to receive it*" (Mal.3:10).

CHAPTER 11

M. The Shocking Decline & Death of Solomon: The Tragic Consequences of Extravagance, Shameful Indulgence, & Compromise, 11:1-43

11:41-43; see 2 Chr.9:29-31

1. The causes of Solomon's shocking decline: A lesson on evil associations
  a. Solomon loved many foreign women (unbelievers): Practiced polygamy & married unbelievers
    1) He defied, disobeyed God's clear command & strong warning
    2) He clung to his wives, became so attached that he put them before the LORD
    3) He had 700 wives (all princesses of royal birth) & 300 concubines
  b. Solomon was led astray by his wives, led into their idolatry & false worship
    1) He was not loyal nor fully devoted, did not trust solely in the LORD
    2) He honored, joined in the worship of false gods: Ashtoreth & Milcom or Molech, 7
    3) He did not follow the LORD completely: Became half-hearted, neutral, double-minded, lukewarm, Re.3:16
    4) He built worship centers on a high hill for the false gods Chemosh & Molech
    5) He built worship centers for all his wives, allowing & encouraging false worship within the promised land

2. The consequences of Solomon's terrible sin: God's chastisement, discipline
  a. The anger of God was aroused
    1) Because of Solomon's apostasy
    2) Because of Solomon's half-hearted commitment, his defiant disobedience
  b. The kingdom was to be divided, split, torn apart
    1) Not to be divided during Solomon's lifetime, but during his son's: For David's sake, Solomon was allowed to continue ruling
    2) Not to be torn completely away from Solomon's son: He would rule one tribe (Judah) for the sake of David & Jerusalem, 2 S.7:1-17
  c. The adversary Hadad the Edomite was raised up to bitterly oppose & cause problems for Solomon
    1) Hadad's early childhood history
      • He had escaped being killed as a boy when David had defeated Edom
      • He had been saved by some Edomite officials who were fleeing to Egypt
      • He was taken from Midian to Paran where others joined him & the officials in their flight
      • He had been well received by Pharaoh, king of Egypt: Given a house, property, & food
    2) Hadad's adulthood
      • He so pleased Pharaoh that the king gave him a sister-in-law to marry
      • He had a son named Genubath, who was brought up with Pharaoh's own sons in the royal household
      • He had heard of David's & Joab's deaths & immediately requested the right to return home to Edom
      • Pharaoh questioned Hadad's request, but granted it, 14

But king Solomon loved many strange women, together with the daughter of Pharaoh, women of the Moabites, Ammonites, Edomites, Zidonians, *and* Hittites;

2 Of the nations *concerning* which the LORD said unto the children of Israel, Ye shall not go in to them, neither shall they come in unto you: *for* surely they will turn away your heart after their gods: Solomon clave unto these in love.

3 And he had seven hundred wives, princesses, and three hundred concubines: and his wives turned away his heart.

4 For it came to pass, when Solomon was old, *that* his wives turned away his heart after other gods: and his heart was not perfect with the LORD his God, as *was* the heart of David his father.

5 For Solomon went after Ashtoreth the goddess of the Zidonians, and after Milcom the abomination of the Ammonites.

6 And Solomon did evil in the sight of the LORD, and went not fully after the LORD, as *did* David his father.

7 Then did Solomon build an high place for Chemosh, the abomination of Moab, in the hill that *is* before Jerusalem, and for Molech, the abomination of the children of Ammon.

8 And likewise did he for all his strange wives, which burnt incense and sacrificed unto their gods.

9 And the LORD was angry with Solomon, because his heart was turned from the LORD God of Israel, which had appeared unto him twice,

10 And had commanded him concerning this thing, that he should not go after other gods: but he kept not that which the LORD commanded.

11 Wherefore the LORD said unto Solomon, Forasmuch as this is done of thee, and thou hast not kept my covenant and my statutes, which I have commanded thee, I will surely rend the kingdom from thee, and will give it to thy servant.

12 Notwithstanding in thy days I will not do it for David thy father's sake: *but* I will rend it out of the hand of thy son.

13 Howbeit I will not rend away all the kingdom; *but* will give one tribe to thy son for David my servant's sake, and for Jerusalem's sake which I have chosen.

14 And the LORD stirred up an adversary unto Solomon, Hadad the Edomite: he *was* of the king's seed in Edom.

15 For it came to pass, when David was in Edom, and Joab the captain of the host was gone up to bury the slain, after he had smitten every male in Edom;

16 (For six months did Joab remain there with all Israel, until he had cut off every male in Edom:)

17 That Hadad fled, he and certain Edomites of his father's servants with him, to go into Egypt; Hadad *being* yet a little child.

18 And they arose out of Midian, and came to Paran: and they took men with them out of Paran, and they came to Egypt, unto Pharaoh king of Egypt; which gave him an house, and appointed him victuals, and gave him land.

19 And Hadad found great favour in the sight of Pharaoh, so that he gave him to wife the sister of his own wife, the sister of Tahpenes the queen.

20 And the sister of Tahpenes bare him Genubath his son, whom Tahpenes weaned in Pharaoh's house: and Genubath was in Pharaoh's household among the sons of Pharaoh.

21 And when Hadad heard in Egypt that David slept with his fathers, and that Joab the captain of the host was dead, Hadad said to Pharaoh, Let me depart, that I may go to mine own country.

22 Then Pharaoh said unto him, But what hast thou lacked with me, that, behold,

d. The second adversary to oppose Solomon, the bandit Rezon, was also raised up by God
   1) He had fled from King Hadadezer of Zobah when David defeated him: Became the leader of a band of raiders or marauders
   2) He conquered & held Damascus
   3) He was a bitter adversary for the remainder of Solomon's life
   4) He roamed about & caused trouble throughout all Israel
e. The rebellion by a third adversary, Jeroboam, also took place: Was one of Solomon's own officials

3. The rebellion of Jeroboam against Solomon & the prophecy of the divided kingdom: The surety of judgment

a. Jeroboam was in charge of a huge work force: Gave him contact—a power base—with a large number of disgruntled people
   1) His work had caught the eye of Solomon
   2) He had been promoted to be labor supervisor over the tribes of Joseph (Ephraim & Manasseh)
b. Jeroboam was dramatically confronted by the prophet Ahijah: Predicted to be the future ruler over the 10 tribes of Israel
   1) Ahijah confronted Jeroboam & presented an object lesson to him: He took a new cloak & tore it into 12 pieces, handing 10 pieces to Jeroboam
   2) Ahijah explained the symbolic message of the torn cloak
      - God was tearing the kingdom away from Solomon & giving ten tribes to Jeroboam
      - God was giving one tribe to Solomon & his son: For the sake of David (the tribe of Benjamin was included in Judah)

thou seekest to go to thine
own country? And he answered, Nothing: howbeit let
me go in any wise.
23 And God stirred him up
another adversary, Rezon the
son of Eliadah, which fled
from his lord Hadadezer king
of Zobah:
24 And he gathered men unto him, and became captain
over a band, when David
slew them *of Zobah:* and they
went to Damascus, and dwelt
therein, and reigned in Damascus.
25 And he was an adversary
to Israel all the days of Solomon, beside the mischief
that Hadad *did:* and he abhorred Israel, and reigned
over Syria.
26 And Jeroboam the son of
Nebat, an Ephrathite of Zereda, Solomon's servant,
whose mother's name *was*
Zeruah, a widow woman,
even he lifted up *his* hand
against the king.
27 And this *was* the cause
that he lifted up *his*
hand against the king:
Solomon built Millo, *and*
repaired the breaches of
the city of David his father.
28 And the man Jeroboam *was* a mighty man
of valour: and Solomon
seeing the young man that
he was industrious, he
made him ruler over all the
charge of the house of Joseph.
29 And it came to pass at
that time when Jeroboam
went out of Jerusalem, that
the prophet Ahijah the
Shilonite found him in the
way; and he had clad himself
with a new garment; and they
two *were* alone in the field:
30 And Ahijah caught the
new garment that *was* on
him, and rent it *in* twelve
pieces:
31 And he said to Jeroboam,
Take thee ten pieces: for thus
saith the LORD, the God of
Israel, Behold, I will rend the
kingdom out of the hand of
Solomon, and will give ten
tribes to thee:
32 (But he shall have one
tribe for my servant David's
sake, and for Jerusalem's sake,
the city which I have chosen
out of all the tribes of Israel:)
33 Because that they have
forsaken me, and have worshipped Ashtoreth the goddess of the Zidonians, Chemosh the god of the Moabites, and Milcom the god of
the children of Ammon, and
have not walked in my ways,
to do *that which is* right in
mine eyes, and *to keep* my
statutes and my judgments, as
did David his father.
34 Howbeit I will not take
the whole kingdom out of his
hand: but I will make him
prince all the days of his life
for David my servant's sake,
whom I chose, because he
kept my commandments and
my statutes:
35 But I will take the kingdom out of his son's hand,
and will give it unto thee,
even ten tribes.
36 And unto his son will I
give one tribe, that David my
servant may have a light alway before me in Jerusalem,
the city which I have chosen
me to put my name there.
37 And I will take thee, and
thou shalt reign according to
all that thy soul desireth, and
shalt be king over Israel.
38 And it shall be, if thou
wilt hearken unto all that I
command thee, and wilt walk
in my ways, and do *that is*
right in my sight, to keep my
statutes and my commandments, as David my servant
did; that I will be with thee,
and build thee a sure house,
as I built for David, and will
give Israel unto thee.
39 And I will for this afflict
the seed of David, but not for
ever.
40 Solomon sought therefore
to kill Jeroboam. And Jeroboam arose, and fled into
Egypt, unto Shishak king of
Egypt, and was in Egypt until
the death of Solomon.
41 And the rest of the
acts of Solomon, and all
that he did, and his wisdom,
are they not written in the
book of the acts of Solomon?
42 And the time that Solomon reigned in Jerusalem
over all Israel *was* forty years.
43 And Solomon slept with
his fathers, and was buried in
the city of David his father:
and Rehoboam his son
reigned in his stead.

   3) Ahijah spelled out the reasons why the kingdom was being divided & the nation Israel torn apart
      - Because the king & people had forsaken God
      - Because they had engaged in false worship
      - Because they had disobeyed, not followed the ways of God
   4) Ahijah reassured Jeroboam that God had chosen him to rule
      - But God would not take the kingdom out of Solomon's hand during the king's lifetime: For David's sake
      - God would take the kingdom from Solomon's son & give Jeroboam 10 tribes
      - God was going to give one tribe (Judah) to Solomon's son: Because of David, that he might have a light (witness) in Jerusalem, the city chosen to honor God's Name
      - God was going to make Jeroboam king, give him rule over all he desired, over Israel
   5) Ahijah declared God's startling promise to Jeroboam, that of a lasting dynasty
      - The strict condition: Obedience—keeping God's commandments
      - The wonderful promise: God's presence & a dynasty that would endure (as much as David's)
   6) Ahijah gave the reason for God's judgment: To humble David's house
c. Jeroboam rebelled & Solomon tried to kill him
   1) He fled to Egypt
   2) He stayed there until Solomon's death

4. The death of Solomon: A legacy of achievement &, tragically, of worldly pleasure

a. The events of his reign were recorded in *The Book of the Acts of Solomon*
b. The reign of Solomon lasted 40 years: But he lost his kingdom due to sin
c. The sad, silent picture of Solomon's death: Due to his shocking decline into sin
   1) Buried in Jerusalem
   2) Succeeded by Rehoboam

DIVISION I

THE RISE AND REIGN OF SOLOMON AS KING: BEGINNING IN GLORY AND ENDING IN SHAME, 1:1–11:43

M. The Shocking Decline and Death of Solomon: The Tragic Consequences of Extravagance, Shameful Indulgence, and Compromise, 11:1-43

(11:1-43) **Introduction**: experiencing pleasure can be wonderful and wholesome—the joy of loving others and of being loved; of sensing purpose, meaning, and fulfillment in life; of setting a goal and attaining it; of leading someone to Christ, and so on. But carried to the extreme, pleasure can lead to indulgence and license and all forms of sinful and immoral behavior. If a person zealously pursues pleasure over and above anything else—above God, above family, above responsibilities, above reason—then pleasure becomes a god to the person. Pleasure becomes the master and the willing participant becomes the slave.

In the same light, luxury, in its purest form, is not sinful. If a person has been blessed materially—never lacking the necessities of life—and keeps a proper perspective on the value of his possessions versus God, family, and responsibilities, then that person does not become the slave of luxury. But far too often, the more a person has or gets, the more he wants. Furthermore, luxury can lead to a life of self-absorption, complacence, indifference, and extravagance, ignoring and neglecting those in need.

Luxury and pleasure became the downfall of King Solomon, the great king of Israel. As we have seen, Solomon had achieved the summit of power and wealth, of luxury and pleasure, and of fame and influence. Up until this point in Scripture, only the crest of his achievements has been seen. But now, shockingly, his story takes a tragic turn. By degrees, Solomon's luxury and pleasure slowly began to eat away at the strength of his character and spiritual commitment to the LORD. Solomon began to travel down the treacherous path of turning away from the LORD and turning to a life of immorality and false worship. This is: *The Shocking Decline and Death of Solomon: The Tragic Consequences of Extravagance, Shameful Indulgence, and Compromise,* 11:1-43.

1. The causes of Solomon's shocking decline: a lesson on evil associations (vv.1-8).
2. The consequences of Solomon's terrible sin: God's chastisement, discipline (vv.9-26).
3. The rebellion of Jeroboam against Solomon and the prophecy of the divided kingdom: the surety of judgment (vv.27-40).
4. The death of Solomon: a legacy of achievement and, tragically, of worldly pleasure (vv.41-43).

1 (11:1-8) **Half-Hearted, Example of—Commitment, Half-Hearted, Example of—Lukewarm, Example of—Neutral, Example of—Double-minded, Example of—Disobedience, Example of—Polygamy, Example of—Evil Associations, Example of—Companions, Evil, Example of—Intermarriage, with Unbelievers, Example of—Company, Evil, Example of—Spiritual Separation, Disobedience - Failure—Solomon, Sin and Decline of**: there were the causes of Solomon's shocking decline. A dramatic transition now takes place. Up until this point, a glowing report has been given on Solomon's life: he had reached the height of spiritual fervor and of international prominence and reputation. He was a man richly blessed by God with wisdom, wealth, and power. And he had established Israel as one of the most powerful and influential nations of the world during his day. But now an alarming descent into depravity takes place. Scripture explains exactly what happened to cause the decline of Solomon:

OUTLINE	SCRIPTURE	SCRIPTURE	OUTLINE
1. The causes of Solomon's shocking decline: A lesson on evil associations a. Solomon loved many foreign women (unbelievers): Practiced polygamy & married unbelievers	But king Solomon loved many strange women, together with the daughter of Pharaoh, women of the Moabites, Ammonites, Edomites, Zidonians, *and* Hittites;	heart was not perfect with the LORD his God, as *was* the heart of David his father.	1) He was not loyal nor fully devoted, did not trust solely in the LORD
1) He defied, disobeyed God's clear command & strong warning 2) He clung to his wives, became so attached that he put them before the LORD	2 Of the nations *concerning* which the LORD said unto the children of Israel, Ye shall not go in to them, neither shall they come in unto you: *for* surely they will turn away your heart after their gods: Solomon clave unto these in love.	5 For Solomon went after Ashtoreth the goddess of the Zidonians, and after Milcom the abomination of the Ammonites. 6 And Solomon did evil in the sight of the LORD, and went not fully after the LORD, as *did* David his father. 7 Then did Solomon build an high place for Chemosh, the abomination of Moab, in the	2) He honored, joined in the worship of false gods: Ashtoreth & Milcom or Molech, 7 3) He did not follow the LORD completely: Became half-hearted, neutral, double-minded, lukewarm, Re.3:16 4) He built worship centers on a high hill for the false gods Chemosh & Molech
3) He had 700 wives (all princesses of royal birth) & 300 concubines	3 And he had seven hundred wives, princesses, and three hundred concubines: and his wives turned away his heart.	hill that *is* before Jerusalem, and for Molech, the abomination of the children of Ammon.	
b. Solomon was led astray by his wives, led into their idolatry & false worship	4 For it came to pass, when Solomon was old, *that* his wives turned away his heart after other gods: and his	8 And likewise did he for all his strange wives, which burnt incense and sacrificed unto their gods.	5) He built worship centers for all his wives, allowing & encouraging false worship within the promised land

a. Solomon loved many foreign women who were unbelievers; that is, he practiced polygamy and married unbelievers (vv.1-3). He had "feet of clay"[1] and was very sensual, obviously being easily attracted and aroused by women. Scripture indicates that Solomon was given over to the flesh. Verse one says that he "loved many strange [foreign] women," and verse two says that Solomon "clung, held fast to these women in love." Note three facts about Solomon's practicing polygamy and marrying unbelievers:

1) Solomon defied, disobeyed God's clear command and strong warning (v.2). God's people—whether they were kings or citizens—were not to intermarry with unbelievers. Why? Because unbelievers would influence the believers and turn their hearts from the LORD, leading believers to participate in their spouses false worship and idolatry (De.17:17; see also Ex.34:12-17; De.7:1-5).
2) Solomon clung to his wives, becoming so attached that he put them before the LORD (v.2). Living with them day by day, he slowly and gradually gave in to their invitations to join them in their false worship. Because of his love, he naturally wanted to please them and to be with them during the joyful occasions and festivals of their religion. Remember that much of the social life of his day and time revolved around the festivities of the people's worship. It is normal and very commendable for a husband to love his wife and to become attached to her. However, Solomon had married the wrong women, and he was clinging to the wrong women. He had married unbelievers; consequently, he was influenced and led astray by them.
3) All together, Solomon had 700 wives who were princesses of royal birth, and he had 300 concubines (v.3). No doubt most, if not all, of these marriages had initially been politically motivated. Seeking peaceful relations with surrounding nations and small territories, Solomon joined in the practice of other nations, that of cementing peace treaties by marrying the royal princesses of the various rulers or kingdoms.

b. Secondly, Solomon was led astray by his wives, led into their idolatry and false worship (vv.4-8). Scripture clearly says that he was neither loyal nor fully devoted to the LORD. He did not trust solely in the LORD as his father David had done (v.4). Solomon honored and joined in the false worship of his wives, worshipping the false gods of Ashtoreth and Milcom or Molech, which is an alternate name for Milcom (vv.5, 7). Ashtoreth was the fertility goddess that was worshipped as the goddess of love (sex) and of war. Milcom or Molech was a national god of the Ammonites that was sometimes worshipped by sacrificing children (Je.7:31-32; 19:5-6; 32:35).

Solomon plainly did not follow the LORD completely as his father David had done (v.6). For when David sinned, he confessed and repented, turning back to the LORD. But not Solomon. He became halfhearted, neutral, double-minded, and lukewarm toward the LORD. When he married his various wives, he did what was a very natural thing for rulers of that day: he built worship centers for them. Two worship centers in particular are mentioned: a high place for their false god Chemosh, who was the detestable god of Moab, and a high place for Molech, the detestable god of the Ammonites (v.7). By building these false worship centers, he encouraged false worship within the promised land. Sadly, many of the people followed the lead of Solomon's wives and became committed worshippers of the false gods (2 K.23:13).

Thought 1. Solomon's character and spiritual commitment declined for one reason: evil associations. He married unbelievers, and his unbelieving wives eventually led him astray. God warns us against evil associations, including marrying unbelievers and keeping company with unbelievers. If we associate and keep company with unbelievers and wicked people, they will influence us no matter how strong we may be spiritually. Eventually they will invite us to join in their worldly behavior or wickedness:

⇒ to join them as they take drugs or drink alcoholic beverages or smoke cigarettes or do something else that will damage the human body
⇒ to join them as they look at pornographic literature or movies or some other lewd, immoral spectacle
⇒ to join them in an immoral act or at an immoral party or function
⇒ to join them in committing an illegal act or crime
⇒ to join them in their worldly conversation or activity
⇒ to join them in their false worship
⇒ to join them in their covetous behavior

It is impossible for any person—no matter how mentally or spiritually strong the person may be—to continually associate with worldly and wicked people and not be influenced by them. Eventually, they will lead us astray. For this reason, God strongly warns us against evil associations:

"If ye were of the world, the world would love his own: but because ye are not of the world, but I have chosen you out of the world, therefore the world hateth you" (Jn.15:19).

"And the servants and officers stood there, who had made a fire of coals; for it was cold: and they warmed themselves: and Peter stood with them, and warmed himself....And Simon Peter stood and warmed himself. They said therefore unto him, Art not thou also *one* of his disciples? He denied *it,* and said, I am not" (Jn.18:18, 25).

"And with many other words did he testify and exhort, saying, Save yourselves from this untoward generation" (Ac.2:40).

"And be not conformed to this world: but be ye transformed by the renewing of your mind, that ye may prove what *is* that good, and acceptable, and perfect, will of God" (Ro.12:2).

"But now I have written unto you not to keep company, if any man that is called a brother be a fornicator, or covetous, or an idolater, or a railer, or a drunkard, or an extortioner; with such an one no not to eat" (1 Co.5:11).

"Be not deceived: evil communications corrupt good manners" (1 Co.15:33).

---

[1] Richard D. Patterson and Hermann J. Austel. *1, 2 Kings*, p.106.

"Be ye not unequally yoked together with unbelievers: for what fellowship hath righteousness with unrighteousness? and what communion hath light with darkness? And what concord hath Christ with Belial? or what part hath he that believeth with an infidel? And what agreement hath the temple of God with idols? for ye are the temple of the living God; as God hath said, I will dwell in them, and walk in *them;* and I will be their God, and they shall be my people" (2 Co.6:14-16).

"Wherefore come out from among them, and be ye separate, saith the Lord, and touch not the unclean *thing;* and I will receive you, And will be a Father unto you, and ye shall be my sons and daughters, saith the Lord Almighty" (2 Co.6:17-18).

"And have no fellowship with the unfruitful works of darkness, but rather reprove *them*" (Ep.5:11).

"Now we command you, brethren, in the name of our Lord Jesus Christ, that ye withdraw yourselves from every brother that walketh disorderly, and not after the tradition which he received of us" (2 Th.3:6).

"By faith Moses, when he was come to years, refused to be called the son of Pharaoh's daughter; Choosing rather to suffer affliction with the people of God, than to enjoy the pleasures of sin for a season" (He.11:24-25).

"Love not the world, neither the things *that are* in the world. If any man love the world, the love of the Father is not in him. For all that *is* in the world, the lust of the flesh, and the lust of the eyes, and the pride of life, is not of the Father, but is of the world" (1 Jn.2:15-16).

"Thou shalt not follow a multitude to *do* evil; neither shalt thou speak in a cause to decline after many to wrest *judgment*" (Ex.23:2).

"Take heed to thyself, lest thou make a covenant with the inhabitants of the land whither thou goest, lest it be for a snare in the midst of thee" (Ex.34:12).

"Blessed *is* the man that walketh not in the counsel of the ungodly, nor standeth in the way of sinners, nor sitteth in the seat of the scornful. But his delight *is* in the law of the LORD; and in his law doth he meditate day and night" (Ps.1:1-2).

"Enter not into the path of the wicked, and go not in the way of evil *men*" (Pr.4:14).

"Be not thou envious against evil men, neither desire to be with them" (Pr.24:1).

"Whoso keepeth the law *is* a wise son: but he that is a companion of riotous *men* shameth his father" (Pr.28:7).

"Depart ye, depart ye, go ye out from thence, touch no unclean *thing;* go ye out of the midst of her; be ye clean, that bear the vessels of the LORD" (Is.52:11).

Thought 2. The commentator Paul R. House gives an excellent exposition on verses one through three that is well worth quoting in its entirety:

After the glowing report in 10:14-29, these verses are the literary equivalent of a blow to the face. Despite all his obvious strengths, the king has a very evident weakness for women, especially foreign women. Besides Pharaoh's daughter, he loves Moabite, Ammonite, Edomite, Sidonian, and Hittite women. Altogether he accumulates "seven hundred wives of royal birth and three hundred concubines." Like the marriage to the Egyptian princess, most of these unions probably were politically motivated. Such linking of nations was intended to foster peaceful relations between normally combative countries. In a straightforward secular kingdom this practice would be good politics.

There are several problems, however, with what Solomon has done. First, he has disobeyed Moses' law for marriage, which constitutes a breach of the agreement Solomon makes with God in 1 Kgs 3:1-14; 6:11-13; and 9:1-9. Moses says in Deut 7:3-4 and Exod 34:15-16 that Israelites must not intermarry with noncovenant nations. Why? Because God says "they will turn your sons away from following me to serve other gods" (Deut 7:4). Judgment will then result. Second, Solomon has broken Moses' commands for kings (cf. Deut 17:14-20). Moses explicitly says, "He must not take many wives or his heart will be led astray" (Deut 17:17). Indeed, all of Moses' dire predictions come true in Solomon's case. His wives do lure him into idolatry. Solomon, however, is responsible for his own actions. He knows better but does not act on this knowledge.

Third, Solomon has evidently fallen into the emotional trap of wanting to be like pagan kings. Moses counsels kings to remain as close to the people as possible (Deut 17:14-20). Kings who become too wealthy desire possessions and women more than they desire to serve God and the people, Moses warns (Deut 17:14-20). Solomon has clearly forgotten this admonition. He has competed with other kings and queens in wisdom and splendor and has won (cf. 1 Kgs 4:29-34; 10:1-13, 23-25). These victories are gifts from God (1 Kgs 3:10-15). Competing in wives is outside of God's will and promise to bless, though, so the process can have no positive result.[2]

2 (11:9-26) **Chastisement, of God, Example of—Discipline, of God, Example of—Consequences, of Sin, Example of—Sin, Consequences, Example of—Solomon, Consequence of Sin—Hadad the Edomite, Adversary to Solomon—Rezon, Adversary to Solomon**: there were the consequences of Solomon's terrible sin. Solomon's shocking sin and spiritual decline were utterly inexcusable, for Solomon had been privileged beyond comprehension. And he had been given two very unique privileges: that of having God appear to him twice and that of being David's very own son. By being David's son, Solomon had been given the privilege of being reared and trained by a man who was fully devoted to the LORD. And he had the privilege of observing a godly king rule the nation, an *ideal example* of what God wanted a ruler to be.

[2] Paul R. House. *1, 2 Kings*, pp.166-167.

But Solomon forgot his upbringing, and the appearances by God slowly diminished from his memory. Consequently, he did the unthinkable: he disobeyed. Slowly but surely he slipped into a sensual, immoral lifestyle, and eventually he participated in the false worship services of his wives. As a result, Solomon was to bear the hand of God's chastisement and judgment. Five consequences of Solomon's terrible sin are spelled out by Scripture:

OUTLINE	SCRIPTURE	SCRIPTURE	OUTLINE
2. The consequences of Solomon's terrible sin: God's chastisement, discipline a. The anger of God was aroused 1) Because of Solomon's apostasy 2) Because of Solomon's half-hearted commitment, his defiant disobedience	9 And the LORD was angry with Solomon, because his heart was turned from the LORD God of Israel, which had appeared unto him twice, 10 And had commanded him concerning this thing, that he should not go after other gods: but he kept not that which the LORD commanded.	of Egypt; which gave him an house, and appointed him victuals, and gave him land. 19 And Hadad found great favour in the sight of Phar- aoh, so that he gave him to wife the sister of his own wife, the sister of Tahpenes the queen.	received by Pharaoh, king of Egypt: Given a house, property, & food 2) Hadad's adulthood • He so pleased Pharaoh that the king gave him a sister-in-law to marry
b. The kingdom was to be divided, split, torn apart	11 Wherefore the LORD said unto Solomon, Forasmuch as this is done of thee, and thou hast not kept my covenant and my statutes, which I have commanded thee, I will surely rend the kingdom from thee, and will give it to thy servant.	20 And the sister of Tahpenes bare him Genubath his son, whom Tahpenes weaned in Pharaoh's house: and Genubath was in Phar- aoh's household among the sons of Pharaoh.	• He had a son named Genubath, who was brought up with Pharaoh's own sons in the royal household
1) Not to be divided during Solomon's lifetime, but during his son's: For David's sake, Solomon was allowed to continue ruling 2) Not to be torn completely away from Solomon's son: He would rule one tribe (Judah) for the sake of David & Jerusalem, 2 S.7:1-17	12 Notwithstanding in thy days I will not do it for David thy father's sake: *but* I will rend it out of the hand of thy son. 13 Howbeit I will not rend away all the kingdom; *but* will give one tribe to thy son for David my servant's sake, and for Jerusalem's sake which I have chosen.	21 And when Hadad heard in Egypt that David slept with his fathers, and that Joab the captain of the host was dead, Hadad said to Pharaoh, Let me depart, that I may go to mine own country. 22 Then Pharaoh said unto him, But what hast thou lacked with me, that, behold, thou seekest to go to thine own country? And he an- swered, Nothing: howbeit let me go in any wise.	• He had heard of David's & Joab's deaths & immediately requested the right to return home to Edom • Pharaoh questioned Hadad's request, but granted it, 14
c. The adversary Hadad the Edomite was raised up to bitterly oppose & cause problems for Solomon 1) Hadad's early childhood history • He had escaped being killed as a boy when David had defeated Edom	14 And the LORD stirred up an adversary unto Solomon, Hadad the Edomite: he *was* of the king's seed in Edom. 15 For it came to pass, when David was in Edom, and Joab the captain of the host was gone up to bury the slain, af- ter he had smitten every male in Edom; 16 (For six months did Joab remain there with all Israel, until he had cut off every male in Edom:)	23 And God stirred him up *another* adversary, Rezon the son of Eliadah, which fled from his lord Hadadezer king of Zobah: 24 And he gathered men unto him, and became captain over a band, when David slew them *of Zobah:* and they went to Damascus, and dwelt therein, and reigned in Da- mascus. 25 And he was an adversary to Israel all the days of Sol- omon, beside the mischief that Hadad *did:* and he ab horred Israel, and reigned over Syria.	d. The second adversary to oppose Solomon, the bandit Rezon, was also raised up by God 1) He had fled from King Hadadezer of Zobah when David defeated him: Became the leader of a band of raiders or marauders 2) He conquered & held Damascus 3) He was a bitter adversary for the remainder of Solomon's life 4) He roamed about & caused trouble throughout all Israel
• He had been saved by some Edomite officials who were fleeing to Egypt • He was taken from Midian to Paran where others joined him & the officials in their flight • He had been well	17 That Hadad fled, he and certain Edomites of his fa- ther's servants with him, to go into Egypt; Hadad *being* yet a little child. 18 And they arose out of Midian, and came to Paran: and they took men with them out of Paran, and they came to Egypt, unto Pharaoh king	26 And Jeroboam the son of Nebat, an Ephrathite of Zere- da, Solomon's servant, whose mother's name *was* Zeruah, a widow woman, even he lifted up *his* hand against the king.	e. The rebellion by a third adversary, Jeroboam, also took place: Was one of Solomon's own officials

a. God's anger was aroused against Solomon (vv.9-10). Two reasons are given for God's anger:

⇒ God was angry because of Solomon's apostasy. Solomon had turned away from the LORD, turned away despite the wonderful privilege God had given him, the privilege of having appeared to him twice (v.9).

⇒ God's anger was aroused because of Solomon's half-hearted commitment to Him, his defiant disobedience to God's clear commandment (v.10; see also v.2).

b. The kingdom of Israel was to be divided, split, torn apart (vv.11-13). A united Israel was never again to be known. But God would show mercy. He would not divide the kingdom during Solomon's lifetime, but rather during his son's reign (v.12). Despite his sin, Solomon would be allowed to continue ruling, but *not for his sake*. Instead, he would continue to rule for his father David's sake. But God's mercy was not to end at Solomon's death: the kingdom would not be torn completely from Solomon's son (v.13). For the sake of David and Jerusalem, Solomon's son would be allowed to rule one tribe, the tribe of Judah.

In granting this concession to Solomon, it must be remembered that it was not granted for Solomon's sake, but for the sake of his father David (see outline and notes—2 S.7:1-17 for more discussion). Because of God's promise to David, the promise to give him a lasting dynasty that would never end, God allowed Solomon to continue ruling for the remainder of his life. Nevertheless, the hand of God's judgment had fallen upon Solomon because of his terrible wickedness. And the judgment was stunning: the unified nation that had reached the pinnacle of power would be ripped, torn apart. And Solomon's son would rule over only one tribe.

c. An adversary, Hadad the Edomite, was raised up to bitterly oppose and cause problems for Solomon (vv.14-22). Although Solomon had been left upon the throne, he was to suffer the consequences of his sins during the latter years of his life. One of the consequences was the bitter opposition caused by Hadad. Note two facts about this adversary:

1) Hadad experienced a suspenseful, life-threatening event during his early childhood (vv.15-18). He barely escaped being killed as a boy when David defeated Edom (vv.15-16). In a mopping up operation, David had left Joab in the land for a period of six months. But Hadad had been saved by some Edomite officials who had escaped and were fleeing to Egypt (v.17). The young boy was taken from Midian to Paran, where others joined the official party in their flight (v.18). After arriving in Egypt, the young boy, apparently of royal blood, was well received by Pharaoh and given a house, property, and food.
2) As an adult, Hadad so pleased Pharaoh that the king gave him his sister-in-law to marry, the sister of his own wife Queen Tahpenes (v.19). Eventually Hadad had a son named Genubath who was brought up with Pharaoh's own sons in the royal household (v.20).

   When David and Joab died, Hadad felt it was safe to return home. So he immediately requested the right to return home to Edom. Pharaoh questioned his request, but granted him permission (vv.21-22).

   Apparently right after returning home, Hadad began to seek revenge against the Israelites. But no specifics of his harassment are given by Scripture. All that is known is that God raised him up to bitterly oppose and harass King Solomon because of Solomon's terrible wickedness.

d. A second adversary, the bandit Rezon, was also raised up by the LORD (vv.23-25). Apparently Rezon had been a commander in the army of Hadadezer, who was king of Zobah. After David had defeated Hadadezer, Rezon escaped and soon became the leader of a band of raiders or marauders. Eventually, he conquered and controlled Damascus, where he and his bandits settled. Scripture says that as long as Solomon lived, Rezon was a fierce adversary of the king's (v.25). He roamed all about, causing trouble for Solomon throughout all Israel.

e. Jeroboam soon arose to become the third significant adversary to oppose Solomon (v.26). Jeroboam had even been one of Solomon's own officials, the labor supervisor over the two tribes of Joseph, Ephraim and Manasseh (see v.28). Jeroboam is discussed in detail in the next point. For now, the fact to see is that God raised up Jeroboam as part of the chastisement against Solomon because of the king's terrible disobedience.

> **Thought 1**. Wickedness damages human life and society and anything else it touches. Think of the harm that can be done when a person lies, steals, cheats, commits adultery, takes drugs, gets drunk, abuses a child, assaults a person, ignores the rules, or violates the law.
>
> **All sin has consequences that damage human life and society. Sin takes its toll on the human body and brings more and more corruption into our neighborhoods and cities.**
>
> **But even though we commit wickedness, God still loves us and wants to save us. To keep us from damaging ourselves further and from hurting other people, God disciplines us when we sin. The hand of God's chastisement seeks to correct us so we will learn to live righteously and morally throughout life. Listen to what God's Holy Word says about chastisement and discipline:**
>
> **"Every branch in me that beareth not fruit he taketh away: and every *branch* that beareth fruit, he purgeth it, that it may bring forth more fruit" (Jn.15:2).**
>
> **"For this cause many *are* weak and sickly among you, and many sleep. For if we would judge ourselves, we should not be judged. But when we are judged, we are chastened of the Lord, that we should not be condemned with the world" (1 Co.11:30-32).**
>
> **"And ye have forgotten the exhortation which speaketh unto you as unto children, My son, despise not thou the chastening of the Lord, nor faint when thou art rebuked of him: For whom the Lord loveth he chasteneth, and scourgeth every son whom he receiveth" (He.12:5-6).**
>
> **"As many as I love, I rebuke and chasten: be zealous therefore, and repent" (Re.3:19).**
>
> **"Thou shalt also consider in thine heart, that, as a man chasteneth his son, *so* the LORD thy God chasteneth thee" (De.8:5).**
>
> **"Blessed *is* the man whom thou chastenest, O LORD, and teachest him out of thy law" (Ps.94:12).**
>
> **"My son, despise not the chastening of the LORD; neither be weary of his correction: For whom the LORD loveth he correcteth; even as a father the son *in whom* he delighteth" (Pr.3:11-12).**

3 (11:27-40) **Judgment, Surety of—Rebellion, Against Solomon—Jeroboam, Rebellion of—Prophecy, Concerning Israel, Divided Kingdom—Israel, Prophecy Concerning, Divided Kingdom—Jeroboam, Appointed by God—Ahijah, Prophecies of, Divided Kingdom**: there was the rebellion of Jeroboam against Solomon and the prophecy of the divided kingdom. By far, this rebellion was the most serious threat faced by Solomon during his reign. For Jeroboam was an Israelite himself and was actually one of Solomon's own officials (see v.26). Moreover, Jeroboam was destined to become the first king of the northern tribes after the split of the nation. Scripture paints a dramatic picture of the uprising and the prophecy predicting the divided kingdom:

OUTLINE	SCRIPTURE	SCRIPTURE	OUTLINE
3. The rebellion of Jeroboam against Solomon & the prophecy of the divided kingdom: The surety of judgment a. Jeroboam was in charge of a huge work force: Gave him contact—a power base—with a large number of disgruntled people 1) His work had caught the eye of Solomon 2) He had been promoted to be labor supervisor over the tribes of Joseph (Ephraim & Manasseh) b. Jeroboam was dramatically confronted by the prophet Ahijah: Predicted to be the future ruler over the 10 tribes of Israel 1) Ahijah confronted Jeroboam & presented an object lesson to him: He took a new cloak & tore it into 12 pieces, handing 10 pieces to Jeroboam 2) Ahijah explained the symbolic message of the torn cloak • God was tearing the kingdom away from Solomon & giving ten tribes to Jeroboam • God was giving one tribe to Solomon & his son: For the sake of David (the tribe of Benjamin was included in Judah) 3) Ahijah spelled out the reasons why the kingdom was being divided & the nation Israel torn apart • Because the king & people had forsaken God • Because they had engaged in false worship	27 And this *was* the cause that he lifted up *his* hand against the king: Solomon built Millo, *and* repaired the breaches of the city of David his fa- ther. 28 And the man Jero- boam *was* a mighty man of valour: and Solomon seeing the young man that he was industrious, he made him ruler over all the charge of the house of Jo- seph. 29 And it came to pass at that time when Jeroboam went out of Jerusalem, that the prophet Ahijah the Shi- lonite found him in the way; and he had clad himself with a new garment; and they two *were* alone in the field: 30 And Ahijah caught the new garment that *was* on him, and rent it *in* twelve pieces: 31 And he said to Jeroboam, Take thee ten pieces: for thus saith the LORD, the God of Israel, Behold, I will rend the kingdom out of the hand of Solomon, and will give ten tribes to thee: 32 (But he shall have one tribe for my servant David's sake, and for Jerusalem's sake, the city which I have chosen out of all the tribes of Israel:) 33 Because that they have forsaken me, and have wor- shipped Ashtoreth the god- dess of the Zidonians, Che- mosh the god of the Moabites, and Milcom the god of the children of Ammon, and have not walked in my ways, to do *that which is* right in mine	eyes, and *to keep* my statutes and my judgments, as *did* David his father. 34 Howbeit I will not take the whole kingdom out of his hand: but I will make him prince all the days of his life for David my servant's sake, whom I chose, because he kept my commandments and my statutes: 35 But I will take the king- dom out of his son's hand, and will give it unto thee, *even* ten tribes. 36 And unto his son will I give one tribe, that David my servant may have a light alway before me in Jerusa- lem, the city which I have chosen me to put my name there. 37 And I will take thee, and thou shalt reign according to all that thy soul desireth, and shalt be king over Israel. 38 And it shall be, if thou wilt hearken unto all that I command thee, and wilt walk in my ways, and do *that is* right in my sight, to keep my statutes and my command- ments, as David my servant did; that I will be with thee, and build thee a sure house, as I built for David, and will give Israel unto thee. 39 And I will for this afflict the seed of David, but not for ever. 40 Solomon sought therefore to kill Jeroboam. And Jero- boam arose, and fled into Egypt, unto Shishak king of Egypt, and was in Egypt until the death of Solomon.	• Because they had disobeyed, not followed the ways of God 4) Ahijah reassured Jeroboam that God had chosen him to rule • But God would not take the kingdom out of Solomon's hand during the king's lifetime: For David's sake • God would take the kingdom from Solomon's son & give Jeroboam 10 tribes • God was going to give one tribe (Judah) to Solomon's son: Because of David, that he might have a light (witness) in Jerusalem, the city chosen to honor God's Name • God was going to make Jeroboam king, give him rule over all he desired, over Israel 5) Ahijah declared God's startling promise to Jeroboam, that of a lasting dynasty • The strict condition: Obedience—keeping God's commandments • The wonderful promise: God's presence & a dynasty that would endure (as much as David's) 6) Ahijah gave the reason for God's judgment: To humble David's house c. Jeroboam rebelled & Solomon tried to kill him 1) He fled to Egypt 2) He stayed there until Solomon's death

a. Jeroboam had been the supervisor of a huge work force that was building the supporting terraces and repairing the walls of Jerusalem (vv.27-28). Supervising a large corps of workers gave him contact—a power base—with a large number of disgruntled people. Sometime earlier, Jeroboam's hard work had caught the eye of Solomon. As a result, the king promoted the young man to be labor supervisor over the tribes of Joseph, that is, the tribes of Ephraim and Manasseh.

b. Soon after his promotion, Jeroboam was dramatically confronted by the prophet Ahijah (vv.29-39). For some reason, Jeroboam was leaving the city of Jerusalem and walking alone in the countryside. Being sent by the LORD to meet with the young man, Ahijah informed him that he was to be the future ruler over the ten northern tribes of Israel after the nation had been torn apart. Ahijah did six things with Jeroboam:

1) The prophet approached Jeroboam and presented an object lesson to him (vv.29-30). He took a new cloak and tore it into twelve pieces, handing ten pieces to Jeroboam.
2) Ahijah then explained the symbolic message of the torn cloak (vv.32-33). Just as he had torn the cloak, so God was tearing the kingdom away from Solomon and giving to Jeroboam ten tribes to rule over. Only one tribe, Judah, was to be given to Solomon and his son, and this only for the sake of David. Keep in mind that the tribe of Benjamin was within Judah and was so small that it was considered to be a part of Judah.

3) Ahijah spelled out the reasons why the kingdom was being divided and the nation Israel torn apart (v.33). Three reasons were given:
   ⇒ because the king and the people had forsaken God
   ⇒ because the king and the people had engaged in false worship, see vv.4-8
   ⇒ because the king and the people had disobeyed God's commandments, refusing to walk in the ways of the LORD

4) Ahijah reassured Jeroboam that God had chosen him to rule (vv.34-37). But for David's sake God was not going to take the kingdom out of Solomon's hand during Solomon's lifetime. God would take the kingdom from Solomon's son and give the ten northern tribes to Jeroboam to rule (v.35). However, Jeroboam must remember that God was going to give one tribe, the tribe of Judah, to Solomon's son. David was always to have a light before the LORD in Jerusalem, the city where God had chosen to honor His Name (v.36). By light is meant the unconditional promise of God in the Davidic covenant: that God would someday establish the throne of David and that his throne would be eternal (see outline and notes—2 S.7:1-17 for more discussion). Of course, this points to the Ideal Son of David, the Eternal King who is appointed by God to rule forever upon the throne of David, the Lord Jesus Christ Himself.

   With these words, Ahijah the prophet reassured Jeroboam that God was going to make him king. The young man would rule over all he desired, over the ten tribes of northern Israel.
5) After reassuring Jeroboam, Ahijah declared God's startling promise to the young man. Just as God had established a lasting dynasty for David, God could establish a lasting dynasty for Jeroboam. But there was one very strict condition: obedience. Jeroboam must keep God's commandments. If he kept God's commandments, God promised to grant His very own presence and to give Jeroboam a dynasty that would endure just as much as David's. What a startling and remarkable promise!
6) Finally, Ahijah gave the reason for God's judgment upon Israel and upon David's descendants (v.39). Israel and David's house were to be humbled, punished in judgment. But note what Scripture says: "not forever." Again, this is a reference to the coming Son of David, the Messiah and Savior of the world, the Lord Jesus Christ.

c. Sometime after being confronted by Ahijah and receiving the prophecy of God, Jeroboam rebelled against Solomon. Nothing is said about how Jeroboam rebelled, but his revolt failed. And he was forced to flee for his life. He fled to Egypt where he stayed until Solomon's death (v.40).

Thought 1. Just as God had foretold to Solomon, His hand of judgment began to fall upon the king. So it is with us: when God predicts judgment, the hand of His judgment does fall. If we continue in sin, we will face the judgment of God. Whether we sin through immorality or engage in false worship as Solomon did, or commit more common sins such as lying, cursing, gossiping, or speaking unkindly, we will face the judgment of God. For sin arises from a heart that is not surrendered to God. And the only answer to sin is repentance, a turning of the heart back to God. The answer to sin, to being set free from the enslavement of sin, is repentance. But if we fail to repent, God has no choice but to condemn us and to send His hand of judgment upon us. This is exactly what Holy Scripture says:

"Marvel not at this: for the hour is coming, in the which all that are in the graves shall hear his voice, And shall come forth; they that have done good, unto the resurrection of life; and they that have done evil, unto the resurrection of damnation" (Jn.5:28-29).

"For the wrath of God is revealed from heaven against all ungodliness and unrighteousness of men, who hold the truth in unrighteousness....Being filled with all unrighteousness, fornication, wickedness, covetousness, maliciousness; full of envy, murder, debate, deceit, malignity; whisperers, Backbiters, haters of God, despiteful, proud, boasters, inventors of evil things, disobedient to parents, Without understanding, covenantbreakers, without natural affection, implacable, unmerciful: Who knowing the judgment of God, that they which commit such things are worthy of death, not only do the same, but have pleasure in them that do them" (Ro.1:18, 29-32).

"Know ye not that the unrighteous shall not inherit the kingdom of God? Be not deceived: neither fornicators, nor idolaters, nor adulterers, nor effeminate, nor abusers of themselves with mankind, Nor thieves, nor covetous, nor drunkards, nor revilers, nor extortioners, shall inherit the kingdom of God" (1 Co.6:9-10).

"Now the works of the flesh are manifest, which are *these;* Adultery, fornication, uncleanness, lasciviousness, Idolatry, witchcraft, hatred, variance, emulations, wrath, strife, seditions, heresies, Envyings, murders, drunkenness, revellings, and such like: of the which I tell you before, as I have also told *you* in time past, that they which do such things shall not inherit the kingdom of God" (Ga.5:19-21).

"But fornication, and all uncleanness, or covetousness, let it not be once named among you, as becometh saints; Neither filthiness, nor foolish talking, nor jesting, which are not convenient: but rather giving of thanks. For this ye know, that no whoremonger, nor unclean person, nor covetous man, who is an idolater, hath any inheritance in the kingdom of Christ and of God" (Ep.5:3-5).

"And as it is appointed unto men once to die, but after this the judgment" (He.9:27).

"The Lord knoweth how to deliver the godly out of temptations, and to reserve the unjust unto the day of judgment to be punished" (2 Pe.2:9).

"But the heavens and the earth, which are now, by the same word are kept in store, reserved unto fire against the day of judgment and perdition of ungodly men" (2 Pe.3:7).

"And Enoch also, the seventh from Adam, prophesied of these, saying, Behold, the Lord cometh with ten thousands of his saints, To execute judgment upon all, and to convince all that are ungodly

among them of all their ungodly deeds which they have ungodly committed, and of all their hard *speeches* which ungodly sinners have spoken against him" (Jude 14-15).

"But the fearful, and unbelieving, and the abominable, and murderers, and whoremongers, and sorcerers, and idolaters, and all liars, shall have their part in the lake which burneth with fire and brimstone: which is the second death" (Re.21:8).

4 (11:41-43) **Legacy, of Solomon—Worldliness, Example of—Death, Surety of—Solomon, Death of**: there was the death of Solomon, a legacy of achievement, but tragically also of overindulgence and worldly pleasure. All the events of Solomon's reign were recorded in a book entitled *The Book of the Acts of Solomon* (v.41). Apparently, this was the source of material drawn upon by the author of 1 Kings. But note: not all the events of Solomon's reign are recorded in Scripture.

The reign of Solomon lasted forty years (v.42). But keep in mind that he was to lose his kingdom due to sin. After his death, the unified nation of Israel that had reached its pinnacle of power and international influence was to be torn asunder. The ten northern tribes were to split off from the tribe of Judah, and never again would the nation be unified. All due to Solomon's terrible wickedness—his disobedience and overindulgence.

Note the sad, silent picture of Solomon's death (v.43). No details are given about his passing away or his funeral. The only facts recorded in Scripture are that he was buried in Jerusalem and was succeeded by his son Rehoboam.

OUTLINE	SCRIPTURE	SCRIPTURE	OUTLINE
4. The death of Solomon: A legacy of achievement &, tragically, of worldly pleasure a. The events of his reign were recorded in *The Book of the Acts of Solomon* b. The reign of Solomon lasted 40 years: But he lost his	41 And the rest of the acts of Solomon, and all that he did, and his wisdom, *are* they not written in the book of the acts of Solomon? 42 And the time that Solomon reigned in Jerusalem	over all Israel *was* forty years. 43 And Solomon slept with his fathers, and was buried in the city of David his father: and Rehoboam his son reigned in his stead.	kingdom due to sin c. The sad, silent picture of Solomon's death: Due to his shocking decline into sin 1) Buried in Jerusalem 2) Succeeded by Rehoboam

Thought 1. In closing, the expositor R. D. Patterson in *The Expositor's Bible Commentary* gives an excellent statement to close the life of Solomon:

Solomon left a big mark in history. His memory and fame live on. He represents the first stage in the fulfillment of the Davidic covenant; and, despite his faults, he foreshadows the coming Christ, the true Son of David. In addition his inspired words of wisdom as recorded in Scripture have challenged, taught, and inspired men throughout the ages.[3]

Thought 2. Also giving an excellent summary of the life of Solomon is the commentator Paul R. House. The summary is well worth quoting in full:

With Solomon's death one of the book's major characters leaves the story. Only Elijah, Elisha, and, perhaps, Hezekiah and Josiah approach Solomon's prominence in the overall scheme of 1, 2 Kings. What kind of man was Solomon? How does the author characterize him? Certainly Solomon has some positive traits. Chief among these good qualities is his wisdom. He has the ability to gather knowledge on a wide range of topics, organize the information gathered, write his conclusions, live by his conclusions, and finally teach others what he has learned (cf. 1 Kgs 4:29-34; 10:1-13). Most importantly, at his best Solomon is able to do all these things in spiritual matters. Early in his career Solomon applies his knowledge of Scriptures and his experiences with God in a way that helps him obey God. He keeps the Lord's commands, judges justly, and builds the temple. Thus, wisdom means the ability to obey God's truth, and Solomon is quite able to be wise.

Three other positive characteristics demonstrate Solomon's wisdom in so-called secular realms. First, he is an organizational genius. He is able to order, tax, and govern a fairly extensive political and financial empire. Solomon's cognitive abilities make this success possible. Second, he implements an effective foreign policy, which demonstrates his adaptability and willingness to compromise and improvise. Third, Solomon is humble enough to ask for God's help and thoughtful enough to pray for Israel, both in his time and in the future, and for other nations as well. Despite his failings in later years these good traits should not be forgotten.

Sadly, no character sketch of Solomon is complete without an analysis of his flaws. He is capable of expressing his ambition to be a great king through the acquiring of vast wealth and numerous wives. Eventually these twin desires for prestige and sensuality lead to his nation's downfall. Solomon is not beyond using oppressive measures to get what he wants, as the institution of forced labor indicates, nor is he beyond cheating a friend, as his giving of worthless towns to Hiram proves. Worst of all, Solomon condones and even practices idolatry. Thus, he is capable of irrational thinking, ingratitude, and covenant infidelity. At his worst, then, this wise leader of Israel acts no better than the most foolish of his subjects. He thereby serves as a warning to those who take their God-given gifts for granted or, worse, come to believe they have achieved greatness on their own.[4]

---

[3] Richard D. Patterson and Hermann J. Austel. *1, 2 Kings*, p.112.
[4] Paul R. House. *1, 2 Kings*, pp.173-174.

PART TWO: THE DIVIDED KINGDOM 12:1–22:53

DIVISION II

THE EARLY HISTORY OF THE DIVIDED KINGDOM: WITNESSING THE AWFUL RISE OF IDOLATRY AND FALSE WORSHIP, 12:1–16:34

(12:1–16:34) **DIVISION OVERVIEW**: tragically, the nation of Israel is split asunder, divided into two kingdoms, the Southern Kingdom of Judah and the Northern Kingdom of Israel. Why? Because of sin, because of the wicked lives of Solomon and the people. In the latter years of Solomon's reign he had...

- become sensual, carnal, fleshly
- given himself up to covetousness and pride, seeking more and more power, wealth, prestige, honor, and fame
- attempted to cheat in paying King Hiram for materials and labor
- begun to oppress the people through instituting a nationwide draft of forced labor
- turned away from the LORD to false gods and false worship
- disobeyed the commandments of God, breaking his covenant with the LORD and living a wicked life

As a result of Solomon's unfaithfulness, the LORD had sent the prophet Ahijah to pronounce judgment upon the people (11:27-40). The judgment was shocking: the union of Israel was to be split asunder. The nation was to be split into two kingdoms. Ten tribes were to rebel against the house of David and form the Northern Kingdom under the leadership of Jeroboam. Only two tribes, the tribes of Judah and Benjamin, would continue to be ruled by the dynasty of David. Because of God's promise to give David an eternal dynasty of descendants, God would make sure the royal line of David continued. Ultimately this promise was to be fulfilled in Christ. But presently, David's royal descendants were to rule only over Judah and Benjamin. However, they would rule only as long as they and the people were faithful to the LORD, obeying His commandments and worshipping Him alone.

In the Northern Kingdom, Jeroboam soon forgot the LORD and His promises. Fearing he might lose the loyalty of his people if they continued to make pilgrimages to the temple in Jerusalem, he established an alternative religion, a false *State religion* to compete with the temple. He built two major worship centers in the Northern Kingdom and encouraged the people to be faithful to the false worship centers (12:25-33). Despite warnings from the LORD's prophets, Jeroboam refused to repent. Consequently, God executed judgment against him that ended his dynasty (13:1–14:20).

During Jeroboam's reign in Israel, three Judean kings ruled: Rehoboam, Abijah, and Asa. After Rehoboam's evil reign in Judah, his son Abijah followed in his wicked steps, but his rule thankfully lasted only three years. Then Rehoboam's grandson Asa assumed the throne. Asa lived and ruled righteously just as his great-grandfather David had. Blessed by God, he executed spiritual and religious reforms throughout the Southern Kingdom of Judah. As a result, he was given a long reign of 41 years by the LORD (15:1-24).

Following the discussion of Jeroboam's evil reign in the Northern Kingdom, the author gives brief biographies of six different kings. The last ruler in the division is Ahab, who becomes the major ruler in the remaining story of *First Kings* (15:25–16:24).

In looking at this division of *First Kings,* one can easily see the seeds of moral and political decline. Politically, the nation is divided and weakened both militarily and economically, destined to be oppressed and overrun by nation after nation. Morally and spiritually, the people of both kingdoms are said to have turned away from the LORD to false gods and false worship. And in the Northern Kingdom, a new religion has even been instituted to compete with the worship of the LORD at the temple in Jerusalem.

The reader is left with a sense of God's judgment lying just over the horizon. It is just a matter of how long God's patience will tolerate His people's wallowing around in the cesspool of wickedness and false worship.

THE EARLY HISTORY OF THE DIVIDED KINGDOM: WITNESSING THE AWFUL RISE OF IDOLATRY AND FALSE WORSHIP, 12:1–16:34

A. The Division of the Kingdom: A Picture of Arrogance and of God's Sovereign Judgment, 12:1-24

DIVISION II
12:1–16:34

B. **The Reign of Jeroboam I in Israel (Part 1): A Picture of Being a Stumbling Block to Others, 12:25–13:34**
C. **The Reign of Jeroboam I in Israel (Part 2): A Prophecy of God's Judgment, 14:1-20**
D. **The Reign of Rehoboam in Judah: A Sad, Detestable Life, 14:21-31**
E. **The Reign of Two Kings in Judah, Abijah (Abijam) and Asa, Father and Son: A Son Who Refused to Walk in the Evil Steps of His Father, 15:1-24**
F. **The Reign of Six Kings in Israel, from Nadab to Ahab: A Downward Spiral of Sin and Destruction, 15:25–16:34**

CHAPTER 12

PART II
THE DIVIDED KINGDOM
12:1–22:53

II. THE EARLY HISTORY OF THE DIVIDED KINGDOM: WITNESSING THE AWFUL RISE OF IDOLATRY & FALSE WORSHIP, 12:1–16:34

A. The Division of the Kingdom: A Picture of Arrogance & of God's Sovereign Judgment, 12:1-24

12:1-24; see 2 Chr.10:1–11:4

1. The coronation of Rehoboam & the revolt against him: A picture of arrogance, pride, & conceit

a. The coronation was held in Shechem

b. The news of Solomon's death & Rehoboam's scheduled coronation reached Jeroboam: He returned from Egypt

c. The northern tribes demanded social reform before they crowned Rehoboam as king
   1) Their leader: Jeroboam
   2) Their specific demand
      • Relief from the compulsory draft into government service, 5:13-18
      • Less taxes

d. The request made by King Rehoboam was for three days to consider the unexpected demand
   1) He consulted the older advisors who had served his father
      • They advised the king to serve the people, to grant the requested social reforms: Would unite the nation & assure their loyalty
      • He rejected their counsel
   2) He sought the advice of contemporaries who were his own age
      • He spelled out the social reform demanded by the northern tribes
      • They suggested he threaten the northern tribes, declaring that he would be harsher, tougher than his father Solomon
      • They also advised that he threaten more taxes & a much heavier demand for government service

e. The demand for social reform was arrogantly rejected by King Rehoboam
   1) The various parties convened
   2) The king rejected the counsel of the elders & followed the course of the younger contemporaries: He declared his harsh decision
      • He would tax them more heavily & make the work load heavier
      • He would even use severe punishment to enforce heavier taxes & labor

2. The rupture, division of the kingdom: A picture of God's sovereignty in working out His judgment upon Israel due to their terrible sin—just as prophesied, 11:27-40

a. The reaction to King Rehoboam's harsh decision was quick, abrupt
   1) The 10 northern tribes revolted, broke off from Judah
   2) The 10 northern tribes marched home
   3) The Israelites of Judah still supported Rehoboam

b. The king made an unwise attempt to either enforce the tax & forced labor law or work out a compromise
   1) His superintendent was killed

And Rehoboam went to Shechem: for all Israel were come to Shechem to make him king.

2 And it came to pass, when Jeroboam the son of Nebat, who was yet in Egypt, heard *of it,* (for he was fled from the presence of king Solomon, and Jeroboam dwelt in Egypt;)

3 That they sent and called him. And Jeroboam and all the congregation of Israel came, and spake unto Rehoboam, saying,

4 Thy father made our yoke grievous: now therefore make thou the grievous service of thy father, and his heavy yoke which he put upon us, lighter, and we will serve thee.

5 And he said unto them, Depart yet *for* three days, then come again to me. And the people departed.

6 And king Rehoboam consulted with the old men, that stood before Solomon his father while he yet lived, and said, How do ye advise that I may answer this people?

7 And they spake unto him, saying, If thou wilt be a servant unto this people this day, and wilt serve them, and answer them, and speak good words to them, then they will be thy servants for ever.

8 But he forsook the counsel of the old men, which they had given him, and consulted with the young men that were grown up with him, *and* which stood before him:

9 And he said unto them, What counsel give ye that we may answer this people, who have spoken to me, saying, Make the yoke which thy father did put upon us lighter?

10 And the young men that were grown up with him spake unto him, saying, Thus shalt thou speak unto this people that spake unto thee, saying, Thy father made our yoke heavy, but make thou *it* lighter unto us; thus shalt thou say unto them, My little *finger* shall be thicker than my father's loins.

11 And now whereas my father did lade you with a heavy yoke, I will add to your yoke: my father hath chastised you with whips, but I will chastise you with scorpions.

12 So Jeroboam and all the people came to Rehoboam the third day, as the king had appointed, saying, Come to me again the third day.

13 And the king answered the people roughly, and forsook the old men's counsel that they gave him;

14 And spake to them after the counsel of the young men, saying, My father made your yoke heavy, and I will add to your yoke: my father *also* chastised you with whips, but I will chastise you with scorpions.

15 Wherefore the king hearkened not unto the people; for the cause was from the LORD, that he might perform his saying, which the LORD spake by Ahijah the Shilonite unto Jeroboam the son of Nebat.

16 So when all Israel saw that the king hearkened not unto them, the people answered the king, saying, What portion have we in David? neither *have we* inheritance in the son of Jesse: to your tents, O Israel: now see to thine own house, David. So Israel departed unto their tents.

17 But *as for* the children of Israel which dwelt in the cities of Judah, Rehoboam reigned over them.

18 Then king Rehoboam sent Adoram, who *was* over the tribute; and all Israel stoned him with stones, that he died. Therefore king Rehoboam made speed to get

2) He himself barely escaped c. The divided kingdom was permanently ruptured d. The 10 northern tribes crowned Jeroboam as king of Israel e. The army of Judah was immediately mobilized by King Rehoboam: 180,000 soldiers 1) The king's purpose: To subject the 10 northern	him up to his chariot, to flee to Jerusalem. 19 So Israel rebelled against the house of David unto this day. 20 And it came to pass, when all Israel heard that Jeroboam was come again, that they sent and called him unto the congregation, and made him king over all Israel: there was none that followed the house of David, but the tribe of Judah only. 21 And when Rehoboam was come to Jerusalem, he assembled all the house of Judah, with the tribe of Benjamin, an hundred and fourscore thousand chosen men, which were warriors, to fight against the house of Israel, to	bring the kingdom again to Rehoboam the son of Solomon. 22 But the word of God came unto Shemaiah the man of God, saying, 23 Speak unto Rehoboam, the son of Solomon, king of Judah, and unto all the house of Judah and Benjamin, and to the remnant of the people, saying, 24 Thus saith the LORD, Ye shall not go up, nor fight against your brethren the children of Israel: return every man to his house; for this thing is from me. They hearkened therefore to the word of the LORD, and returned to depart, according to the word of the LORD.	tribes to his rule, regaining control over the entire kingdom of Israel 2) The intervention of God: He sent the prophet Shemaiah to King Rehoboam & to the leaders of Judah & Benjamin—to declare His Word • Were not to fight • Were to return home • Were to acknowledge that the divided kingdom was of God 3) The king & people obeyed the LORD: Returned home

PART II
THE DIVIDED KINGDOM
12:1–22:53

DIVISION II

THE EARLY HISTORY OF THE DIVIDED KINGDOM: WITNESSING THE AWFUL RISE OF IDOLATRY AND FALSE WORSHIP, 12:1–16:34

A. The Division of the Kingdom: A Picture of Arrogance and of God's Sovereign Judgment, 12:1-24

(12:1-24) **Introduction**: arrogance is a terrible evil, for it puts people down, pushes them away, and treats them as inferior. An arrogant attitude says, "I am superior, better, more qualified and capable, more attractive, and more deserving of attention than you are."

Arrogance can become common behavior for the athlete, the successful manager or businessperson, the highly intelligent or skilled individual, the politician, the excellent speaker or preacher, the successful professional, the famous or highly honored figure.

Arrogance exalts oneself above others, degrading them and often humiliating and shaming them.

But standing opposite the sinful spirit of arrogance is the surety of God's sovereign judgment. God is sovereign, which means that He has the power to execute justice upon the earth. All who are arrogant will stand face-to-face with God when He executes judgment upon the wicked of this earth. For one of the great warnings of God is that of coming judgment. And by His sovereign power, He will move events toward that glorious day when true justice will be executed upon this earth. The righteous will be richly rewarded and the arrogant and unrighteous will face the terrifying hand of God's judgment.

A spirit of arrogance and God's sovereign judgment—these two subjects are the focus of the present chapter. It was the arrogance of Solomon's son Rehoboam that was to cause the divided kingdom of Israel. This is: *The Division of the Kingdom: A Picture of Arrogance and of God's Sovereign Judgment,* 12:1-24.

1. The coronation of Rehoboam and the revolt against him: a picture of arrogance, pride, and conceit (vv.1-14).
2. The rupture, division of the kingdom: a picture of God's sovereignty in working out His judgment upon Israel due to their terrible sin—just as prophesied, 11:27-40 (vv.15-24).

1 (12:1-14) **Arrogance, Example of—Conceit, Example of—Oppression, Caused by—Revolt, Against Rehoboam—Social Reform, Need for, in Israel—Counsel, Example of, Bad**: there was the coronation of Rehoboam and the revolt against him by the ten northern tribes of Israel. Scripture gives the details of the revolt against the son of Solomon:

OUTLINE	SCRIPTURE	SCRIPTURE	OUTLINE
1. The coronation of Rehoboam & the revolt against him: A picture of arrogance, pride, & conceit a. The coronation was held in Shechem b. The news of Solomon's death & Rehoboam's scheduled coronation reached Jeroboam: He returned from Egypt	And Rehoboam went to Shechem: for all Israel were come to Shechem to make him king. 2 And it came to pass, when Jeroboam the son of Nebat, who was yet in Egypt, heard *of it,* (for he was fled from the presence of king Solomon, and Jeroboam dwelt in Egypt;)	that were grown up with him, *and* which stood before him: 9 And he said unto them, What counsel give ye that we may answer this people, who have spoken to me, saying, Make the yoke which thy father did put upon us lighter?	• He spelled out the social reform demanded by the northern tribes
c. The northern tribes demanded social reform before they crowned Rehoboam as king 1) Their leader: Jeroboam 2) Their specific demand • Relief from the compulsory draft into government service, 5:13-18 • Less taxes	3 That they sent and called him. And Jeroboam and all the congregation of Israel came, and spake unto Rehoboam, saying, 4 Thy father made our yoke grievous: now therefore make thou the grievous service of thy father, and his heavy yoke which he put upon us, lighter, and we will serve thee.	10 And the young men that were grown up with him spake unto him, saying, Thus shalt thou speak unto this people that spake unto thee, saying, Thy father made our yoke heavy, but make thou *it* lighter unto us; thus shalt thou say unto them, My little *finger* shall be thicker than my father's loins.	• They suggested he threaten the northern tribes, declaring that he would be harsher, tougher than his father Solomon
d. The request made by King Rehoboam was for three days to consider the unexpected demand	5 And he said unto them, Depart yet *for* three days, then come again to me. And the people departed.	11 And now whereas my father did lade you with a heavy yoke, I will add to your yoke: my father hath chastised you with whips, but I will chastise you with scorpions.	• They also advised that he threaten more taxes & a much heavier demand for government service
1) He consulted the older advisors who had served his father • They advised the king to serve the people, to grant the requested social reforms: Would unite the nation & assure their loyalty • He rejected their counsel 2)He sought the advice of contemporaries who were his own age	6 And king Rehoboam consulted with the old men, that stood before Solomon his father while he yet lived, and said, How do ye advise that I may answer this people? 7 And they spake unto him, saying, If thou wilt be a servant unto this people this day, and wilt serve them, and answer them, and speak good words to them, then they will be thy servants for ever. 8 But he forsook the counsel of the old men, which they had given him, and consulted with the young men	12 So Jeroboam and all the people came to Rehoboam the third day, as the king had appointed, saying, Come to me again the third day. 13 And the king answered the people roughly, and forsook the old men's counsel that they gave him; 14 And spake to them after the counsel of the young men, saying, My father made your yoke heavy, and I will add to your yoke: my father *also* chastised you with whips, but I will chastise you with scorpions.	e. The demand for social reform was arrogantly rejected by King Rehoboam 1) The various parties convened 2) The king rejected the counsel of the elders & followed the course of the younger contemporaries: He declared his harsh decision • He would tax them more heavily & make the work load heavier • He would even use severe punishment to enforce heavier taxes & labor

a. The coronation of Rehoboam was to take place in Shechem (v.1). *The Bible Knowledge Commentary* makes the point that Shechem was an ideal location for the coronation service, for it was at Shechem that the LORD first appeared to Abraham and gave him the wonderful promises of the promised land and the promised seed (Ge.12:1-7). It was also the site chosen by Jacob as a permanent residence, and it was the place where Joseph was buried (Ge.33:18-20; Jos.24:32). After Israel had entered the promised land, it was in the Valley of Shechem between Mt. Ebel and Mt. Gerizim where the Israelites rededicated themselves to the LORD (Jos.24:1-27). Thus, Shechem was a memorable, sacred location that reminded the Israelites of God's very special promises to them.[1]

Apparently Rehoboam had already been acknowledged as, if not crowned, king in the city of Jerusalem (11:43). Hence the coronation service in Shechem was to be the official crowning of Rehoboam over all Israel.

b. But note what had happened: the news of Solomon's death and of Rehoboam's scheduled coronation had reached Jeroboam (v.2). Remember, Jeroboam had fled to Egypt after his attempted rebellion against Solomon (11:27-40). Now, receiving word of Solomon's death, he returned from Egypt. Being aware of God's appointment of him as the future ruler of the northern tribes, Jeroboam sensed the need to make himself available for God to fulfill his predicted promise.

c. As soon as the various delegations arrived in Shechem, the northern tribes demanded social reform before they would crown Rehoboam as king (vv.3-4). Note that the tribal leaders had sent for Jeroboam, probably to be their spokesman. The specific demands made by the northern tribes were twofold: they wanted relief from compulsory government service, and they wanted fewer taxes to pay. Remember, Solomon had instituted the policy of compulsory government service in order to complete his building projects. He had drafted every male Israelite to serve one month in government service and two months at home, making a total of four months a year spent in government service. Compulsory service

[1] John F. Walvoord and Roy B. Zuck, Editors. *The Bible Knowledge Commentary, Old Testament,* p.510.

plus heavy taxation weighed heavily upon the people, placing a harsh, heavy yoke upon their necks. For years the people had been complaining of the harsh labor and yoke of heavy taxation, but to no avail. But now with the succession of a new king upon the throne, the opportunity was ripe to demand social reform for the people. Bear in mind that Jeroboam had been one of the chief supervisors of the massive work force, overseeing the laborers drafted from the tribes of Joseph, Ephraim, and Manasseh (11:28). Therefore, he was very aware of the harsh labor law, the heavy taxation, and the endless complaints of the people (see outline and note—I K. 5:13-18 for more discussion).

d. After receiving the demand for social reform from the northern tribes, King Rehoboam requested three days to consider the unexpected appeal (vv.5-11). Upon returning to Jerusalem, Rehoboam consulted the older advisors who had served his father (vv.6-7). Through the wisdom they had gained in their years of experience, they advised King Rehoboam to consider the duty of the king. The king's duty was to serve the people; for that reason, they recommended that Rehoboam grant the requested social reforms. By granting the requests, the king would unite the nation and assure the loyalty and allegiance of the northern tribes (v.7). But Rehoboam rejected their counsel.

Instead, he sought the advice of contemporaries, sought the counsel of those who had grown up with him and were his own age (vv.8-11). Once summoned into his presence, the young men heard King Rehoboam spell out the social reform demanded by the northern tribes. He then asked for their counsel, exactly how he should answer the demand. With a spirit of arrogance and pride, the young men suggested that Rehoboam threaten the northern tribes, declaring...

- that he would be harsher and tougher than his father Solomon had been
- that if they thought his father had placed a heavy yoke upon them, they knew nothing yet, for his little finger was thicker than his father's waist (v.10)

The young counselors also advised that Rehoboam threaten more taxes, a much heavier demand for government service, and more severe punishment. Although his father had scourged them with whips, he would scourge them with scorpions (v.11).

e. Three days later, when the officials of the northern tribes regathered, Rehoboam arrogantly rejected the demand for social reform (vv.12-14). He refused to heed the counsel of his father's former advisors and instead followed the counsel of the younger contemporaries. He declared his harsh decision:

⇒ He would tax the tribes more heavily and make the workload even more burdensome than his father had ever thought of doing.

⇒ He would even use more severe punishment to enforce heavier taxes and labor: he would scourge the people with whips and with scorpions.

Thought 1. There is one major lesson for us in this passage, the lesson to guard against arrogance and pride. Rehoboam and his young advisors had grown up in the palace with all the luxury and wealth imaginable. They knew nothing of hard work and serious responsibility. On the contrary, they had most likely been pampered and indulged all their lives. Thus they demonstrated a spirit of arrogance and pride against the people of Israel. This evil spirit, as we will see in the next point, tore the nation apart.

An arrogant, prideful spirit exalts us over other people, declaring that we are better than they are:

⇒ better looking	⇒ more wealthy	⇒ more athletic
⇒ more intelligent	⇒ more esteemed	⇒ more educated
⇒ more acceptable	⇒ more skilled	⇒ more socially acceptable

Arrogance and pride exclude others and, carried to the extreme, can lead to such serious abuse as slavery or even war. No sin is any more evil in the eyes of God than the sin of arrogance and pride. Listen to what the Word of God says:

"And whosoever shall exalt himself shall be abased; and he that shall humble himself shall be exalted" (Mt.23:12).

"*Be* of the same mind one toward another. Mind not high things, but condescend to men of low estate. Be not wise in your own conceits" (Ro.12:16).

"And if any man think that he knoweth any thing, he knoweth nothing yet as he ought to know" (1 Co.8:2).

"Love not the world, neither the things *that are* in the world. If any man love the world, the love of the Father is not in him. For all that *is* in the world, the lust of the flesh, and the lust of the eyes, and the pride of life, is not of the Father, but is of the world" (1 Jn.2:15-16).

"And the afflicted people thou wilt save: but thine eyes *are* upon the haughty, *that* thou mayest bring *them* down" (2 S.22:28).

"Be not wise in thine own eyes: fear the LORD, and depart from evil" (Pr.3:7).

"Better *it is to be* of an humble spirit with the lowly, than to divide the spoil with the proud" (Pr.16:19).

"He loveth transgression that loveth strife: *and* he that exalteth his gate seeketh destruction" (Pr.17:19).

"An high look, and a proud heart, *and* the plowing of the wicked, *is* sin" (Pr.21:4).

"Seest thou a man wise in his own conceit? *there is* more hope of a fool than of him" (Pr.26:12).

"He that is of a proud heart stirreth up strife: but he that putteth his trust in the LORD shall be made fat" (Pr.28:25).

"Woe unto *them that are* wise in their own eyes, and prudent in their own sight" (Is.5:21).

"For thou hast said in thine heart, I will ascend into heaven, I will exalt my throne above the stars of God: I will sit also upon the mount of the congregation, in the sides of the north: I will ascend above

the heights of the clouds; I will be like the most High. Yet thou shalt be brought down to hell, to the sides of the pit" (Is.14:13-15).

"The earth mourneth *and* fadeth away, the world languisheth *and* fadeth away, the haughty people of the earth do languish" (Is.24:4).

"Though thou exalt *thyself* as the eagle, and though thou set thy nest among the stars, thence will I bring thee down, saith the LORD" (Obad.4).

2 (12:15-24) **Judgment, Surety of—Sovereignty, of God, Example of—Division, of Israel—Israel, Division of—Kingdom, of Israel, Division—Division, of Israel, Event of—Prophecy, Fulfilled, Concerning Israel**: there was the rupture or division of the kingdom of Israel. This is a clear picture of God's sovereignty using these events to work out His judgment upon Israel—just as He had prophesied (11:27-40). Of course, God foresaw the sins of Rehoboam and his young contemporaries, knowing exactly what they were going to do and the inevitable results that would occur. Their sinful behavior was under the power of God's sovereignty, so He used these events to work out His judgment upon Israel due to Solomon's terrible wickedness. Just as God had prophesied, the nation of Israel were now ruptured, torn apart and divided, never again to be reunited. Scripture gives the tragic details of what happened:

OUTLINE	SCRIPTURE	SCRIPTURE	OUTLINE
2. The rupture, division of the kingdom: A picture of God's sovereignty in working out His judgment upon Israel due to their terrible sin—just as prophesied, 11:27-40	15 Wherefore the king hearkened not unto the people; for the cause was from the LORD, that he might perform his saying, which the LORD spake by Ahijah the Shilonite unto Jeroboam the son of Nebat.	that they sent and called him unto the congregation, and made him king over all Israel: there was none that followed the house of David, but the tribe of Judah only.	
a. The reaction to King Rehoboam's harsh decision was quick, abrupt 1) The 10 northern tribes revolted, broke off from Judah 2) The 10 northern tribes marched home	16 So when all Israel saw that the king hearkened not unto them, the people answered the king, saying, What portion have we in David? neither *have we* inheritance in the son of Jesse: to your tents, O Israel: now see to thine own house, David. So Israel departed unto their tents.	21 And when Rehoboam was come to Jerusalem, he assembled all the house of Judah, with the tribe of Benjamin, an hundred and fourscore thousand chosen men, which were warriors, to fight against the house of Israel, to bring the kingdom again to Rehoboam the son of Solomon.	e. The army of Judah was immediately mobilized by King Rehoboam: 180,000 soldiers 1) The king's purpose: To subject the 10 northern tribes to his rule, regaining control over the entire kingdom of Israel
3) The Israelites of Judah still supported Rehoboam	17 But *as for* the children of Israel which dwelt in the cities of Judah, Rehoboam reigned over them.	22 But the word of God came unto Shemaiah the man of God, saying, 23 Speak unto Rehoboam, the son of Solomon, king of Judah, and unto all the house of Judah and Benjamin, and to the remnant of the people, saying,	2) The intervention of God: He sent the prophet Shemaiah to King Rehoboam & to the leaders of Judah & Benjamin—to declare His Word
b. The king made an unwise attempt to either enforce the tax & forced labor law or work out a compromise 1) His superintendent was killed 2) He himself barely escaped	18 Then king Rehoboam sent Adoram, who *was* over the tribute; and all Israel stoned him with stones, that he died. Therefore king Rehoboam made speed to get him up to his chariot, to flee to Jerusalem.	24 Thus saith the LORD, Ye shall not go up, nor fight against your brethren the children of Israel: return every man to his house; for this thing is from me. They	• Were not to fight • Were to return home • Were to acknowledge that the divided kingdom was of God
c. The divided kingdom was permanently ruptured	19 So Israel rebelled against the house of David unto this day.	hearkened therefore to the word of the LORD, and returned to depart, according to the word of the LORD.	3) The king & people obeyed the LORD: Returned home
d. The 10 northern tribes crowned Jeroboam as king of Israel	20 And it came to pass, when all Israel heard that Jeroboam was come again,		

a. The reaction by the northern tribes to King Rehoboam's harsh decision was quick, abrupt (vv.16-17). They revolted, broke off from Judah. And note: they apparently had been prepared for a harsh decision by King Rehoboam, for they made a formal, defiant statement declaring that they had no share and wanted no part in the dynasty of David. Then they shouted out, "To your tents, O Israel! Look after your own house, O David."

With this formal declaration, the ten northern tribes marched away from Shechem and returned home. But the Israelites of Judah still supported Rehoboam (v.17).

b. Soon thereafter, Rehoboam determined to make one final effort to enforce his control over the northern tribes. This he did by sending Adoniram (or Adoram) either to enforce the tax and labor service law or to work out a compromise with the northern tribes (v.18). Exactly what his purpose was is not stated by Scripture. But regardless of his purpose, his attempt was futile. The labor official was immediately killed and Rehoboam himself barely escaped from the pursuing mob with his life.

c. From that day forward, the kingdom was permanently ruptured. It existed as two kingdoms up until the very day of the author's writing of *First Kings* (v.19).

d. The ten northern tribes immediately crowned Jeroboam as king of what was to become known thereafter as Israel (v.20). Only the tribe of Judah, ruled by Solomon's son Rehoboam, remained loyal to the house or dynasty of David. Keep in mind that the tribe of Benjamin was usually counted as part of Judah because of its small size and its location within the boundaries of Judah's territory.

e. When Rehoboam returned to Jerusalem, he immediately mobilized an army of 180,000 soldiers to invade the northern tribes and to subject them under his rule. Unwisely, he had made the decision to try to regain control of the northern tribes.

But note the intervention of God (vv.22-24). He sent a "man of God" or prophet to King Rehoboam and to the leaders of Judah and Benjamin with a stark warning: they were not to fight against their brothers, the Israelites. Rather, they were to return home, for the ruptured, divided kingdom was of God, the work of His hands. Hearing this from the prophet, the king and the people obeyed the LORD and returned home.

Thought 1. This is a clear picture of God's sovereignty, of how He uses events to work out His will upon earth. In the present instance, God uses the arrogance and pride of Rehoboam and his contemporaries to work out His judgment upon Israel. Still today God uses events and the behavior of men to execute righteousness upon this earth, to accomplish His eternal purposes for mankind. We can rest assured of this one truth: God works all things out for good to those who love Him and are called by Him. In fact, God's ultimate purpose is to work all things together for good, both for Christ and for His dear followers. This is the reason all the evil deeds and terrible wickedness committed by men down through history will be frustrated and eventually overcome by good. No tyrant and no evil nation will last forever.

Look down through the pages of human history: look at the world and society today, the good people who are still living and the good deeds that are still being done; all the love, joy, and peace, and all the beauty of nature that is still existing. Despite all the evil, devastation, and pollution in the world, goodness and beauty still exists upon the earth. This is due to God's sovereignty, to His moving and working all things together for good to those who truly love Him and are called by Him. The ultimate proof of this was the coming of the Ideal Son of David, the Messiah and Savior of this world, the Lord Jesus Christ Himself—whom God sent to deliver man from his sins. The Sovereignty of God is one of the strong teachings of God's Holy Word:

"And lead us not into temptation, but deliver us from evil: For thine is the kingdom, and the power, and the glory, for ever. Amen" (Mt.6:13).

"God that made the world and all things therein, seeing that he is LORD of heaven and earth, dwelleth not in temples made with hands" (Ac.17:24).

"Thou wilt say then unto me, Why doth he yet find fault? For who hath resisted his will? Nay but, O man, who art thou that repliest against God? Shall the thing formed say to him that formed *it,* Why hast thou made me thus? Hath not the potter power over the clay, of the same lump to make one vessel unto honour, and another unto dishonour?" (Ro.9:19-21).

"For he must reign, till he hath put all enemies under his feet" (1 Co.15:25).

"To the only wise God our Saviour, *be* glory and majesty, dominion and power, both now and ever. Amen" (Jude 25).

"The LORD shall reign for ever and ever" (Ex.15:18).

"Because thy rage against me and thy tumult is come up into mine ears, therefore I will put my hook in thy nose, and my bridle in thy lips, and I will turn thee back by the way by which thou camest" (2 K.19:28).

"Both riches and honour *come* of thee, and thou reignest over all; and in thine hand *is* power and might; and in thine hand *it is* to make great, and to give strength unto all" (1 Chr.29:12).

"And said, O LORD God of our fathers, *art* not thou God in heaven? and rulest *not* thou over all the kingdoms of the heathen? and in thine hand *is there not* power and might, so that none is able to withstand thee?" (2 Chr.20:6).

"Behold, he taketh away, who can hinder him? who will say unto him, What doest thou?" (Jb.9:12).

"He leadeth princes away spoiled, and overthroweth the mighty" (Jb.12:19).

"The LORD *is* King for ever and ever: the heathen are perished out of his land" (Ps.10:16).

"For the kingdom *is* the LORD'S: and he *is* the governor among the nations" (Ps.22:28).

"Consume *them* in wrath, consume *them*, that they *may* not *be*: and let them know that God ruleth in Jacob unto the ends of the earth. Selah" (Ps.59:13).

"That *men* may know that thou, whose name alone is JEHOVAH, art the most high over all the earth" (Ps.83:18).

"The LORD reigneth, he is clothed with majesty; the LORD is clothed with strength, *wherewith* he hath girded himself: the world also is stablished, that it cannot be moved" (Ps.93:1).

"The LORD hath prepared his throne in the heavens; and his kingdom ruleth over all" (Ps.103:19).

"Whatsoever the LORD pleased, *that* did he in heaven, and in earth, in the seas, and all deep places" (Ps.135:6).

"The king's heart *is* in the hand of the LORD, *as* the rivers of water: he turneth it whithersoever he will" (Pr.21:1).

"Of the increase of *his* government and peace *there shall be* no end, upon the throne of David, and upon his kingdom, to order it, and to establish it with judgment and with justice from henceforth even for ever. The zeal of the LORD of hosts will perform this" (Is.9:7).

"But I know thy abode, and thy going out, and thy coming in, and thy rage against me. Because thy rage against me, and thy tumult, is come up into mine ears, therefore will I put my hook in thy nose, and my bridle in thy lips, and I will turn thee back by the way by which thou camest" (Is.37:28-29).

"Thus saith the LORD, thy redeemer, and he that formed thee from the womb, I *am* the LORD that maketh all *things*; that stretcheth forth the heavens alone; that spreadeth abroad the earth by myself; That frustrateth the tokens of the liars, and maketh diviners mad; that turneth wise *men* backward, and maketh their knowledge foolish" (Is.44:24-25).

"Behold, the days come, saith the LORD, that I will raise unto David a righteous Branch, and a King shall reign and prosper, and shall execute judgment and justice in the earth" (Je.23:5).

"Daniel answered and said, Blessed be the name of God for ever and ever: for wisdom and might are his" (Da.2:20).

"And all the inhabitants of the earth *are* reputed as nothing: and he doeth according to his will in the army of heaven, and *among* the inhabitants of the earth: and none can stay his hand, or say unto him, What doest thou?" (Da.4:35).

"Now I Nebuchadnezzar praise and extol and honour the King of heaven, all whose works *are* truth, and his ways judgment: and those that walk in pride he is able to abase" (Da.4:37).

"And he was driven from the sons of men; and his heart was made like the beasts, and his dwelling *was* with the wild asses: they fed him with grass like oxen, and his body was wet with the dew of heaven; till he knew that the most high God ruled in the kingdom of men, and *that* he appointeth over it whomsoever he will" (Da.5:21).

"And there was given him dominion, and glory, and a kingdom, that all people, nations, and languages, should serve him: his dominion *is* an everlasting dominion, which shall not pass away, and his kingdom *that* which shall not be destroyed" (Da.7:14).

1. Jeroboam's rule solidified: A picture of idolatry & false worship
a. He fortified & made Shechem his capital & built up Penuel
b. He instituted a new form of religion
1) He feared the people's allegiance to the temple in Jerusalem
• Their religion might arouse them to reunite with Judah & Rehoboam
• They might kill him
2) He sought advice & erected two gold calves as idols: Claimed they represented the gods of their deliverance
• Encouraged the people to worship them instead of going up to Jerusalem
• Set one idol in the south at Bethel & one in the north at Dan
• Worship of the idols was a terrible sin: Broke the first & second commandments, Ex.20:3-6
3) He built local worship sites
4) He appointed a new religious order of priests (non-Levites) from all the tribes to live among the people
5) He replaced the Festival of Tabernacles with a new Fall Festival, changing the date from the 7th to the 8th month
6) He personally officiated as priest, offering sacrifices to the idol calves
7) He appointed priests to serve at the national worship center at Bethel (& most likely at Dan)
8) He personally officiated at the first special religious festival: It was instituted to replace the Festival of Tabernacles for the Israelites

B. The Reign of Jeroboam I in Israel (Part 1): A Picture of Being a Stumbling Block to Others, 12:25–13:34

25 Then Jeroboam built Shechem in mount Ephraim, and
dwelt therein; and went out
from thence, and built
Penuel.
26 And Jeroboam said in
his heart, Now shall the
kingdom return to the house
of David:
27 If this people go up to do
sacrifice in the house of the
LORD at Jerusalem, then shall
the heart of this people turn
again unto their lord, *even*
unto Rehoboam king of Ju-
dah, and they shall kill me,
and go again to Rehoboam
king of Judah.
28 Whereupon the king took
counsel, and made two calves
of gold, and said unto them,
It is too much for you to go
up to Jerusalem: behold thy
gods, O Israel, which brought
thee up out of the land of
Egypt.
29 And he set the one in
Bethel, and the other put he
in Dan.
30 And this thing became a
sin: for the people went *to*
worship before the one, *even*
unto Dan.
31 And he made an house of
high places, and made priests
of the lowest of the people,
which were not of the sons of
Levi.
32 And Jeroboam ordained
a feast in the eighth month,
on the fifteenth day of
the month, like unto the feast
that *is* in Judah, and he
offered upon the altar. So
did he in Bethel, sacrificing
unto the calves that he had
made: and he placed in Bethel the priests of the
high places which he had
made.
33 So he offered upon the altar which he had made in
Bethel the fifteenth day of the
eighth month, *even* in the
month which he had devised
of his own heart; and or-
dained a feast unto the children of Israel: and he offered
upon the altar, and burnt
incense.

CHAPTER 13

And, behold, there came a
man of God out of Judah by
the word of the LORD unto
Bethel: and Jeroboam stood
by the altar to burn incense.
2 And he cried against the altar in the word of the LORD,
and said, O altar, altar, thus
saith the LORD; Behold, a
child shall be born unto the
house of David, Josiah by
name; and upon thee shall he
offer the priests of the high
places that burn incense upon
thee, and men's bones shall
be burnt upon thee.
3 And he gave a sign the
same day, saying, This *is* the
sign which the LORD hath
spoken; Behold, the altar
shall be rent, and the ashes
that *are* upon it shall be
poured out.
4 And it came to pass, when
king Jeroboam heard the saying of the man of God, which
had cried against the altar in
Bethel, that he put forth his
hand from the altar, saying,
Lay hold on him. And his
hand, which he put forth
against him, dried up, so that
he could not pull it in again
to him.
5 The altar also was rent, and
the ashes poured out from the
altar, according to the sign
which the man of God had
given by the word of the
LORD.
6 And the king answered and
said unto the man of God, In-
treat now the face of the
LORD thy God, and pray for
me, that my hand may be restored me again. And the
man of God besought the
LORD, and the king's hand
was restored him again, and
became as *it was* before.
7 And the king said unto the
man of God, Come home
with me, and refresh thyself,
and I will give thee a reward.
8 And the man of God said
unto the king, If thou wilt
give me half thine house, I
will not go in with thee, neither will I eat bread nor drink
water in this place:
9 For so was it charged me by
the word of the LORD, saying,
Eat no bread, nor drink water, nor turn again by the

2. Jeroboam's false religion denounced: A picture of God's judgment against false religion
a. The king was confronted by a young unnamed prophet
b. The prophet prophesied against the altar or false worship of Jeroboam
1) The altar & its priests would be destroyed by a future descendant of David named Josiah (about 300 years later, 2 K.23:15-20)
2) The proof that this prophecy, this event, would take place was to be given that day: The altar was to be split apart & the ashes poured out—by God's power
c. The sign of God's power was immediately seen
1) King Jeroboam—gripped by anger—stretched out his hand, ordering his guards to arrest the young prophet: His hand was immediately paralyzed & withered, shriveling up
2) The altar was immediately split apart & its ashes poured out—just as predicted: God rejected the false worship
d. The terrified Jeroboam pled with the prophet for help
1) He requested that the prophet pray & ask the LORD to heal his hand: The prophet prayed & the LORD answered
2) He requested the young prophet to dine with him & to accept payment
• The young prophet emphatically refused: He would not dine with him nor accept payment, even if the king offered one-half his possessions
• The reason: This was the LORD's command

- The obedience of the young prophet

3. Jeroboam's evil influence & its impact: An example of being a stumbling block to others

a. The evil influence upon an old prophet of Israel
  1) The old prophet heard about the young prophet's confrontation with the king
    - He asked his sons which way the young prophet had gone & asked them to saddle his donkey: He hoped to overtake the young prophet
    - He rode after the young prophet & found him resting under an oak tree
    - He invited the young prophet to return home to dine with him
  2) The young prophet refused
    - He could not fellowship within Israel (among idolaters & false worshippers)
    - He could not come because of God's command
  3) The old prophet lied to persuade the young prophet to accept the invitation
    - Claimed an angel instructed him to bring the young prophet to his house
    - Was lying: An apostate
  4) The young prophet went: Disobeyed—accepted the contradiction of God's Word

b. The young prophet was rebuked & condemned to death by the LORD—through the old prophet
  1) He had disobeyed God's Word, not kept His commandment

same way that thou camest.
10 So he went another way,
and returned not by the way
that he came to Bethel.
11 Now there dwelt an old
prophet in Bethel; and his
sons came and told him all
the works that the man of
God had done that day in
Bethel: the words which he
had spoken unto the king,
them they told also to their
father.
12 And their father said unto
them, What way went he?
For his sons had seen what
way the man of God went,
which came from Judah.
13 And he said unto his
sons, Saddle me the ass. So
they saddled him the ass: and
he rode thereon,
14 And went after the man
of God, and found him sitting
under an oak: and he said unto him, *Art* thou the man of
God that camest from Judah?
And he said, I *am*.
15 Then he said unto him,
Come home with me, and eat
bread.
16 And he said, I may not
return with thee, nor go in
with thee: neither will I eat
bread nor drink water with
thee in this place:
17 For it was said to me by
the word of the LORD, Thou
shalt eat no bread nor drink
water there, nor turn again to
go by the way that thou camest.
18 He said unto him, I *am* a
prophet also as thou *art;* and
an angel spake unto me by
the word of the LORD, saying, Bring him back with thee
into thine house, that he may
eat bread and drink water.
But he lied unto him.
19 So he went back with
him, and did eat bread in his
house, and drank water.
20 And it came to pass, as
they sat at the table, that the
word of the LORD came unto
the prophet that brought him
back:
21 And he cried unto the man
of God that came from Judah,
saying, Thus saith the LORD,
Forasmuch as thou hast disobeyed the mouth of the
LORD, and hast not kept the
commandment which the
LORD thy God commanded
thee,
22 But camest back, and hast
eaten bread and drunk water
in the place, of the which *the
LORD* did say to thee, Eat no
bread, and drink no water;
thy carcase shall not come
unto the sepulchre of thy fathers.
23 And it came to pass, after
he had eaten bread, and after
he had drunk, that he saddled
for him the ass, *to wit,* for the
prophet whom he had
brought back.
24 And when he was gone, a
lion met him by the way, and
slew him: and his carcase
was cast in the way, and the
ass stood by it, the lion also
stood by the carcase.
25 And, behold, men passed
by, and saw the carcase cast
in the way, and the lion
standing by the carcase: and
they came and told it in the
city where the old prophet
dwelt.
26 And when the prophet
that brought him back from
the way heard *thereof,* he
said, It *is* the man of God,
who was disobedient unto the
word of the LORD: therefore
the LORD hath delivered him
unto the lion, which hath torn
him, and slain him, according
to the word of the LORD,
which he spake unto him.
27 And he spake to his sons,
saying, Saddle me the ass.
And they saddled *him.*
28 And he went and found
his carcase cast in the way,
and the ass and the lion
standing by the carcase: the
lion had not eaten the carcase, nor torn the ass.
29 And the prophet took up
the carcase of the man of
God, and laid it upon the ass,
and brought it back: and the
old prophet came to the city,
to mourn and to bury him.
30 And he laid his carcase in
his own grave; and they
mourned over him, *saying,*
Alas, my brother!
31 And it came to pass, after
he had buried him, that he
spake to his sons, saying,
When I am dead, then bury
me in the sepulchre wherein
the man of God *is* buried;
lay my bones beside his
bones:
32 For the saying which
he cried by the word of the

  2) He had fellowshipped in Israel (among idolaters & false worshippers), which had been forbidden by God
  3) He would be judged, die away from home

c. The young prophet died just as predicted
  1) He finished dining & preparations were made for his departure
  2) He began his journey home
  3) He came face-to-face with a lion & was killed

d. The old prophet was informed of the young prophet's death & went after his body
  1) The lion & the young prophet's body were seen by some passersby who reported it in Bethel
  2) The old prophet heard about the death
    - He then knew the LORD's prophetic judgment had been fulfilled
    - He had his donkey saddled
    - He left & found the young man's body lying dead on the road, with the lion & donkey standing close by

e. The old prophet demonstrated renewed faith in the Word of God
  1) He tenderly took care of the corpse
  2) He buried the young prophet in his own tomb & mourned for him
  3) He requested his sons to honor him by burying his own body in the grave right beside the young prophet
  4) He declared his reason: He had a renewed faith in

the Word of God—the prophetic messages of the young prophet would surely come to pass **4. Jeroboam's spirit became even more obstinate: An example of hard-heartedness** a. He refused to heed God's	LORD against the altar in Bethel, and against all the houses of the high places which *are* in the cities of Samaria, shall surely come to pass. 33 After this thing Jeroboam returned not from his evil way, but made again of the lowest of the people	priests of the high places: whosoever would, he consecrated him, and he became *one* of the priests of the high places. 34 And this thing became sin unto the house of Jeroboam, even to cut *it* off, and to destroy *it* from off the face of the earth.	prophetic judgment pronounced upon him & that fell upon the young prophet b. He continued to endorse & strengthen false religion c. He was condemned to face the judgment of God: To suffer the loss of his kingdom & family—his dynasty

DIVISION II

THE EARLY HISTORY OF THE DIVIDED KINGDOM: WITNESSING THE AWFUL RISE OF IDOLATRY AND FALSE WORSHIP, 12:1–16:34

B. The Reign of Jeroboam I in Israel (Part 1): A Picture of Being a Stumbling Block to Others, 12:25–13:34

(12:25-13:34) **Introduction**: What kind of influence are we as individuals having upon other people? A good influence or an evil one? A positive influence or a negative one? Are we living sinful lives, leading others into wrongdoing and shame? Or are we setting good examples by living righteous lives of...

- love
- joy
- peace
- patience
- gentleness
- goodness
- faithfulness
- meekness
- self-control

These qualities are what is known as "the fruit of the Holy Spirit." Take just a moment and think about each of these qualities, how the human heart longs for them:

⇒ to love and to be loved
⇒ to feel joy and to share joy with others
⇒ to experience peace and to pass peace on to others

Every action we take, every word we speak is an influence—either good or bad—upon someone. As believers, we must not be stumbling blocks to other people, influencing them to do evil upon this earth. The present passage of Scripture discusses how King Jeroboam—despite his tremendous opportunity and potential for greatness—planted the seeds of evil that were to destroy the Northern Kingdom of Israel. This is: *The Reign of Jeroboam I in Israel (Part 1): A Picture of Being a Stumbling Block to Others,* 12:25–13:34.

1. Jeroboam rule solidified: a picture of idolatry and false worship (vv.25-33).
2. Jeroboam's false religion denounced: a picture of God's judgment against false religion (ch.13:1-10).
3. Jeroboam's evil influence and its impact: an example of being a stumbling block to others (vv.11-32).
4. Jeroboam's spirit became even more obstinate: an example of hard-heartedness (vv.33-34).

1 (12:25-33) **Idolatry, Example of, Jeroboam—Worship, False, Example of—False Worship, Example of, Jeroboam—Religion, False, Instituted by Jeroboam—Priest, False, Order of, Instituted by Jeroboam—Festivals, False, Instituted by Jeroboam**: Jeroboam immediately set out to solidify his rule over the ten northern tribes of Israel. Remember, the ten northern tribes had just revolted against the harsh demands of Rehoboam, splitting the unified nation of Israel apart. Never again would the nation be united. Rehoboam, the son of Solomon, was now ruling over only Judah. Judah included the small tribe of Benjamin, which was within Judah's territory and thus was counted as part of Judah. The ten northern tribes had just crowned Jeroboam as their king; therefore he immediately set out to strengthen his rule. The two steps taken by Jeroboam to solidify the Northern Kingdom—one of which was most tragic and would eventually lead to the collapse of the Northern Kingdom—are detailed by Scripture:

OUTLINE	SCRIPTURE	SCRIPTURE	OUTLINE
1. Jeroboam's rule solidified: A picture of idolatry & false worship a. He fortified & made Shechem his capital & built up Penuel b. He instituted a new form of religion 1) He feared the people's allegiance to the temple in Jerusalem • Their religion might arouse them to reunite with Judah & Rehoboam	25 Then Jeroboam built Shechem in mount Ephraim, and dwelt therein; and went out from thence, and built Penuel. 26 And Jeroboam said in his heart, Now shall the kingdom return to the house of David: 27 If this people go up to do sacrifice in the house of the LORD at Jerusalem, then shall the heart of this people turn	turn again unto their lord, *even* unto Rehoboam king of Judah, and they shall kill me, and go again to Rehoboam king of Judah. 28 Whereupon the king took counsel, and made two calves *of* gold, and said unto them, It is too much for you to go up to Jerusalem: behold thy gods, O Israel, which brought thee up out of the land of Egypt.	• They might kill him 2) He sought advice & erected two gold calves as idols: Claimed they represented the gods of their deliverance • Encouraged the people to worship them instead of going up to Jerusalem

OUTLINE	SCRIPTURE	SCRIPTURE	OUTLINE
• Set one idol in the south at Bethel & one in the north at Dan • Worship of the idols was a terrible sin: Broke the first & second commandments, Ex.20:3-6 3) He built local worship sites 4) He appointed a new religious order of priests (non-Levites) from all the tribes to live among the people 5) He replaced the Festival of Tabernacles with a new Fall Festival, changing the date from the 7th to the8th month	29 And he set the one in Bethel, and the other put he in Dan. 30 And this thing became a sin: for the people went *to worship* before the one, *even* unto Dan. 31 And he made an house of high places, and made priests of the lowest of the people, which were not of the sons of Levi. 32 And Jeroboam ordained a feast in the eighth month, on the fifteenth day of the month, like unto the feast that *is* in Judah, and he	offered upon the altar. So did he in Bethel, sacrificing unto the calves that he had made: and he placed in Bethel the priests of the high places which he had made. 33 So he offered upon the altar which he had made in Bethel the fifteenth day of the eighth month, *even* in the month which he had devised of his own heart; and ordained a feast unto the children of Israel: and he offered upon the altar, and burnt incense.	6) He personally officiated as priest, offering sacrifices to the idol calves 7) He appointed priests to serve at the national worship center at Bethel (& most likely at Dan) 8) He personally officiated at the first special religious festival: It was instituted to replace the Festival of Tabernacles for the Israelites

a. Jeroboam fortified and made Shechem his capital, the very first capital of the northern tribes (v.25). Shechem was a strategic city, for it sat on one of the major roads running through the northern tribes, a road that was used for both commercial and military traffic. Therefore, it was necessary for Jeroboam to fortify the city in order to control the traffic that ran right through the heart of his kingdom.

He also fortified Penuel, which was located on the east side of the Jordan River. By building this fortress, he was able to protect the northern tribes from being invaded by enemies from the east, including the Gileadites. The Gileadites, who had been loyal to David throughout his reign, might attack the northern tribes in a show of support for Judah, David's dynasty. Penuel also sat on one of the major commercial roads of that day that stretched through the land of Gilead all the way to Damascus.[1] By fortifying these two key cities and choosing Shechem to be the capital, Jeroboam solidified the northern tribes. He strengthened both their military and economic concerns.

b. Jeroboam sought to meet the religious concerns of the people by instituting a new form of religion (vv.26-33). Now split, divided from the Southern Kingdom, the northern tribes no longer had free access to the temple at Jerusalem. Note that Jeroboam began to think about the religious issue, trying to figure out a solution that would help him politically.

1) He feared the people's allegiance to the temple in Jerusalem, that their religion and attachment to the temple might arouse them to seek political reunification with Judah (vv.26-27). Within his mind, he concluded that the people were so loyal and attached to the temple that this might actually happen. If they began to return to worship and offer sacrifices to the LORD at the temple in Jerusalem, he reasoned they might seek political reunification, assassinate him, and return the Northern Kingdom to King Rehoboam.

2) Thus Jeroboam sought advice from his counselors concerning the institution of a new form of religion (vv.28-30). After seeking the advice and receiving confirmation, Jeroboam had two golden calves made and erected as idols (vv.28-30). He then encouraged the people to worship the idols instead of making the long journey to Jerusalem. Note that he proceeded to make an *utterly* foolish and false claim: that these two idols were the gods of the Israelites who had brought them up out of Egypt. Keep in mind that the actual idols of false religions are seldom if ever considered to be gods themselves, but rather representations or symbols of the gods worshipped by the people. Most likely, Jeroboam was claiming that these two idols were symbols of the LORD Himself. Being calves, they were symbols of strong, powerful creatures. Therefore, Jeroboam claimed they were symbols of God's strength and power. These images were only visible representations or images to help the worshipper focus upon God, giving the people something tangible to help stir their faith in the invisible LORD whom they worshipped.

Jeroboam set up one idol in the south at Bethel and the other in the north at Dan (v.29). Choosing these two sights as the religious centers for the northern tribes was a brilliant strategy by Jeroboam, for both sites had a long religious tradition for the Israelites (see outline and notes—Ge.28:10-22; Jud.18:29-31 for more discussion). But establishing these two worship centers resulted in terrible sin, for it was there that the Israelites committed wickedness before the LORD, the wickedness of idolatry and false worship. Of course idolatry and false worship are direct violations of the first and second commandments (Ex.20:3-6). But as stated, the institution of the new form of religion was a brilliant strategy on the part of Jeroboam. In essence, he was saying, "You no longer have to make the long, arduous, and dangerous journey to Jerusalem to worship the LORD, for we have brought the LORD's religion to you."[2]

This fact should be noted: throughout the history of the Northern Kingdom, this false state religion was used by every king to keep the people loyal to the throne. And to their shame, the false worship became so entrenched that there was never an attempt to eliminate it.[3]

3) Jeroboam also built local worship sites all over the territory of the ten northern tribes (v.31). Shrines were most likely built on nearly all of the high hills, enabling the people to easily reach them for daily worship if they wished.

---

1 Paul R. House. *1, 2 Kings*, p.183.

2 *The Nelson Study Bible, NKJV*, I K. 12:29.

3 Matthew Henry. *Matthew Henry's Commentary*, Vol.2, p.774.

4) In a bold move, and in opposition to the clear command of God, he defiled and corrupted the priesthood by appointing a new religious order of priests. These priests were appointed from all sorts of disqualified people, non-Levites, appointed to live in the communities where they could lead the people in the false worship instituted by Jeroboam.

   When Jeroboam instituted the new form of religion and the new order of false priests, the Levitical priests of the Northern Kingdom fled to Jerusalem. It was there that the temple was located and the living and true LORD was still worshipped. The Levitical priests refused to forsake the LORD and to participate in the false state religion initiated by Jeroboam. In addition, many of the genuine believers throughout the ten northern tribes also fled to Jerusalem where they could continue to seek the true and living LORD (2 Chr.11:13-17).
5) In addition to defiling and degrading the holy order of priests, Jeroboam replaced the Festival of Tabernacles with a new fall festival (v.32). He also changed the date for celebrating the festival from the seventh to the eighth month.
6) Note that Jeroboam himself officiated as a priest, offering sacrifices to the idol calves on the altar he had built (v.32). This horrendous sin of assuming the role of a priest and offering up sacrifices was committed at the national worship center in Bethel.
7) After establishing the worship centers at Bethel and Dan, Jeroboam appointed priests to permanently serve at the two national worship sites (v.32).
8) At the very first religious festival, the fact is repeated that Jeroboam himself officiated, offering sacrifices on the altar he had built at Bethel. Note that it is clearly stated: he instituted this special festival for the Israelites of the Northern Kingdom to replace the Festival of Tabernacles (v.33).

Thought 1. The lesson for us is direct, forceful: we must not worship idols nor engage in false worship of any kind. Above all other sins, idolatry and false worship are the most wicked. For when we worship idols, we are worshipping false gods and rejecting the only *living* and *true* God. To reject God is to stand face-to-face *against* God, to throw antagonism and hostility in the face of God. And when we confront God with antagonism and hostility, what kind of reaction can we expect in that day of terrifying judgment? For this reason alone, no evil can compare with the wickedness of idolatry and false worship.

But being antagonistic toward God is not the only evil of idolatry and false worship. When we worship idols and engage in false worship, we influence other people, including our children, friends, neighbors, fellow workers, and all others who have contact with us or hear about us. Through our false beliefs and worship, we mislead people through our bad examples and influence. And millions of people are being misled by those who hold false beliefs and engage in false worship. Listen to the warning of the LORD, the only living and true God:

> **"For the wrath of God is revealed from heaven against all ungodliness and unrighteousness of men, who hold the truth in unrighteousness. Because that which may be known of God is manifest in them; for God hath showed *it* unto them. For the invisible things of him from the creation of the world are clearly seen, being understood by the things that are made, *even* his eternal power and Godhead; so that they are without excuse: Because that, when they knew God, they glorified *him* not as God, neither were thankful; but became vain in their imaginations, and their foolish heart was darkened. Professing themselves to be wise, they became fools, And changed the glory of the uncorruptible God into an image made like to corruptible man, and to birds, and fourfooted beasts, and creeping things. Wherefore God also gave them up to uncleanness through the lusts of their own hearts, to dishonour their own bodies between themselves: Who changed the truth of God into a lie, and worshipped and served the creature more than the Creator, who is blessed for ever. Amen" (Ro.1:18-25).**
>
> **"Know ye not that the unrighteous shall not inherit the kingdom of God? Be not deceived: neither fornicators, nor idolaters, nor adulterers, nor effeminate, nor abusers of themselves with mankind, Nor thieves, nor covetous, nor drunkards, nor revilers, nor extortioners, shall inherit the kingdom of God" (1 Co.6:9-10).**
>
> **"Now the works of the flesh are manifest, which are *these*; Adultery, fornication, uncleanness, lasciviousness, Idolatry, witchcraft, hatred, variance, emulations, wrath, strife, seditions, heresies, Envyings, murders, drunkenness, revellings, and such like: of the which I tell you before, as I have also told you in time past, that they which do such things shall not inherit the kingdom of God" (Ga.5:19-21).**
>
> **"But fornication, and all uncleanness, or covetousness, let it not be once named among you, as becometh saints; Neither filthiness, nor foolish talking, nor jesting, which are not convenient: but rather giving of thanks. For this ye know, that no whoremonger, nor unclean person, nor covetous man, who is an idolater, hath any inheritance in the kingdom of Christ and of God" (Ep.5:3-5).**
>
> **"But the fearful, and unbelieving, and the abominable, and murderers, and whoremongers, and sorcerers, and idolaters, and all liars, shall have their part in the lake which burneth with fire and brimstone: which is the second death" (Re.21:8).**
>
> **"Thou shalt have no other gods before me. Thou shalt not make unto thee any graven image, or any likeness *of any thing* that *is* in heaven above, or that *is* in the earth beneath, or that *is* in the water under the earth" (Ex.20:3-4).**
>
> **"I *am* the LORD: that *is* my name: and my glory will I not give to another, neither my praise to graven images" (Is.42:8).**

DEEPER STUDY #1
(12:31) **High Places**: sometimes the phrase "high places" simply means a place on the mountain side such as in 2 S.22:34: "He maketh my feet like hinds' feet: and setteth me upon my high places." But often the Scripture is speaking of the worship of false gods. In these cases, high places were open-air sanctuaries where altars, shrines, and in some cases enclosed structures were constructed for worship. These open-air sanctuaries were constructed on various hilltops and in the countryside, towns, and cities of the nation. This was in direct violation of God's commandment.

However, God had forbidden the use of pagan altars and high places for worship of the LORD. As the Israelites drove out the Canaanites, they were to completely destroy and remove all places of false worship that had been left behind. (Nu.33:52). God's people were not to allow the infiltration of false beliefs and practices into their lives and into Israel. They were not to participate in the worship of false gods. For this reason, they were not to take over the pagan altars and high places that had been used by the nations they conquered. They were to construct worship centers only at the places chosen by God.

2 (13:1-10) **Judgment, What Is to Be Judged—Religion, False, Judgment of—False Religion, Judgment of—Jeroboam, Rebuked and Denounced**: Jeroboam and his false religion were denounced by a special prophet sent by God. A strong condemnation of Jeroboam could be expected, for his false religion was a terrible evil that would have devastating effects upon the ten northern tribes of Israel. Details of God's rebuke and condemnation are graphically described by the Scripture:

OUTLINE	SCRIPTURE	SCRIPTURE	OUTLINE
2. Jeroboam's false religion denounced: A picture of God's judgment against false religion a. The king was confronted by a young unnamed prophet b. The prophet prophesied against the altar or false worship of Jeroboam 1) The altar & its priests would be destroyed by a future descendant of David named Josiah (about 300 years later, 2 K.23:15-20) 2) The proof that this prophecy, this event, would take place was to be given that day: The altar was to be split apart & the ashes poured out—by God's power c. The sign of God's power was immediately seen 1) King Jeroboam—gripped by anger—stretched out his hand, ordering his guards to arrest the young prophet: His hand was immediately paralyzed & withered, shriveling up	And, behold, there came a man of God out of Judah by the word of the LORD unto Bethel: and Jeroboam stood by the altar to burn incense. 2 And he cried against the altar in the word of the LORD, and said, O altar, altar, thus saith the LORD; Behold, a child shall be born unto the house of David, Josiah by name; and upon thee shall he offer the priests of the high places that burn incense upon thee, and men's bones shall be burnt upon thee. 3 And he gave a sign the same day, saying, This *is* the sign which the LORD hath spoken; Behold, the altar shall be rent, and the ashes that *are* upon it shall be poured out. 4 And it came to pass, when king Jeroboam heard the saying of the man of God, which had cried against the altar in Bethel, that he put forth his hand from the altar, saying, Lay hold on him. And his hand, which he put forth against him, dried up, so that he could not pull it in again to him.	5 The altar also was rent, and the ashes poured out from the altar, according to the sign which the man of God had given by the word of the LORD. 6 And the king answered and said unto the man of God, Intreat now the face of the LORD thy God, and pray for me, that my hand may be restored me again. And the man of God besought the LORD, and the king's hand was restored him again, and became as *it was* before. 7 And the king said unto the man of God, Come home with me, and refresh thyself, and I will give thee a reward. 8 And the man of God said unto the king, If thou wilt give me half thine house, I will not go in with thee, neither will I eat bread nor drink water in this place: 9 For so was it charged me by the word of the LORD, saying, Eat no bread, nor drink water, nor turn again by the same way that thou camest. 10 So he went another way, and returned not by the way that he came to Bethel.	2) The altar was immediately split apart & its ashes poured out—just as predicted: God rejected the false worship d. The terrified Jeroboam pled with the prophet for help 1) He requested that the prophet pray & ask the LORD to heal his hand: The prophet prayed & the LORD answered 2) He requested the young prophet to dine with him & to accept payment • The young prophet emphatically refused: He would not dine with him nor accept payment, even if the king offered one-half his possessions • The reason: This was the LORD's command • The obedience of the young prophet

a. Just as Jeroboam was standing by the altar getting ready to present a false sacrifice, he was suddenly confronted by a young unnamed prophet. Note that he is called a "man of God," which was the way prophets were sometimes addressed. This young prophet had come from Judah, suggesting that no godly prophet could be found by the LORD in the ten northern tribes, not a prophet who was wholeheartedly committed to the LORD and who could be trusted with God's message of condemnation and judgment.

b. The prophecy was against the altar or false worship of Jeroboam (vv.2-3). Shouting to the top of his voice, the young prophet cried out: "O altar, altar! This is what the LORD says."

1) The altar and its priests would be destroyed by a future descendant of David named Josiah (v.2). Note how the very name of the future king was predicted, as well as the destruction of Jeroboam's altar and false worship (2 K.23:15-20). But it would be about 300 years before Josiah would destroy this altar.

2) To prove that this event would take place some 300 years later, the young prophet gave Jeroboam a sign: the altar was to be immediately split apart and the ashes poured out by the power of God Himself (v.3).

c. Immediately after the young prophet's prediction regarding the altar, the miraculous sign was seen (vv.4-5). Infuriated by the prophecy of the altar's destruction, Jeroboam stretched out his hands and ordered his guards to arrest the young prophet. But when he did, his hand was immediately paralyzed and withered, shriveling up. But this was not the only sign of God's power taking place at this moment. The altar was also splitting apart and its ashes pouring out—just as the young prophet had predicted. God had demonstrated that He rejected the false worship of King Jeroboam.

d. Terrified, Jeroboam pled with the prophet for help, begging him to pray for the LORD to heal his hand (v.6). Showing a heart filled with compassion, the prophet did just as the king requested. And the LORD answered, performing a third miracle, healing the king's hand.

Being thoroughly convinced that the prophet had been truly sent by the LORD, Jeroboam requested the young man to dine with him and to accept payment for having healed his hand (vv.7-10). No doubt, Jeroboam hoped to win the favor of the young prophet and perhaps to convince him to join his royal court. Whatever the case, the young prophet emphatically refused the invitation. He would not dine with the king nor accept payment, even if the king offered one-half his possessions. For this was the LORD's command: he was not to eat bread or drink water nor return the same way he had come. The point being made is striking: neither a prophet nor his message is for sale. A prophet must not be put in debt to others. Just why the LORD commanded the prophet to take a different way back to Judah is not stated. Perhaps it was for protection in case Jeroboam decided to retaliate against the young priest. Whatever the reason, the young priest obeyed the instructions of the LORD and took another road back home (v.10).

Thought 1. The lesson for us is again strikingly clear: idolatry and false worship do not please the LORD. God totally opposes idolatry and false worship. But idols are not just images made out of wood, stone, metal, or some other material. We can make an idol out of anything, for idols are anything that captures our heart more than God. We can ignore and forget God, focusing and giving our hearts and primary interests to such people or things as...

- husband, wife, children, or other family members
- girlfriend or boyfriend
- houses, property, cars, planes, or any other possession
- wealth, the making of money, success, or fame
- job, profession, position, authority, or power
- an actor, an athlete, a politician, or even a minister or worship center
- sports (watching or participating in), recreation or leisure activities, television, movies, or computer games

Whatever captivates our hearts, whatever the focus of our hearts is, whatever we give our hearts to—that person or thing becomes our god, our idol. For that person or thing possesses our hearts, our primary interest and attention. As a result, God is either denied or ignored or forgotten. Listen to what God's Holy Word says about idolatry:

"And upon a set day Herod, arrayed in royal apparel, sat upon his throne, and made an oration unto them. And the people gave a shout, *saying, It is* the voice of a god, and not of a man. And immediately the angel of the Lord smote him, because he gave not God the glory: and he was eaten of worms, and gave up the ghost" (Ac.12:21-23).

"For the wrath of God is revealed from heaven against all ungodliness and unrighteousness of men, who hold the truth in unrighteousness....Who changed the truth of God into a lie, and worshipped and served the creature more than the Creator, who is blessed for ever. Amen" (Ro.1:18, 25).

"Little children, keep yourselves from idols. Amen" (1 Jn.5:21).

"Thou shalt not make unto thee any graven image, or any likeness *of any thing* that *is* in heaven above, or that *is* in the earth beneath, or that *is* in the water under the earth" (Ex.20:4).

"Take heed to yourselves, that your heart be not deceived, and ye turn aside, and serve other gods, and worship them" (De.11:16).

"Hear, ye deaf; and look, ye blind, that ye may see" (Is.42:18).

3 (13:11-32) **Stumbling Block, Example of—Influence, Evil, Example of—Jeroboam, Evil Influence of—Prophet, Influenced by, Evil—Example, of Evil**: Jeroboam and his evil had a terrible impact upon others. Tragically, he became a stumbling block to multitudes, even influencing and making an evil impact upon the prophets of his day. What happened to the young prophet of this passage is a strange story. Scripture gives the story in detail:

OUTLINE	SCRIPTURE	SCRIPTURE	OUTLINE
3. Jeroboam's evil influence & its impact: An example of being a stumbling block to others a. The evil influence upon an old prophet of Israel 1) The old prophet heard about the young prophet's confrontation with the king • He asked his sons which way the young prophet	11 Now there dwelt an old prophet in Bethel; and his sons came and told him all the works that the man of God had done that day in Bethel: the words which he had spoken unto the king, them they told also to their father. 12 And their father said unto them, What way went he?	For his sons had seen what way the man of God went, which came from Judah. 13 And he said unto his sons, Saddle me the ass. So they saddled him the ass: and he rode thereon, 14 And went after the man of God, and found him sitting under an oak: and he said unto him, *Art* thou the man of	had gone & asked them to saddle his donkey: He hoped to overtake the young prophet • He rode after the young prophet & found him resting under an oak tree

OUTLINE	SCRIPTURE	SCRIPTURE	OUTLINE
	God that camest from Judah?	slew him: and his carcase	
	And he said, I *am.*	was cast in the way, and the	
• He invited the young	15 Then he said unto him,	ass stood by it, the lion also	
prophet to return home	Come home with me, and eat	stood by the carcase.	
to dine with him	bread.	25 And, behold, men passed	d. The old prophet was informed
2) The young prophet refused	16 And he said, I may not	by, and saw the carcase cast	of the young prophet's death
• He could not fellowship	return with thee, nor go in	in the way, and the lion	& went after his body
within Israel (among	with thee: neither will I eat	standing by the carcase: and	1) The lion & the young
idolaters & false wor-	bread nor drink water with	they came and told it in the	prophet's body were seen
shippers)	thee in this place:	city where the old prophet	by some passersby who
• He could not come be-	17 For it was said to me by	dwelt.	reported it in Bethel
cause of God's com-	the word of the LORD, Thou	26 And when the prophet	2) The old prophet heard
mand	shalt eat no bread nor drink	that brought him back from	about the death
	water there, nor turn again to	the way heard *thereof,* he	• He then knew the
	go by the way that thou camest.	said, It *is* the man of God,	LORD's prophetic judg-
3) The old prophet lied to	18 He said unto him, I *am* a	who was disobedient unto the	ment had been fulfilled
persuade the young proph-	prophet also as thou *art;* and	word of the LORD: therefore	
et to accept the invitation	an angel spake unto me by	the LORD hath delivered him	
• Claimed an angel in-	the word of the LORD, say-	unto the lion, which hath torn	
structed him to bring the	ing, Bring him back with thee	him, and slain him, according	
young prophet to his	into thine house, that he may	to the word of the LORD,	
house	eat bread and drink water.	which he spake unto him.	
• Was lying: An apostate	*But* he lied unto him.	27 And he spake to his sons,	• He had his donkey sad-
4) The young prophet went:	19 So he went back with	saying, Saddle me the ass.	dled
Disobeyed—accepted the	him, and did eat bread in his	And they saddled *him.*	
contradiction of God's Word	house, and drank water.	28 And he went and found	• He left & found the
b. The young prophet was re-	20 And it came to pass, as	his carcase cast in the way,	young man's body lying
buked & condemned to death	they sat at the table, that the	and the ass and the lion	dead on the road, with
by the LORD—through the	word of the LORD came unto	standing by the carcase: the	the lion & donkey stand-
old prophet	the prophet that brought him	lion had not eaten the car-	ing close by
	back:	case, nor torn the ass.	
1) He had disobeyed God's	21 And he cried unto the man	29 And the prophet took up	e. The old prophet demonstrat-
Word, not kept His com-	of God that came from Judah,	the carcase of the man of	ed renewed faith in the Word
mandment	saying, Thus saith the LORD,	God, and laid it upon the ass,	of God
	Forasmuch as thou hast diso-	and brought it back: and the	1) He tenderly took care of
	beyed the mouth of the LORD,	old prophet came to the city,	the corpse
	and hast not kept the com-	to mourn and to bury him.	
	mandment which the LORD	30 And he laid his carcase in	2) He buried the young
	thy God commanded thee,	his own grave; and they	prophet in his own tomb
2) He had fellowshipped in	22 But camest back, and hast	mourned over him, *saying,*	& mourned for him
Israel (among idolaters &	eaten bread and drunk water	Alas, my brother!	
false worshippers), which	in the place, of the which	31 And it came to pass, after	3) He requested his sons to
had been forbidden by	*the LORD* did say to thee, Eat	he had buried him, that he	honor him by burying his
God	no bread, and drink no water;	spake to his sons, saying,	own body in the grave
3) He would be judged, die	thy carcase shall not come	When I am dead, then bury	right beside the young
away from home	unto the sepulchre of thy fa-	me in the sepulchre wherein	prophet
	thers.	the man of God *is* buried; lay	
c. The young prophet died just	23 And it came to pass, after	my bones beside his bones:	
as predicted	he had eaten bread, and after	32 For the saying which he	4) He declared his reason:
1) He finished dining &	he had drunk, that he saddled	cried by the word of the LORD	He had a renewed faith in
preparations were made	for him the ass, *to wit,* for the	against the altar in Bethel,	the Word of God—the
for his departure	prophet whom he had	and against all the houses of	prophetic messages of the
2) He began his journey home	brought back.	the high places which *are* in	young prophet would
3) He came face-to-face with	24 And when he was gone, a	the cities of Samaria, shall	surely come to pass
a lion & was killed	lion met him by the way, and	surely come to pass.	

a. Jeroboam's evil influence apparently had an impact upon an old prophet of Israel who lived in Bethel (vv.11-19). Two sons of this old prophet had witnessed the rebuke of Jeroboam by the young prophet from Judah. As fast as they could, the two sons rushed home to share the news of the confrontation with their father. Immediately after they blurted out the report of the confrontation, the old prophet inquired as to which way the young prophet of Judah had gone. He then asked them to saddle his donkey, for he hoped to overtake the young prophet (vv.12-13). Obviously, the old prophet's heart was longing for fellowship and encouragement from a true "man of God."

As rapidly as he could, the older man rode after the young prophet, eventually catching up and finding him resting under an oak tree (v.14). After greeting one another, the old prophet invited the young man of God to return home to dine with him (v.15). But again, the young prophet refused the invitation to fellowship and dine within Israel (vv.16-17). He was not allowed to mingle and socialize within Israel, that is, among idolaters and false worshippers. The LORD had commanded him not to accept invitations while in the territory of the ten northern tribes.

Hearing this, the old prophet's heart sank, and he lied in order to persuade the young man of God to accept the invitation (v.18). Stating that he was also a prophet just as the young man of God was, the older man claimed that an angel had instructed him to bring the young man of God back to his house for a meal. But note: the old prophet was lying. He was obviously an apostate, a prophet who had turned away from the LORD, having been influenced by the evil religion instituted by King Jeroboam.

Hearing that the instructions had come from an angel, the young man of God was convinced and went with the old prophet (v.19). He disobeyed the clear instructions God had given him earlier. And he accepted that God was now contradicting His own word.

b. But while they were sitting at the table, fellowshipping in the land of idolaters and false worshippers, the young prophet was rebuked and condemned to die by the LORD (vv.20-22). And note the source of the rebuke: the LORD Himself who spoke through the old prophet. Under the inspiration of God's Spirit, the old prophet cried out to the man of God who had come from Judah, cried out that he had disobeyed God's Word, not kept His commandment. He had returned and was now fellowshipping in the Northern Kingdom among idolaters and false worshippers. Consequently, he would be judged, die away from home, never to be buried in the tomb of his family (v.22).

c. Just as predicted, the young prophet died along the road as he traveled back home (vv.23-24). Right after finishing the meal and making preparations to depart, the young man began his journey back home. Not too far away from the old prophet's house, the young man of God came face-to-face with a lion and was killed.

d. Soon thereafter, the old prophet was informed of the young prophet's death and went after his body (vv.25-28). Some passersby had spotted the young man's lifeless form and reported it in Bethel where the old prophet lived. Hearing the news, the old prophet knew that the LORD's prophetic judgment had been fulfilled (v.26). After having his donkey saddled, he immediately left and found the body lying dead on the road as reported, with the lion and the donkey standing close by (vv.27-28). Supernaturally, the lion had neither eaten the prophet's body nor mauled the donkey.

e. Evidently through this experience, the old prophet's faith in the Word of God was renewed (vv.29-32). Tenderly picking up the young prophet's body and laying it on his donkey, he took the corpse back home with him. He buried the young man of God in his own tomb and mourned for him, calling him "my brother!"

Now note what happened: after the burial service, the old prophet made a request concerning his own death and burial in the future: his sons were to honor him by burying his body in the grave right beside the young man of God (v.31). He then stated his reason: he now had a renewed faith in the Word of God. The prophetic messages—the messages preached by the young prophet against the altar in Bethel and against the false worship scattered throughout the northern tribes—would surely come to pass (vv.31-32). And the prophecies were fulfilled—specifically fulfilled, stunningly fulfilled—in the reforms of Josiah some 300 years later (see the accuracy of the predictions, 2 K.23:15-18).

Thought 1. There is a much-needed lesson for us in this point: we must guard against being a stumbling block to others, against being an evil influence upon others. Other people are watching us, listening to what we say and observing what we do. For example, if we use foul, distasteful language or profanity, or grumble and complain, or speak critically, other people hear us. And some people are influenced by our sinful speech, feeling that such speech is acceptable. Therefore, they follow our evil example and speak the same way we do or share the same gossip or criticism we shared. Children *in particular* pick up our evil speaking.

Yet it is not only our sinful speech that influences others. Our behavior, what we do, also becomes a stumbling block. When we lie, steal, cheat, abuse, assault, or murder—these evil behaviors influence people. But not only these. An attitude that reveals a heart of covetousness, greed, or hoarding, or one of arrogance or pride that exalts us and degrades others—all these sinful behaviors influence other people, especially our children.

God's Holy Word teaches that we must not become stumbling blocks. We must not influence other people with evil:

"Ye are the salt of the earth: but if the salt have lost his savour, wherewith shall it be salted? it is thenceforth good for nothing, but to be cast out, and to be trodden under foot of men" (Mt.5:13)

"But woe unto you, scribes and Pharisees, hypocrites! for ye shut up the kingdom of heaven against men: for ye neither go in *yourselves*, neither suffer ye them that are entering to go in" (Mt.23:13).

"Salt is good: but if the salt have lost his saltness, wherewith will ye season it? Have salt in yourselves, and have peace one with another" (Mk.9:50).

"For the name of God is blasphemed among the Gentiles through you, as it is written" (Ro.2:24).

"Let us not therefore judge one another any more: but judge this rather, that no man put a stumblingblock or an occasion to fall in *his* brother's way" (Ro.14:13).

"But if thy brother be grieved with *thy* meat, now walkest thou not charitably. Destroy not him with thy meat, for whom Christ died. Let not then your good be evil spoken of" (Ro.14:15-16).

"Your glorying *is* not good. Know ye not that a little leaven leaveneth the whole lump" (1 Co.5:6).

"For if any man see thee which hast knowledge sit at meat in the idol's temple, shall not the conscience of him which is weak be emboldened to eat those things which are offered to idols" (1 Co.8:10).

"A little leaven leaveneth the whole lump" (Ga.5:9).

"He that loveth his brother abideth in the light, and there is none occasion of stumbling in him" (1 Jn.2:10).

"For it came to pass, when Solomon was old, *that* his wives turned away his heart after other gods: and his heart was not perfect with the LORD his God, as *was* the heart of David his father" (1 K.11:4).

"But there was none like unto Ahab, which did sell himself to work wickedness in the sight of the LORD, whom Jezebel his wife stirred up" (1 K.21:25).

"And he walked in the way of the kings of Israel, like as did the house of Ahab: for he had the daughter of Ahab to wife: and he wrought *that which was* evil in the eyes of the LORD" (2 Chr.21:6).

"And shall say, Cast ye up, cast ye up, prepare the way, take up the stumblingblock out of the way of my people" (Is.57:14).

"Therefore thus saith the LORD of hosts concerning the prophets; Behold, I will feed them with wormwood, and make them drink the water of gall: for from the prophets of Jerusalem is profaneness gone forth into all the land" (Je.23:15).

"For the priest's lips should keep knowledge, and they should seek the law at his mouth: for he *is* the messenger of the LORD of hosts. But ye are departed out of the way; ye have caused many to stumble at the law; ye have corrupted the covenant of Levi, saith the LORD of hosts" (Mal.2:7-8).

4 (13:33-34) **Heart, Hardness of, Example of—Stubborn, Example of—Hardness of Heart, Example of—Jeroboam, Heart of**: Jeroboam's spirit became even more obstinate, hard-hearted than before. No doubt Jeroboam eventually heard what had happened to the young prophet who had confronted him. But nothing—neither the pronouncement of judgment upon him and his false worship nor the execution of judgment against the young prophet because of his disobedience to the LORD's command—turned Jeroboam to repentance and confession. He simply refused to heed God's prophetic judgment. Instead, he continued to strengthen the new form of false religion instituted by him. Consequently, he was condemned to face the judgment of God and to suffer the loss of his kingdom and family, the destruction of his dynasty. The false religion and worship he instituted were to bring destruction upon the Northern Kingdom, and Jeroboam's own name was to live in infamy. Hereafter, it was to be repeatedly said of wicked kings: "He walked in the ways of Jeroboam, the son of Nebat, who made Israel to sin."[4]

OUTLINE	SCRIPTURE	SCRIPTURE	OUTLINE
4. Jeroboam's spirit became even more obstinate: An example of hard-heartedness a. He refused to heed God's prophetic judgment pronounced upon him & that fell upon the young prophet	33 After this thing Jeroboam returned not from his evil way, but made again of the lowest of the people priests of the high places: whosoever would, he consecrated him, and he became *one*	of the priests of the high places. 34 And this thing became sin unto the house of Jeroboam, even to cut *it* off, and to destroy *it* from off the face of the earth.	b. He continued to endorse & strengthen false religion c. He was condemned to face the judgment of God: To suffer the loss of his kingdom & family—his dynasty

Thought 1. Jeroboam heard the pronouncement of judgment upon himself and heard that judgment had actually fallen upon the young prophet for his disobedience, yet he still ignored the warnings and the signs. He continued on in his sins. Likewise, we have commandments and warnings in God's Holy Word to guide and protect us. But we too continue on in our sins. God warns us against hard hearts, against becoming stubborn and stiff-necked toward Him. A person who hardens his heart toward God will face the eternal judgment of the LORD. Our hearts are to be sensitive and open and tender toward the LORD, believing and trusting Him, obeying and serving Him. He and He alone is to be worshipped and honored as the only living and true God, the Creator and Sovereign Majesty of the universe. He is to be praised as the Giver of life, as the One who provides every good and perfect gift upon this earth (Js.1:17).

Scripture says that we are to be sensitive to God and to the leading of the Holy Spirit. We are to follow the direction of His Holy Word, serving God and serving our fellow man, our neighbors upon this earth. God warns us against becoming hard, stubborn, and stiff-necked toward God and toward other people:

"Then began he to upbraid the cities wherein most of his mighty works were done, because they repented not" (Mt.11:20).

"For the heart of this people is waxed gross, and their ears are dull of hearing, and their eyes have they closed; lest they should see with *their* eyes, and hear with *their* ears, and understand with *their* heart, and should be converted, and I should heal them" (Ac.28:27).

"But after thy hardness and impenitent heart treasurest up unto thyself wrath against the day of wrath and revelation of the righteous judgment of God" (Ro.2:5).

"This I say therefore, and testify in the Lord, that ye henceforth walk not as other Gentiles walk, in the vanity of their mind, Having the understanding darkened, being alienated from the life of God through the ignorance that is in them, because of the blindness of their heart: Who being past feeling have given themselves over unto lasciviousness, to work all uncleanness with greediness" (Ep.4:17-19).

"Now the Spirit speaketh expressly, that in the latter times some shall depart from the faith, giving heed to seducing spirits, and doctrines of devils; Speaking lies in hypocrisy; having their conscience seared with a hot iron" (1 Ti.4:1-2).

"Take heed, brethren, lest there be in any of you an evil heart of unbelief, in departing from the living God. But exhort one another daily, while it is called To day; lest any of you be hardened through the deceitfulness of sin" (He.3:12-13).

"Be ye not as the horse, *or* as the mule, *which* have no understanding: whose mouth must be held in with bit and bridle, lest they come near unto thee. Many sorrows *shall be* to the wicked: but he that trusteth in the LORD, mercy shall compass him about" (Ps.32:9-10).

"Harden not your heart, as in the provocation, *and* as *in* the day of temptation in the wilderness: When your fathers tempted me, proved me, and saw my work. Forty years long was I grieved with *this*

[4] Richard D. Patterson and Hermann J. Austel. *1, 2 Kings*, p.120.

generation, and said, It is a people that do err in their heart, and they have not known my ways: Unto whom I sware in my wrath that they should not enter into my rest" (Ps.95:8-11).

"Happy *is* the man that feareth alway: but he that hardeneth his heart shall fall into mischief" (Pr.28:14).

"He, that being often reproved hardeneth *his* neck, shall suddenly be destroyed, and that without remedy" (Pr.29:1).

"Hearken unto me, ye stouthearted, that *are* far from righteousness" (Is.46:12).

"Because I knew that thou *art* obstinate, and thy neck *is* an iron sinew, and thy brow brass....*There is* no peace, saith the LORD, unto the wicked" (Is.48:4, 22).

"And now, because ye have done all these works, saith the LORD, and I spake unto you, rising up early and speaking, but ye heard not; and I called you, but ye answered not; Therefore will I do unto *this* house, which is called by my name, wherein ye trust, and unto the place which I gave to you and to your fathers, as I have done to Shiloh. And I will cast you out of my sight, as I have cast out all your brethren, *even* the whole seed of Ephraim. Therefore pray not thou for this people, neither lift up cry nor prayer for them, neither make intercession to me: for I will not hear thee" (Je.7:13-16).

"I smote you with blasting and with mildew and with hail in all the labours of your hands; yet ye *turned* not to me, saith the LORD" (Hag.2:17).

"If ye will not hear, and if ye will not lay *it* to heart, to give glory unto my name, saith the LORD of hosts, I will even send a curse upon you, and I will curse your blessings: yea, I have cursed them already, because ye do not lay *it* to heart" (Mal.2:2).

1. Jeroboam's deceptive plot to secure help for his sick son: A picture of deceit & lies

a. He sent his wife to Ahijah the prophet, but had her disguise herself: So he would not know the son was Jeroboam's child & refuse to help

b. He sent a gift for Ahijah's help: A modest payment of the common man, again to deceive the prophet

2. Jeroboam's deceptive plot revealed to Ahijah by God: A picture of God's guidance for His servants

a. Ahijah was aged & blind

b. Ahijah was informed by the LORD of two facts:
- That King Jeroboam's wife was coming to ask help for her son
- That she was disguised

c. Ahijah heard her approaching & invited her in
- Identified her
- Asked why the pretense
- Stated he had bad news for her

3. Jeroboam's evil condemned by God: A picture of God's prophetic judgment against Jeroboam

a. The charges

1) Jeroboam had clearly been raised up by God to lead Israel: God had torn the kingdom away from David's house & given it to Jeroboam

2) Jeroboam had not lived righteously as David had: David had obeyed God & followed Him wholeheartedly, living righteously

3) Jeroboam had done more evil than all who had lived before him: Been an idolater, a false worshipper, & a stumbling block to others, misleading them, 15-16; 12:25-33

CHAPTER 14

C. The Reign of Jeroboam I in Israel (Part 2): A Prophecy of God's Judgment, 14:1-20

At that time Abijah the son of Jeroboam fell sick.

2 And Jeroboam said to his wife, Arise, I pray thee, and disguise thyself, that thou be not known to be the wife of Jeroboam; and get thee to Shiloh: behold, there *is* Ahijah the prophet, which told me that *I should be* king over this people.

3 And take with thee ten loaves, and cracknels, and a cruse of honey, and go to him: he shall tell thee what shall become of the child.

4 And Jeroboam's wife did so, and arose, and went to Shiloh, and came to the house of Ahijah. But Ahijah could not see; for his eyes were set by reason of his age.

5 And the LORD said unto Ahijah, Behold, the wife of Jeroboam cometh to ask a thing of thee for her son; for he is sick: thus and thus shalt thou say unto her: for it shall be, when she cometh in, that she shall feign herself *to be* another *woman.*

6 And it was *so,* when Ahijah heard the sound of her feet as she came in at the door, that he said, Come in, thou wife of Jeroboam; why feignest thou thyself *to be* another? for I *am* sent to thee *with* heavy *tidings.*

7 Go, tell Jeroboam, Thus saith the LORD God of Israel, Forasmuch as I exalted thee from among the people, and made thee prince over my people Israel,

8 And rent the kingdom away from the house of David, and gave it thee: and yet thou hast not been as my servant David, who kept my commandments, and who followed me with all his heart, to do *that* only *which was* right in mine eyes;

9 But hast done evil above all that were before thee: for thou hast gone and made thee other gods, and molten images, to provoke me to anger, and hast cast me behind thy back:

10 Therefore, behold, I will bring evil upon the house of Jeroboam, and will cut off from Jeroboam him that pisseth against the wall, *and* him that is shut up and left in Israel, and will take away the remnant of the house of Jeroboam, as a man taketh away dung, till it be all gone.

11 Him that dieth of Jeroboam in the city shall the dogs eat; and him that dieth in the field shall the fowls of the air eat: for the LORD hath spoken it.

12 Arise thou therefore, get thee to thine own house: *and* when thy feet enter into the city, the child shall die.

13 And all Israel shall mourn for him, and bury him: for he only of Jeroboam shall come to the grave, because in him there is found *some* good thing toward the LORD God of Israel in the house of Jeroboam.

14 Moreover the LORD shall raise him up a king over Israel, who shall cut off the house of Jeroboam that day: but what? even now.

15 For the LORD shall smite Israel, as a reed is shaken in the water, and he shall root up Israel out of this good land, which he gave to their fathers, and shall scatter them beyond the river, because they have made their groves, provoking the LORD to anger.

16 And he shall give Israel up because of the sins of Jeroboam, who did sin, and who made Israel to sin.

17 And Jeroboam's wife arose, and departed, and came to Tirzah: *and* when she came to the threshold of the door, the child died;

18 And they buried him; and all Israel mourned for him, according to the word of the LORD, which he spake by the hand of his servant Ahijah the prophet.

19 And the rest of the acts of Jeroboam, how he warred, and how he reigned, behold, they *are* written in the book of the chronicles of the kings of Israel.

20 And the days which Jeroboam reigned *were* two and twenty years: and he slept with his fathers, and Nadab his son reigned in his stead.

b. The prophetic judgment

1) The house—kingdom & family dynasty—of Jeroboam was to be destroyed, cut off
- Was to include all males
- Was to be shamed by not being buried in respect & honor but instead eaten by scavengers

2) The sick son was to die & be buried in honor: Because he alone among Jeroboam's family had a good heart

3) The LORD was to raise up a king over Israel who would soon cut off the family of Jeroboam, 15:27-29

4) The LORD was going to strike Israel, uproot the nation, & scatter the people in exile—beyond the river (Euphrates): Because of their idolatry & false worship

5) The LORD was going to give Israel up: Because Jeroboam sinned & caused all Israel to sin—was a stumbling block

c. The judgment immediately began to fall

1) The child died as soon as Jeroboam's wife returned

2) The child was honored by all Israel: Just as the LORD had prophesied through Ahijah

d. The summary of Jeroboam's reign & his death

1) His reign & achievements: Recorded in the book *The History of the Kings of Israel*

2) His reign: Lasted 22 years

3) His death: Rested with his fathers

4) His successor: His son Nadab

DIVISION II

THE EARLY HISTORY OF THE DIVIDED KINGDOM: WITNESSING THE AWFUL RISE OF IDOLATRY AND FALSE WORSHIP, 12:1–16:34

C. The Reign of Jeroboam I in Israel (Part 2): A Prophecy of God's Judgment, 14:1-20

(14:1-20) **Introduction**: two specific events will take place in the future that are foreordained: death and the judgment of God (He.9:27). We can be certain that both events will happen. Every honest and thinking person knows that he or she will die. But some of us deny the coming judgment of God. Nevertheless, denying a fact does not eliminate or invalidate the fact. Denial never voids or does away with the truth. What we fail to grasp is this fact: there is a tendency within the human heart to believe that if we deny something...

- it ceases to exist
- it goes away
- it is not true
- it can be ignored
- it will not happen

For example, there is the mind-set that if we do not think about death, death will not immediately confront us. This train of thought is a *safety net* for the individual: death is not an immediate concern. It lies out in the future, a long way off. Death is so far away that there is no need to even give it a thought. But the reality is this: death can confront any of us on any day, at any hour, including this very hour.

So it is with the truth of judgment. Some people are not quite sure that God exists or that a future judgment is coming when we will have to give an account before God. Denying God's existence and the coming judgment, they feel their denial will make these truths not so. Nevertheless, no matter what we may deny, claim, or profess, truth is truth. And God has given abundant evidence of His existence and the fact that judgment is coming some day out in the future. He has sent His only Son, the Lord Jesus Christ, into the world to reveal God to us; and no greater revelation of the truth could ever be given. He has also given us His Spirit to live within our hearts, quickening and making alive the truth to us. In addition to God's revelation to us through Christ and through the Spirit of God, God has also given us His Holy Word, the written revelation of His existence and His instructions about how to live. Furthermore, there is the testimony of multitudes of changed lives, lives that have been radically changed by the power of Jesus Christ. No greater evidence could ever be laid out before people to establish the case for God's existence and coming judgment.

As stated above, we will all die and face the coming judgment of God. This is the subject of the present passage of Scripture. It is the prophetic judgment pronounced upon King Jeroboam, who ruled over the Northern Kingdom of Israel. Because of the terrible evil of idolatry and false worship, the king and his people were to face the terrifying judgment of God's condemnation. This is: *The Reign of Jeroboam I in Israel (Part 2): A Prophecy of God's Judgment,* 14:1-20.

1. Jeroboam's deceptive plot to secure help for his sick son: a picture of deceit and lies (vv.1-3).
2. Jeroboam's deceptive plot revealed to Ahijah by God: a picture of God's guidance for His servants (vv.4-6).
3. Jeroboam's evil condemned by God: a picture of God's prophetic judgment against Jeroboam (vv.7-20).

1 (14:1-3) **Deceit, Example of—Lies, Example of—Plot, of Jeroboam**: there was the deceptive plot of Jeroboam to secure help for his sick son. Just what was wrong with his son is not known. But apparently he became critically ill soon after the young prophet had confronted the king and condemned him for instituting a false religion in the Northern Kingdom (13:1-10). At some point during the boy's critical illness, Jeroboam made the decision to seek help from the prophet Ahijah. Remember, Ahijah was the prophet who had suddenly encountered Jeroboam outside Jerusalem. Ahijah had informed Jeroboam that God had chosen him to become the future king of the ten northern tribes after Solomon's death (11:27-40). Interestingly, in Jeroboam's hour of need, he did not turn to one of his own prophets, for he knew they were false prophets and could not help. So he sought help from a prophet in Judah.

Knowing that he was living a wicked life and that he was under the condemnation of God, Jeroboam knew that Ahijah might refuse his appeal to help his sick son. For this reason he convinced his wife to disguise herself as a common citizen and go to Ahijah to appeal for his help. To reinforce the impression that his wife was just a common citizen, Jeroboam sent a modest, not expensive, gift for Ahijah's help.

OUTLINE	SCRIPTURE	SCRIPTURE	OUTLINE
1. Jeroboam's deceptive plot to secure help for his sick son: A picture of deceit & lies a. He sent his wife to Ahijah the prophet, but had her disguise herself: So he would not know the son was Jeroboam's child & refuse to help	**A**t that time Abijah the son of Jeroboam fell sick. 2 And Jeroboam said to his wife, Arise, I pray thee, and disguise thyself, that thou be not known to be the wife of Jeroboam; and get thee to Shiloh: behold, there *is* Ahijah	the prophet, which told me that *I should be* king over this people. 3 And take with thee ten loaves, and cracknels, and a cruse of honey, and go to him: he shall tell thee what shall become of the child.	b. He sent a gift for Ahijah's help: A modest payment of the common man, again to deceive the prophet

Thought 1. There is a very important lesson for us in this point: we must not attempt to deceive people, scheming and lying in order to manipulate them for our own end and benefit. If we lie to people and deceive them, we break

the trust existing between us. For example, if a husband lies to his wife, the trust between them is broken. And if the issue is serious, such as the deception of adultery, it is difficult for the trust to ever be restored. If we deceive and lie to our fellow workers, family, friends, or neighbors, relationships are damaged, frequently beyond repair. If we deceive and lie to an employer, the consequences can be serious—such as getting undeserved praise or promotions—or even disastrous, ruining another person's reputation, endangering someone's safety, or losing our employment. Similarly, if a student deceives and lies by cheating and is then discovered, the student is disciplined, sometimes even expelled from school. Even if the student is not caught, he shortchanges himself from securing more knowledge and better skills to face the world when he leaves school.

Example after example could be given, but the point is well made: the consequences of deception and lies can be catastrophic, causing...

- a destroyed marriage
- huge financial loss
- bankruptcy
- a trail of broken lives and shattered relationships
- false accusations leading to the arrest, imprisonment, and conceivably the execution of an innocent life
- anger between people that leads to hurtful words and sometimes physical harm
- hostility between nations and even the declaration of war

Lies and deception are two of the worst evils that can be committed by the human race. Because of this, God gives severe warnings to all liars and deceivers:

"Wherefore putting away lying, speak every man truth with his neighbour: for we are members one of another" (Ep.4:25).

"Lie not one to another, seeing that ye have put off the old man with his deeds" (Col.3:9).

"But the fearful, and unbelieving, and the abominable, and murderers, and whoremongers, and sorcerers, and idolaters, and all liars, shall have their part in the lake which burneth with fire and brimstone: which is the second death" (Re.21:8).

"Thou shalt destroy them that speak leasing [lies]: the LORD will abhor the bloody and deceitful man" (Ps.5:6).

"But the king shall rejoice in God; every one that sweareth by him shall glory: but the mouth of them that speak lies shall be stopped" (Ps.63:11).

"He that worketh deceit shall not dwell within my house: he that telleth lies shall not tarry in my sight" (Ps.101:7).

"The lip of truth shall be established for ever: but a lying tongue *is* but for a moment" (Pr.12:19).

"Lying lips *are* abomination to the LORD: but they that deal truly *are* his delight" (Pr.12:22).

"A false witness shall not be unpunished, and *he that* speaketh lies shall not escape" (Pr.19:5).

"The getting of treasures by a lying tongue *is* a vanity tossed to and fro of them that seek death" (Pr.21:6).

2 (14:4-6) **Guidance, of God, Example of—Ahijah the Prophet, Guidance of, by God**: Jeroboam's deceptive plot was revealed to Ahijah by God. Ahijah was aged and blind, which was probably the reason Jeroboam felt he could deceive the prophet by disguising his wife. But as was the case in so many events of Jeroboam's life, he foolishly disregarded the LORD. While the king's wife was traveling to see the prophet, the LORD informed Ahijah of two facts: that King Jeroboam's wife was coming to ask for help for her son and that she was disguised. So when Ahijah heard the sound of her footsteps approaching the door, he immediately invited her in and asked why she was disguised, pretending to be a common citizen when she was the wife of the king. Then, without giving her time to respond, note what Ahijah declared: she had not been sent to him, but he the prophet had been sent to her. And the message he had was sorrowful news.

OUTLINE	SCRIPTURE	SCRIPTURE	OUTLINE
2. Jeroboam's deceptive plot revealed to Ahijah by God: A picture of God's guidance for His servants a. Ahijah was aged & blind b. Ahijah was informed by the LORD of two facts: • That King Jeroboam's wife was coming to ask help for her son	4 And Jeroboam's wife did so, and arose, and went to Shiloh, and came to the house of Ahijah. But Ahijah could not see; for his eyes were set by reason of his age. 5 And the LORD said unto Ahijah, Behold, the wife of Jeroboam cometh to ask a thing of thee for her son; for he is sick: thus and thus shalt thou say unto her: for it shall	be, when she cometh in, that she shall feign herself *to be* another *woman.* 6 And it was *so,* when Ahijah heard the sound of her feet as she came in at the door, that he said, Come in, thou wife of Jeroboam; why feignest thou thyself *to be* another? for I *am* sent to thee *with* heavy *tidings.*	• That she was disguised c. Ahijah heard her approaching & invited her in • Identified her • Asked why the pretense • Stated he had bad news for her

Thought 1. Jesus Christ taught us not to fear those who may kill the body, but to fear God who can cast both body and soul into the pit of hell. Jeroboam had much to fear from God for his shameful disobedience. But as believers, we have nothing to fear. God has not given us the spirit of fear, but of power, and of love, and of a sound mind (2 Ti.1:7). God guides His dear people. No matter who may attempt to deceive us and lie to us, God will take care of us. He will guide us, showing us how to walk through the deception and lies of people. He will show us the way

to conquer and overcome the deception. But note this fact: this does not mean that the deception or lie will not hurt us or cause damage to us. It means that God will give us the strength, the power to walk through any terrible circumstance that might result from the lie and deception of people.

Whatever the consequences, God will give us the inner strength to stand tall and fast, enduring and persevering with the promise of victory. No matter how terrible the trial or catastrophe, God will empower us with a conquering spirit. And through it all, God promises to meet the necessities of life. He will always see that we have food, shelter, and clothing—whatever we need to survive. This wonderful promise is always true unless God is calling us to be martyrs as a testimony to His name. Even then God will guide us through it all. He will take care of us, looking after us and delivering us through every step of this life right into the kingdom of heaven itself. And we can rest assured that God will deliver us into His very presence to live with Him eternally. Listen to the wonderful promises of God's guidance, the wonderful promise that He is always with us:

> **"...lo, I am with you alway, *even* unto the end of the world. Amen" (Mt.28:20).**
>
> **"Through the tender mercy of our God; whereby the dayspring from on high hath visited us, To give light to them that sit in darkness and *in* the shadow of death, to guide our feet into the way of peace" (Lu.1:78-79).**
>
> **"Howbeit when he, the Spirit of truth, is come, he will guide you into all truth: for he shall not speak of himself; but whatsoever he shall hear, *that* shall he speak: and he will show you things to come" (Jn.16:13).**
>
> **"And the Lord shall deliver me from every evil work, and will preserve *me* unto his heavenly kingdom: to whom *be* glory for ever and ever. Amen" (2 Ti.4:18).**
>
> **"*Let your* conversation [conduct, behavior] *be* without covetousness; *and be* content with such things as ye have: for he hath said, I will never leave thee, nor forsake thee. So that we may boldly say, The Lord *is* my helper, and I will not fear what man shall do unto me" (He.13:5-6).**
>
> **"And, behold, I *am* with thee, and will keep thee in all *places* whither thou goest, and will bring thee again into this land; for I will not leave thee, until I have done *that* which I have spoken to thee of" (Ge.28:15).**
>
> **"And he said, My presence shall go *with thee,* and I will give thee rest" (Ex.33:14).**
>
> **"When thou goest out to battle against thine enemies, and seest horses, and chariots, *and* a people more than thou, be not afraid of them: for the LORD thy God *is* with thee, which brought thee up out of the land of Egypt" (De.20:1).**
>
> **"The eternal God *is thy* refuge, and underneath *are* the everlasting arms: and he shall thrust out the enemy from before thee; and shall say, Destroy *them*" (De.33:27).**
>
> **"Thou hast also given me the shield of thy salvation: and thy right hand hath holden me up, and thy gentleness hath made me great" (Ps.18:35).**
>
> **"The LORD *is* my shepherd; I shall not want. He maketh me to lie down in green pastures: he leadeth me beside the still waters. He restoreth my soul: he leadeth me in the paths of righteousness for his name's sake. Yea, though I walk through the valley of the shadow of death, I will fear no evil: for thou *art* with me; thy rod and thy staff they comfort me. Thou preparest a table before me in the presence of mine enemies: thou anointest my head with oil; my cup runneth over. Surely goodness and mercy shall follow me all the days of my life: and I will dwell in the house of the LORD for ever" (Ps.23:1-6).**
>
> **"The meek will he guide in judgment: and the meek will he teach his way" (Ps.25:9).**
>
> **"Teach me thy way, O LORD, and lead me in a plain path, because of mine enemies" (Ps.27:11).**
>
> **"For the LORD loveth judgment, and forsaketh not his saints; they are preserved for ever: but the seed of the wicked shall be cut off" (Ps.37:28).**
>
> **"For this God *is* our God for ever and ever: he will be our guide *even* unto death" (Ps.48:14).**
>
> **"Thou shalt guide me with thy counsel, and afterward receive me *to* glory" (Ps.73:24).**
>
> **"*If* I take the wings of the morning, *and* dwell in the uttermost parts of the sea; Even there shall thy hand lead me, and thy right hand shall hold me" (Ps.139:9-10).**
>
> **"And thine ears shall hear a word behind thee, saying, This *is* the way, walk ye in it, when ye turn to the right hand, and when ye turn to the left" (Is.30:21).**
>
> **"Fear thou not; for I *am* with thee: be not dismayed; for I *am* thy God: I will strengthen thee; yea, I will help thee; yea, I will uphold thee with the right hand of my righteousness" (Is.41:10).**
>
> **"And I will bring the blind by a way *that* they knew not; I will lead them in paths *that* they have not known: I will make darkness light before them, and crooked things straight. These things will I do unto them, and not forsake them" (Is.42:16).**
>
> **"...Fear not: for I have redeemed thee, I have called *thee* by thy name; thou *art* mine. When thou passest through the waters, I *will be* with thee; and through the rivers, they shall not overflow thee: when thou walkest through the fire, thou shalt not be burned; neither shall the flame kindle upon thee" (Is.43:1-2).**
>
> **"And *even* to *your* old age I *am* he; and *even* to hoar [gray] hairs will I carry *you:* I have made, and I will bear; even I will carry, and will deliver *you*" (Is.46:4).**

3 (14:7-20) **Judgment, of God, Surety of—Condemnation, of False Worship and Idolatry—Prophecy, of Judgment, of Israel—Israel, Prophecy Concerning, Judgment—Northern Kingdom, Prophecy Concerning, Judgment—Israel, Judgment of, Due to Idolatry and False Worship**: Jeroboam's evil was severely condemned by God.

Bewildered by the prophet's foreknowledge of her disguise and the announcement that he had bad news for her, Jeroboam's wife sat meekly before the prophet, dreading the prophetic message about to be given by Ahijah:

OUTLINE	SCRIPTURE	SCRIPTURE	OUTLINE
3. Jeroboam's evil condemned	7 Go, tell Jeroboam, Thus	to the grave, because in him	
by God: A picture of God's	saith the LORD God of Israel,	there is found *some* good	
prophetic judgment against	Forasmuch as I exalted thee	thing toward the LORD God	
Jeroboam	from among the people, and	of Israel in the house of Jero-	
a. The charges	made thee prince over my	boam.	
1) Jeroboam had clearly been	people Israel,	14 Moreover the LORD shall	3) The LORD was to raise up
raised up by God to lead Isra-	8 And rent the kingdom away	raise him up a king over Isra-	a king over Israel who
el: God had torn the kingdom	from the house of David, and	el, who shall cut off the	would soon cut off the
away from David's house &	gave it thee: and yet thou hast	house of Jeroboam that day:	family of Jeroboam,
given it to Jeroboam	not been as my servant Da-	but what? even now.	15:27-29
2) Jeroboam had not lived	vid, who kept my command-	15 For the LORD shall smite	4) The LORD was going to
righteously as David had:	ments, and who followed me	Israel, as a reed is shaken in	strike Israel, uproot the
David had obeyed God &	with all his heart, to do *that*	the water, and he shall root	nation, & scatter the peo-
followed Him wholehearted-	only *which was* right in mine	up Israel out of this good	ple in exile—beyond the
ly, living righteously	eyes;	land, which he gave to their	river (Euphrates): Because
3) Jeroboam had done more	9 But hast done evil above all	fathers, and shall scatter them	of their idolatry & false
evil than all who had lived	that were before thee: for	beyond the river, because	worship
before him: Been an idola-	thou hast gone and made thee	they have made their groves,	
ter, a false worshipper, &	other gods, and molten imag-	provoking the LORD to anger.	
a stumbling block to oth-	es, to provoke me to anger,	16 And he shall give Israel	5) The LORD was going to give
ers, misleading them, 15-	and hast cast me behind thy	up because of the sins of Jer-	Israel up: Because Jeroboam
16; 12:25-33	back:	oboam, who did sin, and who	sinned & caused all Israel to
b. The prophetic judgment	10 Therefore, behold, I will	made Israel to sin.	sin—was a stumbling block
	bring evil upon the house of	17 And Jeroboam's wife	c. The judgment immediately
1) The house—kingdom &	Jeroboam, and will cut off	arose, and departed, and	began to fall
family dynasty—of Jero-	from Jeroboam him that	came to Tirzah: *and* when	1) The child died as soon as
boam was to be destroyed,	pisseth against the wall, *and*	she came to the threshold of	Jeroboam's wife returned
cut off	him that is shut up and left in	the door, the child died;	
• Was to include all males	Israel, and will take away the	18 And they buried him; and	2) The child was honored by
• Was to be shamed by	remnant of the house of Jero-	all Israel mourned for him,	all Israel: Just as the LORD
not being buried in re-	boam, as a man taketh away	according to the word of the	had prophesied through
spect & honor but in-	dung, till it be all gone.	LORD, which he spake by the	Ahijah
stead eaten by scaven-	11 Him that dieth of Jerobo-	hand of his servant Ahijah	
gers	am in the city shall the dogs	the prophet.	
	eat; and him that dieth in the	19 And the rest of the acts of	d. The summary of Jeroboam's
	field shall the fowls of the air	Jeroboam, how he warred,	reign & his death
	eat: for the LORD hath spoken	and how he reigned, behold,	1) His reign & achievements:
	it.	they *are* written in the book	Recorded in the book *The*
2) The sick son was to die &	12 Arise thou therefore, get	of the chronicles of the kings	*History of the Kings of Is-*
be buried in honor: Be-	thee to thine own house: *and*	of Israel.	*rael*
cause he alone among Jer-	when thy feet enter into the	20 And the days which Jero-	2) His reign: Lasted 22 years
oboam's family had a	city, the child shall die.	boam reigned *were* two and	3) His death: Rested with his
good heart	13 And all Israel shall mourn	twenty years: and he slept	fathers
	for him, and bury him: for he	with his fathers, and Nadab	4) His successor: His son
	only of Jeroboam shall come	his son reigned in his stead.	Nadab

a. The charges of God against Jeroboam were threefold:
   1) Jeroboam had clearly been raised up by God to lead Israel. God had torn the kingdom away from David's house and given the ten northern tribes to Jeroboam.
   2) Jeroboam had not lived a righteous life as God's servant David had (v.8). When he sinned, he confessed and repented and turned away from his sin back to God. Then once again, David began to obey God and follow Him wholeheartedly, living righteously before the eyes of the LORD.
   3) Jeroboam, to his shame, had done more evil than all who had lived before him (v.9). He was an idolater and false worshiper. Furthermore, he had become a stumbling block to all Israel, misleading them to break the first commandment of God, the commandment forbidding the worship of false gods (vv.9; 15-16; 12:25-33; Ex.20:3-4).

b. After making the charges against Jeroboam, the prophet Ahijah spelled out the prophetic judgment that was to fall upon the king. Picture Jeroboam's wife sitting there stunned, overwhelmed with the seriousness of the charges against her husband. She was now to receive the appalling details of the prophetic judgment. Altogether five specific and devastating judgments were spelled out (vv.10-16).
   1) First, the house—kingdom and family dynasty—of Jeroboam was to be destroyed, cut off by assassination (vv.10-11). Every last male member of his family was to be shamed by not being buried in respect and honor, but instead eaten by scavengers, by the dogs in the city and the birds of the air out in the country. (See outline and note—1 K.15:25-34 for more discussion.)

2) Second, Jeroboam's wife heard the sorrowful news that her son was to die as soon as she set foot in the capital city (v.12). But the child, and he alone among Jeroboam's family, would be buried in honor. Note why: because the little child had a good heart.
3) Third, the LORD was to raise up a king over Israel who would kill the entire family of Jeroboam (15:27-29). The man was being prepared even now, at that very moment.
4) Fourth, the LORD was going to strike the nation of Israel, uproot the people and scatter them in exile beyond the Euphrates River (v.15). Why? Because of their idolatry and false worship. They provoked the LORD by making their Asherah poles, their wooden images of false gods.
5) Fifth, the LORD was going to give Israel up to the world, to be captives of the world because of their terrible sin, for they had followed Jeroboam's sin (v.16). It was the king's sin that had become a stumbling block, causing the entire nation to commit idolatry and to engage in false worship.

With the spelling out of these five judgments, the prophetic condemnation of Jeroboam and Israel was completed. Reeling from the news and perhaps in a state of shock, Jeroboam's wife staggered out of the prophet's home and made her way back to the capital city as quickly as she was able to travel.

c. Immediately the judgment of God began to fall, just as the prophet Ahijah had predicted (vv.17-18). As soon as Jeroboam's wife stepped over the threshold of her house, her son died. And just as predicted, the child was buried in honor, being mourned by all Israel.

d. With the passing of Jeroboam's child, the author concludes the account of Jeroboam's tragic, evil life. He simply summarizes Jeroboam's reign and death by stating the following facts:

⇒ His reign and achievements were recorded in the book *The History of the Kings of Israel* (v.19).
⇒ His reign lasted twenty-two years (v.20).
⇒ His death is a silent record: nothing is mentioned of his passing away, only that he rested, was buried with his fathers.
⇒ His successor was his son Nadab.

Thought 1. This is a startling picture of God's prophetic judgment. God predicted that the hand of His judgment would fall upon Jeroboam and upon the Northern Kingdom of Israel. And it did. This will be seen in future Scripture. For now, the lesson for us is striking: God has predicted judgment upon all the ungodly and unrighteous of this earth (Ro.1:18). If we live sinful lives, rejecting God and denying that He exists, claiming to be atheists and agnostics, God declares that the hand of His judgment will fall upon us. Climactically, some day out in the future, He will end the universe as we presently know it and summon every human being to appear before the throne of His judgment. And He will execute perfect justice among all people. When a person is found to have lived an unjust and unrighteous life, the person will face the fierce judgment of God's Holy wrath and condemnation. There will be no escape. No matter what our finite minds may believe, claim, or profess, the truth that the LORD exists and is the only living and true God will be revealed to the entire universe. One day all of us will stand before the throne of the eternal LORD and Creator of the universe, stand to give an account for everything we have done. Denying that God exists and that a Day of Judgment is coming does not do away with God or the Day of Judgment. On the contrary, denying God and the coming judgment only condemns us that much more. The more stiff-necked, obstinate, stubborn, and hard-hearted we become, the more severe the judgment upon us will be. Listen to two facts declared by the Holy Word of God:

(1) Out in the future, there is a Day of Judgment:

"But I say unto you, It shall be more tolerable for Tyre and Sidon at the day of judgment, than for you. And thou, Capernaum, which art exalted unto heaven, shalt be brought down to hell: for if the mighty works, which have been done in thee, had been done in Sodom, it would have remained until this day. But I say unto you, That it shall be more tolerable for the land of Sodom in the day of judgment, than for thee" (Mt.11:22-24).

"And then shall appear the sign of the Son of man in heaven: and then shall all the tribes of the earth mourn, and they shall see the Son of man coming in the clouds of heaven with power and great glory" (Mt.24:30).

"When the Son of man shall come in his glory, and all the holy angels with him, then shall he sit upon the throne of his glory: And before him shall be gathered all nations: and he shall separate them one from another, as a shepherd divideth *his* sheep from the goats. And he shall set the sheep on his right hand, but the goats on the left" (Mt.25:31-33).

"And whosoever shall not receive you, nor hear you, when ye depart thence, shake off the dust under your feet for a testimony against them. Verily I say unto you, It shall be more tolerable for Sodom and Gomorrha in the day of judgment, than for that city" (Mk.6:11).

"And he began to teach them, that the Son of man must suffer many things, and be rejected of the elders, and *of* the chief priests, and scribes, and be killed, and after three days rise again" (Mk.8:31).

"And to you who are troubled rest with us, when the Lord Jesus shall be revealed from heaven with his mighty angels, In flaming fire taking vengeance on them that know not God, and that obey not the gospel of our Lord Jesus Christ" (2 Th.1:7-8).

"And as it is appointed unto men once to die, but after this the judgment" (He.9:27).

"The Lord knoweth how to deliver the godly out of temptations, and to reserve the unjust unto the day of judgment to be punished" (2 Pe.2:9).

"But the heavens and the earth, which are now, by the same word are kept in store, reserved unto fire against the day of judgment and perdition of ungodly men" (2 Pe.3:7).

"And Enoch also, the seventh from Adam, prophesied of these, saying, Behold, the Lord cometh with ten thousands of his saints, To execute judgment upon all, and to convince all that are ungodly among them of all their ungodly deeds which they have ungodly committed, and of all their hard *speeches* which ungodly sinners have spoken against him. These are murmurers, complainers, walking after their own lusts; and their mouth speaketh great swelling *words,* having men's persons in admiration because of advantage" (Jude 14-16).

"Behold, he cometh with clouds; and every eye shall see him, and they *also* which pierced him: and all kindreds of the earth shall wail because of him. Even so, Amen" (Re.1:7).

"And I saw a great white throne, and him that sat on it, from whose face the earth and the heaven fled away; and there was found no place for them. And I saw the dead, small and great, stand before God; and the books were opened: and another book was opened, which is *the book* of life: and the dead were judged out of those things which were written in the books, according to their works. And the sea gave up the dead which were in it; and death and hell delivered up the dead which were in them: and they were judged every man according to their works. And death and hell were cast into the lake of fire. This is the second death. And whosoever was not found written in the book of life was cast into the lake of fire" (Re.20:11-15).

"Also unto thee, O Lord, *belongeth* mercy: for thou renderest to every man according to his work" (Ps.62:12).

(2) God loves the world and every human being in it. He is also long-suffering, not wanting any person to perish or to be separated from Him.

"For God so loved the world, that he gave his only begotten Son, that whosoever believeth in him should not perish, but have everlasting life. For God sent not his Son into the world to condemn the world; but that the world through him might be saved" (Jn.3:16-17).

"But God commendeth his love toward us, in that, while we were yet sinners, Christ died for us" (Ro.5:8).

"Knowing this first, that there shall come in the last days scoffers, walking after their own lusts, And saying, Where is the promise of his coming? for since the fathers fell asleep, all things continue as *they were* from the beginning of the creation....But, beloved, be not ignorant of this one thing, that one day *is* with the Lord as a thousand years, and a thousand years as one day. The Lord is not slack concerning his promise, as some men count slackness; but is longsuffering to us-ward, not willing that any should perish, but that all should come to repentance. But the day of the Lord will come as a thief in the night; in the which the heavens shall pass away with a great noise, and the elements shall melt with fervent heat, the earth also and the works that are therein shall be burned up. *Seeing* then *that* all these things shall be dissolved, what manner *of persons* ought ye to be in *all* holy conversation and godliness, Looking for and hasting unto the coming of the day of God, wherein the heavens being on fire shall be dissolved, and the elements shall melt with fervent heat? Nevertheless we, according to his promise, look for new heavens and a new earth, wherein dwelleth righteousness" (2 Pe.3:3-4, 8-13; esp. v.9).

"If we confess our sins, he is faithful and just to forgive us *our* sins, and to cleanse us from all unrighteousness" (1 Jn.1:9).

"For my name's sake will I defer mine anger, and for my praise will I refrain for thee, that I cut thee not off" (Is.48:9).

D. The Reign of Rehoboam in Judah: A Sad, Detestable Life, 14:21-31
14:21; see 2 Chr.12:13
14:25-28; see 2 Chr.12:9-12
14:29-31; see 2 Chr.12:15-16

1. His background: A man given great opportunity, accountability
   a. He was the son of Solomon & Naamah, an Ammonite (a false worshipper)
   b. He was 41 years old when he became king
   c. He reigned 17 years
   d. He reigned in Jerusalem, the city chosen by the LORD

2. His sad, detestable evil: Apostasy—forsaking & turning away from the LORD
   a. He led the people to commit terrible evil: Aroused God's jealous anger
      1) Built worship shrines on every high place: Sacred stones & Asherah poles
      2) Practiced the religious fertility rituals of prostitution & homosexuality
   b. He led the people to adopt all the detestable, wicked practices of the surrounding nations

3. His defeat by the king of Egypt, Shishak: A picture of God's chastisement
   a. He was forced to pay tribute, to buy off the king: Used the treasuries of the temple & palace, including all the gold shields, as payment
   b. He replaced the shields with less expensive bronze shields
      1) Were assigned to the royal guard
      2) Were used in escorting the king for special functions, when he want to worship

4. His achievements & the summary of his life: A sad, reprehensible life of evil influence
   a. His reign recorded in the book *The History of the Kings of Judah*
   b. His constant warfare with Jeroboam
   c. His death & burial in Jerusalem
   d. His mother reemphasized: An Ammonite, a false worshipper, who influenced him
   e. His successor: Abijah (Abijam)

21 And Rehoboam the son
of Solomon reigned in Judah.
Rehoboam *was* forty and one
years old when he began to
reign, and he reigned seventeen years in Jerusalem, the
city which the LORD did
choose out of all the tribes of
Israel, to put his name there.
And his mother's name *was*
Naamah an Ammonitess.
22 And Judah did evil in the
sight of the LORD, and they
provoked him to jealousy
with their sins which they
had committed, above all that
their fathers had done.
23 For they also built them
high places, and images, and
groves, on every high hill,
and under every green tree.
24 And there were also sodomites in the land:
and they did according to all
the abominations of the nations which the LORD cast
out before the children of Israel.
25 And it came to pass in the
fifth year of king Rehoboam,
that Shishak king of Egypt
came up against Jerusalem:
26 And he took away the
treasures of the house of the
LORD, and the treasures of
the king's house; he even
took away all: and he took
away all the shields of gold
which Solomon had made.
27 And king Rehoboam
made in their stead brasen
shields, and committed *them*
unto the hands of the chief of
the guard, which kept the
door of the king's house.
28 And it was *so,* when the
king went into the house of
the LORD, that the guard bare
them, and brought them back
into the guard chamber.
29 Now the rest of the acts
of Rehoboam, and all that
he did, *are* they not written in the book of the
chronicles of the kings of Judah?
30 And there was war be-
tween Rehoboam and Jero-
boam all *their* days.
31 And Rehoboam slept with
his fathers, and was buried
with his fathers in
the city of David. And his
mother's name *was* Naamah
an Ammonitess. And Abi-
jam his son reigned in his
stead.

DIVISION II

THE EARLY HISTORY OF THE DIVIDED KINGDOM: WITNESSING THE AWFUL RISE OF IDOLATRY AND FALSE WORSHIP, 12:1–16:34

C. The Reign of Rehoboam in Judah: A Sad, Detestable Life, 14:21-31

(14:21-31) **Introduction**: What kind of life are you living? A happy, commendable, constructive life? Or a sad, detestable, destructive life? Every person who is honest will tell you he wants a joyful, loving, and productive life. But despite what we desire, many of us are living sad lives, knowing little love or joy, experiencing little fruit or production, believing ourselves to be failures. Instead of knowing the true joy of life, many are feeling...

• lonely	• disapproved of	• hostile
• empty	• rejected	• bitter
• unfulfilled	• overlooked	• angry
• without purpose	• friendless	• hopeless
• dissatisfied	• unattractive	• discouraged
• insignificant	• low self-esteem	• depressed
• unappreciated	• no self worth	• extreme anxiety

Filled with all sorts of discouraging emotions and thoughts, many people are living sad lives, longing for deliverance from a seemingly hopeless situation, longing for a loving, joyful, and productive life.

But in addition to the sad lives being lived by so many, there are countless others who are living detestable lives, lives of sin and wickedness—lives directly opposed to the clear teachings of God's Holy Word. And keep in mind that wickedness damages and destroys not only the person who is committing the sin, but the person or persons against whom the sin is being committed. Sin damages not only the sinner but also those who surround the sinner. Even society as a whole is affected, for every wicked act adds to the decay and deterioration of society.

For example, every time an act of immorality is committed, another seed of corruption is planted in society. Often the affected families are ripped apart and terrible pain and suffering cut the hearts of the remaining spouses and children. In some cases sexual diseases are transmitted and human suffering results from the one act of immorality that seemed so innocent, so harmless in the beginning. Any sin or act of wickedness can be shown to damage human life and to add to the decay of society. And tragically, there are many people who are living not only sad lives, but also detestable, wicked lives.

Such is the case in the present study of God's Word. The subject now shifts from the Northern Kingdom of Israel to the Southern Kingdom of Judah. Upon Solomon's death, his son Rehoboam took the throne and began a seventeen-year reign. This is: *The Reign of Rehoboam in Judah: A Sad, Detestable Life*, 14:21-31.

1. His background: a man given great opportunity, accountability (v.21).
2. His sad, detestable evil: apostasy—forsaking and turning away from the LORD (vv.22-24).
3. His defeat by the king of Egypt, Shishak: a picture of God's chastisement (vv.25-28).
4. His achievements and the summary of his life: a sad, reprehensible life of evil influence (vv.29-31)

1 (14:21) **Opportunity, Example of—Accountability, Example of—Rehoboam, Opportunity of**: the background of Rehoboam is that of a man who was given great opportunity to succeed and to make a significant contribution to society. Rehoboam was born in the royal palace, the son of King Solomon. Being the son of Solomon, he had the privilege of observing the godly life and wise decisions of his father. He saw the blessings of God poured out upon his father and the nation during the years when Solomon walked closely with the LORD. Then when Solomon began to decline spiritually, Rehoboam witnessed the tragic results of sin upon a life and nation. From all this, he had every chance to learn the importance of following God and of fulfilling one's task upon earth. He had every opportunity to succeed and to make a notable difference in society and in the nation.

Note that Rehoboam was forty-one years old—a fully mature man—when he became king. He was given the unusual privilege of being thoroughly trained and given years of experience before the heavy weight of ruling was placed upon his shoulders. If he failed in the task of ruling the nation, he would be without excuse.

Moreover, Rehoboam ruled as king of Judah for seventeen years, giving him plenty of time to serve and to make a meaningful contribution to the people and nation of Israel. He also was fortunate to reign in Jerusalem, the city chosen by the LORD to be the place where His name was honored. The LORD was anxious to bless Rehoboam as he ruled the nation. Every opportunity imaginable had been given to Rehoboam, that he might succeed and leave a favorable legacy of progress and growth—both materially and spiritually.

OUTLINE	SCRIPTURE	SCRIPTURE	OUTLINE
1. His background: A man given great opportunity, accountability a. He was the son of Solomon & Naamah, an Ammonite (a false worshipper)	21And Rehoboam the son of Solomon reigned in Judah. Rehoboam *was* forty and one years old when he began to reign, and he reigned seventeen years in Jerusalem,	the city which the LORD did choose out of all the tribes of Israel, to put his name there. And his mother's name *was* Naamah an Ammonitess.	b. He was 41 years old when he became king c. He reigned 17 years d. He reigned in Jerusalem, the city chosen by the LORD

Thought 1. Many of us are given unique opportunities to succeed in life, to fulfill our task and purpose on earth. Some of us have had the privilege of...

- being born with above average intelligence
- being born into a family where true love, nurturing, and a sense of responsibility exist
- being born with special talents and gifts
- having a charismatic personality
- being well educated
- being highly trained or skilled
- securing excellent employment
- inheriting wealth
- being led to the LORD and rooted in His Word at a young age

In an unusual and exceptional way, the hand of God has blessed us richly. But we must learn one strong lesson from these opportunities given to us: "To whom much is given, much is required" (Lu.12:48). Listen to what God says about the opportunities given us:

"Therefore is the kingdom of heaven likened unto a certain king, which would take account of his servants" (Mt.18:23).

"For *the kingdom of heaven is* as a man travelling into a far country, *who* called his own servants, and delivered unto them his goods. And unto one he gave five talents, to another two, and to another one; to every man according to his several ability; and straightway took his journey. Then he that had received the five talents went and traded with the same, and made *them* other five talents. And likewise he that *had received* two, he also gained other two. But he that had received one went and digged in the earth, and hid his lord's money. After a long time the lord of those servants cometh, and reckoneth with them. And so he that had received five talents came and brought other five talents, saying, Lord, thou deliveredst unto me five talents: behold, I have gained beside them five talents more. His lord said unto him, Well done, *thou* good and faithful servant: thou hast been faithful over a few things, I will make thee ruler over many things: enter thou into the joy of thy lord. He also that had received two talents came and said, Lord, thou deliveredst unto me two talents: behold, I have gained two other talents beside them. His lord said unto him, Well done, good and faithful servant; thou hast been faithful over a few things, I will make thee ruler over many things: enter thou into the joy of thy lord. Then he which had received the one talent came and said, Lord, I knew thee that thou art an hard man,

reaping where thou hast not sown, and gathering where thou hast not strawed: And I was afraid, and went and hid thy talent in the earth: lo, *there* thou hast *that is* thine. His lord answered and said unto him, *Thou* wicked and slothful servant, thou knewest that I reap where I sowed not, and gather where I have not strawed: Thou oughtest therefore to have put my money to the exchangers, and *then* at my coming I should have received mine own with usury. Take therefore the talent from him, and give *it* unto him which hath ten talents. For unto every one that hath shall be given, and he shall have abundance: but from him that hath not shall be taken away even that which he hath. And cast ye the unprofitable servant into outer darkness: there shall be weeping and gnashing of teeth" (Mt.25:14-30).

"...whomsoever much is given, of him shall be much required: and to whom men have committed much, of him they will ask the more" (Lu.12:48).

"And he called his ten servants, and delivered them ten pounds, and said unto them, Occupy till I come" (Lu.19:13).

"And it came to pass, that when he was returned, having received the kingdom, then he commanded these servants to be called unto him, to whom he had given the money, that he might know how much every man had gained by trading" (Lu.19:15).

"So then every one of us shall give account of himself to God" (Ro.14:12).

"Moreover it is required in stewards, that a man be found faithful" (1 Co.4:2).

"What? know ye not that your body is the temple of the Holy Ghost *which is* in you, which ye have of God, and ye are not your own? For ye are bought with a price: therefore glorify God in your body, and in your spirit, which are God's" (1 Co.6:19-20).

"O Timothy, keep that which is committed to thy trust, avoiding profane *and* vain babblings, and oppositions of science falsely so called" (1 Ti.6:20).

"As every man hath received the gift, *even so* minister the same one to another, as good stewards of the manifold grace of God" (1 Pe.4:10).

"Every man also to whom God hath given riches and wealth, and hath given him power to eat thereof, and to take his portion, and to rejoice in his labour; this *is* the gift of God" (Ec.5:19).

2 (14:22-24) **Apostasy, Described As—Forsaking, God, Example of—Turning Away, from God, by Israel—Idolatry, Example of—False Worship, Example of—Prostitution, Example of—Homosexuality, Example of—Rehoboam, Evil of**: despite the great opportunities given to him, Rehoboam failed to meet his potential. He lived a sad, detestable, and wicked life. He committed apostasy, forsaking and turning away from the LORD to false worship.

OUTLINE	SCRIPTURE	SCRIPTURE	OUTLINE
2. His sad, detestable evil: Apostasy—forsaking & turning away from the LORD a. He led the people to commit terrible evil: Aroused God's jealous anger 1) Built worship shrines on every high place: Sacred	22 And Judah did evil in the sight of the LORD, and they provoked him to jealousy with their sins which they had committed, above all that their fathers had done. 23 For they also built them high places, and images, and	groves, on every high hill, and under every green tree. 24 And there were also sodomites in the land: *and* they did according to all the abominations of the nations which the LORD cast out before the children of Israel.	stones & Asherah poles 2) Practiced the religious fertility rituals of prostitution & homosexuality b. He led the people to adopt all the detestable, wicked practices of the surrounding nations

a. Because of the king's sinful life, the people in turn were led to commit terrible evil. And their evil aroused God's "jealousy," his *jealous anger* (qana) (vv.22-24). His jealousy and anger were justified, for God seeks to protect His people, loving them and caring for them deeply. Just as parents are jealous over their children and become angry if one of their children is threatened, so God is jealous over His people and becomes angry if one of them is threatened. Just as a husband is jealous over the purity and morality of his wife, so God is jealous over the purity and morality of His people.

Thus God's jealous anger against the terrible evil of Rehoboam was justified and righteous. The son of Solomon, who had been given every opportunity to succeed as a righteous king, had led God's people to commit shameful, wicked acts. By following the example of Rehoboam, the people aroused even more anger than their fathers had done.

In addition to living wicked lives, the citizens of the Southern Kingdom built worship centers or shrines on the high hills throughout the land, constructing sacred stones and Asherah poles. Scripture declares there was a shrine on every high hill and under every green tree. Remember that the sacred stones and Asherah poles were visible idols that helped the worshipper focus upon the male or female god they were seeking. Asherah was the mother goddess who symbolized the fruitfulness of the land. She was considered to be the goddess of sex and war, with a strong emphasis on sex or reproduction symbolized in the fruitfulness of the land. In the words of Paul R. House:

> *Asherah was often seen as the female consort, wife or otherwise, of male gods. Obviously, this "coupling" of gods had strong sexual overtones. Thus, the presence of "prostitutes" at sacred Canaanite shrines was not unusual. Such prostitutes were present so worshippers could fulfill their obligations to fertility gods.*[1]

The Israelites also practiced the religious fertility rituals of prostitution and homosexuality (v.24). When a worshipper approached the fertility goddess, a male prostitute was available to help the worshipper reach the summit of emotion that

1 Paul R. House. *1, 2 Kings*, p.194.

symbolized the reproductive fruitfulness of the land. This moral abscess or cancer had been purged from the land during the days of Joshua. But now it has been reintroduced, brought back by King Rehoboam.

b. Rehoboam led the people to adopt all the detestable, wicked practices of the surrounding nations. It was this terrible evil that aroused the LORD's jealous anger against both King Rehoboam and the people of the Southern Kingdom.

Thought 1. When we commit apostasy—forsake the LORD and turn away from Him—His jealous anger is bound to be aroused. For when we come to the LORD seeking salvation, we promise to love and obey the LORD. We promise to follow Him and to live pure, righteous lives. Taking us at our word, that we will worship and serve Him and Him alone, God saves us. And when we are saved, the most wonderful thing happens: God adopts us as His sons and daughters, making us a part of His dear family, the family of God. Furthermore, God gives us the most wonderful promises of His presence, guidance, protection, security, and assurance of living with Him eternally.

We belong to God as His sons and daughters, and God belongs to us as our Father. We have no right to commit apostasy, no right to turn away from God, to worship and follow a false god or any other idol that we set up and consider to be more important than God Himself. Anything that we focus upon and give our hearts to—anything that we put before God—becomes an idol to us. Therefore as sons and daughters of God, we must live holy and righteous lives. We must be responsible and live committed and faithful lives. We must always be on guard against committing apostasy. Listen to what God says about apostasy, about turning away from and forsaking Him:

"And Jesus said unto him, No man, having put his hand to the plough, and looking back, is fit for the kingdom of God" (Lu.9:62).

"This charge I commit unto thee, son Timothy, according to the prophecies which went before on thee, that thou by them mightest war a good warfare; Holding faith, and a good conscience; which some having put away concerning faith have made shipwreck: Of whom is Hymenaeus and Alexander; whom I have delivered unto Satan, that they may learn not to blaspheme" (1 Ti.1:18-20).

"Now the Spirit speaketh expressly, that in the latter times some shall depart from the faith, giving heed to seducing spirits, and doctrines of devils" (1 Ti.4:1).

"Forbidding to marry, *and commanding* to abstain from meats, which God hath created to be received with thanksgiving of them which believe and know the truth. For every creature of God *is* good, and nothing to be refused, if it be received with thanksgiving" (2 Ti.4:3-4).

"For Demas hath forsaken me, having loved this present world, and is departed unto Thessalonica; Crescens to Galatia, Titus unto Dalmatia" (2 Ti.4:10).

"Harden not your hearts, as in the provocation, in the day of temptation in the wilderness: When your fathers tempted me, proved me, and saw my works forty years. Wherefore I was grieved with that generation, and said, They do alway err in *their* heart; and they have not known my ways. So I sware in my wrath, They shall not enter into my rest.) Take heed, brethren, lest there be in any of you an evil heart of unbelief, in departing from the living God" (He.3:8-12).

"For *it is* impossible for those who were once enlightened, and have tasted of the heavenly gift, and were made partakers of the Holy Ghost, And have tasted the good word of God, and the powers of the world to come, If they shall fall away, to renew them again unto repentance; seeing they crucify to themselves the Son of God afresh, and put *him* to an open shame" (He.6:4-6).

"Now the just shall live by faith: but if *any man* draw back, my soul shall have no pleasure in him" (He.10:38).

"Having eyes full of adultery, and that cannot cease from sin; beguiling unstable souls: an heart they have exercised with covetous practices; cursed children: Which have forsaken the right way, and are gone astray, following the way of Balaam *the son* of Bosor, who loved the wages of unrighteousness; But was rebuked for his iniquity: the dumb ass speaking with man's voice forbad the madness of the prophet. These are wells without water, clouds that are carried with a tempest; to whom the mist of darkness is reserved for ever" (2 Pe.2:14-17).

"For if after they have escaped the pollutions of the world through the knowledge of the Lord and Saviour Jesus Christ, they are again entangled therein, and overcome, the latter end is worse with them than the beginning. For it had been better for them not to have known the way of righteousness, than, after they have known *it,* to turn from the holy commandment delivered unto them" (2 Pe.2:20-21).

"Ye therefore, beloved, seeing ye know *these things* before, beware lest ye also, being led away with the error of the wicked, fall from your own stedfastness" (2 Pe.3:17).

"Little children, it is the last time: and as ye have heard that antichrist shall come, even now are there many antichrists; whereby we know that it is the last time. They went out from us, but they were not of us; for if they had been of us, they would *no doubt* have continued with us: but *they went out,* that they might be made manifest that they were not all of us" (1 Jn.2:18-19).

"Nevertheless I have *somewhat* against thee, because thou hast left thy first love" (Re.2:4).

"*Certain* men, the children of Belial, are gone out from among you, and have withdrawn the inhabitants of their city, saying, Let us go and serve other gods, which ye have not known" (De.13:13).

"And yet they would not hearken unto their judges, but they went a whoring after other gods, and bowed themselves unto them: they turned quickly out of the way which their fathers walked in, obeying the commandments of the LORD; *but* they did not so" (Jud.2:17).

"Yet ye have forsaken me, and served other gods: wherefore I will deliver you no more" (Jud.10:13).

"And he went out to meet Asa, and said unto him, Hear ye me, Asa, and all Judah and Benjamin; The LORD *is* with you, while ye be with him; and if ye seek him, he will be found of you; but if ye forsake him, he will forsake you" (2 Chr.15:2).

"Nevertheless they were disobedient, and rebelled against thee, and cast thy law behind their backs, and slew thy prophets which testified against them to turn them to thee, and they wrought great provocations" (Ne.9:26).

"But thou hast not called upon me, O Jacob; but thou hast been weary of me, O Israel" (Is.43:22).

"And I will utter my judgments against them touching all their wickedness, who have forsaken me, and have burned incense unto other gods, and worshipped the works of their own hands" (Je.1:16).

"For my people have committed two evils; they have forsaken me the fountain of living waters, *and* hewed them out cisterns, broken cisterns, that can hold no water" (Je.2:13).

"And it shall come to pass, when ye shall say, Wherefore doeth the LORD our God all these *things* unto us? then shalt thou answer them, Like as ye have forsaken me, and served strange gods in your land, so shall ye serve strangers in a land *that is* not yours" (Je.5:19).

"Thou hast forsaken me, saith the LORD, thou art gone backward: therefore will I stretch out my hand against thee, and destroy thee; I am weary with repenting" (Je.15:6).

"O LORD, the hope of Israel, all that forsake thee shall be ashamed, *and* they that depart from me shall be written in the earth, because they have forsaken the LORD, the fountain of living waters" (Je.17:13).

"And they that escape of you shall remember me among the nations whither they shall be carried captives, because I am broken with their whorish heart, which hath departed from me, and with their eyes, which go a whoring after their idols: and they shall loathe themselves for the evils which they have committed in all their abominations" (Eze.6:9).

"And when they entered unto the heathen, whither they went, they profaned my holy name, when they said to them, These *are* the people of the LORD, and are gone forth out of his land" (Eze.36:20).

3 (14:25-28) **Chastisement, Example of—Rehoboam, Judgment upon—Shishak, King of Egypt, Attacked Jerusalem**: Rehoboam was defeated by King Shishak of Egypt. Shishak founded the twenty-second dynasty of Egypt. Earlier he had allowed Jeroboam to seek safety in Egypt when he was being pursued by King Solomon (11:40). Now, in launching his invasion against Jerusalem, he hoped to conquer and establish Egyptian rule throughout Asia, including Judah, Israel, Edom, and Philistia. Through the military campaign, he ended up conquering roughly 150 cities, but he was unable to subdue all the area as he had planned. His campaigns are inscribed on the exterior of the Amon temple's south wall at Karnak in Egypt.[2] The whole picture is more clearly seen when looking at both this passage and the account in 2 Chronicles below:

"And it came to pass, when Rehoboam had established the kingdom, and had strengthened himself, he forsook the law of the LORD, and all Israel with him. And it came to pass, *that* in the fifth year of king Rehoboam Shishak king of Egypt came up against Jerusalem, because they had transgressed against the LORD, With twelve hundred chariots, and threescore thousand horsemen: and the people *were* without number that came with him out of Egypt; the Lubim, the Sukkiims, and the Ethiopians. And he took the fenced cities which *pertained* to Judah, and came to Jerusalem" (2 Chr.12:1-4; also see vv.5-12)

When Shishak attacked Jerusalem, Rehoboam and his officials humbled themselves and sought the LORD, begging God to rescue them. In compassion and mercy, the LORD heard their request and delivered them from utter destruction. Rehoboam was able to negotiate a payment to the Egyptians for them to retreat and not destroy Jerusalem. To buy off the Egyptian king, Rehoboam used the treasuries of the temple and palace, including all the gold shields, as tribute payment (v.26; 2 Chr.12:7-9). Some time later, Rehoboam replaced the shields with less expensive bronze shields and assigned these to the commanders of his royal guard (vv.27-28). These shields were kept in the guardroom and used only for escorting the king to special functions, such as when he went to worship at the LORD's temple.

OUTLINE	SCRIPTURE	SCRIPTURE	OUTLINE
3. His defeat by the king of Egypt, Shishak: A picture of God's chastisement	25 And it came to pass in the fifth year of king Rehoboam, *that* Shishak king of Egypt came up against Jerusalem:	27 And king Rehoboam made in their stead brasen shields, and committed *them* unto the hands of the chief of the guard, which kept the door of the king's house.	b. He replaced the shields with less expensive bronze shields 1) Were assigned to the royal guard
a. He was forced to pay tribute, to buy off the king: Used the treasuries of the temple & palace, including all the gold shields, as payment	26 And he took away the treasures of the house of the LORD, and the treasures of the king's house; he even took away all: and he took away all the shields of gold which Solomon had made.	28 And it was *so*, when the king went into the house of the LORD, that the guard bare them, and brought them back into the guard chamber.	2) Were used in escorting the king for special functions, when he want to worship

[2] John F. Walvoord and Roy B. Zuck, Editors. *The Bible Knowledge Commentary, Old Testament*, p.518.

Thought 1. The lesson for us concerns discipline, chastisement. When we commit wickedness, God does discipline, chastise us. But when chastised or disciplined, we must always remember one fact: the purpose of chastisement is not punishment, but correction, training, and protection. When we do wrong, we need to be corrected lest we further harm ourselves or damage other people.

⇒ If a husband who commits adultery is not corrected, he will destroy his family, cutting the hearts of his wife and children and causing terrible pain and suffering.
⇒ If a person steals from a neighbor or employer and is not corrected, the person causes loss for the neighbor or business.
⇒ If a person mistreats a fellow worker and is not corrected, the result is a damaged or broken relationship.
⇒ If a person abuses a child or any other person and is not corrected, deep emotional problems and scars result, as well as shattered relationships.

Wrong, sinful behavior must be corrected by God to keep us from harming ourselves and from damaging the lives of other people. Discipline is an absolute essential when we do wrong. By correcting us, God teaches us that we must do right by walking in love and kindness toward others. We learn that we must love our neighbors as ourselves and treat them just as we want to be treated. This is the reason for God's chastisement, His discipline. Listen to what the Word of God says about this great subject:

"Every branch in me that beareth not fruit he taketh away: and every *branch* that beareth fruit, he purgeth it, that it may bring forth more fruit" (Jn.15:2).

"For this cause many *are* weak and sickly among you, and many sleep. For if we would judge ourselves, we should not be judged. But when we are judged, we are chastened of the Lord, that we should not be condemned with the world" (1 Co.11:30-32).

"And ye have forgotten the exhortation which speaketh unto you as unto children, My son, despise not thou the chastening of the Lord, nor faint when thou art rebuked of him: For whom the Lord loveth he chasteneth, and scourgeth every son whom he receiveth" (He.12:5-6).

"As many as I love, I rebuke and chasten: be zealous therefore, and repent" (Re.3:19).

"Thou shalt also consider in thine heart, that, as a man chasteneth his son, *so* the LORD thy God chasteneth thee" (De.8:5).

"He is chastened also with pain upon his bed, and the multitude of his bones with strong *pain*" (Jb.33:19).

"Blessed *is* the man whom thou chastenest, O LORD, and teachest him out of thy law" (Ps.94:12).

"My son, despise not the chastening of the LORD; neither be weary of his correction: For whom the LORD loveth he correcteth; even as a father the son *in whom* he delighteth" (Pr.3:11-12).

"O LORD, correct me, but with judgment; not in thine anger, lest thou bring me to nothing" (Je.10:24).

4 (14:29-31) **Stumbling Block, Example of—Evil Influence, Example of—Life, Evil, Example of—Rehoboam, Evil Influence of**: Rehoboam's achievements and the summary of his life are mentioned in these few verses. As these few facts are read, one truth needs to be kept in the forefront of the reader's mind: Rehoboam lived a sad, reprehensible life of evil, a life that strongly influenced others to do evil. Note the brief summary of his life:

OUTLINE	SCRIPTURE	SCRIPTURE	OUTLINE
4. His achievements & the summary of his life: A sad, reprehensible life of evil influence a. His reign recorded in the book *The History of the Kings of Judah* b. His constant warfare with Jeroboam	29 Now the rest of the acts of Rehoboam, and all that he did, *are* they not written in the book of the chronicles of the kings of Judah? 30 And there was war between Rehoboam and Jero-	boam all *their* days. 31 And Rehoboam slept with his fathers, and was buried with his fathers in the city of David. And his mother's name *was* Naamah an Ammonitess. And Abijam his son reigned in his stead.	c. His death & burial in Jerusalem d. His mother reemphasized: An Ammonite, a false worshipper, who influenced him e. His successor: Abijah (Abijam)

a. The achievements of his reign are recorded in the book *The History of the Kings of Judah* (v.29). This was a book that recorded the important facts and achievements of the various kings of Judah. It was one of the sources the author of First Kings used, although he did use other contemporary sources (2 Chr.12:13-16).

b. Rehoboam was in a constant war with Jeroboam who ruled over the Northern Kingdom (v.30). Most likely, they were not major wars, but rather border skirmishes and disputes (2 Chr.11:1-4).

c. Rehoboam died and was buried in the City of David, that is, Jerusalem. Remember that Rehoboam's grandfather David had captured the city from the Jebusites and made it the capital of Israel. His father Solomon had gone on to enlarge the city. Both his grandfather and his father were buried in the city, just as he was now being buried there.

d. Note that Rehoboam's mother Naamah is reemphasized, the fact that she was an Ammonite. This fact is being stressed because the Ammonites were worshippers of the false god Molech, a detestable god to whom children were sometimes sacrificed (11:7). Naamah obviously had an enormous influence upon Rehoboam, an evil influence.

e. Rehoboam's successor was his son Abijah (Abijam) (v.31).

Thought 1. The lesson for us is straightforward: if we commit evil, our evil will influence others. Our children are always watching what we do, and usually others are as well. Within every school and nation on earth, there are leaders and athletes and teachers whom other students look to and esteem, sometimes very highly. Younger students will even idolize upperclassmen, especially the leaders of various activities, cliques, and clubs. In the adult world, we respect and esteem a fellow worker, friend, neighbor, or anyone else who has a strong trait that we think will help us. But even adults are not above idolizing other adults—sometimes imitating the good in them and sometimes the bad.

We are all being watched by other people, and we all have an influence upon other people. Our influence is either good or evil. If we live moral and upright lives, then our influence is good. But if we live wicked lives, then our influence is evil. We set the example that sinful behavior is acceptable, that the consequences are not really that bad, at least not bad enough to keep us from doing wrong. But God warns us against being a stumbling block, an evil example for sinful behavior. Listen to what the Word of God says:

"But woe unto you, scribes and Pharisees, hypocrites! for ye shut up the kingdom of heaven against men: for ye neither go in *yourselves,* neither suffer ye them that are entering to go in" (Mt.23:13).

"For the wrath of God is revealed from heaven against all ungodliness and unrighteousness of men, who hold the truth in unrighteousness;...Being filled with all unrighteousness, fornication, wickedness, covetousness, maliciousness; full of envy, murder, debate, deceit, malignity; whisperers, Backbiters, haters of God, despiteful, proud, boasters, inventors of evil things, disobedient to parents, Without understanding, covenantbreakers, without natural affection, implacable, unmerciful: Who knowing the judgment of God, that they which commit such things are worthy of death, not only do the same, but have pleasure in them that do them" (Ro.1:18, 29-32).

"For the name of God is blasphemed among the Gentiles through you, as it is written" (Ro.2:24).

"Let us not therefore judge one another any more: but judge this rather, that no man put a stumblingblock or an occasion to fall in *his* brother's way" (Ro.14:13).

"But if thy brother be grieved with *thy* meat, now walkest thou not charitably. Destroy not him with thy meat, for whom Christ died. Let not then your good be evil spoken of" (Ro.14:15-16).

"Your glorying *is* not good. Know ye not that a little leaven leaveneth the whole lump? Purge out therefore the old leaven, that ye may be a new lump, as ye are unleavened. For even Christ our passover is sacrificed for us" (1 Co.5:6-7).

"Know ye not that the unrighteous shall not inherit the kingdom of God? Be not deceived: neither fornicators, nor idolaters, nor adulterers, nor effeminate, nor abusers of themselves with mankind, Nor thieves, nor covetous, nor drunkards, nor revilers, nor extortioners, shall inherit the kingdom of God" (1 Co.6:9-10).

"For if any man see thee which hast knowledge sit at meat in the idol's temple [false worship], shall not the conscience of him which is weak be emboldened to eat those things which are offered to idols; And through thy knowledge shall the weak brother perish, for whom Christ died?" (1 Co.8:10-11).

"Ye did run well; who did hinder you that ye should not obey the truth? This persuasion *cometh* not of him that calleth you. A little leaven leaveneth the whole lump" (Ga.5:7-9).

"He that loveth his brother abideth in the light, and there is none occasion of stumbling in him" (1 Jn.2:10).

"And shall say, Cast ye up, cast ye up, prepare the way, take up the stumblingblock out of the way of my people" (Is.57:14).

"For the priest's lips should keep knowledge, and they should seek the law at his mouth: for he *is* the messenger of the LORD of hosts. But ye are departed out of the way; ye have caused many to stumble at the law; ye have corrupted the covenant of Levi, saith the LORD of hosts" (Mal.2:7-8).

1. **The evil reign of Abijah: Walking in the footsteps of sinful parents**
   a. His background
      1) He reigned 3 years
      2) He was influenced by his mother Maacah's false worship, 13
   b. His evil & failure
      1) He walked in the sins of his father, 14:22-24
      2) His heart was not devoted to the LORD—not like David's had been
   c. His dynasty
      1) The LORD gave him a lamp, a son, to succeed him: For David's sake
      2) The reason: David had genuinely trusted God & lived righteously, always obeying God—except in the case of Uriah & Bathsheba
   d. His continuing war with King Jeroboam of Israel, 14:30; 2 Chr.13:2-20
   e. His achievements & the summary of his life
      1) His reign: Recorded in the book *The History of the Kings of Judah*
      2) His constant war with the Northern Kingdom
      3) His death & burial in Jerusalem
      4) His successor: His son Asa
2. **The righteous reign of Asa: Rejecting the evil influence of parents**
   a. His background
      1) He reigned 41 years
      2) He was not influenced by his grandmother Maacah's false worship, 13
   b. His religious reform: He lived & ruled righteously—just as David had done
      1) He banished the religious or shrine prostitutes, 14:24
      2) He removed all the idols his fathers had made
      3) He even removed his grandmother Maacah from her position as queen mother: Because of her idolatry & false worship
      4) He failed to destroy the high places
   c. His spiritual commitment
      1) He was loyal to the LORD
      2) He supported the temple, replenished the treasury that had been depleted by his father Rehoboam, 14:25-26
   d. His major military engagement: War with King Baasha of Israel
      1) Baasha invaded Judah & began to fortify Ramah: To control all traffic & trade routes
      2) Asa sought a military alliance with Ben-Hadad, king of Syria (Aram): Trusted in man & failed to trust God, 2 Chr.16:7-10
         • He took all the silver & gold in the treasuries of the temple & palace
         • He sent a delegation with the riches to King Ben-Hadad requesting two things: A treaty between Judah & Syria, & the breaking of Syria's treaty with Israel
      3) Ben-Hadad agreed to Asa's proposal: He swiftly invaded northern Israel, conquering a large area that gave him access to major trade routes from Egypt & Phoenicia to Syria
      4) Baasha was forced to retreat from Judah to meet the Syrian invasion
      5) Asa mobilized his forces & retook Ramah: He used the building materials left behind by Baasha to fortify Geba & Mizpah

CHAPTER 15

E. The Reign of Two Kings in Judah, Abijah (Abijam) & Asa, Father & Son: A Son Who Refused to Walk in the Evil Steps of His Father, 15:1-24

15:1-8; see 2 Chr.13:1-22
15:9-24; see 2 Chr.14:1–16:14

Now in the eighteenth year of king Jeroboam the son of Nebat reigned Abijam over Judah.
2 Three years reigned he in Jerusalem. And his mother's name *was* Maachah, the daughter of Abishalom.
3 And he walked in all the sins of his father, which he had done before him: and his heart was not perfect with the LORD his God, as the heart of David his father.
4 Nevertheless for David's sake did the LORD his God give him a lamp in Jerusalem, to set up his son after him, and to establish Jerusalem:
5 Because David did *that which was* right in the eyes of the LORD, and turned not aside from any *thing* that he commanded him all the days of his life, save only in the matter of Uriah the Hittite.
6 And there was war between Rehoboam and Jeroboam all the days of his life.
7 Now the rest of the acts of Abijam, and all that he did, *are* they not written in the book of the chronicles of the kings of Judah? And there was war between Abijam and Jeroboam.
8 And Abijam slept with his fathers; and they buried him in the city of David: and Asa his son reigned in his stead.
9 And in the twentieth year of Jeroboam king of Israel reigned Asa over Judah.
10 And forty and one years reigned he in Jerusalem. And his mother's name *was* Maachah, the daughter of Abishalom.
11 And Asa did *that which was* right in the eyes of the LORD, as *did* David his father.
12 And he took away the sodomites out of the land, and removed all the idols that his fathers had made.
13 And also Maachah his mother, even her he removed from *being* queen, because she had made an idol in a grove; and Asa destroyed her idol, and burnt *it* by the brook Kidron.
14 But the high places were not removed: nevertheless Asa's heart was perfect with the LORD all his days.
15 And he brought in the things which his father had dedicated, and the things which himself had dedicated, into the house of the LORD, silver, and gold, and vessels.
16 And there was war between Asa and Baasha king of Israel all their days.
17 And Baasha king of Israel went up against Judah, and built Ramah, that he might not suffer any to go out or come in to Asa king of Judah.
18 Then Asa took all the silver and the gold *that were* left in the treasures of the house of the LORD, and the treasures of the king's house, and delivered them into the hand of his servants: and king Asa sent them to Benhadad, the son of Tabrimon, the son of Hezion, king of Syria, that dwelt at Damascus, saying,
19 *There is* a league between me and thee, *and* between my father and thy father: behold, I have sent unto thee a present of silver and gold; come and break thy league with Baasha king of Israel, that he may depart from me.
20 So Ben-hadad hearkened unto king Asa, and sent the captains of the hosts which he had against the cities of Israel, and smote Ijon, and Dan, and Abel-beth-maachah, and all Cinneroth, with all the land of Naphtali.
21 And it came to pass, when Baasha heard *thereof,* that he left off building of Ramah, and dwelt in Tirzah.
22 Then king Asa made a proclamation throughout all Judah; none *was* exempted: and they took away the stones of Ramah, and the timber thereof, wherewith Baasha had builded; and king Asa built with them Geba of

e. His achievements & the summary of his life 1) His reign: Recorded in the book *The History of the Kings of Judah* 2) His old age: Had diseased feet	Benjamin, and Mizpah. 23 The rest of all the acts of Asa, and all his might, and all that he did, and the cities which he built, *are* they not written in the book of the chronicles of the kings of Judah? Nevertheless in the time	of his old age he was diseased in his feet. 24 And Asa slept with his fathers, and was buried with his fathers in the city of David his father: and Jehoshaphat his son reigned in his stead.	3) His death & burial in Jerusalem 4) His successor: His son Jehoshaphat, 22:41-50

DIVISION II

THE EARLY HISTORY OF THE DIVIDED KINGDOM: WITNESSING THE AWFUL RISE OF IDOLATRY AND FALSE WORSHIP, 12:1–16:34

E. The Reign of Two Kings in Judah, Abijah (Abijam) and Asa, Father and Son: A Son Who Refused to Walk in the Evil Steps of His Father, 15:1-24

(15:1-24) **Introduction**: just because a parent commits evil does not mean that the child will commit evil. A child does not have to walk in the footsteps of his evil parents. Despite the influence of parents upon their children, a child can break the trend, the tendency of wickedness and evil. No child is doomed to failure or to a life of wickedness because of corrupt or immoral parents. A child can succeed where the parent is unsuccessful and can live righteously where the parent lives dishonorably.

Down through history, many have broken the trend of wickedness and gone on to live righteous and productive lives. Most of us know someone who has done so. One example is in the present passage of Scripture. Two kings will be studied: one, King Abijah, who followed in the evil footsteps of his parents and committed the same evil; and the other, King Asa, who broke the trend of evil and lived a righteous and productive life before the LORD. King Asa chose his path despite the trend of wickedness that had been deeply rooted in his family's history. Against the odds, he stood tall. He broke away from the pattern of the past, choosing to follow in the footsteps of the LORD and His commandments instead of in the footsteps of his wicked parents and grandparents. This is*: The Reign of Two Kings in Judah, Abijah (Abijam) and Asa, Father and Son: A Son Who Refused to Walk in the Evil Steps of His Father,* 15:1-24.

1. The evil reign of Abijah: walking in the footsteps of sinful parents (vv.1-8).
2. The righteous reign of Asa: commitment to the LORD (vv.9-24).

1 (15:1-8) **Parents, Sinful Influence of—Influence, Evil, of Parents—Parental Influence, Evil—Stumbling Block, of Parents—Abijah, Evil Reign of—Judah, Kings of, Abijah**: there was the brief, evil reign of Abijah in Judah. Remember, he was the son of Rehoboam and the grandson of Solomon. Scripture briefly covers his short-lived reign:

OUTLINE	SCRIPTURE	SCRIPTURE	OUTLINE
1. The evil reign of Abijah: Walking in the footsteps of sinful parents a. His background 1) He reigned 3 years 2) He was influenced by his mother Maacah's false worship, 13 b. His evil & failure 1) He walked in the sins of his father, 14:22-24 2) His heart was not devoted to the LORD—not like David's had been c. His dynasty 1) The LORD gave him a lamp, a son, to succeed him: For David's sake	Now in the eighteenth year of king Jeroboam the son of Nebat reigned Abijam over Judah. 2 Three years reigned he in Jerusalem. And his mother's name *was* Maachah, the daughter of Abishalom. 3 And he walked in all the sins of his father, which he had done before him: and his heart was not perfect with the LORD his God, as the heart of David his father. 4 Nevertheless for David's sake did the LORD his God give him a lamp in Jerusalem, to set up his son after him, and to establish Jerusalem:	5 Because David did *that which was* right in the eyes of the LORD, and turned not aside from any *thing* that he commanded him all the days of his life, save only in the matter of Uriah the Hittite. 6 And there was war between Rehoboam and Jeroboam all the days of his life. 7 Now the rest of the acts of Abijam, and all that he did, *are* they not written in the book of the chronicles of the kings of Judah? And there was war between Abijam and Jeroboam. 8 And Abijam slept with his fathers; and they buried him in the city of David: and Asa his son reigned in his stead.	2) The reason: David had genuinely trusted God & lived righteously, always obeying God—except in the case of Uriah & Bathsheba d. His continuing war with King Jeroboam of Israel, 14:30; 2 Chr.13:2-20 e. His achievements & the summary of his life 1) His reign: Recorded in the book *The History of the Kings of Judah* 2) His constant war with the Northern Kingdom 3) His death & burial in Jerusalem 4) His successor: His son Asa

a. Abijah reigned only three years. He began his rule over Judah in the eighteenth year of Jeroboam's rule over the Northern Kingdom. A significant person to note is his mother Maacah, who apparently exercised great influence inside the royal court (v.13). She was the daughter of Uriel of Gibeah (2 Chr.13:2) and Tamar (2 S.14:27), making her the granddaughter of Absalom. Keep in mind that "daughter" or "son" is often used in Scripture to refer to a descendant two or more generations removed. Such is the case in referring to Maacah as the daughter of Absalom.

b. Abijah lived an evil life, and his brief reign over the Southern Kingdom was a failure (v.3). Tragically, he walked in the footsteps of his sinful parents, committing the sins of his father and mother (14:22-24). His father had led the people to commit terrible evil by engaging in idolatry and false worship. Morally, the people were practicing the most vile sins imaginable through the rituals of prostitution and homosexuality. As Scripture says, the people had become very sinful and wicked, arousing God's jealous anger far more than their forefathers had done (14:22). Abijah's heart was clearly not devoted to the LORD, not wholeheartedly, not like the heart of David had been (v.3).

c. Nevertheless, God promised to continue the dynasty of the Southern Kingdom (vv.4-5). But note why: not because of Abijah, but because of David. God had promised to give David a lamp—a son, a dynasty—to succeed him. For David had genuinely trusted God and lived a righteous life, obeying and keeping God's commandments except in the one case of Uriah and Bathsheba. Because of David's faithfulness to the LORD, the LORD had entered a covenant with David, promising that He would be given a lamp, a dynasty that would last forever. Of course, this was fulfilled in the Ideal Son of David, the Messiah and Savior of the world, the Lord Jesus Christ. (See outline and notes—2 S.7:1-17 for more discussion.)

d. Just as his father Rehoboam had done, Abijah was constantly warring with Jeroboam of the Northern Kingdom (v.6; 14:30; 2 Chr.13:2-20). But most likely these were not full-fledged wars, only skirmishes that took place when various raiders or armed forces crossed the border between the Northern and Southern Kingdoms.

e. Abijah's achievements and a summary of his life are very briefly outlined by the author of *First Kings* (vv.7-8).

1) His reign and achievements are recorded in the book *The History of the Kings of Judah* (v.7). Most, if not all, of the facts covered in the Scriptural account of King Abijah were apparently taken from this book.
2) Note that his constant war with the Northern Kingdom under Jeroboam is mentioned again (v.7). In light of constant skirmishes, both kingdoms probably had permanent forces stationed along the border.
3) Abijah died and was buried in Jerusalem, the city where his father Rehoboam, his grandfather Solomon, and his great-grandfather David were buried. Remember that David had conquered Jerusalem and established it as the capital of the former unified nation of Israel. Now that the Northern Kingdom had split off from the Southern Kingdom of Judah, Jerusalem still remained the capital of the Southern Kingdom.
4) Abijah's successor was his son Asa (v.8). It will be seen in the next point that Asa established a righteous reign in the Southern Kingdom.

Thought 1. The lesson for us is compelling: parents must live godly, righteous lives before their children, for children will almost always follow the example of their parents. In fact, children will follow the examples of most adults and older children, including brothers, sisters, other relatives, teachers, coaches, ministers, neighbors, athletes, and many, many others with whom they come in contact or read about. Children are very impressionable. For this reason, parents—and the rest of us, no matter our age—must set an example of love and kindness in dealing with other people. We must help and serve other people who are in need, work hard and diligently at our tasks and jobs, and worship and obey God by living holy, righteous, and moral lives. Such a lifestyle is absolutely essential, for children are observing us. Fathers and mothers, brothers and sisters, teachers and ministers—we are all influencing children by our behavior. Children are walking in our footsteps, whether they be good or evil. In Abijah's case, he was following in the footsteps of his *evil* father. Listen to what God's Holy Word says about the evil influence of parents:

"And she, being before instructed of her mother, said, Give me here John Baptist's head in a charger" (Mt.14:8).

"But fornication, and all uncleanness, or covetousness, let it not be once named among you, as becometh saints; Neither filthiness, nor foolish talking, nor jesting, which are not convenient: but rather giving of thanks. For this ye know, that no whoremonger, nor unclean person, nor covetous man, who is an idolater, hath any inheritance in the kingdom of Christ and of God. Let no man deceive you with vain words: for because of these things cometh the wrath of God upon the children of disobedience" (Ep.5:3-6).

"For I have told him that I will judge his house for ever for the iniquity which he knoweth; because his sons made themselves vile, and he restrained them not" (1 S.3:13).

"And his father had not displeased him at any time in saying, Why hast thou done so? and he also *was* a very goodly *man*; and *his mother* bare him after Absalom" (1 K.1:6).

"And he did evil in the sight of the LORD, and walked in the way of his father, and in the way of his mother, and in the way of Jeroboam the son of Nebat, who made Israel to sin" (1 K.22:52).

"He also walked in the ways of the house of Ahab: for his mother was his counsellor to do wickedly" (2 Chr.22:3).

"The rod and reproof give wisdom: but a child left *to himself* bringeth his mother to shame" (Pr.29:15).

"But have walked after the imagination of their own heart, and after Baalim, which their fathers taught them" (Je.9:14).

"But I said unto their children in the wilderness, Walk ye not in the statutes of your fathers, neither observe their judgments, nor defile yourselves with their idols" (Eze.20:18).

"Thus saith the LORD; For three transgressions of Judah, and for four, I will not turn away *the punishment* thereof; because they have despised the law of the LORD, and have not kept his commandments, and their lies caused them to err, after the which their fathers have walked" (Am.2:4).

2 (15:9-24) **Parents, Influence of—Children, Duty, to Reject Evil Influence—Evil, Influence, Duty, to Reject—Kings, of Judah, Asa**: there was the righteous reign of Asa, a king who was faithful to the LORD. Asa took the throne in Judah in the twentieth year of Jeroboam's reign over the Northern Kingdom. Scripture gives the important facts about his kingship over the Southern Kingdom of Judah:

OUTLINE	SCRIPTURE	SCRIPTURE	OUTLINE
2. The righteous reign of Asa: Rejecting the evil influence of parents	9 And in the twentieth year of Jeroboam king of Israel reigned Asa over Judah.	to Ben-hadad, the son of Tabrimon, the son of Hezion, king of Syria, that dwelt at Damascus, saying,	the temple & palace
a. His background 1) He reigned 41 years 2) He was not influenced by his grandmother Maacah's false worship, 13	10 And forty and one years reigned he in Jerusalem. And his mother's name *was* Maachah, the daughter of Abishalom.	19 *There is* a league between me and thee, *and* between my father and thy father: behold, I have sent unto thee a present of silver and gold; come and break thy league with Baasha king of Israel, that he may depart from me.	• He sent a delegation with the riches to King Ben-Hadad requesting two things: A treaty between Judah & Syria, & the breaking of Syria's treaty with Israel
b. His religious reform: He lived & ruled righteously—just as David had done	11 And Asa did *that which was* right in the eyes of the LORD, as *did* David his father.		
1) He banished the religious or shrine prostitutes, 14:24 2) He removed all the idols his fathers had made 3) He even removed his grandmother Maacah from her position as queen mother: Because of her idolatry & false worship	12 And he took away the sodomites out of the land, and removed all the idols that his fathers had made. 13 And also Maachah his mother, even her he removed from *being* queen, because she had made an idol in a grove; and Asa destroyed her idol, and burnt *it* by the brook Kidron.	20 So Ben-hadad hearkened unto king Asa, and sent the captains of the hosts which he had against the cities of Israel, and smote Ijon, and Dan, and Abel-beth-maachah, and all Cinneroth, with all the land of Naphtali. 21 And it came to pass, when Baasha heard *thereof,* that he left off building of Ramah, and dwelt in Tirzah.	3) Ben-Hadad agreed to Asa's proposal: He swiftly invaded northern Israel, conquering a large area that gave him access to major trade routes from Egypt & Phoenicia to Syria 4) Baasha was forced to retreat from Judah to meet the Syrian invasion
4) He failed to destroy the high places c. His spiritual commitment 1) He was loyal to the LORD 2) He supported the temple, replenished the treasury that had been depleted by his father Rehoboam, 14:25-26	14 But the high places were not removed: nevertheless Asa's heart was perfect with the LORD all his days. 15 And he brought in the things which his father had dedicated, and the things which himself had dedicated, into the house of the LORD, silver, and gold, and vessels.	22 Then king Asa made a proclamation throughout all Judah; none *was* exempted: and they took away the stones of Ramah, and the timber thereof, wherewith Baasha had builded; and king Asa built with them Geba of Benjamin, and Mizpah.	5) Asa mobilized his forces & retook Ramah: He used the building materials left behind by Baasha to fortify Geba & Mizpah
d. His major military engagement: War with King Baasha of Israel 1) Baasha invaded Judah & began to fortify Ramah: To control all traffic & trade routes	16 And there was war between Asa and Baasha king of Israel all their days. 17 And Baasha king of Israel went up against Judah, and built Ramah, that he might not suffer any to go out or come in to Asa king of Judah.	23 The rest of all the acts of Asa, and all his might, and all that he did, and the cities which he built, *are* they not written in the book of the chronicles of the kings of Judah? Nevertheless in the time of his old age he was diseased in his feet.	e. His achievements & the summary of his life 1) His reign: Recorded in the book *The History of the Kings of Judah* 2) His old age: Had diseased feet
2) Asa sought a military alliance with Ben-Hadad, king of Syria (Aram): Trusted in man & failed to trust God, 2 Chr.16:7-10 • He took all the silver & gold in the treasuries of	18 Then Asa took all the silver and the gold *that were* left in the treasures of the house of the LORD, and the treasures of the king's house, and delivered them into the hand of his servants: and king Asa sent them	24 And Asa slept with his fathers, and was buried with his fathers in the city of David his father: and Jehoshaphat his son reigned in his stead.	3) His death & burial in Jerusalem 4) His successor: His son Jehoshaphat, 22:41-50

a. Asa had a long, forty-one year reign over the Southern Kingdom (v.10). And note a significant fact: he was not influenced by his grandmother Maacah's false worship (v.13).

b. On the contrary, Asa carried out a religious reform throughout Judah (vv.11-14). Just as David had done, he lived a righteous life before the LORD and established a just and moral government throughout the land. The first ten years of his rule were peaceful years: no wars or skirmishes threatened the borders of the Southern Kingdom (2 Chr.14:1). This meant that for ten years, he could focus solely upon his religious reforms. Note four significant facts about his efforts to establish a righteous, just government:

1) He banished the religious prostitutes, expelling them from the land of Judah (v.12; 14:24). Engaging in sexual rituals was forbidden throughout the nation.
2) He removed all the idols his forefathers had made and encouraged the people to worship (v.12). Undertaking this task no doubt took an enormous effort, for idolatry and false worship had become embedded in the nation, more so than ever before in the history of Israel (14:22).

3) Asa was even able to depose or remove his grandmother Maacah from her position as queen mother (v.13). For years she had influenced the people to worship the repulsive, obscene image of the Asherah pole. Note that Asa actually cut the pole down and burned it in the Kidron Valley. Removing his own grandmother from her exalted position shows just how deeply committed Asa was to the LORD. Obviously, his love for the LORD was the deepest attachment he had, even deeper than his affection for his family. He loved the LORD above all and he was determined to cleanse the land of idolatry and false worship.
4) But note: Asa did not destroy all the high places (v.14). Keep in mind that some high places had true worship centers where the LORD was genuinely worshipped (3:2; 1 S.9:12), but other high places were used as false worship centers where idolatry was practiced (2 Chr.14:2-3). Most likely, Asa destroyed the high places where idols were worshipped, but he allowed other high places to remain where the LORD Himself was worshipped (v.14).

c. Whatever the case, Scripture says that his heart was perfect. He was fully committed to the LORD *throughout his entire life*. And he was not only committed to the LORD, but also to the temple. Remember that his grandfather had used the wealth of the temple to pay tribute to the king of Egypt in order to keep the Egyptians from destroying Jerusalem (14:25-28). Here King Asa is said to have replenished the treasury that his grandfather had depleted.

d. After enjoying ten years of peace, war broke out between Asa and King Baasha, who was then ruling over the Northern Kingdom (15:33–16:7). This was a major military engagement demanding all-out mobilization for war. Note five facts:

1) King Baasha of the Northern Kingdom invaded Judah, conquering city after city including Ramah, which was only four miles north of Jerusalem itself (v.17). Capturing a town so close to the capital of the Southern Kingdom was a very serious threat to Asa and his people. King Baasha's ambition was perfectly clear, for he began to fortify Ramah in order to cut off all traffic and trade routes leading into Jerusalem. He was determined to conquer the Southern Kingdom.
2) Asa immediately sought a military alliance with Ben-Hadad, who was king of Syria or Aram (v.18). This was a serious failure of Asa's, for he was trusting in man and failing to trust in God (2 Chr.16:7-10). Note the great cost it was to the nation: he emptied the treasuries of the temple and palace and sent a delegation with the riches to King Ben-Hadad requesting two things of the Syrian king. He wanted Ben-Hadad to break his treaty with the Northern Kingdom and to sign a new treaty between Judah and Syria (vv.18-19).

   Sadly, Asa had failed to pray, to ask God for help during this crisis. He was placing his trust in man instead of in God. As a result, he was forced to strip the treasury of his own palace and that of the temple, which he had formerly built up and where he had no doubt dedicated the gifts to God and His service.
3) When the delegation arrived with the enormous treasure and wealth, Ben-Hadad was more than willing to accept King Asa's terms. He could greatly enrich his own wealth by breaking his treaty with the Northern Kingdom of Israel and supporting King Asa against their invasion (v.20). Quickly mobilizing the Syrian forces, he swiftly invaded the Northern Kingdom of Israel and conquered a large area that gave him access to major trade routes running from Egypt and Phoenicia to Syria.
4) As soon as King Baasha heard of the invasion of the Northern Kingdom by the Syrians, he was forced to retreat from Judah in order to block the invaders (v.21).
5) When the army of the Northern Kingdom withdrew, Asa was able to mobilize his own forces, march out, and retake Ramah (v.22). Note that he confiscated the building materials left behind by Baasha and that he used these materials to fortify Geba and Mizpah. These were two major cities that needed to be fortified as military strongholds in order to strengthen the border between the Northern and Southern Kingdoms. By fortifying these cities, Asa hoped to prevent any future invasion by the Northern Kingdom. And he was successful, at least during his reign. For no other invasion occurred during his lifetime.

   But Asa had trusted in man instead of in God. He failed to trust the LORD for deliverance. He had suffered a spiritual defeat that almost led to the conquest of Judah. In another Scripture, God sent His prophet Hanani to rebuke Asa for his unbelief, for having forsaken God and having trusted in man and the power of his military. Instead of receiving the rebuke humbly and in repentance, Asa had the prophet arrested, thrown in prison, and treated harshly. And from this point on, the prophets of God were often to be persecuted, treated harshly by the rulers of Israel (2 Chr.16:7-10; also see 2 K.17:13-14).

e. Asa's achievements and a summary of his life are recorded in the book *The History of the Kings of Judah* (v.23). An interesting fact is that he had diseased feet in his old age. This statement seems disconnected from the context of the passage. Perhaps it is mentioned to indicate what caused his death. After his death he was buried in Jerusalem and succeeded by his son Jehoshaphat (see outline and notes—22:41-50 for more discussion).

Thought 1. A child can reject the evil influence of his or her parents. Asa did, and many others have. Just because a parent lives a wicked life does not mean that the child has to walk in the same footsteps of evil. Just because a parent fails does not mean a child will fail. The trend of evil can be broken, overcome, and conquered. No child can legitimately blame his parents for his own sinful behavior.

⇒ If a parent lives a sinful life, the child can live a righteous life.
⇒ If a parent commits adultery, the child can live a moral life.
⇒ If a parent divorces, the child does not have to divorce. The married child can remain with his or her spouse.
⇒ If a parent is an alcoholic, the child can live a life of sobriety, never touching an alcoholic beverage.
⇒ If a parent is a thief, the child can be honest, respecting the property of others.
⇒ If a parent uses foul, indecent, distasteful language and profanity, the child can reject such vulgar speech and learn to speak kindly, respectfully, and decently.
⇒ If a parent is uneducated and unskilled, the child can educate him or herself and learn a skill.
⇒ If a parent is complacent and lazy, the child can be industrious, working hard and diligently.

No child has to walk in the footsteps of his parents. A child can break the weak or sinful behavior of a parent and walk in strength and righteousness before God. As stated, King Asa broke the deep-seated, ingrained wickedness of his parents. He walked righteously before the LORD—not perfectly, but righteously—throughout his entire life.

Every person is responsible for his own behavior and actions. When we live righteously, we will be rewarded, and the rewards will not be given to someone else. So it is with sinful behavior: when we live wicked lives, we ourselves stand responsible for the wickedness. Neither our mothers nor fathers nor anyone else is to be blamed for our failures and weaknesses. Despite others' harmful or corrupt influence upon us, we are responsible to break the trend of corruption and wickedness. We are responsible for our own personal behavior, whether good or evil. This is the clear teaching of God's Holy Word:

"And thou shalt love the Lord thy God with all thy heart, and with all thy soul, and with all thy mind, and with all thy strength: this is the first commandment. And the second *is* like, *namely* this, Thou shalt love thy neighbour as thyself. There is none other commandment greater than these" (Mk.12:30-31).

"Love worketh no ill to his neighbour: therefore love *is* the fulfilling of the law" (Ro.13:10).

"Awake to righteousness, and sin not; for some have not the knowledge of God: I speak this to your shame" (1 Co.15:34).

"But refuse profane and old wives' fables, and exercise thyself *rather* unto godliness" (1 Ti.4:7).

"But thou, O man of God, flee these things; and follow after righteousness, godliness, faith, love, patience, meekness" (1 Ti.6:11).

"Teaching us that, denying ungodliness and worldly lusts, we should live soberly, righteously, and godly, in this present world" (Tit.2:12).

"Pure religion and undefiled before God and the Father is this, To visit the fatherless and widows in their affliction, *and* to keep himself unspotted from the world" (Ja.1:27).

"The fathers shall not be put to death for the children, neither shall the children be put to death for the fathers: every man shall be put to death for his own sin" (De.24:16).

"And be it indeed *that* I have erred, mine error remaineth with myself" (Jb.19:4).

"If thou be wise, thou shalt be wise for thyself: but *if* thou scornest, thou alone shalt bear *it*" (Pr.9:12).

"Let us hear the conclusion of the whole matter: Fear God, and keep his commandments: for this *is* the whole *duty* of man" (Ec.12:13).

"But every one shall die for his own iniquity: every man that eateth the sour grape, his teeth shall be set on edge" (Je.31:30).

"The soul that sinneth, it shall die. The son shall not bear the iniquity of the father, neither shall the father bear the iniquity of the son: the righteousness of the righteous shall be upon him, and the wickedness of the wicked shall be upon him" (Eze.18:20).

"He hath showed thee, O man, what *is* good; and what doth the LORD require of thee, but to do justly, and to love mercy, and to walk humbly with thy God" (Mi.6:8).

1. The evil reign of Nadab: A lesson on the surety of judgment
   a. His background: Reigned 2 years
   b. His evil life
      1) Walked in the ways of his father Jeroboam, 12:25-33
      2) Was a stumbling block, causing Israel to sin
   c. His death: Assassinated by one of his military commanders, Baasha
      1) Was struck down during the siege of Gibbethon, a Philistine town
      2) Was succeeded by Baasha
   d. His family & relatives (Jeroboam's entire family): All murdered by Baasha to eliminate the dynasty & the threat to his own power
      1) Was a fulfillment of the prophetic judgment by Ahijah, 14:7-16
      2) Was due to sin: The sins of Jeroboam & of Israel
      3) Was bound to face God's judgment
   e. His achievements & the summary of his life: Recorded in the book *The History of the Kings of Israel*

2. The evil reign of Baasha: A legacy, example of terrible evil
   a. His constant war with Asa
   b. His background: Reigned 24 years
   c. His evil life
      1) He walked in the evil ways of Jeroboam, 12:25-33
      2) He was a stumbling block, causing Israel to sin
   d. His scathing condemnation: Confronted by God's prophet Jehu

F. The Reign of Six Kings in Israel, from Nadab to Ahab: A Downward Spiral of Sin & Destruction, 15:25–16:34

25 And Nadab the son of Jeroboam began to reign over Israel in the second year of Asa king of Judah, and reigned over Israel two years.
26 And he did evil in the sight of the LORD, and walked in the way of his father, and in his sin wherewith he made Israel to sin.
27 And Baasha the son of Ahijah, of the house of Issachar, conspired against him; and Baasha smote him at Gibbethon, which *belonged* to the Philistines; for Nadab and all Israel laid siege to Gibbethon.
28 Even in the third year of Asa king of Judah did Baasha slay him, and reigned in his stead.
29 And it came to pass, when he reigned, *that* he smote all the house of Jeroboam; he left not to Jeroboam any that breathed, until he had destroyed him, according unto the saying of the LORD, which he spake by his servant Ahijah the Shilonite:
30 Because of the sins of Jeroboam which he sinned, and which he made Israel sin, by his provocation wherewith he provoked the LORD God of Israel to anger.
31 Now the rest of the acts of Nadab, and all that he did, *are* they not written in the book of the chronicles of the kings of Israel?
32 And there was war between Asa and Baasha king of Israel all their days.
33 In the third year of Asa king of Judah began Baasha the son of Ahijah to reign over all Israel in Tirzah, twenty and four years.
34 And he did evil in the sight of the LORD, and walked in the way of Jeroboam, and in his sin wherewith he made Israel to sin.

CHAPTER 16

Then the word of the LORD came to Jehu the son of Hanani against Baasha, saying,
2 Forasmuch as I exalted thee out of the dust, and made thee prince over my people Israel; and thou hast walked in the way of Jeroboam, and hast made my people Israel to sin, to provoke me to anger with their sins;
3 Behold, I will take away the posterity of Baasha, and the posterity of his house; and will make thy house like the house of Jeroboam the son of Nebat.
4 Him that dieth of Baasha in the city shall the dogs eat; and him that dieth of his in the fields shall the fowls of the air eat.
5 Now the rest of the acts of Baasha, and what he did, and his might, *are* they not written in the book of the chronicles of the kings of Israel?
6 So Baasha slept with his fathers, and was buried in Tirzah: and Elah his son reigned in his stead.
7 And also by the hand of the prophet Jehu the son of Hanani came the word of the LORD against Baasha, and against his house, even for all the evil that he did in the sight of the LORD, in provoking him to anger with the work of his hands, in being like the house of Jeroboam; and because he killed him.
8 In the twenty and sixth year of Asa king of Judah began Elah the son of Baasha to reign over Israel in Tirzah, two years.
9 And his servant Zimri, captain of half *his* chariots, conspired against him, as he was in Tirzah, drinking himself drunk in the house of Arza steward of *his* house in Tirzah.
10 And Zimri went in and smote him, and killed him, in the twenty and seventh year of Asa king of Judah, and reigned in his stead.
11 And it came to pass, when he began to reign, as soon as he sat on his throne, *that* he slew all the house of Baasha: he left him not one that pisseth against a wall, neither of his kinsfolks, nor of his friends.
12 Thus did Zimri destroy all the house of Baasha, according to the word of the

      1) He had been raised up to rule by God Himself
      2) He walked in the evil ways of Jeroboam, 12:25-33; 14:16
      3) He was a stumbling block: Caused God's people to sin
      4) He was to face God's judgment
         • His house—kingdom & family dynasty—was to be destroyed
         • His family was to be shamed: Not buried in respect & honor but instead eaten by scavengers
   e. His achievements & the summary of his life
      1) His reign: Recorded in the book *The History of the Kings of Israel*
      2) His death & burial: In the capital Tirzah
      3) His successor: His son Elah
      4) His tragic legacy
         • A man confronted by God's prophet & God's judgment
         • A man guilty of terrible evil
         • A man guilty of slaughtering the entire house of Jeroboam

3. The evil reign of Elah: A scene of drunkenness & murder
   a. His background: Reigned 2 years
   b. His death: A fulfillment of God's prophetic judgment
      1) The plot by Zimri, a military commander
      2) The scene of the plot: A royal feast where King Elah got drunk
      3) The assassination by Zimri
      4) The takeover of the crown by the commander: His first action was to protect his power
         • By killing all heirs
         • By killing all friends of Elah: To prevent retaliation, revenge
      5) The fulfillment of Jehu's prophecy of judgment, 3-4, 7

c. His evil life
   1) Had committed the same sins as his father Baasha (& Jeroboam), 34; 12:25-33
   2) Had been a stumbling block, causing the people to sin

d. His achievements & the summary of his life: Recorded in the book *The History of the Kings of Israel*

4. The evil reign of Zimri: A picture of hopelessness & suicide

a. His background: Reigned 7 days

b. His desperate & unexpected end
   1) The army heard that the officer Zimri had assassinated the king
      • They immediately proclaimed their commander Omri king of Israel
      • They immediately withdrew from Gibbethon & attacked Zimri at the capital Tirzah
   2) The usurper Zimri saw that the situation was hopeless
      • He set fire to the palace
      • He committed suicide

c. His evil life
   1) Lived a life of sin
   2) Had walked in the ways of Jeroboam, 12:25-33; 14:16
   3) Had been a stumbling block, a bad example for Israel

d. His rebellion & the summary of his life: Recorded in the book *The History of the Kings of Israel*

5. The evil reign of Omri: A spirit of worldly ambition & self-exaltation

a. His background
   1) He had to struggle 4 years for the throne, 15, 23
      • His supporters were stronger than Tibni's
      • His opponent Tibni was either killed or died of other causes
   2) He was crowned over all Israel & reigned 12 years, six of them in Tirzah

LORD, which he spake against Baasha by Jehu the prophet,

13 For all the sins of Baasha, and the sins of Elah his son, by which they sinned, and by which they made Israel to sin, in provoking the LORD God of Israel to anger with their vanities.

14 Now the rest of the acts of Elah, and all that he did, *are* they not written in the book of the chronicles of the kings of Israel?

15 In the twenty and seventh year of Asa king of Judah did Zimri reign seven days in Tirzah. And the people *were* encamped against Gibbethon, which *belonged* to the Philistines.

16 And the people *that were* encamped heard say, Zimri hath conspired, and hath also slain the king: wherefore all Israel made Omri, the captain of the host, king over Israel that day in the camp.

17 And Omri went up from Gibbethon, and all Israel with him, and they besieged Tirzah.

18 And it came to pass, when Zimri saw that the city was taken, that he went into the palace of the king's house, and burnt the king's house over him with fire, and died,

19 For his sins which he sinned in doing evil in the sight of the LORD, in walking in the way of Jeroboam, and in his sin which he did, to make Israel to sin.

20 Now the rest of the acts of Zimri, and his treason that he wrought, *are* they not written in the book of the chronicles of the kings of Israel?

21 Then were the people of Israel divided into two parts: half of the people followed Tibni the son of Ginath, to make him king; and half followed Omri.

22 But the people that followed Omri prevailed against the people that followed Tibni the son of Ginath: so Tibni died, and Omri reigned.

23 In the thirty and first year of Asa king of Judah began Omri to reign over Israel, twelve years: six years reigned he in Tirzah.

24 And he bought the hill Samaria of Shemer for two talents of silver, and built on the hill, and called the name of the city which he built, after the name of Shemer, owner of the hill, Samaria.

25 But Omri wrought evil in the eyes of the LORD, and did worse than all that *were* before him.

26 For he walked in all the way of Jeroboam the son of Nebat, and in his sin wherewith he made Israel to sin, to provoke the LORD God of Israel to anger with their vanities.

27 Now the rest of the acts of Omri which he did, and his might that he showed, *are* they not written in the book of the chronicles of the kings of Israel?

28 So Omri slept with his fathers, and was buried in Samaria: and Ahab his son reigned in his stead.

29 And in the thirty and eighth year of Asa king of Judah began Ahab the son of Omri to reign over Israel: and Ahab the son of Omri reigned over Israel in Samaria twenty and two years.

30 And Ahab the son of Omri did evil in the sight of the LORD above all that *were* before him.

31 And it came to pass, as if it had been a light thing for him to walk in the sins of Jeroboam the son of Nebat, that he took to wife Jezebel the daughter of Ethbaal king of the Zidonians, and went and served Baal, and worshipped him.

32 And he reared up an altar for Baal in the house of Baal, which he had built in Samaria.

33 And Ahab made a grove; and Ahab did more to provoke the LORD God of Israel to anger than all the kings of Israel that were before him.

34 In his days did Hiel the Bethelite build Jericho: he laid the foundation thereof in Abiram his firstborn, and set up the gates thereof in his youngest *son* Segub, according to the word of the LORD, which he spake by Joshua the son of Nun.

b. His significant achievement: He built a new capital, Samaria
   1) It sat on a hill, ideal for a fortress
   2) It was named after the owner Shemer

c. His evil life & reign
   1) He sinned more than all the rulers before him
   2) He walked in the evil ways of Jeroboam, 12:25-33; 14:16
   3) He was a stumbling block: Caused Israel to sin

d. His achievements & the summary of his life
   1) His reign: Recorded in the book *The History of the Kings of Israel*
   2) His death & burial in Samaria
   3) His successor: Ahab

6. The evil reign of Ahab: A life of utter depravity, corruption

a. His background
   1) Was the son of Omri
   2) Reigned 22 years

b. His evil, degenerate life
   1) Did more evil than all the rulers before him
   2) Considered it trivial, a light thing, to sin—even to commit the sins of Jeroboam, 12:25-33; 14:16
   3) Married Jezebel, a priestess of the idol & false god Baal
   4) Served & worshipped Baal
   5) Built a temple for Baal
      • Erected an altar
      • Erected an Asherah pole (a wood image of the goddess Asherah)
   6) Aroused God's anger more than all the other rulers
   7) Charged Hiel of Bethel to rebuild Jericho in defiance of Joshua's curse (Jos. 6:26-27): Caused the death of Hiel's two sons

DIVISION II

THE EARLY HISTORY OF THE DIVIDED KINGDOM: WITNESSING THE AWFUL RISE OF IDOLATRY AND FALSE WORSHIP, 12:1–16:34

F. The Reign of Six Kings in Israel, from Nadab to Ahab: A Downward Spiral of Sin and Destruction, 15:25–16:34

(15:25–16:34) **Introduction**: without question, sin and evil lead to destruction. Whenever we commit an act of evil or sin of any nature, we are contributing to the destruction of some person or some thing. Often the destruction takes place only within our own spirits, making us guilty before God and dooming us to stand before His terrifying judgment—unless we repent of our sins. But often our sin or evil affects the lives of others, and sometimes severely. A drunken driver causes an accident and kills or maims innocent children or adults. Another person steals items of great worth or sentimental value, causing not only loss but also fear and insecurity for the victim.

Picture the physical and emotional damage done to an abused child, wife, or husband, or the pain and destruction done to a family due to separation or divorce. Imagine the loss suffered by corporations because of theft or lazy, incompetent workers. Think of the suffering and unfair treatment of employees by some business owners or supervisors. There is no end to the suffering caused by mistreatment, abuse, anger, violence, lawlessness, immorality, and the unjust deeds done by so many throughout society. All over the world there seems to be a downward spiral of sin and destruction taking place.

In the present passage of Scripture, the story shifts from the Southern Kingdom of Judah to the Northern Kingdom of Israel. As the story now focuses upon the rulers of the Northern Kingdom, one picture stands out above all others: these six leaders all lived evil, wicked lives. They walked in the ways of Jeroboam, the first ruler of the Northern Kingdom. Just as he was a terrible stumbling block to the Israelites, so too were these evil kings. They led the people to continue on in their lives of sin and false worship, giving their allegiance to false gods who had no power to help them in their hour of need. This is: *The Reign of Six Kings in Israel, from Nadab to Ahab: A Downward Spiral of Sin and Destruction,* 15:25–16:34.

1. The evil reign of Nadab: a lesson on the surety of judgment (vv.25-31).
2. The evil reign of Baasha: a legacy, example of terrible evil (ch.15:32–16:7).
3. The evil reign of Elah: a scene of drunkenness and murder (vv.8-14).
4. The evil reign of Zimri: a picture of hopelessness and suicide (vv.15-20).
5. The evil reign of Omri: a spirit of worldly ambition and self-exaltation (vv.21-28).
6. The evil reign of Ahab: a life of utter depravity, corruption (vv.29-34).

[1] (15:25-31) **Judgment, Surety of—Prophecy, Fulfillment of—Stumbling Block, Example of—Parents, Evil Influence of—Children, Following Parental Influence, Evil—Israel, Kings of, Nadab—Nadab, History of—History, of Kings—Nadab**: there was the evil reign of Nadab in the Northern Kingdom of Israel. Nadab was the son of Jeroboam who had committed so much wickedness, setting a terrible example of evil for his son to follow (see outline and notes—12:25–13:34; 14:1-20; 14:21-31 for more discussion). Scripture gives the basic facts of Nadab's brief reign:

OUTLINE	SCRIPTURE	SCRIPTURE	OUTLINE
1. The evil reign of Nadab: A lesson on the surety of judgment a. His background: Reigned 2 years b. His evil life 1) Walked in the ways of his father Jeroboam, 12:25-33 2) Was a stumbling block, causing Israel to sin c. His death: Assassinated by one of his military commanders, Baasha 1) Was struck down during the siege of Gibbethon, a Philistine town 2) Was succeeded by Baasha	25And Nadab the son of Jeroboam began to reign over Israel in the second year of Asa king of Judah, and reigned over Israel two years. 26 And he did evil in the sight of the LORD, and walked in the way of his father, and in his sin wherewith he made Israel to sin. 27 And Baasha the son of Ahijah, of the house of Issachar, conspired against him; and Baasha smote him at Gibbethon, which *belonged* to the Philistines; for Nadab and all Israel laid siege to Gibbethon. 28 Even in the third year of Asa king of Judah did Baasha slay him, and reigned in his stead.	29 And it came to pass, when he reigned, *that* he smote all the house of Jeroboam; he left not to Jeroboam any that breathed, until he had destroyed him, according unto the saying of the LORD, which he spake by his servant Ahijah the Shilonite: 30 Because of the sins of Jeroboam which he sinned, and which he made Israel sin, by his provocation wherewith he provoked the LORD God of Israel to anger. 31 Now the rest of the acts of Nadab, and all that he did, *are* they not written in the book of the chronicles of the kings of Israel?	d. His family & relatives (Jeroboam's entire family): All murdered by Baasha to eliminate the dynasty & the threat to his own power 1) Was a fulfillment of the prophetic judgment by Ahijah, 14:7-16 2) Was due to sin: The sins of Jeroboam & of Israel 3) Was bound to face God's judgment e. His achievements & the summary of his life: Recorded in the book *The History of the Kings of Israel*

a. King Nadab reigned for only two years, becoming king of Israel during the second year of King Asa's rule over the Southern Kingdom of Judah (v.1). But Nadab's *evil* reign was nothing like the *good* reign of Asa's. He undertook none of the social and religious reforms that were taking place in the Southern Kingdom (15:9-24). The name Nadab means "generous" or "noble," but his lifestyle in no way resembled these admirable traits.[1]

b. Nadab lived an evil life, following in the very footsteps of his father Jeroboam. Instead of turning the people back to the only living and true God, Nadab continued to lead the people to follow the new form of idolatrous religion and false worship instituted by his father (12:25-33). Thus he too became a huge stumbling block to the Israelites, causing them to sin.

c. While Nadab was seeking to capture the key Philistine city of Gibbethon, a man named Baasha was plotting to assassinate the king. Baasha was probably one of Nadab's military commanders. But whatever the case, Baasha's plot was successful and King Nadab was assassinated. Thereupon Baasha took the throne for himself.

d. As soon as Baasha took the throne, he killed the immediate family of Nadab and all his relatives, eliminating the entire family of Jeroboam. This ended the dynasty of Jeroboam and all threats to Baasha's claim to power. This was a direct fulfillment of the prophetic judgment by the prophet Ahijah (14:7-16). Judgment fell upon the house of Jeroboam because of his sins and the fact that he had become a terrible stumbling block to Israel. As a result, he had provoked the LORD to anger, arousing the judgment of God. Because of his terrible evil, Jeroboam and his house or dynasty, including his son and successor Nadab, were now suffering the wrath of God's judgment. Jeroboam the father had set an evil example before his household, and his entire family had followed in his wicked footsteps.

e. Nadab's achievements and the summary of his life are simply said to be recorded in the book *The History of the Kings of Israel* (v.31).

Thought 1. God predicted judgment upon Jeroboam because of his sin. God also predicts judgment upon any of us who continue in sin, refusing to repent. Repentance simply means that we turn away from our sin and turn to God, living holy and righteous lives. If we refuse to turn away from sin—denying or neglecting God, walking through life breaking the commandments of God—the hand of God's judgment will fall upon us.

Just as predicted, a future day of judgment is coming. And just as the predicted judgment fell upon Jeroboam and his family, so the future Day of Judgment will come and fall upon us. The judgment of God upon all sin and evil is inevitable. Justice—true justice—will be executed. We will be held accountable for all the injustice, immorality, and evil we do upon this earth. This is the prophecy, the prediction of God's Holy Word. Judgment is a surety; judgment is inevitable:

"For the Son of man shall come in the glory of his Father with his angels; and then he shall reward every man according to his works" (Mt.16:27).

"When the Son of man shall come in his glory, and all the holy angels with him, then shall he sit upon the throne of his glory: And before him shall be gathered all nations: and he shall separate them one from another, as a shepherd divideth *his* sheep from the goats: And he shall set the sheep on his right hand, but the goats on the left" (Mt.25:31-33).

"Whosoever therefore shall be ashamed of me and of my words in this adulterous and sinful generation; of him also shall the Son of man be ashamed, when he cometh in the glory of his Father with the holy angels" (Mk.8:38).

"Marvel not at this: for the hour is coming, in the which all that are in the graves shall hear his voice, And shall come forth; they that have done good, unto the resurrection of life; and they that have done evil, unto the resurrection of damnation" (Jn.5:28-29).

"And to you who are troubled rest with us, when the Lord Jesus shall be revealed from heaven with his mighty angels, In flaming fire taking vengeance on them that know not God, and that obey not the gospel of our Lord Jesus Christ" (2 Th.1:7-8).

"And as it is appointed unto men once to die, but after this the judgment" (He.9:27).

"The Lord knoweth how to deliver the godly out of temptations, and to reserve the unjust unto the day of judgment to be punished" (2 Pe.2:9).

"But the heavens and the earth, which are now, by the same word are kept in store, reserved unto fire against the day of judgment and perdition of ungodly men" (2 Pe.3:7).

"And Enoch also, the seventh from Adam, prophesied of these, saying, Behold, the Lord cometh with ten thousands of his saints, To execute judgment upon all, and to convince all that are ungodly among them of all their ungodly deeds which they have ungodly committed, and of all their hard *speeches* which ungodly sinners have spoken against him" (Jude 14-15).

"Behold, he cometh with clouds; and every eye shall see him, and they *also* which pierced him: and all kindreds of the earth shall wail because of him. Even so, Amen" (Re.1:7).

"And I saw a great white throne, and him that sat on it, from whose face the earth and the heaven fled away; and there was found no place for them. And I saw the dead, small and great, stand before God; and the books were opened: and another book was opened, which is *the book* of life: and the dead were judged out of those things which were written in the books, according to their works. And the sea gave up the dead which were in it; and death and hell delivered up the dead which were in them: and they were judged every man according to their works. And death and hell were cast into the lake of fire. This is the second death. And whosoever was not found written in the book of life was cast into the lake of fire" (Re.20:11-15).

---

[1] *The Nelson Study Bible, NKJV*, 1 K.15:25-26.

2 (15:32-16:7) **Example, of Evil—Influence, for Evil—Stumbling Block, Example of—Legacy, of Evil, Example of—Testimony, of Evil—Kings, of Israel, Baasha—Israel, Kings of—Northern Kingdom, Kings of**: there was the evil reign of Baasha, who left a legacy of terrible evil. Scripture clearly spells out why:

OUTLINE	SCRIPTURE	SCRIPTURE	OUTLINE
2. The evil reign of Baasha: A legacy, example of terrible evil a. His constant war with Asa b. His background: Reigned 24 years c. His evil life 1) He walked in the evil ways of Jeroboam, 12:25-33 2) He was a stumbling block, causing Israel to sin d. His scathing condemnation: Confronted by God's prophet Jehu 1) He had been raised up to rule by God Himself 2) He walked in the evil ways of Jeroboam, 12:25-33; 14:16 3) He was a stumbling block: Caused God's people to sin 4) He was to face God's judgment • His house—kingdom &	32 And there was war between Asa and Baasha king of Israel all their days. 33 In the third year of Asa king of Judah began Baasha the son of Ahijah to reign over all Israel in Tirzah, twenty and four years. 34 And he did evil in the sight of the LORD, and walked in the way of Jeroboam, and in his sin wherewith he made Israel to sin. **CHAPTER 16** Then the word of the LORD came to Jehu the son of Hanani against Baasha, saying, 2 Forasmuch as I exalted thee out of the dust, and made thee prince over my people Israel; and thou hast walked in the way of Jeroboam, and hast made my people Israel to sin, to provoke me to anger with their sins; 3 Behold, I will take away the posterity of Baasha, and the posterity of his house; and	will make thy house like the house of Jeroboam the son of Nebat. 4 Him that dieth of Baasha in the city shall the dogs eat; and him that dieth of his in the fields shall the fowls of the air eat. 5 Now the rest of the acts of Baasha, and what he did, and his might, *are* they not written in the book of the chronicles of the kings of Israel? 6 So Baasha slept with his fathers, and was buried in Tirzah: and Elah his son reigned in his stead. 7 And also by the hand of the prophet Jehu the son of Hanani came the word of the LORD against Baasha, and against his house, even for all the evil that he did in the sight of the LORD, in provoking him to anger with the work of his hands, in being like the house of Jeroboam; and because he killed him.	family dynasty—was to be destroyed • His family was to be shamed: Not buried in respect & honor but instead eaten by scavengers e. His achievements & the summary of his life 1) His reign: Recorded in the book *The History of the Kings of Israel* 2) His death & burial: In the capital Tirzah 3) His successor: His son Elah 4) His tragic legacy • A man confronted by God's prophet & God's judgment • A man guilty of terrible evil • A man guilty of slaughtering the entire house of Jeroboam

a. Baasha was engaged in constant warfare with King Asa of the Southern Kingdom (v.32). Instead of attempting to establish the social and religious reforms as King Asa had done, Baasha was gripped by a spirit of greed. He coveted more and more power, seeking more territory for himself (15:9-24). Keep in mind that he had come to power by assassinating King Nadab, the son of Jeroboam. But he was just the first of several assassins who would take the throne of the Northern Kingdom by murdering the existing ruler (1 K.15:15-16; 2 K.10:1-17; 15:10-13; 15:14-16; 15:25-26; 15:30-31).[2]

b. The long twenty-four-year reign of Baasha began in the third year of King Asa's rule over the Southern Kingdom of Judah (v.33). Baasha ruled from the capital city of Israel, which was Tirzah (v.33).

c. Baasha failed as miserably in his rule as Jeroboam and Nadab had in theirs, for he failed to remove the corrupt, false worship instituted by Jeroboam. Continuing to commit the very same evil as his predecessors, he became a terrible stumbling block. He caused Israel to continue on in their idolatry and false worship (v.34).

d. A scathing condemnation was pronounced upon Baasha by God's prophet Jehu (16:1-14). Jehu was the son of Hanani, who was probably the seer or prophet who issued a warning to King Asa of Judah (2 Chr.16:7-9). God's message to King Baasha through Jehu was direct and to the point:

1) King Baasha had been raised up by God Himself to rule over the Northern Kingdom (although his murderous ways of securing power were not sanctioned by God).
2) But instead of instituting religious and social reforms, he had chosen to walk in the evil ways of Jeroboam (12:25-33; 14:16).
3) Thus, he had become a terrible stumbling block to Israel. He caused God's people to sin and to provoke God to anger by their sins.
4) Consequently, he was to face the hand of God's judgment (vv.3-4). His house—the kingdom and family dynasty—were to be destroyed just as Jeroboam's had been. In addition, his family was to be shamed, not buried with respect and honor. Instead, their dead bodies would be eaten by dogs and birds, scavengers of the earth.

e. A brief statement of Baasha's achievements and a summary of his life are given by the author (vv.5-7). The achievements of his reign are recorded in the book *The History of the Kings of Israel* (v.5). After Baasha's death, he was buried in the capital of Tirzah and succeeded by his son Elah (v.6). Note that his tragic legacy is reemphasized:

⇒ He was a man who had to be confronted by God's prophet to hear a scathing condemnation of God's judgment against himself.
⇒ He was a man who was guilty of terrible evil in the eyes of the Lord, an evil that provoked the Lord to anger.
⇒ He was a man who was guilty of slaughtering the entire house of Jeroboam.

---

2 Paul R. House. *1, 2 Kings*, p.199.

Thought 1. Baasha was a man who set a terrible example for his family and all his generation. He was guilty not only of engaging in false worship and encouraging others to do the same, but also of mass murder in order to secure the throne. Scripture says he did all kinds of evil things, committing all forms of sin and wickedness (v.7). And because of the life he lived, he left behind an appalling legacy of evil.

What kind of legacy are we leaving? What kind of lives are we living before our families, neighbors, fellow workers, friends, communities, and nation? Are we living righteous, holy lives, being positive role models for our families and communities? Or are we living lives of wickedness and evil, showing people that we can ignore God and His commandments and walk through life without any serious consequences? Are we conveying by our sinful behavior the false idea that God does not exist or is unimportant?

People are observing our lives. They pay close attention to how we talk: whether our words are kind and gracious or complaining and grumbling. They pay attention to what we say: whether our speech is pure and honest or off-colored, filthy, distasteful, and full of profanity. Besides this, people observe our behavior: whether we walk righteously and godly or wickedly and sinfully. No matter who we are, we are being watched by someone: a child, a spouse, a sibling, a parent, a friend, a co-worker, or a complete stranger. And, more importantly, our lives are being watched by God. The example we set and the legacy we leave behind for others *matters* to God. Listen to the warning God gives against living ungodly, wicked, and sinful lives:

"For the wrath of God is revealed from heaven against all ungodliness and unrighteousness of men, who hold the truth in unrighteousness....Being filled with all unrighteousness, fornication, wickedness, covetousness, maliciousness; full of envy, murder, debate, deceit, malignity; whisperers, Backbiters, haters of God, despiteful, proud, boasters, inventors of evil things, disobedient to parents, Without understanding, covenantbreakers, without natural affection, implacable, unmerciful: Who knowing the judgment of God, that they which commit such things are worthy of death, not only do the same, but have pleasure in them that do them" (Ro.1:18, 29-32).

"Know ye not that the unrighteous shall not inherit the kingdom of God? Be not deceived: neither fornicators, nor idolaters, nor adulterers, nor effeminate, nor abusers of themselves with mankind, Nor thieves, nor covetous, nor drunkards, nor revilers, nor extortioners, shall inherit the kingdom of God" (1 Co.6:9-10).

"Now the works of the flesh are manifest, which are *these;* Adultery, fornication, uncleanness, lasciviousness, Idolatry, witchcraft, hatred, variance, emulations, wrath, strife, seditions, heresies, Envyings, murders, drunkenness, revellings, and such like: of the which I tell you before, as I have also told *you* in time past, that they which do such things shall not inherit the kingdom of God" (Ga.5:19-21).

"But fornication, and all uncleanness, or covetousness, let it not be once named among you, as becometh saints; Neither filthiness, nor foolish talking, nor jesting, which are not convenient: but rather giving of thanks. For this ye know, that no whoremonger, nor unclean person, nor covetous man, who is an idolater, hath any inheritance in the kingdom of Christ and of God" (Ep.5:3-5).

"But the fearful, and unbelieving, and the abominable, and murderers, and whoremongers, and sorcerers, and idolaters, and all liars, shall have their part in the lake which burneth with fire and brimstone: which is the second death" (Re.21:8).

3 (16:8-14) **Drunkenness, Example of—Murder, Example of—Israel, Kings of—Northern Kingdom, Kings of**: there was the brief, evil reign of Elah over the Northern Kingdom. As soon as his father Baasha had died, Elah assumed the throne, but his reign lasted only two years. In fulfillment of God's prophetic judgment, he was assassinated by Zimri, one of his own military commanders (vv.9-12). However, Elah was not assassinated while on the battlefield, but while attending a *drunken feast* at the home of Arza, his royal official in charge of the royal palace (v.9). While the king was drunk, his commander Zimri joined the drunken party and, at some point, assassinated the king (v.10).

Having taken over the crown for himself, Zimri's first action was to protect his power by killing all of Baasha's heirs (v.11). But he did not stop with the heirs. He also killed all the friends of Elah, anyone who might contest his claim to the throne by seeking retaliation or revenge. Note that Elah's assassination was a fulfillment of Jehu's prophecy of judgment (v.12; see vv.3, 4, 7). And the reason for the judgment is spelled out by Scripture: he had lived an evil life, committing the very same sins as his father Baasha and those of Jeroboam. He was a terrible stumbling block to Israel, causing them to worship empty, worthless idols (v.13).

Elah's achievements and the summary of his life were recorded in the book *The History of the Kings of Israel* (v.14). This was one of the sources used by the author of First Kings.

OUTLINE	SCRIPTURE	SCRIPTURE	OUTLINE
3. The evil reign of Elah: A scene of drunkenness & murder a. His background: Reigned 2 years b. His death: A fulfillment of God's prophetic judgment 1) The plot by Zimri, a military commander 2) The scene of the plot: A royal feast where King	8 In the twenty and sixth year of Asa king of Judah began Elah the son of Baasha to reign over Israel in Tirzah, two years. 9 And his servant Zimri, captain of half *his* chariots, conspired against him, as he was in Tirzah, drinking himself drunk in the house of	Arza steward of *his* house in Tirzah. 10 And Zimri went in and smote him, and killed him, in the twenty and seventh year of Asa king of Judah, and reigned in his stead. 11 And it came to pass, when he began to reign, as soon as he sat on his throne,	Elah got drunk 3) The assassination by Zimri 4) The takeover of the crown by the commander: His first action was to protect

OUTLINE	SCRIPTURE	SCRIPTURE	OUTLINE
his power • By killing all heirs • By killing all friends of Elah: To prevent retaliation, revenge 5) The fulfillment of Jehu's prophecy of judgment, 3-4, 7 c. His evil life	*that* he slew all the house of Baasha: he left him not one that pisseth against a wall, neither of his kinsfolks, nor of his friends. 12 Thus did Zimri destroy all the house of Baasha, according to the word of the LORD, which he spake against Baasha by Jehu the prophet, 13 For all the sins of Baasha,	and the sins of Elah his son, by which they sinned, and by which they made Israel to sin, in provoking the LORD God of Israel to anger with their vanities. 14 Now the rest of the acts of Elah, and all that he did, *are* they not written in the book of the chronicles of the kings of Israel?	1) Had committed the same sins as his father Baasha (& Jeroboam), 34; 12:25-33 2) Had been a stumbling block, causing the people to sin d. His achievements & the summary of his life: Recorded in the book *The History of the Kings of Israel*

Thought 1. In no way was King Elah prepared to defend himself against assassination. He was in a drunken stupor, engaged in revelry and partying, completely caught off guard. He was not watching, was not alert or prepared to guard his life or the welfare of the nation he was ruling. Obviously, he was living a life of sin and indulgence instead of watchfulness and righteousness. He was failing to execute justice and morality throughout the land.

So it is with many throughout the world today: they are living lives of revelry and partying, drunkenness and immorality, indulgence and wickedness. In no sense is there a spirit of watchfulness, of being alert to the commandments of the LORD and His return. Scripture warns us: the LORD can return at any moment. We are to be looking, watching for His return, making sure that we are sober and alert. We are even to be longing for His return. For when He returns, it means that justice will be perfectly executed upon the earth and righteousness will rule and reign from shore to shore, through all the nations of the world. For this reason, God warns us against the sins of drunkenness and murder:

(1) God warns us against drunkenness.

> **"And take heed to yourselves, lest at any time your hearts be overcharged with surfeiting, and drunkenness, and cares of this life, and so that day come upon you unawares. For as a snare shall it come on all them that dwell on the face of the whole earth. Watch ye therefore, and pray always, that ye may be accounted worthy to escape all these things that shall come to pass, and to stand before the Son of man" (Lu.21:34-36).**
>
> **"Let us walk honestly, as in the day; not in rioting and drunkenness, not in chambering and wantonness, not in strife and envying" (Ro.13:13).**
>
> **"Know ye not that the unrighteous shall not inherit the kingdom of God? Be not deceived: neither fornicators, nor idolaters, nor adulterers, nor effeminate, nor abusers of themselves with mankind, Nor thieves, nor covetous, nor drunkards, nor revilers, nor extortioners, shall inherit the kingdom of God" (1 Co.6:9-10).**
>
> **"And be not drunk with wine, wherein is excess" (Ep.5:18).**
>
> **"Woe unto them that rise up early in the morning, *that* they may follow strong drink; that continue until night, *till* wine inflame them!" (Is.5:11).**
>
> **"Woe unto him that giveth his neighbour drink, that puttest thy bottle to *him,* and makest *him* drunken also, that thou mayest look on their nakedness!" (Hab.2:15).**

(2) God warns us against committing murder.

> **"For the wrath of God is revealed from heaven against all ungodliness and unrighteousness of men, who hold the truth in unrighteousness....Being filled with all unrighteousness, fornication, wickedness, covetousness, maliciousness; full of envy, murder, debate, deceit, malignity; whisperers, Backbiters, haters of God, despiteful, proud, boasters, inventors of evil things, disobedient to parents, Without understanding, covenantbreakers, without natural affection, implacable, unmerciful: Who knowing the judgment of God, that they which commit such things are worthy of death, not only do the same, but have pleasure in them that do them" (Ro.1:18, 29-32).**
>
> **"Now the works of the flesh are manifest, which are *these;* Adultery, fornication, uncleanness, lasciviousness, Idolatry, witchcraft, hatred, variance, emulations, wrath, strife, seditions, heresies, Envyings, murders, drunkenness, revellings, and such like: of the which I tell you before, as I have also told *you* in time past, that they which do such things shall not inherit the kingdom of God" (Ga.5:19-21).**
>
> **"Whosoever hateth his brother is a murderer: and ye know that no murderer hath eternal life abiding in him" (1 Jn.3:15).**
>
> **"Whoso sheddeth man's blood, by man shall his blood be shed: for in the image of God made he man" (Ge.9:6).**
>
> **"Thou shalt not kill" (Ex.20:13).**

4 (16:15-20) **Hopelessness, Example of—Suicide, Example of—Northern Kingdom, Kings of—Kings, of Israel, Zimri—Despondency, Example of**: there was the very brief reign of Zimri in the Northern Kingdom, a reign that lasted only seven days. Zimri's reign was the shortest rule in the history of Israel. No sooner had this military officer taken the throne than his *right* to the throne was contested. When the army of the Northern Kingdom heard that Zimri had assassinated the king, they immediately proclaimed their military commander Omri as king over Israel. Then withdrawing from Gibbethon, Omri and his troops marched to Tirzah, laying siege to the capital (vv.16-17). Seeing that the situation was hopeless, the usurper Zimri went into the royal palace and set it on fire, committing suicide (v.18).

Note that Zimri had lived a life of evil, committing sin and following the false worship and idolatry of Jeroboam. All his adult life he had contributed to the sin of misleading Israel into false worship and idolatry, being a terrible stumbling block to the people. A complete record of his rebellion and reign was recorded in the book *The History of the Kings of Israel* (v.20).

OUTLINE	SCRIPTURE	SCRIPTURE	OUTLINE
4. The evil reign of Zimri: A picture of hopelessness & suicide a. His background: Reigned 7 days b. His desperate & unexpected end 1) The army heard that the officer Zimri had assassinated the king • They immediately proclaimed their commander Omri king of Israel • They immediately withdrew from Gibbethon & attacked Zimri at the capital Tirzah	15 In the twenty and seventh year of Asa king of Judah did Zimri reign seven days in Tirzah. And the people *were* encamped against Gibbethon, which *belonged* to the Philistines. 16 And the people *that were* encamped heard say, Zimri hath conspired, and hath also slain the king: wherefore all Israel made Omri, the captain of the host, king over Israel that day in the camp. 17 And Omri went up from Gibbethon, and all Israel with him, and they besieged Tirzah.	18 And it came to pass, when Zimri saw that the city was taken, that he went into the palace of the king's house, and burnt the king's house over him with fire, and died, 19 For his sins which he sinned in doing evil in the sight of the LORD, in walking in the way of Jeroboam, and in his sin which he did, to make Israel to sin. 20 Now the rest of the acts of Zimri, and his treason that he wrought, *are* they not written in the book of the chronicles of the kings of Israel?	2) The usurper Zimri saw that the situation was hopeless • He set fire to the palace • He committed suicide c. His evil life 1) Lived a life of sin 2) Had walked in the ways of Jeroboam, 12:25-33; 14:16 3) Had been a stumbling block, set a bad example for Israel d. His rebellion & the summary of his life: Recorded in the book *The History of the Kings of Israel*

Thought 1. The picture for us in Zimri's reign is that of hopelessness, despair, desperation, and suicide. Sometimes we too face hopeless situations, whether brought on by ourselves, by someone else, or by natural catastrophes. It may be the death of a loved one, financial difficulties, unemployment, a serious accident, disease, divorce, the discovery of unfaithfulness, or some other situation that seems totally devastating and defeating.

But hopelessness is not the way of God. And it is not to be the way we live. The Lord Jesus Christ promises to strengthen us—His true followers—giving us the power to triumph over any hopeless situation. Despair, despondency, and terrible grief—these defeating emotions are not to conquer us. Through the power of Christ, we can and are to conquer the moments of despair and despondency, the hardships and misfortunes that leave us with a sense of desperation. Victory over all adversity by the power of Christ is the promise of God's Holy Word:

"There hath no temptation taken you but such as is common to man: but God *is* faithful, who will not suffer you to be tempted above that ye are able; but will with the temptation also make a way to escape, that ye may be able to bear *it*" (1 Co.10:13).

"And he said unto me, My grace is sufficient for thee: for my strength is made perfect in weakness. Most gladly therefore will I rather glory in my infirmities, that the power of Christ may rest upon me. Therefore I take pleasure in infirmities, in reproaches, in necessities, in persecutions, in distresses for Christ's sake: for when I am weak, then am I strong" (2 Co.12:9-10).

"That at that time ye were without Christ, being aliens from the commonwealth of Israel, and strangers from the covenants of promise, having no hope, and without God in the world: But now in Christ Jesus ye who sometimes were far off are made nigh by the blood of Christ" (Ep.2:12-13).

"That he would grant you, according to the riches of his glory, to be strengthened with might by his Spirit in the inner man" (Ep.3:16).

"Now unto him that is able to do exceeding abundantly above all that we ask or think, according to the power that worketh in us" (Ep.3:20).

"But I would not have you to be ignorant, brethren, concerning them which are asleep, that ye sorrow not, even as others which have no hope. For if we believe that Jesus died and rose again, even so them also which sleep in Jesus will God bring with him. For this we say unto you by the word of the Lord, that we which are alive *and* remain unto the coming of the Lord shall not prevent them which are asleep. For the Lord himself shall descend from heaven with a shout, with the voice of the archangel, and with the trump of God: and the dead in Christ shall rise first: Then we which are alive *and* remain shall be caught up together with them in the clouds, to meet the Lord in the air: and so shall we ever be with the Lord. Wherefore comfort one another with these words" (1 Th.4:13-18).

"For God hath not given us the spirit of fear; but of power, and of love, and of a sound mind" (2 Ti.1:7).

"Who through faith subdued kingdoms, wrought righteousness, obtained promises, stopped the mouths of lions, Quenched the violence of fire, escaped the edge of the sword, out of weakness were made strong, waxed valiant in fight, turned to flight the armies of the aliens" (He.11:33-34).

"If any of you lack wisdom, let him ask of God, that giveth to all *men* liberally, and upbraideth not; and it shall be given him" (Ja.1:5).

"For whatsoever is born of God overcometh the world: and this is the victory that overcometh the world, *even* our faith. Who is he that overcometh the world, but he that believeth that Jesus is the Son of God?" (1 Jn.5:4-5).

"For thou hast girded me with strength to battle: them that rose up against me hast thou subdued under me" (2 S.22:40).

"But they that wait upon the LORD shall renew *their* strength; they shall mount up with wings as eagles; they shall run, and not be weary; *and* they shall walk, and not faint" (Is.40:31).

"Fear thou not; for I *am* with thee: be not dismayed; for I *am* thy God: I will strengthen thee; yea, I will help thee; yea, I will uphold thee with the right hand of my righteousness" (Is.41:10).

"...Fear not: for I have redeemed thee, I have called *thee* by thy name; thou *art* mine. When thou passest through the waters, I *will be* with thee; and through the rivers, they shall not overflow thee: when thou walkest through the fire, thou shalt not be burned; neither shall the flame kindle upon thee" (Is.43:1-2).

5 (16:21-28) **Worldly Ambition, Example of—Self-Exhortation, Example of—Northern Kingdom, Kings of—Kings, of Israel, Omri**: there was the evil reign of Omri, probably the strongest ruler of Israel up to the time of the writing of *First Kings*. However, Scripture gives only a brief record of his rule:

OUTLINE	SCRIPTURE	SCRIPTURE	OUTLINE
5. The evil reign of Omri: A	21 Then were the people of	hill, Samaria.	owner Shemer
spirit of worldly ambition &	Israel divided into two parts:	25 But Omri wrought evil in	c. His evil life & reign
self-exaltation	half of the people followed	the eyes of the LORD, and did	1) He sinned more than all
a. His background	Tibni the son of Ginath, to	worse than all that *were* be-	the rulers before him
1) He had to struggle 4 years	make him king; and half fol-	fore him.	
for the throne, 15, 23	lowed Omri.	26 For he walked in all the	2) He walked in the evil
• His supporters were	22 But the people that fol-	way of Jeroboam the son of	ways of Jeroboam, 12:25-
stronger than Tibni's	lowed Omri prevailed against	Nebat, and in his sin where-	33; 14:16
• His opponent Tibni was	the people that followed Tib-	with he made Israel to sin, to	3) He was a stumbling block:
either killed or died of	ni the son of Ginath: so Tibni	provoke the LORD God of Is-	Caused Israel to sin
other causes	died, and Omri reigned.	rael to anger with their vani-	
2) He was crowned over all	23 In the thirty and first year	ties.	
Israel & reigned 12 years,	of Asa king of Judah began	27 Now the rest of the acts	d. His achievements & the
six of them in Tirzah	Omri to reign over Israel,	of Omri which he did, and	summary of his life
	twelve years: six years	his might that he showed, *are*	1) His reign: Recorded in the
	reigned he in Tirzah.	they not written in the book	book *The History of the*
b. His significant achievement:	24 And he bought the hill	of the chronicles of the kings	*Kings of Israel*
He built a new capital, Sa-	Samaria of Shemer for two	of Israel?	
maria	talents of silver, and built on	28 So Omri slept with his fa-	2) His death & burial in Sa-
1) It sat on a hill, ideal for a	the hill, and called the name	thers, and was buried in Sa-	maria
fortress	of the city which he built, the	maria: and Ahab his son	3) His successor: Ahab
2) It was named after the	name of Shemer, owner of the	reigned in his stead.	

a. After Zimri committed suicide, Omri took the throne of the Northern Kingdom. But almost immediately, there was a split of the Northern Kingdom into two factions, with half supporting Omri and half supporting a leader named Tibni. Just who this leader was is not known beyond what little information is given here. However, he was strong enough to contest the crown of the Northern Kingdom for four long years, struggling for the throne against Omri.

Keep in mind that Omri had the support of the armed forces (v.16), and eventually they were able to conquer the supporters of Tibni. Tibni died, but Scripture does not say how he died. The implication is that he was executed (vv.21-22). After the four-year struggle, Omri was finally crowned king over all the Northern Kingdom where he reigned for twelve years, six of them at Tirzah.

b. One of the most significant achievements by Omri was the building of a new capital in Samaria. Sitting on a hill that was apparently almost impregnable, Samaria became an ideal fortress. For the city controlled the chief commercial routes running through the Esdraelon plain sitting below. Note that the city was named after the property owner Shemer, who perhaps had insisted that the city be named for him if he was going to sell the property to King Omri. Whatever the case, Omri and his descendants ruled from Samaria and became powerful kings who were able to stabilize the government of the Northern Kingdom for some period of time. *The Bible Knowledge Commentary* gives an excellent statement on Omri's dynasty and its relation to other nations throughout the region:

> *Omri was probably the strongest leader of the Northern Kingdom up to that time. Assyrian records dating from over a century later refer to Israel as "the land of Omri." During Omri's reign Ben-Hadad I, king of the Arameans in Damascus...continued to add to his holdings to the north of Israel. Omri's son, Ahab, had difficulty containing these Aramean aggressors. Also the Assyrian Empire was growing stronger and farther to the northeast...and proceeded to expand its territory as far west as the Mediterranean Sea. Faced by these threats on his north, Omri was able to protect Israel well enough to attack and defeat Moab to the southeast at the same time. This victory is referred to on the famous Moabite Stone. Another of Omri's significant achievements was his alliance with the*

Phoenicians which was sealed with the marriage of his son Ahab to Jezebel, a daughter of the Phoenician king, Ethbaal (cf. 1 Kings 16:31).[3]

c. Despite the stability Omri brought to the Northern Kingdom and the fact that he had a successful reign in the eyes of secular history, in the eyes of the LORD his reign was evil for he lived a wicked, sinful life (vv.25-26). In fact, Scripture says that he sinned more than all the rulers before him. His personal behavior was immoral and unjust and he walked in the evil ways of Jeroboam (26; 12:25-33; 14:16). Instead of instituting social and religious reform, he continued to participate in false worship and to lead Israel down the path of idolatry and false worship. He became a terrible stumbling block to the citizens of Israel, causing them to sin and to arouse the anger of the LORD. Both he and the people were worshipping false, empty, worthless gods.

d. Omri's achievements and the summary of his life are recorded in the book *The History of the Kings of Israel* (vv.27-28). After his death he was buried in the capital city of Samaria and was succeeded by his son Ahab.

Thought 1. Omri was a man of worldly ambition and self-exaltation. We know this for he accepted the appointment of the armed forces when they proclaimed him king, and he spent four years struggling to secure the power of the throne. Moreover, Scripture declares that he lived a more wicked life than any of the kings who had ruled before him. His ambition to be exalted as ruler over the Northern Kingdom was not born of a righteous heart that wished to serve, but of a sinful, wicked heart.

Ambition is a good, commendable quality that we should possess. Without ambition, little of significance would be achieved in life. Therefore, a degree of ambition is essential for all of us. But our ambition must be rooted in righteousness, with a desire to serve people. It should not be rooted in deception or insincerity, with the desire to secure power and to exalt self over other people.

Our ambition must be to achieve position or some office in order to serve people and to build them up, not to tear them down or to take advantage of them. Far too many of us who serve in leadership positions attempt to dominate and exercise extreme authority over people, hoping to build up our own name, securing honor and attention for our achievements. But exercising harsh authority over people is forbidden by God and will bring the severest judgment upon the taskmaster. God will never tolerate abuse or harsh treatment of people, nor the subjection or enslavement of people. God warns us against worldly ambition and self-exaltation:

"And whosoever shall exalt himself shall be abased; and he that shall humble himself shall be exalted" (Mt.23:12).

"*Be* of the same mind one toward another. Mind not high things, but condescend to men of low estate. Be not wise in your own conceits" (Ro.12:16).

"Love not the world, neither the things *that are* in the world. If any man love the world, the love of the Father is not in him. For all that *is* in the world, the lust of the flesh, and the lust of the eyes, and the pride of life, is not of the Father, but is of the world" (1 Jn.2:15-16).

"The wicked in *his* pride doth persecute the poor: let them be taken in the devices that they have imagined" (Ps.10:2).

"For the wicked boasteth of his heart's desire, and blesseth the covetous, *whom* the LORD abhorreth" (Ps.10:3).

"*When* pride cometh, then cometh shame: but with the lowly *is* wisdom" (Pr.11:2).

"Pride *goeth* before destruction, and an haughty spirit before a fall" (Pr.16:18).

"He loveth transgression that loveth strife: *and* he that exalteth his gate seeketh destruction" (Pr.17:19).

"An high look, and a proud heart, *and* the plowing of the wicked, *is* sin" (Pr.21:4).

"He that is of a proud heart stirreth up strife: but he that putteth his trust in the LORD shall be made fat" (Pr.28:25).

"For thou hast said in thine heart, I will ascend into heaven, I will exalt my throne above the stars of God: I will sit also upon the mount of the congregation, in the sides of the north: I will ascend above the heights of the clouds; I will be like the most High. Yet thou shalt be brought down to hell, to the sides of the pit" (Is.14:13-15).

"Though thou exalt *thyself* as the eagle, and though thou set thy nest among the stars, thence will I bring thee down, saith the LORD" (Obad.4).

6 (16:29-34) **Depravity, Example of—Corruption, Example of—Kings, of the Northern Kingdom—Ahab, King of the Northern Kingdom—Israel, Kings of**: there was the evil reign of Ahab, who inherited a stable government from his father Omri. From this point to the end of First Kings, Ahab's reign is covered. Unfortunately, this is not because of significant contributions made by the king, but because of his extreme wickedness and the terrible impact he was to have upon both the Northern and Southern Kingdoms. Keep in mind that the purpose of Scripture is not to give a secular history of these kings, but to show how they and the Israelites responded to the LORD. They either lived for the LORD or lived for the world and themselves. They either lived holy and righteous lives or immoral and wicked lives. From the lives they lived, Scripture paints spiritual lessons for every generation of people. These stories show exactly how we should live holy and righteous lives before the LORD (Ro.15:4; 1 Co.10:11).

Although Ahab's evil reign of twenty-two years is one of the major subjects of the remaining chapters of First Kings, the present passage lays the groundwork for his wicked, degenerate life. Under his evil reign, the depth of spiritual decline was reached in the nation. Seven terrible evils committed by Ahab are spelled out by Scripture:

---

[3] John F. Walvoord and Roy B. Zuck, Editors. *The Bible Knowledge Commentary , Old Testament*, p.521.

OUTLINE	SCRIPTURE	SCRIPTURE	OUTLINE
6. The evil reign of Ahab: A life of utter depravity, corruption a. His background 1) Was the son of Omri 2) Reigned 22 years b. His evil, degenerate life 1) Did more evil than all the rulers before him 2) Considered it trivial, a light thing, to sin—even to commit the sins of Jeroboam, 12:25-33; 14:16 3) Married Jezebel, a priestess of the idol & false god Baal 4) Served & worshipped	29 And in the thirty and eighth year of Asa king of Judah began Ahab the son of Omri to reign over Israel: and Ahab the son of Omri reigned over Israel in Samaria twenty and two years. 30 And Ahab the son of Omri did evil in the sight of the LORD above all that *were* before him. 31 And it came to pass, as if it had been a light thing for him to walk in the sins of Jeroboam the son of Nebat, that he took to wife Jezebel the daughter of Ethbaal king of the Zidonians, and went and served Baal, and wor-	shipped him. 32 And he reared up an altar for Baal in the house of Baal, which he had built in Samaria. 33 And Ahab made a grove; and Ahab did more to provoke the LORD God of Israel to anger than all the kings of Israel that were before him. 34 In his days did Hiel the Bethelite build Jericho: he laid the foundation thereof in Abiram his firstborn, and set up the gates thereof in his youngest *son* Segub, according to the word of the LORD, which he spake by Joshua the son of Nun.	Baal 5) Built a temple for Baal • Erected an altar • Erected an Asherah pole (a wood image of the goddess Asherah) 6) Aroused God's anger more than all the other rulers 7) Charged Hiel of Bethel to rebuild Jericho in defiance of Joshua's curse (Jos. 6:26-27): Caused the death of Hiel's two sons

The above list of Ahab's wicked behavior, of his evil, degenerate life is sufficient to get an overview of what lies ahead in the story of his reign over the Northern Kingdom. *The Expositor's Bible Commentary* adds this:

> *The subsequent chapters of 1 Kings show that Ahab was selfish and sullen (20:43; 21:4-5), cruel (22:27), morally weak (21:1-16), and concerned with luxuries of this world (22:39). Though he could display real bravery (ch. 20; 22:1-39) and at times even heeded God's word (18:16-46; 20:13-17, 22, 28-30; 21:27-29; 22:30), nevertheless he was basically a compromiser as far as the will of God was concerned (20:31-34, 42-43; 22:8, 18, 26-28). The divine estimation of his character stands as a tragic epitaph: "There was never a man like Ahab, who sold himself to do evil in the eyes of the LORD" (21:25, cf. 16:33; 21:20).*[4]

Thought 1. The picture of Ahab's reign is that of corruption and the depravity of the human heart. Like Ahab, we have a choice to make in life: we can either live righteously or wickedly. Sitting before us is the Lord Jesus Christ with His commandments: we either follow Him and obey His commandments or we choose to walk through life as we wish, breaking the commandments of God and rejecting the Lord Jesus Christ.

Wherever we set our hearts dictates our course of action. If we focus our hearts upon the Lord Jesus, we will follow and obey Him. But if we focus our hearts upon ourselves and this world with all its wickedness, we will follow the selfishness of our hearts and the evil ways of this world. Our hearts will become corrupted and depraved, and the most horrible acts of lawlessness and violence will take place. Just look around the world at all the crime and hatred, the immorality and acts of injustice that take place every day. But they not only take place around the world, they also take place within our own neighborhoods and far too often within our own families. Picture the depravity, the corruption of the heart of a parent who abuses a child, either sexually, verbally, or physically. Or the heart of a husband who abuses his wife. Or the anger and hostility, the constant turmoil created between spouses in the home.

Picture the murmuring, grumbling, and complaining that take place within the work force of societies every single day. Think of the anger, the disturbed relationships that exist in the factories, shops, and businesses of our communities. Acts of lawlessness, immorality, and violence dominate the headlines of the news media within our own communities. The corruption and depravity of the human heart is incomprehensible, what the Bible even calls the *mystery of iniquity*.

But there is an answer to the corruption and depravity of the human heart. The answer is the Lord Jesus Christ, the Messiah and Savior of the world. The blood of Jesus Christ can cleanse the human heart, and we can be forgiven our sins. All the guilt can be washed away. Then we can stand before God guiltless, free, and acceptable to Him. But God only accepts us if we come to Him through Jesus Christ, the substitute sacrifice who bore our sins upon the cross. Listen to what God's Holy Word says about the corruption and depravity of the human heart and about the wonderful cleansing power of the Lord Jesus Christ:

(1) The human heart is utterly corrupt, depraved.

> **"For from within, out of the heart of men, proceed evil thoughts, adulteries, fornications, murders" (Mk.7:21).**
>
> **"For the invisible things of him from the creation of the world are clearly seen, being understood by the things that are made, *even* his eternal power and Godhead; so that they are without excuse: Because that, when they knew God, they glorified *him* not as God, neither were thankful; but became vain in their imaginations, and their foolish heart was darkened. Professing themselves to be wise, they became fools, And changed the glory of the uncorruptible God into an image made like to corruptible man, and to birds, and fourfooted beasts, and creeping things. Wherefore God also gave them up to uncleanness through the lusts of their own hearts, to dishonour their own bodies between themselves:**

4 Richard D. Patterson and Hermann J. Austel. *1, 2 Kings*, p.136.

Who changed the truth of God into a lie, and worshipped and served the creature more than the Creator, who is blessed for ever. Amen" (Ro.1:20-25).

"This know also, that in the last days perilous times shall come. For men shall be lovers of their own selves, covetous, boasters, proud, blasphemers, disobedient to parents, unthankful, unholy, Without natural affection, trucebreakers, false accusers, incontinent, fierce, despisers of those that are good, Traitors, heady, highminded, lovers of pleasures more than lovers of God; Having a form of godliness, but denying the power thereof: from such turn away" (2 Ti.3:1-5).

"And God looked upon the earth, and, behold, it was corrupt; for all flesh had corrupted his way upon the earth" (Ge.6:12).

"Help, LORD; for the godly man ceaseth; for the faithful fail from among the children of men" (Ps.12:1).

"They are all gone aside, they are *all* together become filthy: *there is* none that doeth good, no, not one" (Ps.14:3).

"And judgment is turned away backward, and justice standeth afar off: for truth is fallen in the street, and equity cannot enter" (Is.59:14).

"But we are all as an unclean *thing,* and all our righteousnesses *are* as filthy rags; and we all do fade as a leaf; and our iniquities, like the wind, have taken us away" (Is.64:6).

"The good *man* is perished out of the earth: and *there is* none upright among men: they all lie in wait for blood; they hunt every man his brother with a net" (Mi.7:2).

(2) The corruption and depravity of the human heart can be cleansed through the blood of the cross, the cross of the Lord Jesus Christ.

"For this is my blood of the new testament, which is shed for many for the remission of sins" (Mt.26:28).

"What then? are we better *than they?* No, in no wise: for we have before proved both Jews and Gentiles, that they are all under sin; As it is written, There is none righteous, no, not one: There is none that understandeth, there is none that seeketh after God. They are all gone out of the way, they are together become unprofitable; there is none that doeth good, no, not one. Their throat *is* an open sepulchre; with their tongues they have used deceit; the poison of asps *is* under their lips: Whose mouth *is* full of cursing and bitterness: Their feet *are* swift to shed blood: Destruction and misery *are* in their ways: And the way of peace have they not known: There is no fear of God before their eyes. Now we know that what things soever the law saith, it saith to them who are under the law: that every mouth may be stopped, and all the world may become guilty before God. Therefore by the deeds of the law there shall no flesh be justified in his sight: for by the law *is* the knowledge of sin. But now the righteousness of God without the law is manifested, being witnessed by the law and the prophets; Even the righteousness of God *which is* by faith of Jesus Christ unto all and upon all them that believe: for there is no difference: For all have sinned, and come short of the glory of God; Being justified freely by his grace through the redemption that is in Christ Jesus: Whom God hath set forth *to be* a propitiation through faith in his blood, to declare his righteousness for the remission of sins that are past, through the forbearance of God; To declare, *I say,* at this time his righteousness: that he might be just, and the justifier of him which believeth in Jesus" (Ro.3:9-26).

"Much more then, being now justified by his blood, we shall be saved from wrath through him" (Ro.5:9).

"In whom we have redemption through his blood, the forgiveness of sins, according to the riches of his grace" (Ep.1:7).

"Neither by the blood of goats and calves, but by his own blood he entered in once into the holy place, having obtained eternal redemption *for us.* For if the blood of bulls and of goats, and the ashes of an heifer sprinkling the unclean, sanctifieth to the purifying of the flesh: How much more shall the blood of Christ, who through the eternal Spirit offered himself without spot to God, purge your conscience from dead works to serve the living God?" (He.9:12-14).

"Forasmuch as ye know that ye were not redeemed with corruptible things, *as* silver and gold, from your vain conversation *received* by tradition from your fathers; But with the precious blood of Christ, as of a lamb without blemish and without spot" (1 Pe.1:18-19).

"Who his own self bare our sins in his own body on the tree, that we, being dead to sins, should live unto righteousness: by whose stripes ye were healed" (1 Pe.2:24).

"For Christ also hath once suffered for sins, the just for the unjust, that he might bring us to God, being put to death in the flesh, but quickened by the Spirit" (1 Pe.3:18).

DIVISION III

THE MINISTRY OF ELIJAH AND OTHER PROPHETS DURING THE REIGN OF AHAB: LEARNING WHO THE LIVING AND TRUE GOD IS, 17:1–22:53

(17:1–22:53) **DIVISION OVERVIEW**: King Ahab married the infamous Jezebel, a domineering and manipulative woman, who deliberately sought to eliminate the worship of the LORD throughout the Northern Kingdom of Israel. Under Ahab's leadership the people became engrossed in wickedness, idolatry and false worship, so engrossed that they turned completely away from the LORD to the worship of the false god Baal. This particular false god was thought to be the god of fertility, the god of the dew and rain and of the sunshine and light—all the ingredients that caused the crops to grow and the lives of men to be productive and fruitful upon the earth.

In these dark days of the Northern Kingdom, God sent forth a prophet to prove that the LORD—not the false god Baal—is the only living and true God. The LORD alone is the only God whom the people should be worshipping and following. The prophet was Elijah, one of the greatest prophets who ever lived. Courageously taking a stand against King Ahab and his infamous wife Queen Jezebel, Elijah proclaimed the Name of the LORD—not Baal—as the only living and true God. Shining like a light in the darkest corner of the universe, Elijah proclaimed the salvation of the LORD in the midst of a dark, corrupt society.

But Elijah was not the only prophet to warn and denounce Ahab and his notorious wife Jezebel. In mercy God sent two other prophets to issue strong warnings to the king, an unnamed prophet (20:35-43) and the prophet Micaiah. It was Micaiah who warned Ahab against attacking Syria and courageously predicted the king's death (22:1-28).

Although the message of these prophets would not stop the flood of wickedness, their message did reach some of the people and slow down the rushing flow of coming judgment. Eventually the wicked would face the consequences of their sinful lives, idolatry and false worship. God and His Word would be proven time and again; nevertheless, the people would continue in their rejection of the LORD and their insane rush to the day when God's patience would no longer tolerate their wickedness. The day of His final judgment was coming. *First Kings* ends with the death of Ahab and the assumption of the throne by his son Ahaziah. But eventually the people's wickedness would lead to the utter destruction of both the Northern and Southern Kingdoms (2 K.1–25).

THE MINISTRY OF ELIJAH AND OTHER PROPHETS DURING THE REIGN OF AHAB: LEARNING WHO THE LIVING AND TRUE GOD IS, 17:1–22:53

A. The Drought Predicted by Elijah: Judgment Due to Idolatry and False Worship, 17:1-24

B. The End of the Drought after Elijah's Contest with the Prophets of Baal: Proving Who the True and Living God Is, 18:1-46

C. The Escape of Elijah from Jezebel: Being Saved by the Living God from Disappointment, Discouragement, and Despair, 19:1-21

D. The Defeat of Syria or Aram by Ahab: Learning That the LORD Alone Is God, 20:1-43

E. The Terrible Crimes Against Naboth by Ahab and Jezebel: Facing Judgment Due to Horrible Evil, 21:1-29

F. The Death of Ahab: Proving the Surety of God's Judgment, 22:1-40

G. The Reigns of Jehoshaphat in Judah, and Ahaziah in Israel: Learning the Importance of Parental Influence, 22:41-53

CHAPTER 17

III. THE MINISTRY OF ELIJAH & OTHER PROPHETS DURING THE REIGN OF AHAB: LEARNING WHO THE LIVING & TRUE GOD IS, 17:1–22:53

A. The Drought Predicted by Elijah: Judgment Due to Idolatry & False Worship, 17:1-24

1. **Elijah predicted the drought & famine: Proof that the LORD is the only living & true God—not Baal (falsely thought to be the god of rain)**
   a. His service for God
   b. His sudden, dramatic appearance before King Ahab
2. **Elijah was fed & protected by God: Proof that the LORD alone—not Baal—is the Provider & Protector of His people**
   a. God's instructions to flee to the Kerith Ravine
      1) Would be safe from Ahab
      2) Would have water & food
   b. God's provision in the wilderness
      1) Elijah obeyed
      2) Elijah witnessed the power of God
         • Was fed by ravens
         • Drank from the brook
   c. God's provision in the city: Through the help of a widow
      1) The brook dried up
      2) The LORD instructed Elijah to go & stay in the city of Zarephath near Sidon: A widow there would feed him
         • He obeyed immediately
         • He saw a widow gathering sticks as he entered the city
         • He tested her to see if she was the widow: Asked her for a little water & a morsel of bread
      3) The widow responded by sharing her desperate situation

And Elijah the Tishbite, *who*
was of the inhabitants of Gilead, said unto Ahab, *As* the
LORD God of Israel liveth,
before whom I stand, there
shall not be dew nor rain
these years, but according to
my word.
2 And the word of the LORD
came unto him, saying,
3 Get thee hence, and turn
thee eastward, and hide thyself by the brook Cherith,
that *is* before Jordan.
4 And it shall be, *that* thou
shalt drink of the brook; and
I have commanded the ravens
to feed thee there.
5 So he went and did according unto the word of the
LORD: for he went and dwelt
by the brook Cherith, that *is*
before Jordan.
6 And the ravens brought him
bread and flesh in the morning, and bread and flesh in
the evening; and he drank of
the brook.
7 And it came to pass after a
while, that the brook dried
up, because there had been
no rain in the land.
8 And the word of the LORD
came unto him, saying,
9 Arise, get thee to Za-
rephath, which *belongeth* to
Zidon, and dwell there: behold, I have commanded a
widow woman there to sus-
tain thee.
10 So he arose and went to
Zarephath. And when he
came to the gate of the city,
behold, the widow woman
was there gathering of sticks:
and he called to her, and said,
Fetch me, I pray thee, a little
water in a vessel, that I may
drink.
11 And as she was going to
fetch *it,* he called to her, and
said, Bring me, I pray thee, a
morsel of bread in thine hand.
12 And she said, *As* the
LORD thy God liveth, I have
not a cake, but an handful
of meal in a barrel, and
a little oil in a cruse: and, behold, I *am* gathering two
sticks, that I may go in and
dres it for me and my
son, that we may eat it, and
die.
13 And Elijah said unto her,
Fear not; go *and* do as thou
hast said: but make me thereof a little cake first, and bring
it unto me, and after make for
thee and for thy son.
14 For thus saith the LORD
God of Israel, The barrel of
meal shall not waste, neither
shall the cruse of oil fail, until the day *that* the LORD
sendeth rain upon the earth.
15 And she went and did according to the saying of Elijah: and she, and he, and her
house, did eat *many* days.
16 *And* the barrel of meal
wasted not, neither did the
cruse of oil fail, according to
the word of the LORD, which
he spake by Elijah.
17 And it came to pass after
these things, *that* the son of
the woman, the mistress of
the house, fell sick; and his
sickness was so sore, that there
was no breath left in him.
18 And she said unto Elijah,
What have I to do with thee,
O thou man of God? art thou
come unto me to call my sin
to remembrance, and to slay
my son?
19 And he said unto her,
Give me thy son. And he
took him out of her bosom,
and carried him up into a loft,
where he abode, and laid him
upon his own bed.
20 And he cried unto the
LORD, and said, O LORD my
God, hast thou also brought
evil upon the widow with
whom I sojourn, by slaying
her son?
21 And he stretched himself
upon the child three times,
and cried unto the LORD, and
said, O LORD my God, I pray
thee, let this child's soul
come into him again.
22 And the LORD heard the
voice of Elijah; and the soul
of the child came into him
again, and he revived.
23 And Elijah took the child,
and brought him down out of

         • She was poverty-stricken: Had no food—only a little flour & oil
         • She was gathering sticks to cook her last meal
         • She & her son would then starve
      4) Elijah challenged the woman to believe, trust the LORD & His provision
         • He told her to go home & make the bread, but to give it to him
         • He told her to then make bread for her & her son: The LORD would replenish the flour & oil miraculously, providing until the day it rained
      5) The widow believed the promise & obeyed
         • The LORD provided food every day
         • The flour & oil never ran dry—as the LORD promised through Elijah
3. **Elijah was used by God to raise the widow's son: Proof that the LORD alone—not Baal—has the power to raise the dead**
   a. The widow's son died: The widow felt a sense of guilt, supposing that God was chastising her because of some sin
   b. The widow's son was raised from the dead
      1) Elijah took the child in his arms & carried him to his own upper room & laid him on the bed
      2) Elijah prayed, cried out to the LORD: Was puzzled, asking God if He had caused the tragedy
      3) Elijah then stretched himself out over the boy three times, crying out in prayer: Asked God to let the boy's soul, life return to him
      4) Elijah witnessed the astounding power of God: The boy's soul, life returned—he revived
      5) Elijah carried the child to his mother with the

wonderful news: "Your son lives" c. The widow's confession of faith	the chamber into the house, and delivered him unto his mother: and Elijah said, See, thy son liveth. 24 And the woman said to	Elijah, Now by this I know that thou *art* a man of God, *and* that the word of the LORD in thy mouth *is* truth.	1) God is the Author of life (just witnessed) 2) Elijah was a man of God 3) God's Word is true

DIVISION III

THE MINISTRY OF ELIJAH & OTHER PROPHETS DURING THE REIGN OF AHAB: LEARNING WHO THE LIVING & TRUE GOD IS, 17:1–22:53

A. The Drought Predicted by Elijah: Judgment Due to Idolatry and False Worship, 17:1-24

(17:1-24) **Introduction**: false worship and idolatry have swept the earth, capturing the hearts and minds of multiplied millions of people. This is most tragic, for false worship and idolatry expose our ignorance and blindness and doom us to destruction. They declare that we would rather follow something false—something created by man's imagination—than follow the only living and true God. Rejecting the living and true God has catastrophic results, leaving us to face the severe crises of life all alone, crises such as...

- sickness or life-threatening illnesses
- crippling or disabling diseases
- physical handicaps or disabilities
- severe depression or other mental problems
- separation or divorce
- serious accidents or disasters
- the loss of friends or loved ones
- loneliness or rejection
- a lack of purpose or meaning in life
- bankruptcy or other financial difficulties
- death, hell, and the judgment to come

False worship and idolatry are grossly misleading. They lull a person into a false sense of security, when in reality they doom a person to the judgment of God. Therefore, no greater danger confronts a person than that of false worship and idolatry.

These two terrible threats are the subject of the present passage of Scripture. The Northern Kingdom of Israel had become engrossed in wickedness, idolatry, and false worship. They became so engrossed that the people turned completely away from the LORD to the worship of the false god Baal. This particular false god was thought to be the god of fertility, the god of rain and sunshine and light—all the ingredients that caused the crops to grow and the hands of man to produce and bear fruit upon this earth. In these dark days of the Northern Kingdom, God sent forth a prophet to prove that the LORD—not the false god Baal—was the only living and true God. The LORD alone was the God the people should be worshipping and following. The prophet was Elijah, one of the greatest prophets who ever lived. And this is the first mention of Elijah in Scripture. He is seen here shining forth as a light in the midst of a dark, corrupt society. This is: *The Drought Predicted by Elijah: Judgment Due to Idolatry and False Worship,* 17:1-24.

1. Elijah predicted the drought and famine: proof that the LORD is the only living and true God—not Baal (falsely thought to be the god of rain) (v.1).
2. Elijah was fed and protected by God: proof that the LORD alone—not Baal—is the Provider and Protector of His people (vv.2-16).
3. Elijah was used by God to raise the widow's son: proof that the LORD alone—not Baal—has the power to sustain life and raise the dead (vv.17-24).

1 (17:1) **God, Proof of—God, Fact—Baal, Weakness of—Drought, Caused by—Famine, Caused by—Elijah, Prophecies of**: suddenly, dramatically, Elijah appeared before King Ahab, predicting a drought and famine upon the Northern Kingdom of Israel. Obviously, for some years the LORD had been preparing Elijah to prove one truth to all Israel: that the LORD (Jehovah-Yahweh) is the only living and true God. In fact, Elijah's very name means "the LORD (Yahweh) is my God." It was his God-given mission to proclaim the message that his name declared: "The LORD is God, He and He alone." His message was to stand against Baal, the false god that most of Israel was now worshipping. Baal was thought to be the god of fertility, the god who controlled the rain and the dew, the crops and the harvest of the fields, and gave man the strength to work and produce with his hands.

OUTLINE	SCRIPTURE	SCRIPTURE	OUTLINE
1. Elijah predicted the drought & famine: Proof that the LORD is the only living & true God—not Baal (falsely	And Elijah the Tishbite, *who was* of the inhabitants of Gilead, said unto Ahab, *As* the LORD God of Israel liveth,	before whom I stand, there shall not be dew nor rain these years, but according to my word.	**thought to be the god of rain)** a. His service for God b. His sudden, dramatic appearance before King Ahab

Appearing out of nowhere, Elijah abruptly confronted King Ahab to pronounce this terrifying drought upon the land of Israel. There would be a drought—neither dew nor rain—for the next few years unless he personally gave the word and reversed the drought. Of course, he was speaking under instruction from the LORD, knowing that the power to hold the rain back and to restart the rains rested solely in the hands of God Himself. But Elijah was the instrument through whom God was working; therefore, the drought was to begin at the word of Elijah and end at his word some years later. Note also that Elijah left Ahab just as quickly as he had appeared.

Just who Elijah was is not known, other than the simple statement that he was from Tishbe, which was located in Gilead, the northern section of East Jordan. No other facts are known about this prophet of God who was to become one of the greatest prophets ever to serve the LORD. For years, Elijah had apparently been observing the wicked lives of the Israelites. Their idolatry and false worship were a constant affront, an offense thrust in the face of God. At some point he became broken before the LORD over the terrible evil of the Israelites. And God moved upon his heart, giving him the mission of proving to the people that the LORD Himself was the only living and true God.

Armed with the mission of God and the promise of God's presence, Elijah marched to the capital of Samaria to confront the evil King Ahab. Abruptly, dramatically, he burst into the royal court, standing face-to-face with Ahab. He declared the message of God: "The LORD God of Israel lives. And because He lives, there will be neither dew nor rain for several years to come."

God had previously predicted that the land would suffer drought and famine if the people rejected Him and turned to idolatry and false worship (Le.26:18-20; De.11:16-17; 28:23-24). Through the drought, the LORD would prove that He, not Baal, was the true God. He and He alone controlled the rain and fruitfulness of the earth.

Thought 1. If the drought and famine prophesied by Elijah actually took place, this would be strong evidence that the LORD is the only living and true God. As seen in the following Scripture, a severe drought and famine did take place.

The LORD (Jehovah, Yahweh) is the only living and true God, the Creator and Sustainer of the universe. He and He alone controls the weather. In fact, He controls all the laws that govern the very existence of the universe and all life throughout the universe, visible or invisible, physical or spiritual.

No matter how much we may deny or question God's existence, or exalt ourselves and science as the ultimate reality of the universe, God does exist. The LORD (Jehovah, Yahweh) is the only living and true God. We are the work of His hands. Denying God's existence does not void God, does not make Him cease to exist. Truth is truth, and God *is* truth. As truth, He is living and longing for all of us to join Him after our sojourn here upon this earth. One of the great proclamations of the Holy Bible is this one truth: the LORD is the only living and true God, the Creator and Sustainer of the universe.

"But Jesus held his peace. And the high priest answered and said unto him, I adjure thee by the living God, that thou tell us whether thou be the Christ, the Son of God. Jesus saith unto him, Thou hast said: nevertheless I say unto you, Hereafter shall ye see the Son of man sitting on the right hand of power, and coming in the clouds of heaven" (Mt.26: 63-64).

"And saying, Sirs, why do ye these things? We also are men of like passions with you, and preach unto you that ye should turn from these vanities unto the living God, which made heaven, and earth, and the sea, and all things that are therein" (Ac.14:15).

"For they themselves show of us what manner of entering in we had unto you, and how ye turned to God from idols to serve the living and true God; And to wait for his Son from heaven, whom he raised from the dead, *even* Jesus, which delivered us from the wrath to come" (1 Th.1:9-10).

"He that despised Moses' law died without mercy under two or three witnesses: Of how much sorer punishment, suppose ye, shall he be thought worthy, who hath trodden under foot the Son of God, and hath counted the blood of the covenant, wherewith he was sanctified, an unholy thing, and hath done despite unto the Spirit of grace? For we know him that hath said, Vengeance *belongeth* unto me, I will recompense, saith the Lord. And again, The Lord shall judge his people. *It is* a fearful thing to fall into the hands of the living God" (He.10:28-31).

"Through faith we understand that the worlds were framed by the word of God, so that things which are seen were not made of things which do appear" (He.11:3).

"Knowing this first, that there shall come in the last days scoffers, walking after their own lusts, And saying, Where is the promise of his coming? for since the fathers fell asleep, all things continue as *they were* from the beginning of the creation. For this they willingly are ignorant of, that by the word of God the heavens were of old, and the earth standing out of the water and in the water: Whereby the world that then was, being overflowed with water, perished: But the heavens and the earth, which are now, by the same word are kept in store, reserved unto fire against the day of judgment and perdition of ungodly men. But, beloved, be not ignorant of this one thing, that one day *is* with the Lord as a thousand years, and a thousand years as one day. The Lord is not slack concerning his promise, as some men count slackness; but is longsuffering to us-ward, not willing that any should perish, but that all should come to repentance. But the day of the Lord will come as a thief in the night; in the which the heavens shall pass away with a great noise, and the elements shall melt with fervent heat, the earth also and the works that are therein shall be burned up" (2 Pe.3:3-10; esp. v.8).

"I am Alpha and Omega, the beginning and the ending, saith the Lord, which is, and which was, and which is to come, the Almighty" (Re.1:8).

"In the beginning God created the heaven and the earth" (Ge.1:1).

"And the LORD God formed man *of* the dust of the ground, and breathed into his nostrils the breath of life; and man became a living soul" (Ge.2:7).

"For I lift up my hand to heaven, and say, I live for ever" (De.32:40).

"The eternal God *is thy* refuge, and underneath *are* the everlasting arms: and he shall thrust out the enemy from before thee; and shall say, Destroy *them*" (De.33:27).

"Thou, *even* thou, *art* LORD alone; thou hast made heaven, the heaven of heavens, with all their host, the earth, and all *things* that *are* therein, the seas, and all that *is* therein, and thou preservest them all; and the host of heaven worshippeth thee" (Ne.9:6).

"The Spirit of God hath made me, and the breath of the Almighty hath given me life" (Jb.33:4).

"My soul thirsteth for God, for the living God: when shall I come and appear before God?" (Ps.42:2).

"My soul longeth, yea, even fainteth for the courts of the LORD: my heart and my flesh crieth out for the living God" (Ps.84:2).

"Know ye that the LORD he *is* God: *it is* he *that* hath made us, and not we ourselves; *we are* his people, and the sheep of his pasture" (Ps.100:3).

"Of old hast thou laid the foundation of the earth: and the heavens *are* the work of thy hands" (Ps.102:25).

"Thy name, O LORD, *endureth* for ever; *and* thy memorial, O LORD, throughout all generations" (Ps.135:13).

"Thy kingdom *is* an everlasting kingdom, and thy dominion *endureth* throughout all generations" (Ps.145:13).

"Have we not all one father? hath not one God created us? why do we deal treacherously every man against his brother, by profaning the covenant of our fathers?" (Mal.2:10).

2 (17:2-16) **Provision, Source, God—Protector, Source, God—God, Proof of, His Provision and Protection—Provision, of God—Protection, of God—Elijah, Provision and Protection of**: Elijah was miraculously fed and protected by God during the years of the drought and famine. Apparently while Ahab was in a state of shock from the appearance and pronouncement by the rugged prophet, Elijah abruptly walked out before he could be arrested. Either immediately or soon thereafter, the LORD instructed Elijah to flee from the king in case Ahab sought retaliation or revenge, in particular after the drought began. Moreover, the prophet needed to be out of Ahab's reach, for the king would be putting undue pressure upon Elijah to stop the drought. Scripture dramatically describes how God protected and provided for His dear prophet:

OUTLINE	SCRIPTURE	SCRIPTURE	OUTLINE
2. Elijah was fed & protected by	2 And the word of the LORD	in a vessel, that I may drink.	& a morsel of bread
God: Proof that the LORD	came unto him, saying,	11 And as she was going to	3) The widow responded by
alone—not Baal—is the Pro-	3 Get thee hence, and turn	fetch *it,* he called to her, and	sharing her desperate situ-
vider & Protector of His people	thee eastward, and hide thy-	said, Bring me, I pray thee, a	ation
a. God's instructions to flee to	self by the brook Cherith,	morsel of bread in thine	
the Kerith Ravine	that *is* before Jordan.	hand.	
1) Would be safe from Ahab	4 And it shall be, *that* thou	12 And she said, *As* the	• She was poverty-strick-
2) Would have water & food	shalt drink of the brook; and	LORD thy God liveth, I have	en: Had no food—only a
b. God's provision in the wil-	I have commanded the ravens	not a cake, but an handful	little flour & oil
derness	to feed thee there.	of meal in a barrel, and a	• She was gathering sticks
1) Elijah obeyed	5 So he went and did accord-	little oil in a cruse: and, be-	to cook her last meal
	ing unto the word of the	hold, I *am* gathering two	• She & her son would
	LORD: for he went and dwelt	sticks, that I may go in and	then starve
	by the brook Cherith, that *is*	dress it for me and my	
	before Jordan.	son, that we may eat it, and	
2) Elijah witnessed the pow-	6 And the ravens brought him	die.	
er of God	bread and flesh in the morn-	13 And Elijah said unto her,	4) Elijah challenged the
• Was fed by ravens	ing, and bread and flesh in	Fear not; go *and* do as thou	woman to believe, trust
• Drank from the brook	the evening; and he drank of	hast said: but make me there-	the LORD & His provision
	the brook.	of a little cake first, and bring	• He told her to go home
c. God's provision in the city:	7 And it came to pass after a	*it* unto me, and after make for	& make the bread, but to
Through the help of a widow	while, that the brook dried	thee and for thy son.	give it to him
1) The brook dried up	up, because there had been	14 For thus saith the LORD	• He told her to then make
	no rain in the land.	God of Israel, The barrel of	bread for her & her son:
2) The LORD instructed Eli-	8 And the word of the LORD	meal shall not waste, nei-	The LORD would replen-
jah to go & stay in the city	came unto him, saying,	ther shall the cruse of oil fail,	ish the flour & oil mi-
of Zarephath near Sidon:	9 Arise, get thee to Zarephath,	until the day *that* the LORD	raculously, providing
A widow there would feed	which *belongeth* to Zidon,	sendeth rain upon the	until the day it rained
him	and dwell there: behold, I	earth.	
	have commanded a widow	15 And she went and did	5) The widow believed the
	woman there to sustain thee.	according to the saying of	promise & obeyed
• He obeyed immediately	10 So he arose and went to	Elijah: and she, and he, and	• The LORD provided food
• He saw a widow gather-	Zarephath. And when he came	her house, did eat *many* days.	every day
ing sticks as he entered	to the gate of the city, behold,	16 *And* the barrel of meal	• The flour & oil never
the city	the widow woman *was* there	wasted not, neither did the	ran dry—as the LORD
• He tested her to see if	gathering of sticks: and he	cruse of oil fail, according to	promised through Elijah
she was the widow: Asked	called to her, and said, Fetch	the word of the LORD, which	
her for a little water	me, I pray thee, a little water	he spake by Elijah.	

a. God instructed Elijah to hide out in the Kerith Ravine, which was east of the Jordan River (vv.2-4). Evidently this was one of the narrow gorges that had a brook running through it from which Elijah would have a plentiful supply of water. In addition, the hideout would give Elijah seclusion and safety from Ahab's frantic search for him. Note God's wonderful promise of supernatural provision: He had personally ordered the ravens to provide food for His dear servant.

b. In obedience Elijah did just as God instructed, and God provided for His dear servant in the wilderness (vv.5-6). Elijah witnessed the power of God as the ravens brought him bread and meat twice a day, morning and evening. And he drank fresh water from the flowing brook. Despite being all alone and being hunted down by the king, Elijah's needs were being met by the LORD Himself. God's dear servant was being protected and provided for day by day.

c. However, God's provision was not only supplied in the wilderness but also in the city through the help of a widow (vv.7-16). Eventually the brook dried up, and the LORD instructed Elijah to go and stay in the city of Zarephath near Sidon. There he would meet a widow whom the LORD had already instructed to supply food for him (vv.8-9). Immediately, Elijah obeyed the LORD and made the trip (v.10). When he entered the city gate, he saw a widow gathering sticks. Elijah decided to test the woman to see if she was the widow appointed by God. He asked her for a drink of water and, as she was going to get the water, he called out and asked her to please bring him a piece of bread as well (vv.10-11).

Turning back toward Elijah, the widow responded by sharing her desperate situation: she was poverty-stricken, having no food whatsoever, only a little flour and oil. In fact, she had been gathering the sticks to cook her last meager supplies, expecting to starve to death along with her son after they had eaten this final small meal.

Hearing the desperate plight of the widow, Elijah challenged her to trust the LORD for His provision (vv.13-14). He told her to go home and bake the bread, but to give him the first part. She could then make bread for herself and her son, for the LORD would replenish the flour and oil miraculously. He would provide for all three of them until the day that it rained (v.14). Note this was a promise based on the authority of God's Word, for Elijah declared that this is what the LORD Himself had promised. Would the widow believe the Word of the LORD? Would she make the bread first of all for Elijah?

The widow did believe the promise. She obeyed the prophet of God, doing exactly what Elijah had instructed her to do. And the result was astounding: the LORD miraculously provided food every day for the woman and her family and, of course, for Elijah the prophet. The flour and oil never ran dry, just as the LORD had promised through His faithful prophet.

Thought 1. Two of the greatest promises in God's Holy Word concern His *provision* and *protection*. God protects and provides for His dear people. But there is a condition: we must trust and obey God's Word. Just as the widow trusted and obeyed the LORD, so we too must trust and obey Him. If we truly believe the LORD and His promises, He will meet our every need. No genuine believer will have his needs unmet nor lack the necessities of life, not unless the LORD is using the experience to strengthen the believer or to take him on home to heaven with Him.

If we seek the LORD and His righteousness first, He promises to provide food, clothing, and shelter for His dear people. He also promises to protect us through all the trials and difficulties of this life, through all the hardships and misfortunes, the temptations and seductions. Note that His protection is not *from* the hardships or trials but *through* them. As believers, we will endure most of the same misfortunes and temptations as unbelievers—and even some that unbelievers will not experience—but God will be with us every step of the way. He will hold our hands, hold us up, and even carry us when needed. This is the clear promise of God's Holy Word.

(1) God promises to provide for His dear people, supplying and meeting their every need.

"Give us this day our daily bread" (Mt.6:11).

"But seek ye first the kingdom of God, and his righteousness; and all these things shall be added unto you" (Mt.6:33).

"And God *is* able to make all grace [supplies, provision] abound toward you; that ye, always having all sufficiency in all *things,* may abound to every good work" (2 Co.9:8).

"But my God shall supply all your need according to his riches in glory by Christ Jesus" (Ph.4:19).

"And ye shall serve the LORD your God, and he shall bless thy bread, and thy water; and I will take sickness away from the midst of thee" (Ex.23:25).

"The LORD *is* my shepherd; I shall not want. He maketh me to lie down in green pastures: he leadeth me beside the still waters. He restoreth my soul: he leadeth me in the paths of righteousness for his name's sake. Yea, though I walk through the valley of the shadow of death, I will fear no evil: for thou *art* with me; thy rod and thy staff they comfort me. Thou preparest a table before me in the presence of mine enemies: thou anointest my head with oil; my cup runneth over. Surely goodness and mercy shall follow me all the days of my life: and I will dwell in the house of the LORD for ever" (Ps.23:1-6).

"The LORD *is* my strength and my shield; my heart trusted in him, and I am helped: therefore my heart greatly rejoiceth; and with my song will I praise him" (Ps.28:7).

"They shall be abundantly satisfied with the fatness of thy house; and thou shalt make them drink of the river of thy pleasures" (Ps.36:8).

"But I *am* poor and needy; *yet* the Lord thinketh upon me: thou *art* my help and my deliverer; make no tarrying, O my God" (Ps.40:17).

"Blessed *be* the Lord, *who* daily loadeth us *with benefits, even* the God of our salvation. Selah" (Ps.68:19).

"Fear thou not; for I *am* with thee: be not dismayed; for I *am* thy God: I will strengthen thee; yea, I will help thee; yea, I will uphold thee with the right hand of my righteousness" (Is.41:10).

(2) God promised to protect His dear people, delivering them through all trials and temptations.

"But there shall not an hair of your head perish" (Lu.21:18).

"And now I am no more in the world, but these are in the world, and I come to thee. Holy Father, keep through thine own name those whom thou hast given me, that they may be one, as we *are*" (Jn.17:11).

"There hath no temptation taken you but such as is common to man: but God *is* faithful, who will not suffer you to be tempted above that ye are able; but will with the temptation also make a way to escape, that ye may be able to bear *it*" (1 Co.10:13).

"For we would not, brethren, have you ignorant of our trouble which came to us in Asia, that we were pressed out of measure, above strength, insomuch that we despaired even of life: But we had the sentence of death in ourselves, that we should not trust in ourselves, but in God which raiseth the dead: Who delivered us from so great a death, and doth deliver: in whom we trust that he will yet deliver *us*" (2 Co.1:8-10).

"For the which cause I also suffer these things: nevertheless I am not ashamed: for I know whom I have believed, and am persuaded that he is able to keep that which I have committed unto him against that day" (2 Ti.1:12).

"And the Lord shall deliver me from every evil work, and will preserve *me* unto his heavenly kingdom: to whom *be* glory for ever and ever. Amen" (2 Ti.4:18).

"Forasmuch then as the children are partakers of flesh and blood, he also himself likewise took part of the same; that through death he might destroy him that had the power of death, that is, the devil; And deliver them who through fear of death were all their lifetime subject to bondage" (He.2:14-15).

"So that we may boldly say, The Lord *is* my helper, and I will not fear what man shall do unto me" (He.13:6).

"The Lord knoweth how to deliver the godly out of temptations, and to reserve the unjust unto the day of judgment to be punished" (2 Pe2:9).

"And, behold, I *am* with thee, and will keep thee in all *places* whither thou goest, and will bring thee again into this land; for I will not leave thee, until I have done *that* which I have spoken to thee of" (Ge.28:15).

"The eternal God *is thy* refuge, and underneath *are* the everlasting arms: and he shall thrust out the enemy from before thee; and shall say, Destroy *them*" (De.33:27).

"And he said, The LORD *is* my rock, and my fortress, and my deliverer" (2 S.22:2).

"For the eyes of the LORD run to and fro throughout the whole earth, to show himself strong in the behalf of *them* whose heart *is* perfect toward him. Herein thou hast done foolishly: therefore from henceforth thou shalt have wars" (2 Chr.16:9).

"Thou hast also given me the shield of thy salvation: and thy right hand hath holden me up, and thy gentleness hath made me great" (Ps.18:35).

"The LORD *is* my strength and my shield; my heart trusted in him, and I am helped: therefore my heart greatly rejoiceth; and with my song will I praise him" (Ps.28:7).

"The angel of the LORD encampeth round about them that fear him, and delivereth them" (Ps.34:7).

"Surely he shall deliver thee from the snare of the fowler, *and* from the noisome pestilence. He shall cover thee with his feathers, and under his wings shalt thou trust: his truth *shall be thy* shield and buckler" (Ps.91:3-4).

"They reel to and fro, and stagger like a drunken man, and are at their wit's end. Then they cry unto the LORD in their trouble, and he bringeth them out of their distresses. He maketh the storm a calm, so that the waves thereof are still. Then are they glad because they be quiet; so he bringeth them unto their desired haven. Oh that *men* would praise the LORD *for* his goodness, and *for* his wonderful works to the children of men!" (Ps.107:27-31).

"Behold, he that keepeth Israel shall neither slumber nor sleep" (Ps.121:4).

"As the mountains *are* round about Jerusalem, so the LORD *is* round about his people from henceforth even for ever" (Ps.125:2).

"Fear thou not; for I *am* with thee: be not dismayed; for I *am* thy God: I will strengthen thee; yea, I will help thee; yea, I will uphold thee with the right hand of my righteousness" (Is.41:10).

"Fear not: for I have redeemed thee, I have called *thee* by thy name; thou *art* mine. When thou passest through the waters, I *will be* with thee; and through the rivers, they shall not overflow thee: when thou walkest through the fire, thou shalt not be burned; neither shall the flame kindle upon thee" (Is.43:1-2).

"And *even* to *your* old age I *am* he; and *even* to hoar [gray] hairs will I carry *you:* I have made, and I will bear; even I will carry, and will deliver *you*" (Is.46:4).

3 (17:17-24) **Life, Source of—Resurrection, Source of—Dead, Raised, by the LORD—Widow of Zarephath, Son Raised from the Dead—Elijah, Miracles of**: Elijah was used by God to raise back to life the widow's son who had died. This miracle is striking proof that the LORD alone—not the false god Baal—has the power to sustain life and to raise the dead. Scripture dramatically paints the scene of this spectacular miracle:

OUTLINE	SCRIPTURE	SCRIPTURE	OUTLINE
3. Elijah was used by God to raise the widow's son: Proof that the LORD alone—not Baal—has the power to raise the dead	17 And it came to pass after these things, *that* the son of the woman, the mistress of the house, fell sick; and his sickness was so sore, that there was no breath left in him.	whom I sojourn, by slaying her son?	
a. The widow's son died: The widow felt a sense of guilt, supposing that God was chastising her because of some sin	18 And she said unto Elijah, What have I to do with thee, O thou man of God? art thou come unto me to call my sin to remembrance, and to slay my son?	21 And he stretched himself upon the child three times, and cried unto the LORD, and said, O LORD my God, I pray thee, let this child's soul come into him again.	3) Elijah then stretched himself out over the boy three times, crying out in prayer: Asked God to let the boy's soul, life return to him
b. The widow's son was raised from the dead 1) Elijah took the child in his arms & carried him to his own upper room & laid him on the bed	19 And he said unto her, Give me thy son. And he took him out of her bosom, and carried him up into a loft, where he abode, and laid him upon his own bed.	22 And the LORD heard the voice of Elijah; and the soul of the child came into him again, and he revived. 23 And Elijah took the child, and brought him down out of the chamber into the house, and delivered him. unto his mother: and Elijah said, See, thy son liveth.	4) Elijah witnessed the astounding power of God: The boy's soul, life returned—he revived 5) Elijah carried the child to his mother with the wonderful news: "Your son lives"
2) Elijah prayed, cried out to the LORD: Was puzzled, asking God if He had caused the tragedy	20 And he cried unto the LORD, and said, O LORD my God, hast thou also brought evil upon the widow with	24 And the woman said to Elijah, Now by this I know that thou *art* a man of God, *and* that the word of the LORD in thy mouth *is* truth.	c. The widow's confession of faith 1) God is the Author of life (just witnessed) 2) Elijah was a man of God 3) God's Word is true

a. Some unknown illness gripped the widow's son, and he died. Sensing guilt, the widow accused Elijah of causing the death of her son. She mistakenly felt that she was being chastised because of some sin in her life and that the holy presence of the prophet had exposed her sin. Thus Elijah's presence was causing God's chastisement to fall upon her son.

b. But wonderfully and miraculously, the widow's son was to be raised from the dead, raised as proof that the LORD alone—not the false god Baal—has the power over the fruitfulness of life. The LORD alone sustains life and has the power to raise the dead (vv.19-23). In response to the widow's accusations, Elijah simply took the child in his arms and carried him up to his own room, laying him on the bed. Puzzled by the child's death, Elijah lifted up his voice in prayer, crying out to the LORD and asking why He had allowed the child to die.

After crying out and expressing his puzzlement, Elijah stretched himself over the boy three times. He cried out in prayer each time, asking God to let the boy's soul, his life return to him (vv.21).

Immediately, Elijah witnessed the astounding power of the LORD (vv.22). The boy's soul, his life returned to the body, and the boy revived. Picking up the child, Elijah carried him to his mother with the wonderful, amazing news: "Your son lives" (vv.23).

c. Taking the child into her arms, no doubt weeping, the widow made a confession of faith declaring three proven truths:

⇒ God is the Author of life, a fact that she had just witnessed.
⇒ Elijah was truly a man of God.
⇒ The LORD's Word is true.

Thought 1. God has the power to raise the dead just as He has the power to create life and the process or law by which every child is born into the world. Whatever processes are involved in the formation of a child from inception to birth—the laws that create life—have been established by God Himself. Life in all its complexity and mystery is given its power by the law of God alone. God holds the power to create life, to take life, and to raise the dead back to life.

Out in the future, a day of resurrection is coming, a day when every human being will be raised from the dead. No matter what the most minuscule particle of human life is, and no matter where the various parts of the human body are scattered through war or disease, these fine particles will be called back together to reform the human body of every individual who has ever lived and died. Even as God created the world by beginning with the most minute particles, so He will revive the most minute particles and reform every human being. And we will all stand before Him in the final judgment of the universe.

After the resurrection, a new heavens and earth will be remade and reformed, so that all the believers of all generations will have the most perfect world imaginable in which to live. This will be the glorious, climactic day of human history when the Lord Jesus will raise the dead to confront Him in judgment. Then He will separate the sheep from the goats, with the sheep being given the glorious privilege of living with Him eternally in the new heavens and earth. But the goats will be doomed to spend eternity in hell, separated from God forever.

Whatever we do in this life, we must make absolutely sure that we trust the Lord Jesus Christ as our Savior and Lord, that we believe His wonderful promises just as the widow believed. For if we believe, the Lord will raise us from the dead to the resurrection of life, to live eternally in the wonderful, glorious presence of God Himself. This is the astounding promise of God's Holy Word:

"Verily, verily, I say unto you, He that heareth my word, and believeth on him that sent me, hath everlasting life, and shall not come into condemnation; but is passed from death unto life. Verily, verily, I say unto you, The hour is coming, and now is, when the dead shall hear the voice of the Son of

God: and they that hear shall live. For as the Father hath life in himself; so hath he given to the Son to have life in himself; And hath given him authority to execute judgment also, because he is the Son of man. Marvel not at this: for the hour is coming, in the which all that are in the graves shall hear his voice, And shall come forth; they that have done good, unto the resurrection of life; and they that have done evil, unto the resurrection of damnation" (Jn.5:24-29).

"And this is the will of him that sent me, that every one which seeth the Son, and believeth on him, may have everlasting life: and I will raise him up at the last day" (Jn.6:40).

"Jesus said unto her, I am the resurrection, and the life: he that believeth in me, though he were dead, yet shall he live" (Jn.11:25).

"And have hope toward God, which they themselves also allow, that there shall be a resurrection of the dead, both of the just and unjust" (Ac.24:15).

"But now is Christ risen from the dead, *and* become the firstfruits of them that slept. For since by man *came* death, by man *came* also the resurrection of the dead. For as in Adam all die, even so in Christ shall all be made alive. But every man in his own order: Christ the firstfruits; afterward they that are Christ's at his coming" (1 Co.15:20-23).

"Behold, I show you a mystery; We shall not all sleep, but we shall all be changed, In a moment, in the twinkling of an eye, at the last trump: for the trumpet shall sound, and the dead shall be raised incorruptible, and we shall be changed. For this corruptible must put on incorruption, and this mortal *must* put on immortality. So when this corruptible shall have put on incorruption, and this mortal shall have put on immortality, then shall be brought to pass the saying that is written, Death is swallowed up in victory" (1 Co.15:51-54).

"Knowing that he which raised up the Lord Jesus shall raise up us also by Jesus, and shall present *us* with you" (2 Co.4:14).

"But I would not have you to be ignorant, brethren, concerning them which are asleep, that ye sorrow not, even as others which have no hope. For if we believe that Jesus died and rose again, even so them also which sleep in Jesus will God bring with him. For this we say unto you by the word of the Lord, that we which are alive *and* remain unto the coming of the Lord shall not prevent them which are asleep. For the Lord himself shall descend from heaven with a shout, with the voice of the archangel, and with the trump of God: and the dead in Christ shall rise first: Then we which are alive *and* remain shall be caught up together with them in the clouds, to meet the Lord in the air: and so shall we ever be with the Lord. Wherefore comfort one another with these words" (1 Th.4:13-18).

"But God will redeem my soul from the power of the grave: for he shall receive me. Selah" (Ps.49:15).

Thought 2. God has proven His power to raise the dead several times throughout Scripture:[1]
(1) He raised the son of the widow who lived in Zarephath.

"And the LORD heard the voice of Elijah; and the soul of the child came into him again, and he revived" (1 K.17:22).

(2) He raised the son of the Shunammite woman.

"Then he returned, and walked in the house to and fro; and went up, and stretched himself upon him: and the child sneezed seven times, and the child opened his eyes" (2 K.4:35).

(3) A dead man was restored to life by touching Elisha's bones.

"And it came to pass, as they were burying a man, that, behold, they spied a band *of men;* and they cast the man into the sepulchre of Elisha: and when the man was let down, and touched the bones of Elisha, he revived, and stood up on his feet" (2 K.13:21).

(4) The daughter of Jairus was raised from the dead by Christ.

"But when the people were put forth, he went in, and took her by the hand, and the maid arose" (Mt.9:25; see also Mk.5:42).

(5) A number of believers who had already died were raised at the time of the Lord's crucifixion.

"And the graves were opened; and many bodies of the saints which slept arose" (Mt.27:52).

(6) The son of the widow of Nain was raised from the dead by Christ.

"And he that was dead sat up, and began to speak. And he delivered him to his mother" (Lu.7:15).

---

[1] *The New Thompson Chain Reference Bible*. (Indianapolis, IN: B.B. Kirkbride Bible Co., Inc., 1964), Reference #2409.

(7) Lazarus, the brother of Mary and Martha, was raised from the dead.

"And he that was dead came forth, bound hand and foot with graveclothes: and his face was bound about with a napkin. Jesus saith unto them, Loose him, and let him go" (Jn.11:44).

(8) A widow named Dorcas was raised from the dead through the ministry of Peter.

"But Peter put them all forth, and kneeled down, and prayed; and turning *him* to the body said, Tabitha, arise. And she opened her eyes: and when she saw Peter, she sat up" (Ac.9:40).

CHAPTER 18

B. The End of the Drought After Elijah's Contest with the Prophets of Baal: Proving Who the True & Living God Is, 18:1-46

1. The end of the drought promised by the LORD, not Baal: God alone has the power to meet desperate needs
- a. God commanded Elijah to go & face King Ahab
- b. Elijah obeyed

2. The encounter between Elijah & Ahab worked out by the LORD, not Baal: God alone is sovereign
- a. God had placed Obadiah—a strong, faithful believer—in Ahab's court: He was manager of the royal palace
  - 1) He had risked his life to save 100 prophets from Jezebel's bloody purge of God's servants
    - Hid them in caves
    - Provided food & water for them
  - 2) He had been sent by Ahab on a desperate search to find pastureland for the royal horses & mules
    - Ahab had assigned the land to be searched
    - Ahab had gone one way, Obadiah the other
- b. God had arranged the events so that Obadiah & Elijah's paths would cross
  - 1) Obadiah, astonished, recognized Elijah & humbled himself
  - 2) Elijah charged Obadiah to go & summon King Ahab to meet him
  - 3) Obadiah was stricken with fear: Saw Elijah's charge as sure death
    - Because Ahab might think he had been hiding Elijah
    - Because Ahab had made a desperate, thorough search for Elijah—in every nation & kingdom
    - Because the Spirit of the LORD might call Elijah to go elsewhere & Elijah not be there when Ahab arrived: The result—Ahab's anger & the possible execution of Obadiah
  - 4) Obadiah pled with Elijah to excuse him from the dangerous task
    - Because he had already risked his life enough by saving the prophets from Jezebel's bloody purge
    - Because reporting Elijah's whereabouts without producing him would mean certain death
  - 5) Elijah assured Obadiah by oath: He would remain there to confront King Ahab that very day
  - 6) Obadiah carried the challenge to Ahab & the king accepted the challenge

3. The vindication of the LORD, not Baal, on Mount Carmel: The LORD alone is the true & living God
- a. Elijah's confrontation with Ahab: A picture of chastisement due to sin
  - 1) He charged Ahab with being the troublemaker & causing the famine: Due to his sin
  - 2) He challenged Ahab to summon the people to a contest on Mount Carmel: Between him (Elijah) & the 850 prophets of Baal
  - 3) Ahab accepted the challenge
- b. Elijah's challenge to the people: A picture of indecision
  - 1) He rebuked the people for wavering between two opinions: Called upon them to make a decision between the LORD & Baal
  - 2) He presented the proposal of a contest to the people: A contest to prove who the true & living God is
    - That the people secure

And it came to pass *after* many days, that the word of the LORD came to Elijah in the third year, saying, Go, show thyself unto Ahab; and I will send rain upon the earth.

2 And Elijah went to show himself unto Ahab. And *there was* a sore famine in Sa-maria.

3 And Ahab called Obadiah, which *was* the governor of *his* house. (Now Obadiah feared the LORD greatly:

4 For it was *so,* when Jezebel cut off the prophets of the LORD, that Obadiah took an hundred prophets, and hid them by fifty in a cave, and fed them with bread and water.)

5 And Ahab said unto Obadiah, Go into the land, unto all fountains of water, and unto all brooks: peradventure we may find grass to save the horses and mules alive, that we lose not all the beasts.

6 So they divided the land between them to pass throughout it: Ahab went one way by himself, and Obadiah went another way by himself.

7 And as Obadiah was in the way, behold, Elijah met him: and he knew him, and fell on his face, and said, *Art* thou that my lord Elijah?

8 And he answered him, I *am:* go, tell thy lord, Behold, Elijah *is here.*

9 And he said, What have I sinned, that thou wouldest deliver thy servant into the hand of Ahab, to slay me?

10 *As* the LORD thy God liveth, there is no nation or kingdom, whither my lord hath not sent to seek thee: and when they said, *He is* not *there;* he took an oath of the kingdom and nation, that they found thee not.

11 And now thou sayest, Go, tell thy lord, Behold, Elijah *is here.*

12 And it shall come to pass, *as soon as* I am gone from thee, that the Spirit of the LORD shall carry thee whither I know not; and so when I come and tell Ahab, and he cannot find thee, he shall slay me: but I thy servant fear the LORD from my youth.

13 Was it not told my lord what I did when Jezebel slew the prophets of the LORD, how I hid an hundred men of the LORD'S prophets by fifty in a cave, and fed them with bread and water?

14 And now thou sayest, Go, tell thy lord, Behold, Elijah *is here:* and he shall slay me.

15 And Elijah said, *As* the LORD of hosts liveth, before whom I stand, I will surely show myself unto him to day.

16 So Obadiah went to meet Ahab, and told him: and Ahab went to meet Elijah.

17 And it came to pass, when Ahab saw Elijah, that Ahab said unto him, *Art* thou he that troubleth Israel?

18 And he answered, I have not troubled Israel; but thou, and thy father's house, in that ye have forsaken the commandments of the LORD, and thou hast followed Baalim.

19 Now therefore send, *and* gather to me all Israel unto mount Carmel, and the prophets of Baal four hundred and fifty, and the prophets of the groves four hundred, which eat at Jezebel's table.

20 So Ahab sent unto all the children of Israel, and gathered the prophets together unto mount Carmel.

21 And Elijah came unto all the people, and said, How long halt ye between two opinions? if the LORD *be* God, follow him: but if Baal, *then* follow him. And the people answered him not a word.

22 Then said Elijah unto the people, I, *even* I only, remain a prophet of the LORD; but Baal's prophets *are* four hundred and fifty men.

23 Let them therefore give us

two bulls
- That he & the Baal prophets prepare a bull for sacrifice & each place his sacrifice on his own altar
- That the Baal prophets call upon their god & he upon the LORD: Whoever sent fire down to consume the sacrifice would be the true & living God

c. Elijah's challenge to the false prophets of Baal: The futility of idolatry & false worship
   1) The false prophets of Baal prepared their sacrifice first & began to pray
      - They prayed—calling on Baal & dancing around the altar—from morning till noon, but there was no answer, no response at all
      - They were mocked, taunted by Elijah: He suggested Baal might be meditating, busy, traveling, or sleeping
      - They became frantic in their ritual, shouting more loudly & cutting themselves
      - They continued their feverish raving until time for the evening sacrifice
   2) The prophets still received no answer, no response whatsoever

d. Elijah's dramatic vindication of the LORD: Proof that He alone is the true & living God
   1) Elijah called the people to him as he rebuilt an altar that lay in ruins
      - Chose 12 stones to represent or symbolize the 12 tribes of Israel
      - Used the stones to build the altar
      - Dug a large trench around the altar

two bullocks; and let them
choose one bullock for themselves, and cut it in pieces,
and lay *it* on wood, and put
no fire *under:* and I will dress
the other bullock, and lay *it*
on wood, and put no fire *under:*
24 And call ye on the name
of your gods, and I will call
on the name of the LORD: and
the God that answereth by
fire, let him be God. And all
the people answered and
said, It is well spoken.
25 And Elijah said unto the
prophets of Baal, Choose you
one bullock for yourselves,
and dress *it* first; for ye *are*
many; and call on the name
of your gods, but put no fire
under.
26 And they took the bullock
which was given them, and
they dressed *it,* and called on
the name of Baal from morning even until noon, saying,
O Baal, hear us. But *there
was* no voice, nor any that
answered. And they leaped
upon the altar which was
made.
27 And it came to pass at
noon, that Elijah mocked
them, and said, Cry aloud:
for he *is* a god; either he is
talking, or he is pursuing, or
he is in a journey, *or* peradventure he sleepeth, and must
be awaked.
28 And they cried aloud, and
cut themselves after their
manner with knives and lan-
cets, till the blood gushed out
upon them.
29 And it came to pass,
when midday was past, and
they prophesied until the *time*
of the offering of the *evening*
sacrifice, that *there was* neither voice, nor any to answer,
nor any that regarded.
30 And Elijah said unto all
the people, Come near unto
me. And all the people came
near unto him. And he re-
paired the altar of the LORD
that was broken down.
31 And Elijah took twelve
stones, according to the
number of the tribes of the
sons of Jacob, unto whom the
word of the LORD came, saying, Israel shall be thy name:
32 And with the stones he
built an altar in the name
of the LORD: and he made
a trench about the altar, as
great as would contain two
measures of seed.
33 And he put the wood in
order, and cut the bullock in
pieces, and laid *him* on the
wood, and said, Fill four bar-
rels with water, and pour *it*
on the burnt sacrifice, and on
the wood.
34 And he said, Do *it* the second time. And they did *it* the
second time. And he said, Do
it the third time. And they did
it the third time.
35 And the water ran round
about the altar; and he filled
the trench also with water.
36 And it came to pass at *the
time of* the offering of the
evening sacrifice, that Elijah
the prophet came near, and
said, LORD God of Abraham,
Isaac, and of Israel, let it be
known this day that thou art
God in Israel, and *that* I *am*
thy servant, and *that* I have
done all these things at thy
word.
37 Hear me, O LORD, hear
me, that this people may
know that thou *art* the LORD
God, and *that* thou hast
turned their heart back
again.
38 Then the fire of the LORD
fell, and consumed the burnt
sacrifice, and the wood, and
the stones, and the dust, and
licked up the water that *was*
in the trench.
39 And when all the people
saw *it,* they fell on their faces: and they said, The LORD,
he *is* the God; the LORD, he *is*
the God.
40 And Elijah said unto
them, Take the prophets of
Baal; let not one of them escape. And they took them:
and Elijah brought them
down to the brook Kishon,
and slew them there.
41 And Elijah said unto
Ahab, Get thee up, eat and
drink; for *there is* a sound of
abundance of rain.
42 So Ahab went up to eat
and to drink. And Elijah went
up to the top of Carmel; and
he cast himself down upon
the earth, and put his face between his knees,
43 And said to his servant,
Go up now, look toward the
sea. And he went up, and
looked, and said, *There is*
nothing. And he said, Go
again seven times.

- Piled wood on the altar
- Cut up the bull & laid it on the wood
- Had the water from four large water jugs poured on the offering three times—12 large water jugs in total
- Had the entire altar soaked & the trench filled with water

2) Elijah stepped forward & prayed to the God of Abraham, Isaac, & Jacob (the covenant God): That He would prove Himself
   - That He alone is God
   - That Elijah is His servant
   - That the LORD hears & answers the prayers of His people: So the people would know that He is the living God & be stirred to repent
3) Elijah was dramatically heard by the LORD
   - Fire immediately fell & consumed the entire altar, even the water in the trench
   - The people were stricken with fear: Fell prostrate & confessed that the LORD is God
4) Elijah immediately commanded the people to seize & execute the false prophets of Baal: Their evil had ruined the nation, De.7:1-26; 13:1-18; 17:2-5
5) Elijah fervently prayed for rain
   - Informed Ahab of coming rain
   - Climbed to the top of Mount Carmel, bowed down & put his face between his knees, then prayed

   Sent his servant to look toward the sea for rain clouds
   - Continued fervently in prayer: Seven times he sent his servant to look

6) Elijah again was dramatically heard by the LORD: The seventh time a small cloud had appeared • He warned Ahab to rush back before the torrential downpour caught him • He & the others witnessed	44 And it came to pass at the seventh time, that he said, Behold, there ariseth a little cloud out of the sea, like a man's hand. And he said, Go up, say unto Ahab, Prepare *thy chariot,* and get thee down, that the rain stop thee not. 45 And it came to pass in the	mean while, that the heaven was black with clouds and wind, and there was a great rain. And Ahab rode, and went to Jezreel. 46 And the hand of the LORD was on Elijah; and he girded up his loins, and ran before Ahab to the entrance of Jezreel.	another proof of the only true & living God: Dark clouds & a strong wind appeared • He was energized by the LORD & ran ahead of Ahab's chariot all the way to Jezreel: A sign to Ahab to repent

DIVISION III

THE MINISTRY OF ELIJAH AND OTHER PROPHETS DURING THE REIGN OF AHAB: LEARNING WHO THE LIVING AND TRUE GOD IS, 17:1–22:53

B. The End of the Drought After Elijah's Contest with the Prophets of Baal: Proving Who the True and Living God Is, 18:1-46

(18:1-46) **Introduction**: Does God really exist? Is there truly a Supreme Being who is living and watching over us at all times? Have this earth and universe been created by a Being with unlimited power (omnipotence) and perfect knowledge (omniscience)? And if there is a true and living God, can we know Him personally? Can we really discover Him and learn about Him?

This much we do know: we cannot enter into the spiritual world, the spiritual dimension of being, in order to discover if God truly exists. We are physical, material beings; and no matter how far or fast we travel, no matter what our state of mind, we are still human beings in the physical world, the physical dimension. We cannot penetrate, go over into the spiritual world, not in these physical bodies.

Something else we know: if there is a god who has left us in the dark, ignorant of his existence, unaware of where we came from and where we are going, not knowing what is expected of us, he is a god of hate. We know this because these very actions would show his lack of attention, consideration, and concern for our welfare. For this reason, we would be doomed to whatever fate he determined, without our ever knowing what to expect.

Conversely, if there is a God of love, He would enlighten us about our existence. He would reveal where we came from and where we are going, reveal what is expected of us. He would also reveal Himself to us, allowing us to know Him personally and to establish a relationship with Him. He would show us the way *through life* and the truth *about life.* And if there was something wrong with our lives, our society, our earth—which we know there is because of sin, lawlessness, and violence—this loving God would provide a way for us to be saved out of the wickedness and death of this world.

There is wonderful news! The God of love *has* revealed Himself to us. He came to this earth in the person of the Lord Jesus Christ, in the form of human flesh, to reveal Himself to us. There is only one true and living God, the Lord God Himself (Jehovah, Yahweh)—the God of perfect love, mercy, and justice. This is the great lesson of the present passage of Scripture. This is: *The End of the Drought After Elijah's Contest with the Prophets of Baal: Proving Who the True and Living God Is,* 18:1-46.

1. The end of the drought promised by the LORD, not Baal: God alone has the power to meet desperate needs (v.1).
2. The encounter between Elijah and Ahab worked out by the LORD, not Baal: God alone is sovereign (vv.2-16).
3. The vindication of the LORD, not Baal, on Mount Carmel: the LORD alone is the true and living God (vv.17-46).

1 (18:1) **Needs, Met - Provided For—Power, of God—God, Power of—Baal, Powerlessness of—Idolatry, Powerlessness of**: the LORD God Himself—not the false god Baal—promised to end the drought and famine. And note, the drought and famine had swept over the land for almost three years. By now the entire nation was in desperate straits with many on the verge of starvation, and perhaps some had already starved to death (5-6; 17:12). But despite the severity of the drought and famine, Ahab and the people of the Northern Kingdom did not turn to the LORD for help. There is no record of their being willing to repent of their sinful, wicked ways; no record of their willingness to turn away from idolatry and false worship and to begin once again to worship the LORD genuinely and wholeheartedly.

Nevertheless, the LORD was ready to prove that He alone—not their false god—could meet their desperate needs. In mercy and compassion, the LORD commanded Elijah to go present himself to King Ahab, for it was time for the LORD to send rain upon the land. It was time for the famine to end and for the needs of the people to be met. In obedience to the LORD, Elijah left to confront the king.

OUTLINE	SCRIPTURE
1. The end of the drought promised by the LORD, not Baal: God alone has the power to meet desperate needs a. God commanded Elijah to go & face King Ahab b. Elijah obeyed	And it came to pass *after* many days, that the word of the LORD came to Elijah in the third year, saying, Go, show thyself unto Ahab; and I will send rain upon the earth.

Thought 1. A lesson that we must learn is this: the LORD alone can meet the desperate needs of man, the agonizing cries of the human heart when confronted with terrible crises. Medical doctors can usually help us when we are sick, even when facing a terminal illness. They can generally help ease the pain and frequently prolong our lives. But only for a while. Their help only delays, never stops, the inevitable day of death.

Counselors and friends can help us when we are facing disability, emotional difficulties, divorce, financial problems, guilt, or some other severe crisis. But counselors and friends can never bridge the gap of alienation between man and God. They can never grant to man the peace and firm assurance of never having to die. This desperate need for reconciliation with God—for being perfectly assured that we are acceptable to Him and will live with Him eternally—can be met only by God. Moreover, only God can meet the cry of the human heart for meaning and purpose and for a sense of security and fulfillment. A conquering, victorious spirit that triumphs over all the hardships, misfortunes, and temptations of this life can come only from the LORD.

When we face the desperate situations of life, the LORD alone can help us. And the wonderful message is just this: the LORD will help us in our hour of need. This is the wonderful promise of His Holy Word:

> **"But as many as received him, to them gave he power to become the sons of God, *even* to them that believe on his name" (Jn.1:12).**
>
> **"And Jesus said unto them, I am the bread of life: he that cometh to me shall never hunger; and he that believeth on me shall never thirst" (Jn.6:35).**
>
> **"I am come a light into the world, that whosoever believeth on me should not abide in darkness" (Jn.12:46).**
>
> **"Let not your heart be troubled: ye believe in God, believe also in me. In my Father's house are many mansions: if *it were* not so, I would have told you. I go to prepare a place for you" (Jn.14:1-2).**
>
> **"And we know that all things work together for good to them that love God, to them who are the called according to *his* purpose" (Ro.8:28).**
>
> **"There hath no temptation taken you but such as is common to man: but God *is* faithful, who will not suffer you to be tempted above that ye are able; but will with the temptation also make a way to escape, that ye may be able to bear *it*" (1 Co.10:13).**
>
> **"For our light affliction, which is but for a moment, worketh for us a far more exceeding *and* eternal weight of glory" (2 Co.4:17).**
>
> **"And he said unto me, My grace is sufficient for thee: for my strength is made perfect in weakness. Most gladly therefore will I rather glory in my infirmities, that the power of Christ may rest upon me" (2 Co.12:9).**
>
> **"Wherefore in all things it behooved him to be made like unto *his* brethren, that he might be a merciful and faithful high priest in things *pertaining* to God, to make reconciliation for the sins of the people. For in that he himself hath suffered being tempted, he is able to succour them that are tempted" (He.2:17-18).**
>
> **"Submit yourselves therefore to God. Resist the devil, and he will flee from you" (Ja.4:7).**
>
> **"Beloved, think it not strange concerning the fiery trial which is to try you, as though some strange thing happened unto you: But rejoice, inasmuch as ye are partakers of Christ's sufferings; that, when his glory shall be revealed, ye may be glad also with exceeding joy" (1 Pe.4:12-13).**
>
> **"And God shall wipe away all tears from their eyes; and there shall be no more death, neither sorrow, nor crying, neither shall there be any more pain: for the former things are passed away" (Re.21:4).**
>
> **"If my people, which are called by my name, shall humble themselves, and pray, and seek my face, and turn from their wicked ways; then will I hear from heaven, and will forgive their sin, and will heal their land" (2 Chr.7:14).**
>
> **"For the oppression of the poor, for the sighing of the needy, now will I arise, saith the LORD; I will set *him* in safety *from him that* puffeth at him" (Ps.12:5).**
>
> **"Many *are* the afflictions of the righteous: but the LORD delivereth him out of them all. He keepeth all his bones: not one of them is broken" (Ps.34:19-20).**
>
> **"Trust in the LORD, and do good; *so* shalt thou dwell in the land, and verily thou shalt be fed" (Ps.37:3).**
>
> **"The LORD will strengthen him upon the bed of languishing: thou wilt make all his bed in his sickness" (Ps.41:3).**
>
> **"And call upon me in the day of trouble: I will deliver thee, and thou shalt glorify me" (Ps.50:15).**
>
> **"Though I walk in the midst of trouble, thou wilt revive me: thou shalt stretch forth thine hand against the wrath of mine enemies, and thy right hand shall save me" (Ps.138:7).**
>
> **"For thou hast been a strength to the poor, a strength to the needy in his distress, a refuge from the storm, a shadow from the heat, when the blast of the terrible ones *is* as a storm *against* the wall" (Is.25:4).**
>
> **"*When* the poor and needy seek water, and *there is* none, *and* their tongue faileth for thirst, I the LORD will hear them, *I* the God of Israel will not forsake them" (Is.41:17).**
>
> **"...Fear not: for I have redeemed thee, I have called *thee* by thy name; thou *art* mine. When thou passest through the waters, I *will be* with thee; and through the rivers, they shall not overflow thee: when thou walkest through the fire, thou shalt not be burned; neither shall the flame kindle upon thee" (Is.43:1-2).**

2 (18:2-16) **Sovereignty, of God—God, Sovereignty of, Example—False Gods, Weakness of—God, Contrasted with False Gods**: the LORD God Himself—not the false god Baal—arranged the encounter between Elijah and Ahab. For some time God had been moving events to arrange the encounter. By working things out for His prophet and the king to meet, God proved that He alone is sovereign, that He alone controls the events of this world and the affairs of men. Nothing happens that is beyond His control, that He does not allow. Scripture shows how God arranged the meeting between His prophet and King Ahab:

OUTLINE	SCRIPTURE	SCRIPTURE	OUTLINE
2. The encounter between Elijah & Ahab worked out by the LORD, not Baal: God alone is sovereign	2 And Elijah went to show himself unto Ahab. And *there was* a sore famine in Samaria.	hand of Ahab, to slay me? 10 *As* the LORD thy God liveth, there is no nation or kingdom, whither my lord	• Because Ahab might think he had been hiding Elijah
a. God had placed Obadiah—a strong, faithful believer—in Ahab's court: He was manager of the royal palace	3 And Ahab called Obadiah, which *was* the governor of *his* house. (Now Obadiah feared the LORD greatly:	hath not sent to seek thee: and when they said, *He is* not *there;* he took an oath of the kingdom and nation, that they found thee not.	• Because Ahab had made a desperate, thorough search for Elijah—in every nation & kingdom
1) He had risked his life to save 100 prophets from Jezebel's bloody purge of God's servants • Hid them in caves • Provided food & water for them	4 For it was *so,* when Jezebel cut off the prophets of the LORD, that Obadiah took an hundred prophets, and hid them by fifty in a cave, and fed them with bread and water.)	11 And now thou sayest, Go, tell thy lord, Behold, Elijah *is here.* 12 And it shall come to pass, *as soon as* I am gone from thee, that the Spirit of the	• Because the Spirit of the LORD might call Elijah to go elsewhere & Elijah not be there when Ahab arrived: The result—Ahab's anger & the possible execution of Obadiah
2) He had been sent by Ahab on a desperate search to find pastureland for the royal horses & mules	5 And Ahab said unto Obadiah, Go into the land, unto all fountains of water, and unto all brooks: peradventure we may find grass to save the horses and mules alive, that we lose not all the beasts.	LORD shall carry thee whither I know not; and so when I come and tell Ahab, and he cannot find thee, he shall slay me: but I thy servant fear the LORD from my youth.	4) Obadiah pled with Elijah to excuse him from the dangerous task
• Ahab had assigned the land to be searched • Ahab had gone one way, Obadiah the other	6 So they divided the land between them to pass throughout it: Ahab went one way by himself, and Obadiah went another way by himself.	13 Was it not told my lord what I did when Jezebel slew the prophets of the LORD, how I hid an hundred men of the LORD'S prophets by fifty in a cave, and fed them with bread and water?	• Because he had already risked his life enough by saving the prophets from Jezebel's bloody purge
b. God had arranged the events so that Obadiah & Elijah's paths would cross 1) Obadiah, astonished, recognized Elijah & humbled himself	7 And as Obadiah was in the way, behold, Elijah met him: and he knew him, and fell on his face, and said, *Art* thou that my lord Elijah?	14 And now thou sayest, Go, tell thy lord, Behold, Elijah *is here:* and he shall slay me.	• Because reporting Elijah's whereabouts without producing him would mean certain death
2) Elijah charged Obadiah to go & summon King Ahab to meet him	8 And he answered him, I *am:* go, tell thy lord, Behold, Elijah *is here.*	15 And Elijah said, *As* the LORD of hosts liveth, before whom I stand, I will surely show myself unto him to day.	5) Elijah assured Obadiah by oath: He would remain there to confront King Ahab that very day
3) Obadiah was stricken with fear: Saw Elijah's charge as sure death	9 And he said, What have I sinned, that thou wouldest deliver thy servant into the	16 So Obadiah went to meet Ahab, and told him: and Ahab went to meet Elijah.	6) Obadiah carried the challenge to Ahab & the king accepted the challenge

a. Sometime earlier God had placed Obadiah—a strong, faithful believer—in Ahab's court (vv.2-6). Obadiah was manager of the royal palace, which meant that he was the chief administrator and steward of the king's properties. It was a position that could be termed *minister of state*, one who served as the personal representative of the king. Some commentators feel that this position was second in command to the king.

To stress Obadiah's commitment to the LORD, Scripture tells us that he had risked his life to save 100 prophets from Jezebel's bloody purge of God's servants (v.4). Remember, the infamous Jezebel was the wife of Ahab. Apparently Jezebel had launched a murderous campaign against the LORD's prophets, seeking to kill them all in order to eliminate the worship of the LORD throughout the land. Doing all he could, Obadiah sought to save 100 of the prophets by hiding them in two caves, fifty in each, and providing food and water for them.

After almost three years, the effects of the famine were reaching into the royal court. For that reason Ahab sent Obadiah on a desperate search to find pastureland for the royal horses and mules to keep them from starving (vv.5-6). Dividing the land between himself and Obadiah, Ahab went in one direction and Obadiah in the other.

b. God had arranged the events so Obadiah's and Elijah's paths would cross (vv.7-16). As Obadiah was walking along, suddenly he saw and recognized Elijah approaching him. He could hardly believe his eyes. When they finally reached other, Obadiah humbled himself by bowing to the ground out of respect for God's prophet. With a sense of urgency, Elijah immediately charged Obadiah to go and summon King Ahab to meet him (v.8). But stricken with fear, Obadiah sensed that Elijah's command would mean certain death for himself (vv.9-11). Obadiah knew that Ahab might think he had been hiding Elijah from the king. For Ahab had been making a desperate and thorough search for Elijah, a search that had reached into every nation and kingdom. Obadiah also knew that the Spirit of the LORD might call Elijah to go elsewhere, and Elijah would not be there when Ahab arrived (vv.11-12). The result would be catastrophic, for Ahab's anger would be aroused and he could possibly execute Obadiah.

Thus Obadiah pled with Elijah to excuse him from the dangerous task (vv.13-16). He informed Elijah that he had already risked his life enough by saving the prophets from Jezebel's bloody purge. Pleading with all his heart, he told Elijah that if he reported the prophet's whereabouts to Ahab then failed to produce him, it would mean certain death for him (Obadiah).

Elijah assured Obadiah by swearing an oath that he would remain there to confront King Ahab that very day (v.15). Being assured, Obadiah carried the challenge to Ahab and the king accepted the challenge. He immediately went to confront Elijah, the LORD's prophet (v.16).

Thought 1. The LORD alone is sovereign. He alone has the power to move events to accomplish His purposes. He alone can work things out to fulfill His promises. God has absolute power throughout the universe, controlling all events, including all the affairs of men. Therefore nothing happens that God does not allow to happen. But in thinking about the sovereignty of God, we must remember three facts: God also gave us a free will. God allows us to exercise our free will, to do what we want when we want. But our free will, our action, is limited. God allows us to go only so far before He steps in and stops us. This means that every movement, every thought, every event that happens to us—although known to God—is not minutely, actively caused or maneuvered by God. Again, God allows us to exercise our free will, to think, to reach out our arms at any given moment, to act within the bounds of our capabilities. But the very source of our mind and body is God. God gave us the mind and the body we have and the free will to do with this body what we desire.

We must remember another fact as well: in the exercise of our free will, we bear the consequences of our actions. One of the basic principles of life ordained by God is this: we reap what we sow. God is in total control, but He has ordained that we have a free will and that when we exercise our free will, certain consequences do occur. Simply stated, God has ordained a framework or bounds within which our free will works.

But in dealing with the sovereignty of God, there is a wonderful truth that God has revealed to us in His Holy Word: that is, He is working out all things for our good, for the good of all who truly love and follow Him (Ro.8:28). And God is moving the whole universe toward the climactic day known as *The Great Day of Redemption*. This is the climactic day when the present heavens and earth will be remade into the new heavens and earth, recreated to be the perfect, eternal home of all believers who truly love and follow the LORD.

God is moving events and working all things out for the good of His dear people. No matter what confronts a genuine believer—hardship or trial, misfortune or accident, disease or suffering—God will strengthen and help His follower. He will work all things out for the believer's good. The sovereignty of God is one of the great truths of this universe. Listen to what God's Holy Word says about His sovereignty:

"But I say unto you, Swear not at all; neither by heaven; for it is God's throne" (Mt.5:34).

"And lead us not into temptation, but deliver us from evil: For thine is the kingdom, and the power, and the glory, for ever. Amen" (Mt.6:13).

"God that made the world and all things therein, seeing that he is Lord of heaven and earth, dwelleth not in temples made with hands" (Ac.17:24).

"And we know that all things work together for good to them that love God, to them who are the called according to *his* purpose. For whom he did foreknow, he also did predestinate *to be* conformed to the image of his Son, that he might be the firstborn among many brethren" (Ro.8:28-29).

"Thou wilt say then unto me, Why doth he yet find fault? For who hath resisted his will? Nay but, O man, who art thou that repliest against God? Shall the thing formed say to him that formed *it*, Why hast thou made me thus? Hath not the potter power over the clay, of the same lump to make one vessel unto honour, and another unto dishonour" (Ro.9:19-21).

"For he must reign, till he hath put all enemies under his feet" (1 Co.15:25).

"Wherefore God also hath highly exalted him, and given him a name which is above every name: That at the name of Jesus every knee should bow, of *things* in heaven, and *things* in earth, and *things* under the earth; And *that* every tongue should confess that Jesus Christ *is* Lord, to the glory of God the Father" (Ph.2:9-11).

"Now unto the King eternal, immortal, invisible, the only wise God, *be* honour and glory for ever and ever. Amen" (1 Ti.1:17).

"And they sing the song of Moses the servant of God, and the song of the Lamb, saying, Great and marvellous *are* thy works, Lord God Almighty; just and true *are* thy ways, thou King of saints" (Re.15:3).

"And I heard as it were the voice of a great multitude, and as the voice of many waters, and as the voice of mighty thunderings, saying, Alleluia: for the Lord God omnipotent reigneth" (Re.19:6).

"And I saw a great white throne, and him that sat on it, from whose face the earth and the heaven fled away; and there was found no place for them" (Re.20:11).

"The LORD shall reign for ever and ever" (Ex.15:18).

"Know therefore this day, and consider *it* in thine heart, that the LORD he *is* God in heaven above, and upon the earth beneath: *there is* none else" (De.4:39).

"Both riches and honour *come* of thee, and thou reignest over all; and in thine hand *is* power and might; and in thine hand *it is* to make great, and to give strength unto all" (1 Chr.29:12).

"And said, O LORD God of our fathers, *art* not thou God in heaven? and rulest *not* thou over all the kingdoms of the heathen? and in thine hand *is there not* power and might, so that none is able to withstand thee?" (2 Chr.20:6).

"He leadeth princes away spoiled, and overthroweth the mighty" (Jb.12:19).

"The LORD *is* King for ever and ever: the heathen are perished out of his land" (Ps.10:16).
"For the kingdom *is* the LORD'S: and he *is* the governor among the nations" (Ps.22:28).
"Who is this King of glory? The LORD of hosts, he *is* the King of glory. Selah" (Ps.24:10).
"The LORD sitteth upon the flood; yea, the LORD sitteth King for ever" (Ps.29:10).
"Thy throne, O God, *is* for ever and ever: the sceptre of thy kingdom *is* a right sceptre" (Ps.45:6).
"For the LORD most high is terrible; he is a great King over all the earth" (Ps.47:2).
"Consume *them* in wrath, consume *them,* that they *may* not *be:* and let them know that God ruleth in Jacob unto the ends of the earth. Selah" (Ps.59:13).
"God shall bless us; and all the ends of the earth shall fear him" (Ps.67:7).
"Yea, all kings shall fall down before him: all nations shall serve him" (Ps.72:11).
"That *men* may know that thou, whose name alone *is* JEHOVAH, *art* the most high over all the earth" (Ps.83:18).
"The LORD reigneth, he is clothed with majesty; the LORD is clothed with strength, *wherewith* he hath girded himself: the world also is stablished, that it cannot be moved" (Ps.93:1).
"The LORD hath prepared his throne in the heavens; and his kingdom ruleth over all" (Ps.103:19).
"Whatsoever the LORD pleased, *that* did he in heaven, and in earth, in the seas, and all deep places" (Ps.135:6).
"The king's heart *is* in the hand of the LORD, *as* the rivers of water: he turneth it whithersoever he will" (Pr.21:1).
"Of the increase of *his* government and peace *there shall be* no end, upon the throne of David, and upon his kingdom, to order it, and to establish it with judgment and with justice from henceforth even for ever. The zeal of the LORD of hosts will perform this" (Is.9:7).
"But I know thy abode, and thy going out, and thy coming in, and thy rage against me. Because thy rage against me, and thy tumult, is come up into mine ears, therefore will I put my hook in thy nose, and my bridle in thy lips, and I will turn thee back by the way by which thou camest" (Is.37:28-29).
"Thus saith the LORD, thy Redeemer, and he that formed thee from the womb, I *am* the LORD that maketh all *things*; that stretcheth forth the heavens alone; that spreadeth abroad the earth by myself; That frustrateth the tokens of the liars, and maketh diviners mad; that turneth wise *men* backward, and maketh their knowledge foolish" (Is.44:24-25).
"Thus saith the LORD, The heaven *is* my throne, and the earth is my footstool: where *is* the house that ye build unto me? and where *is* the place of my rest?" (Is.66:1).
"Behold, the days come, saith the LORD, that I will raise unto David a righteous Branch, and a King shall reign and prosper, and shall execute judgment and justice in the earth" (Je.23:5).
"Daniel answered and said, Blessed be the name of God for ever and ever: for wisdom and might are his" (Da.2:20).
"And all the inhabitants of the earth *are* reputed as nothing: and he doeth according to his will in the army of heaven, and *among* the inhabitants of the earth: and none can stay his hand, or say unto him, What dost thou?" (Da.4:35).
"Now I Nebuchadnezzar praise and extol and honour the King of heaven, all whose works *are* truth, and his ways judgment: and those that walk in pride he is able to abase" (Da.4:37).
"And he was driven from the sons of men; and his heart was made like the beasts, and his dwelling *was* with the wild asses: they fed him with grass like oxen, and his body was wet with the dew of heaven; till he knew that the most high God ruled in the kingdom of men, and *that* he appointeth over it whomsoever he will" (Da.5:21).
"And there was given him dominion, and glory, and a kingdom, that all people, nations, and languages, should serve him: his dominion *is* an everlasting dominion, which shall not pass away, and his kingdom *that* which shall not be destroyed" (Da.7:14).

Thought 2. In the commentary *Mastering the Old Testament,* Russell Dilday has an excellent application dealing with Obadiah that is worth quoting in its entirety:

Obadiah has been described as a good man in a bad place. His firmness and religious zeal did not prevent him from retaining his place of honor and dignity in the royal court. Should godly Obadiah have resigned his post in the wicked court in protest? That is the action some righteous people take as they confront evil situations, but the New Testament makes it clear that at times disciples are to remain in an imperfect environment in order to be salt and leaven for good. Jesus prayed, "I do not pray that You should take them out of the world, but that You should keep them from the evil one" (John 17:15). Sometimes Christian boldness necessitates a costly withdrawal, the resignation from a high-paying job, the cancellation of a contract, the refusal to join a certain organization. But sometimes Christ-like valor means sweetening the sour situation by staying. Like Obadiah, some are called to be "good people in a bad place."[1]

3 (18:17-46) **God, Fact—God, Proof, Is Living and True—God, Existence of, Proof—False Gods, Powerlessness of—Baal, Powerlessness of—Idolatry, Futility of—False Worship, Futility of—God, Vindication of**: the LORD God Himself—not the false god Baal—vindicated His existence on Mt. Carmel. Elijah's confrontation with the prophets of Baal on Mt. Carmel is an exciting, suspenseful story that is high drama at its best. It is a well-known story among Christian circles

[1] Russell Dilday. *1, 2 Kings*, pp.208-209.

and its importance cannot be overemphasized. The purpose of the confrontation between God's prophet and the prophets of the false god Baal is a critical lesson for every generation to learn: to prove that the LORD (Jehovah, Yahweh) is the only living and true God. Scripture gives a descriptive account of the contest:

OUTLINE	SCRIPTURE	SCRIPTURE	OUTLINE
3. The vindication of the LORD, not Baal, on Mount Carmel: The LORD alone is the true & living God a. Elijah's confrontation with Ahab: A picture of chastisement due to sin 1) He charged Ahab with being the troublemaker & causing the famine: Due to his sin	17 And it came to pass, when Ahab saw Elijah, that Ahab said unto him, *Art* thou he that troubleth Israel? 18 And he answered, I have not troubled Israel; but thou, and thy father's house, in that ye have forsaken the commandments of the LORD, and thou hast followed Baalim.	19 Now therefore send, *and* gather to me all Israel unto mount Carmel, and the prophets of Baal four hundred and fifty, and the prophets of the groves four hundred, which eat at Jezebel's table. 20 So Ahab sent unto all the children of Israel, and gathered the prophets together unto mount Carmel.	2) He challenged Ahab to summon the people to a contest on Mount Carmel: Between him (Elijah) & the 850 prophets of Baal 3) Ahab accepted the challenge

a. Elijah's confrontation with Ahab paints a picture of judgment due to sin (vv.18-20). As soon as the two men met face-to-face, Ahab angrily and sarcastically charged Elijah with being a *troublemaker,* the person responsible for the severe drought and famine sweeping the land.

By taking the initiative, Elijah fired back at Ahab that he was really the *troublemaker*, the person who had brought famine upon the land. It was Ahab and his descendants who had sinned, forsaking the commandments of the LORD and committing idolatry and false worship, following the false god Baal (v.18). Then giving Ahab no time to respond, Elijah challenged the king to summon the people to a contest on Mt. Carmel, a contest between himself and the 850 prophets of Baal and Asherah (v.19). Note that 450 of the prophets served the false god Baal and the other 400 prophets served the false god Asherah. Ahab accepted the challenge, no doubt thinking this would be the one way he could get rid of the troublesome prophet and eliminate the worship of the LORD once and for all (v.20). Completely deceived by his faith in and worship of the false god Baal, Ahab excitedly sent word of the contest throughout all the Northern Kingdom, summoning the people to attend. Obviously, there were multiplied thousands who gathered together to witness the contest.

Thought 1. The confrontation between Elijah and Ahab is a clear picture of judgment due to sin. Drought and famine had stricken the land because of the sin and wickedness of both Ahab and the Israelites. Through chastisement or discipline, God was seeking to lead the Israelites to repentance, to arouse them to turn away from lives of wickedness. He was seeking to turn them from false worship and idolatry back to Him.

So it is with us: when we sin, God chastises us just as a parent does when his or her child misbehaves. Through the chastisement, God hopes to arouse us to turn away from our sin and back to Him. If we continue in sin, we will eventually harm ourselves or damage the lives of others. Thus God disciplines us to keep us from destroying ourselves or others. This is the clear teaching of God's Holy Word:

"Every branch in me that beareth not fruit he taketh away: and every *branch* that beareth fruit, he purgeth it, that it may bring forth more fruit" (Jn.15:2).

"For this cause many *are* weak and sickly among you, and many sleep. For if we would judge ourselves, we should not be judged. But when we are judged, we are chastened of the Lord, that we should not be condemned with the world" (1 Co.11:30-32).

"And ye have forgotten the exhortation which speaketh unto you as unto children, My son, despise not thou the chastening of the Lord, nor faint when thou art rebuked of him: For whom the Lord loveth he chasteneth, and scourgeth every son whom he receiveth" (He.12:5-6).

"As many as I love, I rebuke and chasten: be zealous therefore, and repent" (Re.3:19).

"Thou shalt also consider in thine heart, that, as a man chasteneth his son, *so* the LORD thy God chasteneth thee" (De.8:5).

"Blessed *is* the man whom thou chastenest, O LORD, and teachest him out of thy law" (Ps.94:12).

"My son, despise not the chastening of the LORD; neither be weary of his correction: For whom the LORD loveth he correcteth; even as a father the son *in whom* he delighteth" (Pr.3:11-12).

b. As soon as all the people and false prophets had gathered, Elijah stood before them and presented his challenge, explaining the contest (vv.21-24). But first he rebuked the people for wavering between two opinions. No longer could they debate who the true and living God was. No longer could they claim that all gods were equal, that all gods represented the one true and living God. No longer could they serve both the LORD and Baal. It was time to make a decision, time to make a forceful and conclusive declaration that the LORD (Jehovah, Yahweh) was the only living and true God. All other *so-called* gods were false, just the creation of man's imagination. The people could no longer straddle the fence, engaging in the worship of both Jehovah and false gods, no longer limp along between two opinions. They must now decide, take a stand for the LORD and declare the truth, that He and He alone was the true and living God.

But note the response of the people: they stood silent. They said nothing, not a single word. They were completely unwilling to respond to Elijah's challenge. They were unwilling to make a decision for the LORD.

Having presented his call for a decision, Elijah then presented the proposal of a contest to the people, a contest to prove who the true and living God was (vv.22-24). He instructed the people to secure two bulls, one for him and one for the prophets of Baal. Once secured, he and the Baal prophets would prepare their bulls for sacrifice and then place them on the altars. The Baal prophets would then call upon their god and he would call upon the LORD, and whoever sent fire down to consume the sacrifice would be the true and living God (v.24).

Keep in mind that Baal was thought to be the god of fertility and production, the god who controlled the weather, including the clouds, rain, storms, and dew. Of course, if the god of the storm were really the true and living God, he could call down lightning upon the sacrifice to consume it.

OUTLINE	SCRIPTURE	SCRIPTURE	OUTLINE
b. Elijah's challenge to the people: A picture of indecision 1) He rebuked the people for wavering between two opinions: Called upon them to make a decision between the LORD & Baal	21 And Elijah came unto all the people, and said, How long halt ye between two opinions? if the LORD *be* God, follow him: but if Baal, *then* follow him. And the people answered him not a word.	us two bullocks; and let them choose one bullock for themselves, and cut it in pieces, and lay *it* on wood, and put no fire *under:* and I will dress the other bullock, and lay *it* on wood, and put no fire *under:*	two bulls • That he & the Baal prophets prepare a bull for sacrifice & each place his sacrifice on his own altar
2) He presented the proposal of a contest to the people: A contest to prove who the true & living God is • That the people secure	22 Then said Elijah unto the people, I, *even* I only, remain a prophet of the LORD; but Baal's prophets *are* four hundred and fifty men. 23 Let them therefore give	24 And call ye on the name of your gods, and I will call on the name of the LORD: and the God that answereth by fire, let him be God. And all the people answered and said, It is well spoken.	• That the Baal prophets call upon their god & he upon the LORD: Whoever sent fire down to consume the sacrifice would be the true & living God

Thought 1. Note the picture of indecision on the part of the people in this point. This is a strong challenge to us to make a decision for the LORD—in particular if we are engaged in false worship or are attending a church where the Lord Jesus Christ is not honored or the Word of God is not preached. The call of God is for us to make a decision for Christ and to study His Holy Word, learning His commandments and growing into mature believers. God will not tolerate indecision, not for long. It is now time to make a decision for the Lord and to become a follower of His.

(1) God warns us against indecision.

"He that is not with me is against me; and he that gathereth not with me scattereth abroad" (Mt.12:30).

"And Jesus said unto him, No man, having put his hand to the plough, and looking back, is fit for the kingdom of God" (Lu.9:62).

"He that is not with me is against me: and he that gathereth not with me scattereth" Lu.11:23).

"No servant can serve two masters: for either he will hate the one, and love the other; or else he will hold to the one, and despise the other. Ye cannot serve God and mammon" (Lu.16:13).

"A double minded man *is* unstable in all his ways" (Ja.1:8).

"Draw nigh to God, and he will draw nigh to you. Cleanse *your* hands, *ye* sinners; and purify *your* hearts, *ye* double minded" (Ja.4:8).

"And Elijah came unto all the people, and said, How long halt ye between two opinions? if the LORD *be* God, follow him: but if Baal, then follow him. And the people answered him not a word" (1 K.18:21).

"And he did *that which was* right in the sight of the LORD, but not with a perfect heart" (2 Chr.25:2).

"Their heart is divided; now shall they be found faulty: he shall break down their altars, he shall spoil their images" (Ho.10:2).

(2) A decision must be made for the Lord. Now is the time to step forward, professing the LORD and taking a stand for Him.

"Then Jesus beholding him loved him, and said unto him, One thing thou lackest: go thy way, sell whatsoever thou hast, and give to the poor, and thou shalt have treasure in heaven: and come, take up the cross, and follow me" (Mk.10:21).

"Then said Jesus unto the twelve, Will ye also go away?" (Jn.6:67).

"...behold, now *is* the accepted time; behold, now *is* the day of salvation" (2 Co.6:2).

"See, I have set before thee this day life and good, and death and evil" (De.30:15).

"I call heaven and earth to record this day against you, *that* I have set before you life and death, blessing and cursing: therefore choose life, that both thou and thy seed may live" (De.30:19).

"And if it seem evil unto you to serve the LORD, choose you this day whom ye will serve; whether the gods which your fathers served that *were* on the other side of the flood, or the gods of the Amorites, in whose land ye dwell: but as for me and my house, we will serve the LORD" (Jos.24:15).

c. Once the bulls had been brought, Elijah challenged the false prophets of Baal to choose one of the bulls and to prepare it for sacrifice, but not to light the fire under the sacrifice. Accepting the challenge, the false prophets of Baal prepared their sacrifice first then began to pray. Calling on their false god Baal to light the fire, they danced around the altar from morning until noon (vv.25-26). But there was no answer, no response to their prayers. The false god Baal was silent.

Sometime around noon, Elijah began to mock and taunt the false prophets. He suggested they shout louder, for perhaps Baal was meditating, busy at some task, traveling, or off sleeping someplace and needed to be awakened (v.27). Becoming somewhat frantic in their ritual, the false prophets began shouting more loudly and following the ritual custom of cutting themselves and letting their blood flow. This was a symbol of self-sacrifice, which they hoped would arouse their false god Baal to take action. Note that the mutilation of the body, cutting oneself to let the blood flow, was prohibited by the LORD (Le.19:28; De.14:1).

As midday passed, the false prophets continued their frantic, feverish raving until time for the evening sacrifice (v.29).

OUTLINE	SCRIPTURE	SCRIPTURE	OUTLINE
c. Elijah's challenge to the false prophets of Baal: The futility of idolatry & false worship 1) The false prophets of Baal prepared their sacrifice first & began to pray	25 And Elijah said unto the prophets of Baal, Choose you one bullock for yourselves, and dress *it* first; for ye *are* many; and call on the name of your gods, but put no fire *under*.	them, and said, Cry aloud: for he *is* a god; either he is talking, or he is pursuing, or he is in a journey, *or* peradventure he sleepeth, and must be awaked.	suggested Baal might be meditating, busy, traveling, or sleeping
• They prayed—calling on Baal & dancing around the altar—from morning till noon, but there was no answer, no response at all	26 And they took the bullock which was given them, and they dressed *it*, and called on the name of Baal from morning even until noon, saying, O Baal, hear us. But *there was* no voice, nor any that answered. And they leaped upon the altar which was made.	28 And they cried aloud, and cut themselves after their manner with knives and lancets, till the blood gushed out upon them. 29 And it came to pass, when midday was past, and they prophesied until the *time* of the offering of the *evening* sacrifice, that *there was* neither voice, nor any to answer, nor any that regarded.	• They became frantic in their ritual, shouting more loudly & cutting themselves • They continued their feverish raving until time for the evening sacrifice 2) The prophets still received no answer, no response whatsoever
• They were mocked, taunted by Elijah: He	27 And it came to pass at noon, that Elijah mocked		

Thought 1. This is a clear picture of the futility of idolatry and false worship. The prophets of the false god Baal prayed and did all they could to arouse him to action. They even went so far as to mutilate their bodies, shed their own blood in an attempt to propitiate or satisfy the false god Baal. Hoping that the sacrifice of their own blood would make them acceptable to Baal, they continued to mutilate their bodies from noon until midday.

All false gods are just this: false. They are nonexistent, not really living, not possessing life. They are powerless, unable to respond. Being lifeless, they cannot hear prayers nor reach out to help us in our desperate hours of need. False gods are totally incapable of being present with us as we walk day by day. They are unable to guide us or to fulfill any promise ever made by a false prophet. Listen to what the Holy Bible says about idolatry and false worship:

"Forasmuch then as we are the offspring of God, we ought not to think that the Godhead is like unto gold, or silver, or stone, graven by art and man's device" (Ac.17:29).

"Professing themselves to be wise, they became fools, And changed the glory of the uncorruptible God into an image made like to corruptible man, and to birds, and fourfooted beasts, and creeping things" (Ro.1:22-23).

"As concerning therefore the eating of those things that are offered in sacrifice unto idols, we know that an idol *is* nothing in the world, and that *there is* none other God but one" (1 Co.8:4).

"Ye know that ye were Gentiles, carried away unto these dumb idols, even as ye were led" (1 Co.12:2).

"And there ye shall serve gods, the work of men's hands, wood and stone, which neither see, nor hear, nor eat, nor smell" (De.4:28).

"He that *is* so impoverished that he hath no oblation chooseth a tree *that* will not rot; he seeketh unto him a cunning workman to prepare a graven image, *that* shall not be moved" (Is.40:20).

"Who hath formed a god, or molten a graven image *that* is profitable for nothing" (Is.44:10).

"Assemble yourselves and come; draw near together, ye *that are* escaped of the nations: they have no knowledge that set up the wood of their graven image, and pray unto a god *that* cannot save" (Is.45:20).

"They *are* upright as the palm tree, but speak not: they must needs be borne, because they cannot go. Be not afraid of them; for they cannot do evil, neither also *is it* in them to do good" (Je.10:5).

"Every man is brutish by *his* knowledge; every founder is confounded by the graven image: for his molten image *is* falsehood, and *there is* no breath in them" (Je.51:17).

"And now they sin more and more, and have made them molten images of their silver, *and* idols according to their own understanding, all of it the work of the craftsmen: they say of them, Let the men that sacrifice kiss the calves" (Ho.13:2).

"What profiteth the graven image that the maker thereof hath graven it; the molten image, and a teacher of lies, that the maker of his work trusteth therein, to make dumb idols?" (Hab.2:18).

d. Before nightfall, the priests of the false god Baal stepped aside and allowed Elijah to come forth to make his approach to the LORD. Walking to center stage before the massive crowd, Elijah gave a stunning, dramatic vindication of the LORD. He proved that the LORD alone is the living and true God (vv.30-46).

OUTLINE	SCRIPTURE	SCRIPTURE	OUTLINE
d. Elijah's dramatic vindication of the LORD: Proof that He alone is the true & living God 1) Elijah called the people to him as he rebuilt an altar that lay in ruins • Chose 12 stones to represent or symbolize the 12 tribes of Israel	30 And Elijah said unto all the people, Come near unto me. And all the people came near unto him. And he repaired the altar of the LORD *that was* broken down. 31 And Elijah took twelve stones, according to the number of the tribes of the sons of Jacob, unto whom the word of the LORD came, saying, Israel shall be thy name:	sacrifice, and the wood, and the stones, and the dust, and licked up the water that *was* in the trench. 39 And when all the people saw *it,* they fell on their faces: and they said, The LORD, he *is* the God; the LORD, he *is* the God.	• Fire immediately fell & consumed the entire altar, even the water in the trench • The people were stricken with fear: Fell prostrate & confessed that the LORD is God
• Used the stones to build the altar • Dug a large trench around the altar	32 And with the stones he built an altar in the name of the LORD: and he made a trench about the altar, as great as would contain two measures of seed.	40 And Elijah said unto them, Take the prophets of Baal; let not one of them escape. And they took them: and Elijah brought them down to the brook Kishon, and slew them there.	4) Elijah immediately commanded the people to seize & execute the false prophets of Baal: Their evil had ruined the nation, De.7:1-26; 13:1-18; 17:2-5
• Piled wood on the altar • Cut up the bull & laid it on the wood • Had the water from four large water jugs poured on the offering three times—12 large water jugs in total	33 And he put the wood in order, and cut the bullock in pieces, and laid *him* on the wood, and said, Fill four barrels with water, and pour *it* on the burnt sacrifice, and on the wood. 34 And he said, Do *it* the second time. And they did *it* the second time. And he said, Do *it* the third time. And they did *it* the third time.	41 And Elijah said unto Ahab, Get thee up, eat and drink; for *there is* a sound of abundance of rain. 42 So Ahab went up to eat and to drink. And Elijah went up to the top of Carmel; and he cast himself down upon the earth, and put his face between his knees,	5) Elijah fervently prayed for rain • Informed Ahab of coming rain • Climbed to the top of Mount Carmel, bowed down & put his face between his knees, then prayed
• Had the entire altar soaked & the trench filled with water	35 And the water ran round about the altar; and he filled the trench also with water.	43 And said to his servant, Go up now, look toward the sea. And he went up, and looked, and said, *There is* nothing. And he said, Go again seven times.	• Sent his servant to look toward the sea for rain clouds • Continued fervently in prayer: Seven times he sent his servant to look
2) Elijah stepped forward & prayed to the God of Abraham, Isaac, & Jacob (the covenant God): That He would prove Himself • That He alone is God • That Elijah is His servant	36 And it came to pass at *the time of* the offering of the *evening* sacrifice, that Elijah the prophet came near, and said, LORD God of Abraham, Isaac, and of Israel, let it be known this day that thou art God in Israel, and *that* I *am* thy servant, and *that* I have done all these things at thy word.	44 And it came to pass at the seventh time, that he said, Behold, there ariseth a little cloud out of the sea, like a man's hand. And he said, Go up, say unto Ahab, Prepare *thy chariot,* and get thee down, that the rain stop thee not.	6) Elijah again was dramatically heard by the LORD: The seventh time a small cloud had appeared • He warned Ahab to rush back before the torrential downpour caught him
• That the LORD hears & answers the prayers of His people: So the people would know that He is the living God & be stirred to repent	37 Hear me, O LORD, hear me, that this people may know that thou *art* the LORD God, and *that* thou hast turned their heart back again.	45 And it came to pass in the mean while, that the heaven was black with clouds and wind, and there was a great rain. And Ahab rode, and went to Jezreel.	• He & the others witnessed another proof of the only true & living God: Dark clouds & a strong wind appeared
3) Elijah was dramatically heard by the LORD	38 Then the fire of the LORD fell, and consumed the burnt	46 And the hand of the LORD was on Elijah; and he girded up his loins, and ran before Ahab to the entrance of Jezreel.	• He was energized by the LORD & ran ahead of Ahab's chariot all the way to Jezreel: A sign to Ahab to repent

1) Calling the people to come as close as they could, Elijah rebuilt an altar on Mt. Carmel that had been lying in ruins (vv.30-35). Most likely it had been an altar built to worship the LORD Himself, but it had been destroyed during Jezebel's purge. Whatever the case, Elijah chose twelve stones to represent or symbolize the twelve tribes of Israel, and he used the stones to build the altar. Note that he dug a large trench all the way around the altar (v.32). He then piled wood on the altar and cut up the bull and laid it on the wood. With this, the sacrifice would normally have been ready to present to the LORD. But in this case, Elijah surprised the crowd by ordering some men to fill four large water pots and then pour out the water over the offering and the wood. Then, when the men had finished, Elijah instructed them to repeat the procedure. And as if that were not enough, he had them do the same thing a third time. All together, twelve large pots of water had been poured out on the offering and on the wood (vv.33-34). So much water had been poured that the entire altar was soaked and the trench was completely filled with water (v.35).

2) Once the men had completely doused the sacrifice with water, Elijah stepped forward and began to pray to the LORD God of Abraham, Isaac, and Jacob (or Israel); that is, he prayed to the God who had given the covenant to the patriarchs of old (vv.36-37). Note the three things he prayed for:
   ⇒ for the LORD to prove that He alone is God, the God in Israel, the God whom the people of Israel should be worshipping and serving.
   ⇒ for the LORD to prove that Elijah was God's true servant who had been appointed to predict the drought and to presently stand before the people to prove that the LORD was the true and living God.
   ⇒ for the LORD to hear and answer his prayer so the people would know that his God was the living God and be stirred to repent.

3) Suddenly, dramatically, fire fell and consumed not only the sacrifice but also the entire altar, lapping up even the water in the trench. In the most dramatic way possible, the LORD had heard Elijah's prayer and was proving that He and He alone was the living and true God.

   Witnessing the astonishing miracle of the LORD, the people were stricken with a terrifying fear. Falling prostrate upon the ground, the people cried out: "The LORD—He is God! The LORD—He is God!" (v.39).
4) Elijah immediately commanded the people to seize and execute the false prophets of Baal (v.40). Why execute them? Because their terrible sin and evil had ruined the nation and brought catastrophic suffering upon the people. No doubt the prophets were so given over to their false beliefs that they would never repent, never change by turning to the LORD. Instead, they would continue to pollute the land with false beliefs and false worship, deceiving the people and leading them to suffer terrible consequences and eventually eternal doom. (see outline and notes—De.7:1-26; 13:1-18; 17:2-5 for more discussion.)
5) At long last, the drought and famine were to end, for Elijah began to pray fervently for rain (vv.41-43). He instructed Ahab to go off to the side someplace to eat a meal, for there was the sound of a heavy rain off in the distance. While Ahab did as instructed, Elijah climbed to the top of Mt. Carmel. There he bowed down to the ground and put his face between his knees, praying and crying out to the LORD to send rain to end the drought (v.42). Arising, Elijah sent his servant to look toward the Mediterranean Sea for rain clouds. But the servant saw no cloud (v.43). But note what Elijah did: he did not give up; rather, he continued fervently in prayer (v.43). Seven different times he bowed down to the ground and put his face between his knees and continued to cry out to the LORD for rain, to end the drought and famine.
6) After seeking the LORD for the seventh time, Elijah was dramatically heard. The LORD answered his prayer. When the servant returned for the seventh time, he reported that a cloud as small as a man's hand was rising out over the sea (v.44). With this news, Elijah warned Ahab to rush back to the palace before the torrential downpour caught him. As he was speaking, dark clouds began to appear and strong winds began to blow (vv.44-45). Ahab and the massive crowd on Mt. Carmel were witnessing another proof of the LORD'S power and sovereignty: the LORD (Jehovah, Yahweh) was the only living and true God.

   Note that Ahab had jumped in his chariot and headed off toward Jezreel. Running ahead of the chariot was Elijah, who had been energized by the LORD. And he ran all the way to Jezreel which was a distance of thirteen miles. In the words of *The Expositor's Bible Commentary*:

> *What a momentous day it had been for the king! How his head must have reeled with the thoughts of the contest: the pitiful screams of Baal's helpless priests, the calm yet awe-inspiring petition of Elijah, the terrifying and spectacular holocaust that followed, the repentance of the people, and the execution of the pagan prophets! As Ahab rode along through the gathering downpour, the spirit-empowered prophet through whom God had effected his great triumph ran ahead of the royal chariot like a specter (v.46).*[2]

Thought 1. There is no other God but One: the LORD (Jehovah, Yahweh) is the only living and true God. All other gods are false, nonexistent, helpless, and powerless to hear prayers or to answer prayers or to move and act on our behalf. If we are engaged in worshipping false gods, we are left all alone in this world to face the problems and trials, the hardships and misfortunes, the temptations and seductions. We are left all alone to face these difficulties by ourselves. Naturally, if the god we are worshipping is only the god of our imagination, nothing more than a thought in our mind, then that god is lifeless and helpless, unable to save or deliver us in this life and unable to give us life eternal in the next world.

But the LORD (Jehovah, Yahweh) is the living and true God. We know this, for the LORD loves us so much that He has revealed Himself to us. He did not leave us groping and grasping about in the dark, wondering if there really is a true and living God. The LORD is not a God of hate; He is a God of perfect love. And being perfect in love, He has revealed Himself so that we will know the truth, the truth that He exists and has provided salvation for us. God has revealed Himself through the Lord Jesus Christ, by sending Him into the world to save us and to teach us how to live.

Yet God has given us even more than Christ, who is the Living Word. God has given us the written Word, the Holy Bible, which tells us how to live holy and righteous lives. But even this is not all that God has given us: He has also given us His very own Holy Spirit to live within our bodies, once we have accepted Him as our Savior and committed our lives to follow Him. In addition to all these evidences and proofs of the LORD, the LORD has given us changed lives, the testimony of millions of people down through the ages who have been truly and genuinely saved. Millions have experienced a radical change from lives of total wickedness to lives of holiness and righteousness before God.

---

[2] Richard D. Patterson and Hermann J. Austel. *1, 2 Kings*, p.146.

There is only one living and true God, the LORD Himself (Jehovah, Yahweh). Listen to what the Holy Scripture says:

"But Jesus held his peace. And the high priest answered and said unto him, I adjure thee by the living God, that thou tell us whether thou be the Christ, the Son of God. Jesus saith unto him, Thou hast said: nevertheless I say unto you, Hereafter shall ye see the Son of man sitting on the right hand of power, and coming in the clouds of heaven" (Mt.26:63-64).

"And saying, Sirs, why do ye these things? We also are men of like passions with you, and preach unto you that ye should turn from these vanities unto the living God, which made heaven, and earth, and the sea, and all things that are therein" (Ac.14:15).

"God that made the world and all things therein, seeing that he is Lord of heaven and earth, dwelleth not in temples made with hands" (Ac.17:24).

"For they themselves show of us what manner of entering in we had unto you, and how ye turned to God from idols to serve the living and true God; And to wait for his Son from heaven, whom he raised from the dead, *even* Jesus, which delivered us from the wrath to come" (1 Th.1:9-10).

"He that despised Moses' law died without mercy under two or three witnesses: Of how much sorer punishment, suppose ye, shall he be thought worthy, who hath trodden under foot the Son of God, and hath counted the blood of the covenant, wherewith he was sanctified, an unholy thing, and hath done despite unto the Spirit of grace? For we know him that hath said, Vengeance *belongeth* unto me, I will recompense, saith the Lord. And again, The Lord shall judge his people. *It is* a fearful thing to fall into the hands of the living God" (He.10:28-31).

"Through faith we understand that the worlds were framed by the word of God, so that things which are seen were not made of things which do appear" (He.11:3).

"For so an entrance shall be ministered unto you abundantly into the everlasting kingdom of our Lord and Saviour Jesus Christ" (2 Pe.1:11).

"I am Alpha and Omega, the beginning and the ending, saith the Lord, which is, and which was, and which is to come, the Almighty" (Re.1:8).

"In the beginning God created the heaven and the earth" (Ge.1:1).

"For I lift up my hand to heaven, and say, I live for ever" (De.32:40).

"The eternal God *is thy* refuge, and underneath *are* the everlasting arms: and he shall thrust out the enemy from before thee; and shall say, Destroy *them*" (De.33:27).

"Thou, *even* thou, *art* LORD alone; thou hast made heaven, the heaven of heavens, with all their host, the earth, and all *things* that *are* therein, the seas, and all that *is* therein, and thou preservest them all; and the host of heaven worshippeth thee" (Ne.9:6).

"Who knoweth not in all these that the hand of the LORD hath wrought this?" (Jb.12:9).

"He stretcheth out the north over the empty place, *and* hangeth the earth upon nothing" (Jb.26:7).

"When I consider thy heavens, the work of thy fingers, the moon and the stars, which thou hast ordained; What is man, that thou art mindful of him? and the son of man, that thou visitest him?" (Ps.8:3-4).

"The heavens declare the glory of God; and the firmament showeth his handywork" (Ps.19:1).

"My soul thirsteth for God, for the living God: when shall I come and appear before God?" (Ps.42:2).

"My soul longeth, yea, even fainteth for the courts of the LORD: my heart and my flesh crieth out for the living God" (Ps.84:2).

"Of old hast thou laid the foundation of the earth: and the heavens *are* the work of thy hands" (Ps.102:25).

"Thy name, O LORD, *endureth* for ever; *and* thy memorial, O LORD, throughout all generations" (Ps.135:13).

"I will praise thee; for I am fearfully *and* wonderfully made: marvellous *are* thy works; and *that* my soul knoweth right well" (Ps.139:14).

"Thy kingdom *is* an everlasting kingdom, and thy dominion *endureth* throughout all generations" (Ps.145:13).

"He hath made every *thing* beautiful in his time: also he hath set the world in their heart, so that no man can find out the work that God maketh from the beginning to the end" (Ec.3:11).

"I make a decree, That in every dominion of my kingdom men tremble and fear before the God of Daniel: for he is the living God, and stedfast for ever, and his kingdom *that* which shall not be destroyed, and his dominion *shall be even* unto the end" (Da.6:26).

1. Elijah's flight from Jezebel: Discouraged, disappointed
- a. Ahab reported the miraculous events to Jezebel: Failed to stir them to repentance, to turn from Baal to God, 18:17-46
- b. Jezebel became furious: Sent a messenger to Elijah, threatening his life
- c. Elijah fled for his life
  - 1) Fled south to Beersheba & left his servant there
  - 2) Fled into the desert
  - 3) Sat down under a tree
  - 4) Began to pray
    - "Take me: Let me die"
    - "I have had enough": Was worn out, disappointed, discouraged, felt like a failure
  - 5) Lay down—exhausted—& fell asleep
  - 6) Was awakened & fed by an angel
  - 7) Lay down & fell asleep again
  - 8) Was awakened & fed a second time by the angel of the LORD
  - 9) Was strengthened enough to travel 40 days & nights to Mount Horeb or Sinai (where God had called Moses & given the law to Israel, Ex.3-4; 20-24)

2. Elijah's encounter with the LORD: Encouraged, challenged
- a. The LORD confronted Elijah
  - 1) God's question: What was he doing there at Mt. Sinai?
  - 2) Elijah's response: He had faithfully served the LORD, but the people had not responded
    - They had rejected God's

CHAPTER 19

C. The Escape of Elijah from Jezebel: Being Saved by the Living God from Disappointment, Discouragement, & Despair, 19:1-21

And Ahab told Jezebel all
that Elijah had done, and
withal how he had slain
all the prophets with the
sword.
2 Then Jezebel sent a messenger unto Elijah, saying, So
let the gods do *to me,* and
more also, if I make not thy
life as the life of one of them
by to morrow about this time.
3 And when he saw *that,* he
arose, and went for his life,
and came to Beer-sheba,
which *belongeth* to Judah,
and left his servant there.
4 But he himself went a day's
journey into the wilderness,
and came and sat down under
a juniper tree: and he requested for himself that he
might die; and said, It is
enough; now, O LORD, take
away my life; for I *am* not
better than my fathers.
5 And as he lay and slept under a juniper tree, behold,
then an angel touched him,
and said unto him, Arise *and*
eat.
6 And he looked, and, behold, *there was* a cake baken
on the coals, and a cruse of
water at his head. And he did
eat and drink, and laid him
down again.
7 And the angel of the LORD
came again the second
time, and touched him, and
said, Arise *and* eat; because
the journey *is* too great for
thee.
8 And he arose, and did
eat and drink, and went in
the strength of that meat
forty days and forty nights
unto Horeb the mount of
God.
9 And he came thither unto a
cave, and lodged there; and,
behold, the word of the LORD
came to him, and he said unto him, What doest thou here,
Elijah?
10 And he said, I have been
very jealous for the LORD
God of hosts: for the children
of Israel have forsaken thy
covenant, thrown down thine
altars, and slain thy prophets
with the sword; and I, *even* I
only, am left; and they seek
my life, to take it away.
11 And he said, Go forth,
and stand upon the mount before the LORD. And, behold,
the LORD passed by, and a
great and strong wind rent
the mountains, and brake in
pieces the rocks before the
LORD; *but* the LORD *was* not
in the wind: and after the
wind an earthquake; *but* the
LORD *was* not in the earthquake:
12 And after the earthquake
a fire; *but* the LORD *was* not
in the fire: and after the fire a
still small voice.
13 And it was *so,* when Elijah heard *it,* that he wrapped
his face in his mantle, and
went out, and stood in the
entering in of the cave.
And, behold, *there came*
a voice unto him, and
said, What doest thou here,
Elijah?
14 And he said, I have been
very jealous for the LORD
God of hosts: because the
children of Israel have forsaken thy covenant, thrown
down thine altars, and slain
thy prophets with the sword;
and I, *even* I only, am left;
and they seek my life, to take
it away.
15 And the LORD said unto
him, Go, return on thy way to
the wilderness of Damascus:
and when thou comest,
anoint Hazael *to be* king over
Syria:
16 And Jehu the son of Nimshi shalt thou anoint *to be*
king over Israel: and Elisha
the son of Shaphat of Abel-meholah shalt thou anoint *to
be* prophet in thy room.
17 And it shall come to pass,
that him that escapeth the
sword of Hazael shall Jehu
slay: and him that escapeth
from the sword of Jehu shall
Elisha slay.
18 Yet I have left *me* seven
thousand in Israel, all the
knees which have not bowed
unto Baal, and every mouth
which hath not kissed him.
19 So he departed thence,
and found Elisha the son of
Shaphat, who *was* plowing
with twelve yoke *of oxen* before him, and he with the
twelfth: and Elijah passed by

covenant, destroyed His worship centers, & killed the prophets
- He alone was left
- b. The LORD invited Elijah to come out of the cave & to stand in His presence
  - 1) Suddenly, several spectacular events occurred: But God was not present, did not meet Elijah's need through them
    - A ferocious wind split the mountains & shattered the rocks
    - An earthquake struck
    - A fire erupted
  - 2) Some time later, there was a quiet, gentle whisper
    - Elijah heard the whisper
    - Elijah—ashamed, humbled, broken—pulled his cloak over his face
- c. The LORD repeated His question
  - 1) The question: What was Elijah doing there?
  - 2) Elijah's response: Was the same as before
- d. The LORD met Elijah's need: Gave him a new task & encouraged him
  - 1) The task
    - To anoint Hazael as king of Aram or Syria
    - To anoint Jehu as king of Israel
    - To anoint Elisha as his own successor
  - 2) The reason: These three leaders would complete the task that Elijah had begun, the task of purging Baal worship
- e. The LORD corrected & encouraged Elijah even more: Revealed that He had preserved 7000 faithful followers

3. Elijah's call to Elisha: Surrendered, obeyed
- a. Elijah appointed Elisha
  - 1) Found him working
  - 2) Threw his cloak around the unexpectant Elisha: A

symbol of God's call to be Elijah's successor b. Elisha responded immediately to God's call 1) Ran after Elijah & requested time to say farewell to his father & mother 2) Was granted permission, but he must consider his call	him, and cast his mantle upon him. 20 And he left the oxen, and ran after Elijah, and said, Let me, I pray thee, kiss my father and my mother, and *then* I will follow thee. And he said unto him, Go back again: for what have I done to thee?	21 And he returned back from him, and took a yoke of oxen, and slew them, and boiled their flesh with the instruments of the oxen, and gave unto the people, and they did eat. Then he arose, and went after Elijah, and ministered unto him.	3) Returned briefly to his family • Slaughtered his oxen & burned the plowing equipment: A symbol of breaking with his old life & beginning a new life • Enjoyed a final meal with family & friends 4) Set out to join Elijah

DIVISION III

THE MINISTRY OF ELIJAH AND OTHER PROPHETS DURING THE REIGN OF AHAB: LEARNING WHO THE LIVING AND TRUE GOD IS, 17:1–22:53

C. The Escape of Elijah from Jezebel: Being Saved by the Living God from Disappointment, Discouragement, and Despair, 19:1-21

(19:1-21) **Introduction**: How often have you faced disappointment? Discouragement? Despair? At one time or another, every human being faces disappointment. And most of us have felt discouraged at some point in our lives. But despair and despondency are emotions that fewer of us experience. Sometimes a person's despair can be so deep that he or she loses heart and feels utterly hopeless. Under the weight and burden of despair, the person's heart begins to faint and to sense total defeat. Such feelings can lead to long periods of depression and sometimes even to suicide.

This is the practical subject being discussed in the present Scripture. One of the strongest men to ever serve God, the prophet Elijah, was gripped by a spirit of discouragement and despair. But the wonderful news that was proclaimed to him and is still being proclaimed to us today is this: the LORD will meet our need and deliver us from the spirit of discouragement and despair. Empowering us to conquer these crises in life, the LORD will save and deliver us. This is: *The Escape of Elijah from Jezebel: Being Saved by the Living God from Disappointment, Discouragement, and Despair,* 19:1-21.

1. Elijah's flight from Jezebel: discouraged, disappointed (vv.1-8).
2. Elijah's encounter with the LORD: encouraged, challenged (vv.9-18).
3. Elijah's call to Elisha: surrendered, obeyed (vv.19-21).

1 (19:1-8) **Discouragement, Example of—Disappointment, Example of—Distress, Example of—Depression, Example of—Despondency, Example of—Hopelessness, Example of—Elijah, Discouragement of—Jezebel, Evil of, Threatened Elijah**: there was Elijah's flight from Jezebel, a flight filled with deep disappointment and discouragement. Apparently King Ahab and his infamous queen Jezebel had a second home in Jezreel. Remember that Elijah had just confronted the prophets of Baal on Mt. Carmel, proving that the LORD (Jehovah, Yahweh) is the only true and living God. After the LORD had sent a bolt of lightning to set the sacrifice of Elijah ablaze, the fire had burned up not only the sacrifice but also the entire altar. The flame had even lapped up the water that had filled the trench around the altar. Also remember that in answer to Elijah's prayer, the LORD had sent a downpour of rain upon the drought-stricken earth. The closing scene of the former chapter showed Ahab and his chariot rushing back to Jezreel, with Elijah running ahead of the chariot. Now note what happened when Ahab rushed in to tell Jezebel about the spectacular events that had just happened.

OUTLINE	SCRIPTURE	SCRIPTURE	OUTLINE
1. Elijah's flight from Jezebel: Discouraged, disappointed a. Ahab reported the miraculous events to Jezebel: Failed to stir them to repentance, to turn from Baal to God, 18:17-46 b. Jezebel became furious: Sent a messenger to Elijah, threatening his life c. Elijah fled for his life 1) Fled south to Beersheba & left his servant there 2) Fled into the desert	And Ahab told Jezebel all that Elijah had done, and withal how he had slain all the prophets with the sword. 2 Then Jezebel sent a messenger unto Elijah, saying, So let the gods do *to me,* and more also, if I make not thy life as the life of one of them by to morrow about this time. 3 And when he saw *that,* he arose, and went for his life, and came to Beer-sheba, which *belongeth* to Judah, and left his servant there. 4 But he himself went a day's	journey into the wilderness, and came and sat down under a juniper tree: and he requested for himself that he might die; and said, It is enough; now, O LORD, take away my life; for I *am* not better than my fathers. 5 And as he lay and slept under a juniper tree, behold, then an angel touched him, and said unto him, Arise *and* eat. 6 And he looked, and, behold, *there was* a cake baken on the coals, and a cruse of water at his head. And he did eat and drink, and laid him	3) Sat down under a tree 4) Began to pray • "Take me: Let me die" • "I have had enough": Was worn out, disappointed, discouraged, felt like a failure 5) Lay down—exhausted—& fell asleep 6) Was awakened & fed by an angel 7) Lay down & fell asleep

OUTLINE	SCRIPTURE	SCRIPTURE	OUTLINE
again 8) Was awakened & fed a second time by the angel of the LORD	down again. 7 And the angel of the LORD came again the second time, and touched him, and said, Arise *and* eat; because the journey *is* too great for thee.	8 And he arose, and did eat and drink, and went in the strength of that meat forty days and forty nights unto Horeb the mount of God.	9) Was strengthened enough to travel 40 days & nights to Mount Horeb or Sinai (where God had called Moses & given the law to Israel, Ex.3-4; 20-24)

a. Ahab reported the miraculous events to Jezebel, but he attributed the miracles to Elijah instead of to God. Then in an accusing tone he laid the blame for killing all the prophets upon Elijah (v.1). Neither the king nor the queen was moved to repent by the spectacular demonstration of God's power. They were not ready to repent, not ready to turn from their wicked behavior and false worship.

b. Upon hearing the report, Jezebel became furious and immediately sent out a messenger to Elijah, threatening his life (v.2). Hearing from Ahab that the people had now rallied behind Elijah and the LORD, Jezebel was unable to arrest and execute Elijah. But note what she did: she gave him twenty-four hours to leave town or else be killed. By letting Elijah know he was the target of her wrath, she felt he would flee for his life and, by fleeing, would discredit himself before the people. Being unable to kill Elijah, Jezebel concluded that driving him away would be the next best thing. Once Elijah was discredited, she felt that the people would return their loyalty to the king. She could reestablish their loyalty by leading them to return to the worship of her god, the false god Baal.

c. Just as Jezebel had hoped, Elijah fled for his life (vv.3-8). When he had gone as far south as Beersheba, he left his servant there, not wishing to jeopardize his life any further. In addition, Elijah almost certainly wished to be alone, as the following verses indicate.

Elijah traveled another day into the desert and eventually sat down under a broom tree (v.4). Growing to a height of about ten feet, the broom tree provided some shade for the weary traveler. Sitting and resting under its branches, Elijah began to pray for the LORD to take him, to let him die. Note that he told the LORD he had reached the end. He had had enough. Such a confession from a believer is a strong indication of being totally worn out, disappointed, or discouraged. In the case of this dear man of God, all three emotions were obviously being experienced: he was physically and mentally exhausted, and he was disappointed and discouraged at the king's and the people's hard hearts. He felt as though he had failed in his ministry, that he had achieved no more than his ancestors had, which was almost nothing. Consequently, the LORD may as well take him, for his life was of no more value on earth.

Obviously, Elijah had expected a far more positive response from King Ahab and the people. It was only natural for him to expect King Ahab to force Jezebel to withdraw her purge of the LORD'S prophets and the people's worship of the LORD. But in neither case did Ahab act. Refusing to repent before the LORD—the LORD who had given such strong evidence that He alone is the only true and living God—Ahab allowed Jezebel to continue her purge. And now the queen was after his (Elijah's) life.

Utterly exhausted, Elijah could pray no more; thus he lay down and fell fast asleep (v.5). Some time later, an angel awakened him, commanding him to get up and eat. The angel had apparently provided a cake of bread that had been baked over hot coals. In addition, there was a jar of water to quench his thirst. Note how God provided for His dear servant just as He had done earlier, right after Elijah's first confrontation with Ahab when he predicted the drought (17:2-16).

Even after eating, Elijah was still utterly exhausted. So he again lay down and fell asleep (v.6). A short time later, the angel awoke him a second time and fed him (v.7). Strengthened by the additional food, Elijah set out and traveled some forty days and nights to Mt. Horeb, which is Mt. Sinai. This was the very the mountain of God Himself, the mountain where the LORD had called Moses and given the law to Israel (Ex. ch.3-4; 20-24).

Thought 1. One of the hardest feelings for a person to deal with is failure. Whether the failure is real, imagined, or exaggerated, in our eyes alone or in the eyes of many, it is a crushing blow to a person's sense of worth. The sense of having failed can lead someone to despair, to sink into depression, even to contemplate and carry out suicide. Just think of the everyday situations that can bring about a sense of failure:

⇒ being part of a failing marriage
⇒ getting divorced or separated
⇒ being a single parent
⇒ losing employment
⇒ being unable to find employment
⇒ being unable to support your family
⇒ not being recognized or promoted at work
⇒ not having the right kind of job
⇒ failing to make good grades in school
⇒ dropping out of school
⇒ being addicted to drugs, alcohol, or smoking
⇒ feeling powerless to help a loved one who is sick or in trouble
⇒ not being popular enough
⇒ not being attractive enough
⇒ not being athletic enough
⇒ not being smart enough
⇒ not being rich enough
⇒ not being good enough

On and on the list could go. But like Elijah, if we will turn to the LORD in our time of need, God will hear our cry and meet our need.

Elijah had experienced both victory and defeat as God's prophet. But when his life and his task were too heavy to bear, it was to the LORD that he turned. And the LORD met Elijah *where he was* and took care of his every need. Just as the LORD met Elijah and provided for his need during his crisis, so the LORD will meet us and provide for us. If we will just pray as Elijah did, the LORD will meet our need. He will provide for us in our moments of discouragement, despair, and hopelessness. The LORD will not leave us destitute, without help, having to bear the suffering all by ourselves.

"But the very hairs of your head are all numbered. Fear ye not therefore, ye are of more value than many sparrows" (Mt.10:30-31).

"And suddenly there came a sound from heaven as of a rushing mighty wind, and it filled all the house where they were sitting. And there appeared unto them cloven tongues like as of fire, and it sat upon each of them" (Ac.2:2-3).

"For the cloud of the LORD *was* upon the tabernacle by day, and fire was on it by night, in the sight of all the house of Israel, throughout all their journeys" (Ex.40:38).

"Fear thou not; for I *am* with thee: be not dismayed; for I *am* thy God: I will strengthen thee; yea, I will help thee; yea, I will uphold thee with the right hand of my righteousness" (Is.41:10).

"For I the LORD thy God will hold thy right hand, saying unto thee, Fear not; I will help thee" (Is.41:13).

"Fear not: for I have redeemed thee, I have called *thee* by thy name; thou *art* mine. When thou passest through the waters, I *will be* with thee; and through the rivers, they shall not overflow thee: when thou walkest through the fire, thou shalt not be burned; neither shall the flame kindle upon thee" (Is.43:1-2).

"And his feet shall stand in that day upon the mount of Olives, which *is* before Jerusalem on the east, and the mount of Olives shall cleave in the midst thereof toward the east and toward the west, *and there shall be* a very great valley; and half of the mountain shall remove toward the north, and half of it toward the south. And ye shall flee *to* the valley of the mountains; for the valley of the mountains shall reach unto Azal: yea, ye shall flee, like as ye fled from before the earthquake in the days of Uzziah king of Judah: and the LORD my God shall come, *and* all the saints with thee" (Zec.14:4-5).

2 (19:9-18) **Encouragement, Example of—Discouragement, How to Conquer—Disappointment, How to Conquer—Despair, How to Conquer—Needs, Met by, God—Hopelessness, Deliverance from—Word of God, Power of:** there was Elijah's encounter with the LORD, an encounter that encouraged and challenged the dear prophet of God. After arriving at Mt. Sinai, Elijah went into a cave. In the Hebrew, the definite article "the" is used to indicate "the cave." This fact could be significant, for it could be referring to some particular cave that Moses had used when he was confronted by God on Mt. Sinai (see outline and notes—Ex.19:1-25 for more discussion). Whatever the case, Elijah went into a particular cave and spent the night. What then happened is a strong encouragement to the heart of any believer who is experiencing discouragement, despair, or hopelessness. Scripture graphically describes Elijah's experience:

OUTLINE	SCRIPTURE	SCRIPTURE	OUTLINE
2. Elijah's encounter with the LORD: Encouraged, challenged a. The LORD confronted Elijah 1) God's question: What was he doing there at Mt. Sinai? 2) Elijah's response: He had faithfully served the LORD, but the people had not responded • They had rejected God's covenant, destroyed His worship centers, & killed the prophets • He alone was left b. The LORD invited Elijah to come out of the cave & to stand in His presence 1) Suddenly, several spectacular events occurred: But God was not present, did not meet Elijah's need through them • A ferocious wind split the mountains & shattered the rocks • An earthquake struck • A fire erupted 2) Some time later, there was a quiet, gentle whisper	9 And he came thither unto a cave, and lodged there; and, behold, the word of the LORD *came* to him, and he said unto him, What doest thou here, Elijah? 10 And he said, I have been very jealous for the LORD God of hosts: for the children of Israel have forsaken thy covenant, thrown down thine altars, and slain thy prophets with the sword; and I, *even* I only, am left; and they seek my life, to take it away. 11 And he said, Go forth, and stand upon the mount before the LORD. And, behold, the LORD passed by, and a great and strong wind rent the mountains, and brake in pieces the rocks before the LORD; *but* the LORD *was* not in the wind: and after the wind an earthquake; *but* the LORD *was* not in the earthquake: 12 And after the earthquake a fire; *but* the LORD *was* not in the fire: and after the fire a still small voice.	13 And it was *so,* when Elijah heard *it,* that he wrapped his face in his mantle, and went out, and stood in the entering in of the cave. And, behold, *there came* a voice unto him, and said, What doest thou here, Elijah? 14 And he said, I have been very jealous for the LORD God of hosts: because the children of Israel have forsaken thy covenant, thrown down thine altars, and slain thy prophets with the sword; and I, *even* I only, am left; and they seek my life, to take it away. 15 And the LORD said unto him, Go, return on thy way to the wilderness of Damascus: and when thou comest, anoint Hazael *to be* king over Syria: 16 And Jehu the son of Nimshi shalt thou anoint *to be* king over Israel: and Elisha the son of Shaphat of Abelmeholah shalt thou anoint *to be* prophet in thy room. 17 And it shall come to pass,	• Elijah heard the whisper • Elijah—ashamed, humbled, broken—pulled his cloak over his face c. The LORD repeated His question 1) The question: What was Elijah doing there? 2) Elijah's response: Was the same as before d. The LORD met Elijah's need: Gave him a new task & encouraged him 1) The task • To anoint Hazael as king of Aram or Syria • To anoint Jehu as king of Israel • To anoint Elisha as his own successor 2) The reason: These three

OUTLINE	SCRIPTURE	SCRIPTURE	OUTLINE
leaders would complete the task that Elijah had begun, the task of purging Baal worship	*that* him that escapeth the sword of Hazael shall Jehu slay: and him that escapeth from the sword of Jehu shall Elisha slay.	18 Yet I have left *me* seven thousand in Israel, all the knees which have not bowed unto Baal, and every mouth which hath not kissed him.	e. The LORD corrected & encouraged Elijah even more: Revealed that He had preserved 7000 faithful followers

a. Either while he was sleeping or right after he awoke, Elijah was confronted by the LORD with a very specific question: What was he doing there at Mt. Sinai (vv.9-10)? Filled with despair, Elijah responded that he had faithfully served the LORD, but the people had not responded to his challenge. Instead, they had rejected God's covenant, destroying His worship centers and killing the LORD'S prophets. Now only he was left among God's prophets, and the Israelites were trying to kill him too.

Note how Elijah felt all alone, as though he were the only person in the nation who was serving God. He felt defenseless, helpless against the threat of the evil Queen Jezebel. His discouragement was blinding him to the truth of God's presence and His power to deliver His people from the hands of all enemies.

b. Not responding to Elijah's complaint, the LORD invited His dear servant to come out of the cave and stand in His presence (vv.11-13). Once outside, several spectacular events occurred rapidly. But note: God was not present. He did not meet Elijah's need through these spectacular events.

⇒ A ferocious windstorm struck the mountains, a windstorm so fierce that the mountains were split apart and rocks were shattered. But the LORD's presence was not in the wind.

⇒ After the windstorm, an earthquake shook the mountain. But again, the LORD's presence was not in the earthquake.

⇒ After the earthquake, a blazing fire erupted on the mountain. But the LORD was not in the dramatic fire (v.12). In past history, the LORD had used all three of these events to symbolize His presence (Ex.19:16-18; Jud.5:4-5; 2 S.22:8-16; Ps.18:7-15; 68:8; He.12:18). But not this time, not in confronting Elijah. Why? Because Elijah was being used by God to perform spectacular miracles before the people as a demonstration of God's enormous power, events to prove that the LORD is the only true and living God. Obviously, Elijah had begun to depend upon the sensational and to expect repentance due to the amazing events. But it is seldom God's way to reach people through incredible demonstrations of His power. Usually, He moves upon hearts with a still small voice. This, Elijah had to learn.

Some time after the spectacular events, there was the quiet, gentle whisper of God's voice (vv.12-13). During the whisper, Elijah was gripped with shame and humbled himself before the LORD. Broken, he pulled his cloak over his face. Slowly but surely, Elijah was learning the great lesson that God reveals Himself by speaking to the spirit, the heart of man. And it is through the movement of the heart that God convicts and moves a person to repentance. Elijah should not expect people to respond to events such as windstorms, earthquakes, and fires just because they are extraordinary or sensational. For it was the Voice, the Word of God, that convicted people and aroused them to forsake their sin and turn to Him. The lesson was clear: it would be His Word that would change the hearts of the people. Thus, what the people needed was the Word of the LORD proclaimed by Elijah. If Elijah would arise and go forth carrying the voice of God—His Holy Word—to the people, they would respond. At least some of them would.

c. To stir Elijah to arise and return to the people with a new mission, the LORD forcefully repeated His question. Once again He asked Elijah what he was doing there at Mt. Sinai. Still not aroused, Elijah responded the very same as he had before: he had been very zealous in serving the LORD God Almighty, the God of hosts. But the Israelites had rejected God's covenant, destroyed His worship centers, and killed God's prophets (vv.13-14). Then with the same spirit of hopelessness still gripping his soul, Elijah responded once again that he alone was left and that the Israelites were now trying to kill him as well.

d. With compassion and gentleness, the LORD met Elijah's need: He gave him a new task and encouraged him (vv.15-17). With obvious intensity and power in His voice, the LORD instructed Elijah to get up and go back the very same way he had come, going to the Desert of Damascus. There he was to anoint Hazael as king of Aram or Syria. Then he was to anoint Jehu as king over Israel. Finally, he was to anoint Elisha as his own successor. Note why: these three leaders would complete the task that Elijah had begun, the task of purging Baal worship from the land (v.17). What a word of encouragement to God's dear servant! His mission had not been a failure; it was being carried out *step by step* by the power of the LORD Himself as he appointed other leaders to continue the task.

e. Also note that the LORD corrected and encouraged Elijah even more by revealing that he was not alone, not the only believer who was fully and totally committed to the LORD. In fact, there were 7,000 other faithful followers of the LORD who had never bowed the knee to engage in the false worship of Baal (v.18).

Thought 1. Experiencing discouragement, despair, and hopelessness, losing heart and running away from the LORD—all these emotions were flooding Elijah's mind, body, and soul, coursing through his very veins. He desperately needed to be encouraged and rechallenged by the LORD. He needed to know that he had not been a failure in the task assigned to him. And he needed a new task, a renewed purpose in order to continue ministering.

God met Elijah's need and He will meet our need. For no matter what we experience, God never leaves us alone. He is always present to encourage us and to guide us as we walk step-by-step. God will strengthen us to conquer discouragement and all other emotions that break us and pull us down. God will not leave us down, dejected, and defeated, wondering what is the sense of continuing on with life. Therefore, in such discouraging moments, we must learn to turn to the LORD. Crying out to Him in prayer, we must lay the burdens of our heart upon Him. If we will open up and reveal our true emotions to Him, He will bring peace and encouragement to our hearts. Either He will confirm that the path we are walking or the mission we have undertaken is correct or He will give us a whole new mission and purpose in life.

Once we have prayed, we must turn to the Word of God and find out how He tells us to live. And we must live exactly as He says. If we are searching His Word and living as He says, obeying and following His commandments, praying and seeking His face day by day, the LORD will be present with us and guide us step-by-step. We will come to know the victorious life, conquering all the discouraging, despairing trials of life. No hardship or misfortune will overcome us. But through Christ, we will become "more than conquerors" (Ro.8:37).

"But the very hairs of your head are all numbered. Fear ye not therefore, ye are of more value than many sparrows" (Mt.10:30-31).

"Ye have not chosen me, but I have chosen you, and ordained you, that ye should go and bring forth fruit, and *that* your fruit should remain: that whatsoever ye shall ask of the Father in my name, he may give it you" (Jn.15:16).

"There hath no temptation taken you but such as is common to man: but God *is* faithful, who will not suffer you to be tempted above that ye are able; but will with the temptation also make a way to escape, that ye may be able to bear *it*" (1 Co.10:13).

"For the which cause I also suffer these things: nevertheless I am not ashamed: for I know whom I have believed, and am persuaded that he is able to keep that which I have committed unto him against that day" (2 Ti.1:12).

"And the Lord shall deliver me from every evil work, and will preserve *me* unto his heavenly kingdom: to whom *be* glory for ever and ever. Amen" (2 Ti.4:18).

"Casting all your care upon him; for he careth for you" (1 Pe.5:7).

"And, behold, I *am* with thee, and will keep thee in all *places* whither thou goest, and will bring thee again into this land; for I will not leave thee, until I have done *that* which I have spoken to thee of" (Ge.28:15).

"The eternal God *is thy* refuge, and underneath *are* the everlasting arms: and he shall thrust out the enemy from before thee; and shall say, Destroy *them*" (De.33:27).

"For the eyes of the LORD run to and fro throughout the whole earth, to show himself strong in the behalf of *them* whose heart *is* perfect toward him. Herein thou hast done foolishly: therefore from henceforth thou shalt have wars" (2 Chr.16:9).

"Thou hast also given me the shield of thy salvation: and thy right hand hath holden me up, and thy gentleness hath made me great" (Ps.18:35).

"The angel of the LORD encampeth round about them that fear him, and delivereth them" (Ps.34:7).

"He shall cover thee with his feathers, and under his wings shalt thou trust: his truth *shall be thy* shield and buckler" (Ps.91:4).

"The LORD hath been mindful of us: he will bless *us;* he will bless the house of Israel; he will bless the house of Aaron" (Ps.115:12).

"Behold, he that keepeth Israel shall neither slumber nor sleep " (Ps.121:4).

"Fear thou not; for I *am* with thee: be not dismayed; for I *am* thy God: I will strengthen thee; yea, I will help thee; yea, I will uphold thee with the right hand of my righteousness" (Is.41:10).

"For I the LORD thy God will hold thy right hand, saying unto thee, Fear not; I will help thee" (Is.41:13).

"Fear not: for I have redeemed thee, I have called *thee* by thy name; thou *art* mine. When thou passest through the waters, I *will be* with thee; and through the rivers, they shall not overflow thee: when thou walkest through the fire, thou shalt not be burned; neither shall the flame kindle upon thee" (Is.43:1-3).

"And *even* to *your* old age I *am* he; and *even* to hoar [gray] hairs will I carry *you:* I have made, and I will bear; even I will carry, and will deliver *you*" (Is.46:4).

3 (19:19-21) **Surrender, to the LORD, Example of—Call, of God, Surrender to—Elisha, Call of—Elijah, Mission of**: there was Elijah's call to Elisha, a call that demanded surrender and obedience to the LORD. Heeding the command of God, Elijah left Mt. Sinai and struck out to pursue the new mission God had given him. First, he went to Elisha to issue the most important call assigned him, the call of his replacement. When he found Elisha, the young man was not idle but, rather, working hard in the fields plowing (v.19). Walking up to the young man, Elijah unexpectedly threw his cloak around Elisha. And then, instead of stopping, Elijah continued on his journey, leaving it up to Elisha to decide whether or not to follow him. Throwing the cloak around the shoulders of a person was a symbol of God's call. In this case, it was a symbol that the young man was to be Elijah's successor, that he was being chosen to bear the mission of the prophet.

Responding immediately to God's call, Elisha ran after Elijah and requested time to say farewell to his father and mother (vv.20-21). Elijah granted him permission to say his farewells, but he strongly encouraged Elisha to consider God's call, not to change his mind (v.20).

With permission granted, the young appointee returned briefly to his family to celebrate his appointment and departure with a final meal (v.21). Note what else Elisha did: as a symbol of turning from his old life to a new life, he slaughtered his oxen and burned the plowing equipment. He was definitely breaking with his old life and beginning a new service for the LORD. Sitting down with his family and friends, he enjoyed a final meal with them. Then he set out to join Elijah to become his successor-in-training.

OUTLINE	SCRIPTURE	SCRIPTURE	OUTLINE
3. Elijah's call to Elisha: Surrendered, obeyed a. Elijah appointed Elisha 1) Found him working 2) Threw his cloak around the unexpectant Elisha: A symbol of God's call to be Elijah's successor b. Elisha responded immediately to God's call 1) Ran after Elijah & requested time to say farewell to his father &	19 So he departed thence, and found Elisha the son of Shaphat, who *was* plowing *with* twelve yoke *of oxen* before him, and he with the twelfth: and Elijah passed by him, and cast his mantle upon him. 20 And he left the oxen, and ran after Elijah, and said, Let me, I pray thee, kiss my father and my mother, and *then* I will follow thee. And he	said unto him, Go back again: for what have I done to thee? 21 And he returned back from him, and took a yoke of oxen, and slew them, and boiled their flesh with the instruments of the oxen, and gave unto the people, and they did eat. Then he arose, and went after Elijah, and ministered unto him.	mother 2) Was granted permission, but he must consider his call 3) Returned briefly to his family • Slaughtered his oxen & burned the plowing equipment: A symbol of breaking with his old life & beginning a new life • Enjoyed a final meal with family & friends 4) Set out to join Elijah

Thought 1. When God calls us to a particular task, we must surrender to His call. We must obey Him. No greater joy exists upon this earth than the joy of serving the LORD. Think of the joy we experience when we serve or meet the needs of another person:

⇒ The joy of giving a toy to a child who has nothing.
⇒ The joy of visiting a lonely orphan, widow, or widower.
⇒ The joy of encouraging someone who is sick or facing a terminal illness.
⇒ The joy of leading someone to the knowledge of Christ.
⇒ The joy of providing food, clothing, shelter, or money to a needy person.
⇒ The joy of working diligently at one's job and helping to contribute to the success of society and our nation.
⇒ The joy of living an obedient, righteous life and of building up our families, showing and expressing our love for them.
⇒ The joy of being kind, friendly, caring, and helpful to fellow workers and developing healthy relationships with them.

Joy comes through being responsible, responsible in loving God and loving our neighbors as ourselves. When we treat our neighbors as we want to be treated, a sense of fulfillment and satisfaction floods our spirits. And we experience joy, the joy of fulfillment and satisfaction.

Again, there is no greater joy than the joy of serving Christ. For this reason, when the call comes to serve the LORD, we must surrender and obey. We must get up and go forth to do the task He is calling us to do. We must surrender to the call of the LORD:

"For whosoever shall do the will of my Father which is in heaven, the same is my brother, and sister, and mother" (Mt.12:50).

"I beseech you therefore, brethren, by the mercies of God, that ye present your bodies a living sacrifice, holy, acceptable unto God, *which is* your reasonable service" (Ro.12:1).

"I am crucified with Christ: nevertheless I live; yet not I, but Christ liveth in me: and the life which I now live in the flesh I live by the faith of the Son of God, who loved me, and gave himself for me" (Ga.2:20).

"Servants [employees, workers], be obedient to them that are *your* masters according to the flesh, with fear and trembling, in singleness of your heart, as unto Christ; Not with eyeservice, as menpleasers; but as the servants of Christ, doing the will of God from the heart" (Ep.6:5-6).

"Now the God of peace, that brought again from the dead our Lord Jesus, that great shepherd of the sheep, through the blood of the everlasting covenant, make you perfect in every good work to do his will, working in you that which is wellpleasing in his sight, through Jesus Christ; to whom *be* glory for ever and ever. Amen" (He.13:20-21).

"And the world passeth away, and the lust thereof: but he that doeth the will of God abideth for ever" (1 Jn.2:17).

"And thou shalt love the LORD thy God with all thine heart, and with all thy soul, and with all thy might" (De.6:5).

"I delight to do thy will, O my God: yea, thy law *is* within my heart" (Ps.40:8).

"Teach me to do thy will; for thou *art* my God: thy spirit *is* good; lead me into the land of uprightness" (Ps.143:10).

"My son, give me thine heart, and let thine eyes observe my ways" (Pr.23:26).

Thought 2. When the LORD calls us to serve Him, we must surrender to His call. Note the examples given us by Scripture:

(1) Abraham surrendered to the call of God.

"Now the LORD had said unto Abram, Get thee out of thy country, and from thy kindred, and from thy father's house, unto a land that I will show thee: And I will make of thee a great nation, and I will bless thee, and make thy name great; and thou shalt be a blessing: And I will bless them that bless thee, and curse him that curseth thee: and in thee shall all families of the earth be blessed. So

Abram departed, as the LORD had spoken unto him; and Lot went with him: and Abram *was* seventy and five years old when he departed out of Haran" (Ge.12:1-4).

(2) Noah surrendered to the call of God.

"Thus did Noah; according to all that God commanded him, so did he" (Ge.6:22).

(3) Moses surrendered to the call of God.

"Now therefore, behold, the cry of the children of Israel is come unto me: and I have also seen the oppression wherewith the Egyptians oppress them. Come now therefore, and I will send thee unto Pharaoh, that thou mayest bring forth my people the children of Israel out of Egypt" (Ex.3:9-10; see 3:11–4:19).

(4) Gideon surrendered to the call of God.

"And the LORD looked upon him, and said, Go in this thy might, and thou shalt save Israel from the hand of the Midianites: have not I sent thee?" (Jud.6:14; see 6:7-40).

(5) David surrendered to the call of God.

"And Samuel said unto Jesse, Are here all *thy* children? And he said, There remaineth yet the youngest, and, behold, he keepeth the sheep. And Samuel said unto Jesse, Send and fetch him: for we will not sit down till he come hither. And he sent, and brought him in. Now he *was* ruddy, *and* withal of a beautiful countenance, and goodly to look to. And the LORD said, Arise, anoint him: for this *is* he. Then Samuel took the horn of oil, and anointed him in the midst of his brethren: and the Spirit of the LORD came upon David from that day forward. So Samuel rose up, and went to Ramah" (1 S.16:11-13).

"I delight to do thy will, O my God: yea, thy law *is* within my heart" (Ps.40:8).

(6) Elisha surrendered to the call of God.

"And he left the oxen, and ran after Elijah, and said, Let me, I pray thee, kiss my father and my mother, and *then* I will follow thee. And he said unto him, Go back again: for what have I done to thee?" (1 K.19:20).

(7) Isaiah surrendered to the call of God.

"Also I heard the voice of the Lord, saying, Whom shall I send, and who will go for us? Then said I, Here *am* I; send me" (Is.6:8).

(8) Christ Himself surrendered to the call of His Father.

"Jesus saith unto them, My meat is to do the will of him that sent me, and to finish his work" (Jn.4:34).

(9) Paul surrendered to the call of God.

"And he trembling and astonished said, Lord, what wilt thou have me to do? And the Lord *said* unto him, Arise, and go into the city, and it shall be told thee what thou must do" (Ac.9:6).

1. Ahab's confrontation with King Ben-Hadad of Syria: A picture of greed & self-exaltation
- a. The attack of Samaria by King Ben-Hadad
  - 1) Had an alliance of 32 kings
  - 2) Besieged Samaria
- b. The brazen, fleshly demands sent to King Ahab
  - 1) Ben-Hadad demanded silver & gold & slaves, that is, the very best of Israel's wives & children
  - 2) Ahab, outnumbered & sensing a hopeless situation, surrendered—readily agreed to the terms
- c. The additional, greedy demands sent to Ahab
  - 1) Ben-Hadad—because of Ahab's ready surrender—felt he had asked too little: He demanded the right to ransack the royal palace & all the houses of the court officials
  - 2) Ahab became infuriated & summoned the court officials
    - He accused Ben-Hadad of seeking a war, of demanding unreasonable terms in exchange for Syria's withdrawal from Israel
    - He was advised by Israel's officials to reject the new, humiliating demands
  - 3) Ahab sent a twofold reply to Ben-Hadad
    - He would still agree to the first demands
    - He could not accept the disgraceful second demands

CHAPTER 20

D. The Defeat of Syria or Aram by Ahab: Learning That the LORD Alone Is God, 20:1-43

And Ben-hadad the king of
Syria gathered all his host
together: and *there were*
thirty and two kings with
him, and horses, and chariots:
and he went up and besieged
Samaria, and warred against
it.
2 And he sent messengers to
Ahab king of Israel into the
city, and said unto him, Thus
saith Ben-hadad,
3 Thy silver and thy gold *is*
mine; thy wives also and thy
children, *even* the goodliest,
are mine.
4 And the king of Israel answered and said, My lord, O
king, according to thy saying,
I *am* thine, and all that I
have.
5 And the messengers came
again, and said, Thus speaketh Ben-hadad, saying, Although I have sent unto thee,
saying, Thou shalt deliver
me thy silver, and thy gold,
and thy wives, and thy children;
6 Yet I will send my servants
unto thee to morrow about
this time, and they shall
search thine house, and the
houses of thy servants; and it
shall be, *that* whatsoever is
pleasant in thine eyes, they
shall put *it* in their hand, and
take *it* away.
7 Then the king of Israel
called all the elders of the
land, and said, Mark, I pray
you, and see how this *man*
seeketh mischief: for he sent
unto me for my wives, and
for my children, and for my
silver, and for my gold; and I
denied him not.
8 And all the elders and all
the people said unto him,
Hearken not *unto him,* nor
consent.
9 Wherefore he said unto the
messengers of Ben-hadad,
Tell my lord the king, All
that thou didst send for to thy
servant at the first I will do:
but this thing I may not do.
And the messengers departed, and brought him. word
again.
10 And Ben-hadad sent unto
him, and said, The gods
do so unto me, and more also, if the dust of Samaria
shall suffice for handfuls
for all the people that follow
me.
11 And the king of Israel answered and said, Tell *him,*
Let not him that girdeth on
his harness boast himself as
he that putteth it off.
12 And it came to pass,
when *Ben-hadad* heard this
message, as he *was* drinking,
he and the kings in the pavilions, that he said unto his
servants, Set *yourselves in
array.* And they set *themselves in array* against the
city.
13 And, behold, there came
a prophet unto Ahab king
of Israel, saying, Thus saith
the LORD, Hast thou seen
all this great multitude? behold, I will deliver it into
thine hand this day; and thou
shalt know that I *am* the
LORD.
14 And Ahab said, By
whom? And he said, Thus
saith the LORD, *Even* by the
young men of the princes of
the provinces. Then he said,
Who shall order the battle?
And he answered, Thou.
15 Then he numbered the
young men of the princes of
the provinces, and they were
two hundred and thirty two:
and after them he numbered
all the people, *even* all the
children of Israel, *being* seven thousand.
16 And they went out at
noon. But Ben-hadad *was*
drinking himself drunk in the
pavilions, he and the kings,
the thirty and two kings that
helped him.
17 And the young men of
the princes of the provinces
went out first; and Ben-hadad
sent out, and they told him,
saying, There are men come
out of Samaria.
18 And he said, Whether
they be come out for peace,
take them alive; or whether
they be come out for war,
take them alive.
19 So these young men of
the princes of the provinces
came out of the city, and the
army which followed them.
20 And they slew every

- d. The third & final messages sent between the two opposing kings
  - 1) Ben-Hadad—enraged & full of brash self-confidence—threatened the total destruction of Samaria
  - 2) Ahab simply replied with a proverb: Implied Ben-Hadad should not boast of victory until he had won
  - 3) Ben-Hadad—partying & drinking—reacted with vengeance: Ordered the army to prepare for attack

2. Ahab's first defeat of the Syrians: A proof that the LORD alone is God
- a. The LORD's prophet sent to Ahab
  - 1) To announce victory by God
  - 2) To declare God's purpose: To prove He alone is God
  - 3) To lay out God's strategy for victory: A special assault force of young officers was to advance first, to launch a surprise attack
- b. The orders of Ahab to mobilize & begin the advance
  - 1) He had only the 232 young officers of the provinces & 7,000 troops
  - 2) He attached at noon & caught the Syrians off guard
    - Ben-Hadad & the 32 kings were drunk in their tents
    - Ben-Hadad's scouts had seen the 232 young officers advancing, but the king thought they were seeking peace
  - 3) He had the 7,000 troops marching out of sight behind the young officers
- c. The first victory of Ahab

over the Syrian forces
   1) The young officers killed all who immediately faced them
   2) The Syrians fled & Ben-Hadad escaped
   3) The 7,000 Israelite forces—led by Ahab—advanced & overpowered the Syrians, destroying their horses, chariots, & many soldiers
- d. The prophet's warning of a future attack: Because Ahab should have repented, turned to the LORD who had proven Himself on Mount Carmel & had given victory over Syria

3. Ahab's second defeat of the Syrians: A proof that the LORD is sovereign everywhere
- a. The advice of the Syrian officials to King Ben-Hadad
   1) That he fight on the plains: Falsely believed that the LORD ruled only the hills
   2) That he remove the coalition kings from their command & replace them with trained military officers
   3) That he rebuild his army
- b. The springtime mobilization & face-off between the two armies
   1) The huge Syrian army invaded Israel at Aphek
   2) The small Israelite army marched & camped opposite the Syrians
- c. The LORD's prophet again sent to King Ahab: Gave assurance of victory
   1) To prove that the LORD is not one god among many, not just a god of the hills as the Syrians thought, 23
   2) To prove that the LORD alone is God, sovereign over all
- d. The second victory of Israel over the Syrians
   1) The armies began to fight on the seventh day
   2) The Israelites killed 100,000 Syrian foot

one his man: and the
Syrians fled; and Israel pursued them: and Ben-hadad
the king of Syria escaped
on an horse with the horsemen.
21 And the king of Israel
went out, and smote the horses and chariots, and slew the
Syrians with a great slaugh-
ter.
22 And the prophet came to
the king of Israel, and said
unto him, Go, strengthen thyself, and mark, and see what
thou doest: for at the return
of the year the king of Syria
will come up against thee.
23 And the servants of the
king of Syria said unto him,
Their gods *are* gods of the
hills; therefore they were
stronger than we; but let us
fight against them in the
plain, and surely we shall be
stronger than they.
24 And do this thing, Take
the kings away, every man
out of his place, and put captains in their rooms:
25 And number thee an ar-
my, like the army that thou
hast lost, horse for horse, and
chariot for chariot: and we
will fight against them in the
plain, *and* surely we shall be
stronger than they. And he
hearkened unto their voice,
and did so.
26 And it came to pass at the
return of the year, that Ben-
hadad numbered the Syrians,
and went up to Aphek, to
fight against Israel.
27 And the children of Israel
were numbered, and were all
present, and went against
them: and the children of Israel
pitched before them like two
little flocks of kids; but the
Syrians filled the country.
28 And there came a man of
God, and spake unto the king
of Israel, and said, Thus saith
the LORD, Because the Syrians have said, The LORD *is*
God of the hills, but he *is* not
God of the valleys, therefore
will I deliver all this great
multitude into thine hand,
and ye shall know that I *am*
the LORD.
29 And they pitched one
over against the other seven
days. And so it was, that in
the seventh day the battle was
joined: and the children of Israel slew of the Syrians an
hundred thousand footmen in
one day.
30 But the rest fled to
Aphek, into the city; and
there a wall fell upon twenty
and seven thousand of the
men *that were* left. And Ben-
hadad fled, and came into the
city, into an inner chamber.
31 And his servants said unto him, Behold now, we have
heard that the kings of the
house of Israel *are* merciful
kings: let us, I pray thee, put
sackcloth on our loins, and
ropes upon our heads, and go
out to the king of Israel: peradventure he will save thy
life.
32 So they girded sack-
cloth on their loins, and *put*
ropes on their heads, and
came to the king of Israel,
and said, Thy servant
Ben-hadad saith, I pray thee,
let me live. And he said,
Is he yet alive? he is my
brother.
33 Now the men did dili-
gently observe whether *any
thing would come* from him,
and did hastily catch *it:* and
they said, Thy brother Ben-
hadad. Then he said, Go ye,
bring him. Then Ben-hadad
came forth to him; and he
caused him to come up into
the chariot.
34 And *Ben-hadad* said unto
him, The cities, which my father took from thy father, I
will restore; and thou shalt
make streets for thee in Damascus, as my father made in
Samaria. Then *said Ahab,* I
will send thee away with this
covenant. So he made a covenant with him, and sent him
away.
35 And a certain man of the
sons of the prophets said unto
his neighbour in the word of
the LORD, Smite me, I pray
thee. And the man refused to
smite him.
36 Then said he unto him,
Because thou hast not obeyed
the voice of the LORD, behold, as soon as thou art departed from me, a lion shall
slay thee. And as soon as he
was departed from him, a
lion found him, and slew
him.
37 Then he found another
man, and said, Smite me, I
pray thee. And the man
smote him, so that in smiting

soldiers in one day
   3) The other Syrian forces fled into the city of Aphek
      - Part of the wall collapsed, killing 27,000 soldiers
      - Ben-Hadad hid in a secret room
- e. The plea & negotiation of Ben-Hadad for mercy
   1) The Syrian officials suggested they negotiate for mercy
      - Because the Israelite kings were known as being merciful
      - Because Ahab might spare their lives
   2) The officials secured an audience with Ahab
      - Were dressed in the clothing of submission
      - Pled for mercy
   3) The response of Ahab was surprising
      - Ahab called Ben-Hadad "my brother"
      - Ahab's feelings were picked up by the enemy officials: Responded that Ben-Hadad was indeed a fellow king, Ahab's "brother"
      - Ahab sent his chariot for Ben-Hadad
   4) The terms of surrender offered by Ben-Hadad for his life were accepted by Ahab
      - He was to return cities formerly conquered by Syria, 15:20-22
      - He was to grant market places in Damascus

4. Ahab's condemnation by God through an unnamed prophet: A picture of disobedience
- a. The prophet's disguise
   1) He ordered a fellow prophet to strike him, but was refused
   2) He predicted the other prophet's death because of his disobedience: Shows the danger of disobeying God's Word
   3) He asked another man to strike him: This man wounded the prophet—to help with his disguise

b. The prophet's encounter with Ahab 1) He waited by the road for the king: Disguised as a wounded soldier 2) He called out for clemency, a pardon when King Ahab passed by • He pretended that he had accidentally let a prisoner escape—under threat of losing his life or of making a large payment of money • He was condemned by the hard heart of Ahab	he wounded *him.* 38 So the prophet departed, and waited for the king by the way, and disguised himself with ashes upon his face. 39 And as the king passed by, he cried unto the king: and he said, Thy servant went out into the midst of the battle; and, behold, a man turned aside, and brought a man unto me, and said, Keep this man: if by any means he be missing, then shall thy life be for his life, or else thou shalt pay a talent of silver. 40 And as thy servant was busy here and there, he was gone. And the king of Israel	said unto him, So *shall* thy judgment *be;* thyself hast decided *it.* 41 And he hasted, and took the ashes away from his face; and the king of Israel discerned him that he *was* of the prophets. 42 And he said unto him, Thus saith the LORD, Because thou hast let go out of *thy* hand a man whom I appointed to utter destruction, therefore thy life shall go for his life, and thy people for his people. 43 And the king of Israel went to his house heavy and displeased, and came to Samaria.	3) He stripped off his disguise & revealed himself to Ahab, & Ahab recognized him 4) He pronounced God's condemnation: Ahab had condemned himself, for he had let the condemned prisoner Ben-Hadad go free • Ahab would soon die • Israel would be defeated c. The reaction of Ahab: Stubborn, angry, pouting, unrepentant—like a spoiled child

DIVISION III

THE MINISTRY OF ELIJAH AND OTHER PROPHETS DURING THE REIGN OF AHAB: LEARNING WHO THE LIVING AND TRUE GOD IS, 17:1–22:53

D. The Defeat of Syria or Aram by Ahab: Learning That the LORD Alone Is God, 20:1-43

(20:1-43) **Introduction**: there is no God but one. The LORD alone—Jehovah, Yahweh—is God. All other *so-called gods* that are worshipped by people are false, deceptive creations of people's minds and their wild imaginations. Moreover, the idea that all people on earth who worship *a god* are worshipping the *same god* is a totally false idea or belief. There is only one LORD and Creator of the universe, only one true God, not many gods. The living and true God of the universe is the LORD Himself, Jehovah-Yahweh.

This is the major thrust of the present passage, a lesson that was being taught to Ahab, the ruler of the Northern Kingdom of Israel. It was a lesson that he desperately needed to learn, and it is a lesson that every generation of people must learn. For if it is true that there is a true and living God who created the universe, imagine the horrible fate of those who deny or reject Him or worship false gods. This is: *The Defeat of Syria or Aram by Ahab: Learning That the LORD Alone Is God,* 20:1-43.

1. Ahab's confrontation with King Ben-Hadad of Syria: a picture of greed and self-confidence (vv.1-12).
2. Ahab's first defeat of the Syrians: a proof that the LORD alone is God (vv.13-33).
3. Ahab's second defeat of the Syrians: a proof that the LORD is sovereign everywhere and over all nations (vv.23-34).
4. Ahab's condemnation by God through an unnamed prophet: a picture of disobedience (vv.35-43).

1 (20:1-12) **Greed, Example of—Self-Confidence, Example of—Self-exaltation, Example of—Aram, Wars Against Israel—Syria, Wars Against Israel—Israel, Wars of—Ben-Hadad, Wars Against Israel—Ahab, Wars Fought**: there was Ahab's confrontation with King Ben-Hadad of Syria. Remember, Israel had been suffering a severe three-year drought and famine. Knowing this, King Ben-Hadad probably felt that Israel was weak and vulnerable and that Syria could easily conquer and strip Israel of its wealth. This is the first of three battles between Ahab and Ben-Hadad in the book of First Kings (20:13-22; 20:23-34; 22:1-38). In this first battle, Scripture exposes the evil of the human heart, the evil of greed, self-confidence, and self-exaltation:

OUTLINE	SCRIPTURE	SCRIPTURE	OUTLINE
1. Ahab's confrontation with King Ben-Hadad of Syria: A picture of greed & self-exaltation a. The attack of Samaria by King Ben-Hadad 1) Had an alliance of 32 kings 2) Besieged Samaria b. The brazen, fleshly demands sent to King Ahab	**A**nd Ben-hadad the king of Syria gathered all his host together: and *there were* thirty and two kings with him, and horses, and chariots: and he went up and besieged Samaria, and warred against it. 2 And he sent messengers to Ahab king of Israel into the	city, and said unto him, Thus saith Ben-hadad, 3 Thy silver and thy gold *is* mine; thy wives also and thy children, *even* the goodliest, *are* mine. 4 And the king of Israel answered and said, My lord, O king, according to thy saying, I *am* thine, and all that I have.	1) Ben-Hadad demanded silver & gold & slaves, that is, the very best of Israel's wives & children 2) Ahab, outnumbered & sensing a hopeless situation, surrendered—readily agreed to the terms

OUTLINE	SCRIPTURE	SCRIPTURE	OUTLINE
c. The additional, greedy demands sent to Ahab 1) Ben-Hadad—because of Ahab's ready surrender—felt he had asked too little: He demanded the right to ransack the royal palace & all the houses of the court officials	5 And the messengers came again, and said, Thus speak- eth Ben-hadad, saying, Alt- hough I have sent unto thee, saying, Thou shalt de- liver me thy silver, and thy gold, and thy wives, and thy children; 6 Yet I will send my servants unto thee to morrow about this time, and they shall search thine house, and the houses of thy servants; and it shall be, *that* whatsoever is pleasant in thine eyes, they shall put *it* in their hand, and take *it* away.	9 Wherefore he said unto the messengers of Ben-hadad, Tell my lord the king, All that thou didst send for to thy servant at the first I will do: but this thing I may not do. And the messengers depart- ed, and brought him. word again. 10 And Ben-hadad sent unto him, and said, The gods do so unto me, and more al- so, if the dust of Samaria shall suffice for handfuls for all the people that follow me.	3) Ahab sent a twofold reply to Ben-Hadad • He would still agree to the first demands • He could not accept the disgraceful second demands d. The third & final messages sent between the two opposing kings 1) Ben-Hadad—enraged & full of brash self-confidence—threatened the total destruction of Samaria
2) Ahab became infuriated & summoned the court officials • He accused Ben-Hadad of seeking a war, of demanding unreasonable terms in exchange for Syria's withdrawal from Israel • He was advised by Israel's officials to reject the new, humiliating demands	7 Then the king of Israel called all the elders of the land, and said, Mark, I pray you, and see how this *man* seeketh mischief: for he sent unto me for my wives, and for my children, and for my silver, and for my gold; and I denied him not. 8 And all the elders and all the people said unto him, Hearken not *unto him,* nor consent.	11 And the king of Israel an- swered and said, Tell *him,* Let not him that girdeth on *his harness* boast himself as he that putteth it off. 12 And it came to pass, when *Ben-hadad* heard this message, as he *was* drinking, he and the kings in the pavil- ions, that he said unto his servants, Set *yourselves in* *array.* And they set *them-* *selves in array* against the city.	2) Ahab simply replied with a proverb: Implied Ben-Hadad should not boast of victory until he had won 3) Ben-Hadad—partying & drinking—reacted with vengeance: Ordered the army to prepare for attack

a. Ben-Hadad invaded Israel and set up a siege around the capital of Samaria. Note that he had formed an alliance made up of thirty-two kings who were probably rulers of city-states scattered throughout that part of the world.

b. After the army of Syria had set up their camps and armaments around the city, Ben-Hadad sent messengers with his brazen, fleshly demands to King Ahab (vv.2-4). His demands were aroused out of fleshly desires, for he demanded not only silver and gold but also slaves, that is, the very best or loveliest of Israel's wives and children. The reader can just imagine what he and his soldiers would have done with the loveliest or best of the wives and older children. Being outnumbered and sensing a hopeless situation, Ahab surrendered, readily submitting and agreeing to the terms.

c. However when the surrender was reported to King Ben-Hadad, he decided to make additional greedy demands (vv.5-9). Because of Ahab's ready surrender, King Ben-Hadad felt he had asked *too little.* Thus, he demanded the right to ransack the royal palace and all the houses of the court officials.

Infuriated, Ahab immediately summoned his court officials. Before them, he accused the Syrian king of looking for trouble, of seeking a war. Ben-Hadad had changed the terms of payment that Ahab had agreed to in order to end the siege and spare the city. Unanimously, the royal officials rejected the disgraceful demands. Syria was demanding total subjection and the ransacking of the entire city. Such an act would have left the Israelite men with nothing, not even their wives and children. Despite the harsh demands, Ahab controlled his anger and sent a diplomatic reply to the Syrian king. He still had hope that Ben-Hadad would accept the first list of demands when he saw that the Israelites would not accept the new and humiliating demands (v.9).

d. But when Ben-Hadad received the rejection of his new demands, he became infuriated and sent a third and final message to King Ahab. Full of brash self-confidence, he threatened total destruction of Samaria. In response, Ahab simply answered with a proverb. The proverb implied that Ben-Hadad should not boast a victory until he had actually won. When this proverbial response was handed to Ben-Hadad, he was in the midst of partying and drinking. Reacting with a vengeance, he ordered the army to prepare for attack.

Thought 1. In Ben-Hadad, we see a picture of two strong but destructive traits: greed and self-exaltation or boasting. Greed is a burning, overwhelming desire for more and more. No matter how much we may have, if we are greedy, we want more. And if we are greedy, we will rationalize and justify our desire for more. Greed can involve the coveting of anything: money, property, houses, furnishings, automobiles, clothes, toys, or any other item an individual can possess. But in addition to craving material possessions, greed can manifest itself as a burning desire for such things as recognition, praise, honor, position, promotion, power, authority, fame, success, beauty, or any other ambition of the human heart.

There is nothing wrong with having material possessions or seeking the desires of one's heart. But when we allow possessions and desires to consume our lives, then they become wrong. When we are willing to hurt, degrade, or bring misery and pain upon another person in order to secure some possession or to fulfill some desire, then greed has taken over our hearts. Such a greedy spirit focuses upon oneself. It is a spirit that exalts oneself over others, a spirit that is willing to hurt others in order to secure one's own desires. Greed and self-exaltation go hand in hand.

(1) Listen to what the Word of God says about greed and covetousness:

"Then Judas, which had betrayeth him, when he saw that he was condemned, repented himself, and brought again the thirty pieces of silver to the chief priests and elders, Saying, I have sinned in that I have betrayed the innocent blood. And they said, What is that to us? see thou to that. And he cast down the pieces of silver in the temple, and departed, and went and hanged himself" (Mt.27:3-5).

"And he said unto them, Take heed, and beware of covetousness: for a man's life consisteth not in the abundance of the things which he possesseth" (Lu.12:15).

"Mortify therefore your members which are upon the earth; fornication, uncleanness, inordinate affection, evil concupiscence, and covetousness, which is idolatry: For which things' sake the wrath of God cometh on the children of disobedience" (Co.3:5-6).

"But they that will be rich fall into temptation and a snare, and into many foolish and hurtful lusts, which drown men in destruction and perdition. For the love of money is the root of all evil: which while some coveted after, they have erred from the faith, and pierced themselves through with many sorrows" (1 Ti.6:9-10).

"Your gold and silver is cankered; and the rust of them shall be a witness against you, and shall eat your flesh as it were fire. Ye have heaped treasure together for the last days [judgment]" (Js.5:3).

"Thou shalt not covet thy neighbour's house, thou shalt not covet thy neighbour's wife, nor his manservant, nor his maidservant, nor his ox, nor his ass, nor any thing that is thy neighbour's" (Ex.20:17).

"And his [Samuel's] sons walked not in his ways, but turned aside after lucre, and took bribes, and perverted judgment" (1 S.8:3).

"My son, if sinners entice thee, consent thou not. If they say, Come with us, let us lay wait for blood, let us lurk privily for the innocent without cause: Let us swallow them up alive as the grave; and whole, as those that go down into the pit: We shall find all precious substance, we shall fill our houses with spoil: Cast in thy lot among us; let us all have one purse: My son, walk not thou in the way with them; refrain thy foot from their path: For their feet run to evil, and make haste to shed blood. Surely in vain the net is spread in the sight of any bird. And they lay wait for their own blood; they lurk privily for their own lives. So are the ways of every one that is greedy of gain; which taketh away the life of the owners thereof" (Pr.1:10-19).

"He that is greedy of gain troubleth his own house; but he that hateth gifts shall live" (Pr.15:27).

"The desire of the slothful killeth him; for his hands refuse to labour. He coveteth greedily all the day long: but the righteous giveth and spareth not" (Pr.21:25-26).

"He that loveth silver shall not be satisfied with silver; nor he that loveth abundance with increase: this is also vanity" (Ec.5:10).

"Yea, they are greedy dogs which can never have enough, and they are shepherds that cannot understand: they all look to their own way, every one for his gain, from his quarter" (Is.56:11).

"For from the least of them even unto the greatest of them every one is given to covetousness; and from the prophet even unto the priest every one dealeth falsely" (Jer.6:13).

"And they come unto thee as the people cometh, and they sit before thee as my people, and they hear thy words, but they will not do them: for with their mouth they show much love, but their heart goeth after their covetousness" (Eze.33:31).

"And they covet fields, and take them by violence; and houses, and take them away: so they oppress a man and his house, even a man and his heritage" (Mic.2:2).

"The heads thereof judge for reward, and the priests thereof teach for hire, and the prophets thereof divine for money: yet will they lean upon the Lord, and say, Is not the Lord among us? none evil can come upon us" (Mic.3:11).

"Woe to him that coveteth an evil covetousness to his house, that he may set his nest on high, that he may be delivered from the power of evil! Thou hast consulted shame to thy house by cutting off many people, and hast sinned against thy soul" (Hab.2:9-10).

(2) Listen to what the Word of God says about self-exaltation and boasting:

"And whosoever shall exalt himself shall be abased; and he that shall humble himself shall be exalted" (Mt.23:12).

"But now ye rejoice in your boastings: all such rejoicing is evil" (Ja.4:16).

"The wicked in *his* pride doth persecute the poor: let them be taken in the devices that they have imagined" (Ps.10:2).

"For the wicked boasteth of his heart's desire, and blesseth the covetous, *whom* the LORD abhorreth" (Ps.10:3).

"They that trust in their wealth, and boast themselves in the multitude of their riches; None *of them* can by any means redeem his brother, nor give to God a ransom for him" (Ps.49:6-7).

"Pride *goeth* before destruction, and an haughty spirit before a fall" (Pr.16:18).

"Put not forth thyself in the presence of the king, and stand not in the place of great *men:* For better *it is* that it be said unto thee, Come up hither; than that thou shouldest be put lower in the presence of the prince whom thine eyes have seen" (Pr.25:6-7).

"Whoso boasteth himself of a false gift *is like* clouds and wind without rain" (Pr.25:14).

"Boast not thyself of to morrow; for thou knowest not what a day may bring forth" (Pr.27:1).

"How art thou fallen from heaven, O Lucifer, son of the morning! *how* art thou cut down to the ground, which didst weaken the nations! For thou hast said in thine heart, I will ascend into heaven, I will exalt my throne above the stars of God: I will sit also upon the mount of the congregation, in the sides of the north: I will ascend above the heights of the clouds; I will be like the most High. Yet thou shalt be brought down to hell, to the sides of the pit" (Is.14:12-15).

"Though thou exalt *thyself* as the eagle, and though thou set thy nest among the stars, thence will I bring thee down, saith the LORD" (Obad.4).

2 (20:13-22) **God, Proof - Evidence of—Israel, Victories of—Syria, Defeat of—Ahab, Wars of—Proof, God is Living and True**: there was Ahab's first defeat of the Syrians. This supernatural victory would again be a striking proof that the LORD (Jehovah, Yahweh) alone is the true and living God. Remember that Ahab was engaging in the worship of the false god Baal. Thus God, demonstrating His infinite patience and love, sought once again to reach Ahab's heart. Scripture graphically describes just what God did:

OUTLINE	SCRIPTURE	SCRIPTURE	OUTLINE
2. Ahab's first defeat of the Syrians: A proof that the LORD alone is God a. The LORD's prophet sent to Ahab 1) To announce victory by God 2) To declare God's purpose: To prove He alone is God 3) To lay out God's strategy for victory: A special assault force of young officers was to advance first, to launch a surprise attack b. The orders of Ahab to mobilize & begin the advance 1) He had only the 232 young officers of the provinces & 7,000 troops 2) He attacked at noon & caught the Syrians off guard • Ben-Hadad & the 32 kings were drunk in their tents • Ben-Hadad's scouts had seen the 232 young	13 And, behold, there came a prophet unto Ahab king of Israel, saying, Thus saith the LORD, Hast thou seen all this great multitude? behold, I will deliver it into thine hand this day; and thou shalt know that I *am* the LORD. 14 And Ahab said, By whom? And he said, Thus saith the LORD, *Even* by the young men of the princes of the provinces. Then he said, Who shall order the battle? And he answered, Thou. 15 Then he numbered the young men of the princes of the provinces, and they were two hundred and thirty two: and after them he numbered all the people, *even* all the children of Israel, *being* seven thousand. 16 And they went out at noon. But Ben-hadad *was* drinking himself drunk in the pavilions, he and the kings, the thirty and two kings that helped him. 17 And the young men of the princes of the provinces	went out first; and Ben-hadad sent out, and they told him, saying, There are men come out of Samaria. 18 And he said, Whether they be come out for peace, take them alive; or whether they be come out for war, take them alive. 19 So these young men of the princes of the provinces came out of the city, and the army which followed them. 20 And they slew every one his man: and the Syrians fled; and Israel pursued them: and Ben-hadad the king of Syria escaped on an horse with the horsemen. 21 And the king of Israel went out, and smote the horses and chariots, and slew the Syrians with a great slaughter. 22 And the prophet came to the king of Israel, and said unto him, Go, strengthen thyself, and mark, and see what thou doest: for at the return of the year the king of Syria will come up against thee.	officers advancing, but the king thought they were seeking peace 3) He had the 7,000 troops marching out of sight behind the young officers c. The first victory of Ahab over the Syrian forces 1) The young officers killed all who immediately faced them 2) The Syrians fled & Ben-Hadad escaped 3) The 7,000 Israelite forces—led by Ahab—advanced & overpowered the Syrians, destroying their horses, chariots, & many soldiers d. The prophet's warning of a future attack: Because Ahab should have repented, turned to the LORD who had proven Himself on Mount Carmel & had given victory over Syria

a. The LORD sent His prophet to Ahab with a very special message (vv.13-14). Remember that the massive Syrian army was surrounding Ahab's capital city of Samaria. The situation seemed utterly hopeless, for the Syrian alliance was made up of thirty-two kings and their military forces. But the LORD longed to reach the heart of Ahab, longed for Ahab to stop Jezebel's savage purge of God's prophets and the worship of the LORD (18:4; 19:2). Thus the LORD sent an unnamed prophet to Ahab, announcing that God was going to give a miraculous victory to the king. But the LORD had a very specific purpose: to prove that He alone is God, the only true and living God.

In fighting the battle, Ahab was to follow a very specific strategy laid out by God in order to secure the victory (v.14). A special assault force of young officers was to advance and launch a surprise attack against the Syrian alliance. Note that these officers represented the various provinces of the Northern Kingdom. Apparently, Ahab's father King Omri had organized the Northern Kingdom into various provinces after he had assumed the throne (16:21-28).

b. Following the instructions of the unnamed prophet, Ahab mobilized his forces and began the advance (vv.15-19). He had only the 232 young officers of the special assault force and 7,000 troops. Some commentators feel that these 7,000 soldiers were the faithful followers of the LORD revealed to Elijah when the prophet had felt he was the only believer left in the Northern Kingdom (19:18). If so, the LORD was using a force of His own followers to achieve the victory.[1]

Whatever the case, Ahab began the advance at noon and caught the Syrians off guard, for Ben-Hadad and the thirty-two kings were drunk in their tents (vv.16-17). When the scouts reported to the king that a group of young officers was

[1] Russell Dilday. *1, 2 Kings*, pp. 230-231.

advancing, Ben-Hadad thought they were surely seeking peace. Even if they were attacking, they posed no threat. In fact, King Ben-Hadad ordered that the young officers be captured alive. Note that Ahab and the 7,000 troops marched out of sight behind the young officers (v.19).

c. The victory given to Ahab that day by the LORD was quick and decisive (vv.20-21). As soon as the Syrian soldiers confronted the special assault force, the very officers they were sent out to capture killed the entire band of Syrians. Witnessing the fierce, decisive attack and probably being unprepared to respond, the Syrian army was routed, fleeing for their lives. Even King Ben-Hadad barely escaped being captured and killed. Striking quickly, the 7,000 Israelite men led by Ahab advanced, overpowering the horses and chariots and the forces of the Syrians (v.21). After the battle, the heavy losses inflicted upon the Syrians were obvious.

d. Sometime after the victory given by the LORD, the prophet of God was sent again to issue a warning to Ahab. He was to face a future attack by the Syrians (v.22). As a result of the recent victory given by the LORD, King Ahab should have repented and turned back to the LORD. But he had refused. Because of this, he was to be chastised by God again through another invasion by the Syrians. Standing before the king, the prophet warned Ahab of the invasion that was to come the next spring.

Note this fact: even this warning should have aroused Ahab to repent, for God was still reaching out to him in compassion, patiently longing for him to turn from his wickedness. Remember that the LORD had proven that He alone is God on both Mt. Carmel and in the victory recently given over Syria. But Ahab's heart was hard, stubborn, and resistant to the LORD.

Thought 1. The LORD clearly spelled out His purpose for giving Ahab the victory over the Syrian army. His purpose was to prove that He alone is God. There is only one true and living God, only one Creator, only one Sovereign LORD and Majesty of the universe. All other gods are false, deceivers that mislead and entrap human beings and capture their loyalty. And the terrible tragedy is this: if we are deceived into following and worshipping false gods, we condemn and doom ourselves. We condemn ourselves to walk through life without the provision and protection of the living and true LORD. When hardships and misfortunes fall upon us, there is no living God to help us, for we are following false gods that are lifeless and powerless to help.

Moreover, if we are participating in false worship, we never know the supernatural strengthening of the LORD who empowers us to conquer all the trials and temptations of this life. We never know what it is to walk victoriously over all the terrible enemies, hardships, and misfortunes that confront us. And, most tragically, when we come face-to-face with death, if we are following and worshipping false gods, we are doomed to hell. We will never inherit eternal life nor live in the presence of the LORD God Himself, the LORD (Jehovah, Yahweh) who alone is the only living and true God. This is exactly what Holy Scripture says.

"But Jesus held his peace. And the high priest answered and said unto him, I adjure thee by the living God, that thou tell us whether thou be the Christ, the Son of God. Jesus saith unto him, Thou hast said: nevertheless I say unto you, Hereafter shall ye see the Son of man sitting on the right hand of power, and coming in the clouds of heaven" (Mt.26:63-64).

"And saying, Sirs, why do ye these things? We also are men of like passions with you, and preach unto you that ye should turn from these vanities unto the living God, which made heaven, and earth, and the sea, and all things that are therein" (Ac.14:15).

"God that made the world and all things therein, seeing that he is Lord of heaven and earth, dwelleth not in temples made with hands" (Ac.17:24).

"For they themselves show of us what manner of entering in we had unto you, and how ye turned to God from idols to serve the living and true God; And to wait for his Son from heaven, whom he raised from the dead, *even* Jesus, which delivered us from the wrath to come" (1 Th.1:9-10).

"He that despised Moses' law died without mercy under two or three witnesses: Of how much sorer punishment, suppose ye, shall he be thought worthy, who hath trodden under foot the Son of God, and hath counted the blood of the covenant, wherewith he was sanctified, an unholy thing, and hath done despite unto the Spirit of grace? For we know him that hath said, Vengeance *belongeth* unto me, I will recompense, saith the Lord. And again, The Lord shall judge his people. *It is* a fearful thing to fall into the hands of the living God" (He.10:28-31).

"Through faith we understand that the worlds were framed by the word of God, so that things which are seen were not made of things which do appear" (He.11:3).

"For so an entrance shall be ministered unto you abundantly into the everlasting kingdom of our Lord and Saviour Jesus Christ" (2 Pe.1:11).

"I am Alpha and Omega, the beginning and the ending, saith the Lord, which is, and which was, and which is to come, the Almighty" (Re.1:8).

"In the beginning God created the heaven and the earth" (Ge.1:1).

"For I lift up my hand to heaven, and say, I live for ever" (De.32:40).

"The eternal God *is thy* refuge, and underneath *are* the everlasting arms: and he shall thrust out the enemy from before thee; and shall say, Destroy *them*" (De.33:27).

"Thou, *even* thou, *art* LORD alone; thou hast made heaven, the heaven of heavens, with all their host, the earth, and all *things* that *are* therein, the seas, and all that *is* therein, and thou preservest them all; and the host of heaven worshippeth thee" (Ne.9:6).

"He stretcheth out the north over the empty place, *and* hangeth the earth upon nothing" (Jb.26:7).

"When I consider thy heavens, the work of thy fingers, the moon and the stars, which thou hast ordained; What is man, that thou art mindful of him? and the son of man, that thou visitest him?" (Ps.8:3-4).

"The heavens declare the glory of God; and the firmament showeth his handiwork" (Ps.19:1).

"My soul thirsteth for God, for the living God: when shall I come and appear before God?" (Ps.42:2).

"My soul longeth, yea, even fainteth for the courts of the LORD: my heart and my flesh crieth out for the living God" (Ps.84:2).

"Of old hast thou laid the foundation of the earth: and the heavens *are* the work of thy hands" (Ps.102:25).

"Thy name, O LORD, *endureth* for ever; *and* thy memorial, O LORD, throughout all generations" (Ps.135:13).

"I will praise thee; for I am fearfully *and* wonderfully made: marvellous *are* thy works; and *that* my soul knoweth right well" (Ps.139:14).

"Thy kingdom *is* an everlasting kingdom, and thy dominion *endureth* throughout all generations" (Ps.145:13).

"He hath made every *thing* beautiful in his time: also he hath set the world in their heart, so that no man can find out the work that God maketh from the beginning to the end" (Ec.3:11).

"I make a decree, That in every dominion of my kingdom men tremble and fear before the God of Daniel: for he *is* the living God, and stedfast for ever, and his kingdom *that* which shall not be destroyed, and his dominion *shall be even* unto the end" (Da.6:26).

3 (20:23-34) **Sovereignty, of God—Nations, Ruled over by God—Proof, God's Sovereignty—Power, of God, over the Nations—Supremacy, of God, over the Nations—Northern Kingdom, Wars of—Ahab, Wars of—Syria, Wars Against Israel**: there was Ahab's second defeat of the Syrian army. But again the victory was given by God for a very specific purpose, the purpose of proving that His sovereignty is not partial and not limited, but absolute. The LORD is sovereign everywhere and over all nations. Scripture clearly states this purpose of God, and it graphically describes what happened as a result of the victory:

OUTLINE	SCRIPTURE	SCRIPTURE	OUTLINE
3. Ahab's second defeat of the	23 And the servants of the	multitude into thine hand,	alone is God, sovereign
Syrians: A proof that the	king of Syria said unto him,	and ye shall know that I *am*	over all
LORD is sovereign everywhere	Their gods *are* gods of the	the LORD.	
a. The advice of the Syrian of-	hills; therefore they were	29 And they pitched one	d. The second victory of Israel
ficials to King Ben-Hadad	stronger than we; but let us	over against the other seven	over the Syrians
1) That he fight on the plains:	fight against them in the	days. And so it was, that in	1) The armies began to fight
Falsely believed that the	plain, and surely we shall be	the seventh day the battle was	on the seventh day
LORD ruled only the hills	stronger than they.	joined: and the children of Is-	2) The Israelites killed
2) That he remove the coalition	24 And do this thing, Take	rael slew of the Syrians an	100,000 Syrian foot sol-
kings from their command	the kings away, every man	hundred thousand footmen in	diers in one day
& replace them with trained	out of his place, and put cap-	one day.	
military officers	tains in their rooms:	30 But the rest fled to	3) The other Syrian forces
3) That he rebuild his army	25 And number thee an ar-	Aphek, into the city; and	fled into the city of Aphek
	my, like the army that thou	*there* a wall fell upon twenty	• Part of the wall col-
	hast lost, horse for horse, and	and seven thousand of the	lapsed, killing 27,000
	chariot for chariot: and we	men *that were* left. And Ben-	soldiers
	will fight against them in the	hadad fled, and came into the	• Ben-Hadad hid in a se-
	plain, *and* surely we shall be	city, into an inner chamber.	cret room
	stronger than they. And he	31 And his servants said un-	e. The plea & negotiation of
	hearkened unto their voice,	to him, Behold now, we have	Ben-Hadad for mercy
	and did so.	heard that the kings of the	1) The Syrian officials sug-
b. The springtime mobilization	26 And it came to pass at the	house of Israel *are* merciful	gested they negotiate for
& face-off between the two	return of the year, that Ben-	kings: let us, I pray thee, put	mercy
armies	hadad numbered the Syrians,	sackcloth on our loins, and	• Because the Israelite
1) The huge Syrian army in-	and went up to Aphek, to	ropes upon our heads, and go	kings were known as be-
vaded Israel at Aphek	fight against Israel.	out to the king of Israel: per-	ing merciful
2) The small Israelite army	27 And the children of Israel	adventure he will save thy	• Because Ahab might
marched & camped oppo-	were numbered, and were all	life.	spare their lives
site the Syrians	present, and went against	32 So they girded sackcloth	2) The officials secured an
	them: and the children of Is-	on their loins, and *put*	audience with Ahab
	rael pitched before them like	ropes on their heads, and	• Were dressed in the
	two little flocks of kids; but	came to the king of Israel,	clothing of submission
	the Syrians filled the country.	and said, Thy servant Ben-	• Pled for mercy
c. The LORD's prophet again	28 And there came a man of	hadad saith, I pray thee,	3) The response of Ahab was
sent to King Ahab: Gave	God, and spake unto the king	let me live. And he said,	surprising
assurance of victory	of Israel, and said, Thus saith	*Is* he yet alive? he is my	• Ahab called Ben-Hadad
1) To prove that the LORD is	the LORD, Because the Syri-	brother.	"my brother"
not one god among many,	ans have said, The LORD *is*	33 Now the men did dili-	• Ahab's feelings were
not just a god of the hills	God of the hills, but he *is* not	gently observe whether *any*	picked up by the enemy
as the Syrians thought, 23	God of the valleys, therefore	*thing would come* from him,	officials: Responded that
2) To prove that the LORD	will I deliver all this great	and did hastily catch *it:* and	Ben-Hadad was indeed

OUTLINE	SCRIPTURE	SCRIPTURE	OUTLINE
a fellow king, Ahab's "brother" • Ahab sent his chariot for Ben-Hadad 4) The terms of surrender offered by Ben-Hadad for his life were accepted	they said, Thy brother Ben-hadad. Then he said, Go ye, bring him. Then Ben-hadad came forth to him; and he caused him to come up into the chariot. 34 And *Ben-hadad* said unto him, The cities, which my father took from thy	father, I will restore; and thou shalt make streets for thee in Damascus, as my father made in Samaria. Then *said Ahab,* I will send thee away with this covenant. So he made a covenant with him, and sent him away.	by Ahab • He was to return cities formerly conquered by Syria, 15:20-22 • He was to grant market places in Damascus

a. During the winter months, the Syrian officials advised King Ben-Hadad to plan another attack against the Northern Kingdom of Israel (vv.23-25). But this time, they advised he attack on the plains, not in the mountains. For it seemed as though the God of Israel was a god of the hills, that is, His sovereignty and power were much stronger in the hills. If they fought on the plains, the Syrian forces would be much stronger than the forces of Israel.

Moreover, in order to strengthen the king's forces, the officials recommended that he remove all the coalition kings from their commands and replace them with trained military officers. Then they advised him to rebuild his army (vv.24-25). The king agreed, and acted accordingly.

b. When springtime arrived and the weather permitted, King Ben-Hadad once again mobilized his army and marched up to Aphek to attack Israel. This time, however, he believed beyond the shadow of a doubt that he would conquer Israel and be able to ransack the nations wealth and enslave the wives and children. Hearing about the invasion, the small Israelite army was mobilized and marched out to meet the invaders. Camping opposite the Syrians, the Israelite army looked like two little flocks of goats in comparison to the massive forces of the Syrians, which covered the entire countryside (v.27). But again God had other plans for King Ahab and the Israelites of the Northern Kingdom.

c. The LORD sent His prophet to King Ahab once more to announce that He would deliver this vast army into the hands of the Israelites (v.28). Through the victory Ahab was to learn a great truth: the LORD is sovereign; His power is not partial or limited, but absolute. The LORD was going to prove that He was not just one god among many, not just a god of the hills as the Syrians falsely believed (v.23). He alone is the LORD (Jehovah, Yahweh), the only true and living God.

d. Just as He promised, the LORD gave a second victory to Israel over the Syrians (vv.29-30). For seven long days the two armies sat camped opposite each other. The days must have seemed endless and no doubt were filled with anxiety for the soldiers who were waiting to engage in deadly combat. Finally, the seventh day arrived and the two armies began to fight. Somehow, by the sovereign power of the LORD, the Israelites were given the upper hand. They inflicted heavy casualties among the Syrian army. They killed 100,000 foot soldiers in one day. All the other Syrian forces retreated, escaping into the city of Aphek. As the retreating Syrian forces made their way up to the top of the city wall to man their battle stations, they added so much weight to the wall that it collapsed and killed 27,000 of them. In the meantime, King Ben-Hadad quickly hid in a secret room, most likely in a reinforced tower like the ones built in most fortified cities of that day.

e. Hiding in the secret room, he and his officials began to plan a strategy of negotiation to plea for mercy (vv.31-34). The Syrian officials suggested they negotiate for mercy because the Israelite kings were known to be tenderhearted and to extend mercy when people pled for compassion. Note this fact: the world of that day recognized a difference between the Israelites and other people. Even Israelite kings were different from the ruthless Assyrian kings in that they often extended mercy when compassion was requested. Knowing this fact, the Syrian officials suggested they humbly approach Ahab with the plea that he spare their lives.

Securing an audience with Ahab, the officials of King Ben-Hadad carried out their plan. They dressed in the clothing of submission and made their plea for mercy both for themselves and for King Ben-Hadad. The response of Ahab was utterly surprising, for he called Ben-Hadad "my brother."

Picking up on Ahab's tender feelings, the enemy officials responded that Ben-Hadad was indeed a fellow king, a "brother" of Ahab's. After some negotiation, Ahab sent his chariot for the Syrian king. King Ben-Hadad, now standing before Ahab, offered terms of surrender. In return for sparing his life, the Syrian king would return cities formerly conquered by Syria (15:20-22). In addition, he would grant Ahab permission to set up market places in the Syrian capital of Damascus (v.34). On the basis of this agreement, Ahab signed a treaty with the Syrian king and allowed him to go free.

> **Thought 1**. The lesson for us is a much needed one: the LORD's sovereignty (His power) is not limited or partial, but absolute. The LORD is sovereign everywhere, throughout the entire universe. He is sovereign over all nations and kingdoms upon earth and in heaven. No limitation whatsoever hampers God's sovereignty or power. God controls all events and all happenings. It is true that He has given us a free will and that He allows us to act freely within certain limitations and bounds. But God will allow us to choose evil only so often and to carry evil only to a certain point. For example, God would never allow us to destroy the earth.
>
> We may commit all kinds of evil and wicked deeds of immorality, lawlessness, and violence. Nevertheless, God, out of a heart of compassion, is long-suffering and not willing that any of us should perish and be doomed eternally. For this reason, God tolerates the evil that men and women choose to do. He created us with a free will because He longed for the worship of creatures who would freely choose to worship Him and live with Him. But through the centuries, man has chosen to deny, reject, and ignore God, walking selfishly and often wickedly in life. However, as stated earlier, God will allow us to go only so far with our evil and wickedness. He is sovereign, controlling all events and happenings, whether good or evil. Patiently waiting with a heart filled with compassion, the LORD longs for us to return to Him. His sovereign power will eventually end all evil. The climactic day is coming when God will end this corrupted world and create a new heavens and earth, a perfected universe in which all genuine

believers will live eternally, worshipping and serving the LORD. Listen to what God's Holy Word says about the sovereignty of God:

"But I say unto you, Swear not at all; neither by heaven; for it is God's throne" (Mt.5:34).

"And lead us not into temptation, but deliver us from evil: For thine is the kingdom, and the power, and the glory, for ever. Amen" (Mt.6:13).

"God that made the world and all things therein, seeing that he is Lord of heaven and earth, dwelleth not in temples made with hands" (Ac.17:24).

"And we know that all things work together for good to them that love God, to them who are the called according to *his* purpose. For whom he did foreknow, he also did predestinate *to be* conformed to the image of his Son, that he might be the firstborn among many brethren" (Ro.8:28-29).

"Thou wilt say then unto me, Why doth he yet find fault? For who hath resisted his will? Nay but, O man, who art thou that repliest against God? Shall the thing formed say to him that formed *it,* Why hast thou made me thus? Hath not the potter power over the clay, of the same lump to make one vessel unto honour, and another unto dishonour?" (Ro.9:19-21).

"For he must reign, till he hath put all enemies under his feet" (1 Co.15:25).

"Wherefore God also hath highly exalted him, and given him a name which is above every name: That at the name of Jesus every knee should bow, of *things* in heaven, and *things* in earth, and *things* under the earth; And *that* every tongue should confess that Jesus Christ *is* Lord, to the glory of God the Father" (Ph.2:9-11).

"Now unto the King eternal, immortal, invisible, the only wise God, *be* honour and glory for ever and ever. Amen" (1 Ti.1:17).

"And they sing the song of Moses the servant of God, and the song of the Lamb, saying, Great and marvellous *are* thy works, Lord God Almighty; just and true *are* thy ways, thou King of saints" (Re.15:3).

"And I heard as it were the voice of a great multitude, and as the voice of many waters, and as the voice of mighty thunderings, saying, Alleluia: for the Lord God omnipotent reigneth" (Re.19:6).

"And I saw a great white throne, and him that sat on it, from whose face the earth and the heaven fled away; and there was found no place for them" (Re.20:11).

"The LORD shall reign for ever and ever" (Ex.15:18).

"Know therefore this day, and consider *it* in thine heart, that the LORD he *is* God in heaven above, and upon the earth beneath: *there is* none else" (De.4:39).

"Both riches and honour *come* of thee, and thou reignest over all; and in thine hand *is* power and might; and in thine hand *it is* to make great, and to give strength unto all" (1 Chr.29:12).

"And said, O LORD God of our fathers, *art* not thou God in heaven? and rulest *not* thou over all the kingdoms of the heathen? and in thine hand *is there not* power and might, so that none is able to withstand thee?" (2 Chr.20:6).

"He leadeth princes away spoiled, and overthroweth the mighty" (Jb.12:19).

"The LORD *is* King for ever and ever: the heathen are perished out of his land" (Ps.10:16).

"For the kingdom *is* the LORD'S: and he *is* the governor among the nations" (Ps.22:28).

"Who is this King of glory? The LORD of hosts, he *is* the King of glory. Selah" (Ps.24:10).

"The LORD sitteth upon the flood; yea, the LORD sitteth King for ever" (Ps.29:10).

"Thy throne, O God, *is* for ever and ever: the sceptre of thy kingdom *is* a right sceptre" (Ps.45:6).

"For the LORD most high *is* terrible; *he is* a great King over all the earth" (Ps.47:2).

"Consume *them* in wrath, consume *them,* that they *may* not *be:* and let them know that God ruleth in Jacob unto the ends of the earth. Selah" (Ps.59:13).

"God shall bless us; and all the ends of the earth shall fear him" (Ps.67:7).

"Yea, all kings shall fall down before him: all nations shall serve him" (Ps.72:11).

"That *men* may know that thou, whose name alone *is* JEHOVAH, *art* the most high over all the earth" (Ps.83:18).

"The LORD reigneth, he is clothed with majesty; the LORD is clothed with strength, *wherewith* he hath girded himself: the world also is stablished, that it cannot be moved" (Ps.93:1).

"The LORD hath prepared his throne in the heavens; and his kingdom ruleth over all" (Ps.103:19).

"Whatsoever the LORD pleased, *that* did he in heaven, and in earth, in the seas, and all deep places" (Ps.135:6).

"The king's heart *is* in the hand of the LORD, *as* the rivers of water: he turneth it whithersoever he will" (Pr.21:1).

"Of the increase of *his* government and peace *there shall be* no end, upon the throne of David, and upon his kingdom, to order it, and to establish it with judgment and with justice from henceforth even for ever. The zeal of the LORD of hosts will perform this" (Is.9:7).

"But I know thy abode, and thy going out, and thy coming in, and thy rage against me. Because thy rage against me, and thy tumult, is come up into mine ears, therefore will I put my hook in thy nose, and my bridle in thy lips, and I will turn thee back by the way by which thou camest" (Is.37:28-29).

"Thus saith the LORD, thy Redeemer, and he that formed thee from the womb, I *am* the LORD that maketh all *things;* that stretcheth forth the heavens alone; that spreadeth abroad the earth by myself; That frustrateth the tokens of the liars, and maketh diviners mad; that turneth wise *men* backward, and maketh their knowledge foolish" (Is.44:24-25).

"Thus saith the LORD, The heaven *is* my throne, and the earth *is* my footstool: where *is* the house that ye build unto me? and where *is* the place of my rest?" (Is.66:1).

"Behold, the days come, saith the LORD, that I will raise unto David a righteous Branch, and a King shall reign and prosper, and shall execute judgment and justice in the earth" (Je.23:5).

"Daniel answered and said, Blessed be the name of God for ever and ever: for wisdom and might are his" (Da.2:20).

"And all the inhabitants of the earth *are* reputed as nothing: and he doeth according to his will in the army of heaven, and *among* the inhabitants of the earth: and none can stay his hand, or say unto him, What doest thou?" (Da.4:35).

"Now I Nebuchadnezzar praise and extol and honour the King of heaven, all whose works *are* truth, and his ways judgment: and those that walk in pride he is able to abase" (Da.4:37).

"And he was driven from the sons of men; and his heart was made like the beasts, and his dwelling *was* with the wild asses: they fed him with grass like oxen, and his body was wet with the dew of heaven; till he knew that the most high God ruled in the kingdom of men, and *that* he appointeth over it whomsoever he will" (Da.5:21).

"And there was given him dominion, and glory, and a kingdom, that all people, nations, and languages, should serve him: his dominion *is* an everlasting dominion, which shall not pass away, and his kingdom *that* which shall not be destroyed" (Da.7:14).

4 (20:35-43) **Disobedience, Example of—Condemnation, Example of—Ahab, Condemnation of—Prophet, Ministry of**: there was Ahab's condemnation by God through an unnamed prophet. Despite the victory just given, Ahab still refused to repent and turn from his wicked ways and false worship. Moreover, he had just refused to execute King Ben-Hadad, an evil and cruel ruler who was guilty of the most heinous crimes. Ben-Hadad had reached a point where he would never repent or turn from his brutal, savage behavior. The Syrian king should have been executed, but instead Ahab had let him live and had even signed a treaty with him. Scripture graphically describes God's accusation and condemnation of Ahab:

OUTLINE	SCRIPTURE	SCRIPTURE	OUTLINE
4. Ahab's condemnation by God through an unnamed prophet: A picture of disobedience a. The prophet's disguise 1) He ordered a fellow prophet to strike him, but was refused	35 And a certain man of the sons of the prophets said unto his neighbour in the word of the LORD, Smite me, I pray thee. And the man refused to smite him.	aside, and brought a man unto me, and said, Keep this man: if by any means he be missing, then shall thy life be for his life, or else thou shalt pay a talent of	• He pretended that he had accidentally let a prisoner escape—under threat of losing his life or of making a large payment of money
2) He predicted the other prophet's death because of his disobedience: Shows the danger of disobeying God's Word	36 Then said he unto him, Because thou hast not obeyed the voice of the LORD, behold, as soon as thou art departed from me, a lion shall slay thee. And as soon as he was departed from him, a lion found him, and slew him.	silver. 40 And as thy servant was busy here and there, he was gone. And the king of Israel said unto him, So *shall* thy judgment *be;* thyself hast decided *it.* 41 And he hasted, and took the ashes away from his face;	• He was condemned by the hard heart of Ahab 3) He stripped off his disguise & revealed himself
3) He asked another man to strike him: This man wounded the prophet—to help with his disguise	37 Then he found another man, and said, Smite me, I pray thee. And the man smote him, so that in smiting he wounded *him.*	and the king of Israel discerned him that he *was* of the prophets. 42 And he said unto him, Thus saith the LORD, Be-	to Ahab, & Ahab recognized him 4) He pronounced God's condemnation: Ahab had
b. The prophet's encounter with Ahab 1) He waited by the road for the king: Disguised as a wounded soldier	38 So the prophet departed, and waited for the king by the way, and disguised himself with ashes upon his face.	cause thou hast let go out of *thy* hand a man whom I appointed to utter destruction, therefore thy life shall go for his life, and thy people for	condemned himself, for he had let the condemned prisoner Ben-Hadad go free • Ahab would soon die
2) He called out for clemency, a pardon when King Ahab passed by	39 And as the king passed by, he cried unto the king: and he said, Thy servant went out into the midst of the battle; and, behold, a man turned	his people. 43 And the king of Israel went to his house heavy and displeased, and came to Samaria.	• Israel would be defeated c. The reaction of Ahab: Stubborn, angry, pouting, unrepentant—like a spoiled child

a. Under God's instructions, the unnamed prophet sought to disguise himself in order to confront Ahab (vv.35-37). The unnamed prophet ordered a fellow prophet to strike him so that he would appear to be a wounded soldier when he confronted the king. But the fellow prophet refused. As a result, the unnamed prophet predicted the other prophet's death. Note why: because he had explained the LORD'S instructions and the other prophet had not helped carry out the command to confront Ahab. His refusal was equivalent to disobedience. And disobeying the LORD'S Word is a dangerous matter.

Having predicted the other prophet's death by a lion, the unnamed prophet then turned to another man to strike and injure him (v.37). Obediently, this man struck the prophet to help with his disguise.

b. Note the prophet's encounter with Ahab (vv.38-42). Disguised as a wounded soldier, the unnamed prophet waited by the road for the king. When the king finally arrived and was passing by, the unnamed prophet cried out for clemency, for the king to grant him a pardon. He was pretending that he had accidentally let a prisoner escape, that he was under a grave threat from his commanding officer, that if he let the prisoner escape, he would either lose his life or be forced to pay a large payment of money (v.39).

Hearing the case, Ahab demonstrated his hard heart by condemning the man. He pronounced the verdict by simply saying that the man would bear the sentence he had just stated.

As soon as Ahab had issued his verdict, the prophet stripped off his disguise and revealed himself to the king. Immediately Ahab recognized him as one of the prophets. Standing there face-to-face with the king, the prophet pronounced God's condemnation (vv.41-42). With the very verdict that Ahab had just pronounced, he had condemned himself, for the king had let the condemned Ben-Hadad go free. Consequently, Ahab's life was demanded for the life of Ben-Hadad. Both Ahab and the Israelites of the Northern Kingdom would suffer the hand of God's judgment because of their disobedience and wickedness before God.

c. Upon hearing the condemnation of the LORD, Ahab reacted like a spoiled child: stubborn, angry, pouting, and unrepentant (v.43).

Thought 1. The lesson we can learn from this point is that disobedience has consequences. If we disobey God, we stand condemned and will bear the hand of God's judgment. Sin and wickedness cause pain, suffering, and distress; and God will not tolerate our harming and damaging other people.

Just think of the damage adultery causes within a family, the agonizing pain and suffering of the innocent spouse and the precious children. No just person with any sense of compassion would allow the guilty who cause so much pain to go free. Justice will be executed upon the guilty party of immorality.

Just think about the hurt and damage that stealing or embezzlement or cheating causes—the loss of property, the injustice done, and sometimes the terrible suffering due to financial difficulties. God is just, and He will execute justice upon the person who disobeys the commandment that forbids stealing.

Just think about the injury caused by...

- drunken driving
- sexual and physical abuse of children or any other person
- profane verbal attacks by one person against another
- murmuring, grumbling, and complaining
- bitterness, hatred, and hostility
- threats, assaults, and other acts of lawlessness and violence

All such behavior is sinful and wicked, clearly breaking the commandments of God. In giving the commandments, God intended good for us. The commandments tell us how to live good, honorable, and productive lives that are victorious and conquering, lives that prove to be successful and that bring a sense of fulfillment and satisfaction to the human heart. God's commandments are just and good, teaching us how to live lives of love, joy, peace, patience, gentleness, goodness, faithfulness, humility, and self-control. No greater life can be lived than the life that obeys God's commandments. For this reason, God condemns all disobedience. Listen to what God's Holy Word says about disobedience:

"But fornication, and all uncleanness, or covetousness, let it not be once named among you, as becometh saints; Neither filthiness, nor foolish talking, nor jesting, which are not convenient: but rather giving of thanks. For this ye know, that no whoremonger, nor unclean person, nor covetous man, who is an idolater, hath any inheritance in the kingdom of Christ and of God. Let no man deceive you with vain words: for because of these things cometh the wrath of God upon the children of disobedience" (Ep.5:3-6).

"And to you who are troubled rest with us, when the Lord Jesus shall be revealed from heaven with his mighty angels, In flaming fire taking vengeance on them that know not God, and that obey not the gospel of our Lord Jesus Christ: Who shall be punished with everlasting destruction from the presence of the Lord, and from the glory of his power" (2 Th.1:7-9).

"Knowing this, that the law is not made for a righteous man, but for the lawless and disobedient, for the ungodly and for sinners, for unholy and profane, for murderers of fathers and murderers of mothers, for manslayers" (1 Ti.1:9).

"For if the word spoken by angels was stedfast, and every transgression and disobedience received a just recompence of reward; How shall we escape, if we neglect so great salvation; which at the first began to be spoken by the Lord, and was confirmed unto us by them that heard *him*" (He.2:2-3).

"And a curse, if ye will not obey the commandments of the LORD your God, but turn aside out of the way which I command you this day, to go after other gods, which ye have not known" (De.11:28).

"But if ye will not obey the voice of the LORD, but rebel against the commandment of the LORD, then shall the hand of the LORD be against you, as *it was* against your fathers" (1 S.12:15).

"Because thou obeyedst not the voice of the LORD, nor executedst his fierce wrath upon Amalek, therefore hath the LORD done this thing unto thee this day" (1 S.28:18).

"And he cried unto the man of God that came from Judah, saying, Thus saith the LORD, Forasmuch as thou hast disobeyed the mouth of the LORD, and hast not kept the commandment which the LORD thy God commanded thee" (1 K.13:21).

"But if they will not obey, I will utterly pluck up and destroy that nation, saith the LORD" (Je.12:17).

1. The sins of Ahab: Greed & covetousness
- a. His coveting a vineyard owned by Naboth
  - 1) Was in Jezreel
  - 2) Was next to summer palace
- b. His request to purchase the vineyard for a vegetable garden
  - 1) By exchanging a better vineyard for it
  - 2) By paying for it
- c. His offer rejected: Because the vineyard had been part of Naboth's family inheritance for generations
- d. His angry, disappointed, immature reaction
  - 1) He went to bed with his face to the wall
  - 2) He sulked, pouted, & refused to eat

2. The crimes of Jezebel: Revenge & murder
- a. The disgust of Jezebel with Ahab
  - 1) She asked Ahab what was wrong:
    - • He explained his desire for the vineyard & Naboth's refusal to sell
    - • He said nothing about Naboth's reason
  - 2) She became disgusted with Ahab's weak, sulking, immature behavior
    - • Ordered him to get up
    - • Promised to get the vineyard for him
- b. The scheming plot of Jezebel
  - 1) She wrote a command to the city officials to execute Naboth: Used the king's name & imperial seal
  - 2) She made three suggestions
    - • To use the disguise of religion, proclaiming a day of fast: To show concern that a criminal or some evil threatened the city
    - • To use the formality of justice: To bribe two false witnesses to charge Naboth with treason, Ex.22:28; Le.24:16
    - • To stone him
- c. The obedience of the leaders in carrying out the reprehensible orders
  - 1) The disguise of religion, a fast, was used: To show concern that a criminal or some evil threatened the city
  - 2) The formality of justice was used
    - • The two scoundrels made false charges against Naboth
    - • The people executed Naboth, stoning him to death
  - 3) The dreadful murder was reported to Jezebel
- d. The disgraceful possession of the vineyard by Ahab
  - 1) Jezebel immediately instructed Ahab to get up & to take possession of the vineyard
  - 2) Ahab obeyed Jezebel's instructions: Got up, traveled to the vineyard he had so selfishly coveted, & took possession of it

3. The condemnation of Ahab & Jezebel: A picture of God's coming judgment
- a. The summons of God to Elijah: To go & confront Ahab to expose his sins
  - 1) Elijah was to charge Ahab with two crimes
    - • Murder
    - • Theft of property
  - 2) Elijah was to pronounce the coming judgment upon Ahab, 22:37-38

CHAPTER 21

E. The Terrible Crimes Against Naboth by Ahab & Jezebel: Facing Judgment Due to Horrible Evil, 21:1-29

And it came to pass after these things, *that* Naboth the Jezreelite had a vineyard, which *was* in Jezreel, hard by the palace of Ahab king of Samaria.

2 And Ahab spake unto Naboth, saying, Give me thy vineyard, that I may have it for a garden of herbs, because it *is* near unto my house: and I will give thee for it a better vineyard than it; *or,* if it seem good to thee, I will give thee the worth of it in money.

3 And Naboth said to Ahab, The LORD forbid it me, that I should give the inheritance of my fathers unto thee.

4 And Ahab came into his house heavy and displeased because of the word which Naboth the Jezreelite had spoken to him: for he had said, I will not give thee the inheritance of my fathers. And he laid him down upon his bed, and turned away his face, and would eat no bread.

5 But Jezebel his wife came to him, and said unto him, Why is thy spirit so sad, that thou eatest no bread?

6 And he said unto her, Because I spake unto Naboth the Jezreelite, and said unto him, Give me thy vineyard for money; or else, if it please thee, I will give thee *another* vineyard for it: and he answered, I will not give thee my vineyard.

7 And Jezebel his wife said unto him, Dost thou now govern the kingdom of Israel? arise, *and* eat bread, and let thine heart be merry: I will give thee the vineyard of Naboth the Jezreelite.

8 So she wrote letters in Ahab's name, and sealed *them* with his seal, and sent the letters unto the elders and to the nobles that *were* in his city, dwelling with Naboth.

9 And she wrote in the letters, saying, Proclaim a fast, and set Naboth on high among the people:

10 And set two men, sons of Belial, before him, to bear witness against him, saying, Thou didst blaspheme God and the king. And *then* carry him out, and stone him, that he may die.

11 And the men of his city, *even* the elders and the nobles who were the inhabitants in his city, did as Jezebel had sent unto them, *and* as it *was* written in the letters which she had sent unto them.

12 They proclaimed a fast, and set Naboth on high among the people.

13 And there came in two men, children of Belial, and sat before him: and the men of Belial witnessed against him, *even* against Naboth, in the presence of the people, saying, Naboth did blaspheme God and the king. Then they carried him forth out of the city, and stoned him with stones, that he died.

14 Then they sent to Jezebel, saying, Naboth is stoned, and is dead.

15 And it came to pass, when Jezebel heard that Naboth was stoned, and was dead, that Jezebel said to Ahab, Arise, take possession of the vineyard of Naboth the Jezreelite, which he refused to give thee for money: for Naboth is not alive, but dead.

16 And it came to pass, when Ahab heard that Naboth was dead, that Ahab rose up to go down to the vineyard of Naboth the Jez-reelite, to take possession of it.

17 And the word of the LORD came to Elijah the Tishbite, saying,

18 Arise, go down to meet Ahab king of Israel, which *is* in Samaria: behold, *he is* in the vineyard of Naboth, whither he is gone down to possess it.

19 And thou shalt speak unto him, saying, Thus saith the LORD, Hast thou killed, and also taken possession? And thou shalt speak unto him, saying, Thus saith the LORD, In the place where dogs licked the blood of Naboth

	shall dogs lick thy blood, even thine.	shall the fowls of the air eat.	
b. The encounter between Ahab & Elijah 1) Ahab called the prophet, "my enemy" 2) Elijah's response: Ahab had *sold* himself to do evil & only evil	20 And Ahab said to Elijah, Hast thou found me, O mine enemy? And he answered, I have found *thee:* because thou hast sold thyself to work evil in the sight of the LORD.	25 But there was none like unto Ahab, which did sell himself to work wickedness in the sight of the LORD, whom Jezebel his wife stirred up.	f. The reasons for God's judgment: The evil of Ahab surpassed that of all men, was the very epitome of evil 1) Had *sold* himself to do evil: Urged on by his wife Jezebel
c. The judgment of God pronounced upon Ahab 1) He would personally suffer disaster, calamity	21 Behold, I will bring evil upon thee, and will take away thy posterity, and will cut off from Ahab him that pisseth against the wall, and him that is shut up and left in Israel,	26 And he did very abominably in following idols, according to all *things* as did the Amorites, whom the LORD cast out before the children of Israel.	2) Was an idolater, a worshipper of false gods 3) Caused Israel to sin (a stumbling block), 22
2) His descendants, dynasty would be cut off: Just like Jeroboam's & Baasha's had been, 14:10; 15:28-30; 16:3-4, 11-13 • Had angered God • Had caused Israel to sin	22 And will make thine house like the house of Jeroboam the son of Nebat, and like the house of Baasha the son of Ahijah, for the provocation wherewith thou hast provoked *me* to anger, and made Israel to sin.	27 And it came to pass, when Ahab heard those words, that he rent his clothes, and put sackcloth upon his flesh, and fasted, and lay in sackcloth, and went softly. 28 And the word of the LORD came to Elijah the Tishbite, saying,	g. The outward remorse of Ahab: Did not genuinely repent of his wickedness nor turn from idolatry nor return the stolen field h. The LORD's compassion & mercy 1) He summoned Elijah
d. The judgment of God pronounced against Jezebel: To be eaten by dogs	23 And of Jezebel also spake the LORD, saying, The dogs shall eat Jezebel by the wall of Jezreel.	29 Seest thou how Ahab humbleth himself before me? because he humbleth himself before me, I will not bring the evil in his days: *but* in his son's days will I bring the evil upon his house.	2) He informed Elijah that He would delay His judgment • Delay it until the days of Ahab's son • Delay it because of Ahab's humbling himself
e. The judgment of a disgraceful death for many of the evil family	24 Him that dieth of Ahab in the city the dogs shall eat; and him that dieth in the field		

DIVISION II

THE MINISTRY OF ELIJAH AND OTHER PROPHETS DURING THE REIGN OF AHAB: LEARNING WHO THE LIVING AND TRUE GOD IS, 17:1–22:53

E. The Terrible Crimes Against Naboth by Ahab and Jezebel: Facing Judgment Due to Horrible Evil, 21:1-29

(21:1-29) **Introduction**: Can an individual do so much evil that God will condemn the person to hell, to eternal separation from God? Is there in reality a judgment to be faced? Is there even such a place as hell? Many people believe not, for they deny God's very existence. And even some of us who believe in God do not believe in a future day of justice, that God is going to hold all people accountable for their behavior. Interestingly, most people do not think that God would ever reject them, not in the final analysis. Most people feel when the climactic day of judgment comes, God will accept them. Few people believe they deserve hell, that they have committed enough sin to be condemned by God.

Nevertheless, no matter what we believe or think, there is a day of justice coming. And according to the Lord Jesus Christ and Holy Scripture, there is a place called hell, a prison where all the lawless of this earth—all who have rejected the Lord and His commandments—will spend eternity. In fact, Christ Himself referred to hell more than did any other person in Scripture. And probably, He referred to hell more than any person in human history. Think about this fact: one of the major teachings of the Lord Jesus Christ is that there is a place called hell and there is a coming judgment. That day of justice will determine the fate of people, whether they will spend eternity with God or in the dreadful place or prison called hell.

Once again, can a person commit evil worthy of judgment and hell? This is the practical subject painted by the present Scripture. This is: *The Terrible Crimes Against Naboth by Ahab and Jezebel: Facing Judgment Due to Horrible Evil,* 21:1-29.

1. The sins of Ahab: greed and covetousness (vv.1-4).
2. The crimes of Jezebel: revenge and murder (vv.5-17).
3. The condemnation of Ahab and Jezebel: a picture of God's coming judgment (vv.18-29).

[1] (21:1-4) **Greed, Example of—Covetousness, Example of—Behavior, Childish, Example of—Immaturity, Example of—Ahab, Character - Nature of—Ahab, Sins of**: the sins of Ahab included greed and covetousness. Sometime after the victory over Syria, Ahab and his infamous wife Jezebel were spending time in their summer palace located in Jezreel. Next to the palace was a vineyard that caught the eye of the king, and he began to covet the vineyard. Going to Naboth, the owner, Ahab requested the right to purchase the vineyard, offering either to pay for it or else to

exchange a better vineyard for it (vv.1-2). But Naboth rejected the offer because the vineyard had been part of his family's inheritance for generations (v.3). Notice the angry, disappointed, and childish reaction by Ahab: he went home and went to bed, turning his face to the wall, sulking, pouting, and refusing to eat (v.4).

OUTLINE	SCRIPTURE	SCRIPTURE	OUTLINE
1. The sins of Ahab: Greed &	**A**nd it came to pass after	it in money.	
covetousness	these things, *that* Naboth the	3 And Naboth said to Ahab,	c. His offer rejected: Because
a. His coveting a vineyard	Jezreelite had a vineyard,	The LORD forbid it me, that I	the vineyard had been part of
owned by Naboth	which *was* in Jezreel, hard by	should give the inheritance of	Naboth's family inheritance
1) Was in Jezreel	the palace of Ahab king of	my fathers unto thee.	for generations
2) Was next to summer palace	Samaria.	4 And Ahab came into his	d. His angry, disappointed,
b. His request to purchase the	2 And Ahab spake unto	house heavy and displeased	immature reaction
vineyard for a vegetable	Naboth, saying, Give me thy	because of the word which	
garden	vineyard, that I may have it	Naboth the Jezreelite had	
	for a garden of herbs, be-	spoken to him: for he had	
	cause it *is* near unto my	said, I will not give thee the	
1) By exchanging a better	house: and I will give thee	inheritance of my fathers.	1) He went to bed with his
vineyard for it	for it a better vineyard than	And he laid him down upon	face to the wall
	it; *or,* if it seem good to thee,	his bed, and turned away his	2) He sulked, pouted, &
2) By paying for it	I will give thee the worth of	face, and would eat no bread.	refused to eat

Note this fact: Ahab's desire for the vineyard was not wrong, nor was his offer to purchase the property. What was wrong was his coveting the field, the greed that filled his heart. Moreover, his selfish disposition stirred childish and immature behavior within him. Apparently, such shallow and immature reactions were a trait of Ahab's character or personality.

Thought 1. Greed and covetousness are forbidden by God. Covetousness is even named and condemned by one of the Ten Commandments. A person who covets will take advantage of other people in order to get more and more. It is covetousness and greed that cause...

- a landlord to rent property that needs repair or to charge too high a price for the rental property
- a contractor to take shortcuts in his building project
- a repairman to use secondhand replacement parts or to perform a mediocre job
- an employee to abuse his employer by doing personal tasks when he or she is supposed to be on the job
- a man or woman to lust after the wife or husband of someone else
- a person to lie, steal, or cheat in order to get what he desires
- companies to overcharge for their products and to steal ideas, plans, or products from other companies
- politicians and other leaders to make false promises and to misuse their authority for their own personal interests and cravings

Covetousness and greed can affect any area of our lives, for these two terrible evils arise out of the heart. It is from within the heart that lusts and sinful desires originate. Listen to what God's Holy Word says about these two terrible evils:

"And he said unto them, Take heed, and beware of covetousness: for a man's life consisteth not in the abundance of the things which he possesseth" (Lu.12:15).

"But fornication, and all uncleanness, or covetousness, let it not be once named among you, as becometh saints" (Ep.5:3).

"Mortify therefore your members which are upon the earth; fornication, uncleanness, inordinate affection, evil concupiscence, and covetousness, which is idolatry: For which things' sake the wrath of God cometh on the children of disobedience" (Col.3:5-6).

"Not given to wine, no striker, not greedy of filthy lucre; but patient, not a brawler, not covetous" (1 Ti.3:3).

"For the love of money is the root of all evil: which while some coveted after, they have erred from the faith, and pierced themselves through with many sorrows" (1 Ti.6:10).

"*Let your* conversation [behavior, conduct] *be* without covetousness; *and be* content with such things as ye have: for he hath said, I will never leave thee, nor forsake thee" (He.13:5).

"Your gold and silver is cankered; and the rust of them shall be a witness against you, and shall eat your flesh as it were fire. Ye have heaped treasure together for the last days" (Ja.5:3).

"Thou shalt not covet thy neighbour's house, thou shalt not covet thy neighbour's wife, nor his manservant, nor his maidservant, nor his ox, nor his ass, nor any thing that *is* thy neighbour's" (Ex.20:17).

"And his sons walked not in his ways, but turned aside after lucre, and took bribes, and perverted judgment" (1 S.8:3).

"For the wicked boasteth of his heart's desire, and blesseth the covetous, *whom* the LORD abhorreth" (Ps.10:3).

"My son, if sinners entice thee, consent thou not. If they say, Come with us, let us lay wait for blood, let us lurk privily for the innocent without cause: Let us swallow them up alive as the grave; and whole, as those that go down into the pit: We shall find all precious substance, we shall fill our houses

with spoil: Cast in thy lot among us; let us all have one purse: My son, walk not thou in the way with them; refrain thy foot from their path: For their feet run to evil, and make haste to shed blood. Surely in vain the net is spread in the sight of any bird. And they lay wait for their *own* blood; they lurk privily for their *own* lives. So *are* the ways of every one that is greedy of gain; *which* taketh away the life of the owners thereof" (Pr.1:10-19).

"He that is greedy of gain troubleth his own house; but he that hateth gifts shall live" (Pr.15:27).

"The desire of the slothful killeth him; for his hands refuse to labour. He coveteth greedily all the day long: but the righteous giveth and spareth not" (Pr.21:25-26).

"The prince that wanteth understanding *is* also a great oppressor: *but* he that hateth covetousness shall prolong *his* days" (Pr.28:16).

"He that loveth silver shall not be satisfied with silver; nor he that loveth abundance with increase: this *is* also vanity" (Ec.5:10).

"Yea, *they are* greedy dogs *which* can never have enough, and they *are* shepherds *that* cannot understand: they all look to their own way, every one for his gain, from his quarter" (Is.56:11).

"For from the least of them even unto the greatest of them every one *is* given to covetousness; and from the prophet even unto the priest every one dealeth falsely" (Je.6:13).

"As the partridge sitteth *on eggs,* and hatcheth *them* not; *so* he that getteth riches, and not by right, shall leave them in the midst of his days, and at his end shall be a fool" (Je.17:11).

"And they come unto thee as the people cometh, and they sit before thee as my people, and they hear thy words, but they will not do them: for with their mouth they show much love, *but* their heart goeth after their covetousness" (Eze.33:31).

"And they covet fields, and take *them* by violence; and houses, and take *them* away: so they oppress a man and his house, even a man and his heritage" (Mi.2:2).

"The heads thereof judge for reward, and the priests thereof teach for hire, and the prophets thereof divine for money: yet will they lean upon the LORD, and say, *Is* not the LORD among us? none evil can come upon us" (Mi.3:11).

"Woe to him that coveteth an evil covetousness to his house, that he may set his nest on high, that he may be delivered from the power of evil!" (Hab.2:9).

2 (21:5-16) **Revenge, Example of—Murder, Example of—Sins, Listed, Revenge—Jezebel, Sins and Evil of**: the crimes of Jezebel included revenge and murder. Remember that Jezebel was a tyrant who was completely given over to evil. Throughout her reign as queen, she launched a purge to eliminate the prophets and the worship of the LORD from the land of Israel. The depth of her sinful, evil heart is exposed by Scripture in the following event:

OUTLINE	SCRIPTURE	SCRIPTURE	OUTLINE
2. The crimes of Jezebel: Revenge & murder a. The disgust of Jezebel with Ahab 1) She asked Ahab what was wrong: • He explained his desire for the vineyard & Naboth's refusal to sell • He said nothing about Naboth's reason	5 But Jezebel his wife came to him, and said unto him, Why is thy spirit so sad, that thou eatest no bread? 6 And he said unto her, Because I spake unto Naboth the Jezreelite, and said unto him, Give me thy vineyard for money; or else, if it please thee, I will give thee *another* vineyard for it: and he answered, I will not give thee my vineyard.	witness against him, saying, Thou didst blaspheme God and the king. And *then* carry him out, and stone him, that he may die. 11 And the men of his city, *even* the elders and the nobles who were the inhabitants in his city, did as Jezebel had sent unto them, *and* as it *was* written in the letters which she had sent unto them.	false witnesses to charge Naboth with treason, Ex.22:28; Le.24:16 • To stone him c. The obedience of the leaders in carrying out the reprehensible orders
2) She became disgusted with Ahab's weak, sulking, immature behavior • Ordered him to get up • Promised to get the vineyard for him b. The scheming plot of Jezebel 1) She wrote a command to the city officials to execute Naboth: Used the king's name & imperial seal 2) She made three suggestions • To use the disguise of religion, proclaiming a day of fast: To show concern that a criminal or some evil threatened the city • To use the formality of justice: To bribe two	7 And Jezebel his wife said unto him, Dost thou now govern the kingdom of Israel? arise, *and* eat bread, and let thine heart be merry: I will give thee the vineyard of Naboth the Jezreelite. 8 So she wrote letters in Ahab's name, and sealed *them* with his seal, and sent the letters unto the elders and to the nobles that *were* in his city, dwelling with Naboth. 9 And she wrote in the letters, saying, Proclaim a fast, and set Naboth on high among the people: 10 And set two men, sons of Belial, before him, to bear	12 They proclaimed a fast, and set Naboth on high among the people. 13 And there came in two men, children of Belial, and sat before him: and the men of Belial witnessed against him, *even* against Naboth, in the presence of the people, saying, Naboth did blaspheme God and the king. Then they carried him forth out of the city, and stoned him with stones, that he died. 14 Then they sent to Jezebel, saying, Naboth is stoned, and is dead. 15 And it came to pass, when	1) The disguise of religion, a fast, was used: To show concern that a criminal or some evil threatened the city 2) The formality of justice was used • The two scoundrels made false charges against Naboth • The people executed Naboth, stoning him to death 3) The dreadful murder was reported to Jezebel d. The disgraceful possession

OUTLINE	SCRIPTURE	SCRIPTURE	OUTLINE
of the vineyard by Ahab 1) Jezebel immediately instructed Ahab to get up & to take possession of the vineyard	Jezebel heard that Naboth was stoned, and was dead, that Jezebel said to Ahab, Arise, take possession of the vineyard of Naboth the Jezreelite, which he refused to give thee for money: for Naboth is not alive, but	dead. 16 And it came to pass, when Ahab heard that Naboth was dead, that Ahab rose up to go down to the vineyard of Naboth the Jezreelite, to take possession of it.	2) Ahab obeyed Jezebel's instructions: Got up, traveled to the vineyard he had so selfishly coveted, & took possession of it

a. When Jezebel walked into the bedroom of the palace and found Ahab sulking, pouting, and refusing to eat, she became very disgusted (vv.5-7). When she asked her husband what was wrong, Ahab explained his desire for the vineyard and Naboth's refusal to sell the property to him. Note that he said absolutely nothing about Naboth's reason for keeping the property in his family, nothing about its having been in the family inheritance for generations.

Being totally fed up with Ahab's weak, immature, and childish behavior, Jezebel questioned if this were any way for a king to act. She ordered him to get up, eat, and cheer up, for she would get the vineyard for him.

b. Taking immediate action, Jezebel devised a wicked plot against Naboth's life (vv.8-10). She wrote a command to the officials of the city where Naboth lived and ordered them to plot his execution. Note that she used the king's name and the imperial seal to indicate that the command was coming from the king's full authority and power (v.8). In the letters, she suggested that the *pretense of religion* be used by proclaiming a day of fast for the citizens of the city (v.9; Jud.20:26; 1 S.7:5-6; 2 Chr.20:2-4). In ancient times, a day of fasting was sometimes set aside in order to show concern that a criminal or some other evil threatened the city.

But in addition to using the *guise of religion*, Jezebel suggested using the *formality of justice* by bribing two false witnesses to charge Naboth with treason (Ex.22:28; Le.24:16). Finally Jezebel suggested that the officials, after finding Naboth guilty, take him outside the city gates and stone him to death.

c. Just as Jezebel commanded under the king's authority, the officials of the city carried out the reprehensible orders (vv.11-14). They used the false pretext of a religious fast, showing concern that some criminal was loose in the city. Hypocritically—desperately—the officials declared that the hand of God's judgment would fall upon them unless the criminal was exposed. In addition, they used the formality of justice (v.13). Two scoundrels were bribed to make false charges against Naboth, making a mockery of the justice system. As a result, the officials executed an innocent man under the false charges commanded by Jezebel.

The officials then reported their treacherous act of murder—the horrible and unjustified murder—to the queen (v.14). After hearing the report, Jezebel at once instructed Ahab to get up and to take possession of the vineyard. Obeying her instructions, he traveled down to the vineyard and took possession of the field he had so selfishly coveted (vv.15-16).

Thought 1. Jezebel is the very epitome of wickedness. Consumed by evil and corruption, she found it easy to seek revenge and to take the life of an innocent man. It did not matter to her that she took a man's life just to secure a piece of land so her husband could plant a garden. What a shocking abuse of power!

When people strike out against us or fail us or disappoint us, we must seek peace and not retaliation or revenge. As we walk through life day by day—whether at work, in restaurants, in carpools, in retail stores, in businesses, in schools, in church, or anywhere else—we are often offended by what other people say or do. Even on a national level when enemies threaten our country, we must not immediately retaliate and seek vengeance. As Christian believers, we are to first seek peace.

But note this fact: we are never to indulge nor give license to evil. We are always to confront evil with justice, for love demands it. We are not to allow evil to run wild, causing injury, pain, suffering, destruction, or death to any person or animal or business or organization. Peace should always be the objective with our neighbors, whether they are living next door, working beside us, or residing in another nation of the world. But if our neighbors reject the message of peace, we must execute justice without seeking personal retaliation or revenge. God allows us to defend ourselves, but always in a spirit of understanding, love, and justice.

Retaliation and revenge can consume our hearts, causing us to forget peace, love, and justice. As a result, we sometimes find ourselves striking out in bitterness, hostility, and injustice. But a heart that is acceptable to God is one that seeks peace and brotherly compassion and justice among all people everywhere. A godly heart never seeks retaliation or revenge.

(1) Listen to what God has to say about revenge and retaliation.

"But I say unto you, That ye resist not evil: but whosoever shall smite thee on thy right cheek, turn to him the other also" (Mt.5:39).

"Recompense to no man evil for evil. Provide things honest in the sight of all men." (Ro.12:17).

"If it be possible, as much as lieth in you, live peaceably with all men" (Ro.12:18).

"Let us therefore follow after the things which make for peace, and things wherewith one may edify another" (Ro.14:19).

"See that none render evil for evil unto any *man;* but ever follow that which is good, both among yourselves, and to all *men*" (1 Th.5:15).

"Follow peace with all *men,* and holiness, without which no man shall see the Lord" (He.12:14).

"Not rendering evil for evil, or railing for railing: but contrariwise blessing; knowing that ye are thereunto called, that ye should inherit a blessing" (1 Pe.3:9).

"Thou shalt not avenge, nor bear any grudge against the children of thy people, but thou shalt love thy neighbour as thyself: I *am* the LORD" (Le.19:18).

"Say not thou, I will recompense evil; *but* wait on the LORD, and he shall save thee" (Pr.20:22).
"Say not, I will do so to him as he hath done to me: I will render to the man according to his work" (Pr.24:29).

(2) Listen to what God says about murder.

"For this, Thou shalt not commit adultery, Thou shalt not kill, Thou shalt not steal, Thou shalt not bear false witness, Thou shalt not covet; and if *there be* any other commandment, it is briefly comprehended in this saying, namely, Thou shalt love thy neighbour as thyself" (Ro.13:9).
"Now the works of the flesh are manifest, which are *these;* Adultery, fornication, uncleanness, lasciviousness, Idolatry, witchcraft, hatred, variance, emulations, wrath, strife, seditions, heresies, Envyings, murders, drunkenness, revellings, and such like: of the which I tell you before, as I have also told *you* in time past, that they which do such things shall not inherit the kingdom of God" (Ga.5:19-21).
"But let none of you suffer as a murderer, or *as* a thief, or *as* an evildoer, or as a busybody in other men's matters" (1 Pe.4:15).
"Whosoever hateth his brother is a murderer: and ye know that no murderer hath eternal life abiding in him" (1 Jn.3:15).
"But the fearful, and unbelieving, and the abominable, and murderers, and whoremongers, and sorcerers, and idolaters, and all liars, shall have their part in the lake which burneth with fire and brimstone: which is the second death" (Re.21:8).
"Thou shalt not kill" (Ex.20:13).

3 (21:17-29) **Judgment, Surety of—Condemnation, Example of—Ahab, Condemnation of—Jezebel, Judgment and Condemnation of**: Elijah pronounced God's condemnation upon Ahab and Jezebel. The hand of God's coming judgment was to fall upon them. Scripture graphically describes the terrifying fate that was to fall upon both Ahab and Jezebel:

OUTLINE	SCRIPTURE	SCRIPTURE	OUTLINE
3. The condemnation of Ahab & Jezebel: A picture of God's coming judgment a. The summons of God to Elijah: To go & confront Ahab to expose his sins	17 And the word of the LORD came to Elijah the Tishbite, saying, 18 Arise, go down to meet Ahab king of Israel, which *is* in Samaria: behold, *he is* in the vineyard of Naboth, whither he is gone down to possess it.	and made Israel to sin. 23 And of Jezebel also spake the LORD, saying, The dogs shall eat Jezebel by the wall of Jezreel. 24 Him that dieth of Ahab in the city the dogs shall eat; and him that dieth in the field shall the fowls of the air eat.	• Had caused Israel to sin d. The judgment of God pronounced against Jezebel: To be eaten by dogs e. The judgment of a disgraceful death for many of the evil family
1) Elijah was to charge Ahab with two crimes • Murder • Theft of property 2) Elijah was to pronounce the coming judgment upon Ahab, 22:37-38	19 And thou shalt speak unto him, saying, Thus saith the LORD, Hast thou killed, and also taken possession? And thou shalt speak unto him, saying, Thus saith the LORD, In the place where dogs licked the blood of Naboth shall dogs lick thy blood, even thine.	25 But there was none like unto Ahab, which did sell himself to work wickedness in the sight of the LORD, whom Jezebel his wife stirred up. 26 And he did very abominably in following idols, according to all *things* as did the Amorites, whom the LORD cast out before the children of Israel.	f. The reasons for God's judgment: The evil of Ahab surpassed that of all men, was the very epitome of evil 1) Had *sold* himself to do evil: Urged on by his wife Jezebel 2) Was an idolater, a worshipper of false gods 3) Caused Israel to sin (a stumbling block), 22
b. The encounter between Ahab & Elijah 1) Ahab called the prophet, "my enemy" 2) Elijah's response: Ahab had *sold* himself to do evil & only evil	20 And Ahab said to Elijah, Hast thou found me, O mine enemy? And he answered, I have found *thee:* because thou hast sold thyself to work evil in the sight of the LORD.	27 And it came to pass, when Ahab heard those words, that he rent his clothes, and put sackcloth upon his flesh, and fasted, and lay in sackcloth, and went softly.	g. The outward remorse of Ahab: Did not genuinely repent of his wickedness nor turn from idolatry nor return the stolen field
c. The judgment of God pronounced upon Ahab 1) He would personally suffer disaster, calamity 2) His descendants, dynasty would be cut off: Just like Jeroboam's & Baasha's had been, 14:10; 15:28-30; 16:3-4, 11-13 • Had angered God	21 Behold, I will bring evil upon thee, and will take away thy posterity, and will cut off from Ahab him that pisseth against the wall, and him that is shut up and left in Israel, 22 And will make thine house like the house of Jeroboam the son of Nebat, and like the house of Baasha the son of Ahijah, for the provocation wherewith thou hast provoked *me* to anger,	28 And the word of the LORD came to Elijah the Tishbite, saying, 29 Seest thou how Ahab humbleth himself before me? because he humbleth himself before me, I will not bring the evil in his days: *but* in his son's days will I bring the evil upon his house.	h. The LORD's compassion & mercy 1) He summoned Elijah 2) He informed Elijah that He would delay His judgment • Delay it until the days of Ahab's son • Delay it because of Ahab's humbling himself

a. God issued a summons to Elijah the prophet: he was to go and confront Ahab to expose his sins (vv.17-18). And note where Ahab was: in Naboth's vineyard, where the king had gone to take possession of it. Elijah was to charge Ahab with two crimes: murder and theft of property. After laying out the charge, the prophet was to pronounce the coming justice of God upon the king. Dogs were to lick up the blood of Ahab just as they had Naboth's blood. No matter where Ahab was, he would not be able to hide nor to escape the coming judgment.

b. As Elijah was approaching Ahab for the encounter, Ahab called out, addressing the prophet as "my enemy" who had found him (v.20). In a very straightforward response, Elijah declared that, yes, he had found Ahab because the king had sold himself out to do evil. In the eyes of the LORD he had committed the most horrible evil, that of murder and of stealing an innocent victim's property.

c. Then, without hesitating, Elijah pronounced the divine sentence of God upon Ahab (vv.21-22). Disaster was coming upon Ahab personally and upon his descendants and dynasty. Tragedy would consume both him and his descendants. Every last male in Israel who was a descendant of Ahab would be cut off—whether slave or free. His house or dynasty was to suffer just as Jeroboam's and Baasha's had, because he had provoked God's anger by his wickedness and by causing the Israelites to sin (14:10; 15:28-30; 16:3-4, 11-13). By being a stumbling block of evil, Ahab was to suffer the terrifying justice of God.

d. After pronouncing judgment upon Ahab and without giving the king time to respond, Elijah pronounced the judgment of God upon Jezebel (v.23). The queen was to be eaten by dogs beside the wall of Jezreel. Jezebel would not escape the hand of God's justice, for she stood guilty of terrible evil in purging the land of the LORD's prophets and of the worship of His Name.

e. All who belonged to Ahab would suffer disgraceful deaths (v.24). The corpses of all who lived in the city would be eaten by dogs, and those who lived in the country would have their corpses consumed by the birds of the air.

f. Elijah pronounced three reasons for God's judgment upon the king (vv.25-26). The evil of Ahab surpassed that of all men. He was the very epitome of evil:

1) He had sold himself to do evil, and he had allowed his wife Jezebel to influence and urge him on in his wicked ways.
2) He had lived the life of an idolater, a false worshipper just like the Amorites whom the LORD had driven out of the promised land.
3) He had become a stumbling block to the Israelites, causing them to sin and to engage in idolatry and false worship. He had failed to set an example of righteousness before the people and failed to institute social and religious reforms that would have turned the people back to the LORD (v.22).

g. Stricken with utter terror, Ahab showed an outward remorse by tearing off his clothes, putting on sackcloth, and fasting. But note this fact: he was reacting to the divine decree, not genuinely repenting of his wickedness nor turning from his idolatry. Neither was he willing to return the stolen property to the family of Naboth.

h. Nevertheless, the LORD demonstrated compassion and mercy by summoning Elijah and informing him that he would delay His sentence upon Ahab. He would not execute justice upon the house of Ahab until his son took the throne. God's compassion and mercy were being shown because Ahab had humbled himself to some degree before the LORD. Note how this is a strong demonstration of God's eternal mercy and compassion, ever longing for people to repent and return to Him—even those who are terrible sinners living corrupt and immoral lives (2 Pe.3:9).

Thought 1. The major lesson for us is the surety of God's judgment. His judgment is inevitable. If we live lives of sin, wickedness, and evil, we will bear the hand of God's justice. Just as God predicted that judgment would fall upon Ahab and Jezebel, so it fell. Because of their brutality and horrible evil, they both bore the terrifying justice of God. Even today, while this material is being written, Ahab and Jezebel are still suffering eternal separation from God and His holy presence, suffering in a place or prison that the Lord Jesus Christ called hell. And they will suffer there for all eternity. For once we are born into this world, we never cease to exist. First, we exist upon this earth, and then after death, we continue to exist either with God in heaven or without God in hell. In this life there is only one place where we can live: on this earth. But in the next life, there are two places where all of mankind will spend eternity: either in heaven with God or in the prison of hell separated from God.

Where we spend eternity is determined by how we live while upon this earth. If we live wicked and disobedient lives, then we follow in the footsteps of Ahab and Jezebel and will join them in hell. But if we follow after Christ, living righteous and holy lives, we will live in heaven with God throughout all eternity. We will join Elijah and all the other prophets of God and all believers who have trusted the LORD from the beginning of human history. Listen to what God's Holy Word says about the coming judgment:

"I indeed baptize you with water unto repentance: but he that cometh after me is mightier than I, whose shoes I am not worthy to bear: he shall baptize you with the Holy Ghost, and *with* fire: Whose fan *is* in his hand, and he will throughly purge his floor, and gather his wheat into the garner; but he will burn up the chaff with unquenchable fire" (Mt.3:11-12).

"But I say unto you, That whosoever looketh on a woman to lust after her hath committed adultery with her already in his heart. And if thy right eye offend thee, pluck it out, and cast *it* from thee: for it is profitable for thee that one of thy members should perish, and not *that* thy whole body should be cast into hell" (Mt.5:28-29).

"The Son of man shall send forth his angels, and they shall gather out of his kingdom all things that offend, and them which do iniquity; And shall cast them into a furnace of fire: there shall be wailing and gnashing of teeth" (Mt.13:41-42).

"And if thine eye offend thee, pluck it out, and cast *it* from thee: it is better for thee to enter into life with one eye, rather than having two eyes to be cast into hell fire" (Mt.18:9).

"Then shall he say also unto them on the left hand, Depart from me, ye cursed, into everlasting fire, prepared for the devil and his angels" (Mt.25:41).

"And if thy hand offend thee, cut it off: it is better for thee to enter into life maimed, than having two hands to go into hell, into the fire that never shall be quenched" (Mk.9:43).

"But I will forewarn you whom ye shall fear: Fear him, which after he hath killed hath power to cast into hell; yea, I say unto you, Fear him" (Lu.12:5).

"Marvel not at this: for the hour is coming, in the which all that are in the graves shall hear his voice, And shall come forth; they that have done good, unto the resurrection of life; and they that have done evil, unto the resurrection of damnation" (Jn.5:28-29).

"And as it is appointed unto men once to die, but after this the judgment" (He.9:27).

"For if God spared not the angels that sinned, but cast *them* down to hell, and delivered *them* into chains of darkness, to be reserved unto judgment; And spared not the old world, but saved Noah the eighth *person,* a preacher of righteousness, bringing in the flood upon the world of the ungodly; And turning the cities of Sodom and Gomorrah into ashes condemned *them* with an overthrow, making *them* an ensample unto those that after should live ungodly; And delivered just Lot, vexed with the filthy conversation of the wicked: (For that righteous man dwelling among them, in seeing and hearing, vexed *his* righteous soul from day to day with *their* unlawful deeds;) The Lord knoweth how to deliver the godly out of temptations, and to reserve the unjust unto the day of judgment to be punished" (2 Pe.2:4-9).

"But the heavens and the earth, which are now, by the same word are kept in store, reserved unto fire against the day of judgment and perdition of ungodly men" (2 Pe.3:7).

"And Enoch also, the seventh from Adam, prophesied of these, saying, Behold, the Lord cometh with ten thousands of his saints, To execute judgment upon all, and to convince all that are ungodly among them of all their ungodly deeds which they have ungodly committed, and of all their hard *speeches* which ungodly sinners have spoken against him" (Jude 14-15).

"And I saw a great white throne, and him that sat on it, from whose face the earth and the heaven fled away; and there was found no place for them. And I saw the dead, small and great, stand before God; and the books were opened: and another book was opened, which is *the book* of life: and the dead were judged out of those things which were written in the books, according to their works. And the sea gave up the dead which were in it; and death and hell delivered up the dead which were in them: and they were judged every man according to their works. And death and hell were cast into the lake of fire. This is the second death. And whosoever was not found written in the book of life was cast into the lake of fire" (Re.20:11-15).

1. Ahab's alliance with Jehoshaphat: An unholy, worldly union
  a. The three-year peace between Syria & Israel, 20:1-43
  b. The visit of Jehoshaphat with Ahab: During the third year
  c. The concern of Ahab to reclaim the strategic highlands of Ramoth Gilead: Its return had been promised by King Ben-Hadad of Syria when he was defeated by Ahab, 15:20; 20:34
  d. The appeal of Ahab to Jehoshaphat for an alliance to retake Ramoth
    1) Jehoshaphat—a true believer—agreed for political purposes: Was later condemned for the unholy, worldly alliance, 2 Chr.19:2
    2) Jehoshaphat suggested they first seek the LORD's counsel: But he had already agreed to the worldly alliance

2. Ahab's false prophets consulted: A readiness to listen to false teachers
  a. The 400 false prophets of Ahab: When summoned, predicted & assured the kings of victory
  b. The godly desire of Jehoshaphat: Wanted the counsel of a true prophet, a prophet of the LORD
    1) Ahab—somewhat whining—responded that he knew of one such prophet, but he hated him
      • The prophet never prophesied anything good about him, only bad
      • The prophet's name was Micaiah
    2) Jehoshaphat rebuked Ahab & urged him to call Micaiah
    3) Ahab sent an official after Micaiah, the LORD's true prophet
  c. The impressive scene of the dramatic event: The two kings in their royal robes sitting on their thrones by the city gate of Samaria
    1) The false prophets were prophesying before them

CHAPTER 22

F. The Death of Ahab: Proving the Surety of God's Judgment, 22:1-40

And they continued three
years without war between
Syria and Israel.
2 And it came to pass in the
third year, that Jehoshaphat
the king of Judah came down
to the king of Israel.
3 And the king of Israel
said unto his servants, Know
ye that Ramoth in Gilead
is ours, and we *be* still,
and take it not out of
the hand of the king of
Syria?
4 And he said unto Jehoshaphat, Wilt thou go with
me to battle to Ramoth-
gilead? And Jehoshaphat said
to the king of Israel, I *am* as
thou *art,* my people as thy
people, my horses as thy
horses.
5 And Jehoshaphat said unto
the king of Israel, Enquire, I
pray thee, at the word of the
LORD to day.
6 Then the king of Israel
gathered the prophets together, about four hundred men,
and said unto them, Shall I
go against Ramoth-gilead to
battle, or shall I forbear? And
they said, Go up; for the Lord
shall deliver *it* into the hand
of the king.
7 And Jehoshaphat said, *Is*
there not here a prophet of
the LORD besides, that we
might enquire of him?
8 And the king of Israel
said unto Jehoshaphat,
There is yet one man,
Micaiah the son of Imlah,
by whom we may enquire
of the LORD: but I hate
him; for he doth not prophesy good concerning me,
but evil. And Jehosha-
phat said, Let not the king
say so.
9 Then the king of Israel
called an officer, and said,
Hasten *hither* Micaiah the
son of Imlah.
10 And the king of Israel
and Jehoshaphat the king of
Judah sat each on his throne,
having put on their robes, in
a void place in the entrance
of the gate of Samaria; and
all the prophets prophesied
before them.
11 And Zedekiah the son of
Chenaanah made him horns
of iron: and he said, Thus
saith the LORD, With these
shalt thou push the Syrians,
until thou have consumed
them.
12 And all the prophets
prophesied so, saying, Go
up to Ramoth-gilead, and
prosper: for the LORD shall
deliver *it* into the king's
hand.
13 And the messenger that
was gone to call Micaiah
spake unto him, saying, Behold now, the words of the
prophets *declare* good unto
the king with one mouth: let
thy word, I pray thee, be like
the word of one of them, and
speak *that which is* good.
14 And Micaiah said, *As* the
LORD liveth, what the LORD
saith unto me, that will I
speak.
15 So he came to the king.
And the king said unto him,
Micaiah, shall we go against
Ramoth-gilead to battle, or
shall we forbear? And he answered him, Go, and prosper:
for the LORD shall deliver *it*
into the hand of the king.
16 And the king said unto
him, How many times shall I
adjure thee that thou tell me
nothing but *that which is* true
in the name of the LORD?
17 And he said, I saw all Israel scattered upon the hills,
as sheep that have not a
shepherd: and the LORD said,
These have no master: let
them return every man to his
house in peace.
18 And the king of Is-
rael said unto Jehosha-
phat, Did I not tell thee
that he would prophesy no
good concerning me, but
evil?
19 And he said, Hear thou
therefore the word of the
LORD: I saw the LORD sitting
on his throne, and all the host
of heaven standing by him
on his right hand and on his
left.
20 And the LORD said, Who
shall persuade Ahab, that he
may go up and fall at Ra-
moth-gilead? And one said
on this manner, and another
said on that manner.
21 And there came forth a

    2) The leader Zedekiah had made a set of iron horns & claimed to have a special message from the LORD: The kings would gore, defeat the Syrians
    3) The other prophets—all of them—agreed:
      • Urged the two kings to attack Ramoth Gilead
      • Assured them the LORD would give victory
  d. The dramatic scene of the eruption about to take place
    1) The official who had summoned the LORD's true prophet warned him to agree with the other prophets, predicting victory
    2) The prophet Micaiah boldly responded: He would proclaim only what God said—only His Word

3. Ahab's death predicted by the prophet Micaiah: The surety of prophecy, of God's Word
  a. The question of Ahab: Should they attack?
    1) Micaiah responded sarcastically: "Attack—be victorious"
    2) Ahab sensed the sarcasm & demanded the truth
  b. The first prophecy of Micaiah: A prediction exposing Ahab's poor leadership & death
    1) Micaiah saw Israel as sheep with no shepherd (Ahab)
    2) Ahab remarked with half-hearted humor to Jehoshaphat: "See, he never predicts anything good about me, only bad"
  c. The second prophecy of Micaiah: A prediction of Ahab's deception & death
    1) Micaiah saw the LORD sitting on His throne surrounded by the host of heaven
      • The LORD asked who would persuade Ahab to attack Ramoth Gilead so he could be killed: A picture of facing the judgment of God
      • A spirit stepped forth to

volunteer: He would go as a lying spirit in the mouths of Ahab's false prophets
- The LORD agreed, & charged the spirit to go & stir the false prophets to lie & persuade Ahab to attack Syria

2) Micaiah denounced the false prophets, declared they were lying to Ahab: The LORD had decreed disaster, death for him

d. The reaction & rage of the false prophet Zedekiah
1) Zedekiah walked up & slapped Micaiah in the face: Claimed he had God's Spirit as much as Micaiah did
2) Micaiah predicted that Zedekiah would soon be hiding in terror: He would then know the truth

e. The reaction & rage of Ahab
1) He ordered Micaiah to be arrested & imprisoned: By the ruler of the city, his own son
2) He reacted vehemently: Ordered that Micaiah be given nothing but bread & water—until he returned safely from battle

f. The bold declaration of the prophet Micaiah
1) Ahab's death was decreed by God
2) His prophecy was true

4. Ahab's death: The surety of God's judgment

a. Ahab & Jehoshaphat's attack: Despite the warning
1) The two kings dressed differently for battle
- Jehoshaphat wore royal clothing
- Ahab disguised himself: To minimize the chance of the predicted death

2) The king of Syria ordered his 32 chariot commanders to focus their strike force upon killing King

spirit, and stood before the LORD, and said, I will persuade him.

22 And the LORD said unto him, Wherewith? And he said, I will go forth, and I will be a lying spirit in the mouth of all his prophets. And he said, Thou shalt persuade *him,* and prevail also: go forth, and do so.

23 Now therefore, behold, the LORD hath put a lying spirit in the mouth of all these thy prophets, and the LORD hath spoken evil concerning thee.

24 But Zedekiah the son of Chenaanah went near, and smote Micaiah on the cheek, and said, Which way went the Spirit of the LORD from me to speak unto thee?

25 And Micaiah said, Behold, thou shalt see in that day, when thou shalt go into an inner chamber to hide thyself.

26 And the king of Israel said, Take Micaiah, and carry him back unto Amon the governor of the city, and to Joash the king's son;

27 And say, Thus saith the king, Put this *fellow* in the prison, and feed him with bread of affliction and with water of affliction, until I come in peace.

28 And Micaiah said, If thou return at all in peace, the LORD hath not spoken by me. And he said, Hearken, O people, every one of you.

29 So the king of Israel and Jehoshaphat the king of Judah went up to Ramoth-gilead.

30 And the king of Israel said unto Jehoshaphat, I will disguise myself, and enter into the battle; but put thou on thy robes. And the king of Israel disguised himself, and went into the battle.

31 But the king of Syria commanded his thirty and two captains that had rule over his chariots, saying, Fight neither with small nor great, save only with the king of Israel.

32 And it came to pass, when the captains of the chariots saw Jehoshaphat, that they said, Surely it *is* the king of Israel. And they turned aside to fight against him: and Jehoshaphat cried out.

33 And it came to pass, when the captains of the chariots perceived that it *was* not the king of Israel, that they turned back from pursuing him.

34 And a *certain* man drew a bow at a venture, and smote the king of Israel between the joints of the harness: wherefore he said unto the driver of his chariot, Turn thine hand, and carry me out of the host; for I am wounded.

35 And the battle increased that day: and the king was stayed up in his chariot against the Syrians, and died at even: and the blood ran out of the wound into the midst of the chariot.

36 And there went a proclamation throughout the host about the going down of the sun, saying, Every man to his city, and every man to his own country.

37 So the king died, and was brought to Samaria; and they buried the king in Samaria.

38 And *one* washed the chariot in the pool of Samaria; and the dogs licked up his blood; and they washed his armour; according unto the word of the LORD which he spake.

39 Now the rest of the acts of Ahab, and all that he did, and the ivory house which he made, and all the cities that he built, *are* they not written in the book of the chronicles of the kings of Israel?

40 So Ahab slept with his fathers; and Ahaziah his son reigned in his stead.

Ahab of Israel
- The commander mistook King Jehoshaphat for Ahab—because of his royal clothing
- Jehoshaphat cried out, identifying himself: The LORD saved him by causing the chariot commanders to stop their pursuit, 2 Chr.18:31

b. Ahab's death from a random arrow
1) He was struck between the sections of his armor
2) He ordered his chariot driver to wheel around & get him away from the raging battle
3) He had his body propped up in his chariot facing the Syrians: To keep his troops from becoming discouraged
4) He slowly bled to death
5) He died as the sun was setting, & the cry went out to the troops: "Retreat, return home"—just as predicted, 17
6) He was buried in Samaria, the capital of Israel
- His chariot was washed at a pool where prostitutes bathed
- His blood was licked up by dogs—just as predicted, 21:19-24

c. Ahab's achievements & the summary of his life
1) His building projects
- An ivory palace
- Several fortified cities
- All recorded in the book *The History of the Kings of Israel*

2) His successor: Ahaziah, his son

DIVISION II

THE MINISTRY OF ELIJAH AND OTHER PROPHETS DURING THE REIGN OF AHAB: LEARNING WHO THE LIVING AND TRUE GOD IS, 17:1–22:53

F. The Death of Ahab: Proving the Surety of God's Judgment, 22:1-40

(22:1-40) **Introduction**: the surety of God's coming judgment is not a pleasant subject, not a topic that most people want to hear discussed. For the picture of judgment is that of perfect justice being executed by God. It is a picture of being condemned for sin, evil, and wickedness. Judgment is a picture of suffering the penalty for disobedience and lawlessness, for having rejected the LORD and broken His commandments. And no person enjoys such a picture of punishment and inflicted pain.

Nevertheless, God warns every generation of people who live within the universe: there is to be a climactic day of judgment in the future. Every person will give an account of himself before God. God is going to execute justice, straighten out the wrongs that have been done by any of us against Him and against other people:

⇒ all the Hitlers and other mass murderers of this world
⇒ all the judges and leaders who have twisted and taken advantage of the law
⇒ all the citizens of every nation who have lived wicked and sinful lives
⇒ all who have rejected and cursed God and His Son the Lord Jesus Christ

All these will face the condemnation of God and be excluded from His holy presence. Never will they be allowed to live in the new heavens and earth recreated for the Lord and other believers. Heaven, the spiritual world or dimension, is only for those who believe in the Lord Jesus Christ and those who live holy and righteous lives. For this reason, the world must be warned of the coming judgment of God. Every human being must have the opportunity to escape the terror of God's holy wrath. And they must be given the opportunity to live eternally in heaven, the place prepared for believers and the holy angels. The surety of God's coming judgment is the major lesson learned from this Scripture. This is: *The Death of Ahab: Proving the Surety of God's Judgment,* 22:1-40.

1. Ahab's alliance with Jehoshaphat: an unholy, worldly union (vv.1-5).
2. Ahab's false prophets consulted: a readiness to listen to false teachers (vv.6-14).
3. Ahab's death predicted by the prophet Micaiah: the surety of prophecy, of God's Word (vv.15-28).
4. Ahab's death: the surety of God's judgment (vv.29-40).

1 (22:1-5) **Union, Worldly—Associations, Evil, Example of—Separation, Spiritual, Failure in—Alliance, Worldly—Ahab, Alliances—Jehoshaphat, Alliances**: there was Ahab's alliance with Jehoshaphat. This alliance is a picture of an unholy union, of worldly and evil associations. It is the picture of a godly man, Jehoshaphat, failing to remain spiritually separated from the ungodly Ahab. Scripture gives a graphic description of the worldly and unholy alliance:

OUTLINE	SCRIPTURE	SCRIPTURE	OUTLINE
1. Ahab's alliance with Jehoshaphat: An unholy, worldly union a. The three-year peace between Syria & Israel, 20:1-43 b. The visit of Jehoshaphat with Ahab: During the third year c. The concern of Ahab to reclaim the strategic highlands of Ramoth Gilead: Its return had been promised by King Ben-Hadad of Syria when he was defeated by Ahab,	And they continued three years without war between Syria and Israel. 2 And it came to pass in the third year, that Jehoshaphat the king of Judah came down to the king of Israel. 3 And the king of Israel said unto his servants, Know ye that Ramoth in Gilead *is* ours, and we *be* still, *and* take it not out of the hand of the king of	Syria? 4 And he said unto Jehoshaphat, Wilt thou go with me to battle to Ramoth-gilead? And Jehoshaphat said to the king of Israel, I *am* as thou *art,* my people as thy people, my horses as thy horses. 5 And Jehoshaphat said unto the king of Israel, Enquire, I pray thee, at the word of the LORD to day.	15:20; 20:34 d. The appeal of Ahab to Jehoshaphat for an alliance to retake Ramoth 1) Jehoshaphat—a true believer—agreed for political purposes: Was later condemned for the unholy, worldly alliance, 2 Chr.19:2 2) Jehoshaphat suggested they first seek the LORD's counsel: But he had already agreed to the worldly alliance

a. After Ahab's victory over Syria, there was a three-year peace between Syria and the Northern Kingdom of Israel (20:1-43). In fact, the two nations had combined forces to withstand the rising threat of Assyria. The Assyrian king Shalmaneser III had attacked Qarqar in 853 BC. To stop his push into Syria, the Syrians formed a coalition that included Ahab and the Israelite forces. The Syrian coalition was successful in turning back the Assyrian forces.[1,2] The fact to note is that the Assyrian threat apparently occupied the attention of Ahab during the three-year peace and coalition with Syria.

b. During the third year of the peace treaty with Syria, King Jehoshaphat of Judah visited his son's father-in-law Ahab in the Northern Kingdom (v.2). Remember that the families of Jehoshaphat and Ahab were related through the marriage of Jehoshaphat's son Jehoram and Ahab's daughter Athaliah (2 K.8:18, 27). Also keep in mind that Jehoshaphat was a godly ruler, faithful to the LORD (22:41-50).

c. Before the visit of Jehoshaphat, Ahab had become concerned about reclaiming the strategic highlands of Ramoth Gilead (v.3). Many years before, Syria had conquered Ramoth Gilead; but when Ahab defeated King Ben-Hadad three years earlier, the Syrian king promised to return the city to the Israelites (15:20; 20:34). Ramoth was a major city in the tribe of Gad, just 28 miles east of the Jordan River. The city commanded all commercial and military traffic between that section of Israel and the East Jordan nations. Thus it was a very important city for Ahab to reclaim and possess.

d. So when Jehoshaphat visited him, he appealed to the Judean king for an alliance to retake Ramoth (vv.4-5). Despite being a true believer, Jehoshaphat agreed to the alliance for political purposes. But he was later condemned for the unholy, worldly alliance and association (2 Chr.19:2). Remember that Ahab and his infamous wife Jezebel had launched a purge against the prophets of the LORD, no doubt killing many of them. Jezebel was determined to eliminate the worship of the LORD from the land.

---

[1] Paul R. House. *1, 2 Kings*, p. 235.

[2] Richard D. Patterson and Hermann J. Austel. *1, 2 Kings*, p. 163.

Being a true believer, Jehoshaphat suggested that he and Ahab first seek the LORD's counsel before they actually attacked the Syrian stronghold of Ramah (v.5). But note that Jehoshaphat had already agreed to the unholy, worldly alliance.

Thought 1. Worldly unions and evil associations are forbidden by God; for when we associate with evil people on a regular or continual basis, they influence us. Eventually we find ourselves participating in their sinful, evil ways. Consider these examples:

⇒ If a moral person regularly fellowships with an immoral person, he or she is enticed to behave immorally.
⇒ If an honest person associates regularly with thieves, he is eventually influenced to participate in the stealing, whether shoplifting, breaking into homes, holding up shops, embezzling, or defrauding.
⇒ If a person fellowships regularly with gossipers, complainers, grumblers, or talebearers, the person is influenced to take part in the damaging and shameful conversations.
⇒ If a person associates regularly with people who use profanity or distasteful, disrespectful, off-colored, or vulgar language, the person is influenced to use the same kind of language.
⇒ If a person fellowships regularly with a group of people who drink alcoholic beverages, take drugs, smoke, or use any substance that abuses the body, the person is influenced to participate.
⇒ If a person fellowships regularly with those who dress immodestly and expose the human body or participate in revelry and partying, the person is influenced to do the same.

Without question, we are influenced by the people with whom we associate or fellowship. For this reason, God demands that we live lives of separation, lives that are separated from the wicked and evil of this earth. God demands that we set our lives apart to Him and His life of righteousness and holiness. We are *in the world* but we are not to be *of the world*.

As we walk about day by day, we naturally come into contact with people who are living sinful lives: fellow workers, schoolmates, neighbors, relatives, the working public, and a host of other persons. In normal day-to-day contacts we brush shoulders with unbelievers who are living wicked lives. However, we are never to participate in their evil or wickedness. God demands that we not engage in their sinful ways nor participate in their fellowships. We are not to fraternize or socialize with unholy, worldly people on a regular basis. Listen to what God's Holy Word says:

"And take heed to yourselves, lest at any time your hearts be overcharged with surfeiting, and drunkenness, and cares of this life, and *so* that day come upon you unawares" (Lu.21:34).

"If ye were of the world, the world would love his own: but because ye are not of the world, but I have chosen you out of the world, therefore the world hateth you" (Jn.15:19).

"And with many other words did he testify and exhort, saying, Save yourselves from this untoward generation" (Ac.2:40).

"And be not conformed to this world: but be ye transformed by the renewing of your mind, that ye may prove what *is* that good, and acceptable, and perfect, will of God" (Ro.12:2).

"But now I have written unto you not to keep company, if any man that is called a brother be a fornicator, or covetous, or an idolater, or a railer, or a drunkard, or an extortioner; with such an one no not to eat" (1 Co.5:11).

"Be not deceived: evil communications [behavior, conduct] corrupt good manners" (1 Co.15:33).

"Be ye not unequally yoked together with unbelievers: for what fellowship hath righteousness with unrighteousness? and what communion hath light with darkness? And what concord hath Christ with Belial? or what part hath he that believeth with an infidel? And what agreement hath the temple of God with idols? for ye are the temple of the living God; as God hath said, I will dwell in them, and walk in *them;* and I will be their God, and they shall be my people" (2 Co.6:14-16).

"Wherefore come out from among them, and be ye separate, saith the Lord, and touch not the unclean *thing;* and I will receive you, And will be a Father unto you, and ye shall be my sons and daughters, saith the Lord Almighty" (2 Co.6:17-18).

"And have no fellowship with the unfruitful works of darkness, but rather reprove *them*" (Ep.5:11).

"Now we command you, brethren, in the name of our Lord Jesus Christ, that ye withdraw yourselves from every brother that walketh disorderly, and not after the tradition which he received of us" (2 Th.3:6).

"By faith Moses, when he was come to years, refused to be called the son of Pharaoh's daughter; Choosing rather to suffer affliction with the people of God, than to enjoy the pleasures of sin for a season" (He.11:24-25).

"Love not the world, neither the things *that are* in the world. If any man love the world, the love of the Father is not in him. For all that *is* in the world, the lust of the flesh, and the lust of the eyes, and the pride of life, is not of the Father, but is of the world" (1 Jn.2:15-16).

"Thou shalt not follow a multitude to *do* evil; neither shalt thou speak in a cause to decline after many to wrest *judgment*" (Ex.23:2).

"Take heed to thyself, lest thou make a covenant with the inhabitants of the land whither thou goest, lest it be for a snare in the midst of thee" (Ex.34:12).

"Blessed *is* the man that walketh not in the counsel of the ungodly, nor standeth in the way of sinners, nor sitteth in the seat of the scornful" (Ps.1:1).

"Depart from me, ye evildoers: for I will keep the commandments of my God" (Ps.119:115).

"Enter not into the path of the wicked, and go not in the way of evil *men*" (Pr.4:14).

"Be not thou envious against evil men, neither desire to be with them" (Pr.24:1).

"Whoso keepeth the law *is* a wise son: but he that is a companion of riotous *men* shameth his father" (Pr.28:7).

"Awake, awake; put on thy strength, O Zion; put on thy beautiful garments, O Jerusalem, the holy city: for henceforth there shall no more come into thee the uncircumcised and the unclean" (Is.52:1).

2 (22:6-14) **Prophets, False, Dangers of—Counsel, False, Listening to, Example—Ahab, False Prophets of—Jehoshaphat, Sought Godly Counsel**: there was Ahab's consultation with his false prophets seeking godly counsel. This shows just how deeply engrossed Ahab was in idolatry and false worship. Remember that Jehoshaphat had just requested that he and Ahab seek godly counsel before they attacked the Syrian city of Ramah. Ahab was ready to seek godly counsel, but from the false prophets in his court. Scripture vividly describes the scene:

OUTLINE	SCRIPTURE	SCRIPTURE	OUTLINE
2. Ahab's false prophets consulted: A readiness to listen to false teachers a. The 400 false prophets of Ahab summoned: Predicted & assured the kings of victory	6 Then the king of Israel gathered the prophets together, about four hundred men, and said unto them, Shall I go against Ramoth-gilead to battle, or shall I forbear? And they said, Go up; for the Lord shall deliver *it* into the hand of the king.	having put on their robes, in a void place in the entrance of the gate of Samaria; and all the prophets prophesied before them. 11 And Zedekiah the son of Chenaanah made him horns of iron: and he said, Thus saith the LORD, With these shalt thou push the Syrians, until thou have consumed them.	ting on their thrones by the city gate of Samaria 1) The false prophets were prophesying before them 2) The leader Zedekiah had made a set of iron horns & claimed to have a special message from the LORD: The kings would gore, defeat the Syrians
b. The godly desire of Jehoshaphat: Wanted the counsel of a true prophet, a prophet of the LORD 1) Ahab—somewhat whining—responded that he knew of one such prophet, but he hated him • The prophet never prophesied anything good about him, only bad • The prophet's name was Micaiah 2) Jehoshaphat rebuked Ahab & urged him to call Micaiah 3) Ahab sent an official after Micaiah, the LORD's true prophet	7 And Jehoshaphat said, *Is there* not here a prophet of the LORD besides, that we might enquire of him? 8 And the king of Israel said unto Jehoshaphat, *There is* yet one man, Micaiah the son of Imlah, by whom we may enquire of the LORD: but I hate him; for he doth not prophesy good concerning me, but evil. And Jehoshaphat said, Let not the king say so. 9 Then the king of Israel called an officer, and said, Hasten *hither* Micaiah the son of Imlah.	12 And all the prophets prophesied so, saying, Go up to Ramoth-gilead, and prosper: for the LORD shall deliver *it* into the king's hand. 13 And the messenger that was gone to call Micaiah spake unto him, saying, Behold now, the words of the prophets *declare* good unto the king with one mouth: let thy word, I pray thee, be like the word of one of them, and speak *that which is* good.	3) The other prophets—all of them—agreed: • Urged the two kings to attack Ramoth Gilead • Assured them the LORD would give victory d. The dramatic scene of the eruption about to take place 1) The official who had summoned the LORD's true prophet warned him to agree with the other prophets, predicting victory
c. The impressive scene of the dramatic event: The two kings in their royal robes sit-	10 And the king of Israel and Jehoshaphat the king of Judah sat each on his throne,	14 And Micaiah said, *As* the LORD liveth, what the LORD saith unto me, that will I speak.	2) The prophet Micaiah boldly responded: He would proclaim only what God said—only His Word

a. Ahab summoned the 400 prophets of his court and asked them if he and Jehoshaphat should go to war against Ramah (v.6). All the prophets predicted victory, and they assured both kings of success. Not a single one predicted failure.

b. But Jehoshaphat, a genuine believer, had a godly desire aroused within him, a desire to receive counsel from a true prophet of the LORD (vv.7-9). Somewhat whining, Ahab responded that he knew of only one such prophet, but he personally hated the man. He stated that the prophet never said anything good about him but, instead, always predicted evil against the king. The prophet's name was Micaiah.

Notice that Jehoshaphat rebuked King Ahab for making such a negative statement about a prophet of the LORD, and he urged Ahab to summon the prophet. Granting the request, the king of Israel sent an official after Micaiah, the LORD's true prophet.

c. Note the impressive scene of the event about to take place (vv.10-12). The two kings were dressed in their royal robes sitting on their thrones by the city gate of Samaria. Standing before them were the 400 false prophets. Either the leaders among the false prophets or all the prophets one by one stepped forward to give their counsel, assuring the kings of victory. The chief prophet Zedekiah had actually made a set of iron horns and claimed to have a special message from the LORD. With these iron horns he predicted that the two kings would gore the Syrians to death. And in unison, all the other prophets agreed, urging the two kings to attack Ramah and assuring them that the LORD would give victory to Israel.

d. But a dramatic eruption was about to take place (vv.13-14). The official who had summoned the LORD's true prophet warned Micaiah to agree with the other prophets, predicting victory. This was the way to please the kings and to secure their favor. To stand opposed to 400 prophets would be foolish in the eyes of the official. But the prophet Micaiah boldly responded: he would proclaim only what God said. And note, the true prophet swore by an oath that he would only proclaim the Word of God.

Thought 1. Ahab sought the counsel of false prophets, a most unwise step for anyone to take. We must guard ourselves against false prophets and false teachers, for the world is full of both. Far too often the pulpits of the world are filled with false prophets who preach a doctrine other than the doctrine of Christ and of His Holy Word. Their focus is not the Word of God, but some other religious literature or some *feel-good* message. Ignoring the truth of God's Word, they seek the approval of their congregations by tickling their ears with messages of positive thinking and self-esteem, or by placing an overemphasis on healing and miracles or a particular spiritual gift. These messages are important, for positive thinking, self-esteem, healing, miracles, and spiritual gifts are all part of the God's Word. But the *whole counsel* of God's Word is to be proclaimed, including the entire doctrine of the LORD, His salvation, the life of the believer, the coming resurrection and judgment, and all the other teachings of God's Holy Word—both the negative and the positive. Yet false prophets seek merely to *captivate* or *pacify* us, giving us messages they feel will secure our approval while enhancing their honor and recognition.

But we must also guard against false teachers who stand behind the lecterns of our schools, seminars, convention halls, civic clubs, courts, legislatures, and Bible classes of this world. False teachers mislead us into believing half-truths, untruths, and serious doctrinal error. Listen to the strong warning of God's Holy Word against false prophets and teachers:

"Whosoever therefore shall break one of these least commandments, and shall teach men so, he shall be called the least in the kingdom of heaven: but whosoever shall do and teach *them,* the same shall be called great in the kingdom of heaven" (Mt.5:19).

"Beware of false prophets, which come to you in sheep's clothing, but inwardly they are ravening wolves. Ye shall know them by their fruits. Do men gather grapes of thorns, or figs of thistles? Even so every good tree bringeth forth good fruit; but a corrupt tree bringeth forth evil fruit. A good tree cannot bring forth evil fruit, neither *can* a corrupt tree bring forth good fruit. Every tree that bringeth not forth good fruit is hewn down, and cast into the fire. Wherefore by their fruits ye shall know them" (Mt.7:15-20).

"*Ye* hypocrites, well did Esaias prophesy of you, saying, This people draweth nigh unto me with their mouth, and honoureth me with *their* lips; but their heart is far from me. But in vain they do worship me, teaching *for* doctrines the commandments of men" (Mt.15:7-9).

"And many false prophets shall rise, and shall deceive many" (Mt.24:11).

"For false Christs and false prophets shall rise, and shall show signs and wonders, to seduce, if *it were* possible, even the elect" (Mk.13:22).

"I marvel that ye are so soon removed from him that called you into the grace of Christ unto another gospel: Which is not another; but there be some that trouble you, and would pervert the gospel of Christ. But though we, or an angel from heaven, preach any other gospel unto you than that which we have preached unto you, let him be accursed. As we said before, so say I now again, If any man preach any other gospel unto you than that ye have received, let him be accursed" (Ga.1:6-9).

"Neither give heed to fables and endless genealogies, which minister questions, rather than godly edifying which is in faith: *so do.* Now the end of the commandment is charity out of a pure heart, and *of* a good conscience, and *of* faith unfeigned: From which some having swerved have turned aside unto vain jangling; Desiring to be teachers of the law; understanding neither what they say, nor whereof they affirm" (1 Ti.1:4-7).

"Now the Spirit speaketh expressly, that in the latter times some shall depart from the faith, giving heed to seducing spirits, and doctrines of devils; Speaking lies in hypocrisy; having their conscience seared with a hot iron" (1 Ti.4:1-2).

"If any man teach otherwise, and consent not to wholesome words, *even* the words of our Lord Jesus Christ, and to the doctrine which is according to godliness; He is proud, knowing nothing, but doting about questions and strifes of words, whereof cometh envy, strife, railings, evil surmisings, Perverse disputings of men of corrupt minds, and destitute of the truth, supposing that gain is godliness: from such withdraw thyself" (1 Ti.6:3-5).

"For the time will come when they will not endure sound doctrine; but after their own lusts shall they heap to themselves teachers, having itching ears; And they shall turn away *their* ears from the truth, and shall be turned unto fables" (2 Ti.4:3-4).

"For there are many unruly and vain talkers and deceivers, specially they of the circumcision: Whose mouths must be stopped, who subvert whole houses, teaching things which they ought not, for filthy lucre's sake" (Tit.1:10-11).

"But there were false prophets also among the people, even as there shall be false teachers among you, who privily shall bring in damnable heresies, even denying the Lord that bought them, and bring upon themselves swift destruction. And many shall follow their pernicious ways; by reason of whom the way of truth shall be evil spoken of" (2 Pe.2:1-2).

"And that prophet, or that dreamer of dreams, shall be put to death; because he hath spoken to turn *you* away from the LORD your God, which brought you out of the land of Egypt, and redeemed you out of the house of bondage, to thrust thee out of the way which the LORD thy God commanded thee to walk in. So shalt thou put the evil away from the midst of thee" (De.13:5).

"The prophets prophesy falsely, and the priests bear rule by their means; and my people love *to have it* so: and what will ye do in the end thereof?" (Je.5:31).

"Then the LORD said unto me, The prophets prophesy lies in my name: I sent them not, neither have I commanded them, neither spake unto them: they prophesy unto you a false vision and divination, and a thing of nought, and the deceit of their heart" (Je.14:14).

"Thus saith the LORD of hosts, Hearken not unto the words of the prophets that prophesy unto

you: they make you vain: they speak a vision of their own heart, *and* not out of the mouth of the LORD" (Je.23:16).

"Son of man, prophesy against the prophets of Israel that prophesy, and say thou unto them that prophesy out of their own hearts, Hear ye the word of the LORD" (Eze.13:2).

"Her prophets *are* light *and* treacherous persons: her priests have polluted the sanctuary, they have done violence to the law" (Zep.3:4).

"And it shall come to pass, *that* when any shall yet prophesy, then his father and his mother that begat him shall say unto him, Thou shalt not live; for thou speakest lies in the name of the LORD: and his father and his mother that begat him shall thrust him through when he prophesieth" (Zec.13:3).

3 (22:15-28) **Word of God, Surety of—Prophecy, of Judgment, Surety of—Judgment, Prophecy of, Against Ahab, Death Predicted—Micaiah, Predictions of**: there was Ahab's death predicted by the prophet Micaiah. Some commentators feel that Micaiah was probably the unnamed prophet who had earlier been sent by God to condemn Ahab (20:35-43). Whatever the case, he was now being sent by God to predict the hand of God's judgment upon the king. The scene was electrifying and climactic:

OUTLINE	SCRIPTURE	SCRIPTURE	OUTLINE
3. Ahab's death predicted by the	15 So he came to the king.	persuade him.	of Ahab's false prophets
prophet Micaiah: The surety	And the king said unto him,	22 And the LORD said unto	• The LORD agreed, &
of prophecy, of God's Word	Micaiah, shall we go against	him, Wherewith? And he	charged the spirit to go
a. The question of Ahab:	Ramoth-gilead to battle, or	said, I will go forth, and I	stir the false prophets to
Should they attack?	shall we forbear? And he an-	will be a lying spirit in the	lie & persuade Ahab to
1) Micaiah responded sarcas-	swered him, Go, and prosper:	mouth of all his prophets.	attack Syria
tically: "Attack—be victo-	for the LORD shall deliver *it*	And he said, Thou shalt per-	
rious"	into the hand of the king.	suade *him,* and prevail also:	
2) Ahab sensed the sarcasm	16 And the king said unto	go forth, and do so.	
& demanded the truth	him, How many times shall I	23 Now therefore, behold,	2) Micaiah denounced the
	adjure thee that thou tell me	the LORD hath put a lying	false prophets, declared
	nothing but *that which is* true	spirit in the mouth of all	they were lying to Ahab:
	in the name of the LORD?	these thy prophets, and the	The LORD had decreed
b. The first prophecy of Micai-	17 And he said, I saw all Is-	LORD hath spoken evil con-	disaster, death for him
ah: A prediction exposing	rael scattered upon the hills,	cerning thee.	
Ahab's poor leadership &	as sheep that have not a	24 But Zedekiah the son of	d. The reaction & rage of the
death	shepherd: and the LORD said,	Chenaanah went near, and	false prophet Zedekiah
1) Micaiah saw Israel as sheep	These have no master: let	smote Micaiah on the cheek,	1) Zedekiah walked up &
with no shepherd (Ahab)	them return every man to his	and said, Which way went	slapped Micaiah in the face:
	house in peace.	the Spirit of the LORD from	Claimed he had God's Spirit
2) Ahab remarked with half-	18 And the king of Is-	me to speak unto thee?	as much as Micaiah did
hearted humor to Jehosha-	rael said unto Jehosha-	25 And Micaiah said, Be-	2) Micaiah predicted that
phat: "See, he never pre-	phat, Did I not tell thee	hold, thou shalt see in that	Zedekiah would soon be
dicts anything good about	that he would prophesy no	day, when thou shalt go into	hiding in terror: He would
me, only bad"	good concerning me, but	an inner chamber to hide thy-	then know the truth
	evil?	self.	
c. The second prophecy of Mi-	19 And he said, Hear thou	26 And the king of Israel	e. The reaction & rage of Ahab
caiah: A prediction of	therefore the word of the	said, Take Micaiah, and carry	1) He ordered Micaiah to
Ahab's deception & death	LORD: I saw the LORD sit-	him back unto Amon the gov-	be arrested & imprisoned:
1) Micaiah saw the LORD sit-	ting on his throne, and all the	ernor of the city, and to Joash	By the ruler of the city,
ting on His throne sur-	host of heaven standing by	the king's son;	his own son
rounded by the host of	him on his right hand and on	27 And say, Thus saith the	2) He reacted vehemently:
heaven	his left.	king, Put this *fellow* in the	Ordered that Micaiah be
• The LORD asked who	20 And the LORD said, Who	prison, and feed him with	given nothing but bread &
would persuade Ahab to	shall persuade Ahab, that he	bread of affliction and with	water—until he returned
attack Ramoth Gilead so	may go up and fall at Ra-	water of affliction, until I	safely from battle
he could be killed: A	moth-gilead? And one said	come in peace.	
picture of facing the	on this manner, and another	28 And Micaiah said, If thou	f. The bold declaration of the
judgment of God	said on that manner.	return at all in peace, the	prophet Micaiah
• A spirit stepped forth to	21 And there came forth a	LORD hath not spoken by me.	1) Ahab's death was decreed
volunteer: He would go as	spirit, and stood before	And he said, Hearken, O	by God
a lying spirit in the mouths	the LORD, and said, I will	people, every one of you.	2) His prophecy was true

a. As soon as Micaiah entered the royal court, King Ahab questioned him: Should they attack the Syrian city of Ramah (vv.15-16)? At first Micaiah sarcastically mimicked the 400 prophets of Ahab by suggesting that the kings attack, for the LORD would give them victory over the Syrian forces stationed at Ramah. But Ahab sensed the sarcasm in Micaiah's voice and demanded that he speak the truth, exactly what the LORD had said.

b. Heeding the demand of the king, Micaiah gave his first prediction, a prediction that pointed to Ahab's poor leadership and that suggested his death (vv.17-18). He stated that he saw all Israel scattered on the hills like sheep without a shepherd. Why? Because the people had no master. The implication is that the master was dead. Therefore the sheep must find their own way home. Reacting with half-hearted humor to the prophecy, Ahab turned to Jehoshaphat with a statement that the prophet Micaiah never predicted anything good about him, just as he had earlier told his brother-in-law.

c. At this point Micaiah spoke up again and gave a second prophecy, a prediction of Ahab's deception and his coming death (vv.19-23). Micaiah said that he saw the LORD sitting on His throne surrounded by the host of heaven. Suddenly the LORD asked who would persuade Ahab to attack Ramah so the king could be killed there, that is, face the judgment of God. In response to the LORD's call for a volunteer, a spirit stepped forth and said he would go as a lying spirit in the mouths of Ahab's false prophets (vv.20-21). Agreeing, the LORD charged the lying spirit to go and persuade Ahab to attack Syria (v.22).

After describing the heavenly scene, the true prophet Micaiah denounced the false prophets, declaring that they were lying to Ahab. A lying spirit was in the mouths of all these false prophets of the king. The truth was this: the LORD had declared disaster for Ahab. He was to be defeated and die.

d. Standing there listening to the prediction of Micaiah, Zedekiah reacted with rage. Remember, he was the leader of the false prophets. Furious, he walked up and slapped Micaiah in the face, claiming that he had as much of God's spirit in him as Micaiah did (vv.24-25). Immediately responding, Micaiah predicted that Zedekiah would soon be hiding in terror from the enemy troops. He would then know the truth: God had definitely been speaking through him declaring the coming judgment upon the king and the Israelite army. Zedekiah and all the other false prophets would witness the vindication of Micaiah's prophetic ministry.

e. Filled with indignation, Ahab reacted and ordered Micaiah to be immediately arrested and imprisoned. And note who was to imprison the prophet of God: the king's own son Joash (vv.26-27). In addition, Ahab callously demanded that Micaiah be given nothing but bread and water until he, the king, returned safely from battle.

f. Speaking boldly, the prophet of God declared that Ahab's death was decreed by the LORD (v.28). If Ahab ever returned safely, it would be proof that he, Micaiah, was a false prophet, that his prophecy had not come from the LORD, but rather from himself. But everyone present should remember his words, for they were the words of God Himself. The prophecy was true, and they would experience the reality of it.

With these final words, Micaiah finished his ministry before King Ahab. He was then arrested and imprisoned because he proclaimed the Word of God.

Thought 1. God's Word is trustworthy, absolutely trustworthy. Whatever God says will come to pass. Nothing is any more certain than the surety of God's Holy Word. When a prophecy is given in the Word of God, the day always comes when the prediction takes place. So it is with the promises of God. If a believer fulfills the conditions of the promise, the promise takes place in the life of the believer. If we keep God's Holy commandments, living holy and righteous lives, then we can be assured of all God's promises. God gives us His Holy Spirit and empowers us to live fruitful, productive lives. He empowers us to walk through life victoriously, conquering all the trials and difficulties, hardships and misfortunes, temptations and seductions. We become more than conquerors, triumphing over any and all things that attack us, including death itself. God floods our hearts with the fruit of His Spirit:

⇒ love	⇒ patience	⇒ faithfulness
⇒ joy	⇒ gentleness	⇒ meekness
⇒ peace	⇒ goodness	⇒ self-control

Listen to what God says about the surety of God's Holy Word:

"But while he thought on these things, behold, the angel of the Lord appeared unto him in a dream, saying, Joseph, thou son of David, fear not to take unto thee Mary thy wife: for that which is conceived in her is of the Holy Ghost. And she shall bring forth a son, and thou shalt call his name JESUS: for he shall save his people from their sins. Now all this was done, that it might be fulfilled which was spoken of the Lord by the prophet, saying, Behold, a virgin shall be with child, and shall bring forth a son, and they shall call his name Emmanuel, which being interpreted is, God with us" (Mt.1:20-23).

"When he [Joseph] arose, he took the young child and his mother by night, and departed into Egypt: And was there until the death of Herod: that it might be fulfilled which was spoken of the Lord by the prophet, saying, Out of Egypt have I called my son" (Mt.2:14-15).

"And he came and dwelt in a city called Nazareth: that it might be fulfilled which was spoken by the prophets, He shall be called a Nazarene" (Mt.2:23).

"And leaving Nazareth, he came and dwelt in Capernaum, which is upon the sea coast, in the borders of Zabulon and Nephthalim: That it might be fulfilled which was spoken by Esaias the prophet, saying, The land of Zabulon, and the land of Nephthalim, *by* the way of the sea, beyond Jordan, Galilee of the Gentiles; The people which sat in darkness saw great light; and to them which sat in the region and shadow of death light is sprung up" (Mt.4:13-16).

"For verily I say unto you, Till heaven and earth pass, one jot or one tittle shall in no wise pass from the law, till all be fulfilled" (Mt.5:18).

"That it might be fulfilled which was spoken by Esaias the prophet, saying, Himself took our infirmities, and bare *our* sicknesses" (Mt.8:17).

"And they crucified him, and parted his garments, casting lots: that it might be fulfilled which was spoken by the prophet, They parted my garments among them, and upon my vesture did they cast lots" (Mt.27:35).

"Heaven and earth shall pass away: but my words shall not pass away" (Lu.21:33).

"And he said unto them, These *are* the words which I spake unto you, while I was yet with you, that all things must be fulfilled, which were written in the law of Moses, and *in* the prophets, and *in* the psalms, concerning me" (Lu.24:44).

"That the saying of Esaias the prophet might be fulfilled, which he spake, Lord, who hath believed our report? and to whom hath the arm of the Lord been revealed?" (Jn.12:38).

"But *this cometh to pass,* that the word might be fulfilled that is written in their law, They hated me without a cause" (Jn.15:25).

"While I was with them in the world, I kept them in thy name: those that thou gavest me I have kept, and none of them is lost, but the son of perdition; that the Scripture might be fulfilled" (Jn.17:12).

"They said therefore among themselves, Let us not rend it, but cast lots for it, whose it shall be: that the Scripture might be fulfilled, which saith, They parted my raiment among them, and for my vesture they did cast lots. These things therefore the soldiers did" (Jn.19:24).

"But those things, which God before had showed by the mouth of all his prophets, that Christ should suffer, he hath so fulfilled" (Ac.3:18).

"And when they had fulfilled all that was written of him, they took *him* down from the tree, and laid *him* in a sepulchre" (Ac.13:29).

"God forbid: yea, let God be true, but every man a liar; as it is written, That thou mightest be justified in thy sayings, and mightest overcome when thou art judged" (Rom.3:4).

"God *is* faithful, by whom ye were called unto the fellowship of his Son Jesus Christ our Lord" (1 Co.1:9).

"That no man should be moved by these afflictions: for yourselves know that we are appointed thereunto" (1 Th.3:3).

"If we believe not, *yet* he abideth faithful: he cannot deny himself" (2 Ti.2:13).

"Wherein God, willing more abundantly to show unto the heirs of promise the immutability of his counsel, confirmed *it* by an oath: That by two immutable things, in which *it was* impossible for God to lie, we might have a strong consolation, who have fled for refuge to lay hold upon the hope set before us" (He.6:17-18).

"Let us hold fast the profession of *our* faith without wavering; (for he is faithful that promised)" (He.10:23).

"Know therefore that the LORD thy God, he *is* God, the faithful God, which keepeth covenant and mercy with them that love him and keep his commandments to a thousand generations" (De.7:9).

"*He is* the Rock, his work *is* perfect: for all his ways *are* judgment: a God of truth and without iniquity, just and right *is* he" (De.32:4).

"And now, O Lord GOD, thou *art* that God, and thy words be true, and thou hast promised this goodness unto thy servant" (2 S.7:28).

"Blessed *be* the LORD, that hath given rest unto his people Israel, according to all that he promised: there hath not failed one word of all his good promise, which he promised by the hand of Moses his servant" (1 K.8:56).

"Thy mercy, O LORD, *is* in the heavens; *and* thy faithfulness *reacheth* unto the clouds" (Ps.36:5).

"Praise ye the LORD. I will praise the LORD with *my* whole heart, in the assembly of the upright, and *in* the congregation. The works of the LORD *are* great, sought out of all them that have pleasure therein. His work *is* honourable and glorious: and his righteousness endureth for ever. He hath made his wonderful works to be remembered: the LORD *is* gracious and full of compassion. He hath given meat unto them that fear him: he will ever be mindful of his covenant. He hath showed his people the power of his works, that he may give them the heritage of the heathen. The works of his hands *are* verity and judgment; all his commandments *are* sure. They stand fast for ever and ever, and *are done* in truth and uprightness. He sent redemption unto his people: he hath commanded his covenant for ever: holy and reverend *is* his name. The fear of the LORD *is* the beginning of wisdom: a good understanding have all they that do *his commandments*: his praise endureth for ever" (Ps.111).

"Happy *is he* that *hath* the God of Jacob for his help, whose hope *is* in the LORD his God: Which made heaven, and earth, the sea, and all that therein *is:* which keepeth truth for ever" (Ps.146:5-6).

"For I *am* the LORD: I will speak, and the word that I shall speak shall come to pass; it shall be no more prolonged: for in your days, O rebellious house, will I say the word, and will perform it, saith the Lord GOD" (Eze.12:25).

4 (22:29-40) **Judgment, Surety of—Israel, Wars of—Ahab, Death of—Jehoshaphat, Military Alliance of—Judah, Wars of**: there was Ahab's death, just as the prophet Micaiah had predicted. Scripture graphically describes the end of Ahab's reign and his death:

OUTLINE	SCRIPTURE	SCRIPTURE	OUTLINE
4. Ahab's death: The surety of God's judgment a. Ahab & Jehoshaphat's attack: Despite the warning 1) The two kings dressed differently for battle • Jehoshaphat wore royal clothing • Ahab disguised himself: To minimize the chance of the predicted death	29 So the king of Israel and Jehoshaphat the king of Ju- dah went up to Ramoth- gilead. 30 And the king of Israel said unto Jehoshaphat, I will disguise myself, and enter in- to the battle; but put thou on thy robes. And the king of Is- rael disguised himself, and went into the battle.	his chariot, Turn thine hand, and carry me out of the host; for I am wounded. 35 And the battle increased that day: and the king was stayed up in his chariot against the Syrians, and died at even: and the blood ran out of the wound into the midst of the chariot.	driver to wheel around & get him away from the raging battle 3) He had his body propped up in his chariot facing the Syrians: To keep his troops from becoming discouraged 4) He slowly bled to death
2) The king of Syria ordered his 32 chariot commanders to focus their strike force upon killing King Ahab of Israel	31 But the king of Syria commanded his thirty and two captains that had rule over his chariots, saying, Fight neither with small nor great, save only with the king of Israel.	36 And there went a procla- mation throughout the host about the going down of the sun, saying, Every man to his city, and every man to his own country. 37 So the king died, and was brought to Samaria; and they buried the king in Samaria.	5) He died as the sun was setting, & the cry went out to the troops: "Retreat, return home"—just as predicted, 17 6) He was buried in Samaria, the capital of Israel
• The commander mistook King Jehoshaphat for Ahab—because of his royal clothing • Jehoshaphat cried out, identifying himself: The LORD saved him by causing the chariot commanders to stop their pursuit, 2 Chr.18:31	32 And it came to pass, when the captains of the char- iots saw Jehoshaphat, that they said, Surely it *is* the king of Israel. And they turned aside to fight against him: and Jehoshaphat cried out. 33 And it came to pass, when the captains of the chariots perceived that it *was* not the king of Israel, that they turned back from pursu- ing him.	38 And *one* washed the char- iot in the pool of Samaria; and the dogs licked up his blood; and they washed his ar- mour; according unto the word of the LORD which he spake. 39 Now the rest of the acts of Ahab, and all that he did, and the ivory house which he made, and all the cities that he built, *are* they not written in the book of the chronicles of the kings of Is- rael?	• His chariot was washed at a pool where prostitutes bathed • His blood was licked up by dogs—just as predicted, 21:19-24 c. Ahab's achievements & the summary of his life 1) His building projects • An ivory palace • Several fortified cities • All recorded in the book *The History of the Kings of Israel*
b. Ahab's death from a random arrow 1) He was struck between the sections of his armor 2) He ordered his chariot	34 And a *certain* man drew a bow at a venture, and smote the king of Israel between the joints of the harness: where- fore he said unto the driver of	40 So Ahab slept with his fa- thers; and Ahaziah his son reigned in his stead.	2) His successor: Ahaziah, his son

a. Rejecting the warning of the prophet Micaiah, both Ahab and Jehoshaphat launched their attack against the Syrian city of Ramah (vv.29-33). But note that the two kings dressed differently for battle. Jehoshaphat wore the royal clothing of a king, but Ahab disguised himself in order to minimize the chance of death as predicted by the prophet Micaiah (vv.29-30).

Knowing that the key to victory was the killing of Ahab, the King of Syria ordered his 32 chariot commanders to focus their strike force upon slaying the king of Israel (vv.31-33). But as the battle raged, they mistook King Jehoshaphat for Ahab because of his royal clothing. Under fierce attack Jehoshaphat cried out, identifying himself, at which point the chariot commanders stopped their fierce pursuit of him and began anew their search for King Ahab. Another Scripture tells us that it was the LORD Himself who had saved Jehoshaphat by arousing the chariot commanders to stop their pursuit (2 Chr.18:31).

b. During the raging battle, a random arrow found its mark and struck Ahab, inflicting a mortal wound (vv.34-38). The scene shows that Ahab, despite his weaknesses, was courageous in battle. As the random arrow streaked toward him, it struck between the sections of his armor, piercing too deeply to be immediately removed. At once the king ordered his chariot driver to wheel around to get him away from the ferocious battle (v.34). As soon as they were a safe distance away but still within eyesight, Ahab ordered that his weakened body be propped up in his chariot so he would face the Syrians (v.35). This was to keep his troops from becoming discouraged. But ever so slowly, the king bled to death. He died as the sun was setting (v.36). As soon as the word spread throughout the Israelite troops, the cry went out to retreat and return home. Note that this was exactly what had been predicted by the prophet Micaiah (v.17).

Ahab was buried in Samaria, the capital of the Northern Kingdom (vv.37-38). But note what happened: his chariot was being washed at a pool where prostitutes frequented and sometimes bathed. While the chariot was being washed, the dogs actually licked up his blood just as the prophet had earlier predicted (21:19-24).

c. In concluding the biblical history of King Ahab, the author of *First Kings* mentions the fact that he had undertaken several building projects that included an ivory palace and several fortified cities. A record of his achievements and a summary of his life were recorded in the book *The History of the Kings of Israel* (v.39). Ahab's successor was his son Ahaziah (v.40).

Thought 1. God's judgment fell upon Ahab because he had lived a wicked life, disobeying the LORD's commandments and participating in false worship and idolatry. He was condemned to death—not only physical death, but spiritual and eternal death. God could not accept Ahab as long as he lived in wickedness, for Ahab's wickedness would have contaminated the very presence of God and of heaven. His wickedness would have polluted heaven itself, the eternal and perfect home where all believers live. And the one thing God will never allow is the pollution of His presence and of heaven, the very place God has prepared for His dear people.

We must learn this one truth: if we commit wickedness and live sinful lives, we stand condemned before God. The hand of God's judgment will fall upon us; and after death, we will face His judgment. Unless we repent and turn to Christ before the day of our death, we will stand condemned to be eternally separated from God. Never will we be allowed to live in heaven with the Lord and other believers. On the contrary, we will be condemned to spend eternity in the place Christ Himself called *hell*. Listen to what God's Holy Word says about the surety of coming judgment:

> **"And as it is appointed unto men once to die, but after this the judgment" (He.9:27).**
>
> **"When the Son of man shall come in his glory, and all the holy angels with him, then shall he sit upon the throne of his glory: And before him shall be gathered all nations: and he shall separate them one from another, as a shepherd divideth *his* sheep from the goats: And he shall set the sheep on his right hand, but the goats on the left" (Mt.25:31-33).**
>
> **"Marvel not at this: for the hour is coming, in the which all that are in the graves shall hear his voice, And shall come forth; they that have done good, unto the resurrection of life; and they that have done evil, unto the resurrection of damnation" (Jn.5:28-29).**
>
> **"For the wrath of God is revealed from heaven against all ungodliness and unrighteousness of men, who hold the truth in unrighteousness....Being filled with all unrighteousness, fornication, wickedness, covetousness, maliciousness; full of envy, murder, debate, deceit, malignity; whisperers, Backbiters, haters of God, despiteful, proud, boasters, inventors of evil things, disobedient to parents, Without understanding, covenantbreakers, without natural affection, implacable, unmerciful: Who knowing the judgment of God, that they which commit such things are worthy of death, not only do the same, but have pleasure in them that do them" (Ro.1:18, 29-32).**
>
> **"Therefore as by the offence of one *judgment came* upon all men to condemnation; even so by the righteousness of one *the free gift came* upon all men unto justification of life" (Ro.5:18).**
>
> **"Know ye not that the unrighteous shall not inherit the kingdom of God? Be not deceived: neither fornicators, nor idolaters, nor adulterers, nor effeminate, nor abusers of themselves with mankind, Nor thieves, nor covetous, nor drunkards, nor revilers, nor extortioners, shall inherit the kingdom of God" (1 Co.6:9-10).**
>
> **"Now the works of the flesh are manifest, which are *these;* Adultery, fornication, uncleanness, lasciviousness, Idolatry, witchcraft, hatred, variance, emulations, wrath, strife, seditions, heresies, Envyings, murders, drunkenness, revellings, and such like: of the which I tell you before, as I have also told *you* in time past, that they which do such things shall not inherit the kingdom of God" (Ga.5:19-21).**
>
> **"But fornication, and all uncleanness, or covetousness, let it not be once named among you, as becometh saints; Neither filthiness, nor foolish talking, nor jesting, which are not convenient: but rather giving of thanks. For this ye know, that no whoremonger, nor unclean person, nor covetous man, who is an idolater, hath any inheritance in the kingdom of Christ and of God. Let no man deceive you with vain words: for because of these things cometh the wrath of God upon the children of disobedience" (Ep.5:3-6).**
>
> **"And to you who are troubled rest with us, when the Lord Jesus shall be revealed from heaven with his mighty angels, In flaming fire taking vengeance on them that know not God, and that obey not the gospel of our Lord Jesus Christ" (2 Th.1:7-8).**
>
> **"The Lord knoweth how to deliver the godly out of temptations, and to reserve the unjust unto the day of judgment to be punished" (2 Pe.2:9).**
>
> **"But the heavens and the earth, which are now, by the same word are kept in store, reserved unto fire against the day of judgment and perdition of ungodly men" (2 Pe.3:7).**
>
> **"Behold, the Lord cometh with ten thousands of his saints, To execute judgment upon all, and to convince all that are ungodly among them of all their ungodly deeds which they have ungodly committed, and of all their hard *speeches* which ungodly sinners have spoken against him" (Jude 14-15).**
>
> **"But the fearful, and unbelieving, and the abominable, and murderers, and whoremongers, and sorcerers, and idolaters, and all liars, shall have their part in the lake which burneth with fire and brimstone: which is the second death" (Re.21:8).**

1. The good reign of Jehoshaphat: The godly influence of parents

a. His background

1) He was 35 years old when he began to reign

2) He reigned a total of 25 years: Three years as coregent with Asa his father, 15:23

b. His righteous life & the continuation of his father's reforms

1) He walked in the godly ways of his father Asa, 15:9-24

2) He failed to permanently remove the high places: He had once removed them (2 Chr.17:6), but the people restored them & he let them remain, 2 Chr.20:33

3) He established peace with Israel

c. His achievements & the summary of his life

1) His reign: Recorded in the book *The History of the Kings of Judah*

2) His major religious reform: He banished the remaining religious or shrine prostitutes,

G. The Reigns of Jehoshaphat in Judah & Ahaziah in Israel: Learning the Importance of Parental Influence, 22:41-53

41 And Jehoshaphat the son
of Asa began to reign over
Judah in the fourth year of
Ahab king of Israel.
42 Jehoshaphat *was* thirty
and five years old when he
began to reign; and he
reigned twenty and five years
in Jerusalem. And his mother's
name *was* Azubah the
daughter of Shilhi.
43 And he walked in all the
ways of Asa his father; he
turned not aside from it,
doing *that which was* right
in the eyes of the LORD: nevertheless
the high places were
not taken away; *for* the people
offered and burnt incense
yet in the high places.
44 And Jehoshaphat made
peace with the king of Israel.
45 Now the rest of the acts
of Jehoshaphat, and his might
that he showed, and how he
warred, *are* they not written
in the book of the chronicles
of the kings of Judah?
46 And the remnant of the
sodomites, which remained
in the days of his father
Asa, he took out of the
land.
47 *There was* then no king in
Edom: a deputy *was* king.
48 Jehoshaphat made ships
of Tharshish to go to Ophir
for gold: but they went not;
for the ships were broken at
Ezion-geber.
49 Then said Ahaziah the
son of Ahab unto Jehoshaphat,
Let my servants go with
thy servants in the ships. But
Jehoshaphat would not.
50 And Jehoshaphat slept with
his fathers, and was buried with
his fathers in the city of David
his father: and Jehoram
his son reigned in his stead.
51 Ahaziah the son of Ahab
began to reign over Israel in
Samaria the seventeenth year
of Jehoshaphat king of Judah,
and reigned two years over
Israel.
52 And he did evil in the
sight of the LORD, and
walked in the way of his father,
and in the way of his
mother, and in the way of
Jeroboam the son of Nebat,
who made Israel to sin:
53 For he served Baal, and
worshipped him, and provoked
to anger the LORD
God of Israel, according
to all that his father had done.

all who had escaped his father's purge, 14:24; 15:12

3) His subjection of Edom & the rule of his own deputy

4) His building a fleet of trading ships

- The ships wrecked before they ever left port (due to a storm?)
- The king of Israel, Ahaziah, offered to enter a joint venture to build another fleet: Jehoshaphat refused

5) His death & burial in Jerusalem

6) His successor: His son Jehoram

2. The evil reign of Ahaziah: The evil influence of parents

a. His background: He reigned two years

b. His evil

1) He followed the evil examples of his father & mother—Ahab & Jezebel—& of Jeroboam's false religion

2) He served Baal & worshipped the false god

c. His condemnation: He aroused God's anger

DIVISION II

THE MINISTRY OF ELIJAH AND OTHER PROPHETS DURING THE REIGN OF AHAB: LEARNING WHO THE LIVING AND TRUE GOD IS, 17:1–22:53

G. The Reigns of Jehoshaphat in Judah and Ahaziah in Israel: Learning the Importance of Parental Influence, 22:41-53

(22:41-53) **Introduction**: without question, parents influence their children—tremendously so. In fact, the influence of parents upon children cannot be overemphasized. The exceptions to the saying *"as goes the parent, so goes the child"* are few and far between. Hence we influence our children either for good or for bad. Simply stated, if we live productive lives, our children will most likely be successful. But if we live lives that are purposeless and unproductive, the likelihood is that our children will be aimless and unfruitful in life. If we live righteous and holy lives, our children will probably live righteous and holy lives. But if we live sinful and wicked lives, our children will almost certainly live sinful and wicked lives.

This final passage of *First Kings* shows the importance of parental influence. These verses reveal the influence that the parents of two kings had upon their sons. One king had godly parents and the other king had evil parents. Each king followed in the footsteps of his parents, a striking lesson for every generation of people. This is*: The Reigns of Jehoshaphat in Judah and Ahaziah in Israel: Learning the Importance of Parental Influence,* 22:41-53.

1. The good reign of Jehoshaphat: the godly influence of parents (vv.41-50).
2. The evil reign of Ahaziah: the evil influence of parents (vv.51-53).

1 (22:41-50) **Parents, Godly Influence, Followed—Children, Duty—Reforms, Religious, Example of—Religion, Reformed—Jehoshaphat, Godly Reign of**: there was the good reign of King Jehoshaphat in the Southern Kingdom of Judah. Remember Jehoshaphat had formed an alliance with King Ahab in an attempt to conquer Ramoth-Gilead, an attempt that was unsuccessful (22:1-38). Jehoshaphat will appear again in *Second Kings* (2 K.3:12-14) and will remain king throughout all the events up until chapter eight of *Second Kings* (2 K.8:16). In the present passage, a general overview of his life and reign is being covered. From a spiritual and practical perspective, the important lesson to be learned is the godly influence of parents:

OUTLINE	SCRIPTURE	SCRIPTURE	OUTLINE
1. The good reign of Jehoshaphat: The godly influence of parents a. His background 1) He was 35 years old when he began to reign 2) He reigned a total of 25 years: Three years as co-regent with Asa his father, 15:23	41 And Jehoshaphat the son of Asa began to reign over Judah in the fourth year of Ahab king of Israel. 42 Jehoshaphat *was* thirty and five years old when he began to reign; and he reigned twenty and five years in Jerusalem. And his mother's name *was* Azubah the daughter of Shilhi.	how he warred, *are* they not written in the book of the chronicles of the kings of Judah? 46 And the remnant of the sodomites, which remained in the days of his father Asa, he took out of the land. 47 *There was* then no king in Edom: a deputy *was* king.	1) His reign: Recorded in the book *The History of the Kings of Judah* 2) His major religious reform: He banished the remaining religious or shrine prostitutes, all who had escaped his father's purge, 14:24; 15:12 3) His subjection of Edom & the rule of his own deputy
b. His righteous life & the continuation of his father's reforms 1) He walked in the godly ways of his father Asa, 15:9-24 2) He failed to permanently remove the high places: He had once removed them (2 Chr.17:6), but the people restored them & he let them remain, 2 Chr.20:33 3) He established peace with Israel	43 And he walked in all the ways of Asa his father; he turned not aside from it, doing *that which was* right in the eyes of the LORD: nevertheless the high places were not taken away; *for* the people offered and burnt incense yet in the high places. 44 And Jehoshaphat made peace with the king of Israel.	48 Jehoshaphat made ships of Tharshish to go to Ophir for gold: but they went not; for the ships were broken at Ezion-geber. 49 Then said Ahaziah the son of Ahab unto Jehoshaphat, Let my servants go with thy servants in the ships. But Jehoshaphat would not.	4) His building a fleet of trading ships • The ships wrecked before they ever left port (due to a storm?) • The king of Israel, Ahaziah, offered to enter a joint venture to build another fleet: Jehoshaphat refused
c. His achievements & the summary of his life	45 Now the rest of the acts of Jehoshaphat, and his might that he showed, and	50 And Jehoshaphat slept with his fathers, and was buried with his fathers in the city of David his father: and Jehoram his son reigned in his stead.	5) His death & burial in Jerusalem 6) His successor: His son Jehoram

a. Jehoshaphat was 35 years old when he became the sole ruler of Judah. He assumed the throne during the fourth year of Ahab, who was ruler of the Northern Kingdom (v.41). Reigning a total of 25 years, Jehoshaphat ruled three years as co-regent with Asa his father (15:23). Remember that his father Asa had been afflicted with some foot disease in his old age, which probably disabled him and necessitated his son ruling by his side (15:23). Most likely during the latter years of Jehoshaphat's rule, he spent a five year co-regency with his son Jehoram (1 K.22:51-52; 2 K.1:17; 3:1; 8:16-24).[1]

b. Jehoshaphat lived a righteous life and continued his father's social and religious reforms (v.43-44). Scripture clearly says that he walked in the godly ways of his father Asa (15:9-24). His father had instituted religious reforms by removing all the idols throughout the nation and banishing all the religious prostitutes and false prophets. His father had even removed his own grandmother Maacah from her position as queen mother because of her idolatry and false worship. Doing all he could to lead the people back to the LORD, King Asa had set a high standard of righteousness for the nation and for his own family. And his son Jehoshaphat did not disappoint King Asa because Jehoshaphat followed his righteous example, walking in the godly ways of his father. He did what was right in the eyes of the LORD, pleasing the LORD by his righteous life. Only in one area did Jehoshaphat come up short: he failed to permanently remove the high places. Remember that the high places were hills that had been set aside as worship sites, and many of the sites were given over to the worship of idols. At first he had attempted to remove them (2 Chr.17:6), but the people had rebuilt the worship centers. Seeing the people's strong attachment to false gods, he allowed the false worship centers to remain (2 Chr.20:33).

This failure and the fact that he had agreed to the marriage of his son Jehoram to Ahab's daughter Athaliah were the only two serious failures of King Jehoshaphat. The marriage of his son to Ahab's daughter was to result in several crises in Judah (2 K.8:18-19; 11:1-3; 2 Chr.21:6-7, 11).[2] However, through the marriage Jehoshaphat became the brother-in-law to Ahab, and peace was established between the Southern and Northern Kingdoms at least throughout Jehoshaphat's reign (v.44).

c. In discussing Jehoshaphat's achievements and giving a summary of his life, the author lists six facts:

1) His reign and achievements are recorded in the book, *The History of the Kings of Judah* (v.45). Of course, this was one of the primary sources the author used in writing the book of *First Kings*.
2) Jehoshaphat's major religious reform was the banishing of the shrine prostitutes who had escaped his father's purge (14:24; 15:12). Just like his father, he did all he could to turn the people away from their false worship and to turn them back to the LORD, to the worship of the only living and true God.
3) He was also able to subject Edom to the rule and authority of Judah (v.47). Note that he placed his own deputy over the nation.
4) At some point during his reign, he built a fleet of trading ships (vv.48-49). This undertaking was a joint venture with the evil king of Israel, Ahaziah. The commercial alliance was denounced by the LORD's prophet Eliezer (2 Chr.20:36-37). Because of the unholy, worldly alliance, God had sent a storm to destroy the ships before they ever left the port of Ezion Geber. Soon thereafter King Ahaziah offered to enter another joint venture to rebuild the fleet of ships. But this time Jehoshaphat, knowing better, refused.
5) Jehoshaphat died shortly afterwards and was buried in Jerusalem, the capital of the Southern Kingdom of Judah (v.50). Note that all the former rulers of the Southern Kingdom were also buried in Jerusalem (see outline and notes—2 Chr.17:1-21 for a much fuller discussion of Jehoshaphat's reign).
6) Jehoshaphat was succeeded by his son Jehoram.

---

1 Paul R. House. *1, 2 Kings*, p. 241.

2 Richard D. Patterson and Hermann J. Austel. *1, 2 Kings* p. 168.

Thought 1. Jehoshaphat had godly parents, parents who lived righteous lives before their children. As Jehoshaphat was growing up, he was taught the commandments of God and taught to worship the LORD. And most important, he was taught to live what he had learned from the Word of God. The result of his training was wonderful: he obeyed the commandments of God, living a righteous and holy life before the LORD and before the people of the Southern Kingdom. As the head of his own family and the head of the nation, he set a dynamic example for his children and the people to follow.

So it must be with us: we must set a dynamic example of godliness for our children to follow. In most cases, a child will follow in the footsteps of his or her parents. If we live godly and righteous lives, our children will follow our example. They, too, will live righteous and godly lives. If we teach our children the Word and commandments of God, they will follow His Word and obey His commandments. If we teach our children to go to church and worship the LORD, they will go to church and worship the LORD throughout their lives.

As parents, nothing is as important as leading our children to Christ and grounding them in His Holy Word. Listen to what God's Word says about setting a righteous example for children and instructing them in the way of righteousness:

"So when they had dined, Jesus saith to Simon Peter, Simon, *son* of Jonas, lovest thou me more than these? He saith unto him, Yea, Lord; thou knowest that I love thee. He saith unto him, Feed my lambs" (Jn.21:15).

"When I call to remembrance the unfeigned faith that is in thee, which dwelt first in thy grandmother Lois, and thy mother Eunice; and I am persuaded that in thee also" (2 Ti.1:5).

"And that from a child thou hast known the holy scriptures, which are able to make thee wise unto salvation through faith which is in Christ Jesus" (2 Ti.3:15).

"Only take heed to thyself, and keep thy soul diligently, lest thou forget the things which thine eyes have seen, and lest they depart from thy heart all the days of thy life: but teach them thy sons, and thy sons' sons" (De.4:9).

"And *that* their children, which have not known *any thing,* may hear, and learn to fear the LORD your God, as long as ye live in the land whither ye go over Jordan to possess it" (De.31:13).

"And if thou wilt walk before me, as David thy father walked, in integrity of heart, and in uprightness, to do according to all that I have commanded thee, *and* wilt keep my statutes and my judgments: Then I will establish the throne of thy kingdom upon Israel for ever, as I promised to David thy father, saying, There shall not fail thee a man upon the throne of Israel" (1 K.9:4-5).

"And the LORD was with Jehoshaphat, because he walked in the first ways of his father David, and sought not unto Baalim" (2 Chr.17:3).

"And he [Uzziah] did *that which was* right in the sight of the LORD, according to all that his father Amaziah did" (2 Chr.26:4).

"Train up a child in the way he should go: and when he is old, he will not depart from it" (Pr.22:6).

"Whom shall he teach knowledge? and whom shall he make to understand doctrine? *them that are* weaned from the milk, *and* drawn from the breasts" (Is.28:9).

2 (22:51-53) **Parents, Evil Influence of—Influence, of Parents—Children, Tragedy of, Following Evil Influence—Ahaziah, Evil Reign of**: there was the evil reign of Ahaziah, the ruler of the Northern Kingdom of Israel. Only a brief sketch is given of Ahaziah in closing the book of *First Kings*. His reign is picked back up in the first chapter of *Second Kings*.

OUTLINE	SCRIPTURE	SCRIPTURE	OUTLINE
2. The evil reign of Ahaziah: The evil influence of parents a. His background: He reigned two years b. His evil 1) He followed the evil examples of his father &	51 Ahaziah the son of Ahab began to reign over Israel in Samaria the seventeenth year of Jehoshaphat king of Judah, and reigned two years over Israel. 52 And he did evil in the sight of the LORD, and walked in the way of his fa-	ther, and in the way of his mother, and in the way of Jeroboam the son of Nebat, who made Israel to sin: 53 For he served Baal, and worshipped him, and provoked to anger the LORD God of Israel, according to all that his father had done.	mother—Ahab & Jezebel—& of Jeroboam's false religion 2) He served Baal & worshipped the false god c. His condemnation: He aroused God's anger

Ahaziah was crowned king right after his father Ahab died on the battlefield, which was in the seventeenth year of Jehoshaphat's reign over the Southern Kingdom. But Ahaziah had only a brief reign, ruling for only two years (v.51). In a very straightforward manner, Scripture says that he followed the evil example of three persons: his father Ahab, his mother Jezebel, and the founder of the Northern Kingdom, Jeroboam. He walked in the evil ways of these three wicked people whose tragic and terrible examples had been lived out before him. He engaged in false worship, serving and worshipping the false god Baal. As a result, he provoked the LORD God, arousing Him to anger, just as his father and mother had done. Consequently, he was under the condemnation of God. And this fact will be seen in the very first chapter of *Second Kings*.

Thought 1. Setting an evil example before our children is a terrible legacy to leave them. For if we walk in sin and wickedness, most likely our children will follow our example and live sinful and wicked lives. This is a terrible indictment against many of us, for it means that...

- if we live immoral lives, our children will be more prone to commit fornication and adultery
- if we pop pills, take drugs, and drink alcoholic beverages, our children will most likely pop pills, take drugs, and drink alcoholic beverages
- if we lie, steal, and cheat, our children will probably lie, steal, and cheat
- if we live lives of greed and covetousness, ever grasping after more and more, our children will be inclined to live lives of greed and covetousness
- if we complain, grumble, and gossip, undoubtedly our children will complain, grumble, and gossip
- if we curse and use profane, off-colored, and vulgar language, our children will no doubt curse and use profane, off-colored, and vulgar language
- if we overeat and commit the sin of gluttony, in all probability our children will overeat and commit the sin of gluttony

No matter what sin or wickedness we commit, if we continue the pattern of that sin or wickedness, most likely our children are going to follow our example. This is one of the reasons God constantly warns us against living lives of ungodliness and unrighteousness.

(1) Look at the examples given by Holy Scripture of evil parents who influenced their children to do evil:

"And she [Salome], being before instructed of her mother, said, Give me here John Baptist's head in a charger" (Mt.14:8).

"And he [Ahaziah] did evil in the sight of the LORD, and walked in the way of his father, and in the way of his mother, and in the way of Jeroboam the son of Nebat, who made Israel to sin" (1 K.22:52).

"And the inhabitants of Jerusalem made Ahaziah his youngest son king in his stead: for the band of men that came with the Arabians to the camp had slain all the eldest. So Ahaziah the son of Jehoram king of Judah reigned. Forty and two years old *was* Ahaziah when he began to reign, and he reigned one year in Jerusalem. His mother's name also *was* Athaliah the daughter of Omri. He also walked in the ways of the house of Ahab: for his mother was his counsellor to do wickedly. Wherefore he did evil in the sight of the LORD like the house of Ahab: for they were his counsellors after the death of his father to his destruction" (2 Chr.22:1-4).

"And the LORD saith, Because they have forsaken my law which I set before them, and have not obeyed my voice, neither walked therein; But have walked after the imagination of their own heart, and after Baalim, which their fathers taught them: Therefore thus saith the LORD of hosts, the God of Israel; Behold, I will feed them, *even* this people, with wormwood, and give them water of gall to drink. I will scatter them also among the heathen, whom neither they nor their fathers have known: and I will send a sword after them, till I have consumed them" (Je.9:13-16).

"Thus saith the LORD; For three transgressions of Judah, and for four, I will not turn away *the punishment* thereof; because they have despised the law of the LORD, and have not kept his commandments, and their lies caused them to err, after the which their fathers have walked" (Am.2:4).

(2) Listen to what the Word of God says about the duties of parents:

"And, ye fathers, provoke not your children to wrath: but bring them up in the nurture and admonition of the Lord" (Ep.6:4).

"Fathers, provoke not your children *to anger,* lest they be discouraged" (Col.3:21).

"One that ruleth well his own house, having his children in subjection with all gravity" (1 Ti.3:4).

"Let the deacons be the husbands of one wife, ruling their children and their own houses well" (1 Ti.3:12).

"That they may teach the young women to be sober, to love their husbands, to love their children (Tit.2:4).

"And these words, which I command thee this day, shall be in thine heart: And thou shalt teach them diligently unto thy children, and shalt talk of them when thou sittest in thine house, and when thou walkest by the way, and when thou liest down, and when thou risest up" (De.6:6-7).

"Then Adonijah the son of Haggith exalted himself, saying, I will be king: and he prepared him chariots and horsemen, and fifty men to run before him. And his father had not displeased him at any time in saying, Why hast thou done so? and he also *was a* very goodly *man;* and *his mother* bare him after Absalom" (1 K.1:5-6).

"Train up a child in the way he should go: and when he is old, he will not depart from it" (Pr.22:6).

"For the grave cannot praise thee, death can *not* celebrate thee: they that go down into the pit cannot hope for thy truth. The living, the living, he shall praise thee, as I *do* this day: the father to the children shall make known thy truth" (Is.38:18-19).

PRACTICAL BIBLE HELPS & RESOURCES

Solomon's Twelve Districts

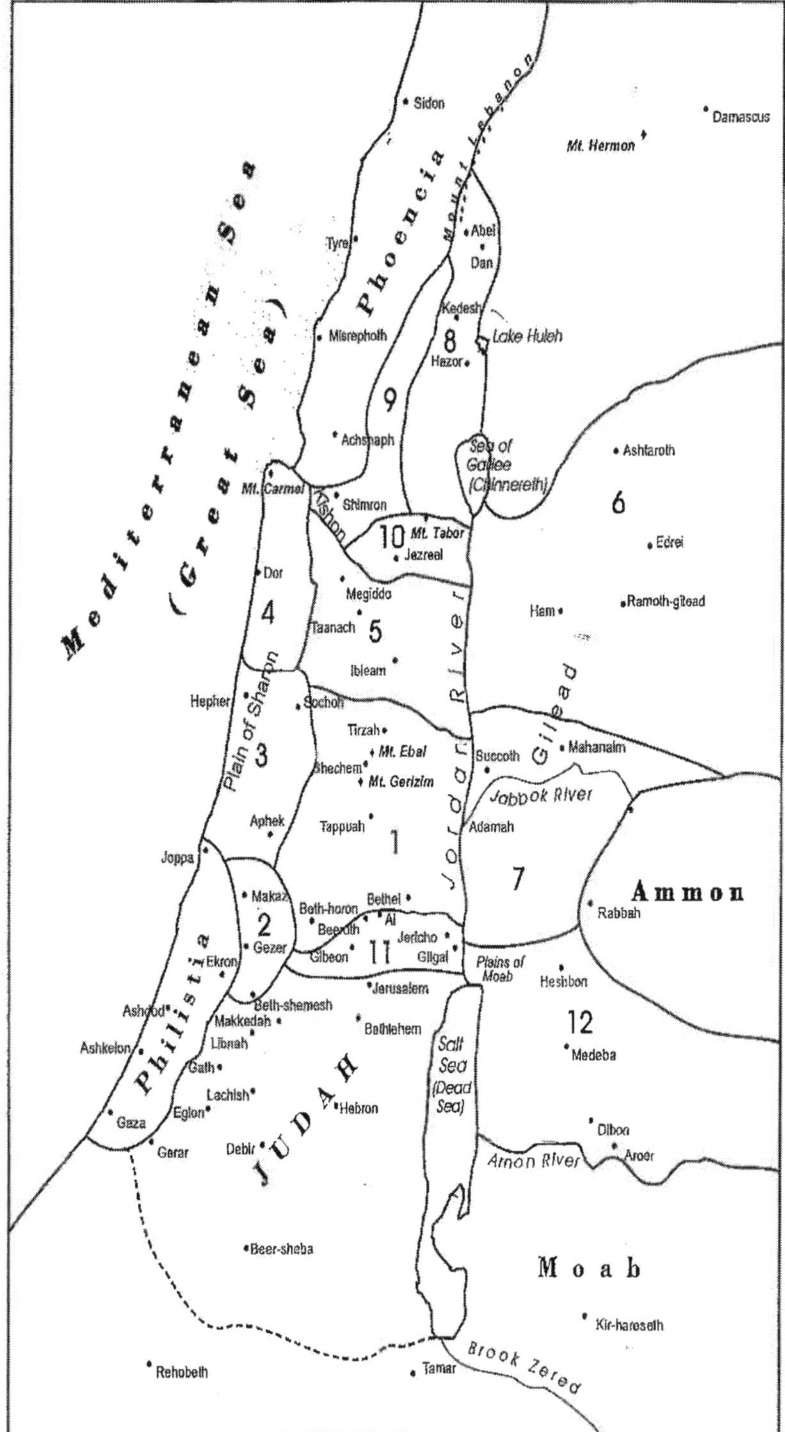

Administratively, the nation of Israel reached its summit under King Solomon. David had expanded Israel's territory and set up an effective political and economic administration. However, he was forced to focus primarily upon the military division of the government due to foreign threats and the territorial expansion of the nation.

Due to the military power David had achieved, Solomon was able to focus upon the political, administrative and economic welfare of the nation. He divided the country into twelve districts or states and appointed governors over them (1 K.4:1-10).

Solomon's 12 Districts

1. **Ben-Hur**: Mountains of Ephraim.
2. **Ben-Deker**: Makaz, Shaalbim, Beth Shemesh, and Elon Beth Hanan.
3. **Ben-Hesed**: Sochoh and land of Hepher.
4. **Ben-Abinadab**: Regions of Dor.
5. **Baana**: Taanach, Megiddo, and all Beth Shean.
6. **Ben-Geber**: Ramoth Gilead.
7. **Abinadab**: Mahanaim.
8. **Ahimaaz**: Naphtali.
9. **Baanah**: Asher and Aloth.
10. **Jehoshaphat**: Issachar.
11. **Shimei**: Benjamin
12. **Geber**: Land of Gilead.

The Empire of David and Solomon

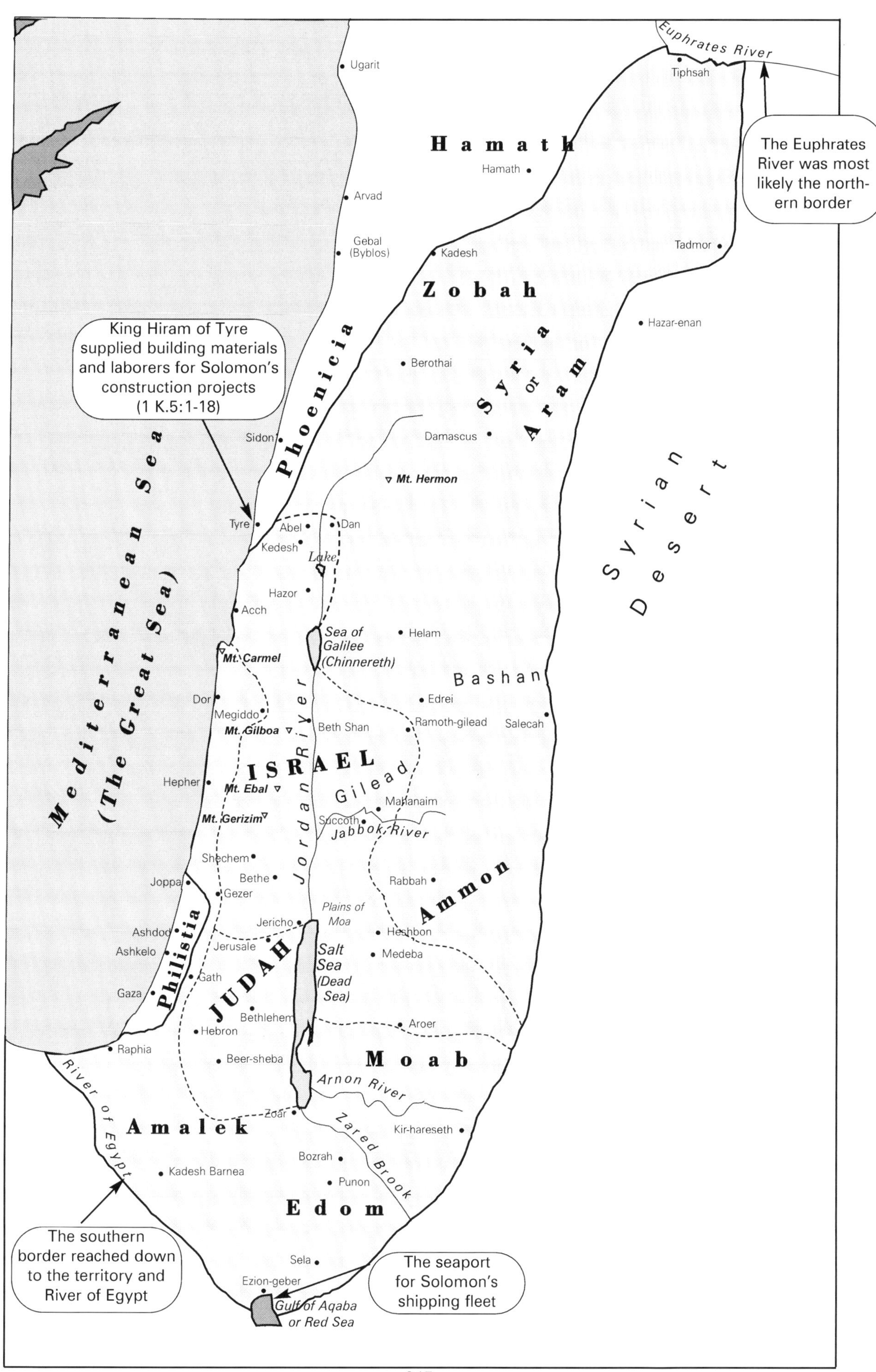

The Divided Kingdom of Israel and Judah

Timeline of Kings, Prophets and History*

The United Kingdom		
Bible Ref.	**Kings** (Years Reigned)	**Prophets**
		Samuel (1095–1015)
1 S.16:1-1 K.2:11; 1 Chr.11:1-30	**David** (40) (1011–971)	**Gad** (1015–950)
		Asaph (1004)
1 K.2:12-11:43; 1 Chr.28:1-2 Chr.9:31	**Solomon** (40) (971–931)	**Nathan** (1003–931) **Heman** (971)

The Divided Kingdom						Date	History	
Southern Kingdom of Judah			Northern Kingdom of Israel					
Bible Ref.	**Kings** (Years Reigned)	**Prophets**	**Bible Ref.**	**Kings** (Years Reigned)	**Prophets**	**BC**	**Foreign Kings**	**World Events**
						1000		**David captures Jerusalem** (1004)
							Ashur-Rabi II (1010–970) *(Assyria)*	
							Hiram (1003–966) *(Tyre)*	**Foundation for the Temple** (966)
						950	**Tiglath-Pileser II** (960–935) *(Assyria)*	**22nd Egyptian Dynasty** (945)
						930		**Kingdom Divided** (930)
I K.12:1-24; 14:21-31; 2 Chr.9:31-12:16	**Rehoboam** (17) (931–913)		I K.12:1-24; 12:25-14:20; 2 Chr.10:1-16	**Jeroboam I** (22) (931–910)	**Ahijah** (931–910)		**Shishak I** (945–924) *(Egypt)*	
1 K.15:1-8; 2 Chr.12:16-14:1	**Abijah** (3) (913–911)				**Man from Judah** (930)			
1 K.15:9-24; 2 Chr.14:1-16:14	**Asa** (3) (911–870)		1 K.15:25-31	**Nadab** (2) (910–909)	**Shemaiah** (927)			**Assyria makes peace with Babylon** (915)
		Iddo (910)	1 K.15:16-16:7; 2 Chr.16:1-6	**Baasha** (24) (909–886)	**Jehu** (886)			
		Azariah (896)	1 K.16:6-14	**Elah** (2) (886–885)		**900**	**Ben-Hadad I** (900) *(Syria)*	**Jehoshaphat leads a revival** (865)
			1 K.16:9-20	**Zimri** (7 days) (885)	**Hanani** (870)		**Eth-Baal** (887–856) *(Sidon)*	**Elijah's contest with prophets of Baal** (857)
			1 K.16:21-28	**Omri** (12) (885–874)				**Elijah's mantle passed to Elisha** (845)
1 K.22:41-50; 2 K.3:6-14; 2 Chr.17:1-21:1	**Jehoshaphat** (25) (873–848)		1 K.16:28-22:40; 2 Chr.18:1-34	**Ahab** (22) (874–853)	**Elijah** (860–845)	**850**		
			1 K.22:49-51; 2 K. 1:1-18; 2 Chr.20:35-37; 22:1-11	**Ahaziah** (2) (853–852)	**Micaiah** (853)		**Hazael** (840) *(Syria)*	
2 K.8:16-24; 2 Chr.21:1-20	**Jehoram** (8) (853–841)		2 K.1:17; 3:1-8:15	**Joram/Jehoram** (12) (852–841)	**Elisha** (850–795)			
2 K.8:25-29; 9:27-29; 2 Chr.22:1-10	**Ahaziah** (2) (841)	**Obadiah** (845)			**Eliezer** (849–48)			**Carthage established** (814)
2 K.11:1-16; 2 Chr.22:10-23:21	**Athaliah** (7) (841–835)		2 K.9:1-10:36; 2 Chr.22:7-9	**Jehu** (28) (841–814)				**Joash repairs Temple** (812)
2 K.11:17-12:21; 2 Chr.22:11-12; 24:1-27	**Joash/Jehoash** (40) (835–796)	**Joel** (830)	2 K.13:1-9	**Jehoahaz** (17) (814–798)		**800**	**Ben-Hadad II** (798) *(Syria)*	**23rd Egyptian dynasty** (800)
2 K.14:1-20; 2 Chr.24:27-25:28	**Amaziah** (29) (796–767)		2 K.13:9-25; 14:8-16	**Jehoash** (16) (798–782)	**Zechariah** (797)			
			2 K.14:23-29	**Jeroboam II** (41) (793–753)	**Jonah** (780–765)		**Ben-Hadad III** (773) *(Syria)*	**Olympic games begin** (776)
2 K.14:21-22; 15:1-7; 2 Chr.26:1-23	**Azariah/Uzziah** (52) (792–740)				**Amos** (750)			**Rome founded** (753)
		Hosea (788-723)	2 K.15:8-12	**Zechariah** (6 mos) (753)				
		Jonah (780-765)	2 K.15:13-15	**Shallum** (1 mo) (752)				
2 K.15:32-38; 2 Chr.26:23-27:9	**Jotham** (16) (750–731)		2.K.15:16-22	**Menahem** (10) (752–742)		**750**	**Rezin** (750) *(Syria)*	**Babylonian and Chinese calendar** (750)

THE DIVIDED KINGDOM

Southern Kingdom of Judah			Northern Kingdom of Israel			Date	History	
Bible Ref.	**Kings** (Years Reigned)	**Prophets**	**Bible Ref.**	**Kings** (Years Reigned)	**Prophets**	**BC**	**Foreign Kings**	**World Events**
			2 K.15:23-26	**Pekahiah** (2) (742–740)			**Tiglath-Pil[n]eser III [or Pul]** (745–727) *(Assyria)*	**Assyria takes control of Northern Kingdom** (745–627)
		Isaiah (740–690)	2 K.15:27-31	**Pekah** (20) (752–732) . (752–740) (ruled only in Gilead) (740–732) (ruled in Samaria)			**Shalmaneser V** (727–722) *(Assyria)*	**Assyria invades Northern Israel** (732)
2 K.15:38-16:20; 2 Chr.27:9-27; Is.7:1-9:1	**Ahaz** (16) (735–715)	**Micah** (735–725) **Oded** (733)	2 K.17:1-23	**Hoshea** (9) (732–722)			**So** (727–716) *(Egypt)* **Sargon II** (710–705) *(Assyria)*	**Fall of Northern Kingdom** (722)
2 K.18:1-20:21; 2 Chr.28:27-32:33; Pr.25:1; Is.36:1-39:8	**Hezekiah** (29) (729–686)					**700**	**Sennacherib** (705–681) *(Assyria)* **Merodach-Baladan** (721–710, 705–704) *(Assyria)*	**Sennacherib defeats Egypt** (701) **Hezekiah's tunnel** (701)
2 K.20:21-21:18; 2 Chr.32:33-33:20	**Manasseh** (55) (696–642)	**Nahum** (663–612)					**Tirhakah** (690–664) *(Egypt)*	**185,000 Assyrians killed by God** (701)
2 K.21:18-26; 2 Chr.33:20-25	**Amon** (2) (642–640)					**650**	**Esarhaddon** (681–669) *(Assyria)*	**Sennacherib destroys Babylon** (689)
2 K.21:26-23:30; 2 Chr.33:25-35:27	**Josiah** (31) (640–609)	**Zephaniah** (640–609)					**Nabopolassar** (626–605) *(Assyria)*	**Josiah's reform** (621) **Nineveh destroyed** (612)
2 K.23:31-33; 2 Chr.36:1-4	**Jehoaz/Jehoahaz** (3 mos) (609)	**Jeremiah** (627–562)					**Neco** (610–595) *(Egypt)*	**Battle of Carchemish** (605) **1st group of exiles from Judah taken to Babylon** (605)
2 K.23:34-24:7; 2 Chr.36:5-8	**Jehoiakim** (11) (608–598)	**Habakkuk** (615–598)				**600**	**Nebuchadnezzar II** (605–562) *(Babylon)*	
2 K.24:8-17; 25:27-30; 2 Chr.36:8-10;	**Jehoiachin** (3 mos) (598–597)	**Daniel** (605–535)						2nd group of exiles from Judah taken to Babylon (597)
2 K.24:18-25:21; 2 Chr.36:10-14; Je.21:1-52:11	**Zedekiah/Mattaniah (11)** (597–586)	**Ezekiel** (593–571)					**Evil-Merodach** (562–560) *(Babylon)*	**Fall of Judah—Third group of exiles from Judah taken to Babylon** (586)
2 K.25:22-26; Je.40:5-41:18	**Gedaliah** (2 mos) (Appointed by Nebuchadnezzar) (586)					**550**	**Cyrus II** (559–530) *(Medo-Persia)*	**Fall of Babylon to Medo-Persian Empire** (539)
							Belshazzar (552–539) *(Babylon)*	**Cyrus II decrees that the Jews may return to the Holy Land** (538) **1st exiles return to Holy Land with Zerubbabel** (537)
		Haggai (520) **Zechariah** (520–518)						**1st Temple foundation laid** (536) **2nd Temple foundation laid** (520)
						500	**Darius I** (521–486) *(Medo-Persia)*	Temple completed (516) Republic of Rome est. (509)
								2nd return under Ezra (458)
		Malachi (430)				**450**	**Artaxerxes** (465–425) *(Persia)*	**3rd return under Nehemiah** (445)

The resources used for the Timeline in addition to the *Bible* are as follows:

[1] Archer, Gleason L. *Encyclopedia of Bible Difficulties*. (Grand Rapids, Michigan: Zondervan Publishing House), 1982.
[2] Freedman, David Noel, ed., et. al. *The Anchor Bible Dictionary*. (New York: Doubleday), 1992.
[3] Grun, Bernard. *The Timetables of History*. 3rd ed. (New York: Simon & Schuster), 1991.
[4] Kaiser, Walter C. *A History of Israel*. (Nashville, Tennessee: Broadman & Holman Publishers), 1998.
[5] Silverman, David P., ed. *Ancient Egypt*. (New York: Oxford University Press), 1997.

*Some dates are approximate.

Solomon's Temple
(Inside)

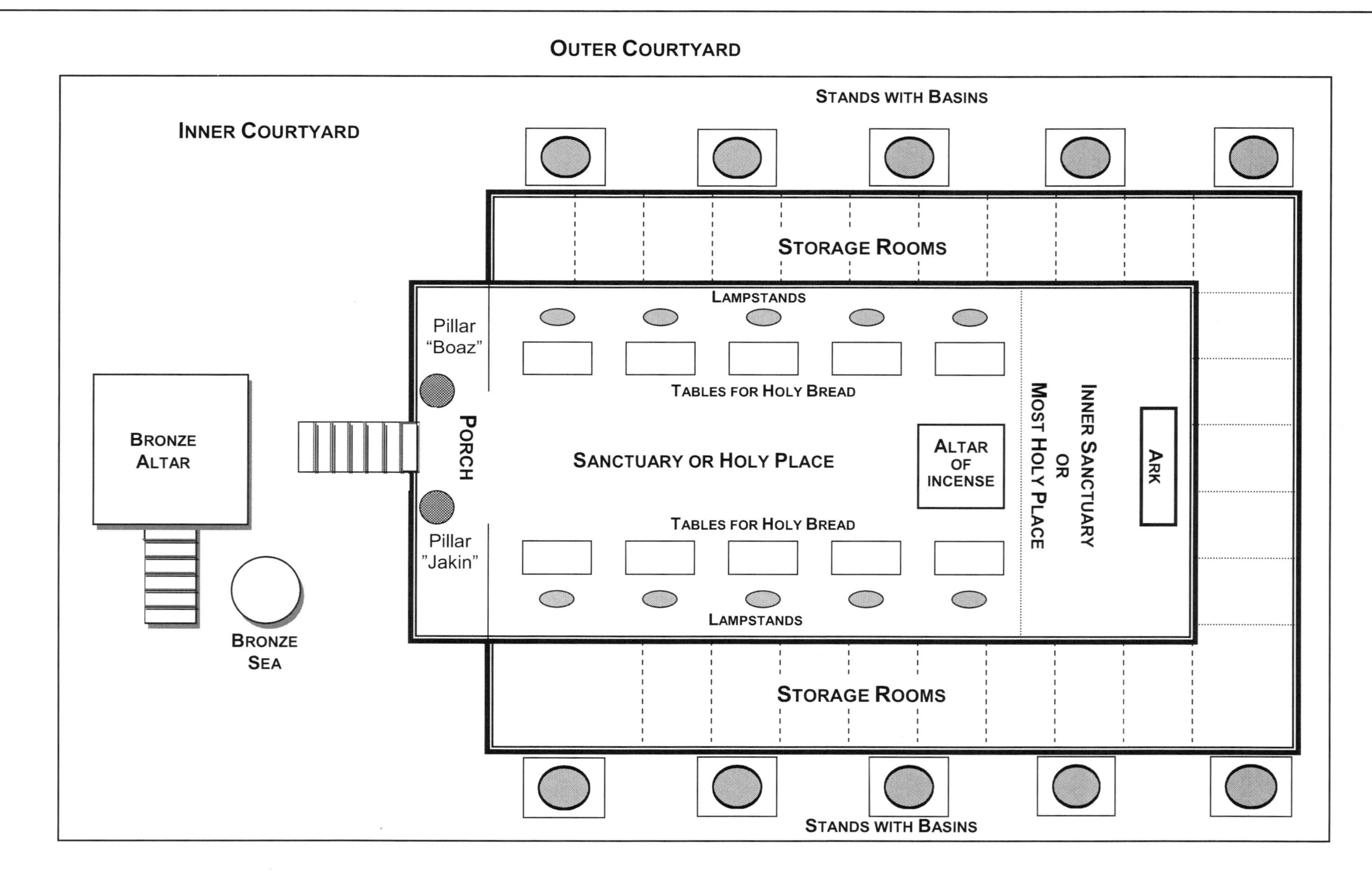

Solomon's Temple
(Outside)

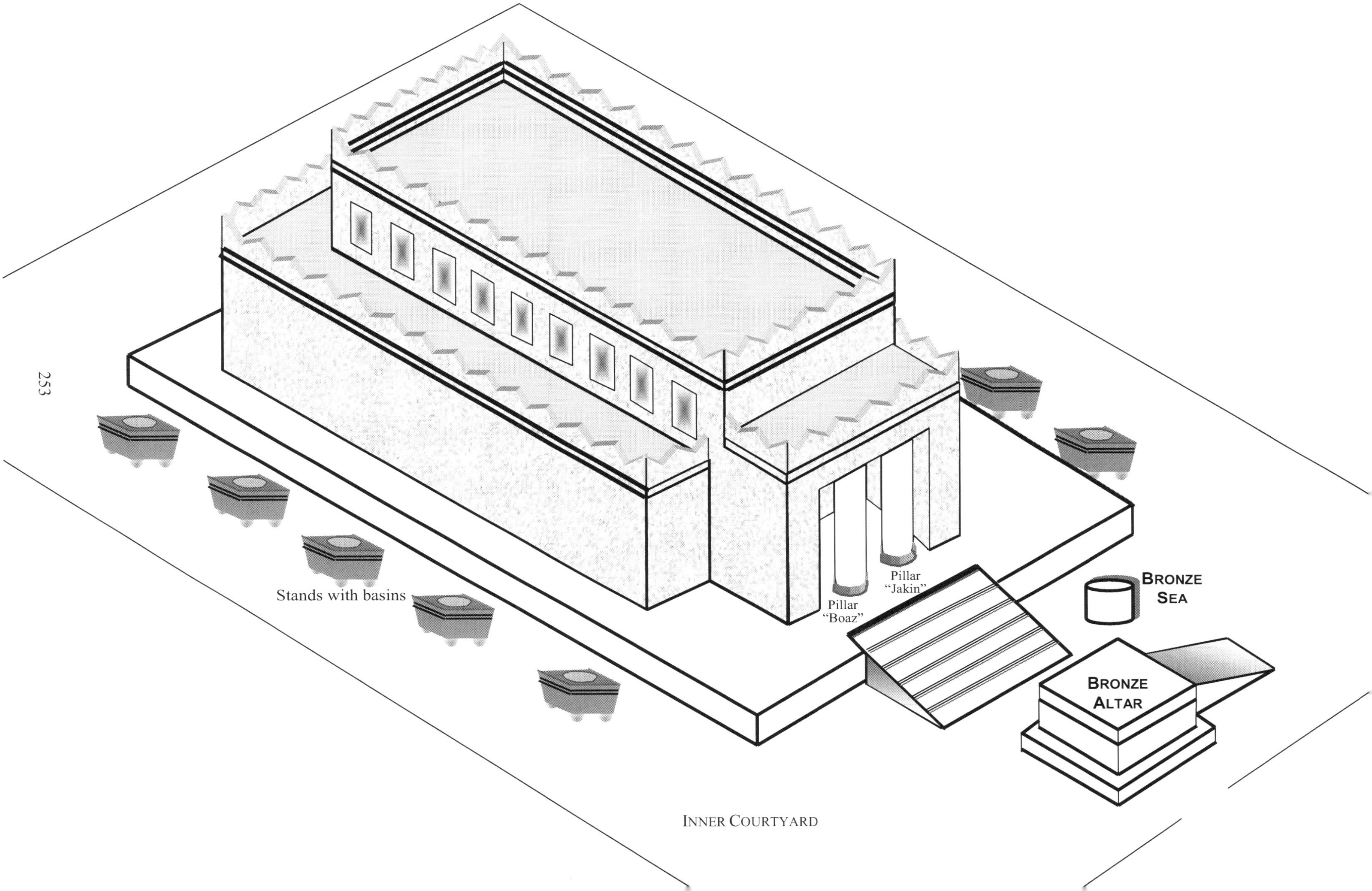

Stands with basins

Pillar "Jakin"

Pillar "Boaz"

Bronze Sea

Bronze Altar

Inner Courtyard

TYPES, SYMBOLS, AND PICTURES
THE BOOK OF 1 KINGS

What is a biblical type or symbol? Simply put, a *biblical type* is a *foreshadowing* of what was to come at a later time in history. Through a person, place, or thing, a biblical type points toward a New Testament fulfillment.

In addition to biblical types, there are what we may call *biblical pictures*. A biblical picture is a lesson that we can see in the Scriptures *without distorting the truth*. The study of biblical types and pictures is a valuable tool in that it helps us apply the truth of the Scriptures in our lives. Scripture itself tells us this:

> **"Now all these things happened unto them for examples: and they are written for our admonition, upon whom the ends of the world are come" (1 Co.10:11).**
>
> **"For whatsoever things were written aforetime were written for our learning, that we through patience and comfort of the scriptures might have hope" (Ro.15:4).**

ALPHABETICAL OUTLINE

PERSON/PLACE/THING	SCRIPTURE, OUTLINE AND DISCUSSION
Adonijah ***Second plot of and his execution***: *A picture of judgment falling upon those who oppose God's kingdom.*	(1 K.2:13-25)
Uprising of. His desperate fear: *A picture of the terror of God's judgment and of God's mercy.*	(1 K.1:41-53)
Anointing. Of Solomon as king: *A type of Christ, the Anointed One of God.*	(1 K.1:38-40)
Ark of the Covenant: *A symbol of the very presence of God Himself.*	(1 K.6:19; 8:10-11)
Bread of the Presence (or Showbread): *A symbol of the Lord Jesus Christ, the Bread of Life.*	(1 K.7:48)
Bronze pillars. At the entrance to the Temple: *A picture of God's power.*	(1 K.7:15-22)
Cherubs. In the Temple: *A symbol of the holiness of God.*	(1 K.6:27)
Condemnation ***Of Ahab. By God through an unnamed prophet***: *A picture of disobedience.*	(1 K.20:35-43)
Of Ahab and Jezebel: *A picture of God's coming judgment.*	(1 K.21:18-29)
Of Jeroboam: *A picture of God's judgment foretold.*	(1 K.14:7-20)
Confrontation. Elijah. Confronted Ahab: *A picture of judgment due to sin.*	(1 K.18:18-20)
Counterplan. Of David and Bathsheba to have Solomon crowned king: *A picture of being willing to work out God's will no matter the cost.*	(1 K.1:11-27)
David: *A type of Christ, the Son of David, the Messiah and Savior of the world.*	(1 K.2:1-9)
Egypt. Slavery in: *A symbol of being bound by the sin of the world.*	(1 K.8:25-53)

TYPES, SYMBOLS, AND PICTURES
ALPHABETICAL

PERSON/PLACE/THING	SCRIPTURE, OUTLINE AND DISCUSSION
Lampstand. Of the Temple: *A symbol of God and of the Lord Jesus Christ, the Light of the world.*	(1 K.7:49)
Laver. Of the Temple: *A symbol of the cleansing from sin that is so desperately needed by us all.*	(1 K.7:23-26)
Prophets. Of Baal: *A picture of the futility of idolatry and false worship—hoping that sacrifice will make a person acceptable.*	(1 K.18:17-46)
Queen of Sheba. Testimony about Solomon: *A picture of seeking truth.*	(1 K.10:1-13)
Rebellion. Of Adonijah against King Solomon: *A picture of rebellion against the King of kings and LORD of lords, God Himself.*	(1 K.2:13-25)
Rehoboam. Defeat by Shishak, king of Egypt: *A picture of God's chastisement.*	(1 K.14:25-28)
Revelation. To Abijah. Of a deceptive plot: *A picture of God's guidance for His servants.*	(1 K.14:4-6)
Revolt. Against Rehoboam: *A picture of arrogance, conceit, and oppression.*	(1 K.12:1-14)
Sacrifice. Of animals by shedding blood: *A type of the coming Ideal Sacrifice, the coming Messiah and Savior of the world, the Lord Jesus Christ.*	(1 K.8:62-66)
Shimei. Execution of: *A picture of judgment, reaping what one sows.*	(1 K.2:35-46)
The Temple ***Gold furnishings of***: *A symbol of prayer and Christ, the most valuable possession a believer has.*	(1 K.7:48-50)
A symbol of the living temple, the believer in whom God's Spirit dwells.	(1 K.6:1-38)
Zimri. Evil reign of: *A picture of hopelessness and suicide.*	(1 K.15:15-20)

TYPES, SYMBOLS, AND PICTURES
THE BOOK OF 1 KINGS

What is a biblical type or symbol? Simply put, a *biblical type* is a *foreshadowing* of what was to come at a later time in history. Through a person, place, or thing, a biblical type points toward a New Testament fulfillment.

In addition to biblical types, there are what we may call *biblical pictures*. A biblical picture is a lesson that we can see in the Scriptures *without distorting the truth*. The study of biblical types and pictures is a valuable tool in that it helps us apply the truth of the Scriptures in our lives. Scripture itself tells us this:

> **"Now all these things happened unto them for examples: and they are written for our admonition, upon whom the ends of the world are come" (1 Co.10:11).**
>
> **"For whatsoever things were written aforetime were written for our learning, that we through patience and comfort of the scriptures might have hope" (Ro.15:4).**

CHRONOLOGICAL OUTLINE

PERSON/PLACE/THING	SCRIPTURE, OUTLINE AND DISCUSSION
Counterplan. Of David and Bathsheba to have Solomon crowned king: *A picture of being willing to work out God's will no matter the cost.*	(1 K.1:11-27)
Anointing. Of Solomon as king: *A type of Christ, the Anointed One of God.*	(1 K.1:38-40)
Adonijah. Uprising of. His desperate fear: *A picture of the terror of God's judgment and of God's mercy.*	(1 K.1:41-53)
Solomon. Power of. Consolidation of: *A picture of justice.*	(1 K.2:1-46)
David: *A type of Christ, the Son of David, the Messiah and Savior of the world.*	(1 K.2:1-9)
Adonijah. Second plot of and his execution: *A picture of judgment falling upon those who oppose God's kingdom.*	(1 K.2:13-25)
Rebellion. Of Adonijah against King Solomon: *A picture of rebellion against the King of kings and LORD of lords, God Himself.*	(1 K.2:13-25)
Shimei. Execution of: *A picture of judgment, reaping what one sows.*	(1 K.2:35-46)
The Temple: *A symbol of the living temple, the believer in whom God's Spirit dwells.*	(1 K.6:1-38)
Ark of the Covenant: *A symbol of the very presence of God Himself.*	(1 K.6:19; 8:10-11)
Cherubs. In the Temple: *A symbol of the holiness of God.*	(1 K.6:27)
Bronze pillars. At the entrance to the Temple: *A picture of God's power.*	(1 K.7:15-22)
Laver. Of the Temple: *A symbol of the cleansing from sin that is so desperately needed by us all.*	(1 K.7:23-26)
The Temple. Gold furnishings of: *A symbol of prayer and Christ, the most valuable possession a believer has.*	(1 K.7:48-50)
Bread of the Presence (or Showbread): *A symbol of the Lord Jesus Christ, the Bread of Life.*	(1 K.7:48)

TYPES, SYMBOLS, AND PICTURES
CHRONOLOGICAL

PERSON/PLACE/THING	SCRIPTURE, OUTLINE AND DISCUSSION
***Lampstand. Of the Temple**: A symbol of God and of the Lord Jesus Christ, the Light of the world.*	(1 K.7:49)
***Egypt. Slavery in**: A symbol of being bound by the sin of the world.*	(1 K.8:25-53)
***Sacrifice. Of animals by shedding blood**: A type of the coming Ideal Sacrifice, the coming Messiah and Savior of the world, the Lord Jesus Christ.*	(1 K.8:62-66)
***Queen of Sheba. Testimony about Solomon**: A picture of seeking truth.*	(1 K.10:1-13)
***Israel. Kingdom of. Division of**: A picture of God's sovereignty.*	(1 K.11:27-40; 12:15-24)
***Revolt. Against Rehoboam**: A picture of arrogance, conceit, and oppression.*	(1 K.12:1-14)
***Revelation. To Abijah. Of a deceptive plot**: A picture of God's guidance for His servants.*	(1 K.14:4-6)
***Condemnation. Of Jeroboam**: A picture of God's judgment foretold.*	(1 K.14:7-20)
***Rehoboam. Defeat by Shishak, king of Egypt**: A picture of God's chastisement.*	(1 K.14:25-28)
***Zimri. Evil reign of**: A picture of hopelessness and suicide.*	(1 K.15:15-20)
***Confrontation. Elijah. Confronted Ahab**: A picture of judgment due to sin.*	(1 K.18:18-20)
***Prophets. Of Baal**: A picture of the futility of idolatry and false worship—hoping that sacrifice will make a person acceptable.*	(1 K.18:17-46)
Condemnation ***Of Ahab. By God through an unnamed prophet**: A picture of disobedience.*	(1 K.20:35-43)
***Of Ahab and Jezebel**: A picture of God's coming judgment.*	(1 K.21:18-29)

INDEX

REMEMBER: When you look up a subject and turn to the Scripture reference, you have not just the Scripture but also an outline and a discussion (commentary) of the Scripture and subject.

This is one of the GREAT FEATURES of *The Preacher's Outline & Sermon Bible®*. Once you have all the volumes, you will have not only what all other Bible indexes give you, that is, a list of all the subjects and their Scripture references, but in addition you will have...

- an outline of every Scripture and subject in the Bible
- a discussion (commentary) on every Scripture and subject
- every subject supported by other Scripture, already written out or cross referenced

DISCOVER THE UNIQUE VALUE for yourself. Quickly glance below to the first subject of the Index:

ABEL-MEHOLAH
Home of Elisha the prophet. 19:16

Turn to the first reference. Glance at the Scripture and the outline, then read the commentary. You will immediately see the TREMENDOUS BENEFIT of the INDEX of *The Preacher's Outline & Sermon Bible®*.

OUTLINE AND SUBJECT INDEX

INDEX

INDEX

Leadership Ministries Worldwide

PURPOSE STATEMENT

LEADERSHIP MINISTRIES WORLDWIDE exists to equip ministers, teachers, and laypersons in their understanding, preaching, and teaching of God's Word by publishing and distributing worldwide ***The Preacher's Outline & Sermon Bible***® and derivative works to reach & disciple all people for Jesus Christ.

MISSION STATEMENT

1. To make the Bible so understandable – its truth so clear and plain – that men and women everywhere, whether teacher or student, preacher or hearer, can grasp its message and receive Jesus Christ as Savior, and...

2. To place the Bible in the hands of all who will preach and teach God's Holy Word, verse by verse, precept by precept, regardless of the individual's ability to purchase it.

The Preacher's Outline & Sermon Bible and derivative works been given to LMW as LMW Resources for printing and distribution worldwide at/below cost, by those who remain anonymous. One fact, however, is as true today as it was in the time of Christ:

THE GOSPEL IS FREE, BUT THE COST OF TAKING IT IS NOT

LMW depends on the generous gifts of believers with a heart for Him and a love for the lost. They help pay for the printing, translating, and distributing of LMW Resources into the hands of God's servants worldwide, who will present the Gospel message with clarity, authority, and understanding beyond their own.

LMW was incorporated in the state of Tennessee in July 1992 and received IRS 501 (c)(3) non-profit status in March 1994. LMW is an international, nondenominational mission organization. All proceeds from USA sales, along with donations from donor partners, go directly to underwrite translation and distribution projects of LMW Resources to preachers, church and lay leaders, and Bible students around the world.

LMW Resources

This material, like similar works, has come from imperfect man and is thus susceptible to human error. We are nevertheless grateful to God for both calling us and empowering us through His Holy Spirit to undertake this task. Because of His goodness and grace, ***The Preacher's Outline & Sermon Bible***® New Testament and the Old Testament volumes have been completed.

LMW Resources include *The Minister's Personal Handbook, The Believer's Personal Handbook,* and other helpful resources available in printed form as well as electronically on various digital platforms.

God has given the strength and stamina to bring us this far. Our confidence is that as we keep our eyes on Him and remain grounded in the undeniable truths of the Word, we will continue to produce other helpful resources for God's dear servants to use in their Bible study and discipleship.

We offer this material, first, to Him in whose name we labor and serve and for whose glory it has been produced and, second, to everyone everywhere who studies, preaches, and teaches the Word.

Our daily prayer is that each volume will lead thousands, millions, yes even billions, into a better understanding of the Holy Scriptures and a fuller knowledge of Jesus Christ the Incarnate Word, of whom the Scriptures so faithfully testify.

You will be pleased to know that Leadership Ministries Worldwide partners with Christian organizations, printers, and mission groups around the world to make LMW Resources available and affordable in many countries and foreign languages. It is our goal that *every* leader around the world, both clergy and lay, will be able to understand God's holy Word and present God's message with more clarity, authority, and understanding—all beyond his or her own power.

Leadership Ministries Worldwide
1928 Central Avenue • Chattanooga, TN 37408
1(800) 987-8790
Email: info@lmw.org
lmw.org

11/22

LEADERSHIP MINISTRIES WORLDWIDE

Product Listing

THE PREACHER'S OUTLINE & SERMON BIBLE® (POSB) ***Available in KJV (44 vols) & NIV (40 vols)***

OLD TESTAMENT

- Genesis I: Chs. 1–11
- Genesis II: Chs. 12–50
- Exodus I: Chs. 1–18
- Exodus II: Chs. 19–40
- Leviticus
- Numbers
- Deuteronomy
- Joshua
- Judges, Ruth
- 1 Samuel
- 2 Samuel
- 1 Kings
- 2 Kings
- 1 Chronicles
- 2 Chronicles
- Ezra, Nehemiah, Esther
- Job
- Psalms I: Chs. 1-41
- Psalms II: Chs. 42-106
  Psalms III: Chs. 107-150
- Proverbs
- Ecclesiastes, Song of Solomon
- Isaiah I: Chs. 1-35
- Isaiah II: Chs. 36-66
- Jeremiah I: Chs. 1-29
- Jeremiah II: Chs. 30-52, Lamentations
- Ezekiel
- Daniel, Hosea
  Joel, Amos, Obadiah, Jonah, Micah, Nahum
- Habakkuk, Zephaniah, Haggai, Zechariah, Malachi

NEW TESTAMENT

- Matthew I: Chs. 1–15
- Matthew II: Chs. 16–28
- Mark
- Luke
- John
- Acts
- Romans
- 1 & 2 Corinthians
- Galatians, Ephesians, Philippians, Colossians
- 1 & 2 Thessalonians, 1 & 2 Timothy, Titus, Philemon
- Hebrews, James
- 1 & 2 Peter, 1, 2, & 3 John, Jude
- Revelation
- Master Outline & Subject Index

Handbooks

- **What the Bible Says to the Believer** —
  The Believer's Personal Handbook
  11 Chapters. – Over 500 Subjects, 300 Promises, & 400 Verses Expounded - Gift leatherette or paperback options
- **What the Bible Says to the Minister** —
  The Minister's Personal Handbook
  12 Chapters. - 127 Subjects - 400 Verses Expounded - Gift leatherette or paperback options
- **What the Bible Says to the Business Leader**—The Business Leader's Personal Handbook
  12 Chapters – Over 100 topics plus hundreds of scriptural values for conducting business in a 21st-century world — Paperback
- **What the Bible Says About Series** —
  Various Subjects

everyWORD

Scripture, Outline, Commentary of the Gospels with ESV Scripture

- everyWORD: Matthew 1–16:12
- everyWORD: Matthew 16:13–28:20
- everyWORD: Mark
- everyWORD: Luke 1–13:21
- everyWORD: Luke 13:22–24:53
- everyWORD: John

- **The Teacher's Outline & Study Bible™** - Various New Testament Books
  Complete 30 - 45 minute lessons – with illustrations and discussion questions
- *Practical Illustrations — Companion to the POSB Arranged by topic and Scripture reference*
- *LMW Resources on various digital platforms Learn more on our website at lmw.org*
- *Contact for resources in other languages*

Contact Us

LEADERSHIP MINISTRIES WORLDWIDE
1928 Central Avenue • Chattanooga, TN 37408
1(800) 987-8790 • E-mail - info@lmw.org
Order online at lmw.org